URBANIZATION IN ASIA

Urbanization in Asia

Spatial Dimensions and Policy Issues

Edited by
Frank J. Costa
Ashok K. Dutt
Laurence J. C. Ma
Allen G. Noble

University of Hawaii Press • Honolulu

Library of Congress Cataloging-in-Publication Data

Urbanization in Asia : spatial dimensions and policy issues / edited
   by Frank J. Costa . . . [et al.].
     p.   cm.
   "Most of the chapters in this book originally were given as papers
at the International Conference on Asian Urbanization held in Akron,
Ohio, in April 1985"—P.
   Includes bibliographies and index.
   ISBN 0-8248-1151-8
   1.   Urbanization—Asia—Congresses.   2.   Urban policy—Asia—
Congresses.   I.   Costa, Frank J.   II.   International Conference on
Asian Urbanization (1985 : Akron, Ohio)
HT384.A78U73   1989   88-29519
307.7'6'095—dc19   CIP

Contents

Acknowledgments

Most of the chapters in this book originally were given as papers at the International Conference on Asian Urbanization held in Akron, Ohio, in April 1985. The editors wish to thank President William Muse and Dean Claibourne Griffin of the University of Akron for their invaluable assistance in planning and carrying out that conference.

In the long and arduous process of working with individual authors and assembling chapter contributions into a coherent manuscript, the editors have many people to thank. Those who gave typing and word processing assistance were Bilkis Banu, Tamara Bauer, Pam Dix, Vijay Gadde, Kim Groves, Hilda Kendron, Arlene Lane, Sharon McKurth, and Barbara Stouffer. A special debt of gratitude must be paid to Alan H. Sommers of the Department of Urban Studies, University of Akron, for supervising the preparation of the final manuscript. We also want to express our thanks to Peter Leahy and John Mulhauser for their willingness to provide resources for the preparation of this manuscript.

The excellent maps and figures throughout this book are due to the skill of Margaret Geib of the Geography Department, University of Akron. She was ably assisted in the statistical compilations by Swati Sinha.

Three of the chapters in this book originally appeared elsewhere. The chapter by William Wood and that by Yue-man Yeung originally appeared in *Geographical Review*. We wish to thank the editor of the *Review*, Douglas McManis, for his kind permission to allow their publication here. Sandra Ward, editor at the East–West Center, has kindly given permission for the chapter by Roland J. Fuchs and Ernesto M. Pernia to appear here.

Finally we want to thank Damaris Kirchhofer of the University of Hawaii Press for her initial encouragement and continued assistance.

Contributors

Swapna Bannerjee-Guha, Bombay University
Thomas K. Chao, National Taiwan College of Marine Science
and Technology
Yong H. Cho, University of Akron
Frank J. Costa, University of Akron
Ashok K. Dutt, University of Akron
Roland J. Fuchs, University of Hawaii
Norton Ginsburg, University of Chicago
Jasmine Irani, University of Akron
Pradyumna P. Karan, University of Kentucky
Young S. Kim, Hanyang University, South Korea
David H. Kornhauser, University of Kentucky
Amrit Lall, University of Windsor
T. G. McGee, University of British Columbia
Laurence J. C. Ma, University of Akron
Charles B. Monroe, University of Akron
V. Nath, Former Deputy Secretary, Planning Commission of India
Allen G. Noble, University of Akron
Clifton W. Pannell, University of Georgia
Ernesto M. Pernia, University of the Philippines
Aktar H. Siddiqi, Indiana State University
Bruce Taylor, Chinese University of Hong Kong
Ramesh Tiwari, University of Manitoba
William B. Wood, University of Hawaii
C. S. Yadav, University of Delhi
Shunzan Ye, Academia Sinica, China
Yue-man Yeung, Chinese University of Hong Kong
Jinggan Zhang, City of Beijing

PART I: INTRODUCTION

1. Trends and Prospects

Frank J. Costa, Ashok K. Dutt, Laurence J. C. Ma, and Allen G. Noble

Patterns of city growth and urban development in Asia are similar to those in other parts of the developing world. In Asia, however, the demographic magnitude of the urban transformation is unusual. The vast populations of China and India have no parallel in other world areas, and countries such as South Korea, Japan, Indonesia, and Bangladesh have rapidly expanding urban systems arising within densely populated countrysides. Thus the peculiar circumstances of city growth in Asia magnify the issues and problems associated with urbanization to an extent never before seen in human history. Asian countries have a living heritage with a rich urban history of over five thousand years. Moreover, the religious, linguistic, and ethnic heterogeneity present in Asian society is unmatched by any other continent.

While Asian urbanization is similar in many respects to Western urbanization, it is quite different as well. Rural–urban migration, high-density urban clusters, social heterogeneity, inadequate economic infrastructure, and social stress are common factors in both environments. But certain elements are different. The compact nature of settlement, the generally greater reliance upon, and development of, basic public transportation, the much greater mixing of land uses and hence the less clearly defined spatial components, characterize the Asian city but not its Western counterpart.

Furthermore, until recently most Asian countries were either directly or indirectly under European colonial domination which generated a port-based, export-oriented urban economy existing largely for the benefit of the manufacturing and mercantile needs of the mother country. In Asia, however, this peculiar urbanization had to occur in areas which were already densely settled: the Ganges Plain, eastern China, Java, and in smaller areas elsewhere. An incipient urban network arising to serve the needs of the peasant and artisan populations of these areas was aborted by the growth of the colonial port/administrative center network.

The depressing physical and social conditions of nineteenth-century European and American cities are reflected today in Asia—and here again the extent of physical and social disorder has not been experienced previously. The rapid growth of London and Paris and other European centers eventually abated because of technological transformations affecting the economy of cities, which required fewer hands. At the same time, the reservoir of surplus population was being depleted by overseas migration. This is not the case today in Asia. Here, except for China, a rapidly growing rural population exceeding its limits and resources of support continues to provide a "rural push" which is far greater than the "urban pull" exerted by social and cultural amenities and economic opportunity. This dynamic creates drastic levels of urban unemployment and underemployment, which in turn contribute to the steady deterioration of physical and social conditions prevalent in many Asian cities. In large part, it was these eroding advantages and amenities which originally acted as the urban magnet drawing rural dwellers from the surrounding countryside.

Urban gigantism and its associated problems are certainly not confined to Asia—witness Mexico City, São Paulo, Lima, and Cairo—but it is most apparent there. Urban growth estimates tell us that by the year 2000, twelve of the fifteen largest urban centers will be in developing countries. Of these twelve, eight will be in Asia.[1]

The implications of this rapid growth of Asian cities are both profound and disturbing—profound because these demographic changes will have an impact on all aspects of the various national societies and disturbing because even today many governments are unable to deal with the flood of new urban dwellers. Unimaginably poor conditions of housing and urban infrastructure are already commonplace in many Asian cities. Millions of people have exchanged an abject rural poverty for an equally abject urban poverty. Major problems of environmental pollution, crime, political violence, and social disorganization are beginning to emerge. Have the great Asian metropolitan centers, places with 10 million and more inhabitants, grown to such a size that they are rapidly becoming so inefficient as to ultimately act as a brake on national development? It is not just a question of the inordinate amount of budget resource which each of these centers demands; it is also a question of maintaining an acceptable quality of life for the rapidly growing millions of inhabitants. In city after city the urban infrastructure is growing much less rapidly than the population it is intended to serve. The Indian novelist Kamala Markandaya recognized the problem a generation ago and created a powerful tale of the frustration and despair which follow the peasant who migrates to the city.[2] Markandaya is not alone in her perception of the social problems which large cities generate.[3]

Although there is an extensive body of literature dealing with urban development in Western nations, Latin America, and Africa, Asian urbanization and urbanism are not only understudied but Asian research is seldom published in any coherent manner. In an effort to fill this gap, an international conference on Asian urbanization was convened in April 1985 at the University of Akron. Some seventy scholars from fourteen countries participated in the conference; they presented their studies, and their views and findings were discussed frankly in small groups of specialists. The studies presented in this volume were selected from those given at the conference either because of their broad spatial dimensions or their implications for urban policy development.

The nineteen studies presented here share certain broad perspectives on urban development. After an overview of the literature on Asian urbanization by Ginsburg (Chapter 2), the studies are divided into four parts. The authors' inquiries cover the spectrum from macrolevel national views to regional studies to microlevel case studies of individual cities. In this introductory essay, we follow the organizational structure of the book and discuss a number of issues essential to the study of urban Asia.

National Urbanization Trends and Processes

Population growth and urbanization in Asia since the end of World War II result primarily from a stable or slowly declining birth rate and a rapidly declining death rate These two factors, in concert, account for nearly all population growth because in-migration, except for the oil-based economies of the Persian Gulf, has been a negligible factor. Urban population growth has outstripped general population growth because of a constantly increasing rate of rural-to-urban migration (see Table 1.1). Such movement is documented for at least one city, Delhi, by Yadav in Chapter 12. He observes that the approximately 100,000 migrants to Delhi each year "have seriously deteriorated its physical, social, and economic environment" because most of the migrants are "marginal farmers, casual laborers, and low social status people" who bring little skills and few resources.

Even though Asian cities are growing rapidly, the Asian nations together still have the smallest proportion of their populations in urban places. In 1980 an estimated 27 percent of Asia's total population lived in urban places compared with 29 percent in Africa and 65 percent in Latin America.[4] Asian rural districts contain the world's largest reservoirs of potential urban migrants. Although Asia's level of urbanization will increase to approximately 40 percent of the total population by the year 2000, the proportion of the urbanized population to the total will

Table 1.1. Asia's Total Population and Rural and Urban
Populations (in millions): 1920-1980

	1920	1930	1940	1950	1960	1970	1980	% Change 1920-1980
Asia								
Total urban	90.0	115.0	160.0	216.3	341.6	482.4	689.3	665.9
Total rural	933.2	1,005.2	1,085.1	1,157.7	1,302.1	1,545.7	1,825.1	95.6
Grand total	1,023.2	1,120.2	1,245.1	1,374.0	1,643.7	2,028.1	2,514.5	145.7

Source: Ved Prakash, "Affordability and Cost Recovery of
Urban Services for the Poor," Regional Development Dialogue
6(2) (autumn 1985), p. 5.

still be lower than anywhere else in the world.[5] For many decades into the future, Asia will be experiencing explosive urban growth. Very little, other than dictatorial population control policies (such as the forceful family planning program attempted by Indira Gandhi's government during the 1975–1977 Emergency Period in India), can curb the anticipated growth. But even draconian policies will not have a noticeable impact for several years.

Asian nations have followed different paths to urbanization. In Part II of this book, the experiences of India and Pakistan are studied by Nath (Chapter 3) and Siddiqi (Chapter 4). Nath notes that "while significant progress has been made in the post-Independence period in devising a strategy of rural economic development, leading to brisk economic growth over several parts of rural India, no suitable strategy has evolved for the management of urban growth." One management technique which Nath discusses is the restriction of urban in-migration. Rural-to-urban migration represents a significant feature of Asian urbanization. Increasingly, such movement is concentrated in migration streams into the capital cities and a few other major urban centers of most Asian nations (Table 1.2). An extreme example of this tendency is found in Thailand, where Bangkok's population approaches 6 million while that of the second largest city, Chiang Mai, is less than 200,000. Not only is the wealth of many Asian nations highly concentrated in a few urban centers, but the socioeconomic and physical development problems of these nations result in large part from this unplanned concentration. In the post-Independence period, significant progress has been made in several parts of rural India. This achievement, however, has not been accompanied by any significant improvement in urban India. The growing pains of the largest cities are intensifying, and the gaps of regional economic development are being widened. In Pakistan, the growth of irrigation agriculture has had a strong impact on urbanization. However, the inability of the cities to provide jobs to the expanding urban population due to the slow tempo of industrialization has resulted in overurbanization.

The urbanization process in India and Pakistan contrasts sharply with that of China. China's emphasis on urban-based industrial development, on the one hand, and the restriction of urban growth through the control of rural-to-urban migration, on the other, have made the Chinese experience of urban development unique. Many of these features of urban China have been presented by Ye in his comprehensive study (Chapter 5). Although Taiwan is not included in Ye's study, the growth of urban areas in Taiwan is analyzed by McGee (Chapter 6). As a result of "economic takeoff" on the island and the development of efficient transportation networks near urban centers, the periurban regions

Table 1.2. Growth of Major Asian Cities (in thousands):
1940-1980

City	1940	1950	1960	1970	1980
India					
Calcutta	3,400	4,490	6,138	7,350	9,166
Bombay	1,660	3,335	4,089	5,100	8,227
Delhi	640	1,737	2,309	3,100	5,714
Madras	765	1,700	2,090	2,600	4,277
China					
Shanghai	3,727	4,995	6,977	10,820	12,000
Peking	1,551	1,940	6,800	7,570	8,500
Tientsin	1,218	1,786	3,278	4,280	7,200[a]
Canton	1,115	1,496		3,000	
Hong Kong					
Hong Kong		1,561	3,075	4,105	5,154[b]
Taiwan					
Taipei		750	1,329	2,150	2,327[c]
South Korea					
Seoul	935	1,467	2,445	4,661	9,204[c]
Japan					
Tokyo	6,779	4,175	9,380	8,841	8,494
Yokohama	968	814	1,375	2,238	2,729
Kyoto	1,090	999	1,285	1,450	1,461
Osaka	3,252	1,559	3,012	2,981	2,700
Nagoya	1,328	853	1,592	2,036	2,086
Indonesia					
Jakarta	1,000	1,452	2,852	4,500	6,500
Philippines					
Manila	900	1,781	2,704	4,000	5,925
Singapore					
Singapore	600	1,022	1,634	2,113	2,334[d]
Thailand					
Bangkok	625	891	1,300	2,100	5,468[b]
Pakistan					
Karachi		1,086	1,884	3,246	5,103[a]
Iran					
Tehran	625	1,073	1,923	3,250	4,496[e]
Iraq					
Baghdad		540	815	1,250	2,183

Sources: 1946, 1951, 1953: Britannica Book of the Year; 1961,
1966, 1973, 1974, 1981: Americana Annual.

[a]1981 estimate.   [c]1983 estimate.   [e]1976.
[b]1982 estimate.   [d]1978.

around the large cities have undergone significant transformations where both urban and rural activities are functionally and spatially mixed. In discussing the process of Taiwan's urban and periurban development, McGee uses the Indonesian word *kotadesasi:* "joining *kota* (town) and *desa* (village) to make up a word which carries the concept of urban and rural activity occurring in the same geographic territory." In *kotadesasi* regions, overlapping urban and rural activities give rise to a dynamic informal sector beyond the regulatory range of municipal government. As a possible tool in national development, *kotadesasi* activities can be fostered by public investment in transportation infrastructure. But such investment must be carefully localized so that *kotadesasi* development does not occur at the perimeters of the giant cities, but rather adjacent to intermediate and small cities in remote or backward regions. In this way several important development objectives can be achieved—including the creation of a balanced national system of urban places, a reduction in migration to the largest cities, and a more efficient use of public revenue in stimulating economic activity.

Regional and Metropolitan Effects of Urbanization

Urban growth has led to the appearance of a number of problems associated with high levels of population concentration. One of the problems is urban pollution, which results largely from too many automobiles. In Part III, Karan and Chao's study of Taipei's pollution (Chapter 7) uses the notion of environmental behavior as a conceptual guide that adds a new dimension to our understanding of urban Taiwan. Comparing these perceptions with similar views held by citizens of Calcutta, the authors conclude that perceptions of environmental problems are largely culture-bound. Thus we need to know more about how decision-makers perceive urban problems and how decisions are made. The policy implications of this type of research are evident.

In the neighboring mountainous nation of Japan, urban growth over the centuries has resulted in an extremely high level of urban concentration in the small coastal plains. But how does one measure urban intensity and distinguish between the urban and less urban prefectures of Japan? Kornhauser's study (Chapter 8) is devoted to this issue and provides a convenient means for urbanists to understand the patterns of spatial variation of Japan's urbanization.

In India, excessive urban concentration has prompted some planners to undertake planned population dispersal, a topic analyzed by Bannerjee-Guha using New Bombay as an example (Chapter 9). New Bombay was envisaged by its planners as a countermagnet to Bombay, and the processes of land acquisition and physical and socioeconomic planning, as well as their problems, are all detailed in the study. Since the first groups of people arrived in 1973, the new town has attracted numerous high and middle-income families. The low-income groups have been excluded because of the high cost of housing. In general, however, New Bombay can be considered an example of population dispersal through new town development for nations that wish to consider this approach as a means to alleviate urban congestion.

Case Studies in Urban Development

In Part IV, several case studies are presented to illustrate the varied nature of Asian urban development. Each study addresses an important topic in a different nation, and the findings may have relevance elsewhere. In Chapter 10, Wood's analysis of the relationship between resource exploitation and urban development calls our attention to the importance of resource management in urban growth. The development of timber and oil in the province of East Kalimantan, Indonesia, the arrival of multinational corporations, and the growing presence of the national government in the timber and oil cities of Samarinda and Balikpapan have brought major changes to the cities. Wood argues that the future of resource frontier cities is more dependent upon government policies aimed at resource management and marketing than it is on policies aimed directly at urban and regional development.

Several nations have had long histories of urban development. Beijing (Peking), the capital of the People's Republic of China, is unquestionably one of the best known and oldest capitals. Since the Communist revolution in 1949, the city has gone through dramatic changes due partly to ideological imperatives and partly to population growth. In the process of change, the tension between preserving tradition and facilitating city growth has always been strong. The city's magnificent historic walls have been leveled to make room for traffic flow, for example, and numerous attractive but space-consuming one-story traditional courtyard houses have been replaced by multistory apartment buildings. These and many other changes are chronicled in Chapter 11 by Zhang, an urban planner in Beijing.

Rural-to-urban migration has been the chief mechanism promoting the growth of large cities in Asia and elsewhere. Yadav's study of migration to Delhi in Chapter 12 is comprehensive—covering such topics as the demographic characteristics of the migrants, their motivation and decision-making process of migration, the spatial patterns of migration, adjustment to city life, and strategies for dealing with the urban problems associated with migration. He argues for the adoption of an urban policy that would facilitate rural development and encourage decentralized urbanization. Following a different line of investigation in Chapter 13, Dutt, Monroe, and Irani discuss patterns of urbanization in India and show how they correlate with occupational and social variables as revealed in census data.

Although many cities in Asia have experienced morphological transformations in the twentieth century, other cities have retained features of the preindustrial city model identified by the sociologist Gideon Sjoberg.[6] Since the publication of *The Preindustrial City* in 1960, the model has been confirmed and criticized by numerous scholars. Tiwari's study of Jaisalmer, India, in Chapter 14 adds to the volume of literature supporting the validity of Sjoberg's model. He does so not only by examining the city's internal structure, but also by going beyond the city to trace the historic forces that have shaped Indian cities.

In China, dramatic changes have taken place in the internal economic structure of the cities since 1949. One major change is that many of the large cities have become primarily industrial centers. Pannell's study (Chapter 15) demonstrates that industrial employment in China's fifty largest cities ranged between 35 and 69 percent in 1984, most of them with above 50 percent. Retail and catering employment was the next most important category, accounting for between 6 and 17 percent of total city employment. No identifiable pattern was found between city size and specific employment share either in industrial or retail activities, but a modest positive relationship existed between city size and industrial output per worker. It seems clear that China's earlier policy of transforming "consumer cities" into "producer cities" has yielded marked results. However, studies are needed to show how this transformation has affected the supply of essential goods for the nation's economy and to reveal how urban industrial development has influenced the quality of life of the Chinese population in general.

Issues and Policies for Urban Development

The lack of a coherent national urbanization policy in most Asian countries is one of the factors contributing to Asia's current urban problems. This policy failure is due to shortcomings associated with an even broader issue: the lack of a national development policy. Urban development and rural development are two sides of the same coin. Each must be viewed as parts of the whole. Economic deprivation in the countryside is the principal reason for continuing high levels of rural-to-urban migration. In an earlier work, Norton Ginsburg called attention

to concentration of national investment in urban areas with the consequence that per capita purchasing power is much greater there than in
the surrounding countryside.[7] Such imbalances represent one of the
most important conditions of urbanization in Asia.

Even though opportunities are greater in urban areas, the ability of
the cities to accommodate new migrants is limited. Migration streams
overpower the capacity of urban authorities to provide services and
facilities, especially housing accommodation. Vast areas of squatter settlements and unmanageable slums spring up in a virtually spontaneous
fashion both within cities on every available piece of unused land and
around the perimeter of cities, pushing it outward into the surrounding
countryside. These peripheral slums have become one of the most characteristic features of the larger Asian cities.

Lack of national urbanization policies in most Asian countries gives
rise to excessive concentration of wealth, and this concentration fosters
continuing growth in the very largest cities. In smaller countries such as
Thailand, Taiwan, and South Korea, the capital city comes to dominate
the entire nation to such an extent that the development of complementary urban centers is effectively stifled. Thailand is the extreme example
of this situation. Larger nations, such as India or China, have not one
but several large cities which function in much the same way for their
vast regions. India's four largest cities, for example, have continued to
grow at the expense of intermediate-sized cities—thus making it difficult to create a functioning and rational urban hierarchy. Ginsburg cites
several causes for the growing dominance of the primate city at the
expense of balanced national and regional development. These great
cities, especially in the small nations, "combine the functions of
national capital, commercial metropole, chief port," and cultural center
for the nation.[8]

Failure to establish a national urbanization policy does not imply,
however, that urban planning is totally lacking in Asian cities. Quite the
reverse. Some cities were established as more or less planned entities.
Sealey has discussed elsewhere the history of the planned city form in
India.[9] Most planned cities function as capitals of a state or nation,
reflecting quite accurately the strong connection between political
administration and planning. Other well-known Asian examples of
planned capital cities include Islamabad, Quezon City, Sri Jayawar-
dhanapura, and Beijing.

In other large cities, great sectors have been subjected to close planning control. But by and large these planning efforts have been too little
and too late. Thus planners are constantly being called upon to remedy
problems grown to such magnitude that only expensive programs will

now correct or counteract them. Even in the planned cities, the planners' scenario has not usually been followed exactly. Unplanned squatter settlements have become an essential feature of most planned cities
—illustrating vividly the inadequacy of these centers to solve modern
urban problems. It is usually not the planners' concept which is at fault,
but rather the scale of development and resource commitment which
fails to keep pace with demand and population growth.

Most Asian nations are aware of the problems associated with unbalanced and extremely rapid growth of their capitals. In some instances,
they have attempted to meet the problem by constructing a new capital
city to drain off administrative activities from the older metropolis. In
other cases, the capital is the subject of strenuous efforts to rationalize
its growth and development—especially by extending the city's effective
control over its surroundings. In his comprehensive survey of policies
for controlling the growth of Asian metropolises, especially Tokyo,
Shanghai, and Seoul, Yeung compares the strategies employed by Asian
planners in terms of physical control, regional planning, and policy
measures (Chapter 16). Although none of the strategies have been
entirely successful, they have fulfilled at least in part the objectives of
restraining urban sprawl or population decentralization. Yeung's review makes it clear that the degree of success in implementing the strategies depends heavily on sound coordination among the implementing
agencies, the availability of funds, and the inclusion of areas surrounding the cities for metropolitan planning.

The role of urban planners in shaping a city's landscape and the quality of life of its residents can be seen clearly in Hong Kong, a city with
more than five million people and the last British colony in Asia. As
Taylor points out in Chapter 17, planners in Hong Kong have made
several significant contributions that have clearly enhanced the quality
of life of the city's residents. The most important accomplishment has
been the construction of subsidized public housing for nearly half of the
population, followed by wise comprehensive land use planning. Other
accomplishments include a well-planned intra-urban transportation
system that has enabled the heavy traffic to flow smoothly and a successful open-space conservation program that has set aside 40 percent of
Hong Kong's land area as permanent parks or green space. On the
other hand, the planners' intervention in Hong Kong development has
fallen short of expectations in several areas, including renewal of older
residential districts, environmental pollution control, new town development, historic preservation, removing incompatible land uses, and
regional planning. Whether the planners in Hong Kong can continue to
make progress and effectively deal with its problems in the future will

depend much on what will happen to the territory's political infrastructure after the colony is returned to China in 1997 and ruled as a special administrative area of China.

One of the major ills of urban growth in Asia and other parts of the developing world is the persistence of squatter settlements that are occupied, often illegally, by migrants in and around the major cities. These settlements have been viewed either as an urban problem characterized by ugly and unsanitary housing development where crime, poverty, and political radicalism abound or as a solution to the complex problems of urban housing shortage and unemployment. Lall's study of such settlements in Chandigarh, India, examines the socioeconomic background and migration behavior of the settlers, their adjustments to new life in the city, their economic activities, and their efforts to improve their living conditions (Chapter 18). He suggests that "migrant colonies" with basic services and amenities be provided to migrants. In view of the fact that the squatter settlements have long existed in Asian cities and their presence strongly affects the visual perception of the urban landscape, it is surprising that they have not been examined more closely by scholars and planners in terms of their functional role in the cities and their long-term future. They seem to have come into existence and thrive largely as a result of the benign neglect of the decision-makers.

One of the issues associated with rapid urbanization is the dramatic escalation of urban land prices, especially in the large cities of the newly industrialized nations such as South Korea and Taiwan. Cho and Kim's report on South Korea (Chapter 19) is a rare contribution to the scant literature on urban land speculation and land price escalation. The authors see land speculation and the resultant windfall profiteering as basically undesirable because the phenomena accentuate unequal income distribution and contribute to a higher cost of living in general. Their study examines land tax policy and practice in South Korea as well as other nations and concludes that South Korea's land tax system has failed to achieve the desired goals due to low tax rates, unrealistic assessment, tax loopholes, and weak tax administration. It would be highly interesting to discover the spatial patterns of urban land prices in Asian cities, a topic of research that has rarely been touched. Particularly intriguing is the innovative approach of the "comprehensive progressive property tax," which levies higher tax rates on large landholdings. In any event, policies providing incentives for development in designated growth-stimulus areas, together with disincentives for present high-growth areas, must take into account the profit expectations of the private and informal sectors of the economy. Government fiscal policy is most effective when it redirects the growth potential of the private firm from areas deemed inappropriate from a national development perspective to areas deemed appropriate for the reasons discussed above. Public policy is seldom successful when it attempts to blunt the growth potential of the private sector or to capture too large a proportion of profits which it may generate.

New areas of research need to be opened from time to time if the study of Asian urbanization is to maintain its vitality. We are fortunate to have the study by Fuchs and Pernia (Chapter 20), who break new ground in research by looking at Japanese investment in Asian cities and their peripheral areas in terms of spatial patterns of investment, industry characteristics, and the implications for urban and regional policies. Japanese investments are highly concentrated in the metropolitan or core regions in some nations but are more diffused in others. The patterns of investment appear to have followed existing patterns of spatial development and industry characteristics. It would be interesting also to study the spatial patterns of investment by multinational corporations in Asian metropolitan regions—an area of inquiry that has already resulted in numerous publications by geographers, economists, and political scientists for other parts of the world.

Urbanization and National Development Policy

The lack of a coherent national development policy—and its policy subset concerning urbanization—is the primary problem facing most Asian countries. Many factors account for this failure, but paramount among them are rapid population growth, inadequate financial resources available to government, and the very structure of government itself. Urban population growth creates vast (and thus far unattainable) requirements for housing and public services—especially water supply, sanitation, and public health. Public planning and the resources of public finance are incapable of developing the necessary infrastructure to accommodate migrants in the cities. Government structure in most Asian nations is highly centralized—which contributes to slow and cumbersome responses by public agencies to steadily worsening problems in the cities, as well as in the countryside.

What are the elements of a national development policy? It is difficult to address such a major issue in this brief space, but a number of components are of such paramount importance that they cannot be ignored. Population control is the single most important element. Population growth must be arrested if economic growth is to be translated into increasing per capita income. Migration streams into urban areas are fueled primarily by a rapidly expanding rural population. Thus population control measures must be fostered in rural areas.

Furthermore, population control measures must be accompanied by agricultural-based, labor-intensive industry in the countryside in order to provide attractive economic conditions which will encourage people to remain in rural areas. A shift in national investment priorities from the present concentration in selected urban areas to a more balanced rural–urban investment pattern is an important step in this process.

Finally, public policy must be used to encourage self-help efforts in housing and public infrastructure development in order to improve physical conditions in the urban centers. Squatter areas must not be viewed entirely as slums to be eventually cleared, but rather as areas which can undergo spontaneous and self-initiated improvement. In the same way that public policy and public investment can be used to stimulate the growth of intermediate and small cities as well as lagging regions, so too can they serve to stimulate grassroots housing and public infrastructure improvements in large cities.

Conclusion

Asia's urban future can be better than its present if well-thought-out and carefully applied measures are undertaken now. If they are not, then we can expect increasing urban social unrest and decreasing standards of human physical conditions. There is a potential for economic and social conflict in Asia's cities if the present living standards and maldistribution of income persist. The traditional social controls that migrants bring with them from the countryside will eventually erode with lengthening tenure in the city, where the stark reality of deprivation coexists with the conspicuous consumption of urban elites. Unchecked and unbalanced, urbanization will result in a further degradation of the physical and social environment for urban life. The alternatives are very clear, and the selection of the appropriate option must be encouraged.

The condition of urban life in Asian cities is not all bleak, however. Economic growth is, in some cases, beginning to transform the lives of many urban dwellers. This is especially true in the high-growth nations of East and Southeast Asia. But many problems of urban and regional development remain even in areas of rapid economic growth. Even in the countries of South Asia, living standards are inching upward, but rapid progress is hindered by population growth.

Although Asian nations differ in their level of economic development, population growth, resource endowment, and political ideology, all are faced with the potentially dangerous problem of excessive urban growth without a high level of national and urban economic development. It is our hope that the facts and ideas presented in this volume will stimulate scholarly research on Asian cities. Understanding a problem is the first step toward finding a solution.

NOTES

1. Phillip M. Hauser and Robert W. Gardner, "Urban Future: Trends and Prospects," in Phillip Hauser and others (eds.), *Population and the Urban Future* (Albany: State University of New York Press, 1982), pp. 1–58.
2. Kamala Markandaya, *A Handful of Rice* (Greenwich, Conn.: Fawcett Publications, 1966).
3. See also Janet P. Gemmill, "The City as Jungle in the Indo-English Novel," in Allen G. Noble and Ashok K. Dutt (eds.), *India: Cultural Patterns and Processes* (Boulder, Colo.: Westview Press, 1982).
4. Hauser and Gardner, "Urban Future."
5. Ibid.
6. Gideon Sjoberg, *The Preindustrial City* (New York: Free Press, 1960).
7. N. Ginsburg, "Reflections on Primacy," paper given at the First International Conference on Asian Urbanization, Akron, Ohio, April 1985.
8. Ibid.
9. Neil Sealey, *Planned Cities of India* (London: School of Oriental and African Studies, University of London, 1982).

2. An Overview of the Literature

NORTON GINSBURG

THIRTY years ago the geographical literature—and indeed the general scholarly planning and social science literature—on urbanization in Asia was slim. To be sure, there were a handful of studies by such figures as E. H. G. Dobby, Shannon McCune, Rhoads Murphey, Joseph Spencer, and myself dealing with specific cities in Asia. There also were several papers of a more systematic nature by Glenn Trewartha, Oskar Spate, Robert B. Hall, Rhoads Murphey, and later John Brush, but they were exceptional. It was over thirty years ago, however, that Donald Fryer's paper on "the million cities" in Southeast Asia appeared in *Economic Geography;* and the next year I published a paper on essentially the same subject in the *American Journal of Sociology* called "The Great City in Southeast Asia." These marked some of the origins of what has become a massive inquiry into comparative urbanization in Asia—an inquiry which continues to this day and is well exemplified by the work of the participants in this conference.

It was shortly thereafter, in 1958, that the Social Science Research Council established its Committee on Urbanization, whose report appeared several years later as *The Study of Urbanization,* edited by Philip Hauser and Leo Schnore. Three chapters, out of the total of fourteen, in that volume were contributed by geographers—by Harold Mayer, Brian Berry, and myself. I would like to believe that this publication, and the extensive discussions that preceded and followed it, gave geographers an opportunity to present their wares in competition with scholars in the other social sciences and led to broadened recognition of the potential contributions of geography to the comparative study of cities.

My paper in that volume dealt with the geographical contributions to the study of cities in "Non-Western Areas." I recall that in reviewing the literature, it was the work on Asian cities that was even then becoming conspicuous by its volume and quality, although, in a sense, the work had just begun. In addition to the names just mentioned, I referred to work on Indian cities by V. L. S. Prakasa Rao, R. L.

Singh, and N. R. Kar among others, and I noted that the Indian urban research output was admirably reviewed by Bert Hoselitz in a still valuable piece in the 1959 *Annals of the AAG* (Association of American Geographers): "The Cities of India and Their Problems."

In the case of Japan, the name of Shinzo Kiuchi loomed large among Japanese geographers, but Douglas Eyre and David Kornhauser had already made important contributions. It is worth mentioning, too, that three Japanese geographers—Hattori, Kagaya, and Inanaga—had performed the first factor analysis of subregionalization in their study of a major metropolitan area, "The Regional Structure of Tokyo's Environs," published in the 1960 *Geographical Review of Japan*. Japanese geographers had been applying central-place theoretical notions to the distribution and functions of Japanese cities in the late 1950s. China's cities too were coming under the scrutiny of such scholars as Sen-dou Chang. The literature on Southeast Asia was, as yet, comparatively sparse, though beginning to appear under the "imprimatur" of Edward Ullman, Hamzah Sendut, Joseph Spencer, and W. A. Withington.

The 1960s, however, saw an enormous proliferation of interest in and publication about urbanization in Asia, not exclusively or even primarily by geographers, but they played an especially conspicuous role in these developments. In 1967, for example, the Pacific Conference on Urban Growth was held in Honolulu, cosponsored by the East-West Center, the Agency for International Development, and the Department of Housing and Urban Development, a conference in which geographers played an important part both in planning and in contributing papers. At that meeting were the ministerial representatives of some sixteen countries in the Pacific region, chiefly from Asian countries. It is of somewhat more than historical interest that it was agreed at the conference, after much debate, that urbanization and great cities were the "engines of growth" in developing countries, including, parenthetically, Japan. Governments were enjoined to focus attention on them and to facilitate their functional roles as the keys to national development and prosperity.

Two years later another meeting was held in Hong Kong, with Denis Dwyer of the University of Hong Kong as host, under the title "The City as a Center of Change in Asia." Again geographers were conspicuous participants and authors of papers. The specific results of that conference were less highly focused than those of the Pacific Conference on Urban Growth, but it was agreed that, despite their problems, cities and city systems were here to stay and needed intensive research into their natures and evolutionary trajectories. It also was agreed that the relationships between urbanization and development were positive and amenable to systematic inquiry.

By this time, the output of research materials on Asian urbanization had greatly increased and had in fact become a veritable flood. This output continued through the 1970s and well into the 1980s. It would be impossible to list the names of all the major contributors to this literature, but it would be inappropriate not to mention the contributions of Terry McGee and his colleagues who, through books, monographs, and articles in a variety of learned journals, put the Asian city on the map, so to speak, and reinforced studies of it in the context of ongoing research on urbanization wherever it might take place. Nor should the distinctive and seminal research of Paul Wheatley on the origins of cities in China, Japan, and Southeast Asia be overlooked, peripheral though these topics might be to the main foci of this conference.

In September 1981, the Fourth Pacific Science InterCongress took place in Singapore and was devoted to the theme "Pacific Basin Cities in the Eighties." Again geographers were extremely well represented, and Yue-man Yeung and I attempted to distill out of all the multidisciplinary papers some of the general findings at the conference and to outline a preliminary research agenda for the future. But before drawing upon our mini-papers prepared for the concluding session of the congress, it might be well to survey what seems to have been accomplished during the twenty years or so preceding it.

A great deal had been learned, of course, about many individual cities in Asia. Not all the studies of them had been as well rounded as, for example, Pannell's study of T'ai-chung in Taiwan, but they have been a welcome addition to our expanding store of knowledge about the physical characteristics and functions of Asian cities in general. We also learned that cities, and urban systems as well, have a distinctive national and regional character. The city is, after all, an artifact of society and it inevitably expresses to a large degree the values of the culture it represents. At the same time, we have come to see in a more discriminating way than in the past how percepts developed within a Western context can be applied to Asian cities. Nonetheless, even in Asia the differences in urban types and systems from country to country, despite great similarities, are striking.

All of us became convinced also of the significance of Europe's expansion into Asia, even in those countries with long-standing and deep urban traditions as in China, Japan, and to a degree India. At the same time, we came to realize that the "colonial city," and its modified forms in those countries, has been transmogrified into something distinctive, national, country-specific, and symbolic of the need, not only in recently independent Asian countries but also in those long independent, for urban symbols of the evolving nation-state and the nationalism that accompanies it.

The remarkable relationship of cities in Asia to the ecumenes of their respective countries also was shown to be remarkable. Unlike much of

Latin America and Black Africa, Asian cities tend to be already associated with the main regions of agricultural production and population in most countries, despite their colonial past and in a few instances (as in Burma) because of it. This association has deep implications for the assessment or reassessment of the significance of nationally or regionally primate cities, which have had a particularly bad press now for years among geographers and nongeographers alike.

In the assessment of such phenomena as primacy, moreover, and the study of urban settlement systems, the technological imperative of Jacques Ellul in the form of changing transportation and communication technologies appeared to be transforming what had been cellular socioeconomic and political systems into more highly integrated ones. Even so, increasingly it had become clear that such assessments of urban, and particularly metropolitan, functions and their regionalization required extranational perspectives. More than ever before—even more than during the height of the colonial period and despite the exception of Burma—the cities of Asia have become integrated into broad regional and global systems far beyond the national.

Moreover, we learned much about the impact of ethnicity and migration upon the population characteristics and spatial structures of cities. Even more, we have gained an impressive understanding of the dualism between formal and informal economic sectors in cities, to an extent barely conceived of thirty years ago or even twenty. This expanded fund of knowledge has forced greater attention upon rural–urban linkages and upon the prospects for town and city development at levels in the hierarchy well below that of the metropoles in each country. In turn, we have become much more sensitive to the pressures which bear upon the location of industry in developing countries everywhere. And this expanded knowledge has stimulated critical appraisal of the utility of both Weberian and central-place concepts concerning the geographical patterning of industrial activity in an increasingly integrated world system of both demand and production. Other knowledge gains have related to housing—one of the great continuing problems of Asian cities —and to the provision of other services essential to the systems maintenance of both larger and smaller cities.

Finally, at least for this brief review, we have become aware of the increasing importance of Asian cities themselves in the decision making concerning national and regional development. And as a concomitant, we have come to realize the importance of understanding the political economies of cities in a part of the world moving inexorably toward greater concentrations of population in cities, particularly the larger ones.

Even as I run through this listing of knowledge we have acquired, I recognize that it constitutes a future research agenda as well. All of us need to know more about the relationships among components of national and regional urban hierarchies; about the role of the informal sector in acculturating urban newcomers and providing employment for those unable to enter the formal sector whether in manufacturing or in services; about how better housing can be provided for the burgeoning populations of the larger cities; about the desirability of spreading the benefits of economic growth more fairly so that the poor, who might always be with us, will not, at least, become more gravely disadvantaged; about the impact of new technologies on urban–rural integration and the production of wealth and the distribution of its benefits both socially and geographically.

These are to a considerable degree, to be sure, policy issues. As such, they underscore an additional understanding which I have thus far neglected—that governments in Asian countries without exception, even Japan, play dominant roles in determining how investment will be allocated among cities and rural areas on the one hand and among urban entities on the other. Urban development is to a striking degree a politically inspired and directed process, even in Japan, let alone China and Malaysia, to cite three important cases. This means that urbanization processes and urban policies, whether formally articulated or not, must be examined in tandem, and this in turn requires an understanding of political processes and structure which may lie beyond the immediate ken of geographers and planners. But then it has never been claimed that the study of urbanization can be other than a multidisciplinary enterprise requiring contributions from all the social sciences, not only those like geography and sociology which have laid claim to major responsibility in the past.

To these broad issues must be added some about which we know comparatively little—such as food for the cities, the impact of international migration on urban development, the ability of cities to raise revenues for their maintenance and growth, the automobile's effect on urban patterns and structures (especially in countries where car ownership is beyond the means of most urban dwellers), and, however indirectly, the effects of rising incomes for many in rural areas where agricultural production has improved.

All of these issues continue to confront us. Even the most immediate and most practical problems have major theoretical implications. Indeed, the research agenda constitutes a charge so formidable that even the most dedicated scholar might hesitate to accept it. And yet the accomplishments of the past thirty years by this community of scholars have been so remarkable that we can accept so imposing a research agenda with optimism and even anticipation.

PART II: NATIONAL TRENDS AND PROCESSES

3. Urbanization in India: Retrospect and Prospect

V. NATH

WHILE significant progress has been made in the post-Independence period in devising a strategy of rural economic development, leading to brisk economic growth over several parts of rural India, no suitable strategy has evolved for the management of urban growth. The Green Revolution of the 1960s has resulted in growth rates averaging 5 or 6 percent a year for almost two decades in Punjab and Haryana and in some districts of Uttar Pradesh and Rajasthan where wheat output has increased rapidly. Increasing agricultural output has been accompanied, particularly in Punjab and Haryana, by growth of small-scale industries and by extensive urbanization along the principal arteries of communication. Similar developments are taking place, although much less advanced, in several other areas.

In urban areas, however, the record of the past thirty to thirty-five years has been one of neglect and inadequate allocation of the resources of public finance and good management required for efficient urban administration and for the expansion of housing and essential services for the rapidly growing urban population. Halfhearted attempts to slow down growth of the large cities, based on such strategies as industrial dispersal to underdeveloped regions, have proved to be ineffective in India, as they have in most other developing countries. The results have been threefold: increasing unemployment and underemployment in the cities and very low productivity in their informal sectors, which have had to absorb most of the in-migrants; acute housing shortages and increasing pressures on urban services, which have led, in turn, to increasing congestion and the proliferation of slums; and progressive deterioration of the physical environment.

Developing suitable strategies for management of rapid urban growth constitutes a major challenge for development planners and policymakers. The strategies must satisfy two essential conditions. First, they must meet the needs for gainful employment, housing, and

essential services of the rapidly increasing urban population at acceptable economic and social costs. Second, they must ensure that urban
growth contributes to national and regional economic growth, particularly through growth-inducing urban–rural interactions. The strategies
will require advances in several directions. Above all, they call for a
spatial pattern of urbanization that is better adapted to the economic
and social conditions of India than the one which has been allowed to
develop during the last several decades; low-cost technologies for construction and for delivery of urban services; and suitable political and
administrative structures for management of large urban systems.

Growth of the Urban Population

Three projections of growth of total population and urban population
for the period 1981–2001, contained respectively in the *World Development Report 1984,* the seventh Five-Year Plan (1986–1990), and in a
recent article by R. Mohan, are presented in Table 3.1. They are close
enough to indicate convergence of views on two major points: progressive reduction in the growth rate of the total population because of
declining fertility and continued rapid increase in the urban population,
due both to natural increase of the resident urban population and rural-
to-urban migration.

The *World Development Report 1984* (WDR) has, on the assumption of
a high rate of rural-to-urban migration, projected a growth rate of the
urban population averaging 4.2 percent a year during the 1980–2000
period.[1] The migration would be rapid enough to bring down the rate of
growth of the rural population by as much as 0.8 percent below the rate
of natural increase of the total population (Table 3.1). The rates of
growth of the urban population in the other two projections are significantly lower. The seventh Five-Year Plan's projection assumes a rate
similar to the average rate of 3.5 percent experienced during the 1961–
1981 period. Mohan, however, projects a sharp slowdown of the urban
growth rate during the 1990s with a similar decline in the growth rate of
the total population.[2]

Under all three projections, the total urban population by the end of
the century would be twice (or more) the 1981 figure of 160 million and
would constitute around one-third of the total population. The WDR's
figures of a total urban population of 353 million and an urban/total
population ratio of 3.5 percent by the year 2000 are the highest.

Both the WDR and the Seventh Plan also assume rapid growth of
gross domestic product (GDP) per capita. The WDR projections are
based on the World Bank's global model under which growth of the
economies of less-developed countries (LDCs) during the decade 1985–

Table 3.1. Projection of Total Population of India (in millions)

	World Development Report		Seventh Five-Year Plan			Mohan		
	1980	2000	1981	1991	2001	1981	1991	2001
Total population	685	994	685	837	986	697	850-856	993-1,018
Average growth rate (%)		1.9		2.0		1.65	2.2[a]	
Urban population	160	353	160	230	326	164	234-236	315-320
Average growth rate (%)		4.2		3.7	3.5		3.8	3.1
Urban population/ total population (%)	23.3	35.5	23.3	27.5	33.1	23.5	27.3-27.5	31.0-31.5
Growth rate of GDP per capita								
High-case Scenario:		3.2[b]	3.2[c]	3.35	—	n.a.		—
Low-case Scenario:		2.5[b]						

Sources: World Development Report 1984, app. table 19, pp. 254-255, and text table 4.3, p. 67; Seventh Five-Year Plan 1986-1990, table 2.1, pp. 11-12; R. Mohan, "Urbanization in India's Future," Population and Development Review 2(4) (December 1985), table 7, p. 630, and table 8, p. 631. Total population is projected under three variables of decline in fertility while urban population is projected under two variants; methodology of the projection is explained on pp. 642-643.

[a] 2.2 percent during 1981-1986 falling to 1.47-1.68 percent during 1996-2001.

[b] 1985-1995.

[c] 1986-1991.

1995 is projected under two scenarios: a high-case scenario, based on the assumption of relatively favorable conditions for growth of the industrial economies and world trade, and a low-case scenario based on the assumption of relatively unfavorable conditions. The economies of the LDCs would grow significantly faster under the high-case scenario than under the low-case scenario. For India, however, the WDR's projection of growth rate of GDP per capita even under the low-case scenario—2.5 percent a year—is almost twice as high as the average rate of 1.3 percent a year experienced during the 1960–1992 period. (See Table 3.2.) The projection of the Seventh Plan approximates the WDR's high-case scenario rate of 3.2 percent a year. The Seventh Plan projects an average growth rate of 5.0 percent a year for total GDP during the

Table 3.2.   Growth Rates of GDP Per Capita in India and Low-Income
             Developing Countries: 1960-1995

	Average Annual Growth Rates of GDP Per Capita (%)				
				1985-1995 (Projected)	
				Low-Case	High-Case
Countries	1960-1973	1973-1979	1980-1985	Scenario	Scenario
Low-income developing countries	3.0	2.9	3.2	2.7	3.4
Low income					
Asia[a]	3.4	3.3	3.7	3.0	3.7
Africa	1.0	-1.0	-1.6	2.5	3.2[c]
India		1.3[b]			

Source: World Development Report 1984, text table 3.2, p. 36, and
app. table 1, p. 218-219.

[a]Includes China, Indonesia, and all the countries of South Asia
(Afghanistan, Bangladesh, Bhutan, Burma, India, Nepal, Pakistan,
and Sri Lanka).

[b]1960-1982.

[c]Assuming India's annual growth rate to be 0.5 percent lower than that
for low-income Asia, as under the low-case scenario.

1986–2000 period—about 50 percent higher than the rate, averaging
3.5 percent, experienced during 1960–1982. The projections of both the
WDR and the Seventh Plan thus assume a radical change in the performance of the Indian economy during the 1985–1995 period from that
during 1960–1982. The growth rate projected under the low-case scenario is almost double the rate actually achieved during the 1960–1982
period.[3]

The performance of the Indian economy during the past five years
has been relatively good. Average economic growth for 1980–1985 is
estimated at around 5.4 percent a year, which translates into a growth
rate of GDP per capita of well over 3 percent a year.[4] But the experience
of five years is simply too short to provide an adequate basis for projection because the Indian economy is still influenced greatly by the mon-
soons and other factors. The second critical factor will be experience
with the economic liberalization policies which have been followed since
the late 1970s but which have been given much greater emphasis by the
new government.

By 1981, more than 60 percent of the urban population was living in
cities with populations of 100,000 or more—a proportion that has gone
up progressively from 38 percent in 1951 (Table 3.3). On the other

Table 3.3.   Distribution of India's Urban Population
             by Size of Urban Places: 1951-1981

Population	Percentage of Urban Population in Urban Places			
	1951	1961	1971	1981
1 million and above	n.a.	22.5	25.1	26.3
500,000-1 million	n.a.	3.1	6.2	13.4
100,000-500,000	n.a.	18.1	17.6	20.7
50,000-100,000	12.2	12.1	13.5	11.6
20,000- 50,000	17.8	20.0	18.3	14.4
Below 20,000	31.9	23.4	19.5	13.6

Source: Population censuses of India: 1951-1981.

hand, the proportion of urban population living in the smallest urban places (population below 20,000) dropped progressively from 32 percent in 1951 to 13.6 percent in 1981. Of the urban population, by 1981 as much as two-thirds were living in the larger cities with population 500,000 or more. The number of such cities went up rapidly from eleven in 1961 to forty-two in 1981.

Data on growth of population during 1961–1981 in urban places of different size classes (Table 3.4) indicate more rapid growth rates for the cities, particularly the larger cities, than for the smaller urban places. The fastest growth rates were recorded by the cities with populations of 500,000 or more, excluding, however, the four metropolitan cities of Calcutta, Bombay, Madras, and Delhi. These cities registered average growth rates of 3.3 percent a year during both decades, lower than the growth rates recorded by most other cities. The lowest growth rates were recorded by the small urban places with populations below 50,000 and especially those with populations below 20,000. The slow growth of the smallest urban places appears to have been due in part to a definitional change—adoption in the 1961 Census of more restrictive criteria for designating a place as urban.[5]

Three factors contributed to rapid growth of the larger urban places: natural increase of the urban population; in-migration from villages or smaller urban places; and expansion of urban boundaries to include adjacent villages and small towns. The third factor appears to have been particularly important in cities with populations of 500,000 or more. The increase in the number of such cities contributed half of the population increase recorded during this period: 20.8 million out of 41.2 million.

Rapid increase in the population of cities, especially the larger cities with populations of 500,000 or more, may be expected to continue. Extrapolation to the year 2000 of the average growth rate of 5.5 percent recorded by the cities during 1961–1981 would take their total popula-

Table 3.4.   Growth Rates of India's Urban Places of Different
             Size Classes: 1961-1981

Urban Places	1961 Population (millions)	Annual Growth Rate (%)	1971 Population (millions)	Annual Growth Rate (%)	1981 Population (millions)
Four metropolitan cities (Bombay, Calcutta, Madras, Delhi)	14.2	3.3	19.8	3.3	27.5
Other cities with population of					
1 million or more	3.5	8.1	7.6	6.0	13.6
500,000-1,000,000	3.9	5.6	6.8	12.0	20.9
100,000-500,000	14.3	2.9	19.6	5.3	32.3
All cities	35.1	4.3	53.4	5.9	94.3
Towns with population of					
50,000-100,000	9.5	4.5	14.7	2.2	18.2
20,000-50,000	15.7	2.4	19.9	1.2	22.4
Below 20,000	18.5	1.3	21.1	0.1	21.3
Total urban population	78.9	3.7	109.1	3.7	156.2
Cities with population of 500,000 or more	20.8 (11)[a]	5.1	34.2 (19)[a]	6.1	61.0 (42)[a]
Population of the 11 cities with populations of 500,000 or more in 1961	20.8	3.1	28.3	3.8	41.1

Source: Population censuses of India: 1951-1981.

[a]Number of cities.

tion to 178 million—more than half the projected total urban population of 353 million.

The Spatial Pattern of Urbanization

During the early 1960s, much discussion took place about the most
appropriate spatial pattern of urbanization for India. The impetus for

the discussion came from industrial planners and economists who were concerned with location of industries and from urban planners who were preparing urban development plans. Industrialization was seen as the key element in urbanization despite mounting evidence that the needs of modern industry for labor were relatively limited—far less than they had been in the nineteenth century when Europe and North America were undergoing industrialization—and that the rate of postwar urbanization in India and most other developing countries was far greater than that required to meet the demands of modern industry.

The consensus was in favor of dispersed development of industries, which would contribute to dispersed urbanization. Several strands of thought converged to form this consensus. First was the realization that urbanization, with a focus on rapid growth of the large metropolitan cities, would involve high costs of expansion. These costs would be much lower, however, in small urban places and on the outskirts of large cities, and there would also be greater scope for use of simple technology and cheap local materials. Self-help by the beneficiaries could reduce the costs further. The data then available indicated that the unit costs of providing housing in the central areas of Bombay and Calcutta were two to three times higher than in small towns.[6] Transportation costs were also much lower with dispersed urbanization because mass transport facilities could be avoided; workers could travel the short distance to their workplace by bicycle or on foot.[7]

The second strand of thought was promotion of small-scale and agro-based industries. The employment potential of such industries was much larger than that of large, capital-intensive industries. Furthermore, growth of small and agro-based industries in medium-sized or small towns would promote growth of entrepreneurship and diffusion of industrial skills. While the relationship between dispersed development of small-scale and agro-based industries and expansion of employment and development of agriculture was clearly seen, the perception of a wider relationship between dispersed urbanization and rural development was not common. Few could envision small towns, such as market centers, serving as foci of economic growth in microregions through their various functions—marketing and processing agricultural produce, distributing consumer goods and agricultural inputs, servicing and repairing implements, and manufacturing a limited range of consumer goods for the microregional market. One reason for lack of interest in the latter relationship was dominance, especially in the states of rural-based, tradition-oriented political leaders who did not see the links between rural and urban development. They viewed towns and villages primarily as competitors for scarce resources of finance and manpower and were concerned with obtaining the maximum resources for the villages, which they believed had long been neglected.

A third consideration was the need to accelerate development of backward regions. The political leaders of these regions first concentrated their efforts on securing large, centrally financed resource development or industrial projects: irrigation and hydroelectric projects in the early 1950s and public-sector industrial projects in the late 1950s and early 1960s. The projects were seen as the nuclei of regional growth which would through their multiple backward and forward linkages set in motion a process of rapid economic growth in the regions.[8] The location of industries supplying the regional market—or the location of "footloose" industries which, though supplying much larger markets, could be sited within the regions—was regarded as an important component of the programs in the late 1960s.

Official intervention for promoting dispersed industrial development included both incentives and sanctions. From the outset the emphasis was on the former. The principal incentives were providing land and various infrastructure facilities needed by the industrial units (electricity, water, road and railway connections, drainage) quickly and at low cost, providing concessional loans and other fiscal incentives for the entrepreneurs, and providing technical assistance—for project appraisal and selection of equipment, for example, or in certain areas of management. These facilities were provided typically for industries locating in the industrial estates or industrial areas which began to be built by the state governments from the mid-1950s under a program sponsored by the central government. While promoting development of small industries and industrial dispersal remained the professed objectives for industrial estates, their actual locations indicated that the state governments attached at least equal importance to promoting the industrial development of the state. Thus while many industrial estates and areas were built in backward regions, or near medium-sized or small towns, some of the largest and most successful ones were located in the vicinity of large cities, including the state capitals and metropolitan cities like Delhi, Madras, and Bombay. In their eagerness to promote development of industry, the state governments were ready to provide these facilities wherever the prospective industrialists wanted them.

Official interest in the strategies of industrial location and urbanization had waned, however, by the late 1960s because the attention of policymakers and planners had shifted to the urgent task of overcoming serious imbalances in the economy, particularly an acute food shortage and large external payments deficits. Growth of agricultural and cereal output, which had been well ahead of the growth of population in the 1950s, had slowed down in the 1960s—partly because agricultural development had not received under the second and third Five-Year Plans (1956–1966) the attention and the resources it had received under the First Plan (1951–1956). The development strategy of the Second and Third Plans had focused on industrialization, particularly development of basic, heavy industries in the public sector. Widespread and severe drought, during both 1965–1966 and 1966–1967, led to a steep fall in agricultural output, and famines were avoided only by massive imports of cereals, (about 10 million tons in each year). The balance of payments deficits were due partly to the large investment needs of the new industrial units. Furthermore, the returns in terms of increased output from these heavy investments and related infrastructures were being delayed because of the nature of the investments and the serious gestation problems that some of the largest units were facing.

Despite this lack of interest, one element of the strategy of industrial location has remained: encouraging location at the outskirts of cities (including satellite towns of the large metropolitan cities) and in backward regions. Such locations have continued to be encouraged through substantial capital investment by the state governments in developing industrial areas and estates and by the other measures mentioned above. Particularly generous fiscal incentives continue to be given, and the powers of the central and state governments for licensing industries have been used to promote location of industries in the backward regions.

On the other hand, there has been little action to check rapid growth of the large cities despite evidence of increasing deterioration in urban conditions. The inevitability of rapid growth of the cities, including the largest like Bombay and Delhi, has been accepted. Indeed, not only has the growth not been discouraged, but it has at times been encouraged by official actions. Thus, in Bombay, the proposals to concentrate further development on the mainland across the bay from the present city (including the progressive shift of offices of the Maharashtra government to this area) in order to relieve the congestion in the central business district, and to connect the two parts by a number of bridges, have not been implemented. On the contrary, further concentration of population and economic activities in the central area of the city was allowed and even encouraged by permitting construction of high-rise residential and commercial buildings and by the Maharashtra government itself selling land reclaimed from the sea in the Nariman Point area for high-rise construction.

The current policy of economic liberalization gives the private sector much greater latitude in industrial decisions, including location of industries. Licensing of industries is now restricted to large industrial units with projected investments of Rs. 250 million or more. This latitude should favor siting industries near the large cities because such location continues to be the most attractive for all entrepreneurs except those wishing to establish huge industrial units. The reasons for the attractiveness of near-city location range from ease of supervision of the unit by the owners or managers from their homes in the cities to access to capital, skilled labor, and the output of ancillary industries. The wider range and higher quality of infrastructure and social services (from telecommunications to education and health) in or near the cities is itself very attractive, because the range of such services is limited away from the cities and their functional efficiency is low. States like Maharashtra may continue their policy of diverting industries away from the overurbanized Bombay–Poona region to the less developed regions of the state, but the dominant trend among the state governments will be toward further back-pedaling on the industrial location issue and encouraging prospective investors to locate industries almost anywhere they want. Indeed, the state governments' efforts to attract industrial investment in their states are expected to become aggressive in the future, culminating at times in intense competition to attract large industrial units.

Resources for Urban Development

At the heart of India's urban problem are grossly inadequate inputs of finance and management needed for efficient functioning of urban government and for expansion of housing and services to keep pace with the rapidly growing urban population. Provision of adequate finance will not be easy because of the great demand. But steady progress toward reducing the present inadequacy can be made if there is greater perception of the interdependence between urban and rural development. The present shortages of urban housing and the inefficiency of urban services not only cause great hardship to the urban population but also result in enormous losses of output. They act as a major disincentive on productive investment. The latter effect is most apparent in the case of services such as electric power, for prolonged cuts and erratic supplies have become a daily occurrence in most cities.

Despite the consensus among planners in favor of promoting dispersed urbanization, the high-cost alternative of increasing concentration of the urban population in the large cities has been allowed to develop. Little progress has been made with respect to the other policy measures also. Thus the Sixth Plan report mentioned:

> A ceiling on urban land, prescribed under the Urban Land [Ceiling and Regulation] Act 1976, was meant to prevent speculation in land and to

Table 3.5. Percentage of Revenue and Capital Expenditures of the State
            Government Financed Through Transfers from the Central
            Government: 1951-1984

	I	II	III	IV	V	VI
			Five-Year Plan			
Revenue transfers as percentage of revenue expenditures of states	22.4	28.2	33.4	35.1	39.5	41.1
Loan transfers as percentage of capital expenditures of states	71.9	58.7	64.5	63.2	83.1	74.6
Aggregate transfers as percentage of aggregate expenditures of states	37.8	39.8	45.7	47.4	42.1	41.6

Source: K. K. George and I. S. Gulati, "Center-State Resource Transfers,
1951-84: An Appraisal," Economic and Political Weekly, 22(7)(16 February
1985), p. 290.

ensure the optimal allocation of land to different users. The implementation of the Act has experienced great difficulties and the State Governments have not been able to implement it effectively. In the meantime,
there is a general feeling that costs of land have increased substantially,
and fears are expressed that urban housing might become too expensive
for a large number of people.[9]

Most of the funds needed to finance expansion or improvement of
urban housing and essential services will have to be provided, as at
present, by grants and loans by the central government and channeled
through the state governments or by loans from financial institutions
which are controlled by the central or state governments. It would be
unrealistic to expect the municipal bodies, even of the largest cities, to
raise more than a small proportion of the funds needed for these purposes. The municipal bodies' powers of taxation are limited; taxes on
property and *octroi,* an indirect tax on goods coming into the city, are
their principal sources of revenue. Table 3.5 gives the distribution of
revenue sources for state governments.

Urban Planning

Formulation of plans for all cities with populations of 500,000 or more
will mean coverage of the largest and most dynamic part of the urban
sector—which moreover is most in need of them. As mentioned earlier,
these cities already had about 40 percent of the total urban population
by 1980 and the proportion is expected to increase to more than 50 per-

cent by the end of the century. Furthermore, the needs for expansion of housing and urban services are higher than in the smaller urban places because of their more rapid growth, and projects involving large expenditures and often requiring solution of complex technical problems have to be undertaken in the big cities.

The plans for individual cities and towns should form part of the five-year and annual plans of the states in which they are located, so that they can be financed as part of the state plans. Preparation of urban plans and their integration with the plans of the states will also give the municipal bodies a strong incentive for greater mobilization of local resources. The practice of matching grants, under which the cost of implementing a project is shared between the state government and local communities, has been successfully used for rural development programs. It can be used even more effectively for urban development programs because the potential for local resource mobilization is greater in the urban areas.

Management

The principal need is for providing high-quality managers and technical officers to run large cities (populations of 500,000 or more) and for implementing development projects and programs. A number of related developments lead us to expect progressive improvement in the availability of high-quality managers and technical officers for urban administration and urban development projects.

Better Political Executives

In the period immediately after Independence, most political talent was drawn into national or state-level politics, which offered the most challenging opportunities for exercise of political power. Municipal bodies were deprived of high-quality political executives, who had been available during the pre-Independence period. Indeed, up to the mid-1930s, before the advent of popular governments in the British-administered provinces, municipal bodies offered some of the few opportunities available to Indians for exercise of political power. Nehru, Sardar Patel, and several other leaders of the Independence movement, who rose to top-level positions in central and state governments after Independence, won their political spurs in municipal administrations. This position of municipal administration as the nursery of national and state-level leaders could be restored in the late 1980s or the 1990s because of the limited opportunities now available in the national and state governments and the increasing importance of urban affairs.

Better Managers and Technical Officers

Similar developments—limited opportunities in the state or national governments and increasingly attractive opportunities in municipal administrations—should attract a growing number of well-trained administrators and professional officers to the latter. Gone is the heady expansion of the public sector, including both the civil service and the public enterprises, which absorbed most of the available managerial and technical personnel in the 1950s and the 1960s and provided exciting opportunities for participating in the formulation of national economic and social policies and the establishment of large public enterprises. Such opportunities will, in future, be available only to a very few members of the higher administrative services, the highly talented or exceptionally lucky. For the great majority, particularly the newcomers to these services, the prospect is merely one of doing routine administrative jobs in various ministries and departments of the state or national governments. Major expansion of public-sector enterprises is not envisaged under the new economic liberalization policies. On the contrary, the trend will be toward divestment by turning over certain units to private or joint-sector companies. The principal remaining challenge in the public sector is that of increasing productivity or reducing the losses of the public enterprises. This challenge will be met, however, by attracting competent executives from both the administrative services and the corporate private sector.

Significant numbers of talented and experienced members of the higher administrative or technical services are already available for secondment to the municipal bodies of the large cities. Most of those who have filled top management or technical positions in these cities find that these posts offer opportunities for achievement which are as good as any available in the state or national governments. The commissioner and the senior technical officers of the municipal corporation of a large city can immediately see the results of their decisions—in expansion of housing, in clearance or improvement of slums, and in improvement of essential services, which translate, in turn, into increases in economic activity or in the welfare of hundreds of thousands of people. Most of their counterparts in the state or national bureaucracies, on the other hand, see themselves as merely cogs in a giant machine who have only a minor role in its functioning.

Increasing Participation of Business Leaders in Urban Affairs

The prospects of expansion—and the consequent growth of opportunities for management and technical personnel—are greater in the private sector (corporate or other) than in the public sector. But the challenges and opportunities in municipal administration will, in the near future, begin to attract a significant number of managers and technocrats from the private sector. One reason for this trend will be the increasing participation of leaders of business and private industry in urban affairs. Such participation had been inhibited earlier—by the antibusiness intellectual climate of the 1950s to the mid-1970s and by "anti-non-Bengali" sentiment such as that expressed in Calcutta, where Bengalis regarded the leaders of business and industry, most of whom are non-Bengalis, as "alien exploiters."

Resentment of "outsiders" will remain an important political force, especially in less developed states such as Assam, where the educated youth (particularly those in low-paid positions or unemployed) keenly resent the dominance of the public services, business, and industry by nonnatives. Nevertheless, even though political agitation such as that in Assam during 1979–1983 may be repeated, the dominant trend in the states will be toward encouraging investment in business and industry by both natives and nonnatives. The courting of business leaders by the present Marxist government of West Bengal is not an aberration; it is part of a nationwide trend. After coming to power, the Marxists realized the vital need for stopping the capital flight from West Bengal and attracting new investments in order to expand employment and income in the state. Consequently, their leaders muted their antibusiness rhetoric and joined governments of other states in actively seeking private investment.

The Problem of the Four Giant Cities

Despite the improved prospects of acquiring the funds and top-level personnel for urban administration and undertaking projects to meet the needs of urban growth, the prospects of the four giant cities, Bombay, Calcutta, Madras, and Delhi, are much less sanguine. Indeed, in the case of Bombay and Calcutta, where the urban systems already show inability to cope with the present populations, it is not at all clear how the pressures created by the projected doubling of the population during the twenty years 1980–2000 will be met.

The *World Bank Report 1984* projected the population growth of the four cities by the year 2000 (Table 3.6). All four cities are included in the twenty-five megalopolises which will have a population of more than 10 million by the year 2000. Except for Delhi, the projected growth rates of the cities are higher than those experienced during 1961–1981. If one assumes that the natural increase of the population already resident would not be significantly different from the national average of

Table 3.6.   Projected Population Growth and Growth Rates of
             Bombay, Calcutta, Madras, and Delhi

	Population (millions)		Annual Growth Rate (%)	
	Actual	Projected	Actual	Projected
City	1980	2000	1961-1981	1980-2000
Bombay	8.2	17.1	3.5	3.7
Calcutta	9.2	16.7	2.3	3.0
Madras	4.3	12.9	4.0	5.7
Delhi	5.7	11.7	4.5	3.7

Source: World Bank Report 1984.

1.9 percent projected in the *World Bank Report* for 1980–2000, less than half the projected increase in their populations would, except in the case of Madras, be due to in-migration.

The potential for and constraints on growth of individual cities appear to have been given some consideration in projecting their growth. The rate projected for Calcutta is significantly lower than the rates projected for the other three cities, but it is still considerably higher than the actual rate for 1961–1981. The problems of managing the urban system and providing essential services are most acute in Calcutta; it suffered capital flight following the industrial and political unrest of the late 1960s, and investor confidence has been slow to return. Keeping these constraints in view, its projected rate for 1980–2000 can well be considered too high.

Projection of rapid growth for Madras can be justified on several grounds. First is a favorable environment for industrial growth, relative freedom from industrial unrest, a disciplined labor force with willingness and aptitude for learning new skills, and moderate wage levels—all leading to lower labor costs per unit of output than in Bombay or Delhi. Second, Madras has a large hinterland with diverse agricultural and mineral resources which has, moreover, been experiencing vigorous growth. And third, except in the case of water, Madras has less difficult problems of expanding the infrastructure than the other three cities. Even so, the projected rate, which will result in trebling of the population in twenty years, appears to be too high.

The growth potential of Delhi, however, may have been underestimated. Growth of employment in the central government will continue to be an important factor for the city. Furthermore, Delhi is the principal city serving a large region, a large part of which, located in Punjab, Haryana, and western Uttar Pradesh, has experienced rapid growth of agricultural production income in the last two decades to reach significantly higher levels than the national average. Furthermore, the region has the potential for maintaining higher rates of growth than the national average.

Growth projections for Bombay are high because of the rapid development of the economies of both the city of Bombay and the state of Maharashtra. Bombay is also the principal city of western India, giving it national importance in the Indian economy. This importance together with the city's developing industrial and services economic base make high population growth rates inevitable.

Without knowing the assumptions and the methodology of the projections, it is impossible to comment on them in detail. The principal questions about the prospects of these cities do not relate, however, to the details of the growth projections; they relate primarily to whether continued rapid growth of their populations to two or three times their present sizes in twenty years can be sustained in the face of existing pressures on housing and essential services. Could such increases not lead to the virtual collapse of the urban administration in one or more of these cities? Alternatively, given the serious resource constraints of the Indian economy and the limitations of the political and administrative systems, is there enough time to undertake the needed reforms of urban administrations and implement the development programs required for the expansion of housing and urban services in these cities?

The questions cannot be answered. The requirements of the cities for both finance and high-quality management for the purposes mentioned above will be very high indeed. Furthermore, in areas of expanding water supply and urban transport where there are major environmental constraints and high cost, technically complex solutions will have to be devised. Procedural delays could also be long—especially in the case of housing, for the intervention of the courts could seriously delay acquisition of land. Finally, the record of the recent past is not reassuring. Problems have been ignored for long periods, and even after major projects have been finally approved, their implementation has often been slow and in many cases fitful.

The answers to the questions will relate, finally, to political judgment and the will to provide the needed resources and ensure that institutional and administrative reforms are undertaken and that projects and programs are implemented with speed and efficiency. Some of the tasks that will need special attention in these cities include housing, food supply, water and electricity, transport, maintenance of peace and security, and restriction of in-migration.

Housing

Expansion and improvement of housing will remain the most difficult problem. The present deficiency is so acute and growing so rapidly, and the costs of expansion of housing are so high in comparison with the incomes of the great majority of urban residents, that the best that can be hoped, even with the most intensive effort, is avoidance of a serious aggravation of the present situation. In Delhi, for instance, the current estimate is of a shortage of 300,000 dwelling units and a requirement of 1.62 million units over the next two decades.[10] In Bombay,

> the shelter problem is theoretically very neatly defined. The demand for shelter works out to 60,000 units each year in the Bombay metropolitan region (45,000 units in Greater Bombay and 15,000 in the metropolitan region). The supply in the formal sector, private and public, is now around 20,000 units each year and the difference between demand and supply has resulted in an accrual to the slum settlements in the metropolis. Not only was 40 percent of the total population in 1976 living in slums but the slum population is growing faster than the overall population.[11]

Acquisition of land for public housing for the poor is itself a most difficult problem. Reference was made earlier to the fact that acquisition of land for such housing was delayed and the area of land available for this purpose was progressively reduced by private interests who obtained political support and used a series of court injunctions against acquisition.[12]

Food Supply

Ensuring both adequate supplies of cereal to the cities and their availability at prices fixed by the government, never easy, should not be unmanageable if the growth rate of cereal output achieved in India during the last twenty years can be maintained. The spread of the wheat revolution from its core area in Punjab, Haryana, and western Uttar Pradesh into eastern Uttar Pradesh, Bihar, and West Bengal and the improvement in the last few years in the rate of growth of rice output give hope of this prospect. But increasing, or even maintaining, the present low levels of consumption of foods rich in proteins, minerals, and vitamins (such as milk, meat, poultry products, and fruits and vegetables) or even such essentials as oils and fats will be very difficult unless there are major improvements in the technologies of producing, processing, and transporting these staples and their prices get more in line with the incomes of the great majority of urban residents.

Water and Electricity

The problem of providing adequate water and electricity could grow even worse unless there are sustained efforts to increase supplies. Large investments in expansion of the systems of supply, transmission, and distribution, as well as progressive improvements in their management, will be needed. Expanding the water supply may present a more complex problem than that of electricity. The customary difficulty and high cost of providing adequate and safe water to cities are multiplied in the four largest cities. The acute shortage of water experienced in Madras in 1984 is an indication of these difficulties. Large and expensive works, involving the transport of water over long distances, will be needed for all four cities. In Calcutta and Delhi, the urgent need for reducing dangerously high pollution levels is expected to be met, however, by the Ganga Cleanup Project.

Transport

Expansion of the transport system to cope with the needs of growth will present special problems in all the cities except Madras. The worst case again is Calcutta, where the transport system is a nightmare. Because the planners for Delhi have never gotten around to conceptualizing an efficient transport system, the existing system is approaching conditions of near chaos. In Bombay, too, the transport system is greatly overloaded and the cost of its expansion will be immense. If a large part of the projected growth takes place on the mainland across the bay from the present city, large investments will be required for construction of bridges and other works linking the transport systems of the two parts of the city. Only in the case of Madras, where the transport system is much less overloaded, would expansion be manageable.

Maintaining Peace and Security

This task will require political and administrative management of a very high order. Above all, the cities must ensure access to the basic needs for food and water, access to other essential services and housing, and opportunities for gainful employment. The tensions ever present below the surface in the Indian cities,[13] tensions which find their outlet in periodic outbreaks of violence, can be kept within manageable limits, and the growth of underworld activities curtailed, only when these fundamental conditions are met.

Restricting In-Migration to the Cities

From time to time there is a demand for curbing in-migration to these four cities, and to smaller cities such as Bangalore, which have experienced very rapid growth during the last two or three decades. The motives for the demand may be political, or they may be techno-admin-

istrative. Thus the Shiv Sena, a militant pro-Maharashtrian organization, threatened in May 1985 to launch an Assam-like agitation to ban
migration into Bombay and reduce the number of "outsiders."[14] Its
motive was purely political; its main support is among the majority
Maharashtrian population of Bombay which has long resented the domination of commerce, industry, and increasingly also the white-collar
services by non-Maharashtrians. They also fear they will lose their
majority status if rapid in-migration to the city continues.

But such a measure has never been seriously considered. Indeed, the
prime minister has ruled out any curb on in-migration,[15] which in any
event would be unconstitutional. Even if the constitutional difficulties
were to be overcome at some future date, the immense task of enforcing
the restrictions would remain. The only solution to the problem of in-
migration to the giant cities is to increase the attraction of alternatives,
including satellite towns.

India's cities and urban regions face a difficult future. Urban infrastructure and housing are inadequate and cannot absorb the massive
numbers of newcomers. Urban economic and social conditions are
deteriorating, which results in higher levels of unemployment and social
unrest. Migration from the countryside continues unabated and in
some cases is accelerating. In these adverse circumstances India's urban
areas must become the focus for new policy initiatives emphasizing population control, rural development, and urban growth containment.

NOTES

1. World Bank, *World Development Report 1984* (Washington, D.C.: World
Bank, 1984).
2. R. Mohan, "Urbanization in India's Future," *Population and Development
Review* 2 (4) (December 1985): 630.
3. Planning Commission, Government of India, *Seventh Five-Year Plan (1985–
1990),* vols. 1 and 2 (New Delhi: Government of India Press, 1985).
4. T. N. Ninan, "The Economy—Buoyant Mood," *India Today* (New
Delhi), 15 March 1985.
5. Ashok Mitra, "Micro Planning of Space," in Allen G. Noble and Ashok
K. Dutt (eds.), *Indian Urbanization and Planning: Vehicles of Modernization* (New
Delhi: Tata–McGraw-Hill, 1978), p. 212.
6. C. B. Wurster, "Urban Living Conditions, Overhead Costs and the
Development Pattern," in Roy Turner (ed.), *India's Urban Future* (Berkeley,
Calif.: University of California Press, 1962), p. 284.
7. Ibid., p. 286.
8. Planning Commission, Government of India, *Third Five-Year Plan,* p. 149.
9. Planning Commission, Government of India, *Sixth Five-Year Plan 1980–
85,* pp. 346–347.

10. "Delhi in 2001," *Overseas Hindustan Times* (New Delhi), 18 May 1985, p. 3.

11. Amrita Abraham, "Housing for the Poor?" *Economic and Political Weekly* 20 (6) (9 February 1985): 226.

12. Ashok K. Dutt and G. Venugopal, "Spatial Patterns of Crime Among Indian Cities," *GeoForum* (London) 14 (9) (1983): 223–233.

13. Ibid.

14. "P.M. Rules Out Curbs on Migration," *Overseas Hindustan Times* (New Delhi), 25 May 1985, p. 3.

15. Ibid.

4. Urban Development in Pakistan

AKHTAR HUSAIN SIDDIQI

THE rise of cities in developing countries often has created a spatial arrangement that is neither functional nor optimal. In traditional societies hierarchical organization was based as much on sacerdotal, juridical, military, or administrative principles as on economic grounds.[1] The status of towns within the hierarchy determines their sphere of influence and depends upon the power residing in their level of the hierarchy. City size remains the simplest and best index to this power. Differences in the number of urban centers in different population-size groups should therefore reveal differences in the nature of power organization, and these in turn should reveal developmental differences and variations in the degree of regional organization and the proportion of population concentrated in large cities.

Most empires have been controlled by holding key cities and strategic points. As the domain expanded, it proved necessary to establish urban posts as administrative and military centers of control to pacify the native population and ensure the orderly collection of agricultural surplus and revenue and their transfer to the central authority, and also as staging areas for further military probes on the frontier.[2] Thus urbanization was a function of the distribution of power, both internally and externally.

In the course of this process, local new elites are produced and rewarded who acquire a growing proportion of the nation's wealth, forcing more and more rural and urban populations to live close to subsistence. The elites' own needs for consumption are met either by imports or by developing industries based on the concept of import substitution. These policies contribute to growing primacy in the distribution of city sizes, because the principal domestic market is concentrated in the cities where the elites reside, tending to sustain accelerated growth at those locations. Because domestic markets are limited, import-substitution industries gradually give way to export-oriented

47

industries. Provincial and regional cities and towns serve primarily as administrative centers for the control of their associated regions and as points for the transshipment of agricultural and mineral products for export. Thus it is the effective political and economic power that, in the end, determines the spatial organization of an urban system and its evolution.[3]

The theory of dependency or "dependent capitalism" seems to account for certain forms of spatial urban development in the developing countries. To understand the role of urbanization properly, one must investigate the conditions of underdevelopment that characterize the developing countries, of which cities are only a part. McGee saw the Third World (primate) city as parasitical on the population in its periphery.[4] He focuses on a sectoral model of the urban economy and renders the basic core/periphery relationship more acceptable by introducing the concept of dependent capitalism. He argues that capitalist enterprise tends to squeeze both the bazaar economy (the indigenous, labor-intensive sector of urban production) and the peasant economy, pushing the surplus labor force into cities while, at the same time, reducing the productive and labor-absorption capabilities of the bazaar economy in competition with the corporate sector. If this process of capitalist penetration could be contained, involution might continue for some time. But if it could not, then the urban bourgeoisie would impose a military dictatorship to gain political control over the country. Thus the urban role is not one of diffusing modernization but one of increasing exploitation, acting on behalf of the distant "metropoles" of the capitalist world.[5]

In light of these theories of urban development and the process of urbanization in the developing countries, the present study aims to point out the processes that resulted in the development of urbanization in Pakistan. It explores the influence of the development of irrigation agriculture, in particular, in creating the country's present urban system.

Historical Background

In Pakistan, the roots of civilization and elite power have been associated with the cities from the earliest times. The remains of the Indus civilization, which evolved at Harappa and Mohenjodaro, show it was a well-organized and prosperous society which owed its existence to the development of irrigation agriculture.[6] But the population of the Indus Basin was never large during the long initial stages of occupancy.

In the well-watered agricultural plain of the Indus Basin, urban settlements were encountered frequently, displaying a linear arrangement along main transportation routes parallel to the Indus River and its tributaries. The Grand Trunk Road, for instance, a great route which passed through the northern part of the basin, was marked with a string of towns commanding river crossings or central positions in the *doabs* (areas between two confluent rivers). Thus most towns were bridge-heads and had military as well as commercial value.

Impact of Colonial Power on Urbanization

Pakistan's urban system is the outcome of a century-long process of social and technical transformation. The dominance–dependence relationship established by the colonial power was primarily restricted to political, military, and administrative functions, providing order and justice and controlling the economy but not generating production. Kiug refers to Castells' perspective on this phenomenon when he discusses the concept of "dependent urbanization."[7] Urbanization occurs in the colonial society, but industrialization, which historically has created urbanization in modern and autonomous societies, takes place only in the metropolitan areas of the developing countries.

The urban settlements initially were designed as military outposts and later developed as centers of administration and collection points for local agricultural materials for export. Many of these sites were dictated by the needs of defense rather than trade and were located at strongly defended sites. Nevertheless, it is obvious that their survival and growth as urban centers depended entirely on their ability to function as regional centers, encouraging little competition with neighboring towns of similar status.

The introduction of the railways in the middle of the nineteenth century added a new element and transformed the structure of the growing urban centers. Although the great majority of towns are still small and have changed little in size over the last hundred years, transportation routes, particularly railroads, undoubtedly have demonstrated a channeling influence on the development of trade centers in the Indus Plains. In the agriculturally productive areas, industries processing agricultural goods for export (rice milling, cotton ginning, and flour milling) have been located on the periphery of the towns with ready access provided by railroad. Large administrative centers were modernized and received a few urban services as time passed. Thus a regional system of cities and towns had the main objective of serving the capital and provincial seats first and the people in the area afterward.

The new railways led to an increase in the trade and population of all the towns along the line. Although railways diverted trade from the

smaller towns, no doubt the result on the whole was to increase the
urban population. Large cities (over 50,000) increased considerably at
the expense of the smaller towns, however; the slackening in the rate of
increase during the period was confined to the smaller towns.[8]

By 1901, small country towns without rail links had become increasingly isolated. Those without established manufacture saw their
through trade diverted to more conveniently located places, and they
recorded population declines.[9] The towns that were *mandis* (trading
posts) for locally produced handicrafts succumbed to the competition of
factory-produced imports. Although the diversion of the old trade
routes caused the decay of many old urban localities, with the administration centralized and the business of the region carried on at the headquarters of the districts, regional towns invariably showed marked
increases. Export trade, however, was the key to their development and
growth. Thus, as is evident from the growth and development of urban
population and towns from 1881 to 1981, the urbanization of Pakistan
is closely connected with the traditional society and the agricultural
basis of its socioeconomic system.

Effect of Irrigation on Urban Growth

Slow early growth in urban population and in the degree of urbanization was associated with the slow expansion of irrigation in the Indus
Plains. By 1911, irrigation in the Punjab area reached a new level of
magnitude. The area produced a grain surplus and exported to the surrounding regions, requiring further extension of the transportation system. The first integrated system connected three of the Punjab rivers in
1907–1914, and the Sutlej Valley project was completed in 1920–1921.
The Panjnad, Bahawalpur, and Haveli projects were completed between 1920 and 1939. The Lloyds Barrage in Sind was completed in
1935. After the opening of these irrigation projects, the towns in the
Indus Basin showed a considerable increase in population. With more
area coming under cultivation, many towns became not only leading
trade centers but also important processing centers for agricultural raw
material. Almost every railway station became a center for export, and
the commerce and trade of these towns contributed to the growth of
population, as well as to industry. The character and importance of various industries in the towns were directly related to the agricultural
areas serving them.

The rapid growth in urban population in Pakistan between 1921 and
1941 reflects not only natural increase but also large-scale migration
from the countryside. The development of irrigation agriculture in
Punjab and Sind involved a radical shift in the use of manpower and

natural resources. Large canal works led to the settlement of all the irrigated sections of the Indus Plains, and the growing requirements of the urban centers were more or less counterbalanced by the opening of new railways that connected all important agricultural tracts with the port of Karachi and larger centers of trade and diverted trade from less favorably located centers to outlying urban centers.[10]

In the six censuses from 1921 to 1981, the general trends in the degree of urbanization and growth in urban population have been upward. Relatively slower growth in the urban population in 1981 indicates three qualifications. First, the periods covered in the last two censuses (1972–1981) are not of equal length. Second, the country experienced economic stagnation and political unrest in the 1970s, with slow internal migration and more people migrating overseas for better economic prospects. Third, because of the general economic difficulties, there may be a "pushback" factor whereby migrants failed to find employment and probably returned home.

Since the administrative structure was designed basically to maintain law and order, places classified as administrative centers were treated as urban regardless of their size. Furthermore, the discretionary power vested in the census organization often introduced an element of subjectivity in its delimitations, and the population size of 5,000 or more required for urban classification was not strictly observed. Thus since 1931 the majority of smaller towns have developed and remained as administrative-cum-local-market centers with little activity to stimulate growth and significant in-migration.

Had it not been for modern irrigation networks, much of what is now the economic heartland of Pakistan would have remained essentially a semidesert. Cultivation of cash crops was stimulated primarily by the extension of canal irrigation. With each new irrigation project, new towns, including *mandis,* were founded along the roads and railways to serve the irrigated hinterland, and a relatively modern infrastructure of transportation and trade developed. Nineteenth-century projects in Punjab and Sind were isolated schemes, but after 1901 efforts were concentrated on integrating the system both within and between the provinces.

The Post-Partition Period

Both old and modern cities have changed in appearance during the past three decades (1951–1981) in Pakistan, and industrial zones have appeared showing a marked concentration of manufacturing enterprises. Unifunctional towns, the most numerous type, are principally small in population and area—and the majority are regional and local centers. Such towns, besides being important at *tahsil, taluka,* or even at district level, play a substantial role as centers for wholesale trade in agricultural produce and have become focal points for the surrounding rural population. Others may be identified as industrial centers, fishing ports, small railway stations, trade and craft centers, mining operations, and military towns.

Rapid urban growth between 1951 and 1981 is associated with periods of intense socioeconomic and political change in Pakistan, resulting in an increase in the number of urban centers of all sizes. Contributing to rapid post-Partition urbanization were internal (rural–urban) and international (India–Pakistan) migrations. Pakistan's urban population has been increased by Muslims displaced from India who have settled in urban areas of Pakistan, and the situation of a particular town relative to the extent of migration depends on its distance from the international frontier.[11] Although the resettlement of displaced persons in larger agglomerations has contributed to rapid urban growth, acceleration in urbanization as a result of this resettlement remains only a special phase in the long and complex history of urban development in Pakistan.[12]

In recent years the larger cities of Pakistan appear to have grown disproportionately in relation to, and apparently at the expense of, the smaller, relatively stagnating urban areas. One explanation is that many small towns in Pakistan have grown and remained *mandi* towns with little if any modern-sector activity taking place to stimulate growth and large-scale immigration.

Urban Typology

In general, the dual economic structure of Pakistan towns may be described primarily in terms of the firm-centered economic sector and the bazaar economy sector. Firm-centered activities include banking, export trade, modern large-scale industry, and some forms of transport; the bazaar economy comprises non-capital-intensive services, trades, and industrial crafts. The majority of enterprises are family-owned industries or retailing firms; most of the labor force of the cities fits clearly into a peasant system of production. In many large cities a "trisectoral" model of the urban economy is also found in which one can distinguish individual operators, family enterprises, and corporate (national and international) production.

There have been three formative influences in the urbanization of Pakistan: the peasant marketing system, an export-oriented industrial commercial system, and a strong local administrative system. At present, interrural and interurban relationships, at the level of the small town communities, are weakly developed if they exist at all. This social and economic relationship has been replaced by big city dominance, which finds expression in the administrative hierarchical structure of Pakistan's cities and in the commercial activities performed by the urban areas.

Urban Growth

Based upon estimates of urban population, about 28 percent of the total population of Pakistan lived in urban concentrations of varying size in 1981.[13] The figures, shown in Table 4.1, reveal accelerated urban population growth, both in relative and absolute terms, and the degree of urbanization during the last eighty years.

The laying out of *mandis* and administrative centers connected by a transportation system was an important adjunct of irrigation–colonization programs in the region. The net growth rates of towns between 1901 and 1941 reveal that the growth rate of population of older cities and towns compared poorly to the growth rate in the new urban centers. Lack of interest in industrial development, however, along with the failure to develop water power and infrastructure in many *mandi* towns, raised serious problems for the urban environment. In most urban localities the population grew at a rate much faster than either total or

Table 4.1. Urban Population Growth of Pakistan: 1901-1981

Year	Total Population (1,000's)	Net Percentage Change in Total Population	Total Urban Population (1,000's)	Urban Population as Percentage of Total Population
1901	16.6	—	1,619	9.8
1911	17.8	7.1	1,689	9.5
1921	18.3	3.1	2,058	11.3
1931	21.3	16.5	2,769	13.0
1941	25.9	21.7	4,015	15.5
1951	33.7	30.2	6,019	17.8
1961	42.9	27.1	9,654	22.5
1972	65.3	52.2	16,698	25.7
1981	83.8	28.3	23,739	28.3

Source: Census of Pakistan Population, 1961, vol. 1: Tables and Reports, Karachi, pp. 11-54, and Census Organization, Population Census of Pakistan, 1972, Islamabad; Pakistan Statistical Yearbook, 1981, p. 6. Computed by the author.

rural populations, ultimately negating the benefits derived from irrigation agriculture.

In comparison with growth in the Indus Plains, urban growth in the
upland areas has been very slow, and many of the so-called towns of the
region have remained just overgrown villages. The degree of urbanization in these areas has been the lowest in Pakistan because of the lack of
any industrial life. With the exceptions of Quetta, Peshawar, and Mar-
den, the total population in upland towns has fluctuated. Basically,
upland towns are unifunctional political and administrative centers.

Impact of Nationhood

Between 1941 and 1951, the total number of urban inhabitants increased by 2 million, almost doubling the urban population. The urban
gains in the following decades, however, have been far greater than the
increase experienced immediately after Partition (3.6 million during
1951–1961 and 14.1 million during the 1961–1981 period), and the
urban population has grown faster than the rural population or the general population. This rapid growth in urban population is due not only
to natural increase but also to large-scale migration from the countryside. The explosion of the urban population has not been experienced
equally in all parts of the country. The distribution of urban population
as a percentage of total population in each district for 1951, 1961, and
1972 reveals that the highest degree of urbanization in these periods was
found in the intensively irrigated areas of Punjab, Sind, and North-
West Frontier Province (NWFP), whereas the lowest concentration of
urban population was associated with less irrigated parts of the Indus
Basin and the upland areas (Figures 4.1 to 4.3). As irrigation facilities
improved in Punjab and Sind between 1961 and 1972, beneficiary districts recorded improvements in their respective degree of urbanization.
There is a considerable difference between the rates of growth of town
population in various parts of the country, however, as well as between
the various size towns. This finding seems to suggest that the nature of
economic development plays an important role in the development of
local urban areas, especially in the agricultural hinterland.[14]

With the adoption of new seed varieties, the beneficiaries of Green
Revolution technology increased their income from agriculture and
were able to buy or rent additional land with a view to mechanizing
farming practices. Burki, basing his findings on Punjab, says that the
small landholders moved out of the agricultural sector because of competition from the middle-sized farmers. They either rented or sold their
land, investing their capital in agriculture-related industries and ser-

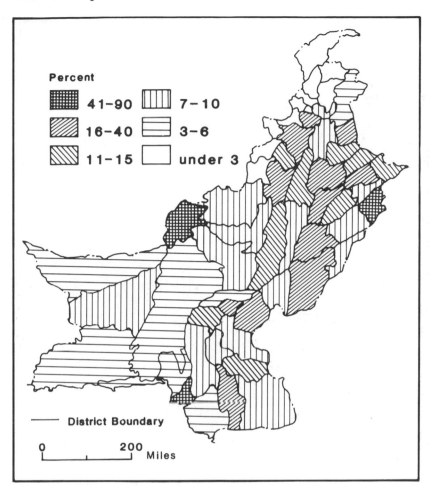

Figure 4.1. Distribution of Urban Population in Pakistan: 1951

vices in various towns.[15] Other Pakistani sociologists have noted that population increases in regions with developed irrigation have reduced per capita agricultural productivity, which in turn has caused farmers' indebtedness to increase and has reduced full-time employment for rural workers. These factors have acted as "push" forces driving rural population into the cities. Cited among the "pull" forces have been the development of new industry and the infrastructure of social life.[16]

The most effective of the various forces responsible for urbanization are rural–urban migration and fundamental economic forces, primarily agricultural development. Although, as indicated earlier, the urban

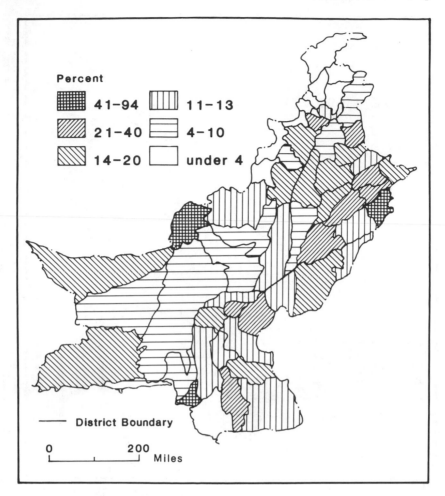

Figure 4.2. Distribution of Urban Population in Pakistan: 1961

population in Pakistan is increasing faster than the rural, there is no information on the natural increase of urban population in Pakistan. A population growth survey does give crude birth rate and death rate figures from 1968 to 1971,[17] but these figures are inadequate and for the most part unreliable, and they pertain to Pakistan's over-all rural and urban population, making no distinctions on a regional basis.

Ahmad estimates that net migration forms a considerable portion of the total decennial increase in urban population.[18] Net migration accounted for 64 percent of the annual increase for 1959, for example. Even if allowance is made for the influx of displaced persons from

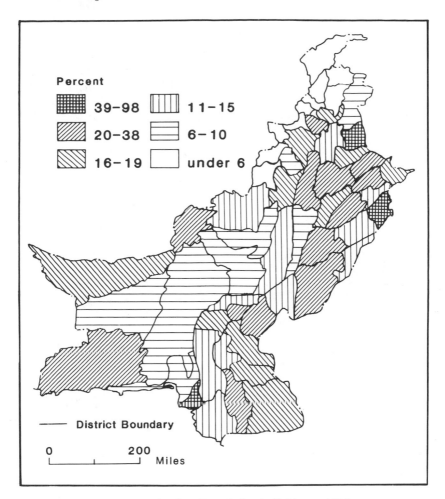

Figure 4.3. Distribution of Urban Population in Pakistan: 1972

India, which should have become very small by 1959, the proportion of rural–urban migration remains high (above 50 percent). Growth rate patterns of the largest cities between 1961–1972 and 1972–1981 reveal that growth rates are dropping in most of the largest cities, reflecting the apparent slowing of rural in-migration to the very largest urban agglomerations. It is very difficult to determine whether the change is due to counterbalancing centrifugal forces of overurbanization or to persistent unemployment, which forces migrants to leave the cities. On the other hand, poorer villages tend to experience greater emigration, especially from the areas where land is poor and rain-fed. The landless laborers seem to prefer cities rather than towns and villages.[19]

Urban Patterns

The distribution of urban centers in Pakistan reveals a regional contrast
(Figure 4.4). About 78 percent of all urban centers are in the Indus
Basin, with 22 percent in the uplands of NWFP and Baluchistan. About
40 percent of the urban localities (in Punjab 28 percent; Sind 54 percent; NWFP about 31 percent; and 74 percent of urban localities of
Baluchistan) are overgrown large villages representing 7 percent of the
total urban population (Tables 4.2 and 4.3).

In the upland region small towns are characterized by a highly dispersed distribution. A tendency toward an aggregated pattern appears
in Sind, however, corresponding to the irrigated tracts of the Lower

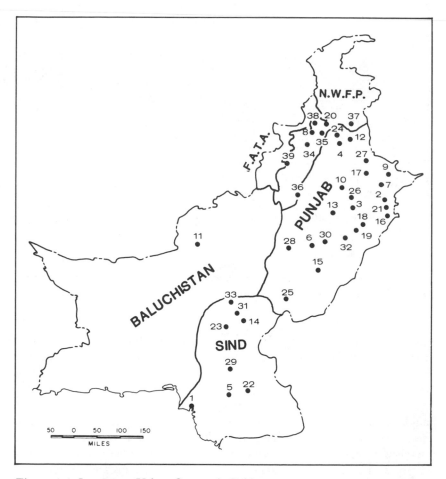

Figure 4.4. Important Urban Centers in Pakistan

Indus Valley. A tendency toward uniform spacing of towns and cities appears in Multan and Lahore divisions of Punjab. These canal colony areas are served by a dense network of highways and railroads, factors that seem conducive to a uniform distribution of urban centers.

Growth of Urban Agglomerations

In 1972, some 59 percent of the total urban population resided in cities of 100,000 people and more, representing 6 percent (twenty-four cities) of all urban centers. Twenty-one cities with populations of 50,000 to 100,000 accounted for 8 percent of the total urban population, and about 33 percent of the total urban population lived in 323 medium (25–50,000) and small (5–10,000 or below) towns. Tables 4.2 and 4.3 reveal marked regional variations in the distribution of towns and cities of all sizes. In the Indus Plains most of the large cities function as regional markets, and many have already passed beyond these relatively simplistic functions to become producers of goods.

Between 1951 and 1972 these cities recorded rapid population increases and growing industrial and agricultural processing industries. During the period from 1950 into the 1970s, many regional planning and development projects were launched to open new resource areas in Punjab and Sind. New public investments resulted in the physical and demographic growth of a few small towns in the Indus Basin. Large cities reported a net increase of 164 percent during the two decades ending 1972, whereas intermediate cities grew 126 percent in the same period. Towns with a population between 25,000 and 10,000 grew 154 percent, but the net growth in other towns ranged from 25 to 88 percent.

There are three demographic components of these increases in cities and towns: natural increase, reclassification of rural areas as urban, and population movements. Of these components, migration is most important. In absolute terms, there has been considerable urbanization —particularly as reflected in the growth of big cities and the creation of small towns as nuclei for agricultural areas. The picture varies from province to province, however.

Considering forty-two large cities with a population ranging from 61,000 to over 5 million in 1981, growth rates in most of these localities between 1901 and 1981 (with the exception of Karachi, Lahore, Hyderabad, Faisalabad, and Gujranwala) is not necessarily a function of the expansion of the industrial base. Between 1901 and 1941, the smaller towns displayed an upward trend that was the reverse of large cities. In fact, the great bulk of the urban population was concentrated in a few

Table 4.2.   Distribution of Pakistan's Urban Population and
            Number of Urban Agglomerations by Group Size

Year	100,000 and over	No.	50-99,999	No.	25-49,999	No.
Pakistan
1951	2,960,890	10	542,667	8	861,581	22
1961	5,275,337	12	872,113	12	1,139,742	31
1972	9,828,007	24	1,437,598	21	1,778,598	52
Punjab
1951	1,553,304	6	409,361	6	471,014	11
1961	2,676,809	7	604,603	8	753,618	21
1972	5,449,504	15	784,549	12	1,079,696	31
Sind
1951	1,297,871	3	77,057	1	176,250	5
1961	2,432,255	4	114,771	2	194,327	5
1972	3,898,125	6	596,032	8	336,975	11
NWFP
1951	109,715	10	0	0	186,223	5
1961	166,273	1	73,246	1	164,657	4
1972	342,719	2	57,296	1	334,256	9
Baluchistan
1951	0	0	56,249	1	28,094	1
1961	0	0	79,493	1	27,140	1
1972	137,659	1	0	0	27,671	1

Source: Government of Pakistan, Statistic Division, Population
Census Organization, Statistical Reports of Punjab, Sind, NWFP
and Baluchistan, 1972, Islamabad.   Computed by the author.

large urban agglomerations, and the regional variations between provinces were prominent (Figure 4.5).

In the pre-Pakistan period, cities grew more rapidly in Punjab than either in Sind or NWFP from 1901 onward. Between 1901 and 1941, the development of irrigation agriculture in the Indus Basin involved a radical shift in agricultural development because of commercial growth. A large influx of rural or small-town inhabitants in the 1901–1941 period occurred in towns located in the intensively irrigated areas of Punjab and Sind. Agricultural underemployment was a strong factor driving people from less irrigated (or *barani*) areas to towns where agricultural raw material processing plants were located, providing constant seasonal demand for unskilled labor. Commercialization of agriculture and new transport systems permitted many towns to achieve the stature of *mandis,* where farmers sold cash crops, such as raw cotton, oil

10-24,999	No.	5-9,999	No.	Below 5,000	No.
769,721	48	574,412	77	150,520	42
1,263,064	83	789,289	106	225,260	67
2,402,161	159	934,223	112	168,438	61
613,988	30	409,845	54	105,855	27
775,790	50	547,407	70	89,838	21
1,431,991	96	438,798	44	60,964	17
131,885	9	73,109	10	12,322	3
225,714	15	130,507	20	70,973	20
461,427	30	341,912	46	61,300	20
122,006	8	78,306	11	5,445	3
236,025	16	65,216	9	29,897	9
378,398	25	90,602	12	10,660	9
11,842	1	13,162	2	26,898	9
25,535	2	46,159	7	34,552	17
130,345	8	62,911	10	35,514	19

seeds, and wheat, for national and international markets. Thus farming together with village-oriented services, administration, and marketing operations expanded job opportunities, increasing in-migration to most towns. In the absence of any defined urban policy, the course of urbanization was determined largely by the cumulative effect of many independent decisions.

Major cities experienced an extraordinary population growth during the 1951–1981 period. In 1951, the major cities of Pakistan housed 4.5 million people; their population rose to 16.8 million in 1981, an increase of 273 percent. Large cities accounted for 75 percent of the total urban population in 1951, but with the development of other small and medium-size towns this proportion dropped to 71 percent in 1981. Apart from natural growth, most of the increase in large cities and towns was due to the in-migration of the rural population. Moreover,

62   *Akhtar Husain Siddiqi*

Table 4.3.   Percentage Distribution of Pakistan's Urban
              Agglomerations by Group Size

Year	100,000 and over Population (%)	No.	50-99,999 Population (%)	No.	25-49,999 Population (%)	No.
Pakistan						
1951	51	5	9	4	15	11
1961	55	4	10	4	12	10
1972	59	6	8	5	11	12
Punjab						
1951	44	5	11	5	13	8
1961	49	4	11	4	14	12
1972	58	7	8	6	12	14
Sind						
1951	73	10	4	3	10	16
1961	77	7	4	3	6	7
1972	69	5	11	7	6	9
NWFP						
1951	22	4	0	0	37	18
1961	23	3	10	3	22	10
1972	28	4	5	2	28	17
Baluchistan						
1951	0	0	41	7	20	7
1961	0	0	37	3.5	13	3.5
1972	35	2.5	0	0	7	2.5

Source: Computed by the author.

many cities have annexed adjoining villages. Important cities such as Karachi, Lahore, Islamabad, Rawalpindi, Hyderabad, Faisalabad, Multan, Gujranwala, and Peshawar have been extremely dynamic in their physical and functional growth. The diversified economic base in these localities, as well as in other large towns, has resulted in large increases in population and proportionate increases in the labor force.

A number of large towns in Punjab and Sind have been chosen by the public or private sector to perform the specific services needed by these areas. Such developments include small-scale labor-intensive industries geared to meet agricultural needs, processing plants, textile mills, and banks. Migration into these urban areas has played a significant role in

| 10-24,999 | | 5-9,999 | | Below 5,000 | |
Population (%)	No.	Population (%)	No.	Population (%)	No.
13	23	9	37	3	20
13	26	8	34	2	22
15	37	6	26	1	15
18	22	12	40	3	20
14	28	10	40	2	12
15	45	6	20	1	8
8	29	4	32	1	10
7	23	4	30	2	30
8	25	6	38	1	16
24	29	16	38	1	11
32	40	9	22	4	22
31	46	7	22	1	9
9	7	10	15	20	64
12	7	22	25	16	61
33	21	16	26	9	48

their absolute growth. There is some evidence that agrotowns of the post-Partition period are experiencing out-migration to the newly developing towns in the agricultural hinterland which have access to capital.

Planners in Pakistan have tried to develop many growth centers with the intention of initiating economic growth in less developed areas, but manufacturing has taken on the character of an economic enclave as reflected in the spatial concentration of industry in a few centers. Despite the initiation of a growth-pole policy, the diffusion of industrial development has been disappointing, and urbanization has exercised limited influence on shifts in the location of industry from highly concentrated areas to less developed areas.[20]

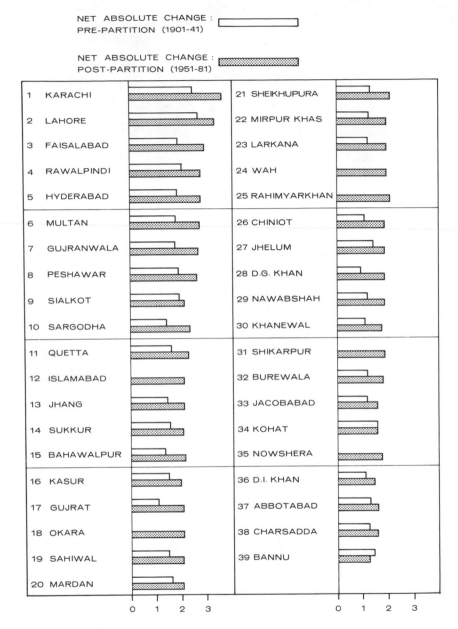

NET ABSOLUTE CHANGE :
PRE-PARTITION (1901-41)

NET ABSOLUTE CHANGE :
POST-PARTITION (1951-81)

1	KARACHI		21	SHEIKHUPURA
2	LAHORE		22	MIRPUR KHAS
3	FAISALABAD		23	LARKANA
4	RAWALPINDI		24	WAH
5	HYDERABAD		25	RAHIMYARKHAN
6	MULTAN		26	CHINIOT
7	GUJRANWALA		27	JHELUM
8	PESHAWAR		28	D.G. KHAN
9	SIALKOT		29	NAWABSHAH
10	SARGODHA		30	KHANEWAL
11	QUETTA		31	SHIKARPUR
12	ISLAMABAD		32	BUREWALA
13	JHANG		33	JACOBABAD
14	SUKKUR		34	KOHAT
15	BAHAWALPUR		35	NOWSHERA
16	KASUR		36	D.I. KHAN
17	GUJRAT		37	ABBOTABAD
18	OKARA		38	CHARSADDA
19	SAHIWAL		39	BANNU
20	MARDAN			

FIGURES ARE LOG-NORMAL

Figure 4.5. Variations in Urban Population in Pakistan

Meanwhile, agricultural resource development policies remained primarily concentrated in areas that were economically active and could provide maximum returns. These policies neglected the western or southwestern areas of Pakistan, and development outside the irrigated areas was limited. Continued channeling of the bulk of investment in these schemes may be economically attractive and perhaps more convenient. Thus the urban role is not one of diffusing modernization but one of increasing exploitation by the distant "metropolis" of the capitalists.[21]

Primate/Intermediate-City Mix

The latest information on the size of cities (1972) reveals the changes that have occurred since 1961 in city-size distribution in Pakistan. Obviously, the distribution of cities does not conform to the requirement of the rank-size rule. The cumulative frequencies obtained were for cities with populations exceeding 20,000 and the cumulation proceeded over six size groups, as shown in Table 4.4.

A comparison of the curves representing Pakistan for the years 1961 and 1972 shows clearly that 1972 has a much more extended section of log-normally distributed sizes. This is evidently due to the fact that during the past intercensus decades, a number of cities have shifted to a higher class size because of abrupt increases in their population. The shape of the curve also indicates a considerable deficiency of cities of intermediate size in the years 1951 and 1961. Berry's study confirms that the city-size distribution of Pakistan in 1951 was intermediate between primate and log-normal distribution, though more primate than log-normal.[22] Friedmann believes that Pakistan falls in the transitional category, possessing a primate/intermediate-city mix.[23]

Table 4.4. Frequency Distribution of Towns in Pakistan by Size

Group	Frequency Number 1972	Frequency Number 1961	Cumulative Number 1972	Cumulative Number 1961	Cumulative Percentage 1972	Cumulative Percentage 1961
20,000-50,000	63	39	63	39	58.3	63.9
50,000-100,000	19	10	82	49	75.9	80.3
100,000-250,000	16	6	98	55	90.7	90.1
250,000-500,000	5	4	103	59	95.3	96.7
500,000-1 million	3	0	106	59	98.1	96.7
Over 1 million	2	2	108	61	100.0	100.0

Source: Computed by the author.

Employment Structure

There are several obstacles to a quantitative evaluation of towns and cities in Pakistan on dominant economic functions. The first major limitation is the unavailability of data. The only statistical information in census volumes is on the civilian labor force. These statistics are not reliable, and the occupational data are not complete in their areal coverage. In the absence of suitable data, personal observation supports the view that urbanization in Pakistan is still in its early stages and that many areas in the country, especially the urban localities, are primarily consumption centers rather than production centers. Although tertiary sectors have expanded markedly during the last two decades, many areas still suffer from inadequate growth and manufacturing development.

In 1961, the gainfully employed labor force in urban localities was about 30 percent of the total urban population, compared to about 33 percent for the entire national population. In 1966–1967, the urban work force dropped to a level of 29 percent, declining to 26 percent in 1974–1975. A manpower survey of Pakistan's major occupational groups (1966–1967) reveals that in the urban areas about 86 percent of the total labor force was employed in manufacturing, public service, trade and commerce, and tertiary services, whereas nonurban functions employed 7 percent of the total labor force. Another 7 percent of workers were not classified by occupation. In 1974–1975, some 85 percent of the labor force was employed in sales, various services, and production-related occupations, whereas nonurban functions employed about 6 percent of the total. The remaining 9 percent was employed in the public service sector.

Since Independence, both private and public investment has encouraged a reorganization of industry resulting in considerable growth and some diversification in the manufacturing sector. In 1971–1976, large-scale manufacturing represented 11.6 percent of the total gross national product compared to 3.4 percent in 1949–1954. In all these years, the annual growth rates in the manufacturing sector have been higher than in any other significant sector of the economy, but manufacturing has been very labor-intensive. Manufacturing has remained the largest employer of the total labor force, followed by commerce and services. In 1974–1975, manufacturing and commerce employed 52 percent of the total labor force; services and transport were other important sectors, employing 30 percent (Table 4.5). Workers in secondary and tertiary sectors are in fact low-wage urban workers carrying out low-skilled tasks. Such a labor force is engaged in tasks that are nominally secondary or tertiary.[24]

Table 4.5. Percentage Distribution of Sectoral Labor
            in Urban Areas of Pakistan

Sector	1966-1967	1974-1975
Manufacturing	29	26
Commerce	26	26
Services	20	20
Transport	10	10
Construction	7	6
Agriculture	7	6
Miscellaneous	1	6

Source: Statistical Yearbook 1981, pp. 17-21.

Service Sector

Censuses of establishments for twenty-four cities and towns of varying population size, conducted by the Central Statistics Office of Pakistan between 1965 and 1970, provide basic data on the number of business and industrial establishments and their related employment. The information reveals that most of the services (with the exception of industrial craft and wholesale dealerships, which were involved to some extent in basic activities) were performing nonbasic functions, were regionally oriented, and were providing services and products locally.

The distribution of the business establishments and their employment shows that industrial crafts, retail dealerships, and personal services were the most important, accounting for 83 percent of the total employment, whereas wholesale trade and community services engaged about 11 percent of the total labor. The remaining 6 percent of employment was found with other services. Average employment in each service was low, ranging from two persons per establishment in personal and retail services to twenty-two persons per establishment in the financial institutions. Big cities had larger establishments and employed more people than small towns. Real estate and insurance services were lacking in many small towns, and the financial, transport, and recreational services were extremely inadequate in most of the small and medium-size towns. These services constituted less than 1 percent of the total establishments in each town (Tables 4.6 and 4.7).

This information can be used to produce an index reflecting the modern commercialization process when all services are properly combined (Figure 4.6). Although comparability of the data set was not achieved through time, it was a basic assumption that the variables together will measure the fundamental thrust in spatial modernization of commercial activities. The problems of reducing the data set, in order to isolate the

Table 4.6. Service Sector Employment in Pakistan by Type

Establishment	Mean Employment	Employment per Establishment	Percentage Distribution Employment
Banks and finance	327	22	1.1
Insurance	131	13	0.4
Real estate	18	3	0.1
Wholesale depots	1,070	5	3.5
Wholesale merchants	1,379	3	4.6
Retail	8,006	2	26.5
Transport	426	13	1.4
Community services	986	3	3.3
Professional services	535	4	1.8
Recreation services	245	11	0.8
Personal services	5,400	2	17.9
Industrial	11,669	8	38.6

Note: Based on twenty-four towns and cities.

Source: Census of Establishments, Central Statistical Office, Government of Pakistan, Karachi (1965-1970). Computed by the author.

Table 4.7. Establishment Distribution in Pakistan by Service

Establishment	Mean	Establishment Standard Deviation	Coefficient of Variation
Banks and finance	327	599	183
Insurance	130	352	271
Real estate	18	57	317
Wholesale depots	1,070	2,419	226
Wholesale merchants	1,379	2,996	217
Retail	8,006	12,502	156
Transport	426	987	232
Community services	986	2,096	213
Professional services	535	1,409	263
Recreation services	245	491	200
Personal services	5,401	11,166	207
Industrial	11,669	19,614	168

Source: Computed by the author.

main dimension of commercialization, was handled through principal component analysis.

Factor analyses revealed one underlying factor both in number of establishments and employment in various service sectors. Inspection of the factor loadings shows that all variables entered in the analyses appeared to be high and indicated an underlying attribute common to

Table 4.8.   Rotated Factor Matrix for Establishment
             and Employment in Pakistan

Variable	Establishment	Employment
Urban population	0.97	0.99
Banks and finance	0.98	0.97
Insurance	0.94	0.99
Real estate	0.79	0.75
Wholesale depots	0.74	0.89
Wholesale merchants	0.98	0.99
Retail	0.99	0.96
Transport	0.97	0.98
Community services	0.99	0.99
Professional services	0.99	0.96
Recreation services	0.91	0.98
Personal services	0.99	0.99
Industrial	0.83	0.97

Source: Computed by the author.

all; that is, all the variables seem to be measures of the service sectors to urban population. Thus this factor is apparently the best index of urban functions or commercialization. Moreover, the pattern of rotated loadings essentially brought out the bipolarity of the dimension (Table 4.8). Although some modernization of commercial activities is spreading to the medium-size and small towns, essentially such development and growth of towns and concomitant expansion of commercialization within these towns is limited in many respects.

The ranking patterns of the factor scores (from positive high to negative high) place the cities and towns into high, medium, and low categories of commercial development. Employment in the service sector has been concentrated in large cities—such as Karachi and Hyderabad in Sind; Lahore, Rawalpindi, Faisalabad, Gujranwala, and Sialkot in Punjab; Peshawar in NWFP; and Quetta in Baluchistan. A lack of growth in service sectors appears in Mirpur Khas, Larkana, and Jacobabad in Sind, in Bahawalpur, Khanewal, and Norowal in Punjab, and in Nowshera in NWFP. This lack is a consequence of unfavorable structural and performance factors. A structural problem may be characterized by a high proportion of unemployment nationally. Many service establishments are understaffed and static, including community service, transport, insurance, and finance. Some small and medium-size towns are experiencing proportional declines in employment in various services (Figure 4.6).

Urban population growth has probably increased the potential for local growth in the demand for various services; industrial crafts, including large-scale manufacture, show some dependence on locally

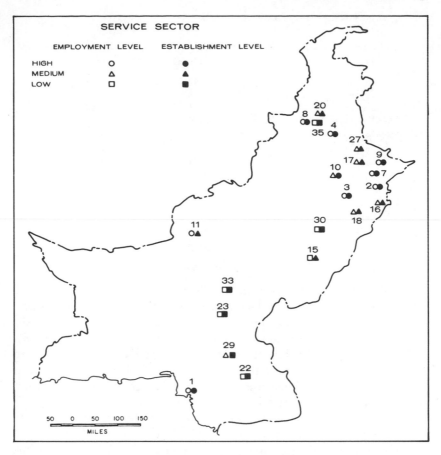

Figure 4.6. Index of Urban Commercialization in Pakistan. Key to Cities: 1, Karachi; 2, Lahore; 3, Faisalabad; 4, Rawalpindi; 7, Gujranwala; 8, Peshawar; 9, Sialkot; 10, Sargodha; 11, Quetta; 15, Bahawalpur; 16, Kasur; 17, Gujrat; 18, Okara; 20, Mardan; 22, Mirpur Khas; 23, Larkana; 27, Jhelum; 29, Nawabshah; 30, Khanewal; 33, Jacobabad; 35, Nowshera

based, tertiary-level, commercial activities, particularly shipping and import–export. Because the urban system has not experienced technological change, labor-intensive administrative and clerical operations have been preserved, providing employment in the nation's large cities. Some growth has occurred in personal and community services provided by local administrations in large and medium-size towns. Often such growth is not tied to that of the local economy. However, quaternary services (banks and financial institutions) have expanded rapidly in large and medium-size cities.

Urban Development and Planning

Initially Pakistan's urban problems were associated with the overall national development programs, and some patchwork schemes, related to urban housing, water supply, sewage, and drainage, were introduced in the metropolitan areas. In the 1970s, many planners and government officials realized that regional and urban development programs had to be spelled out in more positive terms within the national and provincial context, along with the possibilities for decentralization of governmental power and dispersal of economic activities. Moreover, planners asserted that a selection should be made from the existing smaller and medium-size towns that showed potential as growth poles, and their growth should be encouraged. Since there is an urgent need for regional and urban development programs throughout the country, the overall objectives of any plan should be to meet the housing needs of people and to distribute population and facilities for living in urban and rural communities through the growth of economic activities and employment opportunities.

The only outcome of these proposals was the creation of the Environment and Urban Affairs Division, an organization charged with development of programs to help rural–urban migration and the location of additional infrastructure to facilitate "agroville" development schemes in the country. Urban development authorities have been established in the metropolitan areas of Karachi, Hyderabad, Lahore, and Faisalabad, and they have independently executed a few schemes related to housing, water supply, and sewage and drainage. No comprehensive programs of urban development have been designed or executed with a view to evaluating urbanization and industrialization problems. The housing backlog in urban areas has increased. The condition of water and power supplies is even more alarming. Hardly 10 percent of the total population has access to drinkable water; even in large urban areas, not more than 30 percent of the population has access to piped water. Only 7 percent of the urban population has water supplied to their houses. Piped sewage and solid waste disposal is available to 2–4 percent of the total population in the urban areas, while the rest use either the traditional disposal system or open drains. Only 40 to 60 percent of the urban population has access to open drains.

In 1978, policymakers reemphasized that urban and rural development must constitute an integrated whole covering the elements of resource endowment, agricultural production, rural development, industrialization, industrial location policy, urban development, linkage between urban and rural areas, and the interacting sociocultural factors. The implementation of sector policies without attention to their spatial impact, in both rural and urban areas, may have severely damaging effects. The laissez-faire policies of the past already have resulted in continued dominance of the primate city, and the present administration has lost opportunities to guide the pattern of urbanization on sound socioeconomic lines.

Guidelines and policies in relation to population growth should be introduced by promoting a more efficient metropolitan spatial reorganization. Towns and cities must be linked with the metropolitan system to improve regional socioeconomic efficiency and increase their attractiveness for industry and for migrants. Rural conditions must be improved to the point where the rural population reduces its propensity to migrate to the city.

Strategies of development and related programs need to focus on the largest cities in each region, promoting their role as the regional metropolises; at the same time, regional development should be planned to maximize spillovers into the smaller towns of each region. Regional centers should be developed by selecting small towns as growth poles. This action requires not only promotion of backward linkages for the establishment of firms from the smaller cities to the regional centers, but also implementation of a regionwide transportation system and administrative decentralization at the regional and subregional levels.

Conclusions

In the post-Independence years, despite some modification, the basic urban structure has remained unchanged in most cities and still exhibits persistent structural inequalities, services, and spatial standards. The growth of cities has been closely related to the development of agriculture. The process of industrialization and its linkage with agricultural resources has set up intense migration within the labor force, resulting in overurbanization.

As a process of local significance, urbanism continues to be influenced by the tradition of society at large, which is predominantly rural. Development processes should aim at upgrading the living standards of rural residents by improving the economic and living conditions of villages and old towns. Most urban centers in the country are neither functionally diversified nor specialized. The range of economic activity is confined largely to trade, administration, nonurban functions, and some manufacturing. Dualism seems to persist in service sectors, however, ranging from a highly skilled professional subsector, primarily in the large cities, to unskilled labor-intensive economic enterprises characterized by low productivity, underemployment, and seasonal and casual employment. Urban planning has had negligible impact on the amelioration of urban problems, and the institutional framework is woefully inadequate to solve many interurban or regional problems.

For efficient social and administrative services, as well as for overall economic transition, large centers need to be connected with local administrative centers, *mandi* towns, and collection and distribution centers. Such transformation of the society's structure, dominated by agricultural activities on the one hand and service-rendering centers on the other, needs the emergence of new communities as a focal point for an efficient organization regionally oriented to economic functions and for the creation of modern administration and social services.

In short, the problems of urbanization in Pakistan must be studied in a regional context. Despite the deficiences of such studies in different areas of Pakistan, one can sense that the current philosophy of socioeconomic and urban development lags behind suitable planning practice, causing acute regional and urban development imbalances.

NOTES

1. Raanan Weitz, *Urbanization and the Developing Countries: Report on the Sixth Rehovoe Conference* (New York: Praeger, 1971), p. 26.

2. John Friedmann and Robert Wulff, *The Urban Transition: Comparative Studies of Newly Industrializing Societies,* Progress in Geography: International Reviews of Current Research, vol. 0 (New York: St. Martin's Press, 1976), p. 8.

3. G. T. Rozmann, *Urban Networks in Ching China and Tokugawa Japan* (Princeton, N.J.: Princeton University Press, 1973).

4. T. G. McGee, *The Urbanization Process in the Third World: Explorations in Search of Theory* (London: Bell, 1971).

5. D. Hall, *A Spatial Analysis of Urban Community Development Policy in India* (New York: Research Studies Press, 1980), p. 11.

6. S. Piggott, *Prehistoric India* (Middlesex: Penguin Books, 1950), p. 70.

7. A. D. King, *Colonial Urban Development: Culture, Social Power and Environment* (London: Routledge & Kegan Paul, 1976), p. 38.

8. W. W. Drew, *Census of India 1891: Bombay and Its Feudatories, Report,* vol. 7 (Bombay, 1892), p. 72.

9. H. A. Rose, *Census of India 1901: The Punjab, Its Feudatories and the Northwest Frontier Province,* vol. 17 (Simla, 1902), p. 21.

10. P. H. Kaul, *Census of India 1911: Punjab,* vol. 14, pt. 1 (Lahore, 1912), pp. 17–18.

11. M. S. Jilani, "Resettlement of Displaced Persons in Pakistan" (Ph.D. dissertation, University of Chicago, 1962), p. 54.

12. Q. S. Ahmad, "Urbanization in Pakistan" (M.A. thesis, University of Chicago, 1963), pp. 22–23.

13. *Pakistan Statistical Yearbook: 1981,* Government of Pakistan, 1982, p. 6.

14. S. J. Burki, "Development of Towns: The Pakistan Experience," *Asian Survey* 14 (8) (1974): 756–758.

15. Ibid.

16. V. Belokrenitsky, "The Urbanization Processes and the Social Structure of the Urban Population in Pakistan," *Asian Survey* 14 (3) (1974): 251.

17. A. H. Siddiqi, "Regional Inequalities in the Development of Pakistan," *Geojournal* 5 (1) (1981): 17–32.

18. Ahmad, "Urbanization in Pakistan," p. 17.

19. Burki, "Development of Towns," pp. 756–758.

20. A. H. Siddiqi, "Manufacturing and Planning Industrial Development in Pakistan," *Tijdschrift Voor Economishe en Sociale Geographie* 70 (4) (1979): 205.

21. Hall, *Spatial Analysis,* p. 11.

22. B. J. L. Berry, "City Size Distribution and Economic Development," *Economic Development and Cultural Change* 9 (July 1961): 573–587.

23. J. Friedmann, *Regional Development* (Cambridge: MIT Press, 1966), p. 7.

24. M. A. Qadeer, "Do Cities Modernize in Developing Countries?" *Comparative Studies in Society and History* 16 (1974): 266–283.

5. Urban Development Trends in China

SHUNZAN YE

A REVIEW of the literature on Chinese urbanization reveals five major characteristics:[1] pace of urbanization, growth of the urban population, distribution of cities and towns, economic character of cities, and basis of urbanization.

Main Features of Chinese Urbanization

Pace of Urbanization

The process of urbanization in China has progressed slowly, and the level of urbanization is rather low. From 1949 to 1983, the percentage of China's urban population rose from 10.6 to 14.6 percent according to official figures, while that of the world was 42.2 percent around 1980.[2] The average annual increase was only slightly more than 0.1 percent during the thirty-four years. The annual growth rate of China's urban population was 2.79 percent during 1949–1981, but the annual growth rates of the developed countries and the developing countries were 2.1 and 4.5 percent, respectively.[3]

Growth of the Urban Population

The growth of urban population has occurred in the form of expansion of existing cities and towns; urban population is highly concentrated in large cities. China is a densely populated country with a long history of dependence on agriculture. There are numerous cities and towns of different sizes widely distributed in the country, but 90 percent of the new cities (both newly built and those promoted from towns) have evolved from prior towns. All cities and towns have been expanding, but their rates of growth are different. Two-thirds of the small cities have developed into medium-size and large ones, and a few have even evolved into metropolises.[4] In the period 1952–1982, the population increase of

75

Table 5.1. Number and Size of Chinese Cities: 1949, 1965, and 1983

	1949		1965		1982		Increased Number During 1949-1982
City Size	No.	% of Total	No.	% of Total	No.	% of Total	
Metropolises	6	5.2	12	7.0	20	8.2	14
Large cities	8	6.9	19	11.1	28	11.4	20
Medium-size cities	17	14.6	44	25.7	71	29.0	54
Small cities	85	73.3	96	56.2	126	51.4	41
Total	116	100.0	171	100.0	245	100.0	129

Source: Panshou Sun, "The Changes of City Size in New China,"
Acta Geographica Sinica 39(4) (1984): 346.

Table 5.2. Proportion of City Population by City Size in China's
Total City Population: 1952, 1965, and 1982

	1952 (%)	1965 (%)	1982 (%)	Increase of Urban Population (1952-1982)	
City Size				No. (1000's)	%
Metropolises	41.1	43.0	43.3	23,352	45.2
Large cities	19.0	20.5	20.5	11,296	21.9
Medium-size cities	17.4	20.7	22.4	13,811	26.8
Small cities	22.5	15.8	13.8	3,170	6.1
Total	100.0	100.0	100.0	51,629	100.0

Source: See Table 5.1.

China's metropolises, large cities, and medium-size cities totaled 48.46 million, accounting for 93.9 percent of the total urban population increase of the country (51.63 million). Most of the increase occurred in the large cities. Two-thirds of the large cities and metropolises have increased their population by more than 50 percent in the thirty-year period, compared with only one-half of the medium-size cities and less than one-fifth of the small cities.[5]

As Tables 5.1 and 5.2 show, the number of large and medium-size cities increased at a greater rate than the small cities during the past thirty-three years. The number of designated towns decreased from 5,404 in 1953 to 2,786 in 1983, however, because in most cases they were found to have a low proportion of nonagricultural population, although in some cases they have grown into cities.[6] The 1955 resolution of the Chinese State Council defined a designated town as a settlement with 2,000 inhabitants or more, of which at least half are engaged in nonagricultural pursuits. In 1963 the State Council changed this and defined a designated town as a settlement with 3,000 inhabitants or more, of which at least 70 percent are nonagricultural. The city was defined as a settlement with a population of over 100,000, of which the agricultural population does not exceed 20 percent.

As a result, China's urban population is highly concentrated in large cities: 60.6 percent of the total urban population of China is in cities of over half a million and 41.1 percent in metropolises. In 1983 there were forty-eight large cities; twenty of them were metropolises. China has more large cities and metropolises than any other nation in the world.

Distribution of Cities and Towns

Cities and towns in China tend to be unevenly distributed throughout the country. On the basis of socioeconomic development, China can be divided into coastal, interior, and remote regions (Figure 5.1). The coastal region includes Liaoning, Hebei, Beijing, Tianjin, Shandong, Jiangsu, Shanghai, Zhejiang, Fujian, Guangdong, and Guangxi (eleven provinces, autonomous regions, and municipalities under direct jurisdiction of the central government). The interior region includes Shanxi, Shaanxi, Henan, Anhui, Jiangxi, Hubei, Hunan, Sichuan, and Guizhou (nine provinces). The remote region is made

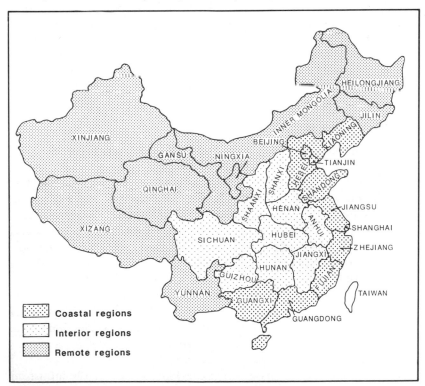

Figure 5.1. Regional Division of China

up of Heilongjiang, Jilin, Nei Monggol, Ningxia, Gansu, Xinjiang, Qinghai, Xizang, and Yunnan (nine provinces and autonomous regions).

The more rapidly growing cities are located in the interior and remote regions, due largely to China's rapid industrial development in the early 1950s in these regions. By 1982, sixty-one new cities had been built in the interior region, compared with thirty-six in the remote region and thirty-two in the coastal region. Tables 5.3 and 5.4 show that the proportion of the number of cities in the coastal region from the country's total had dropped from 49.1 percent (1949) to 36.3 percent (1982). The proportion increased in both the interior and remote regions, however, from 32.8 to 40.4 percent and from 18.1 to 23.3 percent, respectively. During the period from 1952 to 1982, the urban population of the interior region increased by 37.6 percent. In the remote and coastal regions, the growth was 34.4 and 28.0 percent, respectively. As a result, the overconcentration of population in the coastal region was alleviated to some extent between the years 1953 and 1983. The proportion of the urban population in the coastal areas declined from 53.0 to 45.7 percent. Meanwhile the urban proportion of the interior region of the country's total increased slightly, from 31.8 to 32.3 percent. As Table 5.5 shows, most of the urban population increase in the country has happened in remote areas. Due to abundant natural resources for industry, urban development has progressed much faster in northern China. Of the fast-growing cities in China, 68 percent (sixty-three cities) are found in the northern part of the country.

Economic Character of Cities

The economic nature of the Chinese city has been changing from a consumptive to a productive base. In old China the levels of employment in the cities were very low. Many cities and towns were essentially dilapidated and heavily exploited by landlords. Modern industry was nonexistent in many of the cities and towns, and the small and medium-size cities were almost invariably consumer societies with little industry and fewer than 20 percent of the residents employed. Since 1949 the traditional consumer cities and towns have been gradually transformed into industrial/commercial cities and towns. Now 81 percent of working-age city residents are employed,[7] and industrial production in the cities has been multiplied many times. From 1949 to 1983, China's industrial production increased by 20 times, but the industrial production of the cities of Beijing, Shanghai, and Tianjin increased by 248, 30, and 34.6 times respectively during the same period.[8]

Small cities and towns have also experienced remarkable industrial

Table 5.3.   Number of Cities in China by Region: 1949 and 1982

	China		Coastal Region		Interior Region		Remote Region	
Year	No.	%	No.	%	No.	%	No.	%
1949	116	100.0	57	49.1	38	32.8	21	18.1
1982	245	100.0	89	36.3	99	40.4	57	23.3

Source: See Table 5.1.

Table 5.4.   Number of Cities with a Population Increase
of 50 Percent or More: 1952-1982

	China	Coastal Region	Interior Region	Remote Region
Number	93	26	35	32
Percentage	100.0	28.0	37.6	34.4

Source: See Table 5.1.

Table 5.5.   Urban and Total Population by Region (in thousands):
1953 and 1983

	Year	China		Coastal Region		Interior Region		Remote Region	
		No.	%	No.	%	No.	%	No.	%
Urban	1953	75,260	100	39,900	53	23,920	31	11,440	15
population	1983	149,618	100	60,312	46	48,431	32	32,875	22
Total	1953	580,060	100	248,580	43	263,270	45	68,760	11
population	1983	1,020,713	100	420,746	41	448,570	44	151,397	15

Source: State Statistical Bureau.

development, and local industries have increased manyfold. Originally China's towns were primarily commercial centers or marketplaces in rural areas with traditional trades or handicrafts. Now these towns have become local economic centers with small industrial enterprises and cultural/educational facilities at the grass roots level. The proportions of industrial labor are increasing in rural areas. In Shanghai's rural area, for instance, the value of gross industrial output makes up 74 to 80 percent of the total value of industrial and agricultural output, and industrial workers constitute 29 to 32 percent of the total rural labor force. The industry of market towns has absorbed more than one-third of the total rural laborers. Of the total workers in township enterprises,[9] 65 to 75 percent were living in villages but working in nearby towns.[10] Because of rural industrial development, the goods that the towns supplied to the cities are no longer limited to farm products but now also include industrial goods. For a long time the only link between city and countryside was the on-and-off exchange of goods in small quantities. But today, besides the exchange of goods, there are increasing exchanges of technological and other information. Rural enterprises are realizing the importance of technology and have begun to seek technical assistance from urban research institutes.

The policy of converting the consumer cities into productive ones has played a positive role in developing China's economy. Because of ideological confusion about "consumption" and "production," however, the development of tertiary industry has been slow. Persons engaged in tertiary industry make up only 15 percent of China's employed people. This rate is less than that in many developing countries, including India where 20 percent of the employed are in the tertiary sector, compared with 50 to 70 percent in developed countries. About 20 percent of the gross national product is produced by tertiary industry, while it is 40 percent in India and 50 to 65 percent in developed countries. The expenditure on personal services averages 4 percent of the total personal expenditure, considerably lower than the 20 to 30 percent in Hungary and Yugoslavia and 40 percent in developed countries.[11] The backwardness of China's tertiary industry has created many obstacles to industrial and agricultural production, and to the people's daily lives. This effect has been heavily reflected in the widespread deterioration of the quality of urban life throughout the country.

Economic reforms since 1979 have changed the attitude of the Chinese toward tertiary industry. Now it is recognized as an important part of the national economy. At present, China is striving to develop commerce and service trades through economic reform to meet the increasing demand of the people for goods and services in both rural and urban areas. Meanwhile, urban labor surplus is expected to increase because of urban economic reforms and improved labor efficiency in rural areas. As much as one-fourth of the total urban labor force is expected to become unemployed because of these changes.[12] Therefore, the development of tertiary industry has been accelerated to absorb the urban unemployed. This rapid development is an important factor in the faster rate of urbanization in China in the last few years.

Basis of Urbanization

Urbanization has been based on economic growth in both urban and rural areas. Urban economic growth has been proceeding simultaneously with rural economic development. Since 1979, urban–rural integration has aided rural development in many respects. There has been considerable diffusion of urban industry to rural areas as well as the formation of more joint industrial enterprises run by urban and rural interest groups. This is a new way of achieving urban–rural industrial cooperation on the basis of labor division according to specialization of production. Now urban industrial enterprises are extending into rural areas and combining with township enterprises. Joint urban–rural enterprises complement and benefit each other. Cities supply equipment and technology to rural areas, which in turn provide land and labor for production. This new development can contribute to a more balanced form of urbanization, help control the size of the large cities, and promote the development of small cities and towns.

The new economic reform policies being implemented in urban and rural areas since 1979 have helped to narrow the gap between town and country. Since 1979 the peasants' gross income has increased by 1.31 times and that of the urban labor force has increased by 0.67 times. The rural/urban income ratio has changed from 1:2.4 to 1:1.7.[13] Peasants in some parts of Beijing, Tianjin, Shanghai, Jiangsu, and Zhejiang now earn more income than the urban population.

Current Policies Promoting China's Urbanization

Prior to 1979, many towns declined because the state monopolized commercial functions, including the purchasing, marketing, and distribution of major farm products such as grain, cotton, and edible oil. Rural sideline production was kept low because of the lopsided emphasis on grain production. Individual traders almost disappeared after the socialist transformation in the 1950s. The result was a dwindling population in the towns, while the city population expanded and rural areas saw a growing surplus labor force.

Since the Third Plenary Session of the Eleventh Central Committee of the Chinese Communist Party,[14] major changes have taken place. This meeting adopted a series of policies to accelerate the development of agriculture and to motivate the peasants. As a result, China's agriculture is changing from a semi-self-sufficient economy to one of market production using modern methods of farming.

Six major policies are helping to bring about enormous growth in the rural economy, increasing urbanization in rural areas, causing a significant change in the peasant life-style and way of thinking, and promoting further development of the large and medium-size cities. These policies are summarized in the following sections.

The Contract Responsibility System

The contract responsibility system of farming based on households is a powerful stimulus that has greatly motivated individual initiative. It has also resulted in a major increase in agricultural production and, simultaneously, in rural labor surplus—two important elements necessary for urbanization in rural areas.

The contract responsibility system of agricultural production and the diversification of the rural economy have promoted specialization of agricultural production. The creation and vigorous development of specialized households has promoted the division of labor and led to increased productivity. It is estimated that there are 24.82 million specialized households in China (about 14 percent of the total number of peasant households in the countryside). Specialized villages, special markets, and small special economic districts have appeared in some regions. Rural goods entering the market have risen from 51 percent in 1978 to more than 60 percent in 1983.[15] Specialization and commercialization of agricultural production have significantly enriched the rural economy.

As agricultural productivity increases, many villages and towns have also prospered. For instance, Pitiao village (Taihe county, Anhui province) has two newly formed specialized markets for nylon rope. Entertainment and other service trades within the market towns would not have developed without these markets.[16]

The responsibility system in agricultural production has greatly raised production and economic efficiency. According to a sampling study of 198 households by the Zhuxian Committee for Agricultural Regionalization,[17] the labor/days required for a *mu* on average for the county was 40.4 in 1982, compared with 68.6 in 1974 (the most efficient year before introduction of the responsibility system), and the profits from each *mu* on average were 77.60 and 30.00 yuan in the respective years.[18] Consequently, the county saved 60 percent of its labor force. The occupational structure of the county's farmers was as follows: 16 percent in agricultural production, 47 percent in industrial sideline production, and 37 percent surplus in the year of investigation. This should be quite representative of the situation in the North China Plain.

According to Vice-Premier Yao Yilin, the responsibility system created a surplus labor force of about 200 million in China's countryside, but only 100 million farmworkers are needed.[19] As the level of mechanization of agriculture is enhanced in the future, there will be more surplus rural labor. According to estimates made by the Ministry of Agriculture, Animal Husbandry, and Forestry, by the end of this century the agricultural sector will need no more than 50 percent of the total rural labor force (60 percent for farming and 40 percent for animal husbandry, forestry, and fishing). Of this surplus, 20 percent could be absorbed by state-owned enterprises or institutions in urban places and the other 80 percent will be available to do nonagricultural jobs in rural areas. This surplus labor must be used in industry, communications, transport, and service trades, and many small cities and towns are being built to absorb this surplus labor force.[20]

The people's commune system, which had integrated functions of civil administration with economic management, is now ill suited to the present production practices and harmful to further development of the rural economy. To further economic development, the government decided to abolish the commune administrative system. Separation of the political and economic functions of the people's communes led to the reestablishment of townships to assume local administrative functions. These changes began in 1982 and were completed in 1984.

During 1982–1984, new production administrative systems were established to assume the former function of the people's communes. The Huaxiang Agro/Industrial/Commercial Integrated Complex, for example, established in 1983 in the Huangtugang area, a southern suburb of Beijing, has ten companies specializing in such activities as vegetable farming, animal raising, flower and plant growing, machine and transportation services, agrotechnical services, edible fungus growing, commercial services, and engineering and production services. Under each company are management/administrative stations, and under the stations are specialized brigades, groups, households, and individuals. These specialized production administrative systems have greatly increased the economic strength of the area. The total income of 1983, the first year after reorganization, was 28.8 percent more than that of 1982.[21]

Township Enterprises

The development of township enterprises funded by the communes and brigades promises to enrich the life of the peasants and to offer nonfarm jobs to surplus rural labor. It has also increased the prosperity of rural towns.

Although rural industries have developed rapidly since the late 1950s, they have very few ties with the peasant economy. The establishment of factories run by communes and brigades since the early 1970s has brought considerable economic development to rural areas. After the Third Plenum of the Eleventh Party Central Committee held in December 1978, township enterprises have developed more vigorously than ever before. During the years 1978–1983, for example, the total income of township enterprises in the Beijing area increased threefold.[22] Now there are 209 counties in China (or 10 percent of the nation's total counties) which have an annual income of more than 100 million yuan each derived from township enterprises.[23]

The income from the township enterprises has become an important part of the rural economy. For the nation as a whole, township enterprises are producing a quarter of the total rural output.[24] In some economically developed areas like Shanghai municipality, the share of industry is 74 to 80 percent of the total output value of industry and agriculture put together, while the income from township enterprises contributes 64 percent of the total income of the rural economy in the area.[25] In Shunyi county, Beijing municipality, the figure is 70 percent and in Jiangsu province it is 25 percent.[26] The proportions of total peasant income provided by township enterprises are 53 percent in Shanghai municipality[27] and 51 percent in Suzhou municipality.[28] The contribution of township enterprises to the country's income increased by 28 percent in 1984.[29]

In developed regions, township enterprises have been successful in absorbing surplus rural labor into their industrial and commercial sectors. For example, half of the total labor force in Beijing's rural suburbs have gone to work in township factories.[30] The labor force employed by township enterprises in Shanghai's suburbs grew from 124,000 in 1970 to 748,300 in 1981, a sixfold increase.[31] In Jiangsu province, there are nearly 1 million peasants leaving farms for township enterprises every year. By the end of 1982, 4.2 million peasants had left farming.[32] Now one out of every six peasants in Jiangsu is working in a township enterprise.[33] On average, 10 percent of the rural labor force of China has been transferred to township enterprises in the countryside.[34]

Township enterprises in all parts of the country have provided significant funding for the construction of rural towns. Between 1979 and 1982 the total sum of their contribution for that purpose was 7.9 billion yuan.[35] According to the investigation reports, 72 percent of the total investment in capital construction of the town of Xinta (Wujiang county, Jiangsu province) came from funds accumulated by commune-run factories.[36] In Huazhuang (Wuxi county, Jiangsu province), township enterprises have provided money to build a department store, a hotel, a restaurant, a tea shop, a drugstore, a barber shop, a photographic studio, a commune hospital, schools, a storytelling hall, and a theater. The population of the town has grown rapidly. The population of towns in the region of Suzhou municipality increased by 50.8 percent between 1979 and 1982, mainly as a result of the development of township enterprises.[37] In brief, the development of township enterprises is one of the main factors contributing to the prosperity of rural towns.

New Rules on Migration and Designated Towns

Peasants have been permitted to move to towns to engage in industrial and commercial activities and to provide services. They are self-sufficient in food supply. This development has been accompanied by the relaxation of regulations governing the establishment of designated towns.

At the beginning of January 1984, the Central Committee of the Chinese Communist Party issued the "No. 1 Document" on rural economic policies. The document indicates that in appropriate regions, peasants are allowed to move to towns to work or to operate their businesses with their own food supply. They can be registered as nonpermanent or permanent residents in the towns and can rent (but not build) their houses there. The document opened a broad new channel for rural town growth. In October 1984, the State Council published "The Circular on the Movement of Peasants to Towns for Settlement." It urged government at all levels to give firm support to peasants with special skills who were managerially competent to do business in towns (excluding county seats). Township governments are required to protect the lawful rights and interests of peasants with legitimate economic operations. Peasants may transfer their contracted farmlands to others before moving to towns, but they are allowed to return to their home villages permanently if they so desire.[38]

These measures have greatly stimulated the growth of both the economy and the population of towns. Rural towns are thriving again all over the country. The town of Yuantan (Qingyuan county, Guangdong province), for example, has accepted thirty-nine households with seventy-seven peasants who have moved from villages during the first half of 1984 after implementing the policy outlined in the "No. 1 Document." Some of them built houses, and their children were accepted by the local schools.[39]

Another example is the town of Chaopi in Henan province. There were 201 households permitted to engage in private industries and commercial activities before 1984, and the number increased to 374 five months after implementing the document; among them 98 were granted resident status. The daily migratory population, mainly sellers and visitors to the local markets, has increased from about 3,000 to 10,000. The volume of town businesses during the first quarter of 1984 was twice that of the same quarter a year before. In Jiansong, another town in Henan, 64 specialized households had moved into the town by the end of May 1984, and the number was expected to rise to 1,000 by the end of the year. The number of business streets has risen from one to eight, and fourteen bus routes now exist where there were none before.[40]

In terms of distance of migration, the vast majority of the rural households that have moved to small cities and towns do not move beyond their townships, as the migration data on central Hebei province show (Table 5.6). In early 1984, very few households that had moved to the six small cities and towns in central Heibei were from other provinces.

Table 5.6. Number of Peasants and Households Moved to Cities and Towns in Central Hebei Province: January-April 1984

City/ Town	Households	Persons	From Native Township Households	%	From Native Country Households	%	From Native Province Households	%	From Other Province Households	%
Langfang	786	1,572	632	75.7	129	16.4	20	2.5	5	0.6
Sanhe	263	679	155	58.9	89	33.8	3	1.1	16	6.1
Yanjiao	52	115	44	85.0			8	15.0		
Subtotal	1,101	2,366	831	75.5	218	19.8	31	2.8	21	1.9
Baxian	203	1,739								
Gaobeidian	315	1,284								
Hengshui	874	1,293								

Source: Meijin Wang, "Hebei xiaojizhen huji guanli chuyi," in Hebei Learnee Journal (ed.), Xiao chengzhen de fazhan daolu, 1984, pp. 182-189.

Although the rural economy has been booming since 1979, the construction of towns has not caught up with rural development. Indeed, the number of designated towns had been decreasing up to the end of 1983. There are two main reasons for the drop. First, the classification of "nonagricultural population" was based on household registration and not on occupation because it was designed to accompany the system of food rationing; second, the definition of designated town which had been in force since 1963 was clearly outmoded. To suit the needs of rural economic and cultural development, the Ministry of Civil Affairs conducted case studies of rual towns in 1984 and submitted a report on the readjustment of regulations governing the establishment of designated towns to the State Council.[41] The State Council approved the report at the end of November 1984.[42] According to the new regulations, designated towns could be established in the following places:

1. All county seats. Before that, 377 county seats were not designated towns and as such were treated as rural settlements.[43]

2. Township seats with a nonagricultural population of more than 2,000 if the township's total population is less than 20,000; or township seats with a nonagricultural population of more than 10 percent if the township's total population is more than 20,000.

3. Places in minority nationality areas, sparsely populated remote regions or mountainous areas, small mining industrial districts, or small ports, scenic tourist places, frontier trading places, and the like where the nonagricultural population is less than 2,000 but it is necessary to set up designated towns there.

If a township is qualified to establish a designated town, the villages of the township will be under the jurisdiction of the town. In fact, all provinces of the country have a strong desire to establish more designated towns to meet the needs of their regional development. If a rural settlement has been promoted to a designated urban place (town or city), it will be able to obtain more funds from the central and local government for economic development and urban construction. The residents of urban places also enjoy many advantages in terms of employment, migration, and food and materials supplied by the state. According to the Ministry of Civil Affairs, there were 7,469 designated towns by the end of 1984.

Reform of the Administrative System

The reform of the administrative system since 1983 has enabled the city to exercise more direct leadership over the surrounding counties, resulting in closer ties between city and countryside. Under the new administrative system a city has better access to rural agricultural and sideline products as well as land, thus promoting the city's economic and physical development. Meanwhile, the countryside also has better access to urban economic, technical, and cultural support and to funds for establishing industrial facilities and construction in rural towns.

In the past, little direct relationship existed between the large and medium-size cities and the counties in a province. The new system has given the city government the power to administer surrounding counties. In Liaoning and Jiangsu provinces where the economy is well developed, the cities administered nearby counties for many years before 1983 with positive results. Under the new administrative system, the gross output value has increased. For example, Liaoning province's county-run and commune-run industries increased their output by 100 percent between 1976 and 1982.[44] And the output of township enterprises of Wuxi municipality (Jiangsu) increased by 51 percent in 1984.[45]

New Roles for Central Cities

The government has recognized the importance of large and medium-size cities and metropolises in regional economic development. Since 1982, Chinese economists have held three conferences on the role of central cities in facilitating regional economic development. Administrative measures have been taken to enable the central cities to get more involved in regional economic activities on the basis of market forces. This has helped to remove the barrier between regions and those between local authorities and state agencies. Regional trade is thus facilitated and transregional economic zones and networks are gradually being formed. Many large cities such as Chongqing and Qingdao have enlarged their jurisdictions by absorbing nearby counties.

New Economic Zones

Further opening of port cities and coastal areas and the establishment of special economic zones have stimulated considerable development of cities and towns in the coastal region. Special economic zones (SEZs) were established in Shenzhen, Zhuhai, and Shantou in Guangdong province and in Xiamen in Fujian province in 1981 to facilitate technical cooperation and trade with foreign countries. Thus far, fourteen coastal port cities (Dalian, Qinhuangdao, Tianjin, Yantai, Qingdao, Lianyungang, Nantong, Shanghai, Ningbo, Wenzhou, Fuzhou, Guangzhou, Zhanjiang, and Beihai) have been opened to foreign firms for economic development. Moreover, Hainan Island has adopted an open policy similar to that of the four SEZs.

In February 1985, the State Council further opened up the Pearl River Delta, the Yangtze River Delta, and the Southern Fujian Triangle Area centered on Zhangzhou, Quanzhou, and Xiamen as coastal economic zones. The purpose is to produce for the foreign market. Foreign trade has become the top priority in the planning of these zones, followed by industry and agriculture.[46] According to recent information, the State Council may further open up Liaodong and Jiaodong peninsulas as coastal economic zones in the near future.[47]

Conclusion

China has been undergoing rapid economic growth as a result of major reforms instituted since 1979. Policy reforms have greatly relaxed government control of local economic affairs and permitted the use of market forces by all units of production to maximize profit. Improved agricultural production has provided China with a strong base for further urban development. Moreover, large and medium-size cities are expected to play a leading role in promoting regional economic growth while coastal cities and special economic zones have been called upon by the state to attract foreign investment and facilitate export. Such developments represent major departures from the pattern of urbanization prior to 1978. As these changes have been instituted for only a few years, their long-term implications vis à-vis national development in general and urbanization in particular are not entirely clear. In the short run, however, it appears that cities of all sizes in China will grow and the nation's level of urbanization will continue to increase, especially in the coastal region.

NOTES

1. Shunzen Ye, "Urbanization and Housing in China," *Asian Geographer,* 1 (2) (1982): 1–11; Shunn Ye, "Urbanization and Current Issues in Regional Development Plan in China," in D. R. Diamong, K. Hottes, and Chuanchun Wu (eds.), *Regional Planning in Different Political Systems: The Chinese Setting* (Bochum, 1984), p. 1; Xueqiang Xu, "Characteristics of Urbanization of China: Changes and Causes of Urban Population Growth and Distribution," *Asian Geographer* 3 (1) (1984): 15–28.
See also Sen-dou Chang, "Urbanization and Economic Readjustment in China," in Chi-Keung Leung and Steve S. K. Chin (eds.), *China in Readjustment* (Hong Kong: Center of Asian Studies, University of Hong Kong, 1983), pp. 193–215; Sen-dou Chang, "Distribution of China's City Population, 1982," paper for the Workshop on China's 1982 Population Census, December 1984, Honolulu; Anthony Gar-On Yeh and Xueqiang Xu, "Provincial Varia-

tion of Urbanization and Urban Primacy in China," *Annals of Regional Science* 18 (3) (1983): 1–20.

See also Zhang and others, "Shilun Shenzhen jingji tequ renkou fazhan de rougan tezheng" [Discussion on some characteristics of the development of population in the speical economic zone of Shenzhen], *Renkou Yanjiu* [The study of population], no. 2 (1984): 28–31; Sidney Goldstein, "Urbanization in China: New Insights from the 1982 Census," *Papers of the East–West Population Institute* (Honolulu: East–West Center, 1985); Kaihua Hu and Wei Chen, "Woguo chenzhen renkou tongji de youguan wenti" [Issues concerning statistics of city and town population in our country], *Renkou yu Jingji* [Population and economy], no. 3 (1984): 39–42.

2. Urban population, according to these data, excludes the agricultural population in the suburban districts of municipalities. See Xuwei Hu, "Dui woguo chengzhenhua shuiping de boxi" [Analysis of Chinese urbanization level], *Chengshi guihua* [City planning review], no. 2 (1983): 23–26.

3. Xu, "Characteristics of Urbanization of China," pp. 15–28.

4. Chinese cities are classified according to their population as follows: (1) small city, usually with a population of 100,000 to 199,999; (2) medium-size city, with a population of 200,000 to 499,999; (3) large city, with a population between half a million and 1 million; (4) metropolis, with a population of more than 1 million.

5. Panshou Sun, "The Changes of City Size in New China," *Acta Geographica Sinica* 39 (4) (1984): 345–358.

6. Data from the Ministry of Urban and Rural Construction and Environmental Protection.

7. Calculated by the author according to the *Ten Percent Sampling Tabulation on the 1982 Population Census of the People's Republic of China* (Beijing: China Statistical Publishing House, 1983).

8. Data from the statistical bureaus of the municipalities of Shanghai and Tianjin, respectively.

9. The name "commune/brigade-run enterprises" was changed to "township enterprises" after the commune system was changed to the township system in 1983–1984.

10. Shanghai Academy of Social Sciences, *Jizhen Jianshe zai Shanghai jingji fazhan zhong de diwei he zuoyong* [The position and function of market town development in Shanghai's economic development], no. 12, March 1984.

11. *Beijing Ribao,* 19 November 1984.

12. Ibid.

13. *Beijing Ribao,* 13 January 1985.

14. Third Plenary Session, Eleventh Central Committee, Chinese Communist Party, December 1978.

15. *China Daily,* 14 February 1984.

16. Fudong Chen, "Wuge zhuanyecun de diaocha" [An investigation of five specialized villages], *Hongqi* [Red flag], no. 12 (1984): 20–23.

17. Zhuxian Committee of Agricultural Regionalization: *Zhuxian nongye jingji diaocha baogao* [Report on the rural economics of Zhuxian county], working paper, June 1983.

18. 1 *mu* is equal to one-fifteenth hectare and one-sixth of an acre.

19. *China Daily,* 11 October 1984.

20. Central Committee of the Communist Party of China and the State Council of the People's Republic of China, "The Approval of the Report on Starting a New Situation on Commune/Brigade-Run Enterprises, Reported by the Ministry of Agriculture, Animal Husbandry, Fishery and Forestry and the Party Leadership Group," *Renmin Ribao,* 18 March 1984.

21. *Renmin Ribao,* 24 January 1984.

22. *Beijing Ribao,* 9 September 1984.

23. *Beijing Ribao,* 14 April 1984.

24. *Beijing Ribao,* 18 June 1984.

25. Shanghai Academy of Social Sciences, *Jizhen Jianshe zai Shanghai.*

26. *Beijing Ribao,* 19 January and 19 March 1985.

27. Shanghai Academy of Social Sciences, *Jizhen Jianshe zai Shanghai.*

28. Institute of Rural Development, China's Center of Technical Development of Building Engineering, "Suzhoushi xiaochengzhen jianshe qingkuang" [A case study of the construction of small towns in Suzhou municipality], *Jizhen jianshe canko ziliao* [Reference materials for market town construction], no. 10, March 1984.

29. *Beijing Ribao,* 10 December 1984.

30. *China Daily,* 4 December 1984.

31. Yongxing Wu and Yaqun Zhang, "Shanghai jiaoqu jumindian gaizao jianshe he chengzhenhua fangxiang chutan" [Preliminary study of the reconstruction and direction of urbanization in the suburbs of Shanghai], *Jingji fada diqu chengzhenhua duvlu chutan* [Preliminary study on the way of urbanization in economically developed areas], working paper in the Department of Geography, Eastern China Normal University, 1984, pp. 24–29.

32. Xiuzhi Zhang, "Jiaqiang xiao chengzhen jianshe, cujin xiangcun shangpin jingji fazhan" [Enhancing the construction of towns to promote development of commodity economy in rural areas], in Hebei Learned Journal (ed.), *Xiao chengzhen de fazhan daolu* [The direction of developing small cities and towns], 1984, pp. 68–74; Zhonghan Zheng, "Shilun xiaochengzhen" [Discussion on small towns], in Hebei Learned Journal (ed.), *Xiao chengzhen de fazhan daolu* [The direction of developing small cities and towns], 1984, pp. 92–124; Lingbo Zhao, "Zhe meng xiao changzhen jianshe de fazhan zhuangkuang" [The development of towns in the Jerim League], in Committee of Capital Construction, Inner Mongolia (ed.), *Cunzhen guihua yu jianshe* [The planning and construction of towns and villages], no. 1, 1984, pp. 32–42.

33. *Renmin Ribao,* 19 March 1984.

34. Jiusheng Kang, "Yigongyinong renkou yu nongye laodongli zhuanyi" [The population of peasant workers and the transformation of rural laborers], *Renkou Yanjiu* [The study of population], no. 4, 1984, pp. 18–24.

35. Qingyu Ma, "Guanyu jizhen jianshe fazhan wenti" [The development of market towns], working paper, Institute of Geography, Academia Sinica, Beijing, October 1984.

36. Xiaotong Fei, "Prosperity Follows Industrial Development," *Beijing Review* 27 (22) (28 May 1984): 27–29.

37. Institute of Rural Development, "Suzhoushi xiaochengzhen jianshe qingkuang.

38. *Renmin Ribao,* 22 October 1984.

39. According to the investigation report prepared by the Department of Civil Affairs, Government of Guangdong Province, August 1984.

40. Fangting Wei, "Henansheng Nanya pendi Zhenpingxian Chaopi, Jiasong liang zhen qingkuang" [The development of two towns, Chaopi and Jiasong, Zhenping county, Nanyan basin, Henan province], *Jizhen jianshe canko ziliao* [Reference materials on market town development], 30 July 1984.

41. Meijin Wang, "Hebei xiaojizhen huji guanli chuyi" [Preliminary inquiry into management of household registration in small towns, Hebei province], in Hebei Learned Journal (ed.), *Xiao chengzhen de fazhan daolu* [The direction of developing small cities and towns], 1984, pp. 182–189.

42. *Renmin Ribao,* 30 November 1984.

43. Shunza Ye, "Guanyu cunzhen buju de hongguan texing" [Macrocharacteristics of the distribution of villages and towns], in Hebei Learned Journal (ed.), *Xiao chengzhen de fazhan daolu* [The direction of developing small cities and towns], 1984, pp. 190–203.

44. *Beijing Review* 14 (1983): 7.

45. *Beijing Ribao,* 24 January 1985.

46. *Renmin Ribao,* 1 February 1985.

47. *Dagong Bao,* 4 March 1985.

6. *Urbanisasi* or *Kotadesasi?*
Evolving Patterns of Urbanization
in Asia

T. G. McGee

More than twenty years ago, Jean Gottman drew our attention to the emergence of a new and distinctive pattern of urbanization in the United States—namely, the symbiosis of urban and rural activities which occurred in a zone along the Atlantic seaboard, stretching from New Hampshire to North Carolina:

> The symbiosis of urban and rural in Megalopolis, creating new and interesting patterns of multiple-purpose land use over large areas, gives to this region a rather unique character. Like the downtown business districts with powerful skylines, this aspect of Megalopolis will probably be repeated in slightly different but not too dissimilar versions in many other regions of a rapidly urbanizing world.[1]

A major feature of this zone was the growth of large metropolitan regions such as Boston, New York, and Washington, D.C., with extended commuting fields in which rural and urban activity coexist.

My purpose here is to suggest that Gottman's prediction that the Megalopolis process will be repeated in other parts of the world is being proved correct. But I also wish to suggest that there are distinctive facets of the phenomenon in the Asian context which reflect the different patterns of development and incorporation of these countries into the international system.

Definitions and Parameters

Urbanisasi is the term used in Bahasa Indonesia to describe the urbanization process in its broadest sense including the physical, demographic, economic, and sociological processes involved in the growth of urban areas. *Kotadesasi* is a coined word that joins *kota* (town) and *desa*

93

(village) to make up a word which carries the concept of urban and rural activity occurring in the same geographic territory. This is not the same as "urbanization," a term never precise in its meaning, which has generally meant some persistence of rural traditions and values in urban settings.

The central assertion of this chapter is straightforward—namely, that during the last twenty years many countries in Asia, while exhibiting an increase in urbanization levels (in the sense of increases in the proportion of a country's population resident in urban places), have also been characterized by a rapid increase in *kotadesasi* in the sense of regions in which agricultural and nonagricultural activities occur side by side. It should be stressed that this process of *kotadesasi* is not identical with that of emergence of the Megalopolis in the United States which, if I understand Gottman correctly, essentially was a reflection of the growing income generated in the region, increasing economic specialization, the growth of the service sector, increased capacity for personal mobility, and the spatial spread of settlement into rural areas in which the major cities provided the economic impetus. The Megalopolis is a region dominated by the activities of a "central urban system." In many Asian countries, the process of *kotadesasi* is somewhat different, for it is occurring in many different geographic locations. Often it is found in the perimeter regions of the giant cities and sometimes in the form of corridor development adjacent to main roads or railways that link reasonably close, large cities in these countries.

Five main features of the process may be delineated. First, it is generally characterized by an increase in nonagricultural activity in areas which have previously been largely agricultural. These nonagricultural activities are very diverse and include trading, transportation, and industry. This increase in nonagricultural activity is characterized by a great mixture of activities, often by members from the same household. Thus one person may commute to the city to work as a clerk, another engage in farming, a third in industry, and another in retailing in the *kotadesasi* zone. This creates a situation in which the economic linkages within the *kotadesasi* zone may be as important as the dominance of the large cities of Megalopolis which draw the surrounding regions into their orbit.

Second, the *kotadesasi* zones are also characterized by extreme fluidity and mobility of the population. The availability of relatively cheap transport such as two-stroke motorbikes, buses, and trucks has facilitated relatively quick movement over long distances. Thus these zones are characterized not only by commuting to urban centers but also by intense movement of people and goods within the zones.

Third, the *kotadesasi* zones are characterized by an intense mixture of land use with agriculture, cottage industry, and other uses existing side by side. This has both negative and positive effects. On the positive side, nonagricultural activity can utilize farm labor, mainly by recruiting from farm households. Agricultural products, particularly industrial crops, have a ready market. On the negative side, industrial activity can pollute and destroy agricultural land. On the whole, the *kotadesasi* zones are much more intensely utilized than the Megalopolis. Writing of land use in this zone, Gottman comments on the extent of woodland and recreational areas. In the *kotadesasi* zones of Asian countries, pressures of population place greater demands upon the available space.

Fourth, another feature of the *kotadesasi* zones is the increased participation of females in nonagricultural labor. This increase is associated with demand for female labor in industry and other activities, but it is also closely related to changing patterns of agricultural production in the *kotadesasi* regions. Generally, agricultural production shows a shift from monocrop cultivation (principally rice) to an increased diversity with production of livestock, vegetables, fruit, and so forth, sometimes for national and international markets.

Finally, these *kotadesasi* zones are to some extent "invisible" or "gray zones" from the point of view of the state authorities. Urban regulations may not apply in these "rural areas," and it is difficult for the state to enforce them despite the rapidly changing economic structure of the regions. This feature is particularly encouraging to informal-sector and small-scale operators who find it difficult to conform to labor laws or industrial legislation. This lack of authority also permits the proliferation of squatter housing in these regions.

It should be stressed that in suggesting this idea of *kotadesasi,* I am really dealing with the complex question of urban–rural relations—a question which rests primarily upon definitions of urban and rural areas. Virtually all societies have working definitions of urban and rural areas. The problem is that these definitions are highly variable from country to country and often change. Most definitions, however, have common elements such as population size and settlement pattern. In some countries, for instance, all towns over 10,000 in population are regarded as urban; everything else is rural. From a definitional point of view, however, it is more important to know two pieces of economic information: What is the contribution of agricultural and nonagricultural activities to the gross domestic product (GDP) of a given spatial unit (nation, province, and so on)? And what proportion of the labor force is employed in agricultural and nonagricultural work in a given spatial unit (nation, province, and so on)?

If this information were available over given time periods, it would be possible to develop a more precise definition of urban and rural areas. One could conceive a rather simple matrix constructed at the level of small administrative units which would allow a fourfold spatial division of a country (Figure 6.1). The provision of data at this level would create a spatial continuum from the most urban spatial unit (1) to the most nonurban spatial unit (4). Assuming an ideal statistical base, this type of analysis would enable one to estimate the contribution of the urban spatial units to the gross domestic product compared to the non-urban spatial units. If temporal data were available, this would allow one to assess the relative contribution of urban and nonurban areas to the gross domestic product through time as well as the differences in the labor force. This kind of information would provide vital feedback to the government in assessing the spatial impact of its investment policies. Few developing societies possess data permitting analysis at this level, however, so one is forced to use much broader macrodata at a provincial level.

In general, one can approach the problem of investigating rural–urban relationships in two ways. First, the spatial grid of national data can be reassembled in a manner designed to investigate regions of major rural–urban interaction. Second, rural–urban dynamics can be investigated in a sectoral manner analyzing market channels for products (such as rice), population movement, capital and investment flows, and so forth. I have written about these approaches elsewhere and will not discuss them here since they can be consulted in published works.[2] My point here is to suggest that in the *kotadesasi* zones there is no clear-cut division between rural and urban relations; rather, activities in the two sectors are fused and complementary.

Of course, these are only the most salient features of the *kotadesasi* regions. The relationships of the features can only be established after

1. Spatial units with more than 50 percent contribution by non-agricultural economic activities to spatial unit GDP in nonagricultural activities	2. Spatial units with more than 50 percent contribution by non-agricultural economic activities to spatial unit GDP and less than 50 percent in nonagricultural activities
3. Spatial units with less than 50 percent contribution by non-agricultural economic activities to spatial unit GDP and more than 50 percent in nonagricultural activities	4. Spatial units with less than 50 percent contribution by non-agricultural economic activities to spatial unit GDP in nonagricultural activities

Figure 6.1. Spatial Division of a Country at the Level of Small Administrative Units

careful empirical research. In the next section, a case study of Taiwan is investigated as a first step in this direction.

Urbanisasi or *Kotadesasi:* A Case Study of Taiwan

Taiwan presents a polar model where the *kotadesasi* process is well developed. It is occurring in other countries in Asia as well, but at a less rapid rate and subject to the features prevailing in each country. In order to understand the *kotadesasi* process in Taiwan, it is necessary to sketch the broad features of structural and spatial change on the island since the end of World War II.

The island of Taiwan is small, only 36,000 square kilometers in size. This has important implications to the cost of spatial integration. In 1949, the influx of migrants from the Chinese mainland to Taiwan did not find a thriving economy. Wartime bombing had destroyed some of the island's industrial capacity and the managerial class was decimated by the removal of the Japanese, but there was a basic infrastructure of communications set up by the Japanese.[3] The economy was primarily agricultural and there was severe population pressure on the land: 169 persons per square kilometer. This pressure was intensified during the 1950s, mainly because of a rapid decline in infant mortality from 91 per 1,000 in 1952 to 40 per 1,000 in 1960, which increased the pressure to 475 persons per square kilometer. The introduction of a successful birth control program and increased participation of women in the growing industries were important contributors to a rapid fall in the birth rate during the 1960s. Thus it can be argued that during the 1950s, Taiwan had a population pressure on the land of a similar nature to those that characterize other intensely populated regions of Asia.

At that time, rice was the major crop produced in Taiwan. This dominance of rice in the 1950s had much to do with the Taiwanese government's policy of keeping the domestic price of rice roughly 30 percent below international levels in order to lower urban living costs and thereby boost the profitability of manufacturing. This policy was changed after the opening up of the economy in 1961 to bring rice more in line with international prices. While the production of rice has increased considerably over the first thirty years, the share of rice as a proportion of gross agricultural receipts has dropped from 50 percent in 1950 to 34 percent in 1980, whereas livestock products increased from 20 to 36 percent and vegetables and fruits from 7 to 20 percent.[4]

These developments were a manifestation of land reforms introduced between 1949 and 1953 which transferred to tenants 71 percent of the total area of public and private tenanted land, increased the number of owner families from 36 percent of the total farm families in 1949 to 60 percent in 1957, and gave farmers greater opportunity to choose crops, for they were under no obligation to produce rice for rental payments. Improved technological inputs together with higher returns for nonrice crops led to a growth of livestock production, particularly pork and chickens, as well as nuts and vegetables for export.

After import controls were relaxed in the 1960s, industrial growth took over, and with devalued Taiwanese dollars exports were made easier. The government played a considerable role in this industrialization by selling off many of the large-scale industrial plants inherited from the Japanese and creating export zones such as Kaohsiung but leaving the choice of industries to the private sector, which emphasized clothing, electronic goods, rubber goods, and shoes in particular. Since 1976, a tendency toward the production of more capital-intensive goods has developed. Thus this industrial revolution in the 1960s was able to create employment for surplus labor from the agricultural sector as employment in manufacturing rose from 584,000 in 1966 to 2,179,000 in 1981.

The employment of women was particularly significant in this transition, as Table 6.1 shows. This employment increase was concentrated in the age groups between 20 to 49, who show a 10 percent increase in the activity rate for the age groups. This contributed to a decline in birth rates and an increase in income from nonfarm sources.

These developments were accompanied by high rates of gross domestic investment as a percentage of GDP (which averaged 20 percent in the period 1955 to 1978), high rates of internal savings, and considerable foreign investment (average of US$100 million a year between 1965 and 1980). This enabled the government to increase investment in the infrastructure of transportation, which is reflected in the number of private automobiles from 1 per 1,000 persons in 1952 to 32 per 1,000 in 1979 and telephones per 1,000 persons from 4 to 148. Health and educational standards were also greatly improved. In the decade of the sev-

Table 6.1. Female Employment in Taiwan by Industry

Year	Total (%)	Primary Industry (%)	Secondary Industry (%)	Tertiary Industry (%)
1965	100	52.5	18.2	29.3
1970	100	40.6	23.7	35.7
1975	100	31.2	34.3	34.5
1980	100	16.5	43.7	39.8

Source: Shirley W. Y. Kuo, The Taiwan Economy in Transition (Boulder, Colo.: Westview Press, 1983), p. 86.

enties, there has also been a major consumer revolution, as consumption of housing, electronic appliances, motorcycles, and automobiles has grown massively in relation to increased disposable income in the household.

The effects of this economic transformation on the spatial structure of Taiwan can be summarized as follows. First, at the broadest spatial level of the four planning regions designated by the national government there has been a continuing growth of population in the northern region centered on Taipei and the southern region focusing on Kaohsiung. (See Figure 6.2 and Table 6.2.) This growth is reflected in the migration patterns, which show that the northern region absorbed a growing number of migrants in the period between 1966 and 1981. Thus the central, southern, and eastern regions experienced a net migration loss of 1,030,000 people while the northern region gained 952,000.

In fact, these regional shifts were largely the result of the growth of population in the four metropolitan regions of Taipei, Taichung, Tainan, and Kaohsiung, which in the period between 1966 and 1981 increased their proportion of Taiwan's population from 35.6 to 46 percent. Indeed, the building of a north–south freeway from Taipei to Kaohsiung and the electrification of the railway between the two areas is creating a metropolitan corridor similar in character to the corridor between Tokyo and Osaka. The corridor, in which the economy is made up of a great mixture of service, industrial, and agricultural activities, all interconnected by rapid transportation, exhibits all the features of the *kotadesasi* zones outlined earlier.

The emergence of this spatial pattern has, to some extent, been masked by the general patterns of statistical presentation of the Taiwan experience and has led some planners to conclude that Taiwan's industrialization has followed a decentralized pattern. Samuel Ho, for instance, has argued that

Taiwan's industrialization has followed a more decentralized pattern, which has enabled the economy to grow as an organic unit by promoting interaction among its components. In other words, by allowing rural

Table 6.2. Taiwan Population by Four Planning Regions (in thousands)

Region	1966		1971		1976		1981	
Northern	4,271	(32.0%)	5,233	(35.0%)	6,141	(37.0%)	7,161	(39.1%)
Central	3,802	(29.0%)	4,178	(29.0%)	4,429	(27.0%)	4,702	(26.0%)
Southern	4,345	(34.0%)	4,954	(33.0%)	5,299	(32.0%)	5,633	(31.0%)
Eastern	575	(5.0%)	630	(4.0%)	439	(4.0%)	639	(4.0%)

Source: Lung-shen Chang, "Regional Disparity and Regional Development Policies in Taiwan," paper presented at the Conference on Urban Growth and Economic Development in the Pacific Region, Taipei, 1984.

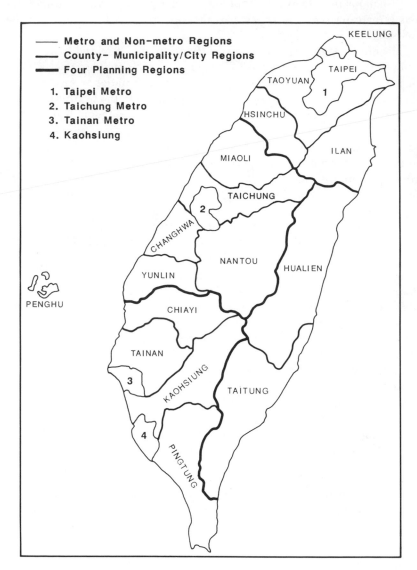

Figure 6.2. Three Types of Spatial Units on Taiwan. (Source: Lung-shen Chang, "Regional Disparity and Regional Development Policies in Taiwan." Paper presented to a conference on urban growth and economic development in the Pacific Region, Taipei, 1984)

industry and agriculture to grow in a more reinforcing manner, decentralized industrialization has created rural employment opportunities and enabled greater numbers of Taiwan's rural population to participate in industry without having to leave the countryside. This has not only reduced the total need for urban housing and infrastructure but also made the transition from agricultural to nonagricultural activity less abrupt, with fewer disruptions of family life and the rural social fabric. The evidence from Taiwan also shows that decentralized and rural industrialization brings to the countryside important income distribution benefits.[5]

Ho bases these assertions on the following evidence:

1. Annual growth rates of manufacturing in Taiwan's rural areas were 7.2 percent in the period 1956–1966 compared to 5.2 percent for nonrural areas.
2. The majority of rural manufacturing establishments were small-scale and capital-intensive.
3. Household data from the 1961 and 1972 household surveys show increased income from manufacturing in farm households.
4. The growth and diversification of agricultural production transformed rural Taiwan into a well-developed market for nonfarm goods and services. Not all market demand can be satisfied in rural areas, but goods with "relatively high income elasticities, such as furniture, household furnishings, and clothing, can be efficiently produced in small-to-medium-sized establishments suitable for location in rural areas."[6] In addition, increased nonfarm income creates needs for services which in turn lead to more activities in the marketing and transportation networks.

While Ho is undoubtedly correct in his analysis of the Taiwanese experience in the 1960s, there are problems in emphasizing the location of these activities in rural areas at the expense of the concept of *kotadesasi* zones of intense rural–urban interaction. Given the small size of Taiwan (an island 380 by 140 kilometers at its extreme points) and a highly developed transportation network in the western part of the island, this idea of maximum accessibility for rural–urban interaction is of major importance.

Recent empirical research on Taiwan gives excellent support to this concept.[7] In his analysis of spatial population change in Taiwan, Tsai recognizes that the zones of intense rural–urban interaction have focused on the major cities. This "living perimeter," as he calls it, is defined as follows: "A living perimeter is drawn from the city nucleus in accordance with required distances for commuting, shopping, administrative divisions, industrial activities, geographical environment, and

potential for city growth."[8] These elements are further defined on the
basis of whether they are located in relationship to metropoles (metropolitan living perimeters) or smaller cities (nonmetropolitan living
perimeters). (See Figure 6.3.)

Utilizing data for Taiwan compiled over the period 1950–1980, Tsai
shows that the population has tended to grow fastest in the metropolitan
living perimeters located from Taipei–Keelung through to Kaohsiung
(see Table 6.3) and, most significantly in the 1970s, in the ring zones
where the greatest amount of rural–urban interaction occurs. When this
analysis is extended to employment, significant findings emerge. For it
can be seen that it is in the ring zone of the metropolitan living perimeters that the greatest increases in manufacturing have occurred, although the nonmetropolitan perimeters still contain a significant component of manufacturing employment (but below their percentage of
total population). (See Table 6.4.)

This growth of manufacturing in the ring zones of the metropolitan
perimeters is of most significance, for it is in these areas that the most
intense mixture of rural and nonrural activities are juxtaposed in a
manner that appears to be very efficient for the Taiwanese economy.
Thus highly productive farm households can send out female workers to
manufacturing jobs or bring assembly activities into the household.
These data therefore support the emergence of *kotadesasi* zones in
Taiwan.

Policy Implications of the Process of *Kotadesasi*

In this final section I wish to discuss the policy implications of this process of *kotadesasi*. From the point of view of planners concerned with
implementing macrospatial strategies, the condition of the *kotadesasi*
zones is often regarded as chaotic. It is impossible for the state authorities to impose more orderly land use policy such as zoning, and the
problems of traffic planning and provision of an adequate physical
infrastructure for these regions are seen as prohibitive. Under such conditions, planners would rather try to direct economic activity into an
urban system—particularly in intermediate-size and small towns where
the decentralization of economic activity is thought to provide employment and income as well as market incentives to agriculture.

Rondinelli has broadly cataloged these policies as follows:[9]

1. Controlling the growth of the largest cities
2. Stimulating the growth of regional metropolitan centers and intermediate cities as "countermagnets" for capital

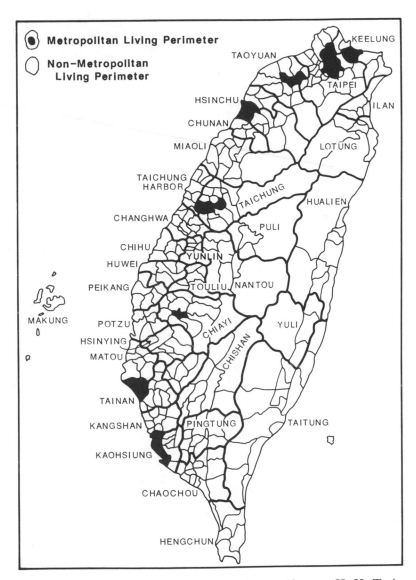

Figure 6.3. Delineation of the Living Perimeter. (Source: H. H. Tsai, "Urban Growth and the Change of Spatial Structure in Taiwan." Paper presented to a conference on urban growth and economic development in the Pacific Region, Taipei, 1984)

Table 6.3. Composition and Change of Population by Metropolitan and Nonmetropolitan Living Perimeter (in thousands)

Zone	1950 Total	%	1960 Total	%	1970 Total	%	1980 Total	%
Metro	3,432	45.41	5,293	49.05	7,953	54.19	10,830	60.83
Core	1,804	23.87	2,964	27.46	4,605	31.38	5,864	32.94
Ring	1,627	21.54	2,329	21.58	3,348	22.81	4,966	27.89
Nonmetro	4,124	54.59	5,499	50.95	6,723	45.81	6,974	39.17
Total	7,555	100.00	10,792	100.00	14,676	100.00	17,804	100.00

Zone	1950-1960 Absolute Change	% Change	% of Total	1960-1970 Absolute Change	% Change	% of Total	1970-1980 Absolute Change	% Change	% of Total
Metro	1,861	54.22	59.32	2,660	50.26	68.49	2,877	36.18	91.98
Core	1,159	64.21	36.95	1,641	55.36	42.25	1,259	27.34	40.25
Ring	702	43.15	22.38	1,019	43.75	26.24	1,618	48.33	51.73
Nonmetro	1,276	30.22	40.68	1,224	22.26	31.51	251	3.73	8.02
Total	3,137	40.98	100.00	3,884	35.99	100.00	3,128	21.31	100.00

Source: H. H. Tsai, "Urban Growth and the Change of Spatial Structure in Taiwan," paper presented at the Conference on Urban Growth and Economic Development in the Pacific Region, Taipei, 1984.

Table 6.4. Composition and Change of Employment in Manufacturing by Metropolitan and Nonmetropolitan Living Perimeter (in thousands)

Zone	1966 Total	%	1971 Total	%	1976 Total	%	1981 Total	%
Metro	426	72.95	901	76.29	1,430	75.54	1,614	74.07
Core	259	44.35	479	40.56	694	36.66	700	74.07
Ring	167	28.60	422	35.73	736	38.88	914	41.95
Nonmetro	158	27.05	280	23.71	463	24.46	565	25.93
Total	584	100.00	1,181	100.00	1,893	100.00	2,179	100.00

Zone	1966-1971 Absolute Change	% Change	% of Total	1971-1976 Absolute Change	% Change	% of Total	1976-1981 Absolute Change	% Change	% of Total
Metro	471	111.50	79.56	529	58.71	74.30	184	12.87	64.34
Core	220	84.94	36.85	215	44.89	30.20	6	0.86	2.10
Ring	255	152.69	42.71	314	74.41	44.10	178	19.47	62.24
Nonmetro	122	77.22	20.44	183	65.36	25.70	102	22.03	35.66
Total	597	102.23	100.00	712	60.29	100.00	286	15.11	100.00

Source: See Table 6.3.

3. Strengthening existing and incipient market towns and small cities as rural service centers

4. Tying decentralized urbanization policy to integrated rural development programs

5. Strengthening the links among settlements in regional and national systems

Apart from the obvious problems of finding capital investment for such strategies, there are major difficulties associated with the timing of their introduction. It has generally been established that some forms of "polarization reversal"—as, for instance, shown in the growth of non-farm income in rural areas—occur without public-sector involvement and begin to stimulate the growth of lower-order centers. Richardson has addressed this problem as follows:

> There is no one key signal, but some of the following changes may guide policymakers: (i) evolution of the industrial structure to the point where branch plants seem feasible; (ii) emergence of scale diseconomies in the primate city; (iii) when the capital restraint has been reached as a result of a strong recent growth record in respect to GNP and investment; (iv) when at least a skeletal national transportation network has been built; (v) when political and social pressures build up for interregional equity and similar spatial objectives; (vi) after the introduction of sound rural development and small-scale industry programs that offer the prospect of demographic stability in peripheral regions; (vii) when per capita incomes in the periphery have risen to levels to justify industries catering for local demand; (viii) when stable export products have been subject to chronic instability; (ix) when the country's supply of administrators, planners, managers, and professional personnel reaches the levels that permit decentralization of planning, economic, and political functions; and (x) when some noncore cities begin to grow faster than the primate city.[10]

In light of the empirical and theoretical arguments concerning *kotade-sasi* zones, the major question for urban strategy is how to incorporate these zones into overall spatial strategies, particularly if they are seen as crucial economic zones in the process of economic development. In the case of Taiwan, it is clear that a number of decisions made by the state and by private investors have had significant effects on the spatial pattern. First, a series of policies with respect to agriculture (pricing, land reform, agroprocessing) created a situation in which rice ceased to be a staple component of agricultural production. Second, a series of decisions encouraged the growth of industrialization and nonfarm employment. Third, a number of social policies (education, health, and welfare) greatly improved the lives of the population. And fourth, considerable investment was put into the physical infrastructure of communications, particularly road and rail, which improved accessibility between urban and rural areas. While one might argue that Taiwan's comparatively small population, the considerable amount of foreign investment, and favorable access to U.S. markets were all special factors which are not duplicated in all other Asian countries, still there are many lessons to be learned from this experience.

There appear to be five priorities for many Asian countries if they are to develop pragmatic strategies which recognize the importance of the *kotadesasi* zones. First, Asian governments will have to make critical decisions with respect to agricultural policy. In most Asian countries, the agricultural labor force is declining and the production of nonrice crops and other nonagricultural activities are increasing. If this trend follows the Taiwanese pattern, the proportion of income from such activities in the total farm income will become increasingly large. The problem will then be: How can these countries supply their population with a sufficient amount of their staple food, rice? If the present trends persist, however, one may expect nonrice agricultural production to accelerate in the areas adjacent to the major urban cores and become the focus of a growing urban–rural interaction.

Second, Asian governments will need to encourage industrialization in the major zones of urban–rural interaction by every means possible. This process will certainly involve increasing institutional effectiveness in the bureaucracy as well as encouraging foreign investment.

Third, Asian governments will have to recognize the reality of these zones of intense urban–rural interaction and direct much of their investment to these areas. This means making hard decisions against fostering small-town development and rural industrialization in less accessible areas, but not neglecting rural integrated development schemes in less accessible areas.

Fourth, Asian governments will need to greatly improve access in these zones of intense rural–urban interaction with better roads and fast railway communication. This is a costly investment, but it will reap developmental rewards.

Fifth, Asian governments should develop new spatial systems of data collection, similar to those of the living perimeters of Taiwan, which enable them to monitor more effectively the impact of these investment decisions on labor force composition, income, and the like.

Of course, the timing of these strategies and the government's fiscal ability to implement them are not easy to gauge. The signals on the "urbanization transition" in Asia are very mixed. But it is equally true that the demographic and economic reality of the growth of *kotadesasi* zones means that planning decisions relating to them cannot be postponed.

NOTES

1. Jean Gottman, *Megalopolis* (Cambridge: MIT Press, 1961), p. 257.

2. See T. G. McGee, *The Southest Asian City* (London: G. Bell and Son, 1967); T. G. McGee, "Rural–Urban Migration in a Plural Society: A Case Study of Malays in West Malaysia," in D. J. Dwyer (ed.), *The City as a Center of Change* (Hong Kong, 1971), pp. 108–124; T. G. McGee, *Hawkers in Hong Kong: A Study of Policy and Planning in the Third World City* (Hong Kong: Center of Asian Studies, University of Hong Kong, 1974); T. G. McGee and others, *Food Distribution Systems in the New Hebrides,* Monograph 25, Development Studies Center, Australian National University, 1980; T. G. McGee, *Labor Markets, Urban Systems and the Urbanization Process in Southeast Asia,* Papers of the East–West Center, no. 81 (Honolulu: Population Institute, East–West Center, 1982); T. G. McGee, and Yeung Yue-man, *Hawkers in Southeast Asian Cities: Planning for the Bazaar Economy* (Ottawa: IDRC, 1977); Warwick Armstrong and T. G. McGee, *Theatres of Accumulation: Studies of Urbanization in Asia and Latin America* (London and New York: Methuen, 1985).

3. For a review of the Japanese control of Taiwan, see Samuel P. S. Ho, *Economic Development of Taiwan: 1860–1970* (New Haven: Yale University Press, 1978).

4. See Shun-yi Shei and Kyon Anderson, "Taiwanese Agricultural Protection in Historical and Comparative Perspective," *Pacific Economic Papers* 104 (Canberra: Australia–Japan Research Center, 1983).

5. Samuel P. S. Ho, "Decentralized Industrialization and Rural Development: Evidence from Taiwan," *Economic Development and Cultural Change* 28 (1) (1979), pp. 77–78.

6. Ibid., pp. 93–94.

7. H. H. Tsai, "Urban Growth and the Change of Spatial Structure in Taiwan," paper presented to the Conference on Urban Growth and Economic Development in the Pacific Region, Taipei, 1984.

8. Ibid., p. 4.

9. See Dennis A. Rondinelli, "Balanced Urbanization, Spatial Integration and Economic Development in Asia: Policy Implications," paper presented to a panel on "Urbanization in Asia: A Conditional Good," Association for Asian Studies annual meeting, Los Angeles, 1979.

10. Harry W. Richardson, *City Size and National Spatial Strategies in Developing Countries,* Working Paper 252 (Washington, D.C.: World Bank, 1977), pp. 21–22.

PART III: REGIONAL AND METROPOLITAN EFFECTS OF URBANIZATION

7. Perception of Environmental Pollution in a Chinese City

Pradyumna P. Karan and Thomas K. Chao

Geographic studies of environmental perception have contributed to the explanation and understanding of a wide variety of problems in human geography—ranging from natural hazard adjustments, residential movement patterns, and shopping behavior to space preferences.[1] The bulk of these studies have been confined to the individual's perception of the environment in North America and Europe. Very few studies have been reported from the non-Western world. Indeed, a recent comprehensive survey of international studies in environmental perception shows only thirteen references to work in Asia, Africa, and Latin America.[2] If human geography is going to develop theories that relate to the totality of human experience, it is essential to study non-Western areas as well.

Here we wish to discuss the perception of environmental pollution in a Chinese city and to compare the results with similar studies in an Indian city in order to offer some generalizations on the perception of environmental pollution in cities in the non-Western world. The generalizations and comparative analyses of environmental perception in the non-Western cities will help in refining the theories of environmental cognition for universal applicability.

Taipei: Urban Growth and Functions

Taipei, with more than 2.38 million people, is one of the largest and most rapidly growing cities in East Asia. During the past thirty-five years, the city has changed from a small market center to a modern metropolitan area in terms of urban functions and structure. Both the city's area and its population have expanded. Serious housing shortages and rapidly increasing environmental problems have resulted from the continuous influx of rural people into the city.

111

Geographically, Taipei is located in an oval-shaped basin surrounded by mountainous areas to the east, south, and north. Toward the north in the urban districts of Peitou and Shihlin, mountains rise to heights of more than 1,000 meters (Figure 7.1). In the west Taipei opens to the northwest coast of Taiwan, which is about 16 kilometers from the city center. The old and densely populated city center occupies a level basin floor about 5 meters above sea level.

The Keelung River, which flows through the city of Taipei, joins the Tamsui River, which marks the boundary of the city. A third river, the Hsintien, forms the southwest boundary of Taipei. The dissection of the area by rivers gives rise to marked variations in relief. The deeply incised valleys do not favor the drainage of stagnant stable air, thus inhibiting the free diffusion of pollutants. During periods of active air circulation, the fragmented relief induces considerable variations in local wind speeds.

The use of the deep-river port for big junks in the eighteenth century was the principal reason for the growth of Taipei on the present site. Mengchia, the site of Taipei's original settlement, became the core of Taipei's historical development. Mengchia, now called Wenhus, was founded by Fukien Chinese. By 1853, big junks from Mainland China sailed upstream from the delta entrance of the Tamsui River to reach the deep-river port of Menchia on the western edge of Taipei. Another group of Fukien immigrants chose a site north of Mengchia on the Tamsui at Tai-Tao-Chen for settlement and commercial activities. By 1860, Tai-Tao-Chen had replaced Mengchia as the economic center and chief port of Taipei.

In 1884, a city wall was built for defense with four gates serving as the main entrances to the city. Within these walls, Tai-Tao-Chen and Mengchia expanded to become one enlarged city with an area of 441 hectares by 1885. The walls have now been replaced by wide streets. The old 1885 city expanded rapidly during the Japanese colonial administration between 1895 and 1945. In 1948, the movement of the central government of the Republic of China to Taipei resulted in a major expansion of the city. In 1968, six small towns located on the outskirts of Taipei—Chingmei, Nankang, Mucha, Neihu, Shihlin, and Peitou—were formally merged into the city. This annexation expanded Taipei's urban area to 27,214 hectares and increased its population to 1,839,641 persons. By 1983, Taipei had grown to more than 2.38 million people.

Morphologically, Taipei comprises two dissimilar areas: the ten districts of the old city and the six peripheral districts added to the city in recent years (Figure 7.2). The ten districts of the old city have only one-fourth of the city's area but contain over three-fourths of its population.

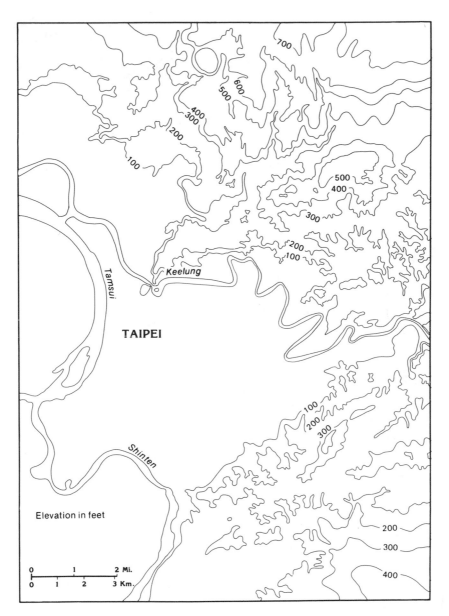

Figure 7.1. The Site of Taipei

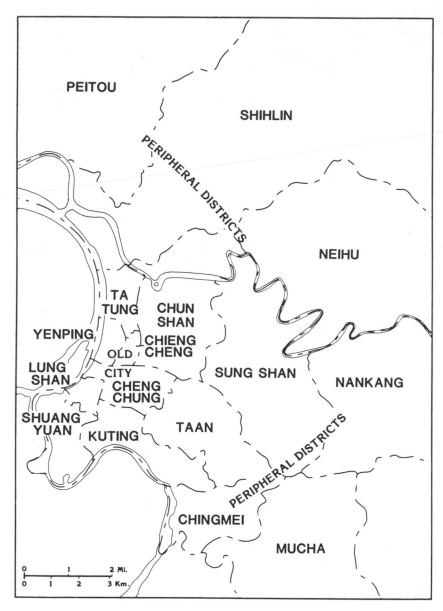

Figure 7.2. Taipei: Urban Districts, Old City, and Peripheral Districts

The four districts added on the south and east contain more than 30 percent of the city area and about 10 percent of the people. The two large northernmost districts—Peitou and Shihlin—contain 41 percent of the area but less than 14 percent of the people (Figure 7.3).

For the city as a whole, the population density in 1983 was 8,775 persons per square kilometer, while there is less than 2 square meters of parks and green space per resident compared to over 12 square meters of green space in New York. The high population density, crowding, and lack of green space aggravate the pollution problem, particularly sanitation. Because of the tremendous increase in population and energy consumption, the rapid development of industry, and major increases in motor vehicles, the environmental problem in Taipei has become more and more serious.[3]

Taipei's land use pattern exacerbates the influence of relief on the pollution concentration. Heavy industry is concentrated in the low-lying areas along the highly congested Keelung riverside, and manufacturing emissions from factories affect the atmospheric particulate concentration (Figure 7.4). Dust from construction, exhaust from vehicles, and the combustion of waste all contribute to air pollution. The numerous small-scale electroplating factories discharge heavy-metal wastewater in rivers. Thus the concentration of heavy metals in the Tamsui and Keelung rivers is relatively high.

Environmental Pollution

A network of environmental monitoring stations in Taipei records the quality of air, water, and noise levels at daily and, in some cases, hourly intervals. Based on these recorded data, it is possible to assign quantitative values to spatial variations in levels of suspended particulates, dust fall, haze, and noise levels throughout the urban area. Pollution records are an objective base against which the attitudes and opinions of Taipei residents may be compared.

Particulates and sulfur dioxide, usually released from the combustion of fossil fuels, have become the main air pollutants in Taipei (Figure 7.5). In fact, the concentration of particulate pollutants in Taipei exceeds the national ambient air quality standards of the Republic of China.[4] Except for 1970, the average monthly dust-fall concentrations in Taipei are between 15 and 17 tons per square kilometer. The average value of suspended particulates in Taipei in 1983 was high (160 to 190 micrograins per cubic meter), frequently entering the human respiratory tract and affecting health (Figure 7.6).

The coefficient of haze, indicated by the opacity measured from the

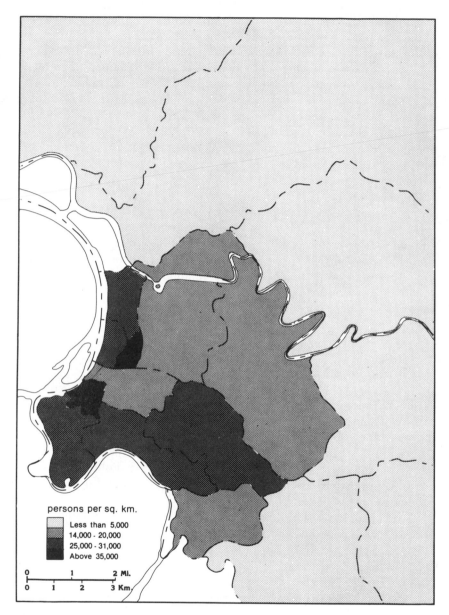

persons per sq. km.

Less than 5,000
14,000 - 20,000
25,000 - 31,000
Above 35,000

0   1   2 Mi.
0   1   2   3 Km.

Figure 7.3. Taipei: Population Density, 1983

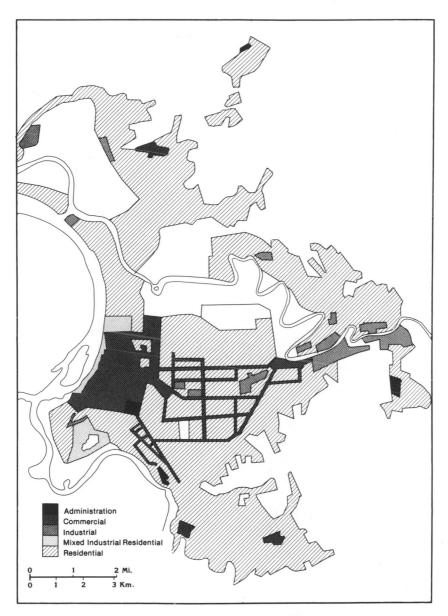

Figure 7.4. Taipei: Land Use, 1984 (Based on Field Survey)

Administration
Commercial
Industrial
Mixed Industrial Residential
Residential

0   1   2 Mi.
0 1 2 3 Km.

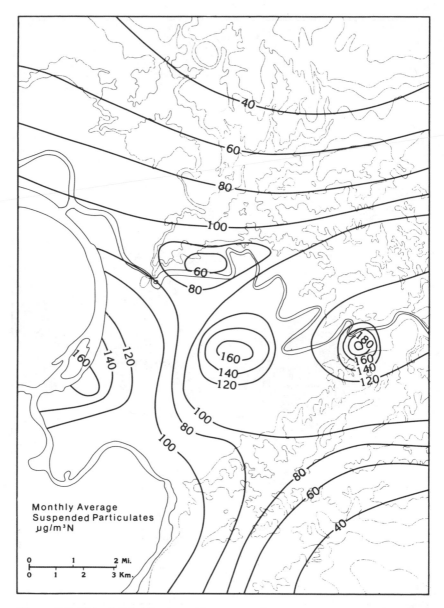

Figure 7.5. Taipei: Distribution of Suspended Particulates (Based on Data from the Department of Environmental Protection)

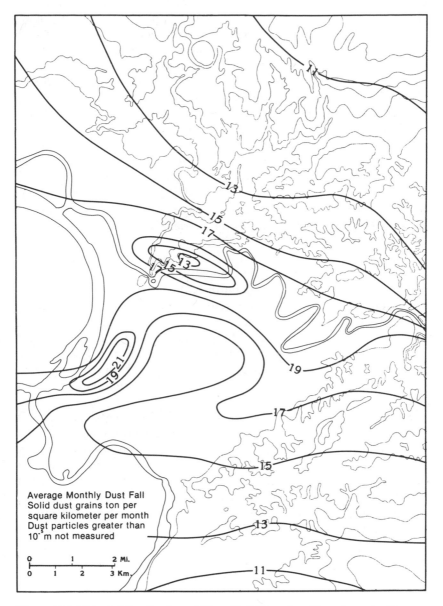

Figure 7.6. Taipei: Distribution of Dust Fall (Based on Data from the Department of Environmental Protection)

suspended particulates in 1,000 feet of air after being filtered, measures the visual dirt in the air and is equivalent to a carbon concentration of 9 $\mu g/m^3$ N. The coefficient of haze in Taipei is particularly high (Figure 7.7). Along major highways, where the main source of carbon is diesel-powered vehicles, the pollution is quite serious.[5] Although the annual average coefficient of haze is decreasing in the major cities of Taiwan, Taipei recorded an increase in 1983 and 1984, which is in accord with the rise in dust fall and suspended particulates.[6]

Pollution from noxious gases is local in nature. Exhaust from automobiles is a serious problem. Near the South Gate in Taipei, the carbon monoxide level exceeds "10 parts per million by 9 A.M. every morning and does not subside until after 8 P.M. At its height, the carbon monoxide level reaches around 20 ppm, and its peak covers a very long time."[7] A close relationship between air pollution and children's asthma has been recorded in Taipei, and the mortality rate from chronic bronchitis shows a large increase in highly industrialized areas compared with rural areas.[8]

Another type of pollution is noise. Taipei's present noise problem is fairly serious—noise in primary shopping and entertainment districts generally exceeds 80 decibels (Figure 7.8). A troubling feature of this noise pollution is that there is no appreciable difference between the daylight and nighttime hours. The rapidly increasing number of motor vehicles and the widespread use of mechanical tools has made noise pollution a significant problem. A 1976 opinion poll revealed that 42 percent of the people interviewed considered noise to be a major problem interfering with normal conversation and causing a temporary hearing loss.[9]

Solid waste disposal is another serious environmental pollutant in Taipei. Along the main streets refuse is picked up regularly, but the alleys and lanes remain a problem. The refuse has been disposed of at landfill sites. Most of the sites are now full, however, and new lots for landfill are not available. Incineration may be an alternative for urban refuse disposal. Often the refuse is dumped into the Tamsui River and its tributaries as it flows through the Taipei urban area, resulting in the decline of dissolved oxygen to zero during the dry period.[10]

Because there is no complete sanitary sewage system in the Taipei area, water pollution has become serious. Waste is discharged into the rivers through storm drains or canals. The zero-dissolved-oxygen portions of the rivers have spread rapidly into the upper stream. In the lower portion of the Tamsui and Keelung rivers, the water is black and highly odorous due to the discharge of raw sewage and industrial wastes from factories, mineral plants, hog pens, and seepage from refuse dumps.[11] Taipei's water supply is drawn from the Hsintien and Kee-

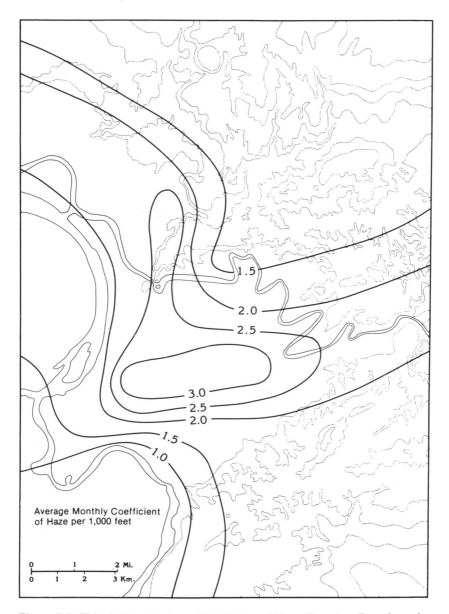

Figure 7.7. Taipei: Distribution of Coefficient of Haze (Based on Data from the Department of Environmental Protection)

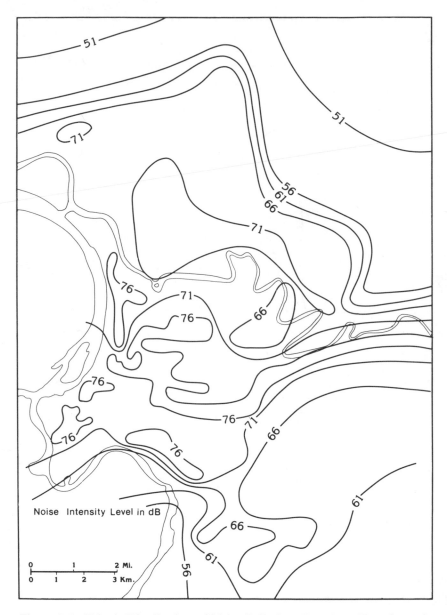

Figure 7.8. Taipei: Distribution of Noise Pollution (Based on Data from the Department of Environmental Protection)

lung rivers and smaller creeks, as well as from springs in Yangmingshan and Shihlin and thirty-six deep wells.[12] The water is cleaned at five water purification plants before it is supplied to the urban area. At present, water must be boiled for drinking.

Institutional Conditions

Public officials in the Republic of China and the city of Taipei are concerned about environmental pollution but have not as yet become significantly involved with the environmental issue. More jobs, economic growth, and a higher standard of living are far more popular causes. Discussions with numerous city, provincial, and national officials, however, indicate that air, water, and solid waste disposal are now beginning to receive significant attention.

Currently, the most effective agencies leading an organized response to the problems are the Bureau of Environmental Protection in the Executive Yuan of the Republic of China, the Bureau of Environmental Protection in the Taiwan provincial government, and the Department of Environmental Protection in the Taipei municipal government. These government agencies monitor environmental pollution, develop regulations, and implement the abatement programs.

In 1975, the Air Pollution Control Act was enacted by the Republic of China. Before this legislation, the Taipei municipal government had attempted to control the combustion of soft coal and the emission of black smoke and other pollutants from factories.[13] Since passing the Air Pollution Act, Taipei has pursued a pollution control policy, but implementing it has been difficult. In addition to the ambient air quality standard, a new emission standard was promulgated on 1 March 1979 for concentrations of SO_2, fluorides, NH_3, H_2S, and other chemicals and organic vapors. The regulations call for penalizing those industries and motor vehicles which emit air pollutants in violation of the standards set by the act.

Under the Water Pollution Control Act of 1974 and the Water Quality Standards of 1976, effluent standards for industrial wastewater have been set to control industrial pollution. In case of violations, the law provides for a penalty. The Water Pollution Control Act was revised in 1983 to ensure effective implementation.

To control noise pollution, the Taiwan provincial government issued an ordinance setting noise limits in 1959. Under this ordinance, industrial noise is regulated by the Labor Bureau of the Ministry of the Interior and the noise from vehicles is regulated by the National Police Administration. There is no single agency responsible for community noise control. Due to the lack of administrative coordination among government agencies, the penalty is not severe enough to enforce noise control in the Taipei area. Specific legislation for noise control is needed.

The Solid Wastes Disposal Act of 1974 regulates the treatment of industrial solid waste, but enforcement has not been completely successful. A major institutional barrier to dealing comprehensively with environmental problems is the lack of adequate government funding to the municipal government of Taipei. Moreover, no national agency now provides capital or tax relief to enterprises interested in introducing new pollution control devices.

Research Methods

We investigated the people's awareness of the pollution hazard and personal adjustments to its existence by using a questionnaire to interview a sample of residents in the city of Taipei in the summer of 1984. The questionnaire was similar to Gilbert White's sample questionnaire for the study of the perception of natural hazards.[14] Although White's questionnaire has been criticized, we chose to follow it in designing our questionnaire in order to facilitate comparison with other surveys based on White's questionnaire.[15] Two major guidelines were used in constructing the interview questionnaire: First, the sequence of questions was from general to specific in order to avoid suggesting answers or problems; second, open-ended questions were provided to capture unanticipated responses.

A grid was placed over a map of each of the sixteen districts of Taipei. These grids were numbered and a sample was drawn using random number tables. Ten sample locations were sought in each district. Each sample location consisted of several households from which one was selected by the probability method for the interview.[16] Either the head of household or the oldest member available at the time of the survey was interviewed. A sample of ten interviews in each of the sixteen districts of Taipei was considered adequate for this study in terms of efficiency, representativeness, and reliability. The sample was small enough to ensure completion within two months and large enough to avoid an intolerable sample error yet yield statistically representative and significant results. The accompanying map (Figure 7.9) shows the locations of the sample interviews in the city of Taipei; these provided a reasonable cross section of the socioeconomic groups in the city.

All interviews were conducted in Chinese by a research assistant under the supervision of the investigators within an eight-week period.

Figure 7.9. Taipei: Location of Sample Household Interviews, 1984

The lack of standardization and variation among interviewers was eliminated by the direct participation of the authors in all interviews. The data were checked for accuracy and completeness by Thomas K. Chao, the co-investigator, and were coded at the computer facilities at the National Taiwan College of Marine Science and Technology, Keelung. The data were analyzed at the University of Kentucky.

Findings

The questionnaires were analyzed with three main objectives. First, we wanted to establish how far the public's perception of environmental pollution in Taipei coincided with the facts as revealed in the pollution data. This task involved a consideration of individual definitions of environmental pollution, the perceived magnitude of the pollution problem, the perceived cost of pollution, and the perceived prospects for the future. Second, we hoped to assess public knowledge of environmental legislation (such as the Air Pollution Control Act of 1975, the Water Pollution Control Act of 1974 and its revision in 1983, the Water Quality Standards of 1976, and the Solid Wastes Disposal Act of 1974) and the respondents' evaluation of its effectiveness in reducing pollution. Third, we wished to investigate attitudes to alternative adjustments to environmental pollution.

Perception of Environmental Pollution

To test the degree and kinds of environmental concerns, the questions were framed in relation to other social and economic issues such as the continued high rates of employment and economic growth. Since an important aspect of our environmental pollution perception survey was to assess the seriousness of the problem to local residents, it was necessary to put environmental pollution into a "general problems" context. A community which is deeply concerned about economic development and industrial growth may be less likely to perceive environmental pollution as serious than would a community whose other problems are less pervasive.

In Taipei, each respondent was told: "I will mention a few problems which different cities are facing. How would you rate each of these problems for your city? Would you rate them 'very serious,' 'somewhat serious,' or 'not serious'?" This inquiry dealt first with the problems of unemployment, air pollution, noise, and refuse collection and disposal; it concluded with traffic congestion, water pollution, lack of open space, and sanitation facilities. At the completion of this series of questions the respondent was invited to indicate any other problem which seemed important in Taipei. We then asked an additional question concerning the relative importance of these items in the respondent's neighborhood. With this information it was possible to place public awareness and concern for environmental problems within a contextual framework as well as to give an overall rating of the environmental quality in the respondent's area of residence.

More than 60 percent of the respondents living in Lungshan, Yenping, Chiengcheng, Tatung, Sungshan, Nankang, and Chungshan (which have the highest recorded levels of air and noise pollution, refuse collection problems, and an overall lower environmental quality) mentioned air, noise, litter, and crowded traffic as serious problems for the entire city and very serious in their neighborhood. Lack of open space, water pollution, and foul odors from rivers were ranked less serious problems for Taipei. As expected, unemployment was not considered a problem by the respondents.

Respondents in old city neighborhoods with high levels of environmental pollution noted convenient shopping, public transportation facilities, and nearby schools as the major advantages of living in the area. The respondents in Peitou, Shihlin, and Mucha—the outer suburban neighborhoods—mentioned the quiet environment, relatively fresh air, and mountain scenery as the major advantages of their areas.

The determination of perception was partly approached through an exploration of the awareness of the geographical distribution of pollution in the city. One early question asked: "Is environmental pollution a problem in this part of town?" The alternatives were specified. Some 90 percent of the respondents in Nankang and 60 percent in Chengchung, Lungshan, and Chingmei perceived high environmental pollution whereas only 1 percent of the respondents in Kuting, Taan, and Chungshan considered pollution high.

Age, sex, education, and length of residency of respondents were compared with an appraisal of local environmental pollution. Respondents between the ages of 15 and 35 (73 percent) and those with a college education (48 percent) saw more significant environmental pollution in their area. We found that perception of environmental pollution varied by the social characteristics of the population of Taipei.[17]

"In which part of Taipei is the air most polluted?" In response to this question, 108 persons replied Nankang, Chengchung, Chingmei, and Lungshan; 52 gave other answers. Recorded pollution data suggest that Nankang, Chengchung, Chingmei, and Lungshan districts have the highest SO_2 particulate matter and noise. All the respondents in Nankang district, and over 60 percent of the respondents in Kuting, Shuangyuan, and Chingmei, cited air pollution as a major problem.

The question "In what part of town is the cleanest air?" resulted in a wide variety of answers. Of the sixteen urban districts, Peitou and Shihlin were frequently mentioned as the cleanest areas.

The findings in Taipei tend to support the view that past experience and frequency of exposure to environmental pollution lead to greater perception and that perception is heightened when the individual lives close to the hazard. Place of residence was of great importance in accounting for differences in the awareness of types and sources of pollution. Once the general attitude and a sense of the relative importance of environmental pollution among the respondents were assessed, the focus of the questionnaire shifted to specific aspects of environmental pollution such as air, water, noise, and solid wastes.

It was assumed that not all respondents would think about air pollution similarly. Therefore, each respondent was asked what he or she meant by the term "air pollution." Our question read: "Would you tell me in as much detail as you can what the words 'air pollution' mean to you?" The answers to this question indicated, in a simple fashion, which aspect of the whole subject was most significant to the individual. Sixty-nine percent of the respondents answered "dust," "black smoke," "air with strange odor," and "automobile exhaust." In Lungshan, Chiencheng, and Chenchung the proportion of respondents answering "dust" or "dirt" increased to 98 percent. Most of them also mentioned "frequent bad smells in the air," "frequent haze," "frequent irritation of the eyes," and "frequent nose or throat irritation."

Once the respondent had made clear his or her ideas about the meaning of air pollution, we proceeded with specific information on how the causality of air pollution is attributed by the sample. Again an open-ended question was asked: "What do you think causes the air pollution that affects this neighborhood?" Emissions from vehicular traffic (automobiles, motorcycles, trucks, and buses) were mentioned by 106 respondents as the principal source of air pollution in Taipei. More than 60 percent of the respondents in Chengchung, Tatung, Chiencheng, Lungshan, Taan, Yenping, Chingmei, Neihu, Chungshan, Kuting, Mucha, Shihlin, and Peitou cited emissions from vehicular traffic as the major source of air pollution in their neighborhoods.

Eleven respondents in Taipei—most of them living in Nankang and Shihlin—cited industry or emissions from factories as the source of air pollution. Twenty-one respondents residing in Shuangyuan, Nankang, Lungshan, Kuting, Mucha, and Chungshan listed industry combined with transportation as sources of air pollution. Fourteen respondents gave various other answers, and eight were unable to provide a precise answer.

Taipei respondents presented a fairly accurate picture of the unique characteristics of the large city. In the central districts, the problems of dust fall, transport exhaust fumes, and odor are a result of concentration of traffic and business establishments and high population density. In the Nankang district the respondents mentioned garbage and refuse dumps ("the Garbage Mountain") plus those factories in the area with highly visible emissions.

The responses to the question "Do you think air pollution is a serious problem for this neighborhood?" have been tabulated (Table 7.1) according to the air quality monitoring station nearest the respondent's residence. Using the total scoring system for measured air quality, the residential areas of Taipei were grouped into eight categories and ranked from "low" to "high" in air pollution. Similarly, the percentages of "serious" responses received in each area were ranked from least to most frequent. We see that the frequency of "serious" responses increases as actual air quality deteriorates—supporting the generalization that there is a direct relationship between the perception of the seriousness of air pollution and the actual ambient air quality in the area of residency.

Respondents were also queried about the possible effect of environmental pollution on their households. Nearly 83 percent of all respondents noted adverse effects on their households. The main worry throughout Taipei was the threat that air pollution would pose to health. Health accounted for 56.8 percent of the effects noted, ranging from 33 percent in Peitou to 69 percent in Chiencheng. Harm to the contents of houses in the form of dirty clothes, more washing, and damage to paint were other major areas of concern. A number of respondents also noted the adverse effect of air pollution on household flowers, plants, and shrubs. Some also mentioned feeling "depressed" during periods of severe air pollution.

In light of these comments, it was not surprising to find that most

Table 7.1. Percentage of Respondents in Taipei who Consider Air Pollution a Serious Problem in Their Own Areas of Residence

Areas Ranked According to Measured Air Pollution	Percentage of "Serious" Air Pollution Responses
1 (lowest)	43.2
2	44.9
3	46.7
4	51.6
5	56.8
6	61.3
7	65.4
8 (highest)	68.2

Source: Calculated by the authors.

respondents felt that air pollution had affected them financially—particularly in Kuting, Chiencheng, Chengchung, Shuangyuan, Yenping, and Mucha, where more people recognized the existence of an air pollution problem. As for the perceived prospects for the future, the residents of Taipei were not very optimistic about substantial improvement in environmental pollution.

Awareness of Environmental Legislation

Most respondents had no knowledge of environmental legislation enacted by the city, province, and republic to control air, water, and noise pollution and solid waste disposal. We asked: "Have you ever heard about specific government legislation to control pollution from any of these sources: newspapers, television, magazines, someone in local government, someone in a community-wide citizens' organization, or from a friend or relative?" Answers to this question, relating awareness of pollution and control programs to exposure by the mass media or in a contact situation, would assist in developing a public information program. The responses in Taipei revealed that the mass media had played a major role in creating an awareness of environmental pollution, but in general the residents were unaware of official legislation to control the problem.

Adjustments to Environmental Pollution

In order to discover patterns of behavior in dealing with the threat of environmental pollution, we asked: "When environmental pollution (air, water, noise, and solid waste) is particularly bad, what can a person do?" Most of the Taipei respondents answered either "don't know" or "nothing." Many doubted that their actions would be effective, indicating a widespread feeling of helplessness in the face of environmental pollution. Several respondents suggested planting more trees in the city to reduce pollution and a temporary move to the countryside during periods of severe air pollution. Leaving the city permanently was not a feasible proposition for respondents.

Many respondents said that they took some direct action to reduce their exposure to pollution, such as closing windows and wearing gas masks. In Shuangyuan, Sungshan, Chungshan, Shihlin, and Peitou, more than 70 percent of the respondents kept windows and other openings closed during periods of severe pollution. In Mucha and Nankang, 50 percent of the respondents wore smog masks to reduce the amount of polluted air they were breathing.

Responses which favored doing something about environmental pollution were influenced by social characteristics and by the perception of environmental pollution. Respondents over the age of 45 tended to consider closing windows and staying indoors during periods of severe air pollution, but they were significantly less willing to complain to the authorities or write to a newspaper. Younger people (under the age of 30) and those who were well educated tended most often to consider leaving their places of residence in Taipei temporarily during periods of severe pollution, but they were least likely to see a doctor or stop using motorcycles or cars.

Only a negligible proportion of the respondents were prepared to admit their own contribution to pollution and to restrict their own level of emissions by not using a car or not burning rubbish outside. Of the sample only twenty-five respondents said they had complained to officials to get some action. Many of the people who were interviewed did not know who to approach and had doubts about the concern and efficiency of those in authority. Only eleven respondents wrote to their local legislator, and only ten wrote to a newspaper to seek relief from the severe environmental pollution in their neighborhood. There appears to be no simple relationship between public concern about environmental pollution, as indicated by the complaints of a small vocal minority, and the spatial patterns of pollution (Figures 7.5 to 7.8) as recorded by monitoring stations.

The study indicates that awareness and concern about environmental pollution did not often result in action of any kind by the respondents themselves. The reluctance to make complaints is found in the answers to the question: "Is there anything that the government can do about the problem of environmental pollution?" Of the 160 respondents, 78 were doubtful of any government action and 42 indicated that the government could not do anything about the problem. Only 40 thought the problem could be reduced significantly by official enforcement of emissions control on factories, motorcycles, and automobiles. Among those few who had any opinion about what could be done, no significant differences could be detected as to preference for control measures.

Though one cannot count on technical expertise in the lay public, knowing the public's attitude toward the role of the city, provincial, or central government in program development would assist planners in making more realistic control program proposals. Public communication is an essential part of a remedial action program, and the release of information about government pollution control programs for press coverage and discussion groups of laymen should be extremely helpful.

In Taipei, most of the forty respondents who indicated a major role for the government in pollution control felt that the central government would take the lead in controlling environmental pollution with the aid of provincial and municipal agencies. Newspaper, radio, and television reports have raised a considerable level of anxiety about environmental pollution in Taipei, for escape from the city is impossible.

There was a feeling of inaction among the respondents, especially when asked about any complaints they had made about pollution. People simply did not complain because they thought little could be done. At the same time, their understanding of the relative contribution of automobiles, motorcycles, factories, noise, and refuse disposal to the total environmental deterioration was highly sophisticated and accurate.

Intensive public education is needed in Taipei to inform the people of what can be done, who is doing it, and what they themselves can do to reduce environmental pollution. The relationship between land use patterns, industrial activity, and human behavior should be taken into consideration in developing concepts of zoning and space allocation in Taipei. Planners must take into account the natural ecology and environment, not merely economic factors.

In general, coping strategies in Taipei depended on the level of exposure to environmental pollution. Unless respondents were adjacent to a major source of pollution, they tended to believe their own homes were relatively unaffected. Two of the most common adjustments in areas of high pollution were closing windows to keep out pollution and not hanging freshly washed clothes outside.

Policy Implications

There is now a general acceptance that public opinion should be included in the formulation of strategies to combat environmental problems. The questionnaire-based survey reflecting public attitudes toward environmental pollution can be a valuable input in the decision-making process for policy planning.[18] Surveys offer a way of taking into account not just the views of highly motivated and unusually articulate public interest groups, but also those who may feel alienated from decision making and those whose opinions might otherwise be ignored. At the same time, it must be recognized that assessments of attitude and perception are difficult to express and record and far from easy to quantify in a meaningful fashion.

These methodological problems are, of course, common to all social science surveys. Nevertheless, it should be pointed out that a number of geographic studies of public attitudes have already been conducted by Auliciems and Burton, Cooke and Saarinen, and Johnston and Hay in North America and Europe[19] and by Bladen and Karan in the industrial areas of South Asia.[20] These surveys give us data concerning the attitudes of the respondents toward the environmental hazards encountered within an area which can then be fed into the decision-making process of environmental planning.[21] A broad review of the scale and nature of environmental pollution, the costs and benefits of regulation, and present attitudes and anxieties concerning pollution may then serve as a basis for informed public debate.

The publication of attitudinal evidence can be invaluable in stimulating public discussion and hence the presentation of considered views and proposals. The feedback relationship between perception studies and decision making can be linked in a constructive fashion to ensure the most advantageous outcome for the policymakers themselves and for the people exposed to the pollutants.

Differences in Perception of Environmental Problems: Taipei and Calcutta

Taipei and Calcutta are two Asian cities affected by serious environmental pollution. A survey of public awareness of environmental pollution was conducted in Calcutta in 1974[22] and again in 1978.[23] A perception-adjustment questionnaire, similar to the one used in Taipei, was used on a stratified sample of 240 respondents in Calcutta to elicit responses and adjustments to the environmental problem. The results of the surveys in Taipei and Calcutta have been compared to discover similarities and differences in the perception of environmental pollution.

A comparison of the perception of environmental hazards in different cities should create a better understanding of the human response to environmental stress in various cultures. By developing data on these personal adjustments to pollution, a wide range of control strategies could be identified for possible use in all cultures. Since this cross-cultural study constituted a pioneer contribution in comparing perceptions to environmental pollution in different cultural milieus, methodological problems were encountered that limited the rigor of analysis but this initial effort is nevertheless valuable.

With a population of over 9.5 million in the metropolitan area, Calcutta is much larger than Taipei in both area and population. It is a diversified urban center with a great variety of commercial and industrial activity. Indeed, Calcutta contains the largest concentration of manufacturing activity in India.[24] Motor vehicle traffic is dense throughout the Calcutta urban area. Although Calcutta and Taipei differ substantially in size and functions, the cities share a serious environmental pollution problem.

Pollution data from the two cities reveal no marked differences between them. Both have continuous monitoring stations which record the concentration of pollutants in the air and in the water. Calcutta experiences more pollution, but concentrations of pollutants are high in both cities. Measures to control pollution are not well implemented in either city. Although both India and the Republic of China have enacted legislation to control environmental pollution, Calcutta has been less effective in its air and water pollution control programs.

Residents of both Asian cities learn about pollution directly from their own exposure and indirectly from other sources, particularly the mass media. In both cities the daily newspapers have directed attention to environmental problems. It can be assumed that the inhabitants of both cities are influenced in their judgment of pollution by secondary information sources.

In order to evaluate the relative importance of environmental pollution, respondents in both cities were asked to list the environmental problems in their own neighborhood. In Calcutta, the city more seriously affected by urban environmental problems, air and water pollution showed up repeatedly among the problems listed by respondents in the 1974 and 1978 surveys.[25] There were significant differences, however, in the awareness levels among respondents living in areas experiencing different pollution levels within each city. In Taipei, for instance, air pollution was less frequently mentioned by the inhabitants of Peitou, which is relatively clean, but was generally acknowledged to be a significant problem in the Keelung Valley and in the old city districts.

The results of the surveys in both Calcutta and Taipei suggest a strong positive correlation between the frequency with which people perceive environmental pollution as a problem in their own neighborhood and the actual level of pollution there. When asked to identify the most and the least polluted areas of their city, respondents of the two cities answered with remarkable accuracy. When asked about the major sources of pollution in their city, respondents usually suggested those sources characteristic of their own residential area. As for the future, respondents in Calcutta and Taipei did not foresee a significant improvement in environmental quality.

A comparison of the public's awareness of environmental pollution reveals a heightened perception in Taipei. The most fascinating difference between the two cultures is that several components that were widely perceived to be part of the environmental problem in Taipei were not so perceived in Calcutta. For example, 53 percent of the Taipei sample said that population growth is central to the environmental problem. In contrast, it is surprising that in Calcutta, which has one of the highest urban population densities in the world, only 12 percent of the respondents perceived population growth as central to the environmental problem. A sizable segment of Calcutta's sample did not perceive noise as part of the environmental problem. Indeed, noise has received little attention in India as an environmental problem. Thus Calcuttans seem to define the environmental problem narrowly as air and water pollution. The broader definition in Taipei includes air, water, and noise pollution and refuse disposal.

To summarize, the environmental issue in Calcutta appears to be perceived as a narrow set of problems, whereas in Taipei a broader range of concerns is included in the public's perception. These marked differences in the definition of the environmental problem were also reflected in the identification of the problem's causes. Industrial activity and traffic were high on the list of causes of environmental pollution in both cities. When one turns to other causes, however, there was a marked divergence in each city.

The policy of rapid economic growth pursued by the Republic of China was noted by some respondents in Taipei as an "important" or "very important" contributor to environmental problems. In Calcutta, people's "carelessness" was mentioned frequently as a source of pollution. The difference here is striking: The Taipei respondents held the policy of rapid growth responsible for enviromental problems, whereas the respondents in Calcutta were much more inclined to blame people like themselves for being careless and causing environmental problems. These responses help to clarify the cultural difference: Indians blame themselves for environmental degradation, but not the industrial development that has polluted the environment, whereas the Taiwanese blame the rapid industrial growth. Both the Calcutta and Taipei surveys reveal that government actions were failing to solve the environmental problem. Most of the Taipei residents rated present programs to combat pollution as inadequate, and half of the Calcutta respondents living in areas of severe pollution were pessimistic about the government's pollution abatement programs.[26]

This preliminary comparison of the perceptions of environmental pollution in Taipei and Calcutta indicates that in order to find solutions to the environmental problem that the people would be willing to accept, it is essential to ascertain the public's perception of the seriousness of the problem, the causes of the problem, and the location of the problem. In other words, causes and solutions are opposite sides of the same coin. In every statement of cause there is an implied solution, and in every expressed preference for a solution there is an implied recognition of the cause.

This review of the similarities and differences between Taipei and Calcutta in perceptions of environmental pollution whets the appetite for a much larger and more closely comparable series of surveys for other Asian cities in various culture areas. Our survey results imply that the perception of the environmental problem is culture-bound, that it is influenced by the mass media, and that one's place of residence is of great importance in accounting for differences in the awareness and sources of environmental pollution. Another survey finding appears to show that we cannot expect people to support strong environmental protection programs by their governments until they themselves perceive a severe environmental degradation.

ACKNOWLEDGMENTS

Fieldwork in Taipei was supported by the Pacific Cultural Foundation. The following persons provided data on air, water, and noise pollution and solid waste disposal problems: C. P. Hsu, commissioner of the Department of Environmental Protection, Taipei Municipal Government; Chuang Chin-Yuan, director of the Bureau of Environmental Protection, Department of Health, Executive Yuan, Republic of China; Shih-Chong Lu, director of the Bureau of Environmental Protection, Taiwan Provincial Government; and Terry Hsu of the Taipei Municipal Government. We wish to express our appreciation to Dr. Jeanne Tchong-Koei Li, president of the Pacific Cultural Foundation; Chen-Chew Pan, director-general of the China Youth Corps; Tze Chi Chao, secretary-general, Policy Coordination Committee, Kuomingtang; and Professor Chang Yu-Sheng for supporting this research. Our efforts were greatly facilitated by the assistance of Yue-Chain Huang, an advanced student at National Taiwan University, who helped conduct all the interviews and made many valuable suggestions during the field surveys.

NOTES

1. T. F. Saarinen and J. L. Sell, "Environmental Perception;" *Progress in Human Geography* 4 (1980): 535–548; T. F. Saarinen and J. L. Sell, "Environmental Perception;" *Progress in Human Geography* 5 (1981): 525–547; T. F. Saarinen, D. Seamon, and J. L. Sell, *Environmental Perception and Behavior: An Inventory and Prospect,* Research Paper 209 (Chicago: University of Chicago, Department of Geography, 1984).
2. T. F. Saarinen, J. L. Sell, and E. Husband, "Environmental Perception;" *Progress in Human Geography* 6 (1982): 515–546.
3. R. M. Selya, "Water and Air Pollution in Taiwan," *Journal of Developing Areas* 9 (1975): 177–202.
4. C. Y. Chuang, *A Review of the Control of Atmospheric Particulate Pollutants in Taiwan* (Taipei: Bureau of Environmental Protection, 1984).
5. Bureau of Environmental Protection, *General Review of Air Pollution Control in 1982* (Taipei: Bureau of Environmental Protection, 1983).
6. Chuang, *Review.*

7. *Central Daily News* (Taipei), 9 July 1980.

8. C. Y. Chuang, "Environmental Quality in Taiwan," paper presented at the Science, Engineering, and Technology Seminar, Houston, Texas, 24–25 May 1980.

9. Ibid.

10. C. Y. Chuang, *Water Pollution in Rivers and Streams of Taiwan, Republic of China, and Its Control* (Taipei: Bureau of Environmental Protection, 1984).

11. Municipal Government of Taipei, *Sewerage Development in Taipei City* (Taipei: Public Works Bureau, Sewerage Engineering Department, 1984).

12. Taipei Water Department, *Taipei Water Supply* (Taipei, 1983).

13. J. S. Chen, "The Control Stratagem of Air Pollutants in Taiwan" (master's thesis, Public Administration and Stratagem graduate, National Chung Hsing University, Taiwan, 1982), p. 43.

14. G. F. White, *Natural Hazards: Local, National, Global* (New York: Oxford University Press, 1974), pp. 6–9.

15. Saarinen, Seamon, and Sell, *Perception and Behavior,* pp. 160–161.

16. Survey Research Center, *Interviewer's Manual* (Ann Arbor: University of Michigan, 1976).

17. This view is supported in a study by Barry Goodchild, "Class Differences in Environmental Perception: An Exploratory Study," *Urban Studies* 11 (1974): 157–169. A recent study by Hwang Rongtsuen and Wu Yin-Chang of National Taiwan University reveals that educated people perceived noise pollution as a more serious environmental hazard than those with less education. See *Free China Journal* (Taipei), 21 April 1985, p. 3.

18. P. Slovic, B. Fischhoff, and S. Lichtenstein, "Why Study Risk Perception?" *Risk Analysis* 2 (1982): 83–93.

19. A. Auliciems and I. Burton, "Perception and Awareness of Air Pollution in Toronto," Natural Hazard Working Paper 13 (Toronto: University of Toronto, 1970); Ronald U. Cooke and Thomas F. Saarinen, "Public Perception of Environmental Quality in Tucson, Arizona," *Journal of the Arizona Academy of Science* 6 (1971): 260–274; R. J. Johnston and J. E. Hay, "Spatial Variations in Awareness of Air Pollution Distributions," *International Journal of Environmental Studies* 6 (1974): 131–136.

20. W. A. Bladen and P. P. Karan, "Perception of Air Pollution in a Developing Country," *Journal of Air Pollution Control Association* 26 (1976): 139–141; W. A. Bladen and P. P. Karan, "Perception of Environmental Problems in Coal Mining Areas of India and the United States," *National Geographer* 10 (1975): 1–8; P. P. Karan, "Changes in the Environmental Perception of Pollution in the Calcutta–Hooghlyside Industrial Strip of India," *International Journal of Environmental Studies* 15 (1980): 185–189; P. P. Karan, "Perception of Environmental Pollution in Chotanagpur Industrial Area, India," *National Geographer* 12 (1977): 17–24; P. P. Karan, "Public Awareness of Environmental Problems in Calcutta Metropolitan Area," *National Geographical Journal of India* 26 (1980): 29–34.

21. Geoffrey C. Smith, "Responses of Residents and Policymakers to Urban Environmental Hazards," *Area* 8 (1976): 279–283.

22. W. A. Bladen and P. P. Karan, "Environmental Pollution and its Per-

ception in the Calcutta-Hooghlyside Area," in A. G. Noble and A. K. Dutt (eds.), *Indian Urbanization and Planning: Vehicles of Modernization* (Delhi: Tata-McGraw-Hill, 1977), pp. 281-293.

23. Karan, "Changes in the Environmental Perception of Pollution."

24. P. P. Karan, "Changes in Indian Industrial Location," *Annals of the Association of American Geographers* 55 (1964): 336-354.

25. Karan, "Public Awareness," p. 32.

26. Bladen and Karan, "Environmental Pollution and its Perception," p. 293.

8. Coefficients of Urban Intensification for Japanese Cities: 1960–1980

DAVID H. KORNHAUSER

THOSE interested in the evolution of Japanese urbanization may be impressed by what appears to be its relatively recent origin. This is probably because, until well after World War II, the main national economic undertaking was overwhelmingly farming or some primary industrial effort. Emphasis on rural activity was also so clearly marked on the landscape that even well-developed and long-flourishing town life, which had many sophisticated elements, and which was a leading influence in the culture, was often slighted. A kind of bucolic impression, one that has been surprisingly persistent, was the standard image.

Rather than rely on the superficial appearance of the landscape, or even on the predominance of certain economic activities, if one were to consider the nature of Japanese prominence in the world, even from a time when this first attracted international attention, it is immediately apparent that the culture has been known for its artistic achievements and other marks of a high civilization that could only have been produced by an urban mode of living that, premodern though it may have been, was surprisingly advanced. Fairly recent revelations, through modern translation of both ancient and modern literature, would bolster the argument that the Japanese descend from a culture that could hardly have been characterized by a nonurban mode of living.

Town and city life, indeed, has roots in Japan dating from the very earliest times—even perhaps from before the advent of documented history. The introduction of Buddhism in the sixth century, and the institutionalization of T'ang-period Chinese influences in the so-called Taika Reforms of the mid-seventh century, led to the creation of Nara and especially Kyoto, a large and resplendent city to this day and the first long-term capital. Historically, Kyoto was the imperial seat from 795 until the Meiji Restoration, and although from 1603 the real center of power and command was Edo, this shogunal headquarters was not retitled Tokyo and designated the capital until the imperial house was moved there in 1868.

From at least the early seventeenth century forward, Japanese cities owe their origins to a feudalistic society dominated by Edo, which saw the molding of a hierarchy of settlements, mainly castle towns, from huge and sprawling Edo (which by the late seventeenth century was the largest city in the world) to burgeoning Osaka, Kyoto, and Nagoya, to the lowliest regional centers, a milieu that included most contemporary cities of note. By the opening of Japan in the mid-nineteenth century, although modernization awaited the establishment of the Meiji government in 1868, city life and urban influences were almost universal.[1]

On these foundations, Meiji modernization simply added such consolidating elements as lines of communication and transportation, around which networks of industrial and commercial might were constructed. By World War I, Japan was still ostensibly rural but the city was growing rapidly more prominent and important to the basic economy. By 1940, Japan was on the threshold of modern urbanization, a process that was interrupted only from the early 1940s to the early 1960s when the proportion of population began to reveal true urban dominance.

Official tabulation of population and the regular publication of the results dates from 1920, although there were census summaries in prior years and often fairly systematic counts even before Meiji times. The recording of urban population was a simple matter of counting residents within a settlement of 30,000 or more. Although programs of urban amalgamation were pursued from time to time and city boundaries tended to swell, until the early 1950s there was little problem in the tabulation of urban versus nonurban population. In the fall of 1953, however, the government embarked on a campaign of major urban expansion on a national scale which was accomplished by enlarging city areas; hence, this process greatly obscured the classification of citizens by residence. In consequence, by the 1960 census the Japanese government's Bureau of Statistics, in reporting data on the state of cities, included a new urban element entitled densely inhabited districts (DIDs).

Until the census of 1960 (standard data have been available every five years since 1920), it was the practice to record only the base population, broken down by sex, age, economic activity, and many other categories and by the area of residence. Supplemental volumes on such matters as commuting were added to complete census reports as time went on. Data were also broadly subdivided into city *(shi)* and county *(gun)*, the latter consisting of towns *(cho ormachi)* and villages *(son ormura)*. Anything other than cities was considered nonurban.

The publication of such material has continued on a quinquennial basis but, as stated and for obvious reasons, the data were importantly supplemented after 1960. Effects of the massive consolidations of cities, towns, and villages can easily be seen in a contrast between the censuses of 1950 and 1955. In the 1950 census, there were only 235 cities, but by 1955 this figure had increased to 490. In every quinquennial figure since, the total has increased: In 1980, there were 647 cities; today there are more than 650.[2]

Since the creation of new cities (and the expansion of older ones) was achieved merely by widening the outer boundaries and incorporating peripheral settlements up to a minimum total population of 30,000, however, by the late 1950s there were many cities that were little more than large towns surrounded by unabashed farmland. The Statistical Bureau, after careful research and advice by population specialists, including urban geographers, inaugurated the DID system, which tended to distinguish, much more clearly, the true urban population. Beginning with the national census of 1960, each census has included double sets of population and area figures, even for places not yet called cities but where DID conditions are known to exist.[3]

Densely Inhabited Districts in Japan

The ratio of the general population and area to DID population and area for each city (multiplied by 1,000) yields a one to four-digit number which indicates urban intensification and which can then be compared through the five census periods since 1960.[4] These numbers represent a hierarchy of places from the least to the most intensively urbanized. The use of a single number is convenient for quickly and clearly demonstrating the phenomenon of urbanization. And since this figure takes into account not only the entire area but also the smaller, more densely urbanized core, this expression has more validity than, say, a simple population density figure which would not consider clearly nonurban population or those for whom nonurban activity is important, yet who are living within the boundaries of a so-called city. To date, published DID data do not go beyond the matter of population and area nor are DID statistics readily available except directly in the census.

In this chapter, statistical compilations of urban coefficients from 1960 to 1980 have been calculated for each of the forty-seven prefectures (Table 8.1, at end of chapter), arranged in nine traditional regions (Hokkaido, Tohoku, Kanto, Hokuriku and Tosan, Tokai and Kinki, Chugoku–Shikoku, and Kyushu–Okinawa, the last two being compound regions), as well as for each of the 647 cities listed in the national census of 1980 (Table 8.2, at end of chapter). In every case, regardless of occasional anomalies, the scores or mean scores show high and low intensification where this might be anticipated—from lows of zero (where DID conditions are still unidentified) to highs of over 1,000, the latter, for all intents and purposes, being saturated.

Prefectures of Japan and Traditional Regions

Incidence of urbanization or the lack of it is obvious from Table 8.1. Hokkaido, where space, by Japanese standards, is uncommonly abundant, shows rather low mean coefficients when one considers the degree of metropolitanization around Sapporo. This tendency is mirrored to a lesser extent in such northern and north-central Honshu prefectures as Iwate, Akita, Yamagata, Fukushima, Ishikawa, Fukui, Nagano, and surprisingly to this writer since it is so near Tokyo, Yamanashi (Figure 8.1). In western Honshu, lack of urbanization, as expected, is noteworthy of Shimane but oddly not of Tottori, for which some explanation is offered later. The Sanyo strip of Okayama, Hiroshima, and Yamaguchi, though they are all increasing as corridors of urbanization to their east and west, is also fairly nonurban but under fast-changing conditions. Shikoku (other than Kagawa) and southern Kyushu also have relatively low urban presence, though often not as much as one finds in northern Honshu and Hokkaido. Okinawa—whose accounting (because it was under American control between 1945 and 1972) dates only from 1970 in modern national censuses—appears an exception, as can be quickly realized in a visit to its crowded cities and suburbs. It is therefore, compared to southern Kyushu, rather in a class by itself.

Conversely, the urban prefectures stand out boldly, beginning with Miyagi in the north and skipping to the Tokaido megalopolitan agglomeration (including the Pacific coastal strip of Shizuoka, Aichi, and the Keihanshin corridor) and finally, more or less skipping again, to Fukuoka in northern Kyushu and ultimately to the hitherto rural prefecture of Kumamoto and perhaps, as stated, even to Okinawa of the Ryukyu Archipelago.

The nine traditional regions, which have no official status but which are often used to present statistical data, clearly reflect the figures for the forty-seven prefectures. In Tohoku, aside from Miyagi which stands out as an exception, the overall mean is low, being surpassed only by atypical Hokkaido. Hokuriku and Tosan, traditionally in the backwash of urban growth, offer few exceptions; nor do Chugoku–Shikoku and Kyushu–Okinawa, unless one takes into account the urban vigor of Kagawa or that of Okinawa itself. Of course, the metropolitan flavor of Fukuoka creates an island of urban intensity in these largely nonurban regions.

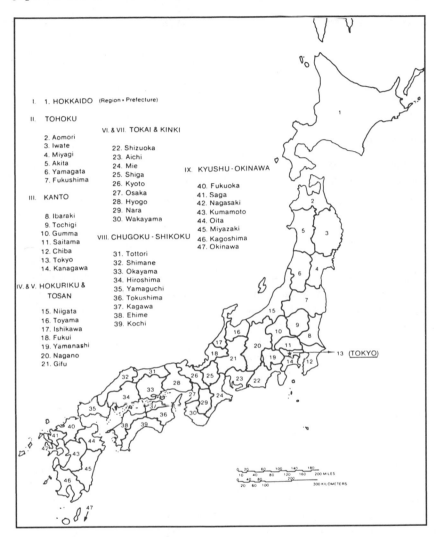

I.   1. HOKKAIDO (Region • Prefecture)

II.   TOHOKU
                        VI. & VII. TOKAI & KINKI
      2. Aomori
      3. Iwate   22. Shizuoka
      4. Miyagi   23. Aichi
      5. Akita   24. Mie   IX. KYUSHU - OKINAWA
      6. Yamagata   25. Shiga
      7. Fukushima   26. Kyoto   40. Fukuoka
                          27. Osaka   41. Saga
III. KANTO   28. Hyogo   42. Nagasaki
                          29. Nara   43. Kumamoto
      8. Ibaraki   30. Wakayama   44. Oita
      9. Tochigi   45. Miyazaki
      10. Gumma   VIII. CHUGOKU - SHIKOKU   46. Kagoshima
      11. Saitama   47. Okinawa
      12. Chiba   31. Tottori
      13. Tokyo   32. Shimane
      14. Kanagawa   33. Okayama
                          34. Hiroshima
IV. & V. HOKURIKU &   35. Yamaguchi
         TOSAN   36. Tokushima
                          37. Kagawa
      15. Niigata   38. Ehime
      16. Toyama   39. Kochi
      17. Ishikawa
      18. Fukui
      19. Yamanashi
      20. Nagano
      21. Gifu

Figure 8.1. Japan: Prefectures by Region

The regions of urbanization are inordinately clear: Kanto is in the lead, followed by Tokai and neighboring Kinki, though one might expect the last two to be juxtaposed in the hierarchy. This order is only for 1980, however. In previous census years, Kinki led over Tokai, or both had the same mean level of urban intensification. Fukuoka, as mentioned, is exceptional, now and historically, and Okinawa is surprisingly urban-oriented, although, as stated, the figures date only from 1970.

Individual Prefectures and Their Cities

This presentation of the twenty-year march of individual cities, by prefecture, allows those with particular interest in the mechanics of modern Japanese urbanization to fully appreciate these overall mean coefficients (Table 8.2).

Hokkaido

In Hokkaido, for example, the demise of former coal mining settlements, of which Yubari is the leader of a sizable group, is all too evident. Odd variations, such as sudden decreases, are also indicative of unstable urban conditions, as is the lack of an upward curve through the years since 1960. Much of this in Hokkaido is attributable to the fading economic importance of coal. Physically cramped sites with little room for expansion are also noteworthy in high coefficients for such places as Muroran, Kushiro, and Hakodate. While the Sapporo coefficients may seem mild for a city so vast, the area is enormous and has been increasing. A low figure for Hokkaido results also from a general population movement, which has steadily quickened since the mid-1960s. In this and other nonurban prefectures, the trend is away from agriculture and toward the city, including Sapporo, but also toward Kanto and other heavily urbanized parts of the country.

Tohoku

Aomori prefecture is traditionally rural and relatively undeveloped, but two cities stand out. Hachinohe was one of the old industrial sites selected in 1962 for inclusion in the program of "New Industrial Cities," and its march to greater prominence can be seen. Likewise, the largely American air base at Misawa and the prosperity surrounding it are reflected in the Misawa figure, which is high compared to most other Aomori places, including the capital city itself.

Iwate prefecture, sometimes called the "Tibet of Japan," appears to live up to the title. The only important urbanization, minor though it may be, follows the Kitakami Lowland from Morioka southward through Mizusawa and Kitakami, as can be seen in Table 8.2. But in the future, thanks to the opening in 1983 of the Tohoku Shinkansen (super-high-speed railway), this area may burgeon. Settlement in Iwate is bifurcated between this lowland and rather isolated coastal cities such as Miyako, Ofunato, Kamaishi, and other struggling communities dependent on fishing, ancient industry, and tourism.

Recent urbanization in parts of Miyagi prefecture is evident from this list. The Sendai–Shiogama agglomeration stands out in vigor, along with suburban, dormitory cities such as Tagajo, a place with roots in prehistoric times. The progression of such cities from coefficients of zero to sudden high numbers is usually indicative of newly opened dormitory cities, often high-rise/single-dwelling combination settlements, adjacent to large urban complexes—a common situation around Tokyo, Nagoya, Osaka, and other metropolises but relatively uncommon in most outlying, formerly rural prefectures.

The cities in Akita, Yamagata, and Fukushima prefectures fully indicate their nonurban status despite minor urban activity in a few places. Fukushima is something of an anomaly as it lies between urbanizing Miyagi and the superurbanized Kanto prefectures and is well connected by rail and highway with the most metropolitan parts of Japan. Thus if urban tentacles continue to reach out toward it from north and south, one might assume that Fukushima is slated for more metropolitan growth in the years ahead.

Kanto

Beginning with Ibaraki and continuing through Tochigi, Gumma, and especially Chiba, Saitama, Tokyo, and Kanagawa prefectures, the list here demonstrates amply the presence of large numbers of cities with high coefficients. It can be noted that in metropolitan Tokyo, certain cities are not only "saturated" in the 1980 census but some, such as Musashino, have been so throughout the scope of this study. Saitama has urbanized more fully and rapidly than any other prefecture adjacent to a major metropolis and now has the highest number of cities of all, a total of thirty-nine.

Hokuriku and Tosan

The prefectures following Kanagawa are, once again, nonurban for the most part, but generally less so than in neighboring Tohoku. Niigata, for example, has several fairly viable cities, though in general the prefectural mean coefficients are low. The cities of Toyama prefecture, on the other hand, demonstrate the importance of the Toyama Plain, whose influence results in a fairly high mean prefectural average, at least since 1970. Ishikawa, Fukui, and Yamanashi, however, are all on the undeveloped side despite the prominence in each prefecture of the capital city. Nagano, though similar to Yamanashi in that it is truly "inland," a rarity in Japan, is more actively linked by major transportation routes to the nation's urban mainstream, which probably accounts for the viability of its four or five leading cities in Table 8.2, even though the prefectural mean coefficients are low. Gifu is ambivalent: Most of its area is decidedly "inland" and nonurban, but a western extremity extends into the Tokaido megalopolis, as reflected in high mean coefficients for the capital of Gifu, as well as for Ogaki, Kakamigahara, and others.

Tokai and Kinki

As the height of the mean prefectural coefficients shows, Shizuoka and Aichi are among the most urbanized prefectures in Japan. In fact, the efficacy of this index system may be justified in the ranking of these and adjacent prefectures in the Kinki district. Comparing these nine prefectures (Shizuoka, Aichi, Mie, Shiga, Kyoto, Osaka, Hyogo, Nara, and Wakayama) in the five census periods, the order (greatest to least urban intensity) shown for 1980 may be reasonably "normal." Osaka is in the lead, followed by Aichi, Hyogo, Nara, and Kyoto and finally by Shiga, Wakayama, Shizuoka, and Mie.

These prefectures could be considered in three groups: (1) Osaka, Aichi, and Hyogo; (2) Nara and Kyoto; (3) Shiga, Wakayama, Shizuoka, and Mie. As leaders in this context, group 1 appears to be fixed for some time to come; but in group 2, Kyoto may continue to increase in urban intensification and may ultimately surpass formerly nonurban Nara. Kyoto itself, considering the size of the capital city, was remarkably nonurban and nonintensified for many years, being situated as the only sizable metropolis within a basically undeveloped, largely rural prefecture that (like Hyogo and even Yamaguchi) straddles western Honshu, even to the extent of having considerable frontage on the Sea of Japan. In more recent years, however, the rapidly increasing urbanization of the Tokaido megalopolis has caused the growth of suburbs, mainly dormitory settlements, adjacent to cities such as Kyoto and Nara. This has exaggerated the urban sphere around the capitals, ordinarily giving these prefectures high coefficients of urban intensification. Group 3 is similar. It seems logical that Mie and Wakayama, being slightly peripheral to the main thrust of metropolitanization, should ultimately be outclassed, especially by Shizuoka but also by Shiga, which are more central to main urban influences.

Chugoku–Shikoku

Beginning with Tottori and running through the prefectures of western Honshu and Shikoku, urban intensification is uniformly low. Although Tottori appears otherwise, its fairly high mean may be attributable to the dearth of cities in the prefecture and to the extraordinarily crowded urban sphere around Yonago. Likewise, Kagawa appears unusually intensified for Shikoku, but again peculiar conditions in the Sanuki Plain of northeastern Shikoku may be responsible. Here Takamatsu is surrounded by other developing, small, coastal cities, all of which are unusually vigorous, either from industry or from local tourism. The configuration of the topography tends also to press these cities toward the sea and arrange them along a corridor of movement and interchange which is backed in the south by high mountains fairly close to the relatively narrow coastal plain. Connections with western Honshu in the present decade also will be vastly improved by new bridges, and these links may further intensify in the years ahead.

Ehime, on the other hand, is a larger prefecture than Kagawa and has much inland and isolated coastal settlement and industry. The predominance of Matsuyama, Imabari, and Niihama—all viable cities located along the Seto Inland Sea west of the Kagawa cities noted above —is insufficient to overcome the general nonurban complexion of the prefecture because of other cities less fortunately placed. Tokushima and Kochi are, of course, affected by their position off the urban mainstream, as can be seen in Table 8.2 in the low figures for both.

Kyushu–Okinawa

Fukuoka, once virtually the lone industrial hub of western Japan, has retained much of its urban intensity, as can be seen in the high prefectural coefficients and in the number of cities with positive mean figures. This intensity exists despite the continued emphasis on primary industry, notably coal mining, which, though much reduced, is still important. Other (usually tertiary) industry has been established here, however, which helps to account for the ascendency of the capital city of Fukuoka over its million-class rival, Kitakyushu. The general viability of Fukuoka cities and their growing intensification over the years is a particular result of the rise and continued health of commercial activity.

Saga and Nagasaki, as their low urban intensification coefficients may indicate, are victims of sagging industrial fortunes, coal mining in the former and shipbuilding in the latter. And while Kumamoto's prefectural coefficients are on the low side, a legacy of its rural heritage, the constantly enhanced commercial activity of the capital city and its suburbs stands out. Oita, again, although it has three viable commercial and industrial centers, including one of the New Industrial City sites in the suburbs of the capital, is too much a product of a nonurban past for the prefecture to show much of an urban intensity average at this time.

Miyazaki and Kagoshima are much the same; vigor shows only in the capital and one or two other cities. But, as stated, Okinawa gives evidence of sizable urban growth and vigor, particularly in and around Naha, the prefectural seat.

Conclusions

This simple means of identifying a complex phenomenon—a single figure representing true urban intensification—may now allow researchers to illustrate some of the details of this process. The reader also must keep in mind the implications of these figures, which might include the augmentation of means of transport by rail, highway, and air and the vast technological improvements in all these modes, as well as the opening of new bridges, tunnels, and other facilities which tend to reduce time and distance between cities and urban agglomerations. There are also the physical effects of radical change in the presence of new housing enclaves, commercial structures of all kinds, even new industrial facilities—all linked by an ever-widening network of highways and railroads—which are fast altering the landscape and introducing new elements into the once traditional Japanese setting.[5]

NOTES

1. For a summary of these conditions, see David H. Kornhauser, *Japan: Geographical Background to Urban-Industrial Development* (London: Longmans, 1982).

2. The statistical data on which this study is based are from the Population Censuses of Japan, vol. 1: Total Population, for 1960, 1965, 1970, 1975, and 1980 (Tokyo: Bureau of Statistics, Office of the Prime Minister, 1961, 1966, 1971, 1976, and 1982. The count of cities in 1955 and 1960 is from Zenkoku Shi, *Cho, Son Yoran National City, Town and Village Handbook 1982,* which is also based on the census (Tokyo: Dai Ichi Hoki Publishing Co., 1982), p. 3.

3. A statement on DIDs is included in each of the bilingual population census volumes mentioned above. In vol. 1 of 1980, p. xxiv, for example, under Densely Inhabited Districts, it is said: "A Densely Inhabited District . . . in this report is defined as an area within a *shi, ku, machi,* or *mura* that is composed of a group of contiguous enumeration districts each of which has a population density of about 4,000 inhabitants or more per square kilometer and whose total population exceeds 5,000 as of 1 October 1980."

4. The formula used to compile the coefficients of urban intensification is: $A/C/B/D \times 1{,}000$, where A = current population, B = current area, C = current DID population, and D = current DID area.

5. I am indebted to my friend and former colleague Dr. Willard T. Chow for suggesting the name of the index. Professor Norton S. Ginsburg, who visited

our department for one semester, read the manuscript and rendered valuable suggestions. Comments by Dr. Donald Fryer led to important revisions of the title. June Yang produced a clear version of my sketch map. Above all, gratitude should be expressed for financial support in my sabbatical year to the University of Hawaii Japan Studies Endowment, funded by a grant from the Japanese government.

Table 8.1. Coefficients of Urban Intensification in Japan
           (means by region and prefecture)

Region and Prefecture	1980	1975	1970	1965	1960	Shi 1980
1. Hokkaido	64	60	57	43	47	32
2. Tohoku						
Aomori	112	99	54	53	40	8
Iwate	42	34	28	23	23	13
Miyagi	208	184	138	81	70	11
Akita	60	53	45	36	31	9
Yamagata	60	49	44	32	29	13
Fukushima	61	53	42	38	78	10
Mean	91	79	59	44	45	64
3. Kanto						
Ibaraki	176	144	106	87	76	18
Tochigi	105	91	64	51	65	12
Gumma	222	189	139	101	95	11
Saitama	466	417	337	211	167	39
Chiba	275	244	199	133	78	26
Tokyo	808	754	667	481	400	27
Kanagawa	524	473	343	241	186	19
Mean	368	330	265	186	152	152
4. Hokuriku						
Niigata	88	76	63	54	48	20
Toyama	134	112	85	74	70	9
Ishikawa	77	63	50	37	35	8
Fukui	67	58	46	39	40	7
Mean	92	77	61	51	48	44
5. Tosan						
Yamanashi	78	71	63	54	28	7
Nagano	84	73	66	57	50	17
Gifu	147	127	101	88	67	13
Mean	103	90	77	66	48	37
6. Tokai						
Shizuoka	151	129	99	78	93	21
Aichi	401	332	247	182	134	30
Mean	276	231	173	130	114	51
7. Kinki						
Mie	128	114	93	74	70	13
Shiga	185	155	114	80	73	7
Kyoto	227	174	133	97	35	11
Osaka	593	543	456	320	252	31
Hyogo	307	289	247	197	167	21
Nara	236	207	158	114	97	9
Wakayama	162	145	116	98	101	7
Mean	263	232	188	140	114	99

150

Table 8.1 (continued)

Region and Prefecture	1980	1975	1970	1965	1960	Shi 1980
8. Chugoku-Shikoku						
Tottori	234	167	123	105	110	4
Shimane	69	61	51	32	29	8
Okayama	116	101	93	89	54	10
Hiroshima	119	106	128	113	106	12
Yamaguchi	167	134	116	97	101	14
Tokushima	146	133	107	97	76	4
Kagawa	238	174	146	126	119	5
Ehime	115	94	75	63	63	12
Kochi	61	54	46	35	30	9
Mean	141	114	98	84	76	78
9. Kyushu-Okinawa						
Fukuoka	276	243	208	181	174	20
Saga	108	92	75	62	56	7
Nagasaki	106	84	81	68	76	8
Kumamoto	132	117	104	88	75	11
Oita	88	75	59	49	93	11
Miyazaki	63	55	44	37	50	9
Kagoshima	63	54	45	43	34	14
Okinawa	267	206	167	0	0	10
Mean	138	116	98	66	70	90
Total no. of shi 1980						647

Source: See note 2.

Table 8.2.   Urban Intensification Coefficients for Japan
by Prefecture and City: 1960-1980

Prefecture and City	1980	1975	1970	1965	1960
1. Hokkaido					
Sapporo	163	131	97	82	180
Hakodate	120	103	97	98	97
Otaru	109	94	88	74	66
Asahikawa	98	76	67	59	72
Muroran	303	401	373	279	253
Kushiro	184	142	117	88	78
Obihiro	60	50	33	26	19
Kitami	52	40	34	25	20
Yubari	16	19	22	18	20
Iwamizawa	73	57	50	44	29
Abashiri	22	16	14	12	12
Rumoi	23	21	21	19	14
Tomakomai	52	45	48	18	14
Wakkanai	11	10	8	5	5
Bibai	36	35	37	45	36
Ashibetsu	9	8	8	8	10
Ebetsu	90	76	55	41	33
Akabira	53	56	62	60	56
Mombetsu	9	7	6	5	4
Shibetsu	15	11	9	8	8
Nayoro	27	20	21	17	20
Mikasa	24	21	22	26	24
Nemuro	16	15	15	12	10
Chitose	63	86	84	12	9
Takikawa	110	92	158	107	79
Sunakawa	127	108	99	75	50
Utashinai	58	55	75	43	58
Fukagawa	16	12	12	17	174
Furano	4	9	9	5	6
Noboribetsu	47	41	35	15	0
Eniwa	31	22	17	12	17
Date	39	33	24	18	17
2. Aomori					
Aomori	57	49	37	27	25
Hirosaki	104	95	78	66	59
Hachinohe	263	222	165	155	90
Kuroishi	36	30	24	22	21
Goshogawara	53	44	33	25	26
Towada	40	33	22	21	22
Misawa	295	283	44	40	35
Mutsu	45	36	32	66	38

Table 8.2 (continued)

Prefecture and City	1980	1975	1970	1965	1960
3. Iwate					
Morioka	96	83	64	50	46
Miyako	32	24	20	17	15
Ofunato	53	36	28	35	39
Mizusawa	107	89	71	58	65
Hanamaki	35	29	22	18	22
Kitakami	83	57	50	44	38
Kuji	35	33	34	30	28
Tono	9	8	7	7	7
Ichinoseki	32	28	22	17	19
Rikuzentakata	0	0	0	0	0
Kamaishi	29	30	23	24	24
Esashi	29	30	23	24	24
Ninohe	34	27	22	0	0
4. Miyagi					
Sendai	377	344	269	190	176
Ishinomaki	177	162	128	133	112
Shigoma	613	572	449	405	347
Furukawa	80	64	57	51	54
Kesennuma	72	54	43	35	30
Shiroishi	30	25	23	18	18
Natori	75	68	36	22	31
Kakuda	49	43	37	35	0
Tagajo	606	509	376	0	0
Izumi	83	60	24	0	0
Iwanuma	129	128	79	0	0
5. Akita					
Akita	111	96	79	65	54
Noshiro	45	41	36	29	32
Yokote	75	64	53	40	50
Odate	39	33	29	27	24
Honjo	47	42	32	25	24
Oga	83	72	51	37	0
Yuzawa	31	29	29	22	23
Omagari	93	81	76	70	58
Kazuno	17	15	16	12	11
6. Yamagata					
Yamagata	104	84	70	56	50
Yonezawa	38	29	27	23	22
Tsuruoka	77	61	57	45	40
Sakata	113	100	84	81	77
Shinjo	34	29	25	23	22
Sagae	67	48	44	42	39

Table 8.2 (continued)

Prefecture and City	1980	1975	1970	1965	1960
Kaminoyama	27	25	23	18	18
Murayama	36	30	27	31	34
Nagai	40	32	29	20	20
Tendo	103	81	68	66	56
Higashine	74	67	60	0	0
Obanazawa	14	12	13	12	0
Nanyo	47	43	42	0	0
7. Fukushima					
Fukushima	66	65	50	45	69
Aizuwakamatsu	62	49	42	34	32
Koriyama	72	61	46	39	423
Iwaki	66	54	42	36	33
Shirakawa	69	64	48	43	41
Haramachi	48	38	32	28	29
Sukagawa	73	67	57	61	45
Kitakata	58	51	42	43	43
Soma	44	36	27	27	31
Nihonmatsu	55	44	33	28	31
8. Ibaraki					
Mito	301	232	178	142	121
Hitachi	274	238	195	167	160
Tsuchira	255	202	142	108	85
Koga	433	418	294	234	209
Ishioka	135	99	86	58	52
Shimodate	121	96	68	56	55
Yuki	154	127	87	66	64
Ryugasaki	101	84	70	63	60
Nakaminato	211	195	162	154	124
Shimotsuma	143	113	0	0	0
Mitsukaido	94	78	72	50	48
Hitachiota	63	55	45	47	37
Katsuta	361	322	222	162	150
Takahagi	33	29	27	29	32
Kitaibaraki	58	44	55	39	38
Kasama	67	54	55	39	38
Toride	262	206	169	156	102
Iwai	100	0	0	0	0
9. Tochigi					
Utsunomiya	233	195	135	98	85
Ashikaga	205	187	114	97	136
Tochigi	114	98	69	53	49
Sano	171	149	113	96	90
Kanuma	53	38	31	25	28
Nikko	23	21	21	21	20

Table 8.2 (continued)

Prefecture and City	1980	1975	1970	1965	1960
Imaichi	38	29	28	22	18
Oyama	178	163	97	66	218
Mooka	88	75	54	57	59
Otawara	81	69	50	38	37
Yaita	48	42	38	27	28
Kuroiso	32	26	20	12	15
10. Gumma					
Maebashi	360	275	222	186	153
Takasaki	412	355	248	176	181
Kiryu	194	183	154	102	97
Isezaki	368	269	187	113	115
Ota	313	284	194	146	177
Numata	59	54	45	39	35
Tatebayashi	232	203	147	114	101
Shibukawa	220	191	143	88	88
Fujioka	93	73	49	35	36
Tomioka	101	89	70	54	57
Annaka	95	99	73	62	0
11. Saitama					
Kawagoe	315	275	206	115	93
Kumagaya	315	248	204	120	100
Kawaguchi	722	659	554	398	370
Urawa	593	506	381	275	266
Omiya	574	492	379	264	212
Gyoda	223	167	124	97	102
Chichibu	92	79	68	54	48
Tokorozawa	417	386	303	108	70
Hanno	90	74	58	37	33
Kazo	150	125	115	80	69
Honjo	263	239	182	122	102
Higashimatsuyama	182	152	124	95	94
Iwatsuki	242	217	170	107	84
Kasukabe	525	395	288	126	87
Sayama	476	442	355	308	313
Hanyu	146	119	92	62	54
Konosu	248	217	167	109	97
Fukaya	269	220	155	102	91
Ageo	512	358	251	152	136
Yono	1,000	944	879	693	545
Soka	888	786	526	238	163
Koshigaya	491	463	313	177	68
Warabi	1,000	1,000	1,000	883	749
Toda	658	605	514	304	274
Iruma	371	354	279	238	282

Table 8.2 (continued)

Prefecture and City	1980	1975	1970	1965	1960
Hatogaya	1,000	1,000	984	668	337
Asaka	673	667	505	419	369
Shiki	692	622	412	280	149
Wako	680	677	665	505	652
Niiza	616	574	380	0	0
Okegawa	315	263	224	123	110
Kuki	278	219	184	128	114
Kitamoto	361	307	253	0	0
Yashio	677	593	608	0	0
Fujimi	389	311	289	133	0
Kamifukuoka	710	644	541	575	195
Misato	527	430	220	0	0
Hasuda	265	234	194	135	81
Sakado	241	192	108	0	0
12. Chiba					
Chiba	405	322	258	179	198
Choshi	157	144	122	121	115
Ichikawa	834	584	464	349	294
Funabashi	591	558	467	268	152
Tateyama	128	96	88	71	73
Kisarazu	169	139	150	160	152
Matsudo	744	604	504	279	141
Noda	239	192	172	131	117
Sawara	79	71	67	56	50
Mobara	160	151	129	79	85
Narita	91	73	52	46	45
Sakura	180	134	110	86	0
Togane	93	83	61	41	0
Yokaichiba	0	0	87	0	0
Asahi	162	155	149	105	0
Narashino	715	939	920	776	391
Kashiwa	382	341	216	134	96
Katsuura	49	45	27	35	34
Ichihara	249	228	111	64	0
Nagareyama	413	323	216	204	0
Yachio	253	204	156	76	0
Abiko	322	252	140	120	0
Kamogawa	35	32	33	31	75
Kamagaya	490	495	342	0	0
Kimitsu	220	128	85	0	0
Futtsu	0	64	52	44	0
13. Tokyo					
Tokyo	1,000	993	957	904	843
Hachioji	273	229	149	103	86

Table 8.2 (continued)

Prefecture and City	1980	1975	1970	1965	1960
Tachikawa	881	824	693	536	1,038
Musashino	1,000	1,000	1,000	1,000	1,000
Mitaka	1,000	1,000	1,000	724	713
Ome	186	163	91	97	94
Fuchu	942	902	820	622	436
Akishima	842	817	724	599	511
Chofu	1,000	993	906	720	437
Machida	496	399	293	172	111
Koganei	1,000	1,000	1,000	875	622
Kodaira	1,000	916	759	519	440
Hino	914	782	514	275	192
Higashimurayama	1,000	895	807	416	351
Kokubunji	1,000	951	899	715	395
Kunitachi	1,000	787	743	515	509
Tanashi	1,000	1,000	952	697	568
Hoya	1,000	1,000	1,000	931	595
Fussa	934	966	918	863	791
Komae	1,000	1,000	1,000	923	776
Higashiyamato	721	584	396	158	0
Kiyose	727	686	566	401	295
Higashikurume	1,000	877	638	232	0
Musashimurayama	629	437	191	0	0
Tama	567	479	487	0	0
Inagi	326	327	262	0	0
Akigawa	378	362	236	0	0
14. Kanagawa					
Yokohama	725	675	565	399	303
Kawasaki	869	811	728	597	481
Yokosuka	607	581	500	409	362
Hiratsuka	518	455	332	238	228
Kamakura	743	698	378	382	330
Fujisawa	662	557	440	309	276
Odawara	292	281	252	169	138
Chigasaki	682	610	493	373	303
Zushi	484	473	429	310	369
Sagamihara	733	631	485	331	250
Miura	194	185	131	88	68
Hadano	178	147	97	55	72
Atsugi	259	195	134	81	70
Yamato	842	680	496	328	214
Isehara	214	173	104	76	62
Ebina	471	371	279	0	0
Zama	688	703	588	427	0
Minamiashigara	107	102	89	0	0
Ayase	688	666	0	0	0

Table 8.2 (continued)

Prefecture and City	1980	1975	1970	1965	1960
15. Niigata					
Niigata	389	336	224	182	163
Nagaoka	107	95	77	69	64
Sanjo	151	128	103	98	76
Kashiwazaki	59	51	56	43	47
Shibata	27	25	21	18	14
Niitsu	121	125	107	87	85
Ojiya	60	58	56	51	37
Kamo	46	39	35	29	29
Tokamachi	46	38	34	29	34
Mitsuke	89	73	60	58	45
Murakami	48	41	38	41	36
Tsubame	180	159	136	93	83
Tochio	30	26	24	18	18
Itoigawa	14	12	12	13	11
Arai	45	42	40	38	31
Gosen	66	55	48	36	30
Ryotsu	10	11	8	10	11
Shirone	72	53	58	50	79
Toyosaka	83	61	48	50	0
Joetsu	110	93	81	71	63
16. Toyama					
Toyama	312	269	217	198	227
Takaoka	233	190	151	128	115
Shinminato	248	194	163	142	149
Uozu	36	32	22	19	22
Himi	42	33	31	27	25
Namerikawa	108	88	84	75	67
Kurobe	97	87	61	0	0
Tonami	74	70	0	45	0
Oyabe	55	44	36	28	28
17. Ishikawa					
Kanazawa	132	103	78	57	57
Nanao	61	61	45	42	35
Komatsu	53	43	37	35	30
Wajima	17	15	15	17	20
Suzu	30	30	0	0	0
Kaga	80	68	67	47	42
Hakui	82	71	62	29	30
Matsuto	162	112	94	66	62
18. Fukui					
Fukui	115	96	79	85	106
Tsuruga	50	43	36	31	32
Takefu	66	58	39	35	27
Obama	32	27	26	23	26

158

Table 8.2 (continued)

Prefecture and City	1980	1975	1970	1965	1960
Ono	14	12	11	15	12
Katsuyama	23	23	14	14	18
Sabae	166	144	115	67	57
19. Yamanashi					
Kofu	178	154	132	96	82
Fujiyoshida	78	72	64	41	38
Enzan	31	29	19	18	23
Tsuru	35	30	27	19	19
Yamanashi	156	152	148	164	0
Otsuki	28	21	23	22	20
Nirasaki	42	41	30	17	16
20. Nagano					
Nagano	149	126	103	133	114
Matsumoto	150	121	107	72	63
Ueda	127	115	105	113	118
Okaya	162	144	130	99	91
Iida	45	40	34	26	37
Suwa	86	72	61	46	44
Suzaka	74	61	138	92	91
Komoro	94	80	70	69	95
Ina	61	47	38	30	33
Komagane	40	32	27	22	18
Nakano	112	112	57	56	56
Omachi	17	14	11	9	8
Iiyama	38	35	41	38	43
Chino	39	37	27	0	0
Shiojiri	80	64	53	45	33
Koshoku	92	75	72	66	0
Saku	70	58	47	46	0
21. Gifu					
Gifu	292	262	210	157	150
Ogaki	306	261	223	187	162
Takayama	65	50	38	26	29
Tajimi	220	164	106	84	71
Seki	98	79	66	42	43
Nakatsugawa	37	32	25	20	15
Mino	42	45	34	39	41
Mizunami	48	42	34	32	32
Hashima	176	145	108	82	80
Ena	39	31	22	21	29
Minokamo	98	88	71	59	60
Toki	133	126	108	79	82
Kakamigahara	360	328	265	320	74

Table 8.2 (continued)

Prefecture and City	1980	1975	1970	1965	1960
22. Shizuoka					
Shizuoka	59	52	40	101	90
Hamamatsu	359	314	240	168	172
Numazu	222	211	174	156	128
Shimizu	181	163	143	128	353
Atami	124	105	95	67	79
Mishima	230	194	137	110	99
Fujinomiya	68	48	38	34	23
Ito	72	62	55	48	37
Shimada	108	123	81	50	65
Fuji	212	191	153	61	252
Iwata	203	169	131	115	118
Yaizu	398	311	198	160	138
Kakegawa	65	56	52	35	37
Fujieda	139	111	81	56	57
Gotemba	65	54	40	31	25
Fukuroi	131	109	91	59	55
Tenryu	27	29	26	40	39
Hamakita	231	203	148	126	98
Shimoda	47	51	39	21	16
Susuno	68	47	34	0	0
Kosai	170	116	82	76	62
23. Aichi					
Nagoya	794	739	645	530	585
Topohashi	198	164	132	97	85
Okazaki	227	166	125	103	93
Ichinoniya	541	499	375	275	208
Seto	163	135	106	84	83
Handa	462	413	416	356	231
Kasugai	488	347	245	184	112
Toyokawa	326	287	245	198	191
Tsushima	355	300	227	159	151
Hekinan	534	372	336	262	250
Kariya	465	389	288	204	160
Toyota	193	181	152	136	124
Anjo	262	217	161	142	89
Nishio	271	203	162	118	129
Gamagori	349	258	241	175	132
Inuyama	207	170	103	86	70
Tokoname	238	222	180	146	157
Konan	450	418	298	231	154
Bisai	558	521	430	352	324
Komaki	375	320	185	93	86
Inazawa	310	266	245	188	0
Shinshiro	52	49	41	39	37

160

Table 8.2 (continued)

Prefecture and City	1980	1975	1970	1965	1960
Tokai	760	277	193	250	190
Obu	380	305	248	157	0
Chita	656	678	113	90	0
Chiryu	419	375	297	167	134
Owariasahi	530	453	262	0	0
Takahama	521	460	483	339	257
Iwakura	487	479	286	306	0
Toyoake	450	286	177	0	0
24. Mie					
Tsu	296	264	261	204	201
Yokkaichi	347	296	226	181	162
Ise	91	80	67	52	50
Matsusaka	90	80	59	50	49
Kuwana	228	245	181	151	128
Ueno	50	44	36	34	33
Suzuka	198	143	112	93	94
Nabari	66	51	33	28	26
Owase	24	30	18	17	18
Kameyama	91	80	68	48	47
Toba	59	50	52	27	26
Kumano	19	22	16	12	11
Hisai	108	95	79	71	71
25. Shiga					
Otsu	125	97	75	70	65
Hikone	188	175	130	123	111
Nagahama	209	202	141	132	111
Omihachiman	139	86	79	70	60
Yokaichi	161	122	80	66	72
Kusatsu	263	228	165	97	92
Moriyama	211	178	130	0	0
26. Kyoto					
Kyoto	224	203	182	156	148
Fukuchiyama	80	35	32	30	24
Maizuru	70	64	55	44	44
Ayabe	29	26	24	23	15
Uji	294	251	209	170	136
Miyazu	30	27	25	20	21
Kameoka	48	46	37	34	0
Joyo	228	184	141	0	0
Muko	710	593	458	382	0
Nagaokakyo	512	483	301	213	0
Yawata	271	0	0	0	0

Table 8.2 (continued)

Prefecture and City	1980	1975	1970	1965	1960
27. Osaka					
Osaka	994	991	989	960	933
Sakai	742	664	552	358	403
Kishiwada	373	346	281	196	158
Toyonaka	1,000	876	709	529	438
Ikeda	506	496	451	338	266
Suita	1,000	923	813	440	297
Izumiotsu	1,000	977	808	677	553
Takatsuki	291	274	209	114	91
Kaizuka	341	348	244	178	129
Moriguchi	1,000	906	883	684	501
Hiratsuka	616	535	401	177	188
Ibaraki	382	301	211	130	101
Yao	739	690	632	463	387
Izumisano	298	276	232	155	92
Tondabayashi	340	250	168	145	105
Neyagawa	795	748	600	361	247
Kawachinagano	113	94	60	48	45
Matsubara	770	765	659	411	304
Daito	671	654	524	271	216
Izumi	177	161	138	115	80
Mino	267	184	140	109	112
Kashiwara	360	275	219	162	147
Hibikino	437	410	348	245	133
Kadoma	1,000	780	659	387	325
Sattsu	699	669	452	241	0
Takaishi	977	1,000	964	728	627
Fujidera	991	899	754	610	505
Higashiosaka	740	704	619	476	362
Sennan	218	172	141	91	69
Shijonawate	245	191	181	126	0
Katano	315	262	164	0	0
28. Hyogo					
Kobe	223	190	156	133	119
Himeji	374	341	280	220	199
Amagasaki	1,000	991	927	877	804
Akashi	654	599	499	385	324
Nishinomiya	398	385	361	343	312
Sumoto	51	44	43	35	38
Ashiya	451	312	395	348	333
Itami	982	926	801	570	323
Aioi	83	71	52	35	31
Toyooka	62	49	42	27	25
Kakogawa	345	380	203	116	114
Tatsuno	145	128	111	119	118

Table 8.2 (continued)

Prefecture and City	1980	1975	1970	1965	1960
Ako	70	58	45	37	45
Nishiwaki	107	94	69	48	51
Takarazuka	232	204	177	126	98
Miki	94	75	49	34	49
Takasago	678	683	661	513	422
Kawanishi	317	271	169	102	79
Ono	89	88	73	49	0
Sanda	28	23	20	15	17
Kasai	69	58	64	0	0
29. Nara					
Nara	210	170	143	83	65
Yamatotakada	561	523	404	297	269
Yamatokoriyama	313	283	162	113	109
Tenri	141	125	101	72	78
Kashihara	401	359	303	198	77
Sakurai	105	104	71	65	59
Gojo	73	65	60	56	50
Gose	114	86	75	77	62
Ikoma	207	146	105	66	0
30. Wakayama					
Wakayama	347	302	237	205	171
Kainan	185	183	164	147	121
Hashimoto	58	55	39	35	36
Arida	285	246	188	126	132
Gobo	103	94	82	76	70
Tanabe	82	65	43	38	122
Shingu	73	68	56	57	54
31. Tottori					
Tottori	97	76	60	51	57
Yonago	246	220	172	132	115
Kurayoshi	59	50	34	37	37
Sakaiminato	533	320	224	199	231
32. Shimane					
Matsue	156	123	102	68	59
Hamada	66	51	42	48	41
Izumo	91	72	59	43	41
Masuda	53	41	35	32	31
Oda	29	22	22	0	0
Yasugi	93	81	60	37	32
Gotsu	0	59	49	0	0
Hirata	60	37	35	25	30
33. Okayama					
Okayama	181	141	186	169	159
Kurashiki	297	358	289	382	93

163

Table 8.2 (continued)

Prefecture and City	1980	1975	1970	1965	1960
Tsuyama	97	79	60	45	37
Tamano	204	176	170	104	117
Kasaoka	104	95	71	57	58
Ibara	84	77	55	63	61
Soja	52	49	57	41	0
Takahashi	19	21	17	17	17
Niimi	18	17	18	14	12
Bizen	0	0	0	0	0
34. Hiroshima					
Hiroshima	174	147	604	572	547
Kure	250	237	210	187	195
Takehara	70	59	49	38	41
Mihara	83	69	55	52	48
Onomichi	136	118	99	70	68
Innoshima	171	166	135	119	137
Fukuyama	210	186	144	112	111
Fuchu	88	76	76	64	48
Miyoshi	35	30	26	27	29
Shobara	26	24	20	0	0
Otake	120	121	118	110	53
Higashihiroshima	63	40	0	0	0
35. Yamaguchi					
Shimonoseki	205	161	143	114	112
Ube	216	190	168	109	91
Yamaguchi	68	54	43	38	61
Hagi	91	86	68	63	65
Tokuyana	73	70	52	62	62
Hofu	202	131	108	75	81
Kudamatsu	202	131	112	107	106
Iwakuni	168	153	141	131	136
Onoda	475	326	306	258	285
Hikari	284	276	250	256	249
Nagato	28	23	21	14	17
Yanai	83	74	63	36	54
Mine	0	0	0	16	13
Shinnanyo	239	202	142	81	84
36. Tokushima					
Tokushima	241	209	159	156	126
Naruto	114	101	75	76	77
Komatsujima	229	170	146	118	101
Anan	0	51	49	37	0
37. Kagawa					
Takamatsu	281	253	215	160	139
Marugame	329	153	123	110	114

Table 8.2 (continued)

Prefecture and City	1980	1975	1970	1965	1960
Sakaide	235	155	135	137	149
Zentsuji	208	186	148	129	118
Kannonji	139	123	111	95	77
38. Ehime					
Matsuyame	232	193	135	110	119
Imabari	288	246	186	157	143
Uwajima	63	60	57	50	52
Yawatahama	59	58	46	36	39
Niihama	249	240	202	159	152
Saijo	64	56	48	35	36
Ozu	36	30	23	22	24
Kawanoe	115	103	85	79	78
Iyomishima	50	42	32	27	34
Iyo	77	61	58	51	49
Hojo	47	34	30	31	30
Toyo	97	0	0	0	0
39. Kochi					
Kochi	296	247	208	163	147
Muroto	23	17	16	21	23
Aki	13	13	12	14	12
Nankoku	65	66	56	71	44
Tosa	70	67	60	0	0
Susaki	29	26	20	19	21
Nakamura	18	16	12	13	11
Sukumo	19	19	12	0	0
Tosahimizu	20	17	14	13	13
40. Fukuoka					
Kitakyushu	344	327	286	251	215
Fokuoka	421	363	400	276	282
Omuta	459	437	402	377	376
Kurume	294	260	206	220	203
Nogata	260	212	163	136	113
Iizuka	238	203	165	137	471
Tazawa	244	225	200	208	162
Yanagawa	206	192	182	192	146
Yamada	145	169	150	145	198
Amagi	50	44	37	33	36
Yame	206	169	142	131	128
Chikugo	268	213	205	204	175
Okawa	263	258	232	207	179
Yukuhashi	176	123	97	71	62
Buzen	95	86	75	67	69
Nakama	488	451	329	382	314
Ogori	175	169	120	0	0

Table 8.2 (continued)

Prefecture and City	1980	1975	1970	1965	1960
Chikushino	102	88	66	46	33
Kasuga	767	624	517	432	317
Onojo	322	252	182	104	0
41. Saga					
Saga	261	229	192	149	130
Karatsu	113	112	93	80	95
Tosu	167	150	126	90	105
Taku	49	0	0	60	0
Imari	47	42	34	22	21
Takeo	52	47	38	36	39
Kashima	64	62	45	0	0
42. Nagasaki					
Nagasaki	212	187	180	150	210
Sasebo	167	151	130	123	138
Shimabara	156	113	104	102	90
Isahaya	94	75	65	54	54
Omura	185	116	105	87	86
Fukue	36	30	27	25	28
Hirado	0	0	33	0	0
Matsuura	0	0	0	0	0
43. Kumamoto					
Kumamoto	452	382	364	300	243
Yatsushiro	187	168	150	137	128
Hitoyoshi	43	36	30	27	27
Arao	318	272	221	176	156
Minamata	60	64	58	53	55
Tamana	114	112	92	100	77
Hondo	60	55	49	30	30
Yamaga	73	63	58	43	53
Ushibuka	45	36	35	31	34
Kikuchi	32	29	25	20	20
Uto	72	65	63	53	0
44. Oita					
Oita	215	159	115	101	458
Beppu	162	138	103	84	73
Nakatsu	230	193	150	121	131
Hita	63	45	39	29	31
Saiki	71	63	55	48	58
Usuki	50	44	41	36	35
Tsukumi	95	76	55	48	47
Taketa	0	27	24	0	0
Bungotakada	41	38	33	42	49
Kitsuki	0	0	0	0	0
Usa	45	41	37	32	142

Table 8.2 (continued)

Prefecture and City	1980	1975	1970	1965	1960
45. Miyazaki					
Miyazaki	147	129	102	79	87
Miyakonojo	96	87	74	68	167
Nobeoka	95	83	71	61	53
Nichinan	50	45	39	35	35
Kobayashi	43	36	32	25	25
Hyuga	111	91	78	52	48
Kushima	0	0	0	0	0
Saito	23	22	0	14	31
Ebino	0	0	0	0	0
46. Kagoshima					
Kagoshima	266	194	152	147	136
Sendai	65	53	46	45	67
Kanoya	115	110	102	114	35
Makurazaki	71	66	60	62	57
Kushikino	64	60	57	64	61
Akune	54	45	34	30	0
Naze	32	26	20	21	17
Izumi	0	0	39	31	31
Okuchi	22	23	22	21	0
Ibusuki	85	78	69	73	68
Kaseda	0	0	0	0	0
Kokubu	81	70	0	0	0
Nishinoomote	26	25	23	0	0
Tarumizu	0	0	0	0	0
47. Okinawa					
Naha	937	866	773	0	0
Ishikawa	119	89	60	0	0
Gushikawa	191	111	80	0	0
Ginowan	495	328	232	0	0
Hirahara	64	49	45	0	0
Ishigaki	21	18	15	0	0
Urasoe	505	319	222	0	0
Nago	31	21	18	0	0
Itoman	106	75	60	0	0
Okinawa	198	182	163	0	0

9. Growth of a Twin City: Planned Urban Dispersal in India

SWAPNA BANNERJEE-GUHA

IN 1950, only thirty-four cities in developing countries had populations of 1 million or more; by 1975 there were ninety such cities and the proportion of urban population living in these massive urban centers has tripled in the last twenty-five years (Table 9.1). This pattern and trend of urbanization of the Third World is in marked contrast with that in the developed nations, where diffusion of development has occurred through a hierarchial system of cities. When analyzing the pattern of urbanization and settlement growth in Third World nations, it is necessary to recall their background of long subservience to an economic system designed for other nations' interests, an infrastructure still often geared to those interests, and a relatively stagnant agriculture, little industry, and export cities dominating the urban scene.[1]

Though there is variation in the levels of economic development and urbanization patterns within countries of the Third World, the overall process reflects a strong bond of similarity. Urbanization in the Third World presents a combination of features that reflect social, political, and economic conditions. Most underdeveloped countries in this group lack sufficient numbers of intermediate cities to stimulate their internal economies.[2] Sixty percent of the urban population in India live in cities of 100,000 or more inhabitants (Class I cities). But even this statistic does not reveal the entire picture. Of the total Class I city population, 45 percent live in cities of more than 1 million.[3]

Many governments in the developing countries have become dissatisfied with the spatial distribution of their population.[4] Of 116 governments surveyed in 1978 by the United Nations, 68 reported that they were strongly dissatisfied, while 42 expressed partial dissatisfaction. In Asia and Latin America, a strong view was expressed against overconcentration in a few metropolitan cities. Thus it is not the pace of urbanization that creates problems but the pattern of urban population concentration as well as the concentration of economic activities and investment. Still the overwhelming majority of the population in many

169

Table 9.1.   Population and Size of Cities of 1 Million or More
              in Developing Countries

Region	1950	1960	1970	1980
Africa				
Population (millions)	3.503	7.482	15.415	36.485
No. of cities	2	8	19	44
Latin America				
Population (millions)	17.376	30.988	56.383	101.301
No. of cities	7	11	17	27
East Asia				
Population (millions)	33.771	62.117	90.495	131.910
No. of cities	14	24	31	42
South Asia				
Population (millions)	19.360	33.267	58.837	105.879
No. of cities	11	16	23	36

Source: United Nations, Pattern of Urban and Rural Population
Growth, Population Studies 68 (New York: U.N. Department of
International Economic and Social Affairs, 1980), tables 20
and 22.

countries such as India is scattered in villages and towns with populations of less than 5,000.

The medium-size cities are insignificant in their economic participation and lack a strong economic base. There is no balanced and hierarchial urban system and no efficient network of central places to integrate the country's economy. The vast majority of the population living in villages, small towns, and medium-size cities suffers from lack of services, facilities, and social infrastructure.

The History of Differential Urban Growth

The present pattern of urbanization in India with dominance of a few metropolitan cities, lack of strong medium-size cities, and lack of integration of the urban and economic system is an expression of the perpetuation of the colonial structure.[5] The spatial concentration and polarization of investment and economic activity in the metropolitan bases continues in the national planning era and hinders wider diffusion of technology, thereby causing stagnation of the countryside.[6]

Urban centers in pre-British India were either economically insignificant in the newly organized economy created by the British or were totally destroyed. Thus inland cities gave way to the three port enclaves of Calcutta, Bombay, and Madras to serve colonial interests. The new cities were oriented toward export promotion and exploitation of the raw materials of the country. Their integration with the regional economies was very tenuous. Their growth was accomplished at the cost of impoverishing the surrounding countryside, as in the cases of Calcutta and Bombay.

In colonial India these three port cities, together with the capital of Delhi, dominated the country's economy. Investment and capital were concentrated in these cities through which raw materials poured out from the country and cheap machine-made goods from Britain poured in. When the British, in order to protect their Indian market from being flooded by goods from other capitalist countries, reluctantly agreed to an industrialization policy for India in the early part of the twentieth century, the production sites were again these cities.

In the post-Independence era the overall pattern did not change despite a policy of promoting urban industrialization in the depressed areas all over the country.[7] Ultimately, urban-industrial growth remained concentrated in the four metropolitan centers and their immediate peripheries. Only gradually did new towns emerge, but they were unable to create any impact on the urban system. Further, as the development of metropolitan settlements in each state was strongly influenced by the state's political, social, and economic conditions and control over capital, there is a wide variation among the states in the proportion of metropolitan to total urban population.[8]

In the last two decades rural–urban migration and migration from small cities have been found to contribute largely toward the population growth of these cities.[9] This has led to a distortion in the metropolitan economic base and also puts a severe strain on public services like housing, transportation, and water supply. As capital is relatively scarce and less easily transferred for investment in the urban infrastructure in countries such as India, the ever-growing population in large cities creates further problems in their distribution. Often the urban poor and semipoor—an integral part of the urban capitalist system but who are not directly employed in it and do not form an effective internal market for consumer goods—are excluded from these material benefits of the urban system.[10]

Following the same process of polarization, a deficiency of social services is pronounced in medium cities and smaller towns where economic diversification, a common feature of the largest cities, declines rapidly and industrial activity is rarely the primary urban specialization. Low proportions of manufacturing employment associated with large proportions of service or tertiary employment lead to lower per capita income and create further problems of capital accumulation. Economic diversification is identified not only with city size but also with income-producing capacity. This ultimately affects the revenue base of the smaller urban centers and leads to diminishing public services.

As a cumulative effect of these processes, the largest cities in India grow larger while medium and small urban settlements either decline or remain stagnant and vast rural areas, barring a few pockets, become impoverished. Increasingly capital and urban population are being concentrated in the disproportionately smaller areas of these core cities, sharpening the core–periphery hiatus.[11] Primate cities and large metropolitan centers have concentrations of national resources and social overhead capital vastly greater than their share of national population and, therefore, benefit a very small percentage. Consequently, they become the favored locations of foreign and corporate investment related to export production, capital-intensive manufacture, and modern infrastructure.[12]

Urban Development Policies of the Government

To correct this distortion, extensive development policies for the backward areas and decentralization of industrial and economic activities were formulated during the third Five-Year Plan in the late 1960s. While the serious problems caused by large-scale urban concentration have been the major reason to promote dispersal, there was also the idea of reviving regional economies through new urban centers which would act as catalysts.

In spite of serious obstacles, attempts toward decentralization and planned urban dispersal have never been abandoned and the planning of new cities and towns has been undertaken by the central, state, and many local governments all over the country. The planned cities can be categorized as follows: administration centers (Chandigarh in Punjab and Gandhinagar in Gujarat); refugee towns (Faridabad in Haryana, Sardarnagar in Gujarat, and Ashokenagar in West Bengal); steel towns (Bokaro in Bihar, Bhilai and Rourkela in Orissa, and Durgapur in West Bengal) sponsored by industrial concerns under the central government; refinery towns (Sindri in Bihar) sponsored by the Fertilizer Corporation of India under the Ministry of Petroleum and Chemicals; government-sponsored model towns (Pimpri near Pune in Maharashtra and numerous towns around New Delhi); and residential suburbs (Kalyani in West Bengal). Most of these towns have been created to provide residence for a particular section of people, such as refugees from Pakistan or employees of the industrial companies sponsoring the projects.

The creation of New Bombay, the twin city of the exploding metropolis of Greater Bombay, is unique, however, in its process of growth, nature of its developers, financing, and the social, political, and economic forces that influence its development. The new metropolis is being developed by the City and Industrial Development Corporation (CIDCO), a limited corporation affiliated with the state government of Maharashtra.

The Urban History of Bombay

Between 1961 and 1971, the population of Greater Bombay rose from 4.15 million to 5.97 million, a rise of 43.8 percent. By 1981, the population had risen to 8.23 million, a doubling from the population of 1961. During the last three decades, a vast urban sprawl has grown up in Bombay, where one person out of every five lives in a slum.

The modern metropolis of Bombay is a coalescence and combination of seven islands. The orientation of the city is provided by two parallel ridges running north–south which have determined the city's suburban extension, transport, and commuting patterns. Restricted by the insular topography, the business community, in order to make use of the proximity of the central business district located in southern Bombay, has been forced to build a skyscraper complex on reclaimed land from the sea in an area called the Back Bay reclamation. This development is the product of the last fifteen years. The central part of Bombay, the industrial heart of the city, lies mostly on eighteenth and nineteenth-century reclamations. Farther north are the post-Independence reclaimed areas housing the large slum and tannery works of Dharavi. Land is still being reclaimed along the railroad corridors pushing development into the tidal marshes along the creeks, where low and middle-income residential apartments are being built. The industrial areas have skirted the central hill complex and spread farther north in the Thane district. A comparatively new industrial area has sprung up in New Bombay known as the Thane–Belapur industrial belt.[13] Land reclamation has resulted in greater erosion in Back Bay in southern Bombay and in Versova in the northwest. Reclamation of lowlands adversely affects natural drainage and increases both sewage problems and erosion of shoreline.

With an ever increasing population, Bombay experiences severe problems of congestion, limited open space, and inadequate housing and other social facilities. In the central part of the metropolis, density of population rises to over 2,000 people per hectare. Though it decreases in the north and northwest, occasional pockets of very high density exist all along the transport corridors: Dadar, Andheri, Jogeshwari, and Borivili in the west; Kurla, Bhandup, and Ghatkopar in the central part; and Chembur and Govandi in the east.

A substantial area of the central city and older suburbs has been undergoing drastic urban renewal in recent decades. Some people, in order to accumulate more capital from real estate, favor urban renewal. Promotion of vertical expansion of residential activity is in constant collision with the social force represented by the Housing Board and the Rent Control Act that protects tenants from unlawful eviction. The landlords, on the other hand, to render the law ineffective, show gross neglect toward the maintenance of buildings and apartments for middle and low-income tenants, and ultimately the buildings either collapse or come down through municipal demolition. The result is a new high-rise, high-rental residential-cum-commercial complex which remains inaccessible to a majority of the older occupants, most of whom satisfy their housing needs in the burgeoning *chawls,* low-cost tenements, or slums *(zopadpattis).* In Bombay, the average numbers of tenements constructed per annum over a recent five-year period by the Maharashtra Housing Board, municipal authorities, state and central governments, statutory bodies, and private societies were 4,200, 1,800, 1,650, 250, and 9,700, respectively—and still the estimate of total housing deficiency in the city in 1981 was 600,000.[14] Two-thirds of the total jobs and job opportunities lie in the central city, and during the peak hours more than 1 million people converge on rail terminals. The average population per bus service is 4,160. The port of Bombay, located in southern Bombay, handles 40 percent of the country's total import volume, thus accentuating further the problem of congestion.[15]

Civic and social services are inadequate. Water and air pollution pose a threat to healthy city life. The average concentration level for trace elements observed in Bombay is the highest among Indian cities and comparable to that of the world's most populated cities.[16]

New Bombay

During the late 1950s a master plan was prepared for the metropolis of Bombay, which by 1960 had already extended its administrative area from 69 to 603 square kilometers. The master plan visualized the necessity of reorganizing neighborhood areas, dispersing the city's population, decentralizing commerce and industry, and improving slum areas and developing urban infrastructure.

In the evolution of New Bombay, the first step was taken in 1958 with the setting up of a study group on Greater Bombay which recommended the construction of a bridge across Thane Creek so that urban development could take place eastward on the mainland. However, political unrest due to the division of Bombay state into Maharashtra and Gujarat delayed implementation. In 1964, the Bombay Municipal Corporation recommended in the Development Plan for Greater Bombay a further northward extension. The plan did not take into consideration the development of the areas outside the city limits. The Bombay Metropolitan and Regional Planning Board in January 1970 published its draft plan and, among other proposals, recommended setting up a "metro-center" on the mainland to act as a countermagnet to the burgeoning growth taking place in Greater Bombay. It was envisaged that the growth of Greater Bombay could best be restrained not by curbing the scale of economic activities but rather with the positive measure of constructing a new center of attraction. The Maharashtra government accepted the proposal and established CIDCO in March 1970. Hence a separate and independent project area evolved within the boundary of the Bombay metropolitan region (Figure 9.1). New Bombay, with a combination of ninety-five villages and vast stretches of submerged marshy land, came into existence.

CIDCO was set up as a public limited company under the Indian Companies Act for the purpose of planning and developing New Bombay and in March 1971 was designated as a New Town Development Authority. CIDCO had various activities under its umbrella: acquiring land, reclaiming land, designing construction, implementing and supervising construction work, and looking after the welfare and community activities of the new settlement.

In developing New Bombay, the government sought the involvement of private capital. To do this, the state government decided to buy land from poor fishermen and peasants at a cheap rate and then leave it in the hands of CIDCO for a lease period of up to sixty years, which would allow enough time to develop the infrastructure and then sell it as a developed area to private capitalists, individuals, and estate agents at a higher price. The development of the nearest nodes of Vashi and Turbhe in this manner had the advantage of proximity to existing industrial areas on the Thane–Belapur road (Figure 9.2). Hence CIDCO could return with interest to the state government the initial loan of Rs. 27 million with which it had acquired the land. This was the financial model behind the project. The cost of acquiring the land rose much higher than first estimated, however, as social and political protest erupted under the leadership of the Peasants and Workers Party when thousands of peasants and fishermen asked for more compensation for

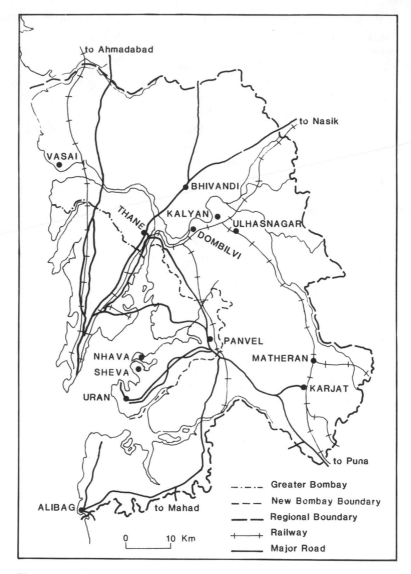

Figure 9.1. Bombay Metropolitan Region

their land. Even the areas which earlier lay submerged and housed no population or cultivation (such as Vashi town) were claimed as private property by the fishermen of nearby villages.

Lying within the Bombay metropolitan region to the east of Thane Creek, the entire project encompasses an area of 343.70 square kilometers in the *talukas* (lowest-level administrative districts) of Thane, Uran,

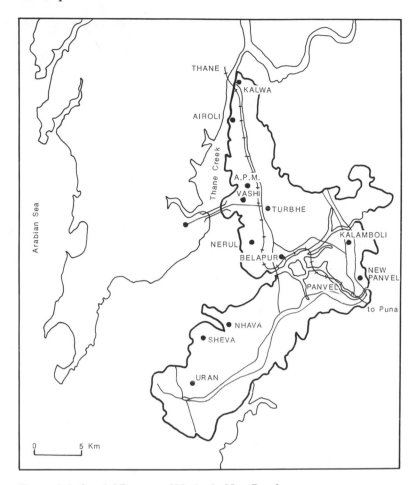

Figure 9.2. Spatial Pattern of Nodes in New Bombay

and Panvel of Thane and Raigad districts. This includes an area of 192.87 square kilometers of private land and salt pans spread over ninety-five villages with a total population of 117,000. The following objectives were laid down by CIDCO:

1. To reduce the growth of population in Greater Bombay by creating an urban center to absorb the migrants and by creating an alternative economic center to shift the concentration of economic activities from Bombay.
2. To provide physical and social services which raise the standard of living and reduce disparities of amenities available to different sections of the population.

3. To provide a better environment which will permit the residents of New Bombay to live fuller and tension-free lives.

4. To undertake intensive rehabilitation of the local population to integrate them in the planned urban development by employing them in the various organizations run by CIDCO.

5. To support the state industrial dispersal policies which will ultimately lead to an efficient and rational redistribution of industries and the growth of new urban centers. In addition to creating New Bombay, CIDCO is developing three other urban centers: New Nasik, New Aurangabad, and New Nanded.

CIDCO decided to adopt a flexible planning strategy which would be subject to change as the need arose. A preliminary development plan proposed by CIDCO in 1973 was accepted by the Maharashtra government in 1975. The major tasks consisted of reclamation of land and provision of necessary infrastructure, construction of houses and business centers, protection and encouragement of commercial and industrial activity in order to provide a sound economic base, effective organization of transport and communication within the new metropolis and to the surrounding areas, and the resettlement of persons displaced by land acquisition (Figure 9.3).

Development of New Bombay envisages a nodal settlement pattern with twenty nodes strung out along principal transport corridors (Figure 9.2).[17] Each nodal center, spread over 400 to 600 hectares of land, was to be further subdivided into sectors, each having about 100,000 to 150,000 population, giving a total population of 2 million for New Bombay. Each center will have a broad mixture of urban functions with residential facilities for different socioeconomic groups. The economic sector of the nodes will include tertiary and service sectors: educational institutions, medical facilities, recreational and religious centers. The plan envisages minimum movement to reach the workplace in order to ensure balanced development of the new city. The major job centers have been planned according to the current and future availability of infrastructure.

CIDCO itself became the principal contractor, and the land it controlled was meant for lease and not for sale. By this means the state government remained owner of the entire property. By 1984, seven nodes had been developed in New Bombay (Figure 9.2): Vashi–Turbhe, Belapur, Nerul, New Panvel, Kalamboli, and Airoli.

Vashi–Turbhe. The pioneer and the leading node in New Bombay is situated just beyond the Thane Creek bridge, developed on a low-lying marshy area facing Vashi village, an old fishing settlement on the other side of the highway. This node is developing as a primarily residential neighborhood area with infrastructural facilities such as shopping cen-

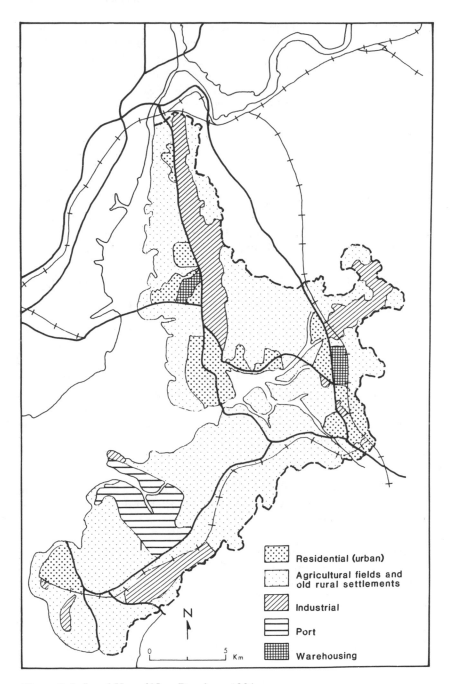

Residential (urban)

Agricultural fields and
old rural settlements

Industrial

Port

Warehousing

N

0   5
|_____| Km

Figure 9.3. Land Use of New Bombay: 1984

ters, schools, colleges, hospitals, and recreational and religious centers. In October 1984, fifteen of thirty-one sectors were fully developed and in five sectors brisk building activity was going on. Five sectors in the township were being developed as commercial and wholesaling areas. A business center for the district was evolving in Sector 17. In 1984, the total population of this node was 80,000.

Belapur. This node lies 8 kilometers south of Vashi. Situated amid beautiful surroundings at the convergence of three hills overlooking the sea to the west, Belapur enjoys a central location in New Bombay and is planned to house the future Central Business District (CBD) of the new metropolis. Belapur also enjoys a nodal advantage in the transport network. Of the thirty-two sectors, twelve had been developed by October 1984 and five were earmarked for the CBD activities. The present population of Belapur is about 35,000.

Nerul. Nerul is situated to the northwest of Belapur and south of Vashi on the Sion–Panvel expressway. Adjoining the old village settlement of Nerul, this node is being developed as a residential area. By 1984, about 4,000 apartments (for middle- and low-income groups) had been constructed by CIDCO. In-migration has just begun in Nerul.

New Panvel. Adjoining the northern limit of the town of Panvel, New Panvel is being developed. This also is primarily a residential area with a small plot earmarked for a medium-scale industrial estate to the north. People began moving into New Panvel in 1983. Ultimately, New Panvel will be linked to the Mankhurd–Panvel railway line via Vashi–Turbhe.

Kalamboli. Situated to the north of New Panvel, Kalamboli is being developed primarily as a wholesale steel market and warehouse center with a small residential area to the northwest.

Airoli. The northernmost node of the new metropolis is situated to the west of the Trans-Thane industrial belt. Development work, which has just started here, is anticipated to house 40,000 population in the future.

The Economic Base of New Bombay

During the early years of growth, CIDCO drew support from the existing industrial base of the Thane–Belapur industrial belt and the Kalwa industrial estate located in the northeastern part of the project area. Set out by the Maharashtra Industrial Development Corporation (MIDC) in the late 1960s, these areas provided jobs to about 50,000 workers in 1984. Industrial operations also got under way in Uran, an old port of the seventeenth century. The Oil and Natural Gas Commission (ONGC) has set up an onshore gas and oil terminal complex. In Nhava–Sheva, which is being developed as a new port, an oil-processing plant has been installed. The new port is said to possess perhaps the best location on the west coast of India.

A large wholesaling market for onions and potatoes has been installed in Sectors 21 and 22 of Vashi township as a result of shifting the wholesaling market from the congested Masjid area of southern Bombay. Installation of a second wholesaling market dealing with spices, dry fruits, edible oil, sugar, and such is imminent. Near the business center for the district being set up in Sector 17 in Vashi, a modern truck terminal and a railway goods yard are being built. A wholesale steel market is being developed in Kalamboli, north of Panvel town, to replace existing markets located at Darukhana and Carnac Bunder in southern Bombay. The Tata Industrial Steel Corporation (TISCO) and the Steel Authority of India, Ltd. (SAIL), together with 1,665 individual steel merchants, have bought spaces in the new market area, the development of which will free 80 hectares of land in southern Bombay and divert 4,000 daily truck trips from Bombay. The complex is expected to result in the shift of 40,000 jobs and provide 7,000 new jobs.

The Central Business District is being developed at Belapur, 8 kilometers southeast of Vashi at a central intersection of road networks. CIDCO envisages this area to provide jobs for up to 60,000 people and accordingly has shifted its head office there. Twelve state government departments, along with a number of banks and private and public offices, are also moving in.

Problems with the Planning Process

In the course of ten years, the planning process in New Bombay has been exposed to manifold social and structural problems resulting in sharp polemics on the validity of urban diffusion and attendant planning strategies. Further, as New Bombay lies within the area of Bombay metropolitan region, the Regional Development Authority still has its say in the planning process, which can create conflicts of ideas.

Social Problems

The creation of New Bombay has been of immense benefit to a large section of people belonging to the urban high and middle-income groups and to some extent to low-income groups. It has had adverse effects, however, on a large section of the rural masses who were the original residents of the ninety-five villages in which they practiced either cultivation or fishing as their major economic activity. Encroachment of industrial areas made up primarily of chemical and petrochemical complexes has posed a constant threat to the livelihood of fishing communities. Thane Creek separating New Bombay from the island city of Greater Bombay, once bustling with fishing activity, now receives industrial effluents and domestic waste. A marked increase of mercury concentration from the harbor to Thane Creek has been noted by environmentalists in recent years.

The problem that has cropped up due to acquisition of agricultural land is even more grave. Various rural-based, as well as urban-based, political parties have gotten involved in the issue, and in early 1984 there was severe social and political unrest in rural communities. Mass movements for more compensation, launched by displaced cultivators in Uran, a southern node where land acquisition is still going on, turned the question of farmland acquisition for urban development into a crucial issue.

The compensation money given to the displaced cultivators was decided on the basis of the prevalent market price of their lands. As the new metropolis grew very fast, it became the only plausible alternative not only for residential location for high and middle-income groups but also for industrialists desiring proximity to the industrial metropolis and for businessmen, service people, professionals, and traders wanting to locate their economic units near Bombay. Thus the price of the developed land and houses became ten to twenty times higher than the original price. The original land was not of very high quality and frequently marshy and uncultivatable, but that has not deterred the displaced cultivators from seeking more compensation. The peasants are also aware that CIDCO has adopted a strategy of cross-subsidization in order to generate revenue from open auction sales of a part of the total area with which to finance its low-income housing schemes. For the rich salt-pan owners and the Bombay-based businessmen who own pleasure villas and weekend cottages in the area, the agitation was a boon: Not only did it give them more time to stall land acquisition proceedings, but (if the peasants succeeded) it could bring about an appreciation of their property value. For the Nhava–Sheva Port Trust project, which is located in the disputed area, the agitation delayed completion of the project for several years. For CIDCO it marked a turning point in the process of dealing with the original residents.

Responsibility for the crisis lay partially with CIDCO, for it delayed the actual acquisition of the lands in question by some thirteen years after the state government had brought them under the notification of the Land Acquisition Act. Meanwhile, the price of land in the surrounding developed areas began rising sharply. But the key issue of the problem lies elsewhere and is much more deeply rooted. As the planned urban dispersal proceeded in this part of the hinterland of Bombay, which was one of the most backward areas, it failed to generate positive socioeconomic change for the original inhabitants. The farmers found no other alternative than to try to maximize the profit from their only source of income: land.

The parts of Raigad and Thane districts that fall in New Bombay are excessively dependent on agriculture of very low productivity. There are very high levels of unemployment and underemployment as well as a near absence of industry, both large-scale and household, and a poor development of the tertiary sector. Most of the areas here are of the one-crop (paddy) economy, binding the adult population as cultivators. There are no big landlords and hardly any who employ wage earners. Extreme fragmentation of land is combined with extremely low capital investment. The percentage of cultivated area under irrigation is less than 10 percent. The state government's expenditure on the Employment Guarantee Scheme for Thane and Riagad districts is among the lowest in the state, and census figures identify workers as being marginal with no permanent occupation during the major part of the year.

Even after the emergence of the new metropolis, cultivation in the surrounding areas is far from intensive and agriculture claims no more than 1 percent of the power consumed in the area. Cooperative societies not only are not developing, they are disintegrating, and loans advanced through cooperatives have decreased by two-thirds. The situation revealed in the employment exchange statistics is dismal, and the ratio of placements to vacancies has actually decreased. The new metropolis has been unable to create a symbiotic relationship with its hinterland by providing jobs to the landless or unemployed from the workers registers of the factories in New Bombay. A majority of the workers come from outside the region; those employed from the region are mostly unskilled casual laborers.

The general decline of the agrarian economy has been associated with uprooting of local people who are not absorbed or integrated into the growing urban economic base. Some 10,000 people have been displaced so far. Unable to find any alternative occupation in the organized sector (individually they received very little compensation as their landholdings were very small and they could not start a business or trade due to the dearth of other financial support), they have joined the informal sector in Vashi township or nearby factories as casual labor.

The planned urbanization thus brings in its wake an overall margin-

alization of the rural people. Caught in a vicious circle of lack of voca-
tional training facilities in the region, on the one hand, and dearth of
unskilled jobs in the modern petrochemical complexes of Thane–Belapur industries or Uran gas projects on the other, they are being reduced
to even greater poverty. Even the industries promoted by the state government agencies have consistently failed in their promise to provide a
permanent job to at least one member of each displaced family.

As a cumulative effect of the breakup of the rural economy, social disruption has also occurred. Large numbers of local rural youths, who
can find only temporary and casual jobs in the factories or work as
domestic servants or coolies, have turned to petty crime, extortion, or
smuggling in the Uran and Mumbra areas.[18]

The new metropolis, it has been argued, is actually not urbanizing
the way of life and the social milieu of the surrounding rural areas.
Rather, the emerging social character of the new metropolis in its different nodes is being shaped around the social and economic class character of the urban in-migrants who come from different urban areas of the
state of Maharashtra (including Greater Bombay) and other states. The
new urban society composed of these heterogeneous groups creates
community organizations based on linguistic divisions on the one side
while the urban complex continues to grow in isolation from the countryside on the other.

Structural and Planning Problems

A large section of the displaced population from the impoverished areas
of Thane and Raigad districts has migrated en masse to different nodes
of the new metropolis, especially Vashi. Some people moved into Vashi
during the early 1970s when the township first started to grow, and
squatter settlements *(zopadpattis)* sprang up in the township to accommodate them. During the later phase of town building, the slums were
cleared by CIDCO and the residents were given (on a hire-purchase
basis) low-cost one-room tenement dwellings without any ventilation
and sanitary facilities in Sectors 21 and 22, close to the wholesaling
zone. As they were not provided with alternative economic opportunities, they had either to work at the lower end of the informal sector or
earn a paltry amount as casual laborers in the nearby factories—not
enough to pay the small monthly installment of Rs. 120 (about $10) and
the service charge of Rs. 25 ($2).[19] The tenements, without the mini-
mum facilities and also without proper plastering, had the appearance
of squalor from the very beginning. Ten years later the whole area,
owing to a complete lack of maintenance by CIDCO, has turned into a
large slum segregated from the residential part of the township by a *nul-*

lah (open drain). Today the slum poses a threat to the salability of the shop premises of the future spice and fruit wholesaling market.

As there is no provision for accommodating the construction workers, they house themselves, together with the continuous stream of rural migrants, in derelict slum quarters, giving rise to pockets of poverty on the otherwise beautifully planned landscape. In October 1984, CIDCO began a drastic cleaning operation of the township by removing the informal-sector units and evicting the poor from the tenements for defaulting in their payment of installments. This move has created considerable tension among the urban poor in Vashi, and demand for economic rehabilitation of the displaced people has become stronger.

The other problems which plague CIDCO stem from its assuming the role of developer, builder, transport authority, civil authority, and water supplier. Maintenance of the townships has declined to a considerable extent, and many areas of Vashi now look old and dilapidated. Heaps of uncollected garbage have become a common sight, and the major roads after every monsoon are full of potholes and depressions. As the town grows larger, the water supply is increasingly strained as CIDCO still depends on MIDC for water. Arguments have been raised that, far from relieving pressure from the older metropolis, New Bombay entails heavy claims on the same source of power and water from the streams of the Sahyadri range (the Western Ghats).[20]

Since Greater Bombay is mostly saturated, New Bombay appears to be the only plausible alternative not only for a large section of high and middle-income groups in search of residences, but also for big business and big capital in search of a new economic base in close proximity to the older metropolis. This has brought private builders, developers, and estate agents on the scene who not only create an artificial demand and inflated prices for the non-CIDCO real estate, but also have led to a price rise in the CIDCO housing stock (which has reportedly gone down in quality). CIDCO still contends that raising the price of houses or arranging auction sale of commercial space ultimately helps it to finance low-income housing for which it gets no return. In reality, due to inordinate price rises, even the cheapest housing stock now lies beyond the reach of the low-income groups.

Recently, following the footsteps of big private builders and developers such as Ansals and Rahejas, CIDCO has begun offering elegant houses and apartments in New Bombay to nonresident Indians abroad, as it is becoming increasingly difficult to get buyers locally.[21] Since a large section of the low-income and middle-income population has become unable to buy property, the only remaining market for CIDCO is the rich. This group, however, despite the overcrowding, still prefers to live in Greater Bombay because of disincentives in the new metropolis. The new city still has no local telephone exchange, no efficient mass transit system, no adequate health-care facilities, and no recreational amenities.[22]

The initial choice of location for New Bombay had raised serious criticism on the grounds that the northeastern part of Vashi township and the whole of Airoli would be exposed to air pollution from existing chemical and petrochemical units and the absence of vegetation would make the threat even greater. CIDCO's promise to create a vegetation screen by means of extensive tree plantations has yet to materialize. Meanwhile, air pollution remains a big health hazard.

Some, however, maintain that one of the greatest obstacles to the proper development of New Bombay is rooted in the rivalries between the four different bodies that share responsibility for the area in some way or other. They are BMRDA and CIDCO, the two district bodies.[23]

Summary

Of late, CIDCO has been trying to decentralize its functions. A new municipal authority has been planned to take over the civic administration of New Bombay. Water supply still rests with MIDC, but distribution has been entrusted to a water management board.

By now it is apparent that New Bombay, if certain structural gaps can be overlooked, is growing rapidly and developing in a way that marks a solid step in planned urbanization for developing countries. But neither the original objectives of the central government laid down in the third Five-Year Plan—to create and develop secondary cities in economically depressed areas in order to achieve widespread economic growth and equitable distribution of benefits—nor the Bombay Metropolitan and Regional Development Authority's plan—to decongest Bombay by creating a countermagnet on the mainland and to revitalize the stagnant economy of the shadow region of Bombay's hinterland—has been realized. The fulfillment of these objectives lies in the symbiotic relation between the new city and the countryside. I believe that the central government, in deciding to deconcentrate urbanization and industrialization from the overinvested primate metropolises of India during the third Five-Year Plan, had already taken its stand on the question of benefits of the economies of scale in agglomerations. Hence the planned cities are expected to help accomplish deconcentration.

The success of planning and developing New Bombay, therefore, lies not just in its evolution as a challenging countermagnet to Greater Bombay and a lucrative base for investors but in becoming integrated into the economy of the surrounding region by creating a sound economic base for thousands of local people, especially those displaced by land acquisition. CIDCO may find ready allies among big business and among those of the urban residential population who in the course of the last ten years have become property owners in New Bombay. These groups will support the present nature of growth of the new metropolis, and its alienation from the immediate rural hinterland may be subdued. But the real problem remains. In a developing country such as India, where most people are rural and poor, projects like New Bombay, instead of integrating them in the mainstream of development, simply promote exploitative urban development. Equity and justice in the distribution of benefits remain elusive in Indian planning.

NOTES

1. Barbara Ward, *Rich Nations and Poor Nations* (New York: Norton, 1968).

2. T. Rauch, "Regional Policy in Nigeria," *Geoforum* 13 (2) (1982): 151–161; S. Brugger, "Regional Policy in Costa Rica: The Problems of Implementation," *Geoforum* 13 (2) (1982): 177–192.

3. Census of India, General Population Tables, 1981.

4. D. A. Rondinelli, *Secondary Cities in Developing Countries,* Sage Library of Social Research, no. 145 (Beverly Hills: Sage Publications, 1983).

5. S. Banerjee and N. Dasgupta, "The Geography of Socio-Economic Well-Being in Maharashtra and West Bengal: Positive and Normative Approaches," in A. B. Mukerji and A. Ahmad (eds.), *India—Culture, Society and Economy* (New Delhi: Inter-India Publications, 1985).

6. S. M. Alam, "Distortions in Settlement System of India," *Geographical Review of India* 42 (4) (1980): 305–322.

7. P. Rosenstein-Rodan, "Problems of Industrialization in Eastern and Southeastern Europe," *Economic Journal* 53 (1943): 202–211.

8. S. M. Alam, "The National Settlement System of India," in L. S. Bourne, R. Sinclair, and K. Dzieworiski (eds.), *Urbanization and Settlement Systems* (New York: Oxford University Press, 1984).

9. Ashish Bose, "Urbanization in the Face of Rapid Population Growth and Surplus Labor," paper submitted to the Asian Population Conference, New Delhi, December 1983. Bose estimates that migration accounted for 50 percent of the increase in urban population.

10. B. Roberts, *Cities of Peasants* (London: Edward Arnold, 1978).

11. N. Dasgupta, "The Geography of Socio-Economic Well-Being in India" (unpublished M.Phil. dissertation, Department of Geography, University of Bombay, 1984).

12. Rondinelli, *Secondary Cities.*

13. C. D. Deshpande and B. Arunachalam, "Bombay," in M. Pacione (ed.), *Problems and Planning in Third World Cities* (New York: St. Martin's Press, 1981), pp. 187–217.

14. Ibid.

15. K. S. Keswani, "Traffic and Transportation Problems in the Bombay Metropolitan Area," in Institute of Town Planners (ed.), *Selected Papers in Urban and Regional Planning* (Bombay: Blackie & Sons, 1977).

16. S. Gopalkrishnan, B. S. Negi, and G. C. Mishra, "Trace Element Concentration in the Urban Environment in India," in *Proceedings of International Symposium on Management of the Environment* (Bombay, 1980).

17. CIDCO, *An Outline of Activities* (Bombay, 1983).

18. P. Bidwai, "Flexing City Uproots Rurals," *Times of India* (Bombay), 18 February 1984.

19. Since a civic administrative body has yet to take charge of the new metropolis, CIDCO continues to look after maintenance, for which it collects a monthly service charge in lieu of tax.

20. Deshpande and Arunachalam, "Bombay."

21. CIDCO, *India To-day* (Bombay, 1985).

22. Deshpande and Arunachalam, "Bombay."

23. Ibid.

PART IV: CASE STUDIES IN URBAN DEVELOPMENT

10. Intermediate Cities on the Resource Frontier: A Case Study from Indonesia

WILLIAM B. WOOD

STUDIES of urbanization in the Third World have tended to focus on primate cities within national frameworks. This study departs from this tradition to focus on intermediate cities within an international framework.[1] The cities studied here are located in a "resource frontier" region which has recently experienced the large-scale extraction and export of natural resources demanded by the world economy. A broad world-systems framework is adopted in this study to highlight the critical function of international linkages in the development of resource frontier cities.[2]

The intermediate cities of Samarinda and Balikpapan are located in the province of East Kalimantan, Indonesia, a resource-rich region well known for its export of exotic forest products, timber, and, perhaps most important, petroleum. Both cities have populations of over 260,000 and have experienced population growth rates of over 7 percent a year during the 1970s, when timber and petroleum exports from the province increased dramatically. Samarinda is the provincial capital and center of timber processing and exports, while Balikpapan is the regional headquarters and refining center for the state-owned petroleum company, Pertamina. This study argues that these cities have become "growth centers" not because of government fiat but because of world market demand for regional resources.[3]

The function of international economic linkages in the growth of resource frontier cities has important policy implications. Many national governments have expressed strong interest in the growth of intermediate cities as a means of directing rural-to-urban migration away from the primate city and as a means of stimulating regional development.[4]

Adapted, by permission of the American Geographical Society, from *Geographical Review* 76 (2): 149–159 (April 1986). Further reproduction without written consent of the society is prohibited.

Most governments, however, have been unsuccessful in their attempts to influence population distribution and limit the growth of their largest cities.[5] One reason for their failure is that explicit population policies are often undermined by the unforeseen spatial consequences of national economic policies. Thus the promotion of intermediate cities, as an explicit policy of population distribution, needs to be judged in relation to other national policies as well as macroeconomic conditions. The study of Samarinda and Balikpapan underlines the relevance of national economic policies and international market conditions to the development of intermediate cities.

This study integrates several disparate lines of academic research. The first line concerns the functions and roles of intermediate cities in regional development.[6] The second is the study of cities within a world-systems framework.[7] The third analyzes how resource exploitation affects the regions in which these resources are located and the towns and cities to which they are linked.[8] The final line attempts to devise a qualitative methodology for analyzing urban change.[9] The product of these lines is a study of how two intermediate-size cities, with different resource bases, have reacted to the drastic changes brought about by the increased world demand for their respective resources.

East Kalimantan

The province of East Kalimantan covers an area of about 202,440 square kilometers athwart the equator in the eastern half of the island of Borneo. The equatorial climate and relatively flat terrain support vast expanses of broadleaf evergreen and swamp forest, developed on generally infertile soils and dissected by an extensive network of rivers. The harsh environment has discouraged sedentary agricultural practices and has allowed indigenous shifting cultivators to live in relative isolation until recent times.

East Kalimantan's population of 1.3 million is concentrated in the coastal areas and along the major rivers; the population density for the province as a whole is less than six persons per square kilometer. The province contains a mixture of peoples from the Indonesian archipelago and beyond and includes indigenous Dayaks and Kutai, Bugis, Banjarese, Japanese, and Chinese. During the 1960s and 1970s East Kalimantan experienced a sharp increase in in-migration from other provinces, particularly East and Central Java.

Politically, East Kalimantan is under the jurisdiction of the Republic of Indonesia. Prior to Indonesian independence from the Dutch in 1949, the area consisted of separate sultanates. The most powerful sultanate was the Kutai, which controlled the resource-rich region in which Samarinda and Balikpapan are located. In the two decades following independence, the political autonomy of the province was abrogated by the Jakarta-based national government. The granting of provincial status to East Kalimantan in 1957 effectively undermined the traditional power base of the sultanates, which were then reduced to subprovincial regency status. At the same time, Samarinda and Balikpapan received municipal status which placed them on the same political level as the sultanates to which they were once subordinate (see Figure 10.1). In 1965, the state-owned petroleum company, Pertamina, took over control of the Royal-Dutch Shell refinery in Balikpapan. By 1970, the national forestry administration had taken over almost all important functions relating to the regulation of provincial timber resources, a domain previously regulated by the sultanates. All provincial governors and most of the senior administrative personnel have been appointed by the national government, many from the armed forces.

During the 1970s East Kalimantan's timber and petroleum exports increased dramatically in both volume and value. The volume of raw log exports increased from 2.7 million cubic meters in 1969–1970 to 9.2 million cubic meters in 1978–1979, while the value of these exports jumped from US$7.2 million to US$512.2 million. Similarly, crude oil production grew from 7.2 million barrels in 1971 to 150.1 million barrels in 1978, about 25 percent of Indonesia's total oil production. In addition, production of liquefied natural gas, which began in 1977, reached 9 million cubic meters by 1980.[10]

East Kalimantan's export-based growth during the 1970s arose primarily from the participation of large multinational corporations who funded and managed resource extraction activities from exploration to processing and export. Timber multinationals, such as Georgia-Pacific and Weyerhauser, received concession rights to millions of hectares of forest in "joint ventures" with Indonesian partners. Petroleum multinationals, such as the American-based Union Oil and Roy M. Huffington Company (called "Huffco") and the French-based Total Indonesia, operated as "service contractors" with Pertamina.

Exports of raw logs fell after 1978 because of restrictions imposed by the national government regulations aimed at encouraging local processing of logs into plywood. The world demand for Indonesia's plywood was low, however, and many timber companies either went bankrupt or chose to withdraw from the region rather than risk investing in plywood factories. To make matters worse, in 1983 a forest fire covering over 3 million hectares destroyed many valuable timber concessions. By 1984, Georgia-Pacific and Weyerhauser had sold out to local partners.

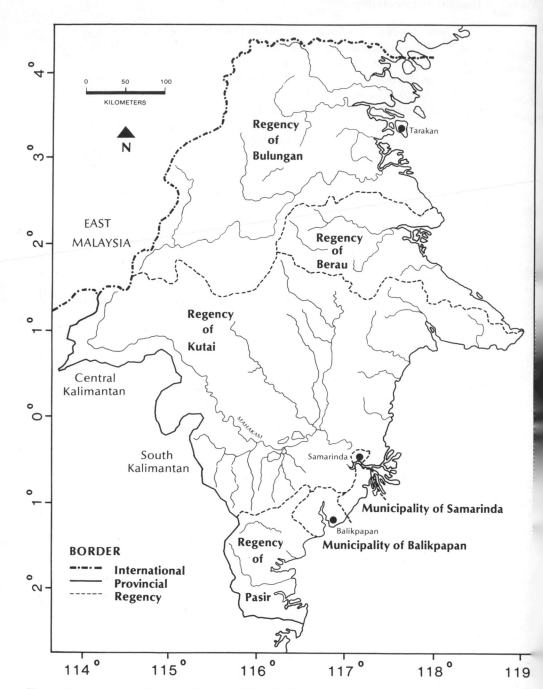

Figure 10.1. Resource Frontier Region of East Kalimantan

Petroleum production in the region continues at a high level, although crude oil production by 1983 was down to 103.2 million barrels from a high of 151.5 million barrels in 1977. In 1982, Pertamina completed a billion-dollar expansion of its Balikpapan refinery and constructed a large-capacity liquefied natural gas plant in the Bontang area north of Samarinda. Oil discoveries have slumped since the peak year of 1974, however, despite extensive exploration efforts, which suggests a possible decline in the region's oil exports within the next decade regardless of world demand.

Urban System Model

The effects of resource extraction activities on Samarinda and Balikpapan appear rather obvious to visitors. Both cities are undergoing building booms and seem to have thriving commercial enterprises. The rapid demographic and economic growth of the cities has made it difficult for their municipal governments to provide basic public services such as electricity and piped drinking water. The municipal governments engage in a variety of urban development projects, including road construction and upgrading of their airports and wharves, in an effort to keep up with the increased pressure on urban infrastructure. All these activities are directly or indirectly the result of three factors: the in-migration of people working, or hoping to work, for resource-based industries or in services arising from these enterprises; the increased wealth of residents associated with the new commercial enterprises; and the national government's commitment to further resource exploitation. The problem, then, is not in identifying the major catalysts of change in the cities but in documenting how the cities have responded to the catalysts.

One solution to the problem of analyzing complex urban changes with limited data is offered by Peter Nijkamp. Nijkamp's "integrated systems approach to qualitative assessment" seeks to determine the spatial implications of urban policies. He divides an urban area into six subsystems which interact with each other. The effects of a given policy can be traced through the "integrated system" and qualitatively analyzed. The main attributes of Nijkamp's model are its relative simplicity and limited demand for quantitative data bases that in most Third World contexts are nonexistent.

In the study of Samarinda and Balikpapan, I have modified Nijkamp's model by rearranging his subsystem categories (see Figure 10.2). Nijkamp's subsystem categories are reorganized to emphasize socioeconomic rather than spatial urban changes and to accommodate

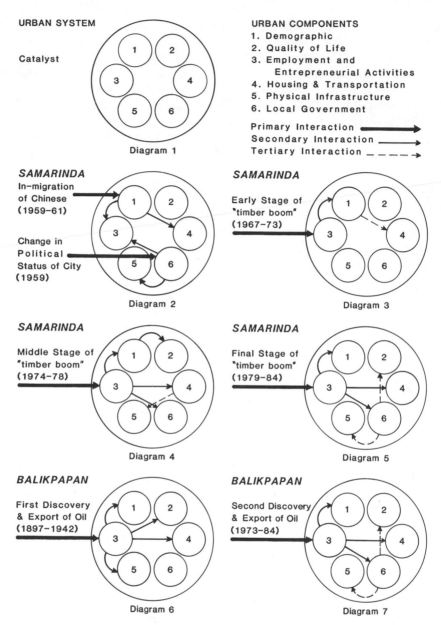

Figure 10.2. Urban System Model with Changing Components for Samarinda and Balikpapan During Conjunctural Period

the availability of data in the two cities. The six system components in the revised model are demography, employment and entrepreneurial activities, physical infrastructure, housing and transportation, quality of life, and local government. Each of these system components has indicators for which data can be collected and at least qualitatively measured over a period of time. Primary, secondary, and tertiary effects can thereby be traced for each catalyst to the urban system. In the case of Samarinda, the principal catalyst was the timber boom and arrival of multinational timber companies in the early 1970s; in Balikpapan the principal catalyst of the 1970s was the discovery of offshore oil reserves and the economic involvement of multinational petroleum companies. These two catalysts established a period of "conjuncture" during which the urban systems underwent structural alterations.[11]

Samarinda

The municipality of Samarinda straddles a bend in the Mahakam River about 60 kilometers from the coast. The 400-kilometer-long river has played a central role in the history of the city and the Kutai region, as it is the major artery between the coast and the interior. Although the earliest recorded evidence for civilization in the area dates back to the fifth century A.D., the original settlement of the present-day city was in 1668 by Bugis from South Sulawesi. The Bugis effectively controlled trade through the river port town for several hundred years as Samarinda slowly grew in importance as a center of trade in exotic forest products, such as birds' nests, resins, rattan, and reptile skins.[12] The abundance of these products brought Chinese and Banjarese merchants who soon established trading links to China and other ports throughout insular Southeast Asia. The Dutch defeated the sultan of Kutai's army in 1844 and set up an assistant residency post in Samarinda; for the next hundred years, however, they maintained only superficial contact with the interior of the region. After independence from the Dutch and the subsequent decline of the Kutai Sultanate, Samarinda became the provincial capital and received a large land area (approximately 2,727 square kilometers) at the expense of the Kutai Sultanate (now Kutai Regency).

Two events in 1959 helped set the stage for Samarinda's conjunctural period. The first was the arrival of Chinese traders and their families into Samarinda from the interior of the region because of Proklamasi Presiden 10, a law adopted in 1959 by President Sukarno forcing all "aliens" (meaning Chinese) in Indonesia to reside only in urban areas. Many of these Chinese moved into the urban neighborhood along Samarinda's waterfront and built two-story shop-houses, thereby creating Samarinda's business district. These Chinese merchants were now situated in the ideal place to control trade into Samarinda's vast hinterland and to take advantage of the early stages of the timber boom. The second event that paved the way for Samarinda's conjunctural period was the designation of municipal status and provincial capital. Municipal status gave Samarinda political autonomy from the Kutai Regency, while the selection of Samarinda as provincial capital ensured that it would be the point of interaction between the national government and the various provincial administrations. By the mid-1960s, Samarinda was the center of both trading activities and political control for East Kalimantan.

Samarinda's conjunctural period began about 1967 with the arrival of East Asian timber buyers who came to purchase tropical hardwood logs for export to processing plants in Japan, South Korea, and Taiwan. Local entrepreneurs took advantage of this new market demand for the seemingly endless supply of East Kalimantan's trees by cutting logs and floating them downriver to Samarinda. The increased wealth of local timber entrepreneurs and the sudden demand for timber cutting supplies, which included everything from canned goods to outboard motors, created a commercial bonanza for Samarinda's shopkeepers and traders, most of whom were Chinese.

The scale of Samarinda's timber industry shifted in the early 1970s away from local entrepreneurs toward timber multinationals and away from provincial management of forest reserves toward national-level management. Multinational corporations had the technology, labor skills, management, and marketing networks to carry out timber cutting on an unprecedented scale in the region. The national forestry administration had the authority to negotiate with the multinationals over concession rights and, at the same time, force out local entrepreneurs who could not fulfill the new requirements for officially sanctioned timber cutting. The result was the arrival of foreign timber experts and relatively sophisticated equipment needed to cut and export logs on a major scale. The volume of exports from the port of Samarinda, which consisted mostly of logs, jumped from 1.2 million metric tons in 1969 to 15.7 million metric tons in 1978. From an enterprise dominated by local entrepreneurs and local officials, timber became an industry dominated by multinationals and the central government.

Toward the end of the 1970s the national government became concerned about the lack of local timber processing and imposed restrictions on the export of raw logs. Timber enterprises reluctantly responded with the construction of numerous sawmills and plywood factories. By 1984, nineteen plywood factories and twenty-seven sawmills were in operation in and around Samarinda. Problems with quality control and limited foreign and domestic demand for the inferior-grade plywood produced in Samarinda's factories severely reduced the profits of many timber exporters and even forced some into bankruptcy. To make matters worse, the catastrophic forest fire of 1983 in Samarinda's hinterland curtailed the supply of raw logs on which the city's timber industry depends. All of these factors have accelerated the withdrawal of timber industry multinationals, such as Georgia-Pacific and Weyerhauser, from Samarinda.

The major changes occurring in Samarinda during the 1960s and 1970s can be generalized using the urban system model. The first changes, brought about by the in-migration of Chinese merchants and the change in political status, primarily affected the demographic and local government system components with secondary effects on employment and entrepreneurial activities, housing and transportation, and physical infrastructure (Figure 10.2, Diagram 2). The next three major changes in Samarinda's urban system all had primary effects on employment and entrepreneurial activities, as this component was directly involved in the timber boom (Figure 10.2, Diagrams 3, 4, and 5). The employment and entrepreneurial component also responded quickly to the rising incomes of the local population through the expanding variety and volume of retail commodities. While the national government and multinational companies consolidated their control over the timber industry, other urban system components were affected by the timber boom through secondary linkages—most notably the demographic component as the city's foreign and Japanese population increased; the housing and transportation component as Western-style housing was built and traffic became more congested; and the local government component as it tried to respond to the increased demand for physical and social infrastructure. The timber boom indirectly affected the physical infrastructure and quality of life through the growing urban population.

The government has responded to this new growth stress by investing in basic public services such as schools and health care centers. The city's urban system is still undergoing major changes despite the decline of the regional timber industry. For example, many of the numerous Western-style houses built for foreigners in the mid to late 1970s now stand empty while there is a shortage of adequate low-cost housing for the continuous stream of Indonesian in-migrants.

Balikpapan

Unlike Samarinda, Balikpapan has always been associated with multinational resource extraction industries. Prior to the discovery of high-

grade oil, Balikpapan was an isolated Bugis fishing village. The first oil
well was drilled in the Balikpapan area in 1897 and was soon followed
by a small refinery. After Dutch petroleum companies moved in, the village of Balikpapan was transformed as roads, wharves, warehouses,
office buildings, barracks, and bungalows were built to facilitate the
extraction of petroleum and to accommodate the arrival of Dutch super-
visors and Indonesian laborers. Royal-Dutch Shell, an English–Dutch-
owned multinational corporation, operated the Balikpapan refinery
until it fell to the invading Japanese army in 1942. After the war Royal-
Dutch Shell repaired the extensive damage done to the refinery and
continued its drilling and refining operations, despite the victory of
Indonesian nationalists over the Dutch in 1949. In 1965, Royal-Dutch
Shell sold out its petroleum interests in the Balikpapan area to Pertamina, the Indonesian army-controlled petroleum company.

In the early 1970s, multinational petroleum companies were awarded
exploration and drilling contracts by Pertamina, which lacked the technology, skilled manpower, and capital to explore the region's potential
petroleum reserves. These foreign companies soon discovered significant onshore and offshore petroleum reserves in the East Kalimantan
region. Balikpapan, as Pertamina's regional headquarters and the site
of the region's only refinery, became the center of a revitalized regional
petroleum industry. Within a few years, a number of petroleum-related
companies had set up branch offices in Balikpapan and hundreds of
petroleum industry employees and their families had arrived. By 1980,
Pertamina was sufficiently confident of its regional petroleum exports to
begin upgrading its Balikpapan refinery—a project reportedly employing several thousand laborers, many from Java. The municipality of
Balikpapan, meanwhile, continued to grow around the large urban core
controlled by Pertamina.

Balikpapan's urban system has undergone two distinct conjunctural
periods based on the same catalyst—the discovery of petroleum—which
primarily affected the same urban component, employment and entrepreneurial activities. The first conjunctural period began in 1897 with
the first oil well and ended with the occupation of Balikpapan by the
Japanese army (Figure 10.2, Diagram 6). The second conjunctural
period began about 1973 with the arrival of multinational petroleum
companies and their subsequent discovery of large offshore and onshore
oil reserves; the urban system is still in the midst of this second conjunctural period (Figure 10.2, Diagram 7). Both conjunctural periods saw
the arrival of a numerically small but influential group of foreigners
employed as managers and engineers by the petroleum companies and
the in-migration of Indonesians from other parts of the archipelago
employed (or hoping to be employed) as semiskilled and unskilled

laborers in petroleum-related industries and services. Moreover, both periods witnessed a building boom as the industries and local entrepreneurs rushed to meet the demands of increased petroleum production as well as the housing needs of petroleum industry employees. The first conjunctural period was perhaps the more revolutionary in that all components but local government were drastically altered by the industrialization implemented by Royal-Dutch Shell. The second conjunctural period essentially repeated this industrialization process but with the infrastructural foundations already established. The second period also included the direct participation of the national government in both the local government and the major industrial employer, Pertamina.

Comparative Urban Systems

A comparison of the urban system diagrams of Balikpapan and Samarinda emphasizes the importance of the employment and entrepreneurial component as the primary channel of change during their conjunctural periods. In both cases this component is primarily influenced by a resource extraction industry which is, in turn, dependent upon the international market system. Both cities are thus products of the world economy.

Samarinda and Balikpapan share common characteristics that go beyond their close proximity and municipal status. Both have experienced rapid demographic and economic growth over the last fifteen years, primarily as a result of their function as processing centers for their respective resource industries. They are both boom towns or, more appropriately, given their large populations, "boom cities." Samarinda and Balikpapan, however, have some important differences from boom towns associated with resource extraction activities in the First World: The population of these two cities is not in the hundreds or even thousands typical of First World boom towns but in the hundreds of thousands; Samarinda and Balikpapan have become international centers of resource processing, not just resource extraction; and the national government itself, rather than just a private company, is committed to the success of the resource extraction activities and the continued growth of the cities. In brief, the Indonesian government has too much invested in Samarinda and Balikpapan for them to be allowed to deteriorate into desolate ghost towns as was the fate of many First World boom towns.

Prior to 1915, Samarinda and Balikpapan had less than 6,000 people each; today their populations are each over 260,000. Although the total land area of both municipalities is more than 2,500 square kilometers, most of their populations live in built-up urban areas of less than 250 square kilometers. Population densities within the municipalities, therefore, vary widely. The average population density for Samarinda, as of 1980, was 97 persons per square kilometer while for Balikpapan it was 110 persons per square kilometer. Samarinda, however, has an urban neighborhood with more than 10,000 persons per square kilometer while Balikpapan has one with more than 8,000 persons per square kilometer. Sex ratios for both cities are more than 110, which is typical of male-dominated boom towns in other regions. Interestingly, the age group with the lowest sex ratio is between 15 and 24 years—which suggests a relatively high in-migration of young women, who might be entering secondary schools or some type of urban employment, and perhaps an out-migration of young men, who might be employed in rural-based resource industries such as timber concessions or oil fields. The age structure of both municipal populations is young: over 41 percent of the population is under 14 and only 7 percent is over 50.

Both cities have active commercial districts characterized by two-story shop-houses occupied by Chinese merchants. The Chinese, although a small minority of the municipal population, play an influential economic role and help to define the character of urban core areas within each municipality. The Chinese provide many services to resource extraction industries and control the import and retail selling of consumer goods to growing urban and rural populations.

Urban development in Samarinda and Balikpapan is heavily influenced by the government—not indirectly through land use plans (which do exist but remain unenforced) but directly through government grants and construction projects. The national, provincial, and municipal governments play leading roles in urban development projects, such as road widening, school and marketplace construction, housing for public employees, and *kampuna* (village) improvement. Private developers, working on a smaller scale, have had only marginal effects on the spatial growth patterns of the two cities. Many private developers, however, capitalized on the in-migration of foreign resource industry employees in the mid to late 1970s by engaging in land speculation, building Western-style houses and offices, and renting these properties out to timber and petroleum companies for exorbitant prices.[13] Many of the houses built less than ten years ago now stand empty.

The municipal governments of the two cities have grown rapidly over the past decade, both in budget and staff. Their budgets, for example, although slightly different from each other, went from less than US$0.5 million in 1969–1970 to more than US$8 million by 1982–1983. As Samarinda and Balikpapan grew during the 1970s, however, the demands on municipal government services far surpassed the government's ability to meet them. Neither municipal government has been able to administer a tax collection system that could even begin to meet government expenses; in both cities entertainment and hotel and restaurant taxes provide over half of the total taxes collected. During the latter part of the 1970s, the national government began to absorb a greater percentage of the municipal budgets through subsidized development projects.

Politically, the municipal government operates as a "top-down" hierarchy: The governor appoints the mayors who, in turn, appoint department heads. The municipal governments of Samarinda and Balikpapan have little influence on decisions concerning resource extraction activities even though many of those activities profoundly affect the two cities. The municipal governments can, therefore, only react to changes already imposed on the urban systems by resource-related activities instead of planning for expected future changes. Land use and planning decisions within the municipalities are coordinated through the local planning offices (BAPPEDA), which have rudimentary master plans but virtually no authority to implement them. Although community participation in the municipal government is limited, suggestions for development projects at the village level are accepted and, if deemed worthy, passed on to the national planning board (BAPPENAS) in Jakarta for possible funding.

The municipal and national governments have, however, been relatively successful in providing primary and secondary schooling to the cities' young population and have implemented a network of basic health care centers, many of which emphasize child nutrition. The national government, with financial support from international development agencies, has carried out a successful Kampung Improvement Program and has completely rebuilt many ramshackle marketplaces. Both municipal planning offices are aware of the problems their cities face due to regional resource extraction activities and are trying to bring about improvements to the urban environment within their limited means.

Physical infrastructure is a continual problem in both cities. Squatter settlements built on marginal land within the urban area have resulted in mudslides and large-scale soil erosion, especially after rainstorms. Drainage canals are often filled with silt and garbage, which contributes to frequent flooding during the rainy season (October through May). Inadequate firefighting equipment and crowded housing have led to widespread outbreaks of fire, the most recent occurring in November 1984 with almost 700 houses destroyed. Neither municipality has been able to supply piped water or electricity to growing populations in the urban fringe areas.

Changes in the quality of life are difficult to determine, partly because of the ambiguity of the term "quality of life." The inflated regional economy has driven up prices for most commodities, although some basic staples, such as rice, salted fish, and fruit, remain relatively cheap. Both cities have serious problems with public sanitation, especially the disposal of human waste. The growing congestion of families living in the urban core areas makes traditional disposal methods inadequate, but there are, as yet, no alternatives. Refuse collection from roadside containers is sporadic, particularly in the poorer areas, and there is still no workable mosquito control program. Finally, the limited access to piped drinking water forces many residents to rely on possibly contaminated sources. During periods of drought the rivers, which serve as bathroom and source of drinking water to many poor urban residents, become polluted pools and stagnant streams. Poor public sanitation has led in the past to epidemics of malaria and cholera and could easily do so again.

Conclusion

The urban system components I have described here are only general reflections of complex interrelationships within the cities of Samarinda and Balikpapan. These broad observations, however, provide an overview from which to study current planning problems in the cities. The qualitative analysis of changes during the cities' conjunctural periods strongly supports the contention that, in resource frontier regions, international economic linkages play the principal role in urban development. Regional and national linkages, though important to the continued growth and management of the cities, are secondary to the cities' major function as gateways between the world economy and regional resources.[14]

The cities of Samarinda and Balikpapan are two of the fastest-growing cities in Indonesia. The factors responsible for their rapid growth need to be studied by national-level policymakers interested in their continued growth as well as in the growth of similar cities located in other resource frontier regions. The relative economic prosperity of Samarinda and Balikpapan facilitates resource extraction and migration to East Kalimantan, both of which activities the central government has deemed to be in the national interest. The economic growth of these cities, however, has been largely due to international market demand for timber and petroleum—a demand which could fall as quickly as it once rose. Indonesia's simultaneous commitment to an export-based economy, dependent upon international economic conditions, and to regional development and population redistribution, dependent upon stable growth of the Outer Islands, could thus be in conflict.

The future of Samarinda and Balikpapan, as gateways between the world market and regional resources, depends more on the international marketplace than on government policy. The dwindling prospects of Samarinda's timber industry might be partially offset by the national government's investments in its provincial capital, but the government can hardly afford to match the contribution of timber exports to the regional and municipal economies. Balikpapan's petroleum industry has a somewhat brighter future, as long as regional oil reserves are not depleted too quickly and the price of oil does not drop significantly. If the Indonesian government wishes to ensure continued growth in these two cities, or other resource-based "growth centers," it must first control the extraction and marketing of its natural resources—an unlikely prospect given the important role of multinational corporations in the capitalist world economy and the fluctuating demands of the international marketplace.

NOTES

1. I have defined an intermediate city as being a principal city in a region with intermediary economic and political functions between the national capital and smaller regional cities and towns. Intermediate cities usually have a population between 100,000 and 500,000. For a general review of this type of city, see Dennis Rondinelli, *Secondary Cities in Developing Countries: Policies for Diffusing Urbanization* (Beverly Hills: Sage Publications, 1983).

2. "World-systems" theory, at a general level, attempts to explain the current inequalities between rich and poor countries as the product of a growing world-capitalist economy which has its origins in sixteenth-century Europe. Perhaps the best summary of this theory is Immanuel Wallerstein's *The Capitalist World-Economy* (Cambridge: Cambridge University Press, 1979).

3. This study is based on research carried out in Samarinda and Balikpapan in the spring of 1984 as part of a dissertation submitted to the Department of Geography, University of Hawaii, Manoa. Research was funded by a grant from the Population Institute, East–West Center, Honolulu.

4. United Nations, *Population Distribution Policies in Developing Countries* (New York, 1981).

5. Roland Fuchs, "Government Policy and Population Distribution," in John Clarke (ed.), *Geography and Population: Approaches and Applications* (New York: Pergamon Press, 1984).

6. Rondinelli, *Secondary Cities*.

7. Christopher Chase-Dunn, "Urbanization in the World Economy: New Directions for Research," *Comparative Urban Research* 9 (2) (1983): 41–46.

8. Gary Malamud, *Boomtown Communities* (New York: Van Nostrand Reinhold, 1984).

9. Peter Nijkamp, "Qualitative Impact Assessments of Spatial Policies in Developing Countries," *Regional Development Dialogue* 4 (Spring 1983): 44–65.

10. These figures are taken from the *East Kalimantan Statistical Guide 1980* compiled by the Transmigration Area Development Project, based in Samarinda.

11. This study presents only a general summary of the structural changes that occurred in each city. A more detailed analysis appears in my dissertation.

12. Nancy Peluso, "Markets and Merchants: The Forest Products Trade of East Kalimantan in Historical Perspective" (master's thesis, Cornell University, 1983), pp. 30–35.

13. Some of these "private developers" are in fact public employees who have used their government connections to make large profits on land development projects.

14. The concept of "gateway" cities is discussed by J. H. Bird in "Gateways: Slow Recognition But Irresistible Rise," *Tijdschrift voor Economische en Sociale Geografie* 74 (3) (1983): 196–202.

11. Beijing: Yesterday, Today, and Tomorrow

Jinggan Zhang

Beijing is situated on the northwestern fringe of the great North China Plain. To its west lie the Western Hills that are connected with the Shanxi Plateau; to its north stand the Yanshan Mountains that border the Mongolian Plateau; and to the southeast is a plain that drops gently to the Bohai Sea. The Yongding, the Chaobai, and a few other small and medium-size rivers flow through the Beijing area.

Early in Chinese history, the Han (Chinese) people gradually moved northward along the Taihang Mountains to the small plain from their birthplace in Central China (comprising the middle and lower reaches of the Yellow River). Further north of the city are high mountains where minority peoples have lived for centuries. There are three routes leading from ancient Beijing, known then as Ji, to the north. The first goes through Nankou and Juyongguan passes between the Taihang and Yanshan mountains, then extends to the basins of Huailai and Xuanhua in Hebei province, and eventually reaches the Mongolian Plateau. The second stretches through Gubeikou to the mountains in northern Hebei, and the third reaches the Songliao Plain in northeastern China through the Shanhaiguan Pass.

In ancient times, many minority nationalities in northern China had frequent economic and trade contacts with the Han in the Central Plains, but armed conflicts between them were also frequent. Historically, Beijing always served as a hub of transportation for these three routes that were often used by trade caravans and military forces moving between central and northern China (Figure 11.1).

An Ancient Capital with a Long History

Kublai Khan, founder of the Yuan dynasty (1279–1368), established his capital in Beijing in 1260. In 1264 he built the Daning Palace northeast of the original Zhongdu city that had served as the capital of the Jin

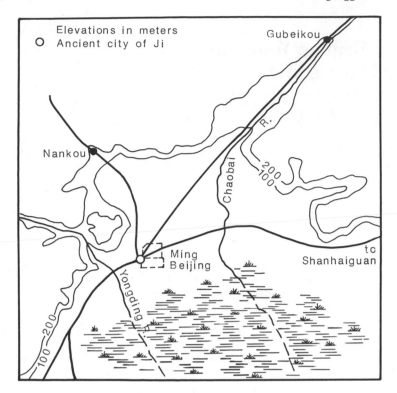

Figure 11.1. Location of Ancient Beijing

dynasty (1115–1235) since 1153. In 1267, construction of a new capital for the Yuan was begun which resulted in the renowned Great Capital (or Dadu) of the Yuan dynasty. The scale of Dadu was much larger than that of Zhongdu, and its location was approximately north of today's Chang'an Avenue. The Great Capital was an extremely busy city with bustling merchants both local and foreign, and goods were brought into or sent out of the city in endless streams. In the silk trade alone, a thousand loaded carts were brought into the city every day. The city was not only a great capital of China but also an important trade center of the Orient.

In 1368, Zhu Yuanzhang, leader of a peasant uprising, declared himself emperor and founded the Ming dynasty (1368–1644) in Nanjing, Jiangsu province. In the same year, his senior general Xu Da made a northern expedition and captured Dadu and renamed it Beiping. The Ming rulers systematically destroyed portions of the Yuan capital, including its northern city wall, and rebuilt the city according to a new city plan. In 1403, Zhu Di, King Yan of Beiping, inherited the throne

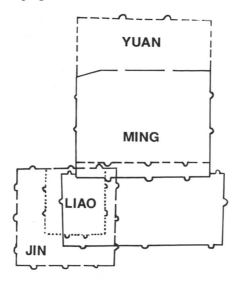

Figure 11.2. Site of Beijing During the
Liao, Yuan, and Ming Dynasties

and moved the capital from Nanjing to Beiping and at the same time changed its name to Beijing. The name Beijing originated from that time. The construction of new palaces and city walls and moats started in 1406 and reached completion in 1420. The new Ming capital is what is known as the Inner City today. An outer city was added in 1553, and the basic structure of the capital remained unchanged until the Communist revolution in 1949 (Figure 11.2).

The Great Capital of the Yuan dynasty was about 6.5 kilometers from east to west and about 7.5 kilometers from north to south, and its wall had a total of eleven gates. The main streets in the city went through all the gates and intersected like a chessboard. The Imperial City, built at the center of the city's southern part, contained three groups of palaces, Wansui Hill (today's Jingshan Hill), and Taiye Pond (now called Beihai and Zhonghai lakes).

The most splendid buildings of Ming Beijing were the palaces situated along the city's central axis. The Lizhengmen Gate facing the south at the center was magnificent. According to traditional layout, the Imperial Ancestral Temple was built north of the Qihuamen Gate in the eastern part of the city, the Altar of Land and Grain was located north of the Pingzemen Gate in the west, and most of the commercial centers were found north of the Imperial City. Government offices, temples, and pavilions were scattered all over the city. The other areas of the city were all residential quarters, divided into fifty blocks (Figure 11.3).

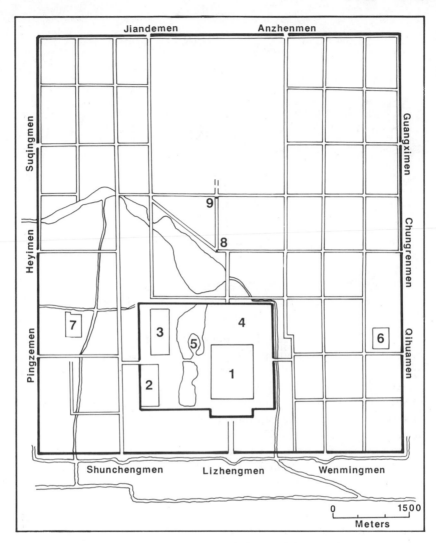

Figure 11.3. Dadu During the Yuan Dynasty: 1, Inner Palace; 2, Fulong Temple; 3, Xingsheng Palace; 4, Imperial Garden; 5, Qionghua Island; 6, Imperial Ancestral Temple; 7, Altar of Land and Grain; 8, Drum Tower; 9, Bell Tower

The city of Beijing during the Ming dynasty (1368–1644) was renovated and expanded. The city's north wall was moved southward, and the Forbidden City was built slightly to the south of the old site of the palace of the Yuan dynasty. The Imperial Ancestral Temple and the Altar of Land and Grain were built east and west of the central axis in the Forbidden City. The Nanhai Lake was dug south of Taiye Pond.

Meanwhile, the Tongzi Moat was dug around the Forbidden City, and the present-day Jingshan Park (Coal Hill) was built with silt dug up from the Nanhai Lake and the Tongzi Moat. The Drum Tower and Bell Tower were built north of Jingshan Park.

The Imperial City, which was 9 kilometers in circumference and covered an area of 7 square kilometers, was built to protect the Forbidden City at the center of Beijing. Outside the Imperial City is the present Inner City of Beijing. The Outer City to the south of the Inner City contained the Temples of Agriculture and Heaven and the commercial and residential areas of the city dwellers (Figure 11.4).

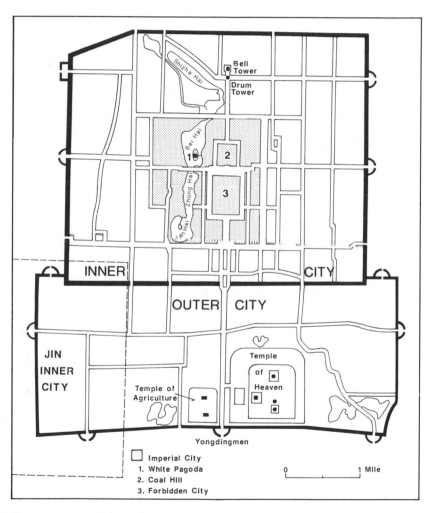

Figure 11.4. Beijing During the Ming Dynasty

Beijing during the Ming and Qing dynasties covered an area of 62 square kilometers and was bigger than the Great Capital of the Yuan dynasty. The city was constructed in a traditional style marked by an obvious central axis, neat symmetry, compactness, and solemnity. The magnificence of the 8-kilometer-long central axis, starting from the Yongdingmen Gate in the south and ending at the Bell Tower in the north, was unmatched by any capital in historic times. Geometric relationships exist among the city wall, city gates, main streets, and important buildings in Beijing. Coal Hill is the highest point of the city, for example, and therefore is located in the center of the Inner City at the intersection of the city's two diagonal lines (Figure 11.5).

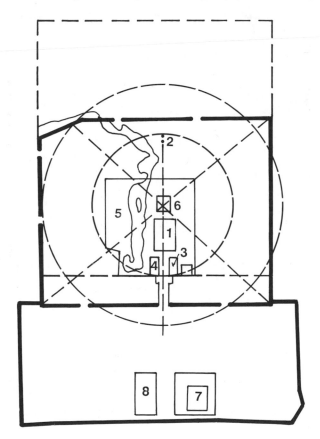

Figure 11.5. Physical Layout of Beijing During the Ming and Qing Dynasties: 1, Forbidden City; 2, Bell and Drum Towers; 3, Ancestral Hall; 4, Altar of Land and Grain; 5, Imperial City; 6, Jing Hill; 7, Temple of Heaven; 8, Temple of Mountain and River

Recent Construction and Renovation

At the time of liberation in 1949, there were only 20 million square meters of housing in Beijing's urban areas and in the neighborhoods outside the city gates, and three-fourths were the typical one-story local houses with courtyards left over from the Ming and Qing dynasties. They had not been repaired for many years and were in a ramshackle state. The basic urban facilities were extremely backward and the city looked shabby.

The city expanded rapidly after its liberation. By the end of 1983, the city's administrative area had grown from 707 square kilometers in 1949 to 16,800 square kilometers. The city's registered population had increased from 2 million in 1949 to 9.3 million in 1983, and the urban space had risen from 109 square kilometers in the early postliberation days to the present 360 square kilometers. The city now has ten newly built and comparatively independent housing areas in the suburbs. Besides, four sizable satellite towns—Huangcun, Changping, Tongzhen, and Yanshan—have successively been built in the outlying suburban counties.

In the past thirty-five years, various kinds of housing with a combined floor space of more than 100 million square meters have been built—five times the floor space of all the city's residential housing that existed shortly after liberation. Of that total, the floor space of the newly built housing was 48.8 million square meters, over three times the figure for 1949. In the newly developed suburban areas, nearly sixty residential districts, each with a residential floor space of more than 100,000 square meters, have been set up. Many living quarters have also been built in towns and industrial districts on the outskirts. At the same time, a large number of buildings have been built to accommodate central government institutions or to meet the needs of foreign governments and international trade. Various other public facilities have also been constructed for use by businesses and service trades and for cultural, sports, medical, and health purposes. These buildings have given the city a completely new look. Moreover, great advances have been made in the construction of such facilities as roads, traffic signals, water supply and sewerage, electric power, gas, heating, communication, parks, and open space.

There was hardly any modern industry in Beijing before 1949, and the few enterprises existing at the time of the city's liberation were at a standstill. Beijing's industry today is fairly diversified with more than 4,000 large, medium-size, and small industrial enterprises dealing with food, textiles, daily consumer goods, paper making, printing, arts and crafts, electronics, machinery, metallurgy, electric power, coal, petro-chemicals, and building materials.

After 1949, part of old Beijing was renovated. The old north–south city axis was retained and extended, and the east–west Chang'an Avenue was widened and extended, forming a new east–west axis. The two axes meet at Tiananmen Square. The square, after expansion on a number of occasions, has been extended from the original 11 hectares to the present 40 hectares. It is the largest public square in the world and the central square for activities of the people in Beijing (Figure 11.6).

In the past thirty-five years, great efforts have been made to improve the city's environment and strengthen its infrastructure. A number of factories and storehouses dealing with inflammable, explosive, or unsanitary products have been moved out of the city. Dilapidated houses have been rebuilt block by block and street by street. Mean-

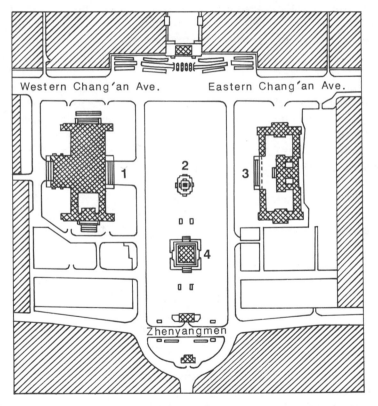

Figure 11.6. Tiananmen Square: 1, Great Hall of the People; 2, Monument of People's Heroes; 3, Museums of Chinese Revolution and History; 4, Chairman Mao's Memorial Hall

while, the remaining cultural relics and historic buildings have been preserved and numerous trees have been planted. These developments have infused vigor into this ancient city.

Residential Housing and Public Service Facilities

Great advances have been made in the construction of residential housing since 1949. As a result, the people's living conditions have improved. There is still a housing shortage, however, chiefly because of the rapid increase in the city's urban population. Between 1949 and 1983, the city's residential population rose by 3.4 percent annually, while the living floor space for the city's residents increased by 3.6 percent yearly. Therefore, people's housing conditions have improved only slowly. The construction of residential quarters has been speeded up in recent years, though, and an average of 4 million square meters of living space has been added each year. Housing construction coupled with controlled growth of the city's population have resulted in more living space in the city. The per capita living space was 5.68 square meters in 1983, as opposed to 4.75 square meters in 1949 and 4.79 square meters in 1980.

The new residential areas are equipped with department stores, drugstores, groceries, food stores, restaurants, barbershops, public bathrooms, laundries, photo studios, tailor shops, repair centers, clinics, post offices, banks, bookstores, recycling centers, and other service facilities. Generally, these facilities have a service radius of 250 meters.

At present, the city has about 10,000 state-operated shops, 9,700 collective shops, and 29,000 shops run by individual households. Besides, the city has also opened some 100 retail outlets run by industrial enterprises to sell their own products. Moreover, 100 warehouses and 24 supermarkets, and 139 fairs and markets, have been opened. By 1983, the city's total volume of retail sales amounted to 8.36 billion yuan, twenty-eight times the figure for 1949.

The city's service trade also has over 2,900 restaurants, hotels, barbershops and beauty salons, public baths, photo studios, laundries, and repair facilities, with a combined work force of 75,000 people. At the same time, the number of collective shops and networks in the urban area has increased to 7,100 employing some 350,000 people. A number of educational and cultural facilities have also been set up since 1949. There were 57 colleges and universities with more than 100,000 students in 1984, and some 100 secondary technical schools with 27,000 students. The city also has 191 research institutions. Beijing now has 37 theaters and 2,700 film-showing teams, 22 public libraries, 19 exhibition centers and museums, 370 cultural centers and stations at all levels, and nearly 300 sports facilities. Great achievements have also been made in the construction of medical and health facilities. The city now has a total of 4,300 medical centers at various levels.

Generally speaking, the number of tertiary activity units in Beijing is insufficient and their distribution is overconcentrated in the old city. Further expansion and readjustment of the tertiary sector is needed.

Urban Transport and Communications

In 1949, Beijing's roads were mostly narrow and unpaved, except for a dozen low-quality asphalt roads totaling 215 kilometers. There were only forty-nine old-fashioned tramcars and five buses in use. Since 1949, much has been done to improve the roads and urban traffic. By the end of 1983, the combined length of roads in both the city's urban and suburban areas amounted to 2,437 kilometers, eleven times that in 1949. Sixty percent of these roads were of relatively high quality.

In the past thirty-five years, five east–west and two north–south truck roads have been opened or widened, and a third ring road, 23.7 kilometers long, has been built to connect the suburban areas. Part of a fourth ring road has also been completed. At the same time, a dozen radial highways leading to the Great Wall at the Badaling section, the Summer Palace, and the Peking Man site at Zhoukoudian have been built, and more than forty overpasses of various types have been erected. More-over, 3,562 kilometers of roads have been added in the mountainous areas of the city. These roads have greatly improved the city's traffic conditions. On the basis of the existing checkerboard-style road pat-terns, a new road system comprising the ring roads and radial highways has been taking shape (Figure 11.7).

Beijing now has more than 200,000 motor vehicles and 4.73 million bicycles, and its mass transit system has expanded greatly. By the end of 1983, there were 3,225 buses and 528 trolley buses in the city, more than twenty-two times the figure of 1949. The length of the newly opened routes totaled 1,800 kilometers, and the annual ridership in the urban and suburban areas reached 3 billion person-trips. Moreover, two subway lines have been built in Beijing reaching a total length of approximately 40 kilometers. Shortly after 1949, Beijing had only three trunk rail lines leading to Shanhaiguan, Baotou, and Shanghai. Since then, five new trunk railways have been built, stretching from Beijing to the cities of Chengde, Qinhaungdao, Fengtai, and Shacheng in Hebei province, Yuanping city in Shanxi province, and Tongliao city in Liaoning province. Meanwhile, the Beijing Railway Station, the Yong-dingmen Railway Station, a marshaling yard to the west of Fengtai, and two auxiliary marshaling yards in Beijing have been built. The 7,906 kilometers of highway built is twenty times that in early postliber-

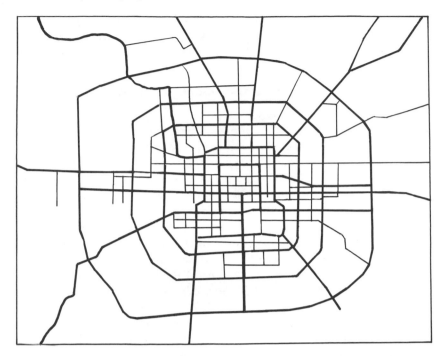

Figure 11.7. Beijing's Road System

ation days. On the whole, every township in Beijing municipality now has asphalt roads and every village is accessible to buses. Beijing airport has opened forty-six domestic and international air routes.

Urban traffic remains a problem, however, because of the low density of roads in the city proper and a rapid increase in the flow of passengers, motor vehicles, and bicycles. With the expansion of the urban and rural economy and tourism, the present traffic facilities are unable to keep pace with the demand.

Great progress has been made in postal service and telecommunications. The Telegram Service Building, the Long-Distance Telecommunications Building, a ground satellite telecommunications station, and other projects have been built in Beijing. The city has thirty-five telephone exchanges and branch exchanges with a capacity of 158,000 lines, more than six times that available shortly after liberation. Coaxial cables, a microwave and telecommunications satellite, and other means have been introduced for long-distance communication and transmissions. There are now 398 post offices and postal agencies in Beijing, nearly ten times the figure from the early postliberation days. These postal establishments have daily mail service to more than 2,000 cities and towns in China, distribute newspapers and publications to over

5,000 cities and towns, and have mail service to 150 cities in 112 countries and regions. Although the city's present communications facilities are still very backward, great efforts are being made to improve them.

Environmental Protection, Parks, and Open Space

Environmental protection agencies were set up in Beijing in the early 1970s. By the end of 1983, the city had more than 4,000 people employed as professional environmental protection workers. The citywide environmental protection and management system and monitoring network have basically been formed. A series of regulations and standards on environmental protection have been promulgated through legislative procedures. As a result, great achievements have been made in this field.

Beijing has little rain and is quite windy in winter and spring, and sometimes dust storms darken the sky in the spring. Citywide drives for afforestation have been carried out since 1949 to reduce dust. By 1983, nearly half the 6,000 square kilometers of land in the city's suburbs suitable for tree planting had been covered with trees. The wooded area within Beijing has been raised from 1.3 percent in the early 1950s to 16.6 percent in 1983. The soil erosion area has been reduced by 55 percent. In 1981–1983, government functionaries, students, workers and staff members, and soldiers of the People's Liberation Army planted 47.7 million trees in seven scenic spots, two source areas of water supply, and five dust-storm–affected zones.

A series of measures have also been taken to reduce and control atmospheric pollution—including renovating boilers, using cleaner fuels, promoting central heating, extending the city's greenery, using more closed garbage bins, and improving the management of construction sites. Compared with 1971, the annual consumption of coal in 1983 rose by 3 million tons, but the suspension rate of coal dust in the air did not increase and the sulfur dioxide content in the atmosphere dropped. Thanks to the prevention and treatment of water pollution at the source, the quality of water in Miyun and Guanting reservoirs has met the standards set by the state for drinking water. The quality of water has been improved and the ecological balance restored gradually in the lower reaches of the Wanquan River, the Northern Moat, and the Liangma River, and people are seen angling along the rivers where fish and shrimp had disappeared earlier. By 1983, more than 800 polluting sources had been eliminated or reduced and 322 polluting factories and workshops had been closed. The noise in the thirty-seven major streets of the urban area has been reduced by 1 to 6 decibels owing to the ban on horn blowing of motor vehicles. The amount of organic chlorine pesticide in use dropped from 9,000 tons in 1975 to 1,000 tons in 1983, and use of the pesticide was banned completely in 1984. The city's present annual volume of garbage is about 1.26 million tons. Dustbins and enclosed garbage trucks have gradually been introduced since the early 1970s along with mechanized handling and transportation of garbage. Even so, the city's environmental pollution remains a serious problem.

Apart from the existing renowned parks, gardens, and scenic spots, twenty-five parks and a dozen open spaces have been opened since 1949. The public green space in the city proper and suburbs now amounts to 2,751 hectares—more than triple the figure for the early postliberation days—averaging 5.14 square meters per person as against 3.6 square meters in 1949. More than 1,800 kilometers of roads and riverbanks have been lined with trees, a twentyfold increase over that of 1949. Thirty residential areas have attained garden-type standards and some 150 others have also been greened. In the past thirty-five years, workers, government functionaries, soldiers, and students have planted 4.4 million trees within the compounds of their own units, and the newly planted areas amount to 7,000 hectares. As a result, a number of garden-type factories and government compounds have emerged. The greenery rate has reached 27 percent in the compound of the Capital Iron and Steel Company on Beijing's western outskirts, for example, and its per capita share of green space has reached 32.33 square meters. Today, ninety-four sculptures of educational significance have been erected in the green areas and parks of Beijing. Diverse in national styles, they help make the capital's environment more attractive.

Beijing's General Development Plan

The city of Beijing differs from other Chinese cities in that it is the political and cultural center of the nation. As such, Beijing's urban growth should always take into consideration the city's role as national center. While visitors from other parts of China and abroad must be able to carry out their business with minimum inconvenience, at the same time efforts must be made to raise the working and living conditions of the city's population. Throughout its history, Beijing, as one of the ancient capitals of Chinese civilization, has always been a cultural and educational center. Thus economic development in Beijing must take into consideration the city's political and cultural role. The development of the city's industry will focus mainly on tapping its existing potential and on technological innovation. The growth of heavy industry—especially those demanding large amounts of energy, water, and land, those adding more burden to the city's transportation system, and those posing environmental threats—will be discouraged. Instead, the development of light and clean industries such as food processing and electronics will be promoted. In agricultural development, the city's suburban areas will be gradually built into bases which will enable Beijing to become self-sufficient in such major foods as vegetables, milk, eggs, meat, and fruits.

The population of the city, already too large, must be strictly controlled. To limit its growth, family planning policies will be continued and the policy of population dispersal will be gradually carried out. Construction projects will not be allowed to increase, and construction permits will be granted only to those projects which fit Beijing's existing urban characteristics. The very few projects that will be built will be located in satellite towns in the outer suburbs. Government departments and enterprises in Beijing, both centrally and locally owned, are not encouraged to hire workers and staff from places outside of Beijing, and their demand for personnel will be met locally as much as possible. Moreover, technical staff will be sent to other parts of the country to assist in construction. By the year 2000 the registered population of the municipality is targeted to be around 10 million with 4 million within the city's built-up areas.

Improving the City's Environment and Physical Layout

In order to improve Beijing's environment, work must be done to afforest the mountains and green the land, harness the rivers, and reduce pollution. More than 660,000 hectares of mountain land are expected to be reforested. This project, together with the windbreak forest belts in Bashang of Hebei province and in Inner Mongolia, will form a large windbreak zone along the northern outskirts of Beijing that may help to reduce sandstorms and prevent water loss and soil erosion. Areas of low hills will be converted into orchards. Mountainous areas circling the western, northern, and northeastern outskirts of Beijing will be fringed with forests which, with the development of scenic spots, will form a scenic forest belt. It has been suggested that windbreak forest belts be set up at the three wind gaps of the Yongding River valley, Chaobai River valley, and the open space between Kangzhuang and Nankou. Planners have also considered transforming hills, rivers, lakes, abandoned brick kilns, and sand pits and enlarging old parks and adding new ones to make Beijing a garden city. The renovation of cultural and historical sites is considered to be an important aspect of the expansion and creation of parks. By the year 2000 the forest coverage rate is expected to reach around 28 percent from today's 16.6 percent. Pollution sources are expected to be brought under strict control or eliminated. Garbage removal will be mechanized with the use of refuse trucks and rubbish bins and modern garbage treatment plants. These efforts will turn the capital into one of the cleanest and most beautiful cities in China.

Over the past three decades, planned growth has given Beijing's urban area a clear general layout (Figure 11.8). Future development will follow certain principles: gradually renovating and reconstructing the old city; developing adjacent suburban areas into housing and industrial areas complete with urban facilities and services; and developing the outer suburbs into satellite towns.

Before 1949, Beijing was almost entirely confined to an area which serves as the urban center of the present-day city and which is now known to planners as the "old city." The old city's functions will have to be readjusted as it undergoes renovation to reflect Beijing's role as the nation's political and cultural center.

Development within the city area will be limited to residential dwellings and related services, municipal infrastructure facilities, and a limited number of government offices which cannot be located elsewhere. Other units which either need to be set up or demand space for expansion will all be placed in the outer suburbs. To achieve this goal, the short-term plan will concentrate on major construction projects at Huangcun, Changping, Tongzhen, and Yanshan. While facilities are reorganized in suburban areas around the city proper, residential buildings, shops, schools, cultural and sports facilities, medical centers, and other utilities will be built around industrial districts and other centers of employment. Many such facilities will be set up in the eastern, southeastern, southern, western, northwestern, and northern suburbs, forming a multicentered and self-contained system of settlements, each complete with commercial and service establishments as well as cultural activities. This multicenter pattern will aid in dispersing the population of the old city.

With progress made in the agricultural economy, a considerable number of small market towns with modern facilities will be constructed in the vast rural areas surrounding Beijing. These will serve as local economic and cultural centers and will become an integral part of the urban system in the entire region of Beijing. The present plan calls for the establishment of a network of large, medium, and small cities and towns located around Beijing.

The City Center

The physical structure and architecture of the old city of Beijing are characterized by symmetry with a prominent central axis. Moreover, many buildings, parks, and gardens in the city are very attractive. But

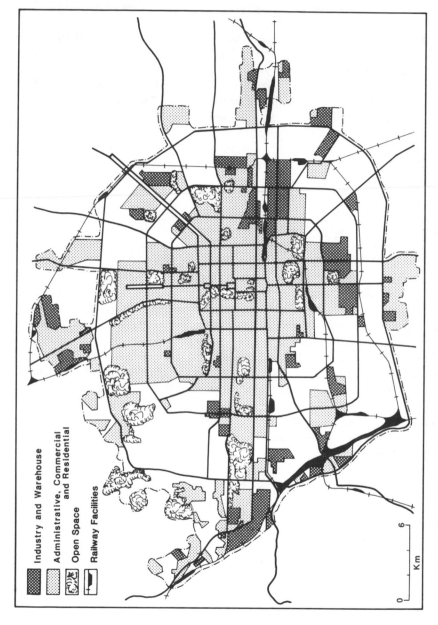

Industry and Warehouse

Administrative, Commercial
and Residential

Open Space

Railway Facilities

Km
0   6

Figure 11.8. Beijing's Master Plan: 1983–2000

as Beijing was built in historic times, its housing conditions as well as urban infrastructure are now quite inadequate. These inherent restrictions make it difficult to meet the demands of the ever increasing population.

Although the old city, which became the center of the capital after liberation, has undergone partial renovation, its general backward appearance still remains. Work must be done to gradually improve the present situation, and certain principles should be followed in doing so. The unique historic flavor of the old city must be retained, carried forward, and developed while attempts should be made to modernize its facilities. Initiative must be encouraged to preserve old traditions while creating a new design suitable for a capital of the socialist era which reflects the great achievements of the nation and the creative power of its people. To fulfill these conditions, ten basic tasks are planned.

First, renovation work on Tiananmen Square and along East and West Chang'an Avenue will continue. Central party and government offices as well as certain major public buildings will be located here. Tiananmen Square will continue to be a solemn and impressive square, and Chang-'an Avenue will serve as a main boulevard in the city's road system.

Second, the second ring road circling the old city will be turned into a parkway planted with trees and grass, thus improving the environmental quality of the areas through which it runs. Areas on both sides of it will be developed into residential districts.

Third, construction is expected to be speeded up in areas of dilapidated housing and in places where water gathers in the rainy season.

Fourth, to reflect Beijing's role as an ancient cultural center, more buildings with traditional Chinese architectural styles will be added to Wusi and Wenjin streets. Liulichang, a street of traditional cultural heritage, will also be renovated and developed.

Fifth, the city's commercial centers at Qianmen, Wangfujing, and Xidan will be further developed and expanded.

Sixth, planners of Beijing have recognized the necessity of preserving the city's cultural relics and historic sites and their surrounding areas. The original Imperial City has been recognized as a high-priority protection district. Areas flanking the city's north–south axis beginning at Qianmen and ending at the second ring road, as well as the areas adjacent to such ancient structures as the Temple of Heaven, Imperial Academy, Confucian Temple, and Lama Temple (Yonghegong), will also be zoned for protection.

Seventh, buildings in the old city will be kept under six stories in height, although a few higher structures may be permitted. In the areas between Xidan/Xisi Street and Dongdan/Dongsi Street, the height limits will be strictly controlled.

Eight, the work of preserving cultural and historic relics will be done in connection with the dredging of Beijing's rivers and lakes and with the expansion of green space and parks. Grass and trees will be planted in areas surrounding Jishuitan, Houhai, and Shichahai to expand the existing green areas. These areas together with Beihai, Zhongnanhai, Jingshan Park, the Palace Museum, Zhongshan Park, and the People's Cultural Palace will form a system of lakes and green space. The northern and southern city moats will be embanked; trees and flowers will be planted along these embankments to form a greenbelt.

Ninth, to improve traffic flow within the old city, some existing roads will be widened and new roads opened to help facilitate north–south and east–west traffic through the city center. To improve the urban environment, underground pipes and cables will have to be renovated, and new ones added. Gradually the city will have to make more use of gas and central heating systems.

Finally, systematic planning and construction will be followed to save time and resources. When old buildings are pulled down and new structures are built, consideration must be given to entire streets, areas, and districts instead of individual structures.

When these ten tasks are accomplished, Beijing will have a neat and orderly appearance. The old as well as the new structures together will give the city a variety of architectural styles. With improvement in the traffic system and municipal facilities, it is expected that the capital will become a clean and efficient urban center.

Improving Housing Conditions

Construction of residential dwellings and service facilities will be expanded. New residential districts will be built close to industrial districts and in areas where government and institutional organizations, universities and colleges, as well as scientific research institutions, are concentrated. This will help save commuting time and also eliminate unnecessary traffic. Facilities to be used for commercial and service trade, for culture and education, and for sports and health purposes will be constructed in the new districts and in the satellite towns in Beijing's outer suburbs.

Expanding Urban Infrastructure

Construction of the city's road system is expected to be speeded up. To facilitate traffic flow in the city center, the master plan calls for a high-speed road system which includes four ring roads, nine major and fourteen subordinate radial roads, and six east–west and three north–south arterial streets.

Improvement in Beijing's railway service will include the renovation of the Xizhimen and Yongdingmen stations, expansion of the Beijing Railway Station, and construction of the West Beijing Railway Station near Lianhuachi in the southwest.

Water is in short supply in Beijing. To make full use of the city's water resources, equal weight will be given to finding new sources of water, protecting existing sources, and minimizing consumption. All of Beijing's water comes from limited sources located within its administrative region. Apart from constructing Zhangfang Reservoir, water conservation represents a major thrust in the city's planning work. Planners would like to see the enactment of water protection codes and the demarcation of water source areas for protection. The city is planning to build large waterworks tapping surface water and to erect several large secondary sewage treatment plants.

In order to reduce air pollution caused by coal burning, gas is expected to become the basic fuel both for residential and for commercial and service uses. Centralized heating systems should be constructed and large boilers used to save heat.

Implementing the General Development Plan

Successful implementation of this general development plan hinges on whether the city's legal and administrative authorities can provide strong support to the city's planners. There is a need to reform the system of capital construction in the city and to produce a detailed plan for the city's future growth. Such a plan should be implemented in stages. Coordinated efforts are required from all institutions, enterprises, and residents in Beijing to transform the capital into a modern socialist metropolis.

12. Migration and Urbanization in India: A Case Study of Delhi

C. S. Yadav

THE magnitude, incidence, and significance of urban population growth in developing nations have evolved as topics of major interest among social scientists during the last three decades. The growth of urban population is due to three factors: natural increase, rural–urban migration, and the reclassification of urban boundaries to include rural hinterland. A recent U.N. report stated that approximately 61 percent of the urban population growth in developing countries is due to natural increase and 39 percent to rural–urban migration.[1] Thus rural–urban migration, one of the most dramatic occurrences of recent decades, has fostered the urbanization of large numbers of peasants.

The growth of literature on rural–urban migration over the last two decades has significantly improved our understanding of the behavior of human movements. A review of the literature demonstrates the complexity of the rural–urban population shift and the challenges associated with its interpretation. These discussions offer differing perspectives on urbanization and migration processes and lead to diverse interpretations of rural–urban migration.[2] They tell us that rural–urban migration is a complex phenomenon and that its incidence and consequences are multidimensional. Bogue and Zachariah contend that rural–urban migration is by far the most important component of the urbanization process and the chief mechanism by which all the world's great urbanization trends have been initiated.[3] It is not merely a mechanical process, however, but is governed by economic, social, and political forces. Nor does rural–urban migration simply imply a redistribution of population from one ecological setting to another. It is also a redistribution of the attitudes, behavior, and customs of the people, a process which has profound effects on the whole spatial patterning of human activity, the repercussions of which may be felt long after the migrations themselves have taken place.

The study of rural–urban migration is a multidisciplinary study. Nevertheless, there are various reasons why geographers in particular devote attention to the study of migration. For one, the territorial redistribution of population is an attractive theme for a spatially oriented discipline. Moreover, geographers are interested in the dynamic aspects of spatial processes and spatial interactions. The following range of questions characterizes the quest of geographers in studying migration: Who migrates? Why does migration occur? What are the patterns of migration? What are the effects of migration on the areas, communities, and societies of destination? The objective of geographers is to evaluate spatial flows with interaction between different places and with areal variations between the places of origin and destination.

Rural–Urban Migration in Delhi

The purpose of this study is to examine the geographical impact of rural–urban migrants in Delhi. In this effort I deal comprehensively with the magnitude, incidence, and process of migration. In particular I examine the way in which a migrant's perceptions affect the decision to migrate. Migrants frequently hold an erroneous view of their environment, and it is this mistaken view which they act upon rather than the objective real-world situation. Normative explanations of migration as a response to economic wage rate fluctuations are only partial generalizations, for they always fail to consider the perceptions prevalent among the potential migrants.[4] This chapter explores the subjective appraisals of migrants whose perceptions of the spatial differentiation of opportunities for different geographic locations offer different levels of potential well-being to various migrants.

It is these perceived differences between places that are important rather than any "push" or "pull" mechanism propounded by economic model-builders. My generalizations are based on the presumption that so long as migrants perceive differences in the utility of places, there is likely to be a greater volume of migration from rural to urban areas. This field of study owes much to behavioral psychology and to the work of Julian Wolpert, of course, who introduced certain behavioral concepts to a wider geographical audience.[5] The behaviorist approach to the process of migration has provided a useful set of concepts, but it has not yet provided a satisfactory set of predictive models. Nevertheless, the analysis of the importance of the individual decision-maker in migration provides satisfactory clues to the understanding of the selectivity of migration.

The Data Set

The present study relies entirely upon field data I collected during 1980–1981. The interpretation is made on the basis of a sample of 1,000 heads of household systematically distributed among the five types of colonies in urban Delhi which receive the largest number of rural migrants: urban villages, squatter settlements, regularized colonies, old resettlement colonies, and new resettlement colonies.

There is an unchecked flow of rural migrants from villages to the small and medium-class towns and from these to metropolitan cities. The migrants have brought with them a variety of intractable problems to cities like Delhi, Bombay, and Calcutta. In Delhi, the problems are unprecedented and pertain to increasing squatter settlements, spiraling land values, speculation on land and rental values, congestion of traffic, shortage of housing, and inadequate basic amenities. Planners now believe that the unabated flow of rural migrants to Delhi frustrates the orderly growth and maintenance of the capital. To manage growth, some of these migrants must be diverted from Delhi to other towns.

Trend of Population Growth

Very few cities in India, or for that matter even in the world, have grown as fast as Delhi.[6] Over a period of seventy years, the population has increased ten times—for example, in 1901 it was 405,000 while in 1971 it was 4,065,000.[7] The bulk of this increase, however, has occurred during the last three decades (Table 12.1). The population of Delhi between 1941 and 1951 recorded the highest increase over the previous census records: 106 percent. This sudden spurt was due primarily to the large-scale migration of population during the partition of India, when Delhi was the destination of innumerable migrants because it provided extraordinary economic possibilities after becoming the capital of independent India. In the subsequent two decades, 1951–1961 and 1961–1971, there was a more or less similar rate of increase (Table 12.1). The primary factors responsible for Delhi's rapid growth of population included a burst of new jobs in government and semigovernment offices and an increasing concentration of the transportation network and wholesale trade and commerce in the city. These forces, coupled with push factors operating in the rural areas, have been responsible for the rising crescendo of in-migration to Delhi, an influx which is damaging its physical, social, and economic environment.

Table 12.1.   Growth of Population in Delhi:
1901-1971

Decade	Population of Urban Delhi	Percentage Increase Over Previous Decade
1901	214,115	—
1911	237,944	11.13
1921	304,420	27.94
1931	447,422	46.98
1941	695,688	55.49
1951	1,437,134	106.58
1961	2,359,408	64.17
1971	3,647,023	54.57

Source: Census of India, Delhi, 1971.

Components of Urban Growth

Migration to Delhi has played a dominant role in accelerating the growth of population in the city. The contribution of net migration to the total population growth of Delhi has always been more than that of natural increase. During the 1961–1971 period the growth of population due to natural increase was 44.62 percent (Table 12.2). The proportional increase due to extension of urban boundaries was only 5.48 percent. The contribution of migration was 49.90 percent. The total migrants counted in 1971 in Delhi were 1,504,286 (Table 12.3). The bulk of migrants to Delhi poured in from four adjoining states: Uttar Pradesh, Haryana, Punjab, and Rajasthan, which together contributed 77.96 percent of the total migrant stream. Uttar Pradesh sends by far the largest contingent of migrants to Delhi, 42.95 percent. Haryana provides 13.98 percent, Punjab 12.92, and Rajasthan 8.11. Migrants from the remaining states of India accounted for only 22.04 percent (Table 12.3).[8] Approximately 150,000 migrants per year pour into Delhi.

Process of Migration

Before we discuss the perceptions of migrants, it is essential to know their premigration social and spatial status. There is enough evidence to prove that migration is a selective process in terms of the demographic characteristics of those who move.

The character of immigrants to Delhi is complex and heterogeneous. They vary, for example, in terms of social experience. Most of the migrants to Delhi belong to the "have not" group—the poorest of all

Table 12.2.   Growth of Delhi's Population Due
             to Various Components: 1961-1971

Component	Absolute Increase	Percentage of Total
Natural Increase	587,878	44.62
Extension of urban boundary	72,278	5.48
Net migration	657,459	49.90
Addition in population	1,317,615	100.00

Source: Town and Country Planning Organization.

Table 12.3.   Migrants in Delhi: 1971

Source Region	No. of Migrants in Delhi	Percentage of Total Migrants
Uttar Pradesh	646,073	42.95
Haryana	210,311	13.98
Punjab	194,403	12.92
Rajasthan	121,951	8.11
Total from four adjoining states	1,172,738	77.96
Total migrants from other states	331,548	22.04
Total migrants from all India	1,504,286	100

Source: Compiled from the Census Records, 1971.

the poor, socially deprived, destitute and economically underemployed, illiterate casual laborers. The largest stream of migrants comprises marginal farmers and sharecroppers (40 percent) who are unable to earn enough to support their families. The other prominent sector of migrants comprises landless laborers (35 percent) and the artisan class (15 percent) such as carpenters, weavers, barbers, potters, cobblers, street sweepers, and manual laborers. Rural migrants are made up primarily of the lowest social classes. Approximately 70 percent of all migrants belong to the scheduled castes and 15 percent to "backward classes." The higher-status migrants constitute a very small proportion.

Migration is a selective process in terms of the demographic characteristics of those who move. In general, the propensity to move is great-est among young adults. This is the most widely demonstrated proposi-tion to emerge from the survey. Broadly speaking, persons aged 15 to 30 predominate and comprise 75 percent of all migrants. The flow of migrants in this age group suggests that there will be social and eco-nomic depression or decline in rural settings.

Males participate more frequently than do females in migration to Delhi, and the difference is pronounced (80 percent males and 20 per-cent females). The differentiation by marital status is also great: Single male adults are more prone to move (60 percent unmarried and 40 per-cent married). And, finally, approximately 65 percent of migrants were illiterate when they left their villages.

All these aspects of the premigration status of migrants clearly reveal that migration from rural areas to the city is highly selective. The most deprived choose to leave the familiar environment of the village. Young unmarried male adults are most mobile.

Ninety percent of the migrants to the unplanned colonies or localities of Delhi come from rural areas, and only 10 percent come from small cities. The regional affinities of the migrants have already been dis-cussed. However, migrant streams from Uttar Pradesh confirm that the majority of migrants come from the districts which are close to Delhi, from the most economically backward districts, from districts where natural calamities (such as floods and droughts) occur frequently, and from districts where there is agricultural stagnation.

The study of sources of migration confirms that there is a relationship between migration and distance. A change of residence necessarily involves spatial considerations and cost of transportation. The study of Delhi supports one of the most familiar "laws" of migration pro-pounded by Ravenstein: The great body of migrants journey a short distance.[9] As a corollary, the longer the distance of migration, the less the number of people migrating. The study of Delhi supports the con-cept that poor migrants travel short distances or to places which mini-mize the cost of transportation. Those with higher incomes move a greater distance to look for desirable jobs or opportunities, while poor migrants move to nearby locations for less desirable opportunities. Thus distance is a critical factor. Delhi recruits more of its migrants from the nearby hinterland than from the remote areas because short journeys are much simpler and less costly than long ones. Clearly, the nearer areas are likely to have experienced an early and faster rate of economic development and their people tend to have greater contacts and hold a better image of the opportunities available in the city.

Thus the process of migration brings in its wake much more than mere population redistribution. It also leads to a redistribution of social and cultural attributes from rural areas to the city—age, sex, family status, occupation, educational attainment—which ultimately results in a spatial structure neither rural nor urban.

Process of Decision Making

In studies of migration, the accent has generally been placed on dissatisfaction with one's social and economic environment. From the survey of Delhi, it is obvious that a majority of migrants (80 percent) were initially dissatisfied with the conditions prevalent in their villages, including insufficient food, shelter, and clothing (Table 12.4). Approximately 40 percent of the respondents revealed that they were seasonal laborers, so it was difficult for them to earn enough money to support a family. Seventy percent of the respondents were worried about repaying debts to moneylenders. Seventy-five percent were dissatisfied because they were landless laborers. Sixty-five percent reported low wages as the cause of dissatisfaction. Fragmentation of landholdings caused dissatisfaction in the minds of 42 percent. The other reasons for dissatisfaction (Table 12.4) were lack of medical facilities (20 percent), harassment by upper-caste people (21 percent), crop failure (13 percent), insecurity (17 percent), fear of famine and drought (20 percent), and unemployment (30 percent).

The decision to migrate involves a change in place of employment

Table 12.4.   Dissatisfaction with Native Place

Reason for Dissatisfaction	Composite Percentage of Respondents
Insufficient food, shelter, clothing	80
Seasonal employment	40
Caste discrimination	45
Indebtness	70
No medical facilities	20
No land to cultivate	75
Low wages	65
Large family	35
Division of land	42
Crop failure	13
Fear of dacoits	17
Flooding	14
Drought/famine	9
Unemployment	38
Insufficient price for goods	11

Source: Compiled from Field Survey, 1980-1981.

Table 12.5.   Source of Motivation for Migration

Source of Motivation	Percentage of Respondents
Family members	25
Villagers	15
Friends	10
Relatives	18
Agents	10
Voluntary	20
No response	2
Total	100

Source: Compiled from Field Survey, 1980-1981.

and residence. Thus migrants take the decision very seriously. In rural communities, there is a customary resistance against mobility. If migration does occur, kinship plays an important role in guiding the decision-maker. The source of information about the job opportunities prior to migration is a significant contributing factor. Such information may take the form of recollection of personal visits, letters from past migrants, conversation with friends who have visited other places, or books, newspapers, and broadcasts. The informal system of information is more operative, however (Table 12.5). This flow of information enables migrants to develop a good idea of the destination. The migrants were not only motivated; they were also provided financial help in their move and their search for jobs and housing by relatives already living in the city. About 60 percent received such financial help; of these, 90 percent received help from relatives and 10 percent from contractors.

The causes and motivations of migration of the rural poor to Delhi may be many, but six reasons predominate: perceived employment opportunities in the city, dissatisfaction of laborers in their native place, encouragement by relatives in the city, offers of employment by professional contractors, long-standing social injustices suffered in "backward" rural communities, and aspirations for a better life in the city.

Mode and Patterns of Migration

The rural migrants in Delhi come from all areas. They leave their villages because there are very few opportunities there. The patterns of migration vary not only between communities but also over time. Any argument that either step or chain or circular migration represents the correct model is clearly misconceived. A hypothetical example may clarify this point. It is customary in India for a weekly market to be organized where villagers from nearby areas gather. Most of the stalls in these markets are run by artisans who were the first emigrants to go to the nearby towns. They returned after a few months to continue their traditional mode of life. Thus a pattern of circular or seasonal migration is established. Some of these artisans, however, instead of returning home, ventured further afield and eventually reached the capital city. These men have experienced step migration. Of these, a few succeeded and reports of their good fortune drifted back to the village, encouraging others to come to the city directly. Gradually the link between village and city intensifies. As the new arrivals seek better living in the city, they encourage their kin to follow them and the chain movement increases by geometric progression.

The survey of Delhi's rural migrants demonstrates that cityward migration involves a series of spatial movements. There are various escape routes adopted by migrants (Figure 12.1). Often their journey to Delhi is not straight from their village; for some, indeed, Delhi is the last stage. Many wander from one city to another led by the pressure of events. This is step migration. A step migration is postulated when the migrants successively move from village to small towns and then to provincial towns and thence to the capital city. The survey of Delhi confirms that approximately 55 percent of the migrants experienced this process.

A substantial number of migrants (40 percent) have experienced a process of chain migration. The chain process postulates the integration of rural communities and urban communities. Relatives and friends who had migrated earlier and established themselves in the city stimulate others to come to the city. These new aspirants, who are torn rapidly away from the traditional cultural framework of their lives, find themselves thrown too quickly as strangers into a cultural environment which is unfamiliar and thus the danger of disorganization is great. The newcomers to the city treat the immigrant community as the beachhead from which they advance with strength and establish themselves. This explains why new migrants tend to go to the same places where earlier migrants live.

Ninety percent of the migrants in the survey spent some period of their lives in the city, returned home, and, perhaps after a further period, returned to the city. The artisans or traders always seek expansion of their activity into a larger and wealthier community. They set off tentatively to try their luck. If successful, they will stay in the city; if they fail to establish themselves, they will try again, later, in some other place, thus becoming circular migrants. The movement to cities by migrants from rural areas, who return to the rural areas at certain intervals, is a paramount factor in the urbanization of rural folk.

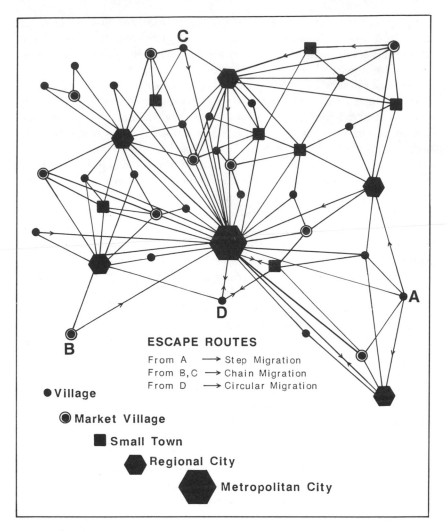

Figure 12.1. Patterns of Migration

Preference for Delhi

The migrant's choice of city is based entirely on the individual's evaluation of anticipated utility, which is derived from information flows.
Thus a large number of prospective migrants have selected Delhi as
their destination. Before making a final decision, migrants go through a
complex process of decision making. Initially, potential migrants gather
precise knowledge about job opportunities, places to stay, and financial
support needed at the destination. In this process, they are helped by

Table 12.6.   Reasons Migrants Prefer Delhi as
              Their Destination

Reasons for Preference	Composite Percentage
Better opportunities in Delhi	62.2
Nearest place from village	8.3
Glamour of city	2.2
Relatives or friends in Delhi	22.8
Higher wages	26.5

Source: Compiled from Field Survey, 1980-1981.

relatives who have already migrated to Delhi. It is their links with fellow migrants and their perception of Delhi as a convenient center of job opportunities that attracts them to select Delhi as their destination. Some 62.2 percent of the migrants chose Delhi as a place of migration because of better job opportunities (Table 12.6). Approximately 26 percent prefer Delhi because of the higher wages offered. A very large section of migrants (23 percent) consider the presence of their relatives as an additional reason for migrating to Delhi.

Migrant Adjustment to City Life

Adjustment of rural migrants to urban life takes many forms. Physically, adjustment is a search for shelter and jobs through assimilation into the complex system of the city. Economically, the migrants must adjust to changed occupation and rhythm of work. Culturally, they undergo a revolution in motivation, values, and ideology. While busy with these activities, the migrants shape the culture of the city as much as they adjust to it. Their action is neither traditional nor citylike. They are ruralizing the culture of Delhi. Many aspects—such as duration of stay, occupational mobility, links with the native place, remittances sent to the native place, desirability of keeping contacts with the native place, comparison of city life with village life, and attitude toward city life—reflect how migrants adjust to the city.

The enormous expansion of Delhi through the construction of houses and roads, and development of commerce and industry, provides a wide range of job opportunities for migrants. Most are engaged in unskilled low-paid jobs, so their status in the city remains marginal. The classification of migrants in various jobs is given in Table 12.7. A relatively low proportion (8.3 percent) is engaged in industrial establishments. Workers in traditional trades constitute only 11.5 percent. The other sectors of employment for these migrants are semiprofessional and petty

Table 12.7. Occupational Status of Migrants in Delhi

Occupation	Percentage of Respondents
Hawkers and vendors	12.2
Construction laborers	39.8
Loading and unloading	0.2
Household workers	5.2
Laborers in industrial and commercial establishment	8.3
Workers in traditional trade	11.5
Semiprofessional workers	5.7
Petty shopkeeper	9.1
Others	8.0
Total	100.0

Source: Compiled from Field Survey, 1980-1981.

Table 12.8. Duration of Employment for Migrants

Duration of Employment	Wages	Percentage of Respondents
10 days a month	Rs. 150	8.5
15 days a month	Rs. 225	15.8
20 days a month	Rs. 300	12.7
25 days a month	Rs. 375	40.2
Full month but semipermanent	Rs. 400	22.8

Source: Compiled from Field Survey, 1980-1981.

trades. The survey shows that about 37 percent of the migrants are casual laborers, whereas 52 percent are semipermanent. Only 23 percent are permanently engaged (Table 12.8). The low monthly wages earned by these workers confirm them as marginal workers who cannot earn enough to support themselves from their wages.

When migrants enter the city, their immediate task is to seek shelter which normally they share in their initial stage with their host. Nearly 80 percent of migrants sought assistance from relatives during this transitional period. Seventy percent of migrants live in groups of four or five persons, usually in one-room accommodations devoid of basic amenities. Often low-paid laborers select accommodations which are even cheaper and less desirable.

Process of Stabilization

Migrants are active participants in the development of the city. They serve the city by rendering various services; they are the source of cheap labor which is essential for the city's efficient functioning. In fact, they are essential for the survival of its more affluent segments.

The rural migrants adopt different mechanisms to cope with urban life. Earlier arrivals provide assistance to later ones in finding jobs and shelter. Information links with senior migrants play an important role in the socialization, stabilization, and acculturation of migrants in the city. In the process of stabilization the affinity for the village seems to be weakening even though these migrants visit their native place, send remittances, and retain property and kinship there.

Migrants keep close contact with kin and family members in the village. Frequency of visits to the home village is one measure of the strength of ties with native communities. The migrants report that on average they visit their villages twice a year. In general, these visits are made on the occasion of important festivals and social ceremonies or in connection with the management of their property.

Village residents usually visit their kin in the city. In Delhi about 60 percent of the migrants received visitors in the year previous to the survey. Some of these visitors came to see family members; others came to explore chances of migration at some future date. Approximately 40 percent of migrants also keep a close link with their native place by sending remittances.

Upon leaving their native place, migrants face a transition in which there is loss of one context and gradual acceptance of the other. The poor migrants of Delhi have documented the complex emotional problems involved in such a transition. The obvious question is: Have they left behind the old and prepared themselves for assimilation into the new? A large majority of migrants (70 percent) have decided to settle permanently in Delhi. The longer the stay, the stronger the migrant's desire to live permanently in the city.

In effect, to make a clear distinction between the perceived and objective environment it is essential to discover how migrants react to their immediate surroundings. In the sample survey, respondents were asked to describe the prevailing living conditions in their own locality. This question is designed to reveal how rural migrants perceive their own environment and how they evaluate living conditions in their own localities.

Only 20 percent described their localities as poor whereas 60 percent regarded their localities as either good or satisfactory. The analysis emphasizes that nearly 78 percent of migrants to Delhi feel quite satisfied there and have no sense of disappointment and dejection (Table 12.9). Indeed, the migrants to Delhi show a high degree of adjustment to a difficult environment.

Some migrants, however, feel dissatisfied with Delhi in several ways.

Table 12.9.   Reasons for Satisfaction with Delhi

Reason for Satisfaction	Composite Percentage Satisfied
Good transportation	93.4
Good water	55.0
Good electricity	74.5
Own a house	88.2
Low rent	41.0
School facilities for children	65.0
Market facilities	82.0
Closer to kin	87.0
Living for long time	42.0
No interference in life-style	78.0
No sense of dejection	78.0
Better job opportunities	90.0
Higher wages	87.0
Better social status	60.0

Source: Compiled from Field Survey, 1980-1981.

Table 12.10.   Reasons for Dissatisfaction with Delhi

Reason for Dissatisfaction	Composite Percentage Dissatisfied
House far from workplace	80.0
Congestion	20.0
Lack of sanitation	60.0
High prices in market	77.0
Administrators ignore our conditions	40.0
Conditions in Delhi favor affluent sector of city	30.0
No response	10.0

Source: Compiled from Field Survey, 1980-1981.

These migrants reported that their main resentment is that they live too far from their place of work. The migrants are also aware of the prevailing congestion and poor sanitation (Table 12.10) in the city. Most of the migrants found Delhi a costly place. Fully 30 percent saw Delhi as a city meant for an affluent society. They also feel that planners and administrators do not pay attention to their problems.

The magnitude of migration in Delhi, the process of migration, the patterns and their links with Delhi—all point to the prospect that for some decades large-scale migration will be inevitable. The study of migration to Delhi confirms Rondinelli's concept that rural-to-urban migration patterns have tended to reinforce the growth and dominance of primate cities in India.[10] India is overurbanized and its primate cities are manifestations of a pseudo-urbanization which relies primarily upon tertiary-sector activities rather than on productive economic activities. Moreover, migration from rural areas, which is frequently considered an evil of urbanization, is not itself necessarily bad. In fact, rural–urban migration is an essential condition of both rural and urban development and can be a sign of healthy economic change. A certain level of rural-to-urban migration is inevitable and must be accommodated in the cities. However, as may be the case in Delhi, unabated streams of migration, combined with a high rate of population increase in both rural and urban areas, have led India to search for an urbanization policy which will lower overall population growth rates and migration. If no solution is found for the unguided flow of migrants, administrators and planners will face a difficult task because these unabated streams will simply add to existing problems. The remedy lies with policies for urban unemployment, dispersed urbanization, and housing.

Policies to Deal with Urban Problems

The most obvious means for dealing with urban unemployment is to fix minimum wages for casual laborers. The government can help by providing wage subsidies to urban employees and by encouraging and subsidizing industrial investment to expand urban employment. Another effective means lies in government restriction of rural–urban migration and the establishment of government-run labor exchanges in which job openings in urban centers are matched with an equal number of workers permitted to migrate to cities to fill those jobs.

The most promising policy seems to be dispersed urbanization and population planning, which will aim at lowering overall population growth rates. Measures should be taken to increase the productive capacity of rural areas by encouraging the growth of market centers, small cities, and regional urban centers. In India, this policy is feasible because there is an articulated national spatial hierarchy of urban centers (Figure 12.1).

Since planners and administrators have failed to strengthen the economies and promote the growth of secondary cities, rural migrants have nowhere to go for better economic opportunities but to already overcrowded primate cities. Thus Delhi is receiving large numbers of migrants and is unable to absorb additional migrants. A crisis has arisen. If government would provide better infrastructure to already existing intermediate and small towns in the vicinity of Delhi, migrants will move toward smaller towns and medium-size cities. This study of Delhi supports the contention that rural people always move to places offering a wide variety of services, facilities, and potential employment.

If intermediate cities and small towns around Delhi are provided with these facilities, they will stimulate the economies of surrounding rural areas and help curb migration to Delhi—and the backward regions will receive the benefits of economic growth. The growth of secondary cities will alter the overall patterns of rural–urban migration to Delhi.

Another strategy that can check rural–urban migration is to foster a comprehensive national development plan which will involve an integrated urban and rural development strategy. Plans should be prepared to make rural life productive and attractive. All efforts should be made to provide better facilities to villagers. In order for laborers to get higher wages, they could be absorbed in such developments as construction of roads. So long as there is a wide gap between the development of cities and villages, the rural–urban migration will continue.

A large proportion of migrants to Delhi live in slums and squatter settlements. The slums are "transitional" settlements in the sense that their inhabitants are undergoing a social and economic change from rural to urban life. This transition, however, is associated with much human deprivation. In the process of searching for jobs and basic shelter, many marginal rural migrants occupy public and private land and build slum settlements or housing composed of makeshift substandard material in areas devoid of basic amenities. Urban housing policies should be based on the economic needs of the poor migrants.[11] The essence of these policies is that they emphasize help to the migrants rather than offering complete solutions. They emphasize housing services rather than public housing and a gradual rather than a precipitate approach.[12]

A solution of the housing problem can be advanced on the basis of the following strategies. The first step is to ensure security of land tenure and eliminate the threat of eviction—as was done in Delhi in 1976, when migrants were given land titles in resettlement colonies. Second, government can encourage self-help construction of houses by poor migrants through assistance in management, design, and execution. In this way house construction will require less capital, create valuable skills, and encourage community cooperation.[13] The proper role of the government is to ensure that those who are best able to build, either for themselves or for their neighbor, have access to the tools, materials, and basic resources for the job.

Conclusion

Rural–urban migration has been one of the most dramatic occurrences of recent decades and has urbanized large numbers of peasants. The process of urbanization in India is slow and concentrated. Primate cities receive most migrants. In Delhi, 150,000 migrants are pouring in each year. They have seriously impaired the city's physical, social, and economic environment. A close view of rural–urban migration in Delhi provides a useful perspective on the process as a whole. Theoretically rural–urban migration is not a shift of a random segment of the population but a deliberate move of certain people with certain characteristics; the social, economic, and demographic elements of both the sending and the receiving societies are affected. This mechanism should lead to a regional balance in terms of distribution of income and labor. In reality, however, this does not happen because rural migration creates underemployment in the city and the selective out-migration of the labor force hampers the development of rural areas.

The migration of poor laborers into Delhi is selective in terms of sex, age, education, and social status. The largest number of migrants constitute marginal farmers, casual laborers, people of low social status. Young males predominate. Delhi receives migrants from four neighboring states. Each migrant brings with him certain attributes—for example, age, sex, family status, occupation, educational status, regional origins, attitudes, customs, and behavior. Thus migration also leads to a redistribution of these attributes from rural areas to the city.

The decision to migrate demonstrates a conscious desire among migrants for economic and social betterment. They seek better jobs, higher income, and less social discrimination. The migrants possess a dual outlook which is neither completely traditional nor completely urban. It is transitional.

An integrated plan of rural and city development, guided migration, and population planning may help to redirect the streams of migration from primate to other cities. So long as migrants perceive better job opportunities in cities, they will migrate. Hence migration is inevitable. To slow down the rate of migration, efforts are needed to develop rural areas with job opportunities and satisfactory services and amenities.[14]

NOTES

1. U.N. Population Division, *Patterns of Urban and Rural Growth* (New York: Department of Economic and Social Affairs, 1980).

2. Lawrence Brown and David B. Longbrake, "Migration Flows in Intra Urban Space: Place Utility Considerations," *Annals of the Association of American Geographers* 60 (1970): 368–389; Richard J. Cebulla and Richard K. Vedder, "A Note on Migration, Economic Opportunity and the Quality of Life," *Journal of the Regional Science Association* 13 (1973): 205–211.

3. D. J. Bogue and K. C. Zachariah, "Urbanization and Migration in

India," in Roy Turner (ed.), *India's Urban Future* (Oxford: Oxford University Press, 1962), p. 27.

4. Paul White and Robert Woods (eds.), *The Geographical Impact of Migration* (New York: Longmans, 1980).

5. Julian Wolpert, "Behavioral Aspects of the Decision to Migrate," *Papers of the Regional Science Association* 15 (1965): 159–169.

6. Town and Country Planning Organization, *National Capital Regional Plan Summary and Recommendation* (Delhi: Town and Country Planning Organization, 1962).

7. *Census of India* (Delhi, 1971).

8. Ibid.

9. E. G. Ravenstein, "The Laws of Migration," *Journal of the Royal Statistical Society* 48 (1885): 167–227.

10. Dennis A. Rondinelli, "Balanced Urbanization, Spatial Integration and Economic Development in Asia," *Urbanism Past and Present* 9 (Winter 1979–1980): 20.

11. White and Woods, *Geographical Impact of Migration.*

12. United Nations, *Report on Habitat: United Nations Conference on Human Settlements, Vancouver, 31 May–11 June 1976* (New York: United Nations, 1976).

13. Samuel Avoni, "Housing Policies: A Development World Perspective," *Housing Science* 2 (4) (1978): 299–334.

14. J. F. C. Turner, "Approaches to Government-Sponsored Housing," *Ekistics* 41 (242) (January 1976): 4–7; J. F. C. Turner and R. Fitcher (eds.), *Freedom to Build* (New York: Macmillan, 1972); J. F. C. Turner, "A New Universe of Squatter Builders," *UNESCO Courier* (Paris), June 1976, pp. 12–33.

13. India's North–South and Rural–Urban Correlates for Urbanization

ASHOK K. DUTT, CHARLES B. MONROE, AND JASMINE IRANI

THE concept of north versus south in regional economic development has been studied for many nations of the world, including a number of works focusing on north/south differences in development in the United States, Italy, and Britain. In India, however, many studies have analyzed urbanization and economic development, but none has focused on differences between the North and South regions. This study analyzes the correlation between urbanization and occupational and social variables, comparing results between the North and South regions of India. The 1981 census data at the district level were used for the study.

Historical Development of North and South

In India, North–South regional variation is more a sociocultural phenomenon than an economic one. Historical differences do exist between the North and South regions in language, customs, racial and cultural heritage, caste, and structural and behavioral aspects.[1] The Tamil Plains, the heart of South Indian culture, were never controlled by the North; similarly, no southern kingdom penetrated northward into the Ganges Plain.

The historical evolution of North India has differed greatly from that of the South. While the South has enjoyed relative tranquility throughout much of its history, North India has been subjected to a series of foreign invasions, often on a grand scale such as the various Muslim invasions. As a result of these events, the administrative structure of North India was repeatedly destroyed, its society often deprived of leadership, and its religious faith shaken. Unlike the North, southern India enjoyed an almost uninterrupted series of Hindu kingdoms.

The British rule imposed on India in the eighteenth century eventually was accompanied by Western secular education which provided the training for Indian elites. These elites migrated to urban centers for employment in educational, professional, administrative, and commercial activities and thus became divorced from the rural masses. Hence the polarization between the rural people and the urban elites, already deeply rooted in North Indian society, was further accentuated during British rule.

Factors Determining Urbanization

Numerous studies have established the correlates of urbanization.[2] Most such studies have used aggregate data at the national, state, or city level without focusing on overall North–South regional patterns.[3] They have shown significant relationships between occupation and the degree of urbanization at the national level. The fact that cultivation of land is a rural activity and a high percentage of individuals are dependent on agriculture has been repeatedly documented.[4] It has also been shown that the proportion of gainfully employed population in agricultural occupations declines progressively in urban areas.[5]

The urban occupational structure is as closely related to manufacturing and service as the rural function is to cultivation and agriculture.[6] Contrary to expectation, though, Bose found no association between overall level of urbanization and the level of industrialization in the economy.[7] Sovani, however, found that people employed in nonagricultural pursuits have a positive correlation with urbanization—that is, the higher the nonagricultural employment, the higher the urbanization.[8] The level of literacy was also found to be closely related to urban development.[9] A high literacy rate correlates strongly with a high degree of modernization in agriculture.

This study examines occupational and social patterns based on the distribution of rural, urban, and intermediate population at the district level for the North and South macroregions of India. The Planning Committee of India has divided India into five main regions: North, South, East, West, and Northeast. On the basis of this division, the two macroregions of North and South India are studied. The North includes the states of Rajasthan, Punjab, Himachal Pradesh, Haryana, Uttar Pradesh, and the union territories of Delhi and Chandigarh. The South includes the states of Karnataka, Andhra Pradesh, Kerala, Tamil Nadu, and the territories of Andaman and Nicobar islands, Lakshadweep, Minicoy, and Amindivi islands, and Pondicherry.

The 1981 census defines urban areas in the following way: all places with a municipality, corporation, cantonment board, or a notified town area committee; and all other places with a minimum population of 5,000 (of which at least 75 percent of the working male population is engaged in nonagricultural activities) and a minimal population density of 400 persons per square kilometer. The urban classification also includes other areas such as major development-project colonies, intensive industrial zones, and important tourist sites.

Methodology

In total, 174 districts from the North and South regions were studied. The state of Jammu and Kashmir was excluded as the data were not available. Districts were classified into one of three categories based on the degree of urbanization. Because the average urbanization of India was 23.7 percent in 1981, districts with an urban proportion of less than 0.5 standard deviation below this mean (16 percent) were defined as rural. Districts with greater than 0.5 standard deviation above the mean (32 percent) were defined as urban. Districts with urban proportions between 17 and 31 percent were called intermediate (Figure 13.1). Using this classification, the North has a total of 100 districts of which 18 are urban, 40 intermediate, and 42 rural. The South has 74 districts of which 16 are urban, 76 intermediate, and 22 rural.

The percentage of workers engaged at the district level in five occupations (cultivators, agricultural laborers, household industry workers, other workers, and marginal workers), as well as the percentage of nonworkers, literacy rate, population density, and male/female ratio are the census data used for the study. All variables (except the last two) are further disaggregated by sex into male, female, and total components. Mean values of the occupational and demographic variables were calculated for each of the categories of districts (urban, intermediate, and rural). Relationships among the relative sizes of work force and demographic variables among the three urbanization categories are displayed graphically with bar charts and analyzed statistically using the t test. Moreover, Pearson's correlation is used to determine the relationship between the percentage of urban population and each of the twenty-three occupational and demographic variables (Table 13.1). The correlation was also tested for statistical significance. Further, t values were computed for the North and South regions to determine the significance and direction of the variables (Table 13.2).

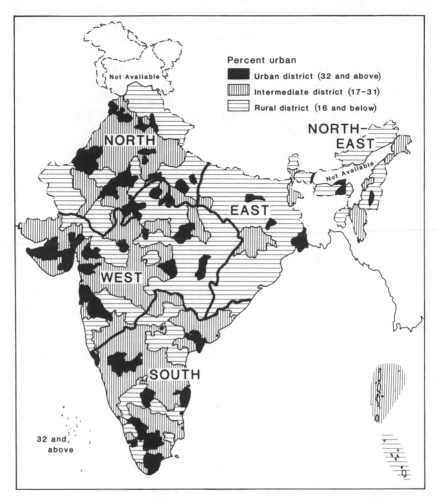

Figure 13.1. Classification of Rural and Urban Districts in India: 1981

Correlates of Urbanization

Cultivators

In the northern districts, male cultivators form a higher percentage of their working population than female cultivators do of their working population in all three categories: urban, intermediate, and rural (Figure 13.2*a*). Comparatively, the southern districts have a significantly lower percentage of male and female cultivators than the North in all the categories. In the South, male cultivators represent a higher percentage of their working population than female cultivators in the rural

Table 13.1. Pearson's Correlation Between Urbanization and Occupational
and Demographic Variables for North and South India

	Dependent Variable			
	Urbanization (Urban Population as Percentage of Total Population)			
	North		South	
Variable	Pearson's Correlation	Signifi- cance	Pearson's Correlation	Signifi- cance
Literacy				
Total literates as % of total literate population	0.4043	0*	0.2632	0.012**
Male literates as % of total male population	0.2643	0.004**	0.3044	0.004**
Female literates as % of total female population	0.4635	0*	0.2186	0.031**
Cultivators				
Total cultivators as % of total working population	-0.0668	0.254***	-0.2170	0.032***
Male cultivators as % of male working population	-0.0158	0.438***	-0.2159	0.032**
Female cultivators as % of female working population	-0.2316	0.010**	-0.1837	0.059***
Agricultural laborers				
Agricultural laborers as % of total working population	0.2233	0.013**	-0.1591	0.088***
Male agricultural laborers as % of male working population	0.2258	0.012**	-0.1541	0.095***
Female agricultural laborers as % of female working population	0.0355	0.363***	-0.1556	0.093***
Household industry workers				
People engaged in household industry as % of total working population	0.5512	0*	0.0527	0.328***
Males engaged in household industry as % of male working population	0.5573	0*	0.0716	0.274***
Females engaged in household industry as % of female working population	0.3926	0*	0.0235	0.421***

Table 13.1 (continued)

	Dependent Variable			
	Urbanization (Urban Population as Percentage of Total Population)			
	North		South	
Variable	Pearson's Correlation	Signifi- cance	Pearson's Correlation	Signifi- cance
Other workers				
Other workers as % of total working population	0.6920	0*	0.6438	0*
Other male workers as % of male working population	0.5944	0*	0.6572	0*
Other female workers as % of female working population	0.6698	0*	0.4800	0*
Marginal workers				
Total marginal workers as % of total working population	-0.0873	0.194***	-0.1501	0.101***
Male marginal laborers as % of male working population	-0.1688	0.047**	-0.0431	0.358***
Female marginal laborers as % of female working population	-0.1561	0.060***	-0.1966	0.047**
Nonworkers				
Total nonworkers as % of total population	0.5295	0*	0.3170	0.003**
Male nonworkers as % of male population	0.5296	0*	0.3029	0.004**
Female nonworkers as % of female population	0.5275	0*	0.3237	0.002**
Density				
Density of population/sq km	0.7701	0*	0.6992	0*
Male/female ratio				
Females/1000 males	-0.4587	0*	-0.3140	0.003**

Source: Computed by authors.

  * Highly significant.
  ** Significant.
*** Not significant.

and urban categories, but in the intermediate category the females form a higher proportion than males.

The percentage of male cultivators in the North and female cultivators in the South declines from rural to intermediate to urban categories respectively. However, the intermediate districts have a lower percentage of cultivators than either the rural or urban districts. This anomaly may be attributed to relatively greater female participation in the labor force in the South compared to the North.

Because cultivators are involved with tilling, sowing, harvesting, and processing of crops, they are essentially rural residents. Consequently, the number of cultivators should have a negative correlation with urbanization. This holds for both North and South India, although the correlation is not significant in the South (Table 13.1). In the North, female cultivators are a better indicator of urbanization than male cultivators; that is, an absence of female cultivators indicates a higher level of urbanization.

Agricultural Laborers

As shown in Figure 13.2*b*, the South has relatively more agricultural laborers than the North in each of the rural, intermediate, and urban categories. This relationship is especially strong for females in the South, reflecting a far greater female labor participation in this region compared to the North. Female agricultural laborers in the South constitute a higher percentage of the work force in all the categories compared to northern male and female agricultural laborers, as well as the southern male agricultural laborers in all the categories. In the North, the percentage of male agricultural laborers is slightly higher than the percentage of female agricultural laborers in all the categories. In general, the percentage of agricultural laborers is higher in the intermediate category for both males and females in the North as well as the South. This proportion is much higher for males in the North, however, which may reflect the migration of male agricultural laborers into the Green Revolution areas of the North. These migrants come primarily from the East region.

Although agricultural laborers are assumed to be a rural group, Pearson's correlation indicates the opposite (Table 13.1). The percentage of agricultural laborers has a positive correlation with urbanization in the North and an insignificant negative correlation in the South. In the North, male agricultural laborers are more strongly associated with urbanization than are female agricultural laborers, which is also seen in the results of the *t* test (Table 13.2).

Table 13.2. t̲ Test Showing Differences Between Occupational and
            Demographic Variables for India's Urban Districts
            by North and South Regions: 1981

Rank	Variable
1	Male cultivators as % of male working population
2	Female cultivators as % of female working population
3	Male agriculture laborers as % of male working population
4	Female agriculture laborers as % of female working population
5	Males engaged in household industry as % of male working population
6	Females engaged in household industry as % of female working population
7	Other male workers as % of male working population
8	Other female workers as % of female working population
9	Male marginal labor as % of male working population
10	Female marginal labor as % of female working population
11	Male nonworkers as % of male population
12	Female nonworkers as % of female population
13	Male literates as % of male population
14	Female literates as % of female population
15	Density of population/sq km
16	Females/1000 males

Source: Computed by authors.

  * Highly significant ($p < 0.001$).
 ** Significant ($0.001 < p < 0.05$).
*** Not significant ($p > 0.05$).

Household Industry Workers

The percentage of male and female household industry workers shows
that this group forms a lower proportion of the work force (Figure
13.3*a*). Also, the percentage of people engaged in household industries
increased with urbanization in the North, but in the South the intermediate category has a higher concentration of household workers than the
urban or rural categories. Activities such as weaving, country cigarette
(bidi) making, and pottery could possibly engage substantial numbers of
the work force in the intermediate districts of the South.

Workers engaged in household industries are either self-employed or
employed by others in small industrial operations. Although the handi-
craft-oriented household workers are found in rural and urban areas,
the small industrial operations are essentially urban. Household workers have a positive correlation with urbanization in the North and the
South, but the correlation is not significant in the South (Table 13.1). In
the North, male household industry correlates more strongly with urbanization than does female household industry. Correlations between
male and female household workers and urbanization in the South are

	North			South	
Direction	t Value	Significance	Direction	t Value	Significance
Rural	8.41	0*	Rural	3.76	0.001**
Rural	3.34	0.001**	Rural	2.04	0.048**
Urban	-2.64	0.011**	Rural	1.35	0.187***
Urban	-1.63	0.107***	Rural	0.40	0.691***
Urban	-5.71	0*	Urban	-0.02	0.988***
Urban	-1.37	0.176***	Urban	-0.98	0.332***
Urban	-6.22	0*	Urban	-4.36	0*
Urban	-5.96	0*	Urban	-2.18	0.036**
Rural	1.49	0.143***	Rural	1.41	0.167***
Rural	1.61	0.113***	Rural	2.07	0.045**
Urban	-2.26	0.027**	Urban	-0.94	0.354***
Urban	-3.48	0.001**	Urban	-1.72	0.094***
Urban	-2.36	0.021**	Urban	-2.00	0.053***
Urvan	-3.43	0.001**	Urban	-1.18	0.248***
Urban	-3.37	0.001**	Urban	-1.68	0.102***
Rural	3.53	0.001**	Rural	1.77	0.086***

not significant. (Again these findings are corroborated by the *t*-test results in Table 13.2.)

Other Workers

"Other workers" is the category containing essentially a combination of manufacturing and service sectors. As expected, urban districts have a higher concentration of both male and female other workers than do the rural and intermediate districts in the North (Figure 13.3*b*). In the South, for both the male and the female subgroups, the urban districts have the highest percentage of their total workers in the other worker class, followed by the rural districts and then the intermediate districts. Such an anomaly needs more research for explanation.

Other workers have the highest positive correlation with urbanization in both the North and the South (Table 13.1). Economic development almost invariably results in an accentuation of the process of urbanization and implies a change in the occupational structure of the work force in favor of nonagricultural activities. In the North, female other workers have a higher positive correlation with urbanization than male other

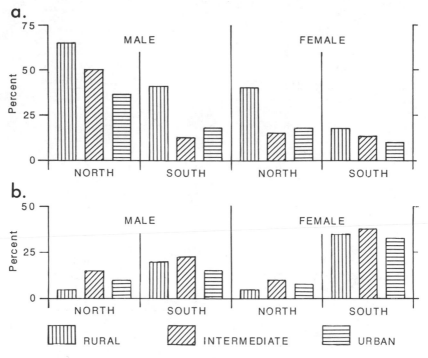

Figure 13.2. Percentage of Total Work Force: *a,* Cultivators; *b,* Agricultural Workers

workers. In the South, the opposite is true: Other male workers have a higher positive correlation with urbanization than other female workers. The *t* values, though significantly larger in the urban direction, show males with a slightly higher statistical significance than the females, both for North and South (Table 13.2).

Marginal Workers

The percentage of female marginal workers (Figure 13.3*c*) in the North in all the categories forms the highest concentration compared to the South's percentage of male and female marginal workers in all the categories. The general trend seems to be greater for female marginal workers than for male marginal workers as a percentage of their respective work forces in both North and South in the categories. A very large component of the North's female labor force in the marginal group indicates this region's general reluctance to use females in regular productive work. Those females who desire to supplement their family income end up being casual or part-time workers for whom greater opportuni-

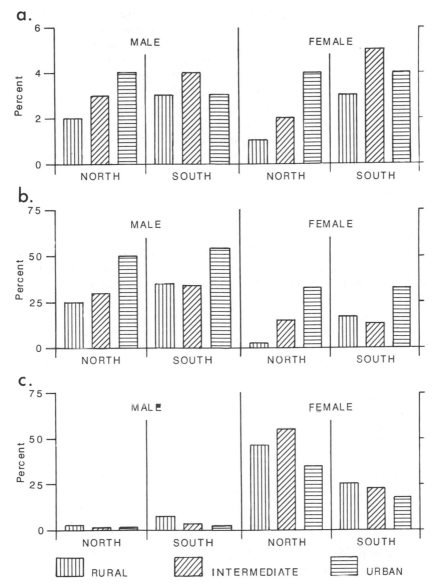

Figure 13.3. Percentage of Total Work Force: *a*, Household Workers; *b*, Other Workers; *c*, Marginal Workers

ties exist in the intermediate districts where the Green Revolution demands more of their work, particularly during harvesting and sowing.

Both the North and South regions have a negative correlation of marginal workers with urbanization, but the results are not statistically significant (Table 13.1). In the South, female marginal workers are a better indicator of rural districts than the male category. The opposite holds for the North, where male marginal workers are a better indicator of rural districts. The t values, although showing larger rural values, are not significant except for the females in the South (Table 13.2), which validates the findings with Pearson's correlation.

Literacy

The percentage of total male and female literates (Figure 13.4a) indicates a higher literacy rate in urban rather than rural districts. The male literacy rate is higher than the female literacy rate in all the categories in both the North and South. The South is distinctive, however, as it has the highest concentration of literates in all the categories for both males and females when compared to the North. In the North, the male literacy rate is lowest in the intermediate category, even lower than the rural counterpart, which reflects the concentration of male agricultural laborers (largely illiterates) in the intermediate category.

The general level of literacy is higher among the urban population than the rural dwellers. This is shown by the significant positive correlation with urbanization both in the North and the South (Table 13.1). In the North, female literates are better indicators of urbanization than males; in the South, male literates have a higher correlation to urbanization than females.

The t test also indicates that the level of literacy is higher among the urban population than among the rural dwellers (Table 13.2). In the North there is a greater difference in female literacy between the rural and urban districts, while in the South there is a greater difference in male literacy between the rural and urban districts. The difference in female literacy between rural and urban districts is not statistically significant in the South. Female illiterates in the North are higher in proportion than males; this is true in the South to a lesser degree.

Male/Female Ratio

The South has a more equitable male/female ratio than the North (Figure 13.4b). The North has a relatively greater percentage of males compared to the South. The North–South urban male/female disparity is greatest, whereas rural districts have the least disparity. In the North,

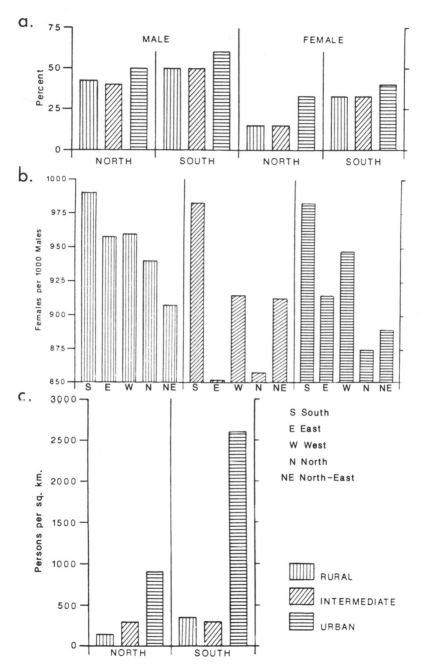

Figure 13.4. *a,* Literates as Percentage of Total Population; *b,* Male/Female Ratio; *c,* Density of Population

the percentage of females declines from rural to intermediate to urban categories, respectively, whereas in the South, although the percentage of females in rural areas is higher than in the intermediate and urban areas, there is no percentile difference between the latter two areas.

The ratio of females per 1,000 males is a reliable characteristic that shows a negative correlation with urbanization, more so in the North than in the South (Table 13.1). The lower urban sex ratio can be attributed to the large number of males who seek urban employment and the limited opportunities for females in cities due to traditional societal attitudes. The increased cost of family housing in urban areas is also an important factor that discourages male migrants from taking their families. Moreover, the purdah system, widely prevalent in North India, limits female migration to cities. Consequently, males migrate for education, employment, or both. Male urban dominance may also be related to the economic bases of modern urbanization, on the one hand, and to Hindu and Muslim attitudes toward female employment on the other. Women are economically productive in rural areas as agricultural laborers.

Density

As expected, density of population shows a strong positive correlation with urbanization both in the North and the South (Table 13.1). The urban South has a higher than expected density (Figure 13.4c). The location of the city of Madras in the South, which has a very high density, further accentuates the density count. This statistical count indicates the polarized economic development in a country where cities tend to offer more opportunities for the labor force. The same results were found with the *t* test (Table 13.2).

Rural–Urban Continuum

The findings of this study are summarized in a descriptive model indicating a rural–urban continuum (Figure 13.5). In the North (Figure 13.5a), agricultural laborers, particularly males, occur in both rural and intermediate areas, but they are more dominant in intermediate areas. Female cultivators and male and female marginal workers are prime indicators of rurality. Other workers are primarily urban. In the North, female literates are better indicators of urbanization than male literates. Male household workers are more highly correlated with urbanization than female household workers.

In the South (Figure 13.5b), the household workers, male and female, correlate strongly with the intermediate districts. The indicators

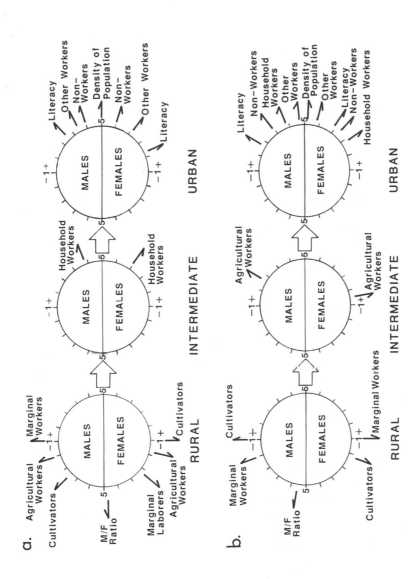

Figure 13.5. Rural–Urban Continuum: *a*, North India; *b*, South India

of rurality are male cultivators, female marginal workers, and both male and female agricultural laborers. Again, as in the North, other workers and nonworkers are primarily urban. In contrast to the North, male literates in the South are better indicators of urbanization.

For both North and South, density of population has a positive correlation with urbanization, whereas the females/1,000 males ratio is negatively correlated with urbanization.

One can, therefore, evolve a rural–intermediate–urban continuum. In the North, at one end, is the rural area with a high proportion of male and female cultivators and marginal workers. The intermediate area has a high proportion of male agricultural laborers. At the other extreme, the urban area has a high proportion of male other workers, a high population density and high male literates, and a moderate proportion of household workers and nonworkers. In the South, by contrast, the rural end has a high proportion of male cultivators, female marginal workers, and agricultural laborers. The intermediate areas have a high proportion of household workers. At the other end, in urban areas there is a high proportion of female literates, other workers, and nonworkers and a high population density.

Conclusion

When Dutt, Monroe, and Vakamudi studied rural–urban correlates of urbanization for India, their findings did not consider regional variation of patterns within the country.[10] The present study, which divides the districts into two large North and South regions, produces results which correspond in some cases with the original study but differ in others. Patterns which show up at the national scale may appear in both the North and South regions, or sometimes in only one region. For example, "other workers" are associated strongly with urbanization both for the North and South regions and for the country as a whole. The same is true of the male/female ratio, which is strongly and negatively correlated with urbanization in both regions and the country. Male agricultural laborers are associated with rural areas for India and the North region only, while in the South they are associated with the intermediate areas. Similarly, household workers, both males and females, are associated with urban areas in the South, while in the North (and the country as a whole) they are associated with the intermediate areas. Thus when the district-level statistics are analyzed for the country of India, the results can differ by region. Therefore a regional analysis provides a much clearer picture of urbanization.

NOTES

1. A. G. Noble and A. K. Dutt (eds.), *India: Cultural Patterns and Processes* (Boulder: Westview Press, 1982), pp. 5–9.

2. N. V. Sovani, *Urbanization and Urban India* (London: Asia Publishing House, 1966), p. 32; Ashish Bose, *India's Urbanization 1901–2000* (New Delhi: Tata McGraw-Hill, 1978), p. 3; D. K. Bose, "Urbanization, Industrialization and Planning for Regional Development," *Economic and Political Weekly* 4 (1969): 1169.

3. Kingsley Davis, *The Population of India and Pakistan* (Princeton, N.J.: Princeton University Press, 1951); Quazi Ahmad, *Indian Cities: Characteristics and Correlates* (Chicago: University of Chicago Press, 1965); Debnath Mookerjee and Richard C. Morrill, *Urbanization in a Developing Economy: Indian Perspectives and Patterns* (Beverly Hills: Sage Publications, 1973).

4. David M. Schneider (ed.), *India: The Social Anthropology of a Civilization* (Englewood Cliffs, N.J.: Prentice-Hall, 1971), p. 38.

5. Sovani, *Urbanization and Urban India,* pp. 4–59.

6. Davis, *Population,* p. 139.

7. A. Bose, *Urbanization 1901–2000.*

8. Sovani, *Urbanization and Urban India.*

9. S. Gosal Gurdev, "Spatial Variation of Literacy," in A. G. Noble and A. K. Dutt (eds.), *India: Cultural Patterns and Processes* (Boulder: Westview Press, 1982), pp. 36–40.

10. Ashok K. Dutt, Charles B. Monroe, and Ramesh Vakamudi, "Rural-Urban Correlates for Indian Urbanization," *Geographical Review* 76 (2) (1986): 173–183.

14. The Preindustrial City Reexamined: The Cases of Jaipur and Jaisalmer

RAMESH TIWARI

THE classic models of city structure—the concentric zone, the sector, and the multiple nuclei—are considered models of North American industrial cities and can also serve as three observations in time in the life history of American cities (Figure 14.1). The cities of South Asia have been in existence much longer than North American cities. Sjoberg has developed a model for preindustrial cities everywhere.[1] Such cities display strikingly similar social and ecological structures, not necessarily in specific cultural content but certainly in basic form.

Throughout Sjoberg's work is the concept of an underlying scale with the preindustrial city at one end and the industrial city at the other. Many scholars have taken this scale to be evolutionary in that most of the industrial cities have had a preindustrial past. As a result, testing of Sjoberg's model has been largely confined to the preindustrial stage of later industrial cities.[2]

A model is a generalized simplification of reality. In deriving a model, a number of observations are taken into account and each observation (which can be equated to a fact) is split into two parts: the unique and the general. By combining a number of generalized parts, a model is developed. In testing the model, social scientists tend to forget that their example (a city) may be totally dominated by "unique characteristics"; hence testing a model may result in its rejection. If the city has more "generalized characteristics," however, the model can easily be validated. Figure 14.2 explains this process of model formation.

Sjoberg's Model

Although Sjoberg's model covers all aspects of the preindustrial city, the emphasis is basically on intra-urban relationships. Nevertheless, inferences about the external relations of the preindustrial city can be drawn from his earlier article of the same title.[3] A city, especially a preindustrial city, has an organic relationship with its hinterland, and as technol-

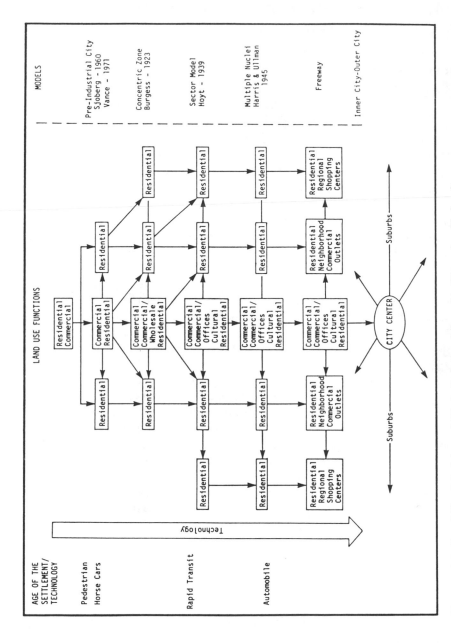

Figure 14.1. Land Use Models and Their Relationships with Changing Technology

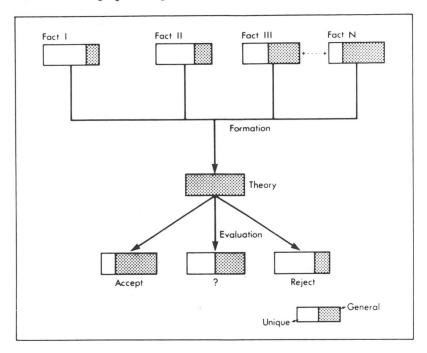

Figure 14.2. Formulation and Explanatory Power of Theory

ogy forms the determinant variable in Sjoberg's analysis, primitive technology has a controlling effect on the size of the preindustrial city. In other words, the growth and the size of the preindustrial city are closely related to the spatial extent of its hinterland. The land use patterns and the hierarchy of functions observed within the city can be understood only if the city–hinterland relationships are taken into account. Sjoberg discusses the preconditions for urbanization and then surveys the earliest cities from Mesopotamia, the Nile Valley, the Indus Valley, the valley of the Hwang Ho, and the cities of Meso-America. His basic assertion is that "certain structural elements are universal for all urban centers." Extending this argument would allow us to conclude that if the internal structural elements of these cities are similar, then the external structural elements responsible for the city's existence must also be fairly similar. Based on this argument the following axioms regarding the external (or intercity) relationships can be advanced:

1. The city acts as a central place for the surrounding area.
2. The rural/urban ratio indicates that urban population forms a small proportion of the total population.
3. The city's rate of growth is fairly slow.

4. Because of the interdependence between the city and its hinterland, the whole region remains unchanged for a long time.

Furthermore, if one applies the concept of centrality of functions and examines the role it plays in the spatial organization of land use within the city, it becomes clear that if a city came into existence as a religious center then the religious buildings will occupy the most accessible locations and these locations are usually in the center of the city. If a city has functioned as the capital of a feudal state, the palace/administration complex will dominate the central area. If a city comes into existence as a market center, the market functions will occupy the most accessible locations. The hierarchy of functions is not static, however, and land use in the central area of the city will change as the centrality of functions changes.

Intra-Urban Relationships

Sjoberg described the land use patterns within the preindustrial city. These patterns, which are in complete contrast to what one would observe in the industrial city, include:

1. The preeminence of the "central area" over the periphery, especially as portrayed in the distribution of social classes
2. Certain fine spatial differences according to ethnic, occupational, and family ties
3. The low incidence of functional differentiation in other land use patterns[4]

This model of the preindustrial city forms only one end of the urban continuum; at the other end is the industrial city. Berry has summarized the differences between them (Table 14.1).

Spatial Aspects of the Model

Sjoberg's model attempts to cover most aspects of the preindustrial city, but as Mumford observed the work lacks "topological reference."[5] Consequently, geographers tend to draw inferences about the spatial aspects of the model. Although it is beyond the scope of this discussion to describe Sjoberg's model in its entirety, an attempt is made here to describe its spatial aspects and state them as hypotheses to be tested:

1. The distribution of social status within the preindustrial city is a distance decay function—that is, the elite lives in the center while the lower classes occupy the peripheral areas. This relationship is opposite

Table 14.1.   Polar Distinctions Between Preindustrial and
               Urban-Industrial Society

Dimension	Preindustrial Society	Urban-Industrial Society
Demographic	High mortality, fertility.	Low mortality, fertility.
Behavioral	Particularistic, prescribed. Individual has multiple roles.	Universalistic, instrumental. Individual has specialized role.
Societal	Kin-group solidarity, extended family, ethnic cohesion. Cleavage between ethnic groups.	Atomization. Affiliations secondary. Professional influence groups.
Economic	Nonmonetary or simple monetary base. Local exchange. Little infrastructure. Craft industries. Low specialization.	Pecuniary base. National exchange. Extensive interdependence. Factory production. Capital intensive.
Political	Nonsecular authority. Prescriptive legitimacy. Interpersonal communication; traditional bases.	Secular polity. Elected government. Mass media participation. Rational bureaucracy.
Spatial	Parochial relationships. Close ties to immediate environment. Duplication of sociospatial groups in a cellular net.	Regional and national interdependence. Specialized roles based on major resources and relative locations in urban spatial system.

Source: B. Berry, The Human Consequences of Urbanization (New York: St. Martin's Press, 1981), p. 13.

to what is now considered the typical distribution in a Western industrial city.

2. There exists a high degree of correlation between social status and occupation. In India this axiom can be restated to mean that a high degree of correlation exists between castes and occupations. In spatial terms this leads to the agglomeration of one occupational group in one residential area or to spatial segregation in residential areas.

3. Such a city displays a haphazard organization of land use—that is, the town lacks functional specialization in terms of land use.

Urban Development in India

At present the population of India is estimated to be about 700 million of which 24 percent is considered urban. An urban population of 24 percent in 1981 makes a staggering total of about 168 million people. Though the majority of India's population resides in rural areas, in prehistoric times the subcontinent was a center of urban-based civilizations, including Harappa and Mohenjodaro. The history of urban development can be divided into four overlapping stages: the early period (towns in independent states); towns in dominant–dependent states; the British period; and Independence and after.

Early Period: Towns in Independent States

Urban centers on the subcontinent of India are very old. Indeed, the oldest culture, the Harappan, was essentially a city culture.[6] Initially a city collects the agricultural surplus from its hinterland; moreover, the boundaries of the hinterland may be taken as the administrative/political limits of "the state" of which the city forms the capital. The city in return provides the countryside with protection. During an emergency people from the countryside take refuge in the city. Except for this protection, the city does not cater much for the countryside and the dominant spatial linkages are economic transactions in which agricultural surplus is moved into the city. Furthermore, the city receives "human surplus" from the countryside, thus accelerating the process of urbanization.

The main decision making lies with the ruler, who also organizes the space within the city. Thus organization of the space is in the best interest of the organizer. The most defensible location is occupied by the ruler and the least defensible sites are left to the workers. The city is usually protected by a wall, so that during an emergency "the *praja*" or dependent public from the countryside can find refuge within the city walls. Figure 14.3 describes these spatial relationships.

Towns in Dominant–Dependent States

A powerful ruler and state may subjugate other states and bring them into their governing sphere of influence. The new administrative linkage does not necessarily change the economic ties between a town and the countryside, however, because this new linkage is now between two capitals: the dominant capital and the dominated capital. The dominated capital continues to collect the agricultural surplus, but it is now subservient to the larger state and occupies a lower position in the settlement hierarchy. Such a settlement pattern was characteristic of Indian feudalism.[7]

The administrative hierarchy of settlements in Mughal India shows

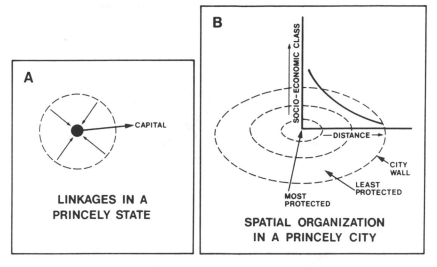

Figure 14.3. *A,* Linkages in a Princely State of India; *B,* Spatial Organization in a Princely City of India

these dominant–dominated linkages. Although commercial and other ties exist, these are relegated to secondary importance relative to the administrative linkages. Furthermore, not only do the dominated states pay tribute to the dominant power, but they also lose their creative talent, which moves to the dominant capital. (See Figure 14.4.)

The British Period

Although historians of the British period continue to debate whether or not the Mughal system was the forerunner of the British system, for the purpose of governing cities the dual administration continued. Like the Mughals, the British left the internal administration of the princely states to ruling princes. Consequently, two types of administration coexisted on the subcontinent, giving rise to different types of cities. The internal organization of cities under the princes continued, as shown in Figure 14.3, but in the areas which came under direct British rule, two points can be made. First, the center of administration moved from the inland towns like Lahore, Delhi, and Agra to the coastal city of Calcutta. Second, the economic linkages changed: The coastal city no longer collected just agricultural surplus; now it required the countryside to produce goods which were to be exported. In other words, the powerful colonial economic system had extended its "peripheral" areas from

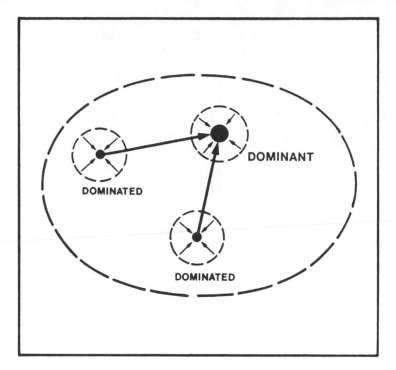

Figure 14.4. Linkages in Dominant–Dominated States

which it collected goods. (See Figure 14.5.) The British administrative/commercial interest did not use the same urban space but added to the existing town. The major functions of the precolonial town were taken over by the new rulers. The resultant spatial patterns are shown in Figure 14.6.

Independence and After

At the time of Independence in 1947, two separate administrative systems existed in India: British India, which after 1857 was ruled by administrators appointed by the government of Great Britain, and Princely India, where Indian feudalism was to continue until the princely states were incorporated into larger administrative units. The capitals of the princely states were the primate cities of those states, and the internal organization of space within these cities remained as depicted in Figure 14.3. The only visible change was the location of new palaces. The treaties between the British and the princes had made "the

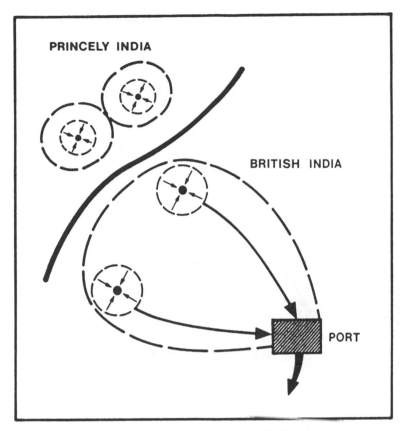

Figure 14.5. Changing Linkages: Colonial Era, India

most protected location" superfluous; consequently new palaces could be built outside the city walls.

Figure 14.7 shows the spatial distribution of the British states and the princely states. On the eve of Independence there were 582 princely states and estates, of which 115 were "gun salute" states (Table 14.2). The number of gun salutes reflected the importance of individual princes and had little to do with the area of the state or the ruler's income. Figure 14.8 shows the hierarchy of princely capitals based on the three highest levels of gun salutes.

The reorganization of states in 1950 and again in 1956 (with subsequent adjustments) has led to the formulation of linguistic states. In this process of merger, the princely cities lost their primacy, their prestige, and their princes. Since cities are the product of their socioeconomic and political environments, the capitals of the princely states have

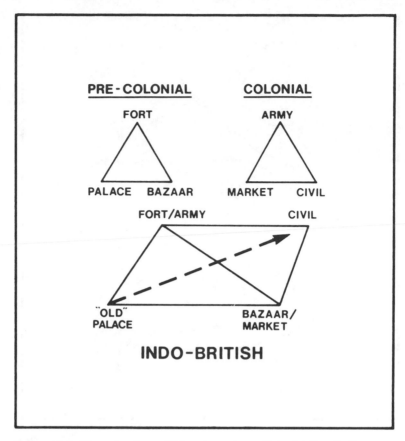

Figure 14.6. Changing Intra-Urban Locations: Colonial Era, India

remained more or less important Indian cities. During the reorganization of states, the princes (especially those of the larger states) lobbied
hard on behalf of their capital cities. However, only five ex-princely
capitals are at present the capitals of the new states: Bhopal in Madhya
Pradesh, Hyderabad in Andhra Pradesh, Jaipur in Rajasthan, Srinagar
in Jammu and Kashmir, and Trivandrum in Kerala. The incorporation
of princely states into the Republic of India and the subsequent reorganization of states have altered spatial relationships. Figure 14.9 shows
urban growth rates for India and compares them with the growth rates
of urban areas in Princely India. The figure also shows the growth rates
of Class I cities (those of 100,000 or more inhabitants) with princely
capitals which also qualify as Class I cities. As can be seen, the growth
rates are in the process of merging, as the princely capitals are now on
their way to finding their place in the national urban system.

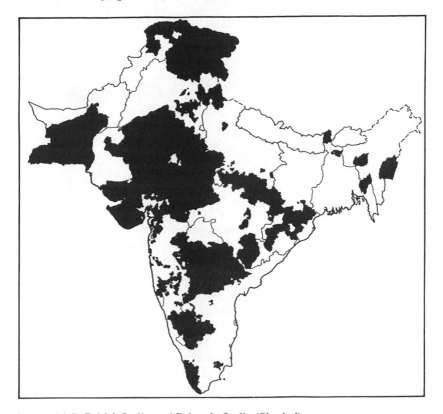

Figure 14.7. British India and Princely India (Shaded)

Testing Sjoberg's Model

Sjoberg uses the term "city" rather loosely and does not indicate the number of persons required to make a settlement a city. In India the definition of a city is fairly precise. An urban area with a population of 100,000 or more is considered a city. Two kinds of Indian cities can be identified: the planned and the unplanned city. There are very few examples of the former. Jaipur, the capital of Rajasthan, is a planned city which came into existence in 1727. The chief planner of the city was the ruler Maharaja Jai Singh—hence the name Jaipur. The king may have followed a city planning model laid down by Kautilya in his work *Arthasastra*. Kirk has reconstructed Kautilya's model (Figure 14.10) and provided a description of the distribution of social classes along with other urban functions.

Ideally, Kautilya's city was of geometrical form, normally square, to allow its layout to conform to the cosmological principles of urban plan-

Table 14.2.   Gun Salutes by Number of
             Princely States in India

No. of Gun Salutes	No. of Princely States
21	5
19	6
17	13
15	17
13	15
11	29
9	30
105	115

ning. It was surrounded by a series of moats, fed by a perennial source of water and containing crocodiles, and by an earthen rampart surmounted by brick parapets and towers. On each side it is recommended that three gates should be located, allowing three royal roads to run east–west and three north–south, thereby dividing the interior of the city into sixteen wards. The king's palace, with its internal courtyards, was to occupy the two north-central wards, and around it the houses of the four castes were to be arranged—the northern quarter allocated to Brahmans, the eastern to Kshatriya (warriors), the southern to Vaishya (merchants), and the western to Sudra (serfs and manual laborers). In the northern area were to be located, as well as the homes of Brahmans, the residences of ministers to the crown, the royal tutelary deity of the city, artificial ponds, monasteries, ironsmiths, and jewelers. In the eastern area were to be located the elephant stables, storehouses, the royal kitchen, expert artisans, troops, and the treasury. To the south the substantial houses of merchants, warehouses and workshops, restaurants, lumber yards, stables, and the arsenal were to be located; while in the west, as well as the houses of the lower classes, there were to be various groups of artisans working on textiles, skins, mats, weapons, and other goods required by the court and other inhabitants of the city. Around the central crossroads of the city, temples to various gods were to be built and commemorative pillars erected to successive kings. Between the houses and the defensive rampart, a road encircles the city to facilitate movement of troops, chariots, and so forth. Temples of guardian deities were to be located at each corner of the built-up area.

The city as thus described functioned primarily as an administrative center. Most of its activities centered on the needs of the royal palace, the court, the priests, the army, and the considerable bureaucracy with which the king surrounded himself. The development of craft industries and commerce was geared in the main to this internal urban market

Figure 14.8. Pre-Independence India: Capitals of Princely States

rather than servicing the surrounding rural areas. The city had some
impact on the immediate countryside insofar as villages clustered under
its protection and the roads leading to the city gates had wayside shrines
and inns for pilgrims. Burial grounds were located there, as were troop
encampments and exercise grounds, and agricultural production (particularly milk and fruit) was stimulated by the urban markets. But
beyond this inner zone, contact with other towns or rural areas was on
an administrative basis.[8]

Figure 14.11 shows the city of Jaipur and environs in 1865. The
maharaja at that time was well known as an astronomer and scholar. He
had also served as governor of Malwa, where his headquarters were at
Ujjain. He may also have used Kautilya's *Arthasastra* in planning the
city. If the model drawn in Kirk's article is compared to the basic layout
of Jaipur, its adaptation by the maharaja becomes quite plausible. The
model, it seems, is better fitted to plains with an adequate water supply;
in Jaipur, where the conditions are different, the major area of land use

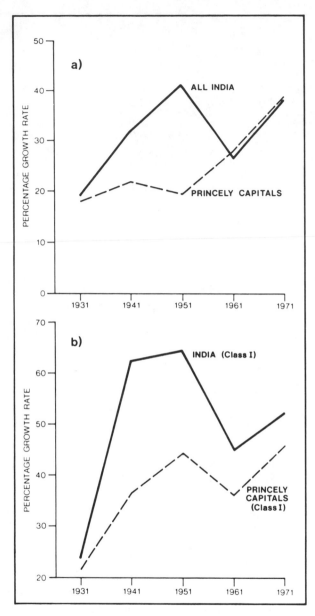

Figure 14.9. Urban Growth Rates: India (1921–1971):
a, Includes All Cities and Princely Capitals; b, Includes Class I Cities and Class I Princely Capitals

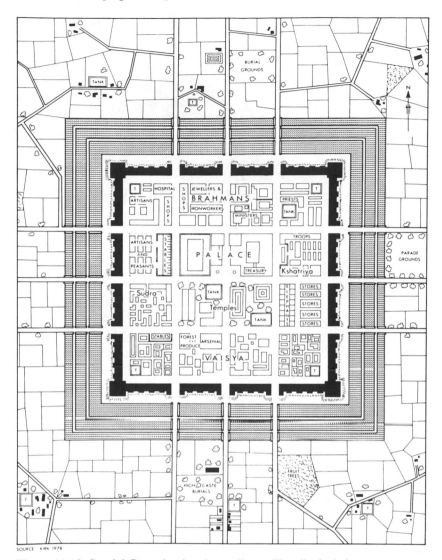

Figure 14.10. Spatial Organization According to Kautilya's *Arthasastra*

is given over to artificial ponds. At present only vestiges of these tanks are visible; the remainder have become residential land. As the city was founded by the prince, the space within the city was allocated by him on the basis of caste and occupation.[9] Consequently Sjoberg's hypothesis dealing with socioeconomic status and spatial location when applied to the city of Jaipur holds true.

To test Sjoberg's hypothesis fully, Jaisalmer, which was isolated in

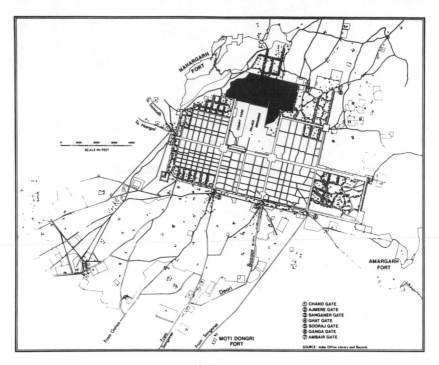

Figure 14.11. City and Environs of Jaipur in Rajputana: 1865

space and arrested in time, has been chosen. Before the reorganization
of Indian states in 1950, Jaisalmer was the capital of the state of
Jaisalmer. The reorganization led to the loss of power, prestige, and the
prince, and the town was relegated to obscurity. Subsequent improvements have brought railways, and now the Tourist Corporation of
Rajasthan has constructed tourist bungalows. The town's main attraction is its fossilized nature. Furthermore, the nearness of the town to the
Indo–Pakistan border adds to its importance.[10]

The town's isolated nature can be easily inferred from its slow population growth (Table 14.3). The main period of growth was 1961–1971,
which saw an increase of 98.25 percent. Most of the growth was due to
increases in the "other service" sector. This category as defined by the
census of India includes the occupational groups which fall under public
utility services, central and state government employees, and trade and
labor associations. This group grew by 166.26 percent during the decade 1961–1971. Most of the buildings constructed to accommodate
these functions are located outside the town wall.

Jaisalmer is divided into nine wards, and three variables are chosen
to show the domination of social groups: the distribution of scheduled

Table 14.3. Population Growth
of Jaisalmer

Year	Total
1931	7,120
1941	7,340
1951	8,026
1961	8,362
1971	16,578
1981	20,355

Source: Censuses of India.

castes and scheduled tribes, female literacy rates, and persons in trade (Table 14.4). The index of concentration of scheduled castes and scheduled tribes shows a complete absence of this group from the center of town, indicating that the traditional elite still lives in the center. The state of Rajasthan has one of the lowest rates of female literacy in India, and the district of Jaisalmer has the lowest female literacy rate in Rajasthan. Consequently, these rates are a significant indicator of modernization. Tables 14.4 and 14.5 show the wardwise distribution of these variables in 1971 and 1961, respectively. The high concentration of scheduled castes and scheduled tribes in some wards is accompanied by low concentrations of female literacy and low numbers in trade. A comparison between the tables indicates that scheduled castes were far more concentrated in 1961 than in 1971.

Figure 14.12 shows the distribution of dominant caste or social groups in Jaisalmer. (Numbers indicate *mohallas*, or neighborhoods, and narrow streets.) Although there is some mixing of castes, this has been the result of the location of a number of administrative functions. Most of the public-sector jobs tend to provide residential quarters, but due to the greater demand for these residences, the older part of town had an influx of people who would normally reside outside the town wall—that is, in the newer part of town. As hypothesized by Sjoberg, the traditional elite still lives in the center of town and the agglomerations due to caste and occupation are clearly visible: Blacksmiths, goldsmiths, shoemakers (or dealers in hides and skins), and *malis* (gardeners) all have separate *mohallas*.

Sjoberg's hypothesis that the city displays a haphazard organization of land use really means mixing of land use and mixing of functions, which is no longer common in the industrial city. The organization of functions is not without logic, however (Figure 14.13). An explanation lies in the concepts of order of goods, the hierarchy of goods, and the centrality of functions. The organization of these functions in the preindustrial city does have a logic which in the industrial city may seem to

Table 14.4.   Distribution by Ward of Selected
              Demographic Variables in Jaisalmer:
              1971

1971 Ward	Index[a]	Female Literacy (%)	Persons in Trade (%)
1	0.50	31.81	7.07
2	1.14	14.13	8.12
3	1.65	10.68	5.25
4	0.59	24.09	21.33
5	0	38.85	20.34
6	2.50	11.70	9.50
7	0	56.90	27.19
8	0.14	27.14	12.60
9	1.54	21.68	5.01

Source: Census of India, 1971.

[a] Index of concentration of scheduled castes and
scheduled tribes.

Table 14.5.   Distribution by Ward of Selected
              Demographic Variables in Jaisalmer:
              1961

1961 Ward	Index[a]	Female Literacy (%)	Persons in Trade (%)
1	0.04	28.32	8.20
2	0.67	5.10	15.91
3	2.69	1.94	6.67
4	0	15.85	29.60
5	0	33.33	43.41
6	2.62	4.07	15.56
7	0	45.58	42.65
8	0	9.98	12.71
9	1.45	14.96	13.57

Source: Census of India, 1961.

[a] Index of concentration of scheduled castes and
scheduled tribes.

be utterly irrational. Perhaps a certain combination of food habits, different clothing requirements, and other cultural traits leads to a very different pattern of shopping habits, unlike those seen in industrial cities or for that matter in the larger cities of India, and consequently to a very different type of "daily urban system." Lack of transport facilities means that the distance between home and shops or home and work has

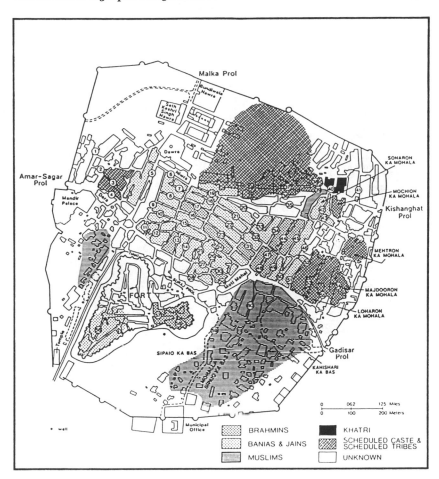

Figure 14.12. Dominant Caste and Social Groups: Jaisalmer (1983)

to be minimized—hence the mixed land use. The persistence of this pattern is due to the slow rate of change. Present-day life is only a slight improvement over what had gone before. Thus Jaisalmer's morphological form confirms the basic assumptions of Sjoberg's model. With a relative absence of modernization pressures, traditional residential and land use patterns provide a close approximation of the model's outlines.

Conclusions

Since the publication of Sjoberg's hypothesis on the preindustrial city, a number of studies have tested the model. Reviewers have objected to

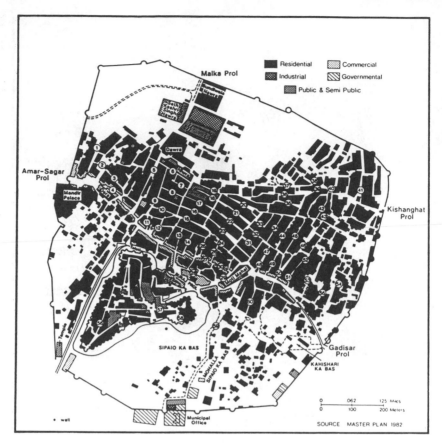

Figure 14.13. Generalized Land Use: Jaisalmer (Walled City), 1980

the simplicity of the preindustrial/industrial dichotomy upon which the arguments rest and the dubious spatial and temporal claims for the model's validity.[11] Although social scientists who have tested Sjoberg's ideas on the "preindustrial stage" of a later industrial city tend to question the validity of his model, scholars who work on Third World cities, such as Janet Abu-Lughod, recognize the significance and basic application of Sjoberg's preindustrial city.[12] The only way to validate a model is to use statistical tests which may tell us how much confidence to place in the model. But quantitative information on the preindustrial city is in short supply. This study of Jaisalmer has had to rely on limited quantitative information, but Sjoberg's model does seem to apply. Perhaps more studies of ex-princely capitals, especially of those states below the fifteen-gun-salute level, may prove Sjoberg's model appropriate, and deviations from the model may be taken as signs of modernization.

NOTES

1. G. Sjoberg, *The Preindustrial City: Past and Present* (New York: Free Press, 1960).

2. O. C. Cox, "The Preindustrial City Reconsidered," in P. Meadows and E. H. Mizruchi (eds.), *Urbanism, Urbanization and Change: Comparative Perspectives* (London: Addison-Wesley, 1969); J. Langton, "Residential Patterns in Preindustrial Cities: Some Case Studies from Seventeenth Century Britain," *Institute of British Geographers Transactions* 65 (July 1975): 1–27; John P. Radford, "Testing the Model of Preindustrial City: The case of Ante-Bellum Charleston, South Carolina," *Institute of British Geographers Transactions,* new series, 4 (3) (1979): 392–410.

3. G. Sjoberg, "The Preindustrial City," *American Journal of Sociology* 60 (1955): 438–445; also published in G. Gmelch and W. P. Zenner (eds.), *Urban Life* (New York: St. Martin's Press, 1980).

4. G. Sjoberg, "Theory and Research in Urban Sociology," in P. M. Hauser and L. F. Schnore (eds.), *The Study of Urbanization* (New York: Wiley, 1965).

5. A. Hawley, "Review of L. Mumford's *The City in History,*" *American Sociological Review* 26 (1961): 791–792.

6. R. A. Thapar, *History of India,* vol. 1 (Baltimore: Penguin Books, 1966), p. 24.

7. Ibid., pp. 241–265.

8. W. Kirk, "Town and Country Planning in Ancient India According to Kautilya's Arthasastra," *Scottish Geographical Magazine* 94 (2) (September 1978): 67–75.

9. Indra Pal, "Jaipur City Region, Jaipur and Its Environ," *Proceedings of an Interdisciplinary Conference on Human Ecology* (Jaipur: University of Rajasthan, 1979); R. A. E. Benn, *Notes on Jaipur* (Jaipur, 1916); A. K. Roy, *History of Jaipur City* (Delhi: Monohar, 1978).

10. R. Bala and G. Krishnan, "Urbanization in a Border Region: A Case Study of India's Border District Adjoining Pakistan," *Geographical Journal* 148 (1) (March 1982): 43–49.

11. Radford, "Testing the Model," n. 2, p. 392.

12. J. Abu-Lughod, "The Legitimacy of Comparisons in Comparative Urban Studies," in J. Walton and L. H. Masotti (eds.), *The City in Comparative Perspective* (New York: Wiley, 1976).

15. Employment Structure and the Chinese Urban Economy

CLIFTON W. PANNELL

ANALYSIS of China's cities and their growth during recent years has typically depended on a demographic approach and focused mainly on net natural growth rates with some attention to migration as the main determinant of city growth.[1] Migration, however, has been difficult to analyze because the quantity and quality of migration data from China have been modest. Some local information has been available, and considerable data have been provided about the nature of policy and regulations regarding residential changes. Despite a number of reviews of these policies and issues,[2] we still know precious little about the aggregate numbers of people involved in population shifts, the specific location of the shifts, and the forces that propel these movements.

The focus of this chapter is on certain determinants of growth in large Chinese cities. Rather than basing the study on population growth over time, here the approach will be on a partial investigation of the urban economy in some of China's large cities. The primary goal will be to establish the main elements in the urban economy of these cities as defined by their employment structures. It may then be possible to identify some of the key determinants of urban growth as they have evolved during recent years. This study makes no attempt to present a full and exhaustive treatment of the economy of China's cities. On the contrary, it represents an initial effort to investigate a limited aspect of China's urban economy and some of the regional variation in the economy of China's large cities. The subject is enormous, and there remains a serious dearth of data on which to proceed with an empirically based analysis of China's cities. But the situation is improving, and enough information is now available to begin studying various aspects of the economy and economic geography of these cities.

Studies have begun. Chang surveyed labor structure in major cities in his study of urbanization and economic development.[3] Sit has a brief discussion of the urban economy of China's fifteen largest cities in which he surveys their employment structure and comments on their economic performance based on both the industrial and agricultural output of these cities and the national revenue they generated.[4] Tang and Ma examined in detail the role of urban collective enterprises and their significance in the production systems of China's cities since 1952.[5] Today these enterprises account for almost one-quarter of the employment in urban enterprises in China and are, therefore, vitally important in terms of their labor absorption role in urban areas.

On the whole, however, little is known outside China about the nature of the urban economy and the specifics of employment generation associated with different sectoral activities such as industry and its various types, retail and catering activities, and other service activities such as education and scientific research. Finally, little attention has been paid to the regional questions that can help us determine whether there are significant differences in urban production systems and employment structure in different parts of China. The suspicion is that, as in other aspects of China's economic, physical, and cultural geography, significant differences among cities do exist in various regions of the country based on the nature of the surface terrain, climate, and drainage patterns along with the historical development and recent patterns of economic growth and change. My assumption is that regional variations are indeed significant and may form the basis for posing hypotheses or at least serious questions on the nature of regional development in China.

Concepts, Postulates, and Approaches

How should one approach the study of urban economics and urban economic geography in China? Conceptually it seems most logical to begin with an approach that has been tried with success in the Western industrial context to see if it might be useful in China. I recognize that historical periodicity is not the same, that the cultural context is different, and that new technologies have altered the nature of industrial production in many cases and therefore conditions may be different. Indeed, it may be argued that technologies of industrial production have rendered many production processes more capital intensive, thereby offsetting one of the key advantages of production that China has always had: its abundance of low-wage labor. To what extent this capital intensification has affected the nature of industrial production and the industry mix in China's cities is a challenging question. Clearly one would assume almost without questioning that the labor absorption capacity of specific industries would be an important ingredient in the industrializing cities of China. It may be well to approach that question cautiously, however. Between 1978 and 1984, for example, between 5.4 and 9.03 million new workers were entering the urban labor force annually. Why there should be such annual variation, and which cities and which industries were involved, is not clear from the data I have examined.

Western theory on the analysis of urban economics had early focused on a city's employment structure as a fundamental key to understanding how its economy operates and how one city's employment structure and therefore economic activity compares with those of other cities in a system.[6] Economic or export-base studies essentially divide the economic activities of a city into two types—those that serve consumers beyond the boundaries of the city and are therefore "exported" and those that remain local and aim at serving the local population. A variety of approaches to the study of the economic base of cities followed. Essentially, most researchers concluded that service activities such as retailing, beauty shops, and laundries tend to focus on satisfying the demands of local consumers, whereas industrial and manufacturing activities, or at least the major share of such activities, tend to serve consumers beyond the local scene and are thus exported and come to be viewed therefore as city-building activities.

Such an approach, especially in its view of industrial activity, has been criticized in advanced industrial states. There are several reasons for this criticism. One is that, due to maturation of the economic system, manufacturing and other industrial enterprises are no longer seen as the key employment-generating activities they once were. Today much greater emphasis is seen in service and informational activities in advanced economic systems. Moreover, complex analytic approaches and techniques are now available which make traditional export-base studies appear unsophisticated. For example, input-output analysis of the economic structure of a large metropolitan area based on extremely detailed information and involving very large quantities of data and extensive machine processing have become routine in the United States.[7] Such studies provide a highly realistic means for replicating and modeling the conditions of economic activity, change, and growth in our cities.

Such data are simply not available for the study of Chinese cities, at least not available outside China. Therefore, a more straightforward approach based on the available data seems appropriate. The data available on the employment patterns in China's cities offer only a few broad categories: industrial, retail, catering, and a few other service activities such as education, technical work, and medical services. These data are provided in a format that permits them to be examined systematically against the total employment of these cities (Table 15.1).

Table 15.1. Big-City Labor Force in China (in thousands): 1984

City	State-Owned Enterprises	Collective Enterprises	Total[a]
Over 2 million			
Shanghai	292.89	80.69	373.53
Beijing	287.81	66.59	354.50
Tianjin	196.15	66.83	262.98
Shenyang	119.33	76.93	196.26
Wuhan	130.35	49.91	180.26
Guangzhou	115.17	37.87	153.04
Harbin	83.78	54.40	138.18
Chongqing	89.11	33.82	122.93
1 million-2 million			
Nanjing	76.27	33.55	109.82
Xi'an	80.28	25.15	105.43
Chengdu	79.40	20.23	99.63
Changchun	56.87	29.54	86.41
Taiyuan	71.15	21.16	92.31
Dalian	50.51	28.74	79.25
Lanzhou	60.56	8.73	69.29
Qingdao	46.87	20.18	
Jinan	49.46	21.39	70.85
Anshan	42.98	30.36	73.34
Fushun	38.49	29.08	67.57
500,000-1 million			
Hangzhou	46.55	18.53	65.08
Zhengzhou	42.80	12.40	55.20
Qiqihar	29.66	18.99	48.65
Kunming	46.69	11.09	57.78
Urumqi	41.88	11.90	53.78
Tangshan	46.31	14.27	60.58
Changsha	40.65	16.91	57.56
Shijiazhuang	47.49	11.99	59.48
Jilin	34.89	17.53	52.42
Nanchang	36.55	16.97	53.52
Guiyang	37.26	13.44	50.70
Baotou	36.20	16.81	53.01
Zibo	31.01	12.32	43.33
Yichun	22.22	15.03	37.25
Fuzhou	29.66	16.10	45.76
Handan	44.75	7.74	52.49
Xuzhou	37.69	12.32	50.01
Wuxi	30.42	12.34	42.76
Datong	33.44	10.93	44.37
Benxi	25.70	14.77	40.47

Table 15.1 (continued)

City	State-Owned Enterprises	Collective Enterprises	Total[a]
Jixi	18.16	11.50	29.66
Luoyang	29.36	7.97	37.33
Suzhou	22.64	14.27	36.91
Huainan	24.60	11.00	35.60
Hefei	28.61	8.51	37.12
Jinzhou	22.73	10.58	33.31
Nanning	25.81	6.49	32.30
Fuxin	19.12	13.10	32.22
Hohhot	25.66	8.64	34.30
Liuzhou	23.79	9.34	33.13
Daqing	25.04	2.26	27.30

Source: State Statistical Bureau, 1985.

[a] Does not include individually employed citizens.

Although the employment categories are not always clear, enough information is provided to examine some basic issues. Inasmuch as a considerable amount of the employment data are provided for industrial activities, it seems that this provides a good opportunity to explore the relationship between industrial employment and activities and other fundamental characteristics of the city. Because it is important to say what the industrial employment share means to the city, this study will focus on the size of the city since population data, at least for the same time period, are also available (Figure 15.1).[8] In this way it may be possible to identify the elements in city size and, implicitly, city growth that appear most promising for future examination. Population data for China's fifty largest cities (administrative area and city only figures) are provided in Table 15.2.

Using this somewhat crude approach seems reasonable because the Chinese have in recent years made a clear distinction between "producer" versus "consumer" cities. In all cases it seems clear that their distinction—which is drawn from political economy ideas associated with Marxist and Maoist rhetoric—translates to basic, city-forming (producer) versus nonbasic, city-serving (consumer) activities.[9] From the ideological and polemical perspective, the notion of a producer city is attractive and positive—a city typically possessing a large industrial base which is contributing to the economic well-being and production of the entire nation. Consumer cities, by contrast, are seen as negative—a typical representative of the consumerist attitudes of capitalism as experienced especially in the treaty ports with their past service and trading functions and foreign, imperial connections. Such a city is viewed as

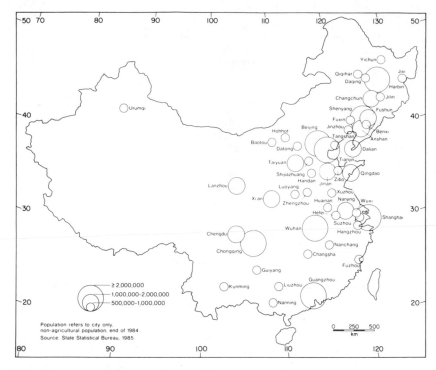

Figure 15.1. Major Cities of China: 1984

serving itself mainly and, in the Maoist view, as contributing little to the national good. Thus two contrasting prototypes may be identified in socialist parlance.

Although most of China's larger cities and many of the treaty ports had industrial facilities prior to 1950, treaty ports such as Canton and Shanghai were regarded as consumer cities. A great effort was made during the 1950s and 1960s to promote industrial activity in all cities in order to ensure that all were producer cities and therefore ideologically compatible with the direction of socialist China. Converting the city's economic base to a substantial industrial function and altering its employment structure to the point where a large share of the city's labor force was employed in industry were the methods for achieving this goal.

Considerable contradiction in this policy followed. For example, since 1952 both Shanghai and Tianjin have lost their shares of national industrial output despite a great deal of critical rhetoric directed against Shanghai as the archetype of an evil, sin-filled treaty port. In fact, Shanghai has throughout the socialist period been the major center of

Table 15.2. Big-City Population and Industrial Efficiency in China

City	Nonagricultural Population (City Only) (10,000)	Total 1984 Population (City Administrative Area) (10,000)	Net Output/Worker (Efficiency of Industrial Enterprise) (City Only)
Over 2 million			
Shanghai	672.57	1,204.78	13,438
Beijing	498.30	945.18	10,484
Tianjin	412.38	798.89	8,853
Shenyang	317.32	526.16	6,276
Wuhan	289.90	600.59	7,319
Guangzhou	248.61	698.89	9,758
Harbin	221.73	377.09	5,403
Chongqing	203.08	1,394.48	6,052
1 million-2 million			
Nanjing	186.51	460.75	8,881
Xi'an	168.63	544.56	5,329
Chengdu	152.34	853.99	6,391
Changchun	142.45	584.23	6,688
Taiyuan	133.59	299.68	5,474
Dalian	133.43	480.76	10,236
Lanzhou	114.45	243.36	7,162
Qingdao	114.00	623.91	9,347
Jinan	111.05	343.60	7,750
Anshan	108.89	258.34	10,459
Fushun	107.73	208.34	10,459
500,000-1 million			
Hangzhou	97.34	537.49	10,354
Zhengzhou	96.25	480.04	6,682
Qiqihar	95.52	565.11	4,926
Kunming	95.00	326.82	7,574
Urumqi	94.70	114.73	5,644
Tangshsn	92.11	603.33	5,484
Changsha	91.92	496.95	5,527
Shijiazhuang	90.20	171.82	7,767
Jilin	88.27	394.37	8,781
Nanchang	87.13	135.27	6,390
Baotou	86.62	157.96	5,039
Zibo	76.25	273.20	3,161
Yichun	75.82	124.51	3,161
Fuzhou	75.45	482.65	5,266
Handan	72.75	124.86	5,985
Xuzhou	70.91	700.04	5,539

Table 15.2 (continued)

City	Nonagricultural Population (City Only) (10,000)	Total 1984 Population (City Administrative Area) (10,000)	Net Output/Worker (Efficiency of Industrial Enterprise) (City Only)
Wuxi	69.63	388.48	9,657
Datong	68.82	98.10	7,203
Benxi	67.85	142.26	5,985
Jixi	62.63	106.23	3,343
Luoyang	62.40	255.91	6,023
Suzhou	60.32	432.38	8,160
Huainan	60.32	159.01	2,833
Hefei	59.42	343.66	6,701
Jinzhou	58.48	457.21	8.360
Nanning	57.94	244.49	5,351
Fuxin	55.13	171.79	3,838
Hohhot	54.28	124.92	4,494
Liuzhou	50.10	139.75	7,494
Daqing	50.09	80.21	48,905

Source: State Statistical Bureau, 1985.

industrial output in China. Beijing, the nation's capital and leading administrative center, was also criticized during the 1950s and 1960s as not having enough producer or basic economic activities. Industrial production statistics show that in fact Beijing did enlarge its industrial base to the point that its share of national industrial output more than doubled between 1952 and 1974. Since then its share of national industrial output has declined, and there seems to be a growing view that Beijing perhaps developed more of an industrial base than was appropriate for a great national capital city.[10] A tabulation of the gross value of industrial output of China's fifty largest cities indicates the relative shares in 1984 (Table 15.3).

Big-City Employment and the Industrial Sector

The bulk of employment in China's large cities today is industrial employment (see Table 15.4). Industrial activity in large Chinese cities typically accounts for more than 45 percent of total employment, and this share ranges to more than 65 percent. Industrial employment, as defined by the gross value of industrial output in China, includes the value of finished and semifinished products, processing of certain primary goods, and repairing of industrial and transport equipment. The

Table 15.3. Big City Gross Value of Industrial Output
(in 1980 RMB 10,000) in China: 1984

City	Total	Light	Heavy
Over 2 million			
Shanghai	5,604,762	3,059,103	2,545,659
Beijing	2,637,439	1,127,514	1,510,925
Tianjin	2,454,208	1,384,609	1,069,599
Shenyang	1,309,815	468,639	841,176
Wuhan	1,293,359	596,612	696,747
Guangzhou	1,198,255	767,359	421,866
Harbin	675,728	303,855	371,873
Chongqing	794,930	364,864	430,066
1 million-2 million			
Nanjing	873,595	317,032	556,563
Xi'an	988,399	481,694	506,329
Chengdu	666,423	506,645	397,916
Changchun	490,558	268,507	313,939
Taiyuan	535,109	145,054	390,055
Dalian	705,439	120,346	454,371
Lanzhou	497,076	120,346	376,730
Qingdao	687,008	424,365	262,643
Jinan	505,402	276,873	228,529
Anshan	621,919	91,074	530,845
Fushun	517,334	72,370	444,964
500,000-1 million			
Hangzhou	669,579	431,515	238,064
Zhengzhou	364,951	210,590	154,361
Qiqihar	290,951	92,433	188,358
Kunming	378,209	191,090	187,119
Urumqi	187,525	64,523	123,002
Tangshan	349,373	100,882	248,491
Changsha	267,791	166,980	109,811
Shijiazhuang	493,274	326,193	167,081
Jilin	398,439	119,629	278,810
Nanchang	275,416	151,102	124,314
Guiyang	250,693	121,681	129,012
Baotou	267,111	54,106	213,005
Zibo	464,174	119,174	344,859
Yichun	87,620	23,925	63,695
Fuzhou	284,418	197,750	586,668
Handan	338,703	117,590	221,113
Xuzhou	311,806	140,948	170,858
Wuxi	654,387	415,145	239,242
Datong	211,705	40,443	171,262
Benxi	240,518	53,304	187,214

Table 15.3 (continued)

City	Total	Light	Heavy
Jixi	82,329	15,304	67,003
Luoyang	258,043	65,340	192,703
Suzhou	446,226	294,828	151,398
Huainan	144,101	44,258	99,843
Hefei	244,857	141,310	103,547
Jinzhou	282,040	93,432	188,608
Nanning	154,887	113,133	41,754
Fuxin	109,924	28,350	81,574
Hohhot	117,857	75,089	42,768
Liuzhou	241,733	141,691	100,042
Daqing	796,640	16,543	780,097

Source: State Statistical Bureau, 1985.

gross value of industrial output is the sum of the value of all industrial enterprises in a city. Inasmuch as we are using statistics based on the "city only" definition, the share of industrial employment outside of manufacturing and closely related activities is believed to be very small. By this measure, then, China would appear to have transformed the economic structure of its large cities to accord closely with the socialist ideal of the producer city.

It can be argued that Chinese cities reflect China's recent economic condition as a society converting its economy from rural to urban, from a farming economy to an industrial, city-based economy. In terms of sectoral contribution to national income, such a structural shift is indeed indicated with industrial activities increasing their share steadily up to 1979, although this share slowed from 1980 to 1984. The employment picture is different, however. Agricultural employment on the national level (Table 15.5) accounted at the end of 1984 for almost 70 percent of the nation's employment. Admittedly many of these agricultural employees were not in field cultivation, yet the large bulk of China's people continue to derive their livelihood from rural-based activities. Cities present a sharp contrast, for there is a remarkably high percentage of workers in industrial activities in all of China's large cities. Large cities in the United States, even in the period of greatest industrial expansion, rarely exceeded 35 to 40 percent of their employed in industrial activities except in a few special cases such as Providence or Detroit.[11] As Buck has indicated in his historical study of a Chinese city, Jinan in the mid-1920s had less than 10 percent of its labor force employed in industrial activities.[12]

Perhaps a more instructive example and comparable model for Chinese cities and economic change is the case of Japan. Miyakawa has

Table 15.4. Big-City Industrial Employment in China (in 10,000s): 1984

City	State-Owned Industries	Collective Industries	Total Industrial Labor Force	% of Total Labor Force
Over 2 million				
Shanghai	160.68	46.75	207.43	55.53
Beijing	104.35	35.11	139.46	39.35
Tianjin	91.13	42.21	133.34	50.70
Shenyang	63.72	50.78	114.50	58.34
Wuhan	59.88	32.22	92.10	51.09
Guangzhou	43.90	23.27	67.17	43.89
Harbin	41.17	28.96	70.13	50.75
Chongqing	49.49	19.53	69.02	56.15
1 million-2 million				
Nanjing	36.08	19.87	55.95	50.95
Xi'an	39.66	13.53	53.19	50.45
Chengdu	37.07	11.65	48.72	48.90
Changchun	26.28	18.61	44.89	51.95
Taiyuan	35.27	13.39	48.66	52.71
Dalian	23.51	18.74	42.25	53.31
Lanzhou	32.11	4.78	37.09	53.52
Qingcao	27.80	14.11	41.91	62.51
Jinan	23.11	15.03	38.14	53.83
Anshan	27.74	20.34	48.08	65.56
Fushun	25.51	18.45	43.96	65.06
500,000-1 million				
Hangzhou	22.53	12.25	34.78	53.44
Zhengzhou	21.00	7.80	28.80	52.17
Qiqihar	17.40	10.69	28.09	57.74
Kunming	19.51	6.25	25.76	44.58
Urumqi	14.92	3.73	18.65	34.68
Tangshan	25.97	9.11	35.08	57.90
Changsha	14.59	11.04	25.63	44.52
Shijiazhuang	22.43	8.24	30.67	51.56
Jilin	18.45	9.58	28.03	53.47
Nanchang	17.43	11.42	28.85	53.91
Guiyang	17.11	6.77	23.88	47.10
Baotou	20.96	10.52	31.48	59.39
Zibo	21.28	8.78	30.06	69.37
Yichun	15.75	6.14	21.89	58.76
Fuzhou	12.33	10.53	22.86	49.95
Handan	27.15	5.00	32.15	61.25
Xuzhou	21.75	8.77	30.52	61.00
Wuxi	20.64	7.81	28.45	66.35
Datong	19.56	5.00	24.56	60.12
Benxi	15.16	9.17	24.33	60.12

Table 15.4 (continued)

City	State-Owned Industries	Collective Industries	Total Industrial Labor Force	% of Total Labor Force
Jixi	13.13	5.51	18.64	62.84
Luoyang	16.58	4.62	21.20	56.79
Suzhou	13.30	10.47	23.77	64.39
Huainan	14.58	7.76	22.34	62.75
Hefei	13.78	3.77	17.55	47.27
Jinzhou	12.74	7.12	19.86	59.62
Nanning	9.70	3.08	12.78	39.56
Fuxin	11.94	8.93	20.87	64.72
Hohhot	9.32	3.44	12.76	37.20
Liuzhou	11.40	5.46	16.86	50.89
Daqing	11.53	0.29	11.82	43.29

Source: State Statistical Bureau, 1985.

noted that the share of industrial employment in Tokyo fell from 36.4 to 24.1 percent between 1963 and 1975, and there was an absolute decline in the number of industrial jobs.[13] At the same time, however, he noted that industrial employment in many of the smaller, satellite cities in the Tokyo metropolitan area during the 1970s had shares of more than 40 percent. In 1975 the national average of Japanese industrial employees to the total number of employees was 34.7 percent. In the same year there were thirty-four cities with an industrial employment share greater than the average national industrial employment share of 34.7 percent. In some of the "company towns" where one industry dominated the employment structure, industrial employment has exceeded 50 percent of the city's total employment picture. Such cities tend to be small, however. In Japan, as in other advanced market economies, the conventional view today is one of declining industrial employment share as cities get larger and their industry mix and economic base diversify.

Another useful comparison is with Soviet cities. As Harris has demonstrated, a large number of Soviet cities had industrial employment shares of more than 50 percent in 1959, and in the same year a number of the USSR's largest and most important cities such as Leningrad, Novosibirsk, Sverdlovsk, Riga, and Omsk had industrial employment shares greater than 40 percent. The comparison among socialist cities may in fact be the most instructive in this case.[14]

Most of China's large cities have a pattern of industrial employment that ranges between 45 and 60 percent of the total employment of the cities; there is no clear pattern among these cities, either by size or location, as to the industrial share of their population. While there is no

Table 15.5.   National Labor Force Employed by Sector of the
              National Economy in China (in 10,000s): 1984

Sector	Total	% of Total
Industry	6,338	13.3
Construction and prospecting	1,858	3.9
Agriculture and forestry	32,538	68.4
Transport and telecommunications	1,080	2.3
Commerce, catering service, and trade	2,354	4.9
Scientific research, education, and public health	1,779	3.7
Parties, people's organizations, and other	1,650	3.5
Total all sectors	47,597	100.0

Source: Statistical Yearbook of China, 1985.

clear spatial pattern regarding the location of major industrial employment in China, there exists an interesting and complex pattern of variation in industrial employment among these large cities (Figure 15.2).
Industrial employment as a share of total city employment ranges from
a low of 35 percent in Urumqi (Xinjiang province) to a high of 69 percent in Zibo (Shandong province). All cities over 1 million in the city-
only or city proper zone, with the exception of Beijing (39 percent) and
Chengdu (49 percent), had more than half of their total employment
share in industrial activities. Compared with industrial employment in
large cities and metropolitan areas in advanced industrial market economies, where the estimated average is probably between 17 and 28 percent and declining, especially in the United States, this is an extraordinarily large share of urban employment in industrial activities. It also
suggests an aspect of urban structure and process that is fundamentally
different between contemporary large Chinese cities and cities in advanced market economic systems.

City Size and Economic Efficiency

The question of the relationship between city size and economic efficiency in China's large cities (Table 15.2) is especially intriguing in view
of the World Bank's recommendation that China should pursue industrialization policies that take advantage of scale and urbanization economies.[15] Figure 15.3 depicts the plot of net industrial output per worker
against urban population (city only) for China's fifty largest cities. A
relationship would appear to exist suggesting that the larger the city, the
more efficient its industrial labor force will be. As the plot indicates, this
is not a strong relationship, and the pattern in all three size classes of
China's large cities is ambiguous. It may well reflect the different mix of

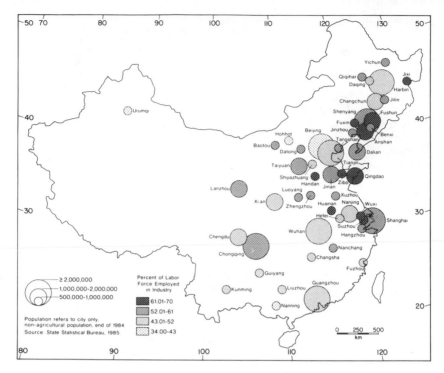

Figure 15.2. Big-City Industrial Employment: 1984

industries in these cities or their diverse developmental histories. It is puzzling to see relatively high per capita output in Anshan and Fushun, centers of heavy industry, as well as in Hangzhou, a city of equivalent size but noted for its handicraft industries and tourism. Shenyang, the leading center in southern Liaoning, has a much lower per capita output than Anshan and Fushun. Obviously there is much complexity here, both in structural and in spatial terms, and further study of specific cities will be necessary to shed light on these questions.

Emerging Regional Foci of Industrial Centers

A few patterns of industrial employment are obvious. The large northeastern cities of Anshan, Fushun, Benxi, Fuxin, and Jixi all had industrial employment of more than 60 percent, for example, and the share of Shenyang, the most industrial of China's eight largest metropolises, was 58.34 percent. Yet there were seven other cities with an industrial employment share greater than 60 percent, and these were in Jiangsu

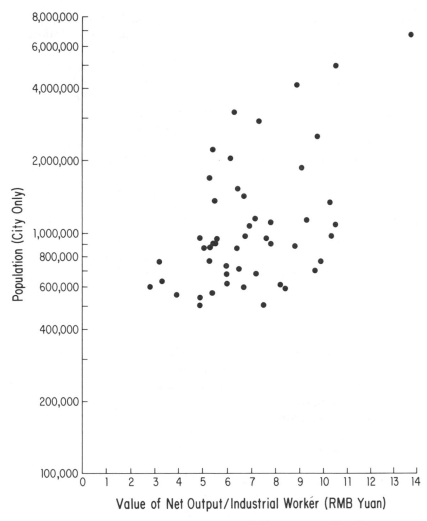

Figure 15.3. Relationship Between Economic Efficiency and City Size

(three cities), Shandong (two), Anhui (one), and southern Hebei (one). Aside from Beijing, the national capital, the only two large cities with industrial shares under 40 percent were in border regions: Urumqi (35 percent) in Xinjiang and Hohhot (37 percent) in Inner Mongolia.

Policy is obviously very important, and all cities no doubt have been under pressure to expand their industrial base and thereby increase their industrial/producer role. Yet why do some cities have a larger industrial share and higher percentage of industrial employment than others, and what can we conclude from the existing pattern of structural and spatial variations? The answers are complex. Historical factors of development in the Northeast, where a strong tradition of industrial cities has existed, help to explain the strong industrial showing there. Some of the smaller cities around Shanghai, such as Suzhou and Wuxi, suggest some overspill or deconcentration of Shanghai's industrial role to these satellite cities, analogous to the Tokyo pattern of the 1960s, but it is in fact too early to know how this trend is evolving. Clearly the lower Chang Jiang region is developing rapidly as one of China's great industrial metropolitan regions, but the role of specific cities in that region is still not well understood, at least outside China. Great clusters of industrial activity in China seem likely given recent trends and policies which are building on a historic pattern of development as well. In this case three dynamic centers of industrial activity and urban/regional development may be identified: the Shanghai–Nanjing–Hangzhou region, the Liaoning region in the Northeast, and the Beijing–Tianjin region. In these three industrial regions is concentrated almost one-third of the industrial employment of China's 295 cities.

Retail and Catering Activities

Retail and catering employment generally reflects the size of a city, although there are important exceptions. The city with the largest employment share in retail and catering activities (17.39 percent) in 1984 was Nanjing; the city with the smallest share (5.83 percent) was Nanchang in Jiangxi province (Table 15.6). There is no apparent spatial or size pattern, however, as only nine of the fifty largest cities had more than 10 percent of their employed persons engaged in retail and catering activities. The overall patterns are complex and difficult to interpret (Figure 15.4). It might be easy to say that Guangzhou has a long tradition of commercial activity and thus one is not surprised to see that it has 10.5 percent of its workers in retail and catering or that Nanjing, with a strong tradition as an administrative and marketing center, has 17.4 percent of its workers in retail and catering and represents the maximum for a large city. Why Zibo has 15.5 percent and is the second leading retail city in terms of employment share, however, is not quite so clear. Given that service activities, of which retail and catering are major facets, still have a certain opprobrium attached to them, it is not surprising that cities make no attempt to publicize or promote their service activities. For this reason, perhaps, it is hard to obtain additional information about retail service activities and their role in the economic structure of large cities.

Table 15.6. Big-City Retail and Catering Employment in China: 1984

City	Retail	Catering	Total	% of Total Labor Force
Over 2 million				
Shanghai	224,957	52,329	277,286	7.42
Beijing	186,493	49,178	235,671	6.64
Tianjin	150,462	32,953	183,414	6.97
Shenjin	121,317	28,833	150,150	7.65
Wuhan	87,518	27,481	114,999	6.37
Guangzhou	119,791	40,629	160,420	10.48
Harbin	116,009	26,429	142,508	10.31
Chongqing	58,755	16,363	75,118	6.11
1 million-2 million				
Nanjing	88,985	26,892	190,995	17.39
Xi'an	100,263	19,681	119,944	11.38
Chengdu	65,709	17,999	83,708	8.40
Changchun	91,616	19,579	111,195	12.87
Taiyuan	41,989	17,860	59,849	6.48
Dalian	52,380	11,739	64,119	8.09
Lanzhou	49,810	16,496	66,306	9.57
Qingdao	32,656	11,522	44,178	6.79
Jinan	49,494	16,093	65,587	9.26
Anshan	38,428	8,803	47,231	6.44
Fushun	31,398	10,001	41,399	6.13
500,000-1 million				
Hangzhou	32,834	10,406	43,240	6.64
Zhengzhou	61,905	13,215	75,120	15.61
Qiqihar	34,325	10,218	44,453	9.14
Kunming	35,666	13,742	49,408	8.55
Urumqi	28,399	8,870	37,269	6.93
Tangshan	37,345	9,442	46,787	7.72
Changsha	44,098	9,262	53,360	9.27
Shijiazhuang	40,529	10,775	51,304	8.63
Jilin	33,271	10,225	43,496	8.29
Nanchang	25,184	6,041	31,225	5.83
Guiyang	37,359	9,175	46,534	9.18
Baotou	36,020	8,566	44,586	8.41
Zibo	50,730	16,236	66,966	15.45
Yichun	22,140	4,619	26,759	7.18
Fuzhou	36,405	7,941	44,346	9.69
Handan	38,164	9,881	48,045	9.15
Xuzhou	19,720	6,419	26,139	5.23
Wuxi	21,577	7,280	28,857	6.75
Datong	39,177	7,674	46,851	10.56
Benxi	19,883	5,446	25,279	6.24

Table 15.6 (continued)

City	Retail	Catering	Total	% of Total Labor Force
Jixi	18,317	5,510	23,827	8.03
Luoyang	24,631	7,745	32,376	8.67
Suzhou	17,106	5,567	22,673	6.14
Huainan	25,680	7,119	32,799	9.21
Hefei	23,058	6,634	29,692	7.98
Jinzhou	22,836	4,209	27,035	8.12
Nanning	26,241	8,133	34,374	10.64
Fuxin	16,408	7,653	24,061	7.44
Hohhot	25,500	5,346	30,846	8.99
Liuzhou	16,146	4,130	20,276	6.12
Daqing	13,620	3,984	17,604	6.44

Source: State Statistical Bureau, 1985.

Employment Structure and City Size

In beginning this study I had hoped to use employment data as a basis for predicting something about the size, economic health, and growth trends of China's cities. At this point I can only argue that a few trends emerge. Moreover, the data do not yet permit a sufficiently deep analysis to be able to say a great deal about growth trends in population and employment as a driving force in city growth. Wilbur Thompson claimed, "Tell me your industry mix and I will tell you your fortune." Unfortunately, the nature and precision of Chinese urban data do not yet tell us much about the industry mix. Nor are the urban population data sufficiently consistent for one to establish growth trends for different urban administrative and definitional units.[16]

After reviewing the data in the report *China: Urban Statistics 1985,* I set out to examine several relationships for large cities (500,000 city-only population) in China: the relationship between city size and industrial employment share, the relationship between city size and retail employment share, and the relationship between city size and economic efficiency as measured by the per-capita value of output of industrial workers. While there appeared to be a modest trend indicating that the larger the city the greater its economic efficiency, there was no discernible relationship between city size and the specific employment function (either industrial or retail) among these fifty largest cities in China.

From these findings I conclude that the impact of structural shift in the economy of socialist China has led to remarkably different urban employment patterns than exist in cities in market economies. The findings also suggest that economic transformation in socialist systems generally, and China specifically, proceeds at a different pace than in

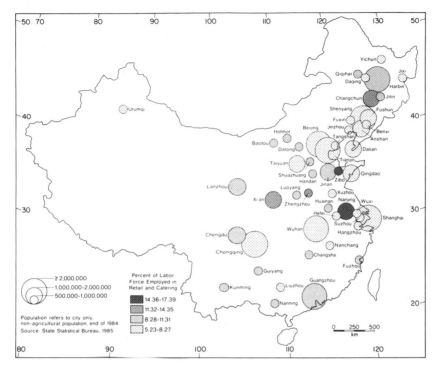

Figure 15.4. Big-City Retail and Catering Employment: 1984

advanced industrial nations and has different effects on urbanization and urban change. At what point urban statistics begin to indicate growth in their service economies remains to be seen. For now, essentially all we have is a baseline from which to track future trends in urban employment.

A second goal of my study was to look for spatial patterns to determine if there were significant regional patterns of growth and development among the largest of China's cities and to discover to what extent these patterns were related to specific patterns of employment structure or economic efficiency. A few patterns seemed reasonable and logical given the historic development of specific areas of China—for example, the great industrial cities of Liaoning and the petroleum city of Daqing in Heilongjiang. Again there was not enough information to establish clear regional patterns about size, growth, or economic efficiency. At this point each city needs to be examined on its own merits and an urban profile drawn that can be used for comparative purposes and future studies. Such case profiles for purposes of analyzing the urban economy and economic geography will require thorough and consistent data sets on existing industrial structure, urban population change over time, and urban employment. This latter requirement may indeed be the most difficult of all to fill, but it will be necessary if we are to have serious analytical studies of the economic structure and geography of China's cities. In the next section I illustrate this approach with three urban profiles.

Urban Profiles: A Tale of Three Cities

To achieve better understanding of the urban economy of China's cities, I describe here some aspects of three cities. These details provide a clearer picture of the employment and economic structures of these cities which may in turn provide clues that will help us to project their future patterns of growth and change. Shenyang, Nanjing, and Kunming represent the three size classes for China's large cities used in the preceding analysis.

Shenyang: Major Industrial City of the Northeast

Although an ancient city that was once the capital for a Manchu emperor in A.D. 1625, Shenyang has had its greatest growth in the twentieth century as an industrial city. It forms the core of a cluster of great industrial and mining cities in southern Liaoning which together comprise one of China's greatest concentrations of industrial output. Today Shenyang is the provincial capital of Liaoning and the largest metropolis in the Northeast. Its population, including the surrounding counties of its administrative district, was 5.26 million in 1984. The nonagricultural population in the city proper was 3.17 million at the end of 1984. Shenyang has been the focus of large-scale industrial development during recent years. Especially important is the machine building industry, but mining, coking, steel making and rolling, metal and mining equipment, aircraft, automobiles, electronics, and plastics are also significant. Almost half the value of industrial output in 1984 was accounted for by the machine building sector. In 1984 there were 151 large and medium-size industrial enterprises in the city, and these employed 1.22 million workers. This number represented 58 percent of the city's labor force, although no data were reported on employment by specific industry. Despite a large share of workers in industry, the net output per industrial worker was less than half that of workers in Shanghai.

Shenyang is also an important trade, commercial, educational, and service center. Almost 200,000 people were employed in retail and catering activities in 1984, although this was less than 8 percent of the city's labor force. In brief, despite its great size, Shenyang continues to earn its living as a producer city, and its diversified mix of industries, including those whose products are in great demand such as machinery, suggests a promising future for this key industrial center.

Nanjing: Diversified City on the Lower Yangzi

Nanjing is one of China's oldest cities and was the site of the national capital from the third to the fifteenth centuries. It later served as the capital of Republican China from 1912 to 1949, and today it is the capital of Jiangsu province. Its total population in 1984 was 4.61 million, of whom 1.86 million were non-agriculture-related citizens in the city proper. Since 1950 its economic base has been substantially diversified, and Nanjing has become an important industrial center. In 1984 more than half a million workers were employed in its industries, and this number comprised 51 percent of the city's total employment.

The industrial base of Nanjing is diversified; chemicals, petroleum, machine building, electronics, and building materials are the most important industries. The city is especially well known for its high-quality precision machines and equipment and for its electronic goods. Of its 9.74-billion-yuan gross industrial output value in 1984, 62 percent originated in heavy industry. The efficiency of its industrial workers in net output was about two-thirds that of Shanghai's workers, the nation's most productive.

Nanjing has long been an important commercial and trade center and employed more than 200,000 business people in 1984. This number represents over 17 percent of the city's labor force and was the highest percentage share of any large city in China. Nanjing is also an important educational and scientific center, and there were more than 180,000 scientific workers in 1984. The science function is apparently vital to the city as a center of high-tech and knowledge-intensive industries, a focus that would appear to augur well for the future of technology-related industries and industrial growth. Despite the lack of employment data by specific industrial type, the broad mix with emphasis on scientific and technically based industries would appear to be a good blend for Nanjing to ensure its future prosperity as an industrial and diversified city.

Kunming: Gateway to Southwest China

Kunming, young by Chinese standards, has grown rapidly in recent decades and has become the major city of southwest China, a leading industrial, transportation, and service center. Kunming's 1984 total population was 3.27 million with a nonagricultural population in the city proper of 950,000. Major industries include machine building (which accounts for one-quarter of the output value of industrial goods), food processing, metallurgy, chemicals, and textiles. More than 250,000 workers were employed in industrial activities, and these accounted for about 45 percent of the city's labor force. The efficiency of its industrial workers as measured in per capita output was about 0.56 that of Shanghai's industrial workers. Retail activities employed about 50,000 workers in 1984, and this number represented about 9 percent of the city's workers.

Compared with Shenyang (60 percent) and Nanjing (40 percent), Kunming is not only considerably smaller but has a much smaller share (26 percent) of its total population identified as nonagricultural and living in the city proper. Such a figure may simply be a quirk of the city's administrative organization and area. (The enormous expansion of Chongqing's administrative boundaries in 1985 increased that city's total population to more than 13 million and made it the nation's largest city in what is the most egregious illustration of administrative overbounding.) However, these figures may also indicate that Kunming is less "urban" than the larger two cities with which it is being compared. Agricultural and rural-based activities continue to play a much more prominent role in its urban economy and the daily life-style of a much larger share of the city's total population.

Much insight into the nature of Chinese urbanization and urban growth processes can be gained from examining the changes going on in the periurban zones of China's great cities. Although the employment statistics are not clear, the share of the city's population that is classified as agricultural or nonagricultural permits a basic division. Within periurban agriculture, however, there are many activities ranging from fishing, forestry, and cropping to sideline production and industry. Here is an important aspect of the metropolitan economy of all of China's large cities that holds significant clues to the nature of urban change and growth processes and the very essence of China's urbanization process. Unless we understand this sector of the urban economy, we will not understand an important segment of the quasi-urban population of the metropolitan area of China's cities. Therefore, our ability to analyze the metropolitan economy and predict likely patterns of its growth and change will also be impeded.

Conclusion

The search for improved understanding of the Chinese urban economy has seen substantial gains during the 1980s with the publication of considerably more population, employment, and output data on China's cities. Yet the details of the published data remain elusive, and one is still unable to identify employment by specific type within major sectoral categories. Today we know more, it is true, but at this point we are tantalized more than satisfied by the available data. We will need more information if we are to answer fundamental questions about the nature of urban rise and decline and the prospects for specific cities.

The initial goal of this investigation was to examine the relationship between city size and specific employment sectors to determine what effect, if any, city size has on specific employment structure or sectoral activity. No relationship could be clearly discerned among the employment categories examined—industrial and retail services—which were the two largest employment categories. It is clear, however, that Chinese cities have remarkably large shares of their urban employment in industrial activity, and this is true for large as well as medium-size cities. This finding suggests that the government's effort to make these cities "producer" centers to comport with the ideological maxims of socialism have succeeded remarkably well. Without better and more detailed data on industry mix and type, employment growth, and the overall growth of cities, however, it is not possible to offer any but the most general projections about the economic vitality, health, and prospects of the various cities.

It was initially postulated that a relationship was likely to exist between a city's size and its economic efficiency on the assumption that workers produce more efficiently in large urban agglomerations as Western theory of urban economy indicates. Although such a pattern was found to exist, the strength of the relationship is modest. There was enough variation in that pattern to suggest that individual cities will have to be studied in order to examine their developmental histories and their pattern of industrial growth and industry mix.

Spatial patterns of city growth and employment structure were also examined to ascertain whether any regularity existed. Major clusters of industrial cities were identified in three major regions—Liaoning, eastern Hebei, and Shanghai–Jiangsu—but almost all of China's big cities have large industrial bases. The clustering effect seems significant, but without knowing the specific industrial types and growth in demand and employment in these types, it is difficult to offer projections with confidence. We know more about the employment base and economic structure of China's cities than we did ten years ago, but we still do not have enough details to analyze these urban economies in any depth.

NOTES

1. Mei-ling Hsu, "Growth and Control of Population in China: The Rural Urban Contrast," *Annals of the Association of American Geographers* 75 (2) (1985):

241–257; Judith Banister, "An Analysis of Recent Data on the Population of China," *Population and Development Review* 10 (2) (1984): 241–271.

2. See Martin King Whyte and William L. Parish, *Urban Life in Contemporary China* (Chicago: University of Chicago Press, 1984); Marc Blecher, "Peasant Labour for Urban Industry: Temporary Contract Labour, Urban Rural Balance and Class Relations in a Chinese County," in N. Maxwell and B. A. MacFarlane (eds.), *China's Changed Road to Development* (Oxford: Pergamon Press, 1984), pp. 109–123; S. Goldstein and Alice Goldstein, "Population Movement, Labor Force Absorption, and Urbanization in China," *Annals of the Academy of Political and Social Science* 476 (1984): 90–110; R. J. R. Kirkby, *Urbanization in China: Town and Country in a Developing Economy, 1944–2000* (New York: Columbia University Press, 1985).

3. Sen-dou Chang, "Urbanization and Economic Readjustment in China," in Chi-keung Leung and Steve S. K. Chin (eds.), *China in Readjustment* (Hong Kong: University of Hong Kong, Center of Asian Studies, 1983).

4. Victor F. S. Sit, *Chinese Cities: The Growth of the Metropolis Since 1949* (Hong Kong: Oxford University Press, 1985), pp. 41–46.

5. Jianzhong Tang and Laurence J. C. Ma, "Evolution of Urban Collective Enterprises in China," *China Quarterly* 104 (December 1985): 614–640.

6. Wilbur Thompson, *A Preface to Urban Economics* (Baltimore: Johns Hopkins University Press, 1968); Raymond Vernon, *Metropolis 1985* (New York: Anchor Books, 1963); Edgar Hoover, *An Introduction to Regional Economics* (New York: Knopf, 1971).

7. Walter Isard, *Introduction to Regional Science* (Englewood Cliffs, N.J.: Prentice-Hall, 1975).

8. State Statistical Bureau, *China: Urban Statistics 1985* (Hong Kong: Longman Group, 1985).

9. Mao Tse-tung, *On the Correct Handling of Contradictions Among the People* (London: Farleigh Press, 1957).

10. State Statistical Bureau, *Statistical Year Book of China* (Hong Kong: Economic Information Agency, 1985).

11. Thomas J. Stanback and Thiery J. Noyelle, *Cities in Transition* (Totowa, N.J.: Allaheld, Osmun, 1982).

12. David Buck, *Urban Change in China: Policies and Development in Tsinan, Shandong, 1890–1949* (Madison: University of Wisconsin Press, 1978), p. 141.

13. Yasuo Miyakawa, "The Location of Modern Industry in Japan," *Geography of Japan,* Special Publication no. 4 of the Association of Japanese Geographers (Tokyo: Teikoku-Shoin, 1980), pp. 265–298.

14. Chauncy D. Harris, *Cities of the Soviet Union,* Association of American Geographers Monograph Series no. 5 (Washington, D.C.: Association of American Geographers, 1970).

15. World Bank, *Long Term Development Issues and Options* (Baltimore: Johns Hopkins University Press, 1985).

16. See, for example, Kam Wing Chan and Xueqiang Xu, "Urban Population Growth and Urbanization in China Since 1949: Reconstructing a Baseline," *China Quarterly* 104 (1985): 583–613; Kirkby, *Urbanization in China;* Leo A. Orleans and Ly Burnham, "The Enigma of China's Urban Population," *Asian Survey* 24 (7) (1984): 693–707.

PART V: ISSUES AND POLICIES FOR URBAN DEVELOPMENT

16. Bursting at the Seams: Strategies for Controlling Metropolitan Growth in Asia

Yue-man Yeung

During the two decades before 1980, Asia witnessed very rapid urbanization in every subregion. Although the increase was differential, it was generally true of every country. By 1980, three subregions of Asia—East, Southeast, and South—provided empirical support to the oft-stated close relationship between the level of economic development and urbanization (Table 16.1).[1] With the exception of China, all East Asian countries are urbanizing rapidly and have reached a level of urbanization markedly above the developing country norm. South Asian countries, at the other extreme, can be distinguished by their slower-growing economies and their lower than average level of urbanization. Southeast Asian countries may be placed in between these two extremes, with levels of urbanization and economic development intermediate between the other two subregions.

Another way of highlighting the subregional contrasts in urbanization between 1960 and 1980 is to examine the growth rate of urban population in relation to the growth of the largest city in each country. While urban populations more than doubled in eleven of the seventeen countries, the largest cities grew at even faster rates in nine cases (Table 16.2). Specifically, these are Tokyo, Seoul, Taipei, Jakarta, Kuala Lumpur, Manila, Bangkok, Dacca, and Karachi. Despite Dacca's growth by more than 500 percent in the study period, it is primarily in East Asia where mega-cities such as Tokyo and Shanghai are found. This chapter extends a recent study and examines the ways in which large cities in East and Southeast Asia have coped with recent population growth, changes in socioeconomic structure, and the problems they have engendered.[2]

Metropolitan growth in Asia has been widespread and rapid over the

Adapted, by permission of the American Geographical Society, from *Geographical Review* 76 (2): 125–137 (April 1986). Further reproduction without written consent of the society is prohibited.

Table 16.1. Levels of Urbanization in Asia and the World: 1960-2000

Country	1960 (%)	1970 (%)	1980 (%)	1990 (%)	2000 (%)
China	18.7	21.7	28.7	31.5	39.1
Hong Kong	89.1	89.7	90.3	91.4	92.6
Japan	62.8	71.4	78.3	83.0	88.9
N. Korea	40.2	50.1	59.7	67.4	72.9
S. Korea	27.7	40.7	54.8	65.2	71.4
Taiwan	58.4	62.4	66.8		
Burma	19.3	22.8	27.2	33.2	40.9
Indonesia	14.6	17.1	20.2	25.2	32.3
Malaysia	25.2	27.0	29.4	34.2	41.6
Philippines	30.3	32.9	36.2	41.6	49.0
Singapore	77.6	75.3	74.1	75.1	78.5
Thailand	12.5	13.2	14.4	17.5	23.2
Bangladesh	5.2	7.6	11.2	16.1	22.2
India	18.0	19.8	22.2	26.8	33.9
Nepal	3.1	3.9	5.0	6.8	9.8
Pakistan	22.1	24.9	28.2	33.6	41.1
Sri Lanka	17.9	21.9	26.6	32.9	40.6
World	33.9	37.4	41.1	45.8	51.2
More developed regions	60.3	66.4	70.6	75.6	77.8
Less developed regions	21.4	25.2	29.4	36.8	40.4

Source: United Nations, "Estimates and Projections of Urban, Rural and City Populations, 1950-2025: The 1980 Assessment," 1982, table 1; and for Taiwan, Paul K. C. Liu, "Factors and Policies Contributing to Urbanization and Labor Mobility in Taiwan," Industry of Free China (May 1983), p. 3.

past two decades, so that large cities have loomed increasingly large in the national life of many nations. Whereas in 1970 the developing world had altogether seventy-two cities in excess of 1 million inhabitants each, by 1980 East and Southeast Asia alone had sixty "million cities."[3] Equally significant, the share of the largest city in the total urban population of each country is so large that much of the economic wealth, political power, and service facilities is concentrated in the large cities. Bangkok, for example, where 72 percent of Thailand's urban population was concentrated in 1980, is an extreme case of the primate city (Table 16.2). Its dominance over the economic, social, political, and cultural life of the country is virtually complete.

Bangkok is not the only large city whose overarching influence is felt widely in its country. Shanghai, Tokyo, Jakarta, Seoul, and Manila exhibit the same tendency. Moreover, other large cities in the region share the same experience of growing too rapidly and too large without commensurate fiscal and physical provisions. Consequently, the problems that afflict these large cities include chronic housing shortages, snarled traffic, deteriorating basic services, increasing social inequality, omnipresent squatter settlements and slums, widespread poverty, and limited employment opportunities. In order to alleviate problems of metropolitan governance and to forestall a deteriorating urban environment, several cities have experimented with a number of planning, policy, and administrative strategies to control, divert, and decelerate future metropolitan growth. It is instructive to review and compare these strategies, which may be grouped by their nature and intent into physical control strategies, regional planning and management, and policy measures.

Physical Control Strategies

The first group of development strategies are those intended to contain, restrain, and control physical metropolitan growth. One way of reaching this planning objective is to design and build a number of satellite towns within a wider regional context, so that these "new towns" will absorb additional growth in population and economic activities that would otherwise spill over the immediate boundaries of the metropolitan area. The satellite towns ideally are self-contained and balanced communities, reflecting the influence of British new towns, and are placed near enough the metropolis to be under its influence but distant enough to discourage commuting.

In Seoul, proposals for the development of new towns and growth poles at distances of 45 to 120 kilometers from the city were made in the Seoul Metropolitan Area Plan in 1964. The first serious attempt at developing a satellite town, however, occurred in the late 1960s by establishing Sungnam, some 25 kilometers to the south of Seoul, primarily to relocate squatters from the city. Sungnam soon proved to be ineffective in meeting its original objectives, as its lack of industrial employment forced many squatters gradually to move back to Seoul or to commute daily to Seoul. The Seoul authorities shifted the administration of Sungnam to the neighboring province of Kyonggi in 1973, a measure which placed administrative distance between the new town and the capital but did little to solve the basic economic problems. The 1971 basic guidelines for the capital region proposed the development of ten satellite towns within a radius of 30 kilometers from Seoul. In 1978, five medium-size cities, each with a population between 200,000 and 1 million, were designated priority investment centers to provide alternative migration destinations to Seoul. These five centers have expanded rapidly, with populations largely of low-skilled, poorly educated youths, on account of their strong industrial economies.[4]

Table 16.2.   Total Urban and Largest-City Population, Growth Rates, and
               Share of Urban Population in Largest City: Asia, 1960-2000

Country	Urban Population (in millions)			Growth Rate[a] %		Largest City (in millions)		
	1960	1980	2000	1960-1980	1980-2000	1960	1980	2000
China	127.5	256.0	491.9	100.7	92.2	7.7	15.0	25.9
Hong Kong	2.7	4.6	6.5	68.4	40.0	—	—	—
Japan	58.8	91.3	111.1	55.3	21.7	10.7	20.0	23.8
N. Korea	4.2	10.7	19.9	152.4	86.0	0.6	1.3	2.2
S. Korea	6.9	21.1	36.2	204.1	72.0	2.4	8.5	13.7
Taiwan	6.3	11.9	—	88.2	—	1.1	2.2	—
Burma	4.3	9.6	22.5	123.6	135.0	1.0	2.2	4.7
Indonesia	14.3	29.9	64.1	109.9	114.3	2.9	7.0	14.3
Malaysia	2.1	4.1	8.8	100.5	114.1	0.4	1.1	2.6
Philippines	8.5	17.8	37.8	109.3	112.0	2.3	5.7	10.5
Singapore	1.3	1.8	2.3	39.6	31.5	—	—	—
Thailand	3.4	6.8	15.9	98.5	135.2	2.2	4.9	9.9
Bangladesh	2.6	9.9	33.0	274.1	232.9	0.5	2.8	10.2
India	78.9	152.1	325.9	92.8	114.3	5.6	8.9	15.9
Nepal	0.3	0.7	2.2	145.2	210.3	0.1	0.2	0.5
Pakistan	10.9	24.5	57.5	124.3	134.8	2.0	5.0	11.4
Sri Lanka	1.8	3.9	8.6	122.1	117.4	0.5	0.6	1.1

Sources: United Nations, Patterns of Urban and Rural Population Growth,
1980, table 48; United Nations, "Estimates and Projections of Urban,
Rural and City Populations, 1950-2025: The 1980 Assessment," 1982,
tables 2 and 8; Paul K. C. Liu, "Labor Mobility and Utilization in
Relation to Urbanization in Taiwan," Industry of Free China (May
1982), p. 4, and Paul K. C. Liu, "Factors and Policies Contributing
to Urbanization and Labor Mobility in Taiwan," Industry of Free
China (May 1983), p. 3.

In Shanghai, satellite town development has been pursued vigorously
since the late 1950s, and its successful implementation has been largely
responsible for maintaining Shanghai's remarkable population stability
over the past twenty-five years. Shanghai's urban population stood at
11.8 million in 1982 compared with 10.8 million in 1964, a mere 9.6
percent increase in eighteen years.[5] A satellite town policy has been
adopted in the planning for the Shanghai City Region since 1958, when
its area was expanded ten times to 6,000 square kilometers. Satellite
towns are planned at a distance of 20 to 70 kilometers from the city to
accommodate 50,000 to 200,000 inhabitants (Figure 16.1). It is envisaged that at this distance, satellites will not be absorbed by the parent
city and will retain mutual advantages in industrial production and
other functional linkages. By 1974, between sixty and seventy satellites

Growth Rate[a] %		Share of Urban Population[a] %			
1960-1980	1980-2000	1960	1980	2000	City
94.8	72.7	6.0	5.9	5.3	Shanghai
—	—	—	—	—	
87.6	19.0	18.2	22.0	21.4	Tokyo
102.0	74.6	15.0	12.0	11.3	Pyongyang
254.4	61.2	34.1	40.3	37.9	Seoul
102.1	—	17.5	18.8	—	Taipei
123.4	117.3	22.8	22.9	21.1	Rangoon
141.4	104.3	20.3	23.4	22.3	Jakarta
198.9	130.7	18.0	26.9	28.9	Kuala Lumpur
147.6	84.2	26.9	31.8	27.8	Manila
—	—	—	—	—	
126.4	102.0	65.1	72.0	62.3	Bangkok-Thonburi
446.4	264.3	19.6	28.7	30.9	Dacca
58.9	78.7	7.3	5.6	4.9	Calcutta
61.0	164.7	41.4	26.8	22.8	Kathmandu
150.3	128.0	18.3	20.4	19.8	Karachi
32.0	73.9	27.7	16.4	13.2	Colombo

[a]Computed from source tables, not from rounded figures presented here.

had been established in suburban Shanghai.[6] Since 1957, highway construction, as well as other infrastructure development, has proceeded hand in hand with satellite town growth.[7] One can only conclude that planned spatial redistribution of population within the city region of Shanghai has been achieved through satellite town planning. The success of Shanghai's satellite communities is due partly to their being self-contained and designed with a number of separate independent neighborhoods. Each neighborhood is clustered around a factory or major commercial center, hence minimizing travel between home and workplace. Other essential services and facilities are also provided within the neighborhood. Each satellite town in the city region may be distinguished by its type of industrial production.[8]

With the explosive growth that Tokyo experienced in the postwar

Figure 16.1. Satellite Towns in the Shanghai City Region

period, the pressure of population congestion and inadequate services began to be felt in the late 1950s. In the 1956 development plan, satellite towns were identified as potential population growth areas to accommodate decentralized population and employment. These towns were designated at distances of 27 to 72 kilometers from central Tokyo. Among the more developed of these is Tama New Town, built and planned by the Tokyo metropolitan government in cooperation with the Japan Housing Corporation. Tama New Town is developing as a commuter city, with a projected population of 400,000, in the Tama Hills in the western suburbs of the capital. It extends in an east–west direction for 13 kilometers at a site which is 29–40 kilometers west of Toyko. The new city is being created in the only large rural area remaining in the Tokyo region and is linked to the city center by extensions of two railway lines. The town's construction is expected to be completed by 1990.[9] Partly the result of effective commuter railway transportation, Tokyo's satellite communities have never developed a self-contained status as in Shanghai. As a result, the commuting radius in Tokyo has been progressively extended, now reaching as far as 50 kilometers (Figure 16.2).[10] This is reflected in the low nighttime population compared to daytime population in the central area of Tokyo. Tokyo has been extending its sphere of influence rather than decentralizing population and employment outside the direct influence of the metropolis.

On a much smaller scale, the city-states of Hong Kong and Singapore also have decentralized population and employment from con-

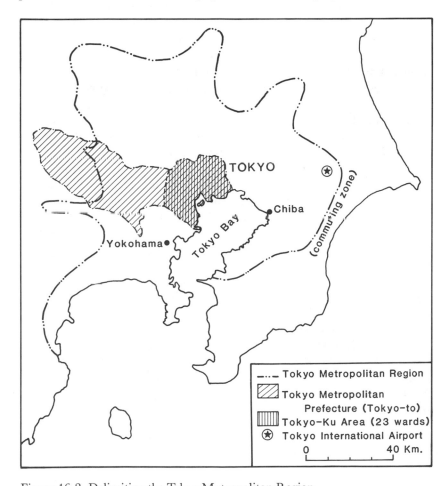

Figure 16.2. Delimiting the Tokyo Metropolitan Region

gested core areas through the development of new towns since the early 1960s. In both cases, public housing has been a salient component in this development, resulting in improved living conditions in these communities. The program in Hong Kong has been pursued in earnest since 1972, when the governor announced an ambitious ten-year housing program, essentially through the development of new towns in the New Territories. A measure of the decentralization program's success can be gained by studying the relative distribution of population. In 1971, some 81.1 percent of the total population of Hong Kong lived in the main urban area, compared with 72.9 percent in 1981. Conversely, the proportion of the population living in the new towns increased from 9.8 percent in 1971 to 18.8 percent in 1981.[11]

Another widely applied planning tool to contain metropolitan growth is the use of greenbelts, and several large Asian cities have adopted this strategy to limit undesirable expansion. In Tokyo, an 11-kilometer-wide greenbelt was delineated in the 1956 development plan beyond the defined built-up area which extended 16 kilometers in all directions from Tokyo Central Station. Unable to curb development without commensurate legal power, the strategy was abandoned a decade later to be replaced in 1965 by a new suburban development area beginning 48 kilometers from the city center.[12] The new suburban growth area was physically contiguous with the existing urban area, but open space was preserved where possible. In 1968 the concept of distinguishing urban promotion areas and urban control areas was introduced. The former consisted of those areas which were already urbanized or which would be preferentially and systematically urbanized within ten years or so. The latter consisted of those areas where urbanization had to be restricted. This distinction is made in the present plans for Tokyo's future development.[13]

In Seoul the greenbelt was formally instituted to contain physical growth in 1972 through the revision of the City Planning Act. The concept was later extended to thirteen other major urban areas in South Korea. By 1980, a total of 5,420 square kilometers had been designated as greenbelts representing 11 percent of the total urban area in the country. For Seoul alone, 369.5 square kilometers was designated greenbelt, of which 66.5 percent was development-restricted.[14] Likewise, in Bangkok greenbelts covering agricultural land 12 kilometers wide along the eastern and western flanks of Bangkok's built-up areas were introduced in 1981, and building was prohibited more than 100 meters from either side of the existing roads.[15] Somewhat different in purpose, but not in function, has been the preservation of a vegetable production belt around the central city and satellite communities in Shanghai.[16] Food production for the city has therefore been safeguarded. In 1959 Shanghai itself produced 75 percent of the fruit and 97 percent of the vegetables its inhabitants consumed.[17]

A third planning strategy often considered, but not yet widely adopted, is the construction of new capital cities to relieve pressure on existing ones. In 1976, among the plans drawn up for the dispersal and redistribution of Seoul's population was the proposal for a new administrative capital. Such a project has long been considered by South Korea's policymakers, as Seoul is seen to appeal to some in-migrants because of its ready access to political power and opportunities for upward social mobility. The new capital city is envisaged to reduce the sociopolitical attraction of Seoul by removing from the city the central administrative and executive functions of the government. The new capital would also be seen as a symbol of South Korea's postwar development and prosperity.[18] The construction plan has been permanently shelved, however, since the assassination of President Park Chung Hee in 1979. The latest proposal for twin cities comes from Malaysia, where the present capital, Kuala Lumpur, does not suffer the same degree of congestion and concentration as some other large Asian capitals. The Malaysian government recently revealed plans for constructing a new city at Janda Baik, at present a quiet retreat 31 kilometers from Kuala Lumpur. Initially the new city will be under the administration of Kuala Lumpur, but it will grow to become a city of 100,000 by 1990 and 500,000 by the year 2000.[19]

Regional Planning and Management

Implicit in growth restraint strategies is an increasing awareness of spatial interdependence between the metropolis and the wider region of which it is part. It is increasingly recognized that metropolitan growth problems cannot be tackled on their own within a restricted geographical setting. A large region surrounding the metropolis must be incorporated into its planning and development if growth is to proceed in an orderly manner and along preconceived lines. This explains the tendency for the progressive expansion of the region that is considered during the planning of the metropolis or in relation to it.

Among the large Asian cities, Tokyo is probably the first to adopt a regional planning approach in order to come to terms with its remarkable postwar population growth and economic development. When the National Capital Region was proclaimed in 1956, planning for the Tokyo metropolitan government, three whole prefectures, and parts of four other prefectures came under the National Capital Region Development Commission. The new metropolitan region encompasses an area 97 to 120 kilometers from central Tokyo. Over the years, new laws have been enacted to empower implementation agencies to carry out their plans, the administrative structure has been reorganized and streamlined, and more concrete plans have been formulated for regional decentralization. But the principle of a regionwide approach to deal with Tokyo's manifold problems arising from rapid growth and concentrated development has been adhered to as Tokyo plans for the remaining years of this century.[20]

Similarly, immediately after the massive annexation of territory by the city of Shanghai, the City Region was established in 1958. One of the major objectives behind this move was to provide a wider range of cities to be selected for industrial development and new satellite towns. The measure permitted planners to locate future satellite towns and industrial production at optimal distances from the central city, generally considered to be between 20 and 70 kilometers (Figure 16.1). Satellite towns were proposed, wherever possible at existing town sites, and industrial districts were proposed at sites with easy access to water and rail transportation. In order to minimize capital investment, preference was given to suburban towns already possessing a basic urban infrastructure. An intensification of agricultural land use and large-scale conversion of urban fringe cropland into market gardens accompanied the development of satellite towns. All in all, Shanghai has succeeded in holding its growth and development within manageable limits, and population growth and new industrial production have been effectively dispersed to many preselected localities within a large region.[21]

Although decentralization objectives were embodied in development plans for the Seoul Metropolitan Area in 1964 and subsequent years, relentless population pressure and economic growth continued to add to Seoul's unwanted size. Only in the late 1970s did the rates of growth in concentration indices begin to moderate. The Capital Region Plan was adopted in 1981 and covered a ten-year period. Under the plan, a region of 12,489 square kilometers is seen to interact spatially with Seoul. Interdependencies are especially important in land use, transportation, jobs, and housing location, as the plan specifically allows intraregional decentralization to take precedence over interurban dispersal. The plan envisages five subregions in the Capital Region, each with a specific land use plan and development strategy. The subregions consist of a restricted development region (Zone I), a controlled development region (Zone II), an encouraged development region (Zone III), an environmental conservation region (Zone IV), and a special development region (Zone V) (Figure 16.3). More than half of the total region is to be reserved as open space for national security purposes, and future population growth will be accommodated primarily in Zones

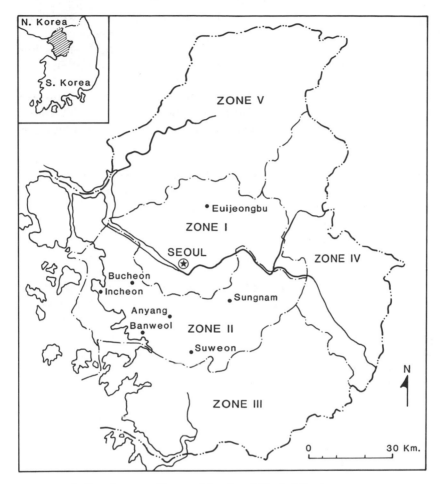

Figure 16.3. Development Zones of the Seoul Capital Region

II and III, consisting of 45 percent of the total area. The plan appears to be well conceived but without detailed implementation guidelines. Coordinated among the thirty local and provincial governments affected by the regional land use plan may prove to be a serious obstacle in translating the plan into reality.[22] Hwang further observes that the ultimate success of the plan depends upon strict preservation of the greenbelt around Seoul, more stringent control of office development (which so far has counteracted some of the positive results of the policy of population and industrial decentralization), and successful development of growth centers in other regions of the country.[23]

Within Southeast Asia there also have been attempts to improve and enlarge metropolitan planning and development on a regionwide basis, notwithstanding efforts made on a smaller scale. The most noteworthy administrative innovation has been the creation of the Metropolitan Manila Area, also referred to as the National Capital Region, in 1975. With a presidential decree, the Metro Manila Commission (MMC) was created out of four cities and thirteen municipalities possessing an area of 636 square kilometers and a population of 6 million in 1980. One of the operational goals of the MMC is the integration of planning and improved delivery of basic services within its service area in order to rectify the previous inefficiency of metropolitan services such as flood control, police and fire protection, traffic management, and water supply. Consequently, one of the MMC's first achievements was the adoption in 1976 of a structure plan for Metro Manila. The plan makes provisions for the relative location of activities, the spatial arrangement of functional areas, and the desired pattern of metropolitan growth. The metropolitan region is divided into an inner core of high-density development, an intermediate area of low-density residential development, and an outer area extending 50 kilometers beyond the inner core.[24] The reorganization of metropolitan government in Manila is the first step in reducing bureaucratic redundancy and fiscal competition, but a real assessment of the accomplishments of the new style of governance is overdue.

Kuala Lumpur provides an example which demonstrates time lag in legal provisions relating to metropolitan planning in the face of rapid development. In 1974 the Federal Capital of Kuala Lumpur annexed an area almost twice its own size and expanded to a total of 243 square kilometers (the Federal Territory). By virtue of an amendment, the City of Kuala Lumpur (Planning) Act of 1973 was extended to cover the whole Federal Territory. A problem developed, however, because, in the absence of a comprehensive development plan outside the original 93-square-kilometer Federal Capital, development control had to be carried out on a piecemeal basis. Meanwhile, Parliament passed in 1976 the Town and Country Planning Act, which provided a new legal framework for planning and development control in peninsular Malaysia outside the Federal Territory. The act introduced the "structure plan system," with its emphasis on social, economic, physical, and other issues, as opposed to the "comprehensive development plan" system, which is physically oriented. The Federal Territory adopted the same system with the enactment of the Federal Territory (Planning) Act in 1982. A structure plan, to be reviewed periodically, envisages development of a modern and different Kuala Lumpur over the next twenty years.[25] The plan has followed faithfully the policy guidelines of the New Economic Policy and has been criticized as unduly favoring *bumiputras* (Malays).[26]

Elsewhere, in the metropolitan area of Bangkok, the Department of Town and Country has drawn a development plan for the year 1990. The plan follows the 1971 Development Plan of Greater Bangkok covering an area of approximately 732 square kilometers. The planning area includes the four municipalities of Greater Bangkok and a certain proportion of the surrounding nonmunicipal land. The innovative feature of the plan is that it gives recognition to the influence of the large hinterland on the development of the city of Bangkok. Specifically the plan delineates an "inner area of absolute influence," measuring 4,150 square kilometers with a population of 2.8 million, a "middle area" broadly corresponding to the area encompassed by a circle with a radius of 75 kilometers centered on Bangkok, and an "outer area of absolute influence" consisting of an area of some 50,000 square kilometers with Chainat, Hua Hin, Kanchanaburi, and Nakhon Nayok on the periphery marking the outer limits of the city region of Bangkok. Each of these zones is roughly defined by a concentric circle around Bangkok with a decline in influence away from the city.[27]

Finally, in Indonesia the interminable north–south sprawl of Jakarta has led to such horrendous problems with service provision and uncoordinated development that planners have come up with an innovative solution. It involves basically the extension of Jakarta's planning and development context to a wider region by inclusion of a few adjacent cities. Given the name of Jabotabek, this city region is to encompass Jakarta, Bogor, Tangerang, and Bekasi, an area projected to have a population of 25 million by the year 2003. For Repelita IV (1984–1988), the central government has earmarked Rp. 900 billion (US$904.5 million) to be spent on Jabotabek, with another 25 percent of the projected expenditure to be raised by new taxes. The likelihood that many of the projects in the Jabotabek master plan will be implemented depends critically on the ability of Jakarta and its associated cities to devise a new revenue structure to finance development.[28] In the absence of adequate financial provisions, the new city region plan may merely diffuse Jakarta's growing pains to a wider region.

Policy Measures

Some important policies have been invoked to control metropolitan growth in various parts of East and Southeast Asia. Each of these measures was born in an ideological and sociological context befitting the particular city. First is the mass movement of reverse migration from Chinese cities, or *hsia-fang* (sending down), of urban dwellers to the countryside. To a degree, the movement contributed to stabilizing the size of China's urban population—witness Shanghai's remarkable population stability at about the 10 million level since 1959. One estimate identifies some 20 million urban dwellers throughout the country as involved in this movement during the period 1961 to 1963 alone.[29] The rustication program that spanned approximately two decades beginning with the mid-1950s was motivated by several goals both ideological and practical: narrowing the differences between city and countryside and between labor and mental work, alleviating the threat of urban unemployment, and mobilizing educated city youths to serve as catalysts for rural transformation. Generally speaking, the movement succeeded in meeting its objectives owing to the Chinese government's strong administrative controls (travel permits and ration cards), mass media propaganda, and political exhortation. The program did encounter opposition from the farmers, the rusticated youths, and their families, however. Thus the campaign was heavily toned down after 1974 and eventually was abandoned.[30]

Another quite different policy decision that affected only one city, rather than the whole country, is Jakarta's "closed city" policy, implemented since August 1970 for new jobless settlers. This drastic policy reflects the futility of other alternatives in stemming the tide of rural–urban migration. Under the policy, in-migrants are required to show evidence of employment and housing accommodation before they are issued residence permits. Further, migrants must deposit with the city government for six months the equivalent of the return fare to the point of origin. The policy was intended primarily to produce a psychological impact rather than to physically prevent people from coming to Jakarta.[31] The evidence to date indicates that the policy has produced mixed results. On the one hand, Suharto and colleagues suggest that there has been no noticeable diminution of the rate of growth from migration.[32] An average of 648 migrants have continued to enter Jakarta every day. On the other hand, Papanek has found that since a high "price" is attached to the residency card, the lowest-income groups tend to ignore the regulation altogether whereas others who need the card engage in bribery and corruption.[33]

Of the large cities in East and Southeast Asia, Seoul experienced the fastest growth during the period 1960–1980 and best exemplifies the range of possible policy measures to control metropolitan growth. In 1960, Seoul had 2.4 million inhabitants, but by 1980 its population had soared to 8.5 million—a 254 percent increase (Table 16.2). The growth was particularly rapid in the 1960s, when in-migration was the principal factor contributing to population growth. In five years alone between 1966 and 1970, of 1.7 million inhabitants added to Seoul, 82 percent were migrants from rural areas.[34] The Seoul government recognized the gravity of the situation and began to apply, beginning in 1969, a battery of policy instruments that left scarcely any aspect of urban life untouched. The primary objectives of these measures, which are summarized in Table 16.3, are to check further uncontrolled growth of Seoul and to disperse population and economic activities to other parts of the country.

To highlight some of these policy measures, a new tax called the citizen tax was introduced in 1973, making tax rates discriminatory against people living in Seoul. At the same time, differential property tax rates were applied to newly established factories in Seoul, which had to pay three times the normal rate. In the sphere of education, policies in place since the early 1970s were aimed at decentralizing both institutions and students. The measures included the application of differential school fees, the introduction of preliminary college entrance examinations with regional quotas, the adoption of professor exchange programs, and the strict control of expansion in Seoul of existing universities. Thus, in the period 1973–1976, some 69 percent of the 11,565 additional places for college students went to universities outside the Seoul region.[35]

By 1975, when Seoul's population reached 6.8 million, or 41 percent of South Korea's urban population, there were few signs of slackening in the rate of growth.[36] The Seoul government thus attempted to attack the problem of too-rapid growth more systematically along two fronts: population and industries. In 1977 the Basic Plan for Redistribution of the Population of the Capital Region was announced. The plan includes proposals to redistribute population to other areas of South Korea over a ten-year period, as well as short-term measures to achieve a reduction in Seoul's population. These short-term measures included restriction of in-migration to Seoul, encouragement of out-migration, and accommodation of the dispersed population in other regions. For the first time, Seoul's population and planning problems were viewed in a national context and tied to industrial relocation and national land use plans. The plan is new in its preventive and development-oriented approach.[37] The target population figure for Seoul of 7.4 million in 1986 has been a matter of debate, however. The government proposed to hold Seoul's population steady at its 1977 level of 7.4 million, but with the projected population reaching 11.4 million by 1986, some 4 million inhabitants will have to be diverted. Critics have viewed this population decentralization policy, if carried to its logical conclusion, as going too far and having every risk of jeopardizing the planned economic growth of the country.[38]

Concomitant with the population redistribution plan was the industrial relocation plan, initiated by the Distribution of Industry Act of 1977, for creating employment opportunities in outlying regions in accordance with South Korea's fifteen-year (1977–1991) economic and

Table 16.3. Policy Measures for Guiding Seoul's Controlled Growth

Policy Measure	Concerned Agencies and Period	Remarks
Economic and industrial		
Enactment of regional industry development	1969	
Designation of industrial parks	MOCI (1970)[a]	11 industrial parks designated
3 years tax exemption for corporation income	MOCI	
Restricting new construction and expansion of facilities in Seoul	Seoul (1975)[a]	
Reducing semi-industrial zones within Seoul north of Han River	Seoul (1972)	
Urban planning and development		
Amendment of Urban Planning Law; designated greenbelt surrounding Seoul (143 sq km)	MOC (1972)[a]	Amended in 1972; environment conservation, military strategic consideration as well as development of restricted area amended
Amendment of Construction Law; implementing urban renewal programs	Seoul (1972)	Banned substandard housing construction
Construction of satellite city of Seongnam	Seoul (1972)	Resulted in expansion of Metropolitan Seoul
Education		
Restricting student transfers into Seoul	MOE (1970)[a]	To reduce educational population in Seoul
Imposing school fees according to city size	MOE (1970)	Limited to public schools

Policy	Agency (year)	Comments
Allotting regional quotas for college applicants	MOE (1973)	To reduce education as cause for immigration
Restricting new establishment and expansion of college departments in Seoul	MOE (1973)	
Starting program of exchange professors between Seoul and other regions	MOE (1973)	To reduce quality gap in college education
Restricting new middle and high schools in Seoul, particularly north of Han River	MOE (1974); Seoul	
Administrative and tax		
Amendment of Local Tax Law; creation of residence tax	MHA (1973)[a]	Amendment applied to metropolitan residents
Transfer of central administrative functions to local offices (except policymaking functions)	PGO[a]	Presidential Decree No. 4710
Gradual removal of state-run firms and other public agencies from Seoul to other regions	1972	
Enactment of Local Industry Tax Regulation (discriminatory tax) for factories constructed in Seoul)	MHA (1973)	Regulation by MHA

Source: Kim and Donaldson, "Dealing with Seoul's Population Growth," Asian Survey 19(7) (July 1979): 664-665.

[a]MOCI = Ministry of Commerce and Industry; Seoul = Seoul Municipal Government; MOC = Ministry of Construction; MOE = Ministry of Education; MHA = Ministry of Home Affairs; PGC = Department of Personnel and General Office.

land development plan. As many in-migrants flock to Seoul in search of better economic opportunities, industrial location is seen as a key variable that can be redesigned to serve the purposes of population redistribution.[39] Spatial rearrangement of manufacturing can thus be a most effective policy instrument. The experience to date shows that the more relocatable industries are the pollution-causing, footloose enterprises, bigger rather than smaller, which are in need of space for expansion, more mobile (such as textiles, food, and machinery), and characterized as economically robust. The policy criteria for identifying relocatable industries vary with the size of firms, the type of production, interindustry links, the distribution of market and supply areas, and labor's availability and cost.[40]

It is too early to assess fully the effectiveness of the various policy measures that Seoul has adopted with such determination in order to control its metropolitan growth. Nevertheless, the annual average rate of 7 to 9 percent population increase in previous years had slowed to approximately 4 percent by the late 1970s. Over the past fifteen years, Seoul's share in many indices of industrial employment and economic production has also decreased markedly. In 1973, Seoul accounted for 7.3 percent and 23.4 percent, respectively, of the area and number of firms in South Korea's industrial estates. By 1978, the corresponding figures had decreased to 1.9 percent and 13.1 percent, respectively.[41] Nevertheless, a major destabilizing factor that runs counter to the decentralizing tendency has been the rapid growth of the service sector, in particular office development. This, too, has to be controlled if the decentralization policy is to be given a fair chance of reaching its desired goals.[42]

Conclusion

The foregoing review of strategies designed to control metropolitan growth in Southeast and East Asia is concerned only with macrolevel policies. Coping mechanisms geared to alleviating or solving problems within the cities are equally important but have been studied elsewhere.[43] None of the strategies has been entirely successful, but most of them have fulfilled, in varying degrees, the restraint or decentralization objectives for which they are designed. In reviewing the policies, several factors seem to play a critical role in determining their success or failure.

The first is the need for coordination among implementation agencies, most vividly illustrated by the case of Seoul. Successful decentralization policies since the early 1960s failed to slow Seoul's unremitting growth because of the lack of coordination among the agencies charged with different functions and spheres of activity. Without an effective implementation plan, thoughtfully designed plans to curb metropolitan growth may be rendered meaningless. The problem of coordination and implementation is especially acute when the metropolitan area is saddled with competing administrations stemming from numerous independent municipal authorities, as was the case in Manila prior to 1975. Metro-wide services and facilities should have improved with the creation of the Metro Manila Commission, but a careful assessment has not yet been undertaken.

Second, even the best-conceived growth control plans cannot be translated into reality if the city is short of funds. Tokyo, Jakarta, and Bangkok, to cite only a few examples, have not been able to carry out some of their development plans due to financial constraints. Not surprisingly, therefore, Tokyo has been called a city of paradoxes: Although it is probably the most technologically advanced city in Asia, its inhabitants often live at a level below lesser cities in the region. The problem came to a head in 1976 when Tokyo was characterized as a world city in a financial crisis.[44] Similarly, much to the benefit of the individual but to the detriment of the city, property, land, and cars are grossly undertaxed in Jakarta and Bangkok, resulting in a dependence on the central government for meeting a substantial proportion of the city expenditure and in a situation with deteriorating urban services.

Third, the cities reviewed in this study provide empirical evidence for the increasingly current planning philosophy that, in order for metropolitan growth restraint policies to succeed, a large region must be included in the planning and operational strategies. Shanghai, Seoul, Tokyo, and Jakarta have all followed this approach. In fact, to ensure success and integration of the large city with other cities and regions in the country, city–region development plans should be articulated with a national urbanization policy. In this way, development in the large city can be related not only to its immediate region but to the national setting as well.

Whatever the effectiveness of metropolitan growth control strategies in Asia, they are vitally necessary in the light of recent development and urbanization trends. Although most of the control strategies have been employed in a different manner in other regions of the world, several peculiarly Asian policies have been reviewed. These need to be continually improved and refined while innovative solutions are sought. Already some large urban agglomerations have appeared in Asia, and present population growth trends suggest continuation of rapid urbanization to the end of this century, when eighteen of the twenty-five largest cities in the world probably will be in Asia. The better these Asian cities can manage their growth and devise dispersal strategies, the sooner they will be prepared for the more urban world projected for the next century.

NOTES

1. For illustrative purposes, the level of economic development in the three subregions may be reflected in the GNP per capita figures in several selected countries. In 1980, according to the World Bank, the GNP per capita for the Republic of Korea, the Philippines, and Pakistan was, respectively, US$1,490, $710, and $310.

2. See Yue-man Yeung, "Great Cities of Eastern Asia," in Mattei Dogan and John D. Kasarda (eds.), *The Metropolis Era: A World of Giant Cities* (Newbury Park: Sage Publications, 1988), pp. 155–186.

3. Ibid.

4. Hyung-koon Kim, "Social Factors of Migration from Rural to Urban Areas with Special Reference to Developing Countries: The Case of Korea," *Social Indicators Research* 10 (1) (January 1981): 29–74.

5. Shanghai Shehui Kexue Yuan, *Shanghai Jingji: 1949–1982* [The economy of Shanghai, 1949–1982] (Shanghai: Renmen Chubanshe, 1983), p. 1232.

6. Ka-iu Fung, "Satellite Town Development in the Shanghai City Region," *Town Planning Review* 52 (1) (January 1981): 26–46.

7. Shanghai Shehui Kexue Yuan, *Shanghai Jingji: 1949–1982,* p. 720.

8. Fung, "Satellite Town Development," p. 34.

9. Masahiko Honjo, "Tokyo: Giant Metropolis of the Orient," in H. W. Eldredge (ed.), *World Capitals: Toward Guided Urbanization* (New York: Anchor Press, 1975), pp. 340–387.

10. Tokyo Metropolitan Government, *Long-Term Plan Tokyo Metropolis: "My Town Tokyo" Heading into the 21st Century* (Tokyo: TMG Municipal Library 18, 1984), p. 33.

11. Anthony G. O. Yeh and Peter K. W. Fong, "Public Housing and Urban Development in Hong Kong," *Third World Planning Review* 6 (1) (February 1984): 83.

12. Peter Hall, *The World Cities* (New York: McGraw-Hill, 1977), p. 236.

13. Tokyo Metropolitan Government, *Plain Talk About Tokyo: The Administration of the Tokyo Metropolitan Government,* 2d ed. (Tokyo: TMG, 1984), p. 69.

14. Suo Young Park, "Urban Growth and National Policy in Korea," paper presented at the Pacific Science Association Inter-Congress in Singapore, September 1981, p. 35; Seoul Metropolitan Government, *Seoul: Metropolitan Administration* (Seoul, 1983), p. 50.

15. Sidhijai Tanphiphat, "Thailand Country Study: Urban Land Management Policies and Experience," paper presented at International Seminar on Urban Development Policies in Nagoya, UNCRD, October 1982, p. 36.

16. Ka-iu Fung, "The Spatial Development of Shanghai," in C. Howe (ed.), *Shanghai: Revolution and Development in an Asian Metropolis* (Cambridge: Cambridge University Press, 1981), pp. 292–294.

17. Lynn T. White, "The Suburban Transformation," in C. Howe (ed.), *Shanghai: Revolution and Development in an Asian Metropolis* (Cambridge: Cambridge University Press, 1981), p. 260.

18. Son-Ung Kim and Peter Donaldson, "Dealing with Seoul's Population Growth: Government Plans and Their Implementation," *Asian Survey* 19 (7) (July 1979): 671.

19. Michael Specter, "The 'Small Town' Big City," *Far Eastern Economic Review* 125 (39) (27 September 1984): 23–30.

20. Hall, *World Cities,* pp. 233–237.

21. Fung, "Spatial Development," pp. 269–300.

22. Won Kim, "Land Use Planning in a Rapidly Growing Metropolis: The Case of Seoul," *Asian Economies* 3 (January 1983): 3–21.

23. Myo-chang Hwang, "A Search for a Development Strategy for the Capital Region of Korea," in Y. H. Rho and M. C. Hwang (eds.), *Metropolitan Planning: Issues and Policies* (Seoul: Korea Research Institute for Human Settlements, 1979), p. 18.

24. L. A. Viloria, "Manila: Creation of a Metropolitan Government," in M. Honjo (ed.), *Urbanization and Regional Development* (Singapore: Maruzen Asia, 1981), p. 295.

25. Dewan Bandaraya, *Kuala Lumpur Draft Structure Plan* (Kuala Lumpur: Dewan Bandaraya, 1982).

26. Specter, "The 'Small Town' Big City."

27. Wolf Donner, *The Five Faces of Thailand: An Economic Geography* (New York: St. Martin's Press, 1978), pp. 872–875.

28. Michael Specter, "A Sprawling, Thirsty Giant," *Far Eastern Economic Review* 123 (13) (29 March 1984): 23–30.

29. Jan S. Prybyla, "*Hsia-Fang:* The Economics and Politics of Rustication in China," *Pacific Affairs* 48 (?) (Summer 1975): 153–172.

30. P. H. Chang, "China's Rustication Movement," *Current History* (September 1975): 85–89; Pi-chao Chen, "Overurbanization, Rustication of Urban-Educated Youths, and Politics of Rural Transformation," *Comparative Politics* (April 1972): 361–386.

31. R. Critchfield, "The Plight of the Cities: Jakarta, the First to 'Close'," *Columbia Journal of World Business* 6 (4) (July–August 1971): 89–93.

32. Suharso and others, *Migration and Education in Jakarta* (Jakarta: LEKNAS, 1975).

33. G. V. Papanek, "The Poor of Jakarta," *Economic Development and Cultural Change* 24 (1) (October 1975): 1–28.

34. Won-yong Kwon, "A Study of the Economic Impact of Industrial Relocation: The Case of Seoul," *Urban Studies* 18 (1) (February 1981): 73–90.

35. Hwang, "Search for a Development Strategy," p. 8.

36. Kwon, "Economic Impact," p. 79.

37. Kim and Donaldson, "Dealing with Seoul's Population Growth."

38. Hwang, "Search for a Development Strategy."

39. Kim and Donaldson, "Dealing with Seoul's Population Growth."

40. Kwon, "Economic Impact."

41. Hwang, "Search for a Development Strategy," pp. 12–13.

42. Myo-chang Hwang, "Planning Strategies for Metropolitan Seoul," in W. Kim (ed.), *The Year 2000: Urban Growth and Perspectives for Seoul* (Seoul: Korea Planners Association, 1980), pp. 31–53.

43. Yeung, "Great Cities."

44. Hall, *World Cities,* p. 237.

17. Planning in Hong Kong: Accomplishments and Failures

BRUCE TAYLOR

A STRICT interpretation of the term "planning," when applied to governmental activity in an urban area, would have it be synonymous with the activity known more fully as land use planning or town planning—that is, the purposeful arrangement of different land uses into a pattern that best provides for the needs of those who make use of the land. By setting appropriate policies to shape urban development, which traditionally have taken the form of a master plan or comprehensive plan for the area, the land use planner guides the growth (or, sometimes, the decline) of a city or region so as to produce a spatial pattern of land uses reflecting the functions that society attaches to its cities, efficiency of operation being prominent among these functions in modern planning doctrine. The profession of urban planning grew up in recognition of the need for trained practitioners who could analyze land use problems affecting cities or regions and suggest appropriate remedies. From its origins in the Western industrialized nations, the planning profession has spread to much of the rest of the world. An identifiable group of professional planners, carrying out the activities normally associated with land use planning, has been part of the government administrative machinery in Hong Kong since the early 1950s.[1]

There is, however, another and broader way to apply the term "planning" in relation to an urban area. The term may relate to a process of foreseeing the future needs or aspirations of residents in the area and intervening in its ongoing development in order to meet them. "Planning" here refers not only to activities which lead to production of a specific product, such as a land use plan, or even to those concerned with ordering the built environment, but to any intervention which seeks to influence the process of change in the area in order to create a desirable outcome. The cast of characters involved in planning-related work under this interpretation extends well beyond the professional land use planners to encompass many other officials: finance officers who draw up a program for capital works expenditures, engineers who design a highway, managers who administer a housing rehabilitation program, and a host of others too numerous to list. Even judges can be said to be involved in planning if, as in the United States, disputes over contentious issues related to urban development tend to find their way into the court system.

It is this usage which is implied by K. S. Pun, a prominent planner in the Hong Kong civil service, when he defines his task and that of his colleagues not in relation to producing a product but to creating an outcome: "Urban planning aims at providing the necessary physical setting and facilities in which to build an optimum living and working environment so as to enable present and future citizens to lead a satisfactory and satisfying life."[2] Pun's definition suggests that the work of officials who have guided the course of Hong Kong's development (including the territory's professional land use planners) might best be evaluated according to the outcomes that have resulted from it: Have their actions resulted in better living conditions for the residents of Hong Kong? Deriving an answer to this question is the fundamental purpose of this study.

This chapter is divided into three sections. A brief background section touches on elements of Hong Kong's physical setting and governmental system which affect the context in which the territory's planners operate. Following this, five areas of accomplishment and six areas of failure by planners in Hong Kong are enumerated and closely examined in the last two sections.[3] The listing of accomplishments and failures is not intended to be exhaustive; rather, it is illustrative of the outcomes from planned intervention in the urban development process that have had a bearing on the quality of life experienced by the territory's residents.

The Context of Planning in Hong Kong

As in any other area, Hong Kong's setting has led to special difficulties in planning its continuing development, while the territory's governmental system has an important bearing on the rationale for officially sanctioned interventions in the development process. This section touches on a few of the significant local conditions affecting planning in Hong Kong and sets the context for the later evaluations of accomplishment and failure.

Hong Kong is, first, a small territory with an area of only about 1,070 square kilometers (413 square miles). Much of the land is not easily developable owing to its steepness or, in the far northwest, to its swampiness; hence the bulk of the territory's 5.6 million residents are crowded onto only a small proportion (about one-sixth) of the available land.[4] The consequence is a very high population density by world standards in the built-up areas, perhaps most noticeable in the lower-income communities of Kowloon (see Figure 17.1), where density rises to as high as 165,000 persons per square kilometer. Some of the most pressing problems confronting planners in Hong Kong are traceable to overcrowding in these older parts of the built-up area. Virtually all residents of Hong Kong, however, including the wealthiest, have their lives affected in some fashion by high density and its associated traffic congestion, high noise levels, and limited access to green space and other amenities.

The growth of Hong Kong in the past has not followed the smooth and steady trajectory that is typical of cities in Western industrialized nations. Rather, Hong Kong since World War II has experienced periodic waves of mass immigration from China reflecting changing circumstances in that country.[5] The most important were in the late 1940s and early 1950s, when many Chinese fled the civil war and, later, the new Communist government, and again in the late 1970s for mostly economic reasons. In these periods of rapid immigration the demand placed by the newcomers on the housing stock, the educational system,

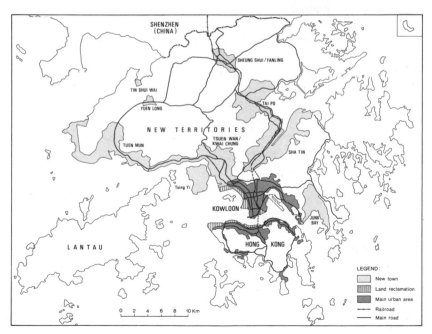

Figure 17.1. Hong Kong's Urban Areas, New Towns, and Reclaimed Land

and the network of social welfare services has stretched the community's resources to the limit. Hong Kong officials have had to face the unpleasant fact that planned development programs in such areas as housing could not keep pace with the demands made upon them. Timetables for attainment of planning objectives have had to be adjusted in light of new demands made by the community; priorities have had to be reshaped to fit the needs of a changing population. The process has not been painless and, in fact, has at times created considerable rancor as various interest groups have fought to maintain their "share of the pie."[6]

With no natural resources to speak of other than its harbor, the economic mainstays of Hong Kong are export manufacturing (notably of garments, electrical goods, toys, and other consumer products), entrepôt trade (most notably the fast-growing reexport trade with the People's Republic of China), business and financial services (including an expanding regional headquarters function), and tourism.[7] One of the prime tasks for Hong Kong's planners is to anticipate the needs for additional facilities and infrastructure resulting from the territory's economic growth and to set into motion a program to supply them as economic circumstances dictate they are needed. For instance, expansion of the container port is being carefully studied in light of a rapid growth in container throughput that is taxing the capacity of the present facility.[8] The job is made more difficult by the fact that, taken as a group, the economic activities that dominate in Hong Kong tend to be cyclical. Moreover, the territory's economic performance is highly dependent on the state of the world economy and in particular on the domestic economies of Hong Kong's major trading partners. Economic fluctuations outside of Hong Kong thus have a disproportionate effect on the timing of local economic expansion, which in turn affects the timing of the need for new infrastructure and facilities. Shortages in boom times are balanced by an embarrassing oversupply in lean years when the takeup rate of, say, industrial land is low.

Much has been made of Hong Kong's philosophy of "nonintervention" (sometimes a bit misleadingly characterized as laissez-faire) under which government officials intervene as little as possible in the workings of the private economy.[9] This philosophy does not mean that urban development ever has proceeded in a completely unregulated manner; in fact, the two areas of land development and infrastructure provision are among those where the government in Hong Kong has always taken a more interventionist approach. Nor does the tilt toward nonintervention mean that the government gives no attention to community welfare, although much of its involvement is channeled indirectly through charitable groups. Rather, the prevailing philosophy of minimizing government involvement in the territory's economic life has meant that forceful intervention in the urban development process tends to occur only when serious problems associated with urban growth threaten Hong Kong's continued prosperity—a planning style that Roger Bristow has termed "planning by demand."[10] Problems of such magnitude occurred, to give two examples, in the late nineteenth century in relation to public health and sanitation, leading to the adoption of Hong Kong's first building regulations, and in the 1950s in relation to squatter settlements, leading to the earliest government involvement in large-scale public housing.

Accomplishments

It is appropriate first to single out several areas where intervention by Hong Kong officials into the process of urban development in the territory has resulted in significant accomplishments that have gone a long way toward enhancing the quality of life presently enjoyed by residents of Hong Kong. The following paragraphs examine five areas where the outcome of planned intervention has been highly favorable for Hong Kong's population.

Construction of Public Housing

The single greatest accomplishment traceable to government intervention in urban development in Hong Kong is the provision of subsidized public housing for nearly half of the territory's population. Since 1954 the Hong Kong government has built public housing of increasingly high quality, in line with the increasing expectations among Hong Kong residents, at a pace which is probably unequaled anywhere in the world except in Singapore, where the physical environment and social climate are very similar.[11]

A few statistics can give an indication of the magnitude of this achievement. In April 1986 there were 2,350,000 Hong Kong residents living in more than 550,000 rental housing units managed by the Hong Kong Housing Authority.[12] New housing units were going up at the rate of more than 35,000 per year, a rate that has been sustained each year since 1980–1981. Almost 70,000 units had been made available since 1979 under a "home ownership scheme" designed to encourage public housing tenants to buy their own homes. More than 1 million residents of public housing units lived in the New Territories, in what has amounted to a major spatial redistribution of Hong Kong's population. (Most of these had congregated in the eight new towns under

development by the government since the early 1970s; the locations of
these new towns are shown in Figure 17.1.) Redevelopment programs
in progress were to rehouse more than 35,000 people in better-quality
accommodations; further redevelopment would eliminate by the early
1990s the oldest housing units, now considered substandard, from the
Housing Authority's rental stock.[13]

A number of factors have contributed to the results achieved in Hong
Kong with a capital and technology-intensive program for public housing—a direction not normally recommended for the needs of developing countries.[14] One of the most important is the leading role that the
housing sector receives in physical planning; the major planning task of
developing new towns was motivated in the first place by the need to
find locations outside the main urban area for public housing construction.[15] The emphasis given to housing management and building maintenance has enabled standards of quality in public housing to be maintained at levels well above low-rent tenement buildings in the private
sector. The Housing Authority has over the years become highly experienced in mass housing construction and benefits from significant economies of scale in its development activity. Finally, housing provision in
Hong Kong remains one of the few government activities for which
specified targets are set. Over the past several years resources have been
made available to meet those targets even at times when Hong Kong's
overall economy was in recession and other public works expenditure
was cut back.

The accomplishments of the Hong Kong authorities in developing
public housing come, of course, at a significant cost. In fiscal 1985–
1986, the capital expenditures on housing in Hong Kong amounted to
HK$3.31 billion (US$424 million), which was fully 30 percent of total
government capital expenditures in that year. An additional HK$2.2
billion (US$280 million) was spent on recurrent expenditures (opera-
tions and maintenance).[16] Clearly the benefits derived from Hong
Kong's mass housing program have only come about because of the
willingness of the territory's leaders to plow a very large proportion of
public revenues into the construction and maintenance of housing.
Such willingness may owe a lot to the fact that Hong Kong's policymakers are unelected and need not answer to a political party or an
interest group constituency which might question their judgment on
this matter.

Anticipating Demands for Land

The rapid economic growth of Hong Kong, together with its swelling
population, has resulted in great demand for building sites to accommo-

date all types of development from luxury housing to transport terminals to amusement parks. Public housing and manufacturing industry are the two largest consumers of new building sites in Hong Kong, but sites for other uses are equally critical in supporting the territory's continued economic growth. The central business district on Hong Kong Island, for instance, has expanded to the east and west in response to a boom in office construction stimulated by the growing needs of Hong Kong's financial and business services sector. Officials in Hong Kong have for the most part been quite successful in anticipating these demands for land arising from various segments of the community.

The accomplishments of Hong Kong's planners in this regard are not due to a sustained effort at preparing a "comprehensive" land use plan for the territory. No such plan was in existence until the past few years. Rather, they are the result of wise projections by groups of planners working in individual government departments (the Housing Authority, for one), together with other findings related to Hong Kong's land use needs. Concern within top government circles over the possible detrimental effect that land scarcity might pose for economic growth led to the appointment of a Special Committee on Land Supply in the late 1970s, charged specifically with studying community (particularly industrial) needs for building sites. This committee's reports provided detailed breakdowns to the government of land requirements for a variety of urban functions.[17] In the new towns, close cooperation between government departments responsible for site formation and those in charge of capital works programming have kept site formation well ahead of actual development needs.

The Territorial Development Strategy (TDS), a territory-wide plan for future urban development completed over the period 1980–1984, will provide guidance to Hong Kong's planners on directing growth into the 1990s (that is, in the period after completion of the new town development program). Recommendations of the TDS were based on careful consideration of the community's need for additional land and services, coupled with a close look at the development potential in each of Hong Kong's major subregions. The team of planners responsible for the TDS concluded that new land should be reclaimed off the coast of the main urban area to accommodate, among other things, new public housing for an additional 310,000 people, an expanded central business district, and additional open space to serve the densely built-up urban areas of western Kowloon and northwestern Hong Kong Island.[18] The locations of these proposed land reclamations, which are the latest evidence of planners' continuing efforts to meet the community's land needs, are shown in Figure 17.1.

Coping with Transport Needs

The high density of development in Hong Kong has led to extraordinary demands being placed on the territory's transport network. Vehicle density per unit of road space in Hong Kong—more than 240 vehicles per kilometer of road—is one of the highest in the world. In these circumstances, maintaining a relatively smooth and well-regulated flow of traffic in Hong Kong should be counted as a significant accomplishment for the territory's traffic planners.

The transport system in Hong Kong incorporates a wide variety of modes, somewhat bewildering initially to the first-time user.[19] Buses form the mainstay of the public transport system; between them the two large government-franchised bus companies carry nearly 4 million passengers each day. Buses are supplemented by "minibuses" and "maxicabs" (fourteen-seat vehicles) and by a large taxi fleet. Rail transport (the underground Mass Transit Railway, or MTR, and the surface Kowloon–Canton Railway) is the fastest-growing mode in terms of patronage, though rail remains a distant second to buses. Ferries and the historic tramway (streetcar) on Hong Kong Island complete the public transport network.[20] The government's policy is to coordinate the services of the various public transport modes, allowing them to complement each other, while restraining competition which might prove wasteful. All transport operators except the two rail systems are privately managed and thus are able to make their own business decisions regarding such questions as staffing or modernization of their vehicle fleets—subject to the authority of government transport regulators who reserve the right to intervene into decisions affecting, say, the frequency or quality of service.

The private car plays a rather poorly defined role in the local transport system. Official policy is to discourage rapid growth in private car ownership, which is increasingly difficult in an increasingly affluent society like Hong Kong. Priority in use of the roadways is granted to public transport vehicles, and planners hope that by making public transport more attractive and efficient, growth in car ownership might be forestalled. The government, however, especially since 1982, has had to resort to heavy taxation on car licenses, car registration, and fuel in order to restrain the growth in car ownership to what it views as an acceptable level.

Hong Kong's achievements in the transport sector can be linked to several factors. A comprehensive study of Hong Kong's future transport needs was completed in 1976, creating a blueprint for the future development of the transport network that, while not infallible, proved very useful in guiding capital works expenditures over the succeeding decade.[21] Widespread use is made of traffic engineering techniques to maximize the capacity of the present road network. The efficient management of public transport operators is another contributing factor, allowing fares to be kept at what by world standards are very reasonable levels, as is the willingness for the most part of the different operators to cooperate with planners' attempts to coordinate their activities and maximize the integration of the transport system.

As with housing, the government's willingness to invest heavily in capital facilities for transport plays a significant role in the success of transport planning. The Mass Transit Railway alone has carried a price tag of over HK$25 billion (US$3.2 billion) to date; the size of this investment necessitated one of Hong Kong's few forays into the international capital markets. The willingness of Hong Kong officials to make unpopular decisions in relation to transport is another factor contributing to the achievements of transport planners. While the sharp increases in taxation on private cars and on gasoline in 1982 provoked a storm of protest, the measures had an immediate benefit in reducing levels of road congestion. An attempt in 1985 to replace these fiscal measures with an electronic road pricing scheme was scrapped, however, when it proved politically unpopular.[22]

It is an indication of the intensity of demand for transport facilities in Hong Kong that despite the best efforts of local traffic planners, the system as a whole can barely cope with the ever expanding local needs. A small disruption in the system—a vehicle breakdown in a tunnel, say, or a minor accident—is enough to provoke a major traffic tie-up; a failure on any of the railway systems creates disruption on a massive scale. A new comprehensive transport study now under way will be counted on to point out those aspects of the transport system where further capital expenditures will have the greatest beneficial effect into the 1990s.

Countryside Conservation

Despite the small size of Hong Kong, and despite the high-density environment that prevails in the built-up areas, fully 40 percent of Hong Kong's land area is set aside as permanent open space. Figure 17.2 shows the distribution of these so-called country parks, which cover not only the more remote reaches of the territory but also include some land surprisingly near to urban areas, albeit mostly land which is difficult to develop owing to its steepness.

The country parks are a relatively new addition to Hong Kong's landscape, appearing only since 1976. They serve a variety of roles benefiting the community. The parks provide facilities for outdoor recreation which are increasingly in demand in Hong Kong as the population

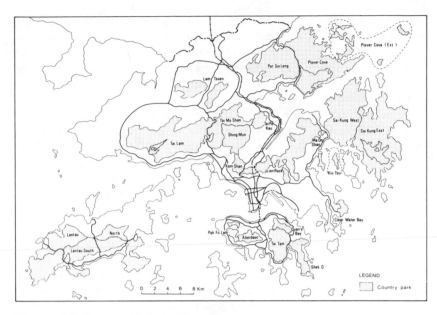

Figure 17.2. Country Parks in Hong Kong

enjoys higher disposable income and more leisure time. They serve as greenbelts surrounding the major population centers, including the new towns, thus bringing the countryside within close range of most urban dwellers. They aid in wildlife conservation efforts and in the maintenance of Hong Kong's local water supplies. (Much of the country park land serves a dual function as a water catchment area.) Significantly, the country parks provide a psychological escape from the pervasive concrete canyons of the built-up area and the fast-paced urban life-style which dominates most residents' day-to-day existence in Hong Kong.

The rest of Hong Kong's rural land, however, is not under the same degree of protection as the country parks. Agricultural land, in particular, is being abandoned at a rapid rate or turned over to squatter factories or other urban-oriented uses, all with little hindrance from land use planners.[23] Countryside conservation in Hong Kong thus should be viewed as only a partial success; nonetheless, the accomplishments that have been made in the area of parkland management are significant achievements which would not have happened without forceful government action.

Coping with High Densities

As already noted, high-density living is inevitable in Hong Kong: Most residents of the main urban area (except the very wealthiest individuals) and the majority of New Territories dwellers live in high-rise buildings. It is a significant accomplishment that planners have helped to insulate Hong Kong residents from the worst of the social and psychological problems which are potentially inherent in high-density living.[24]

Increasing the allocation of residential space to households is one way in which planners have alleviated some of the harmful effects of high density. In the public housing sector, standards for space allocation have increased from an initial 2.2 square meters per adult in the earliest "resettlement estates" of the 1950s to the present figure of more than double that amount. Another way is to emphasize proper layout of buildings and attractive landscape design. Here the newer public housing developments in the new towns have made great strides; attempts to create a tranquil and attractive environment through landscaping in the midst of the high-rise structures have been successful enough to earn architectural awards for the Housing Authority design staff. In the built-up urban area, planners have created localized amenities (vest-pocket parks, plazas, and promenades) which provide restful oases from the bustle of the surrounding city.

Not all urbanized districts in Hong Kong enjoy the amenities which permit residents an escape, however temporary, from their high-density living environment. In planning for the use of newly reclaimed land in Hong Kong, special attention is given to how pieces of that land might be able to alleviate the worst of the space shortages in adjacent areas too overcrowded and densely developed to enjoy local open spaces of their own.[25] Urban renewal, if successfully implemented in the future, also holds out promise for increasing the availability of local open spaces to the residents of urban Hong Kong.

Failures

The preceding paragraphs point to undeniable progress over the past fifteen years in shaping Hong Kong's urban development so that the increasing affluence of the territory's residents is matched by an improved quality of life. It would be wrong, however, to gloss over other areas where the effects of planned intervention in the urban development process have fallen short of expectations or where planners have avoided addressing critical questions. In this section the picture given previously is balanced by pointing to several areas where the outcome of planners' actions (or inaction) has been far less favorable for Hong Kong's residents.

Renewal of Older Districts

Hong Kong's planners have failed in their attempts at comprehensive redevelopment of older residential districts in the main urban area of Hong Kong. These neighborhoods are built up with privately owned residential and commercial buildings, sometimes used partly for workshops or small factories, ranging in age from prewar structures to some built as recently as the 1960s. Though movement to the New Territories has reduced the population of the older districts somewhat, they remain fearfully overcrowded and owing to limits on space lack the public amenities provided elsewhere (in, for instance, the new towns). Many of the buildings offered poor-quality shelter even when first built and cannot be rehabilitated economically to provide acceptable living conditions. Clearance and redevelopment are the preferred methods for renewal in all but a few locations.

Many difficulties face officials in their attempts to institute a renewal program in these areas.[26] Ownership of most buildings is fragmented among many different individuals or companies, any one of whom may obstruct plans to acquire the building for redevelopment purposes. Some owners who have died or left Hong Kong may not be traceable at all. Building lots are small, and acquiring a site large enough for economical development necessitates buying several properties, adding to the length of time consumed by negotiations. Typically there is little chance for rehousing owners and tenants affected by redevelopment in the same general area. Operators of factories, unable to find new sites nearby, may be forced to quit business.

Though these difficulties are very real, the Hong Kong government has contributed to its own problems in past attempts at urban renewal through poor coordination, underfinancing, overreliance on the private sector, and uncertainty as to the aims of the programs. There is no single government department in Hong Kong which can take charge of implementing a comprehensive redevelopment program. Financing of an urban renewal effort must be spread over a period of years, and in the past government financial officers could not guarantee that the funds needed to carry out renewal on a timely basis would continue regardless of the territory's economic ups and downs. Renewal sites created by past government action have for the most part been sold to private builders who have carried out the actual redevelopment work; this means that the timing of redevelopment has depended on fluctuations in the Hong Kong property market as much, or more, than it has on the community's social needs. Finally, although renewal is justified on the basis of improving living conditions for people in the affected districts, government actions in relation to the location and timing of redevelopment suggest that renewal serves a financial purpose—that is, bringing in revenue to the government from the sale of new land—as well as, or perhaps in place of, a social one.[27]

It is not surprising that in the face of these conditions most redevelopment has taken place on a piecemeal basis, as individual owners pull down old buildings and replace them with taller ones on the same small lots. The resulting "pencil development," as one official has termed it,[28] may alleviate the worst of the poor housing conditions, but it contributes nothing toward improving community facilities and actually worsens traffic flow owing to the overloading of the old streets with more pedestrian and vehicular traffic.

A new proposal for a separate quasi-independent corporation to conduct urban renewal activities, the "Land Development Corporation," was introduced and passed into law in Hong Kong's legislature in October 1987.[29] Thus, it appears that Hong Kong will have for the first time a body with a specific mandate to come to grips with the problems affecting older residential districts and with the powers to cut through many of the obstacles which have hindered the progress of renewal in the past. Serious questions remain, however, concerning the effectiveness of the proposed corporation in achieving the social objectives which underlie urban renewal. In particular, there is concern that to ensure its financial viability the corporation will be forced to undertake profit-making redevelopment projects first, leaving other areas with perhaps an even greater need for redevelopment in limbo until some unspecified future date when its finances are sound.

Planning for Pollution Control

Planners in Hong Kong have been very slow to recognize that, in the words of a recent government report, "today's bad planning decision is tomorrow's environmental problem."[30] Consequently, Hong Kong's residents face serious problems of water and noise pollution and more localized but still significant problems with air pollution and solid waste disposal.

Water pollution is the single most damaging form of environmental degradation affecting Hong Kong; according to some analysts the problem is becoming so severe that it poses a major public health threat.[31] Most of the dwelling units in the main urban area, although sewered, are not connected to waste treatment plants, and their effluent is dumped without treatment into Hong Kong's coastal waters. Only the flushing effect of tides and currents in the main Victoria Harbor have kept that body relatively clean, though water quality in some of its coastal embayments has deteriorated badly. Elsewhere, in more land-locked harbors without the same degree of tidal flushing, the level of degradation is far more serious. Disposal of pig and poultry waste into New Territories streams means that Hong Kong's countryside is as affected by water quality problems as are the built-up areas. Even the comprehensively planned new towns are not immune from water pollution problems. In both Sha Tin and Tuen Mun, channelized river courses (known locally as *"nullahs"*) running through the center of the built-up area have become little better than open sewers for industrial wastes from factories in the town and agricultural wastes from farms in the surrounding area.

Noise pollution problems in Hong Kong stem from many different sources, a diversity which hinders efforts to enforce control over the level of noise emissions. The pace of construction activity in Hong Kong has meant that much of the urban area is affected by noise from piledrivers and other construction equipment, noise which is largely unrestricted although some controls are applied at night. Industrial establishments located near (or often in) residential buildings operate day and night with little control over their activities. Kai Tak Airport, in the heart of Kowloon, has its advantages in terms of accessibility and convenience for travelers but creates a serious nuisance for more than half a million people living within its flight path. The high density of population in Hong Kong neighborhoods exacerbates the noise problem: Not only are more residents exposed to noise from any one source, but the high-rise urban environment intensifies the effect of any noise that is generated.

The failure to limit environmental degradation resulting from Hong Kong's urban growth is traceable to a number of factors:[32] a feeling, common before the 1980s, that environmental protection is a "luxury" that merits a low priority compared to, say, economic development; an approach to environmental protection which stresses waste disposal rather than waste management; delays in creating an appropriate legislative framework for pollution control, due partly to the complexity of the subject and partly to the need to consult affected interest groups, including industrialists; and limited opportunity for public consultation on environmental matters and, hence, limited expression of public concern. The effects of previous planning mistakes are, of course, both cumulative and difficult to reverse; it is virtually impossible to retrofit older industrial buildings, occupied by many different manufacturers having very different waste disposal needs, with proper pollution control equipment.

As in the case of urban renewal, efforts are now being made to address this previous failure and specifically to ensure that future urban growth is planned so as to prevent the appearance of future environmental problems. Since 1985 a set of planning guidelines relating to the environment has appeared in the government's internal working manual *Hong Kong Planning Standards and Guidelines,* alerting land use planners to the possible environmental problems linked with different kinds of development activity.[33] New legislation on disposal of agricultural wastes was enacted by Hong Kong's legislature in late 1987. Plans are also afoot to centralize policymaking relative to environmental protection in a single Environment Branch within the government.[34] Yet critics can easily argue that these initiatives are far too little and too late, appearing only after environmental problems created by earlier inadequately planned development have reached a critical state, and promising only to alleviate the effects of new development rather than to reverse the environmental deterioration that already has taken place throughout Hong Kong.

Development of New Towns

The original intention of Hong Kong's planners was to develop Hong Kong's new towns (see Figure 17.1) in line with the twin objectives of balance and self-containment. The former objective, balance, refers to the social structure of the new towns. A mixture of public and private and of owned and rented housing was intended to attract groups of residents of different ages and income levels into the new settlements, giving them a population similar in composition to Hong Kong taken as a whole. Self-containment relates to the planners' desire to minimize the need to commute between the new towns and the main urban area; achieving this end required that a suitable range of employment opportunities and community facilities be provided in the new towns so that residents might satisfy their daily needs within the town's boundaries.[35]

In reality neither of these planning ideals has been achieved in new town developments in Hong Kong. "Balanced" development has been hindered by the dominance of public housing in the new towns; typically 60 percent or more of the housing stock in each new town comprises low-cost public housing estates. As there are income ceilings which constrain eligibility for these housing units, the new towns are being populated mainly by working-class and low-income families. Of more immediate import is the age structure of families attracted to the new towns, which is skewed toward younger families with school-age children. This unanticipated imbalance has meant a serious shortage of classrooms in some of the new towns—particularly Tuen Mun and Sha Tin, which have been the fastest growing—and has led to some children traveling long distances to schools in the urban area.

"Self-containment" is an even more problematic objective to attain in Hong Kong's new towns. Though officials in Hong Kong have considerable control over the location of new residences, owing to the dominant role played by public housing, there is no similar control over the location of job opportunities. Nor is it likely that any future attempts will be made to steer employment toward the new towns, either through compulsion or through subsidy, given the government's general nonintervention policy toward the economy. Those industrial jobs that have decentralized to the new towns are not necessarily filled by new town residents, who often hold onto their jobs in Kowloon or Hong Kong Island. In nonmanufacturing sectors, notably the white-collar office sector, employers remain firmly entrenched in the main urban area. Cross-commuting by new town residents to the urban area is made more difficult by inadequate transport links to the urban area; long traffic jams of Kowloon-bound workers are a fixture of most Hong Kong workday mornings.

Failure of the new towns to develop in the manner envisioned has occurred mainly because attaining the objectives of balance and self-containment—objectives that were lifted initially from new town planning practice in Britain—was simply an unrealistic expectation in the context of Hong Kong.[36] The small size of the territory made self-containment, at least, a debatable proposition from the start. The fact that planners do not have the authority to induce the relocation of facilities other than housing into the new towns exacerbates the difficulties. Failure to attain these planning ideals would not in itself create a problem, except that planners in Hong Kong clung to the concepts long after it should have become evident that they were unattainable. The true failure in Hong Kong's new town development program lies in this inflexibility of vision. The lack of adequate external transport links to the new towns is one indication that when making the hard decisions on investment priorities for the new towns, the planners' abstract objectives have tended to override the obvious reality.

Officially, balance and self-containment remain development objectives for the new towns, although it is now admitted that they will be achieved only in the very long term.[37] In the meantime, many new town dwellers must put up with settings where housing is plentiful and cheap but other urban amenities appear in painfully short supply or are difficult to reach.

Retaining Historic Character

Hong Kong's planners have failed to retain the man-made features of the territory's environment which give it any claim to unique character or visual distinctiveness. Structures of historic value, whether colonial or traditional Chinese, have been demolished and replaced by undistinguished residential or office/commercial buildings in a derivative quasimodernistic style which appear very much like similar buildings anywhere else. The presence of an architectural tour de force here and there, such as the Hong Kong and Shanghai Bank headquarters building, does not compensate for the sterile character of much of the rest of Hong Kong's newly built environment.

The intense pressure on developable land is the major culprit behind this process which leads to the obliteration of Hong Kong's heritage. Historic buildings seldom utilize the full development potential of their sites, which makes them ripe for replacement if they are privately owned. Although much of the destruction has been at the hands of private developers in the name of economic efficiency, the government has itself been responsible for consigning historic public buildings to oblivion—either in the course of its program for developing new public facilities or to clear an important piece of land for eventual private sale.[38] The natural beauty of Hong Kong's physical setting may compensate somewhat for the loss of important landmarks in the built environment; yet certain elements of the territory's ambiance, such as its lively traditional street life, cannot be replicated once the built environment is redeveloped.

The failure of planners in this regard must be viewed as a failure of intentions. Hong Kong officials have never given priority to developing a program aimed at preserving the territory's architectural heritage. The limited efforts at preservation supervised by the Antiquities and Monuments Board have dealt mostly with sites in the remote New Territories or with publicly owned buildings (which in itself is no guarantee of preservation). Almost none of the listed monuments are on sites where there is intense development pressure. Unlike some of the problems noted above, there is no evidence to this point promising a greater degree of success for heritage conservation efforts in Hong Kong in years to come.

Removing Incompatible Land Uses

Haphazard planning or inconsistent enforcement of land use regulations in the past has led to many instances where incompatible land uses uneasily coexist side by side in Hong Kong. Housing has been built near oil and gas storage facilities in places such as Tsing Yi Island (Figure 17.1); incinerators vital to the territory's solid waste disposal program are sited near densely built-up residential areas; noise from aircraft operations at Kai Tak Airport affects schools, homes, and businesses over much of Kowloon. Some land uses, of course, are undesirable neighbors wherever they are sited; in respect to these the NIMBY (not in my back yard) attitude is as prevalent in Hong Kong as it is elsewhere. In other cases, though, the incompatibilities are mainly the consequence of historical inertia and have no valid reason to exist. Occasionally new land use proposals even add to the incompatibility problem. Despite complaints from the affected residents, only very slow progress is being made in dealing with these incompatible uses, and this glacial pace of change can be viewed as a significant failure of planning in Hong Kong.

Hong Kong's small size is, of course, a factor contributing to this failure; there simply are not enough sites far removed from populated areas to segregate all incompatible land uses. Another factor is that land use controls in Hong Kong are not strong enough to enforce changes in established land use patterns once they take shape—to relocate, say, an entrenched industry (even a polluting one) normally requires the government to lay out cash to acquire the site and compensate the operator for relocation expenses. But a major part of the problem, particularly when new incompatibilities are introduced, is traceable to an inadequate mechanism for coordination between government departments with potentially conflicting interests. One agency may find a site ideal for a certain use (for instance, the storage of hazardous wastes) on the basis of particular site characteristics it finds appealing (for instance, proximity to a deep-water anchorage). A second agency may find a nearby site suitable for an unrelated purpose (a public housing estate) and begin its own plans for development. All too often in the past the juxtaposition of unsuitable land uses was caught too late in the implementation process; even today the pressing need for a specific type of facility (again, hazardous waste storage is an example) may override concerns about the potential effects it might have on its neighbors.

As a result, makeshift solutions to incompatibility problems are adopted with unfortunate regularity—limiting the operating hours of Kai Tak Airport, for instance, or installing scrubbers on incinerator smokestacks to lower the quantity of particulate emissions. Other cases slip through the coordinating machinery and are never dealt with at all, or at least not until the complaints begin. Undoubtedly Hong Kong's land use planners do their best to reconcile potential incompatibilities at the planning stage, but it is an uphill struggle to reverse more than thirty years of less-than-comprehensive planning for the territory's industrial growth or to reconcile the competing needs of government departments and special interest groups.[39] Some degree of incompatibility among land uses in Hong Kong is therefore likely to persist.

Planning for Regional Development

Hong Kong will come under control of the People's Republic of China in 1997 as a "Special Administrative Region" with a high degree of administrative autonomy.[40] Yet planners in Hong Kong have failed to consider the potential future growth of the territory in relation to growth taking place in the broader South China or Pearl River Delta region of which Hong Kong is a part (Figure 17.3).[41] Specifically, they have paid scant attention in their long-range planning to the implications that the emergence of the Shenzhen special economic zone across the Chinese border might hold for the future urban development of Hong Kong. Nor have they given much thought to how Hong Kong could best make use of the resources found in China to benefit its own population.

Several reasons might be advanced for this situation, reasons related to both pragmatic and political considerations.[42] Decision-makers in Hong Kong identify with the territory rather than with China or the Pearl River Delta, and in any event they only exert control over the development of land and resources found on the Hong Kong side of the border. As China's policy toward the special economic zones has under-

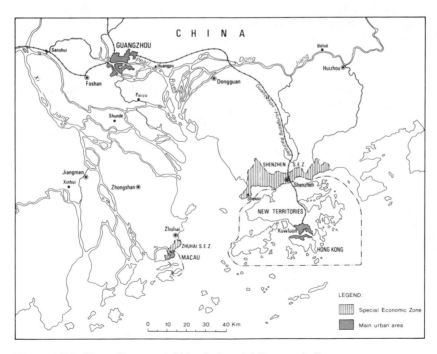

Figure 17.3. Hong Kong and China's Special Economic Zones

gone marked fluctuations over the years, it might be inexpedient to tie Hong Kong's development over the long term to resources managed by China, the availability of which cannot be assured in the long run (or at least before 1997). As a center for export manufacturing and business services, the facilities needed by Hong Kong to support its economic growth (telecommunications, container berths, conference and exhibition centers) are very much different from those needed almost everywhere else in the Pearl River Delta, where communities are only in the initial stages of building up their infrastructure.

All of these pragmatic considerations are important, but the political elements leading up to the fragmented regional planning situation should not be overlooked. Hong Kong has been promised administrative autonomy after 1997 according to the terms of the Sino-British Joint Declaration signed in 1984, and the planning of Hong Kong's urban development in isolation from China can be interpreted as one way of preserving some of the autonomy or freedom of action for future administrators in the territory. At a time when many Hong Kong residents harbor doubts as to the willingness of the Chinese to grant the territory its promised autonomy, Hong Kong's present administration may be especially reluctant for symbolic reasons to enter into a planning dialogue which, rightly or wrongly, may be viewed as yielding partial control over Hong Kong's development to an outside party.

There are initial signs that officials in Hong Kong are beginning to take account of the broader region in considering the future development of the territory. In July 1987, nine top Hong Kong officials exchanged views on future infrastructure projects with counterparts from Guangdong province during a visit to Guangzhou—the first time contacts have taken place at such a high level. This visit is likely to be a harbinger of further contacts in years to come. Until Hong Kong's political future is settled, however, any cooperative arrangements with the Chinese will probably be limited to noncontroversial issues such as the integration of utility networks across the region.

NOTES

1. For a comprehensive look at the historical development of the planning profession in Hong Kong and planners' activities in the territory, see Roger Bristow, *Land-Use Planning in Hong Kong* (Hong Kong: Oxford University Press, 1984), especially chap. 2–4.

2. K. S. Pun, "Urban Planning," in T. N. Chiu and C. L. So (eds.), *A Geography of Hong Kong,* 2d ed. (Hong Kong: Oxford University Press, 1986), p. 223.

3. The imbalance has no significance; it certainly is not intended to imply a

judgment that planners in Hong Kong have failed more often than they have succeeded.

4. For an analysis of land areas under various uses in Hong Kong, see Hong Kong Government, *Hong Kong 1987* (Hong Kong: Government Printer, 1987), p. 95.

5. C. P. Lo, "The Population: A Spatial Analysis," in Chiu and So, *Geography of Hong Kong,* pp. 148–184.

6. One instructive example relates to the territory's trunk road system. Despite pressure from motorists' groups such as the Hong Kong Automobile Association, the government has not made funds available to complete the planned arterial road network despite a commitment in 1979 to expedite its construction.

7. Comprehensive summaries of Hong Kong's economic activity in the preceding year appear in the annual reports of the Hong Kong government. See also Y. P. Ho, "Hong Kong's Trade and Industry: Changing Patterns and Prospects," in Joseph Y. S. Cheng (ed.), *Hong Kong in Transition* (Hong Kong: Oxford University Press, 1986), pp. 165–207.

8. See David K. Y. Chu, "The Container Port of Hong Kong: Problems and Prospects," in P. L. Y. Choi and others (eds.), *Planning and Development of Coastal Open Cities* (Hong Kong: Center of Urban Studies and Urban Planning, University of Hong Kong, 1986), pp. 145–158.

9. One of the most comprehensive discussions of Hong Kong's system of governance is Norman Miners, *The Government and Politics of Hong Kong,* 4th ed. (Hong Kong: Oxford University Press, 1986); see especially chap. 4, pp. 47–54.

10. Roger Bristow, "Planning by Demand: A Possible Hypothesis About Town Planning in Hong Kong," *Hong Kong Journal of Public Administration* 3 (2) (December 1981). 199 223.

11. Housing policies and programs in Hong Kong are very well documented. See, for instance, E. G. Pryor, *Housing in Hong Kong,* 2d ed. (Hong Kong: Oxford University Press, 1983); Peter K. W. Fong, "Public Housing Policies and Programmes in Hong Kong: Past, Present, and Future," in Choi and others, *Coastal Open Cities,* pp. 97–112. For a comparison with Singapore, see Y. M. Yeung and D. W. Drakakis-Smith, "Public Housing in the City States of Hong Kong and Singapore," in J. L. Taylor and D. G. Williams (eds.), *Urban Planning Practice in Developing Countries* (Oxford: Pergamon, 1982), pp. 217–238.

12. Hong Kong Housing Authority, *Annual Report 1985/86* (Hong Kong: Hong Kong Housing Authority, 1987), pp. 106–111.

13. Ibid., pp. 114–115.

14. This discussion draws heavily from a presentation I made to the American Planning Association National Planning Conference, New York City, April 1987.

15. Peter Hills and Anthony G. O. Yeh, "New Town Developments in Hong Kong," *Built Environment,* 9 (3–4) (1983): 226–277.

16. Hong Kong Government, *Hong Kong 1987,* p. 318.

17. See, for instance, Special Committee on Land Supply, *Report to His Excel-*

lency the Governor by the Special Committee on Land Supply (Hong Kong: Government Printer, 1985).

18. E. G. Pryor, "An Overview of Territorial Development Strategy Studies in Hong Kong," *Planning and Development* 1 (1) (1985): 8–20; Anthony G. O. Yeh, "Urban Planning and Development in Hong Kong: Now and in the 1990s," in Choi and others, *Coastal Open Cities*, pp. 1–23. For a critique of the TDS planning strategy, see Bruce Taylor, "Rethinking the Territorial Development Strategy Planning Process in Hong Kong," *Asian Journal of Public Administration* 9 (1) (June 1987): 25–55.

19. For a concise description, see C. K. Leung, "Urban Transportation," in Chiu and So, *Geography of Hong Kong*, pp. 305–327.

20. For patronage statistics see Hong Kong Government, *Hong Kong 1987*, p. 341.

21. Wilbur Smith and Associates, *Hong Kong Comprehensive Transport Study* (Hong Kong: Wilbur Smith and Associates, 1976).

22. On electronic road pricing, see Peter K. W. Fong and Peter Hills, "Urban Transport Problems in Hong Kong," in Choi and others, *Coastal Open Cities*, pp. 127–144. Strong opposition to the scheme by Hong Kong's neighborhood advisory councils (known as District Boards) finally killed it.

23. On the shrinkage in agricultural land, see C. T. Wong, "Land Use in Agriculture," in Chiu and So, *Geography of Hong Kong*, pp. 185–206.

24. Research into these social and psychological effects is summarized in Rance P. L. Lee, "High Density Effects in Urban Areas: What Do We Know and What Should We Do?" in Ambrose Y. C. King and Rance P. L. Lee (eds.), *Social Life and Development in Hong Kong* (Hong Kong: Chinese University Press, 1981), pp. 3–19.

25. See Edmund C. W. Lo and Lawrence W. C. Lai, "A Location Quotient Approach for Open Space Investment Decisions in Metropolitan Hong Kong," *Planning and Development* 2 (2) (1986): 42–46.

26. Edmund C. W. Lo and Michael C. T. Ma, "Urban Redevelopment in Hong Kong," *Planning and Development* 2 (1) (1986): 2–10; J. R. Todd, "Why We Need a Land Development Corporation," *Hong Kong Business Today* 5 (43) (January 1986): 26–28.

27. Bristow, *Land-Use Planning*, pp. 218–230.

28. Todd, "Land Development Corporation," p. 27.

29. The concept was first proposed by the Special Committee on Land Supply several years earlier. See Peter K. W. Fong, "Issues in Urban Development: The Land Development Corporation," *Built Environment* 11 (4) (1985): 284–294.

30. Environmental Protection Agency, *Environment Hong Kong 85* (Hong Kong: Government Printer, 1985), p. 18.

31. Thorough discussions of Hong Kong's environmental planning policy and the state of Hong Kong's environment are given by K. C. Lam, "Environment Problems and Management," in Chiu and So, *Geography of Hong Kong*, pp. 350–393; Peter Hills, "Environmental Protection in Hong Kong," in Choi and others, *Coastal Open Cities*, pp. 64–81; Environmental Protection Agency, *Environment Hong Kong 85*.

32. This discussion draws from the insights of Lam, "Problems and Management," and Hills, "Environmental Protection."

33. Environmental Protection Agency, *Environment Hong Kong 85,* pp. 138–140.

34. Sa Ni Harte, "Wilson Orders New Attack in Pollution War," *South China Morning Post,* 16 August 1987.

35. Hills and Yeh, "New Town Developments"; Anthony G. O. Yeh, "New Towns in Hong Kong," in Choi and others, *Coastal Open Cities,* pp. 113–126; Town Planning Division, *Town Planning in Hong Kong* (Hong Kong: Government Printer, 1984), pp. 26–27.

36. Bristow, *Land-Use Planning,* provides an explanation of the historical background for the decision to undertake new town development.

37. Town Planning Division, *Town Planning,* p. 26.

38. One example is the demolition of the original terminal building of the Kowloon–Canton Railway in 1975 to make way for a cultural center which had yet to be completed in 1987.

39. For a thorough discussion of the planning problems created by Hong Kong's small-scale industries, including potential incompatibility problems, see D. J. Dwyer and V. F. S. Sit, "Small-Scale Industries and Problems of Urban and Regional Planning," *Third World Planning Review* 8 (2) (1986): 99–119.

40. For a lengthier discussion of this point, see Bruce Taylor, "Development by Negotiation: Chinese Territory and the Development of Hong Kong and Macau," in Frank J. Costa and others (eds.), *Asian Urbanization: Problems and Processes* (Stuttgart: Gebrüder Borntraeger, 1988), pp. 103–116.

41. The development of the Shenzhen special economic zone is well documented in English; see K. Y. Wong and D. K. Y. Chu (eds.), *Modernization in China: The Case of the Shenzhen Special Economic Zone* (Hong Kong: Oxford University Press, 1985). For a mainland Chinese view, see "Shenzhen Experiment," a special issue of *China City Planning Review* 3 (1–2) (March 1987).

42. This discussion draws from an earlier paper of mine, "Regional Planning for Reciprocal Benefit in South China," presented at the International Conference on China's Special Economic Zones and Open Policy: Development and Perspective, Hong Kong, April 1987.

18. The Role of Squatter Settlements in Chandigarh

AMRIT LALL

ONE OF the most pervasive and visually disturbing features of rapid urbanization in India, as in several other developing countries in recent decades, has been the sprawling growth of squatter settlements around and in the major cities. Perceived variously by outsiders as peripheral, unauthorized, uncontrolled, temporary, and spontaneous,[1] these settlements constitute major points of concentration of poor, underprivileged rural migrants and are a striking feature of the urban environment.[2] These settlements are seen as the most challenging problems of cities in India.[3] Spatially cramped, marginal in site and location, these substandard habitations, with little or no services, have earned numerous derogatory titles from social scientists, planners, and administrators as "growing virus or fungus," "creeping paralysis," and "ugly blots" on the fair face of the cities. Their inhabitants have been looked upon as land-grabbers suffering from acute material deprivation and social and personal disorganization.

Such negative perceptions, grounded in the purely legalistic approaches of law enforcement authorities and sociological traditions of "culture of poverty" and "folk culture,"[4] have been increasingly challenged by Mangin, Leacock, and several others and more recently by Majumdar in his studies of Delhi's squatter settlements.[5] Though forming unauthorized and disorderly clusters of dismal structures, some, though not all, of these settlements can be viewed as socially vibrant and economically functional communities. In many cases, they represent an effective solution to the complex problems of housing and employment for an ever-growing stream of poor in-migrants, the new urbanites, operating in an environment of severe socioeconomic, spatial, and administrative constraints, neglect, and even hostility. The settlers in some of these settlements show a remarkable spirit of enterprise and endurance. They offer a variety of low-cost skills and services in the informal sector that plays, and will continue to play, a meaningful role in an urban economy and life that is still largely dependent on low-tech and low-energy inputs and poor intra-urban mobility.

This study of a squatter settlement in the planned city of Chandigarh, before its demolition in 1975–1976 during the national emergency in India, examines the socioeconomic background of the in-migrants settled in the colony, their postmigration adjustments, and their efforts to become functionally integrated into the planned urban complex. The evidence produced here reinforces certain positive images and evaluations. In conclusion it is suggested that a demolition-eradication approach, even when it is followed by resettlement within a planned framework as was the case with this settlement, is materially wasteful and socially disorganizing—especially when this approach is adopted several years after such settlements have been allowed to take root, grow, and mature, as was the case with this particular settlement. In concluding I outline some alternative strategies.

This study is based on pertinent information about a so-called labor colony in Chandigarh gathered through a series of interviews conducted during 1973–1974 for a study whose primary focus was on spatial and temporal dimensions of migration of the urban poor and their migration decision-making process, involving a 20 percent randomly selected sample from more than 1,100 households with a population of over 5,000.

Ironic as it might appear, unplanned squatter settlements, both residential and work-related, have been an essential component of new planned towns in India right from their inception. This seems to indicate a serious failure of the planned town concept. The planners of Chandigarh, the dream city of the architect Le Corbusier, in failing to recognize the crucial role of the massive and ongoing in-migration of the poor skilled and unskilled working population from small towns and rural areas, did not provide for them any affordable residential and work-related accommodation in their blueprints. Isolated from many of the primary problems of India's planning, the planners of Chandigarh duplicated the Western City in the formulation of housing, public utility, and civic amenity concepts and thus made housing for the really poor almost impossible.[6] When the work on various construction sites, both public and private, and other infrastructural projects started in the early 1950s and gained momentum, Chandigarh's hunger for low-wage construction workers appeared insatiable. The result was a flood of in-migrants who, left to themselves to find shelter, built clusters of crude shanty huts in close proximity to work sites. As their numbers multiplied, partly as a result of chain migration, a variety of low-cost basic commercial and service establishments began to huddle together within these residential clusters, catering not only to the low-wage working population but also to the growing population in the planned sectors that had as yet not been provided with an adequate base of commercial and service functions.

In the late 1950s, even when some of the planned sectors began to fill up and major projects were nearing completion, the growth of unsightly "Jhuggi–Jhompri" clusters showed no sign of abatement, and the planners decided to move them to certain peripheral sites that were not to be brought under any planned growth in the near future. With a minimum of layout planning and infrastructure development, small lots measuring 9 × 6 feet, arranged in rows and standing wall to wall and back to back with narrow streets facing them, were allocated to the settlers at a nominal rent on which they built their frugal structures through their own efforts. Some rows of huts formed rectangles or squares around common open spaces; others faced narrow streets with open drains running through them. The self-built huts, often flimsy structures in the beginning and containing a small multipurpose room, went through a gradual process of upgrading and enlargement. Depending on the resources and influence of the allottees, some acquired more than one adjacent lot and constructed additional rooms, kitchens, baths, and porches, as well as some rental accommodation. Moreover, as closely packed residential areas, these settlements acquired some semblance of a mature community with a bazaar street and "chowk" and an increasing variety and number of service and commercial establishments. Electric supply for authorized houses and streets and some public latrines and hydrants were obtained through organized lobbying—particularly when politicians came to seek support at election time.

These authorized settlements attracted in turn several clusters of unauthorized tenements around them to accommodate a constantly growing stream of new in-migrants attracted by the city's expanding employment potential not only in construction trades but also in a variety of secondary and tertiary trades and services. Some settlers built even more unauthorized structures just for the sake of rental income or to acquire some stake in the claims for resettlement—if and when the planner-administrators decided to resettle them again from these sites, which were not being accorded a permanent status. Thus four major labor colonies, or migrant settlements, had become quite firmly established by the 1960s adjacent to residential Sectors 14, 25, 26, and 30 (Sector 30 had three separate clusters of its own) with a total population of over 19,500 forming almost 9 percent of the city's population.[7] The colony we examined had a population of over 4,346 persons in about 1,043 occupied houses.[8]

The settlers in this colony were drawn mainly from the adjacent states of Punjab (26 percent), Haryana (24 percent), Uttar Pradesh (18 percent), Rajasthan (11 percent), and Himachal Pradesh and Kashmir (6 percent). Over 58 percent had come a distance of 50 to 250 kilometers and another 23 percent were drawn from a distance of 250 to 550 kilometers. A rather unusually large proportion of in-migrants, about

14 percent, had come a distance of over 2,000 kilometers from the South Arcot district of Tamil Nadu—a migration that involved years of intervening steps by individuals and family groups through several old and new urban centers that were undergoing brisk development, such as Hyderabad, Bangalore, Rourkela, Bhilai, Kanpur, and Delhi. While more than half of the in-migrants from Punjab were from urban areas, having strong association with trade, commerce, and skilled service jobs, in-migrants from other states, particularly from more distant areas, were more heavily drawn from rural areas that have been chronically underdeveloped and overpopulated—such as the South Arcot district of Tamil Nadu, the Mohindergarh, Jind, and Rohtak districts of Haryana, unserved by the new irrigation and other development schemes, the adjacent districts of Alwar and Jhunjhunu, and eastern districts of Uttar Pradesh along with some northern parts of western Uttar Pradesh.

The inflow of migrants, slow in the beginning, rapidly gained momentum and remained strong until the end of the 1960s, when it tended to slow down again. The major force behind this migration was not the pull of city life but the deeply felt influence of strong push factors, particularly for migrants coming from the depressed or stagnant rural areas, as identified earlier. Most migrants (58 percent) were drawn from landless farmworkers and marginal farming families, while 14, 10, and 8 percent had backgrounds in caste-related crafts, personal and miscellaneous services, and retail trade, respectively. Among the 108 scheduled-caste migrants, 70 percent perceived very strong or strong push factors in their areas of origin as opposed to 52 percent among 103 non-scheduled-caste migrants (including all religions). A balance between push factors and pull factors was perceived by only 22 percent of the scheduled-caste in-migrants against 28 percent of the others. It was also found that in-migrants from rural and urban Punjab as well as from urban Haryana, who also belonged largely to the non-scheduled-caste group, perceived push factors to be weaker in comparison with those from other states with larger proportions of scheduled castes, landless farmworkers, and craft workers.

Postmigration Changes

Most migrants did not have to wait long to find employment after arriving in Chandigarh. They were primarily absorbed in the construction industry through links with relatives, friends, or building contractors. This factor not only boosted the morale of the newcomers but also sent a signal to others who were still in the source areas. Moreover, the migrants with some spirit of enterprise soon became aware of earning potentials in a number of urban activities. Thus a rapid occupational transformation and upgrading was witnessed as more and more people, particularly new entrants with some skills or education, moved rapidly into a chain of diversified services and trades in the informal sector that seemed to have a significant role in the growing city's underserviced economy.

Several migrants shifted from their family occupational background into craft industries (shoemaking and repairing, cabinet and furniture-making, tailoring, pottery making, quilt making, repair services for small household gadgets, small machines, bicycles, scooters), numerous small trades in shops in the settlement, street-corner and door-to-door vending of numerous low-cost consumer goods (*raddi* dealers, buying old newspapers and other reusable goods, formed an important link in the recycling of waste materials), and a variety of personal and miscellaneous services (barbershops, domestic help jobs mostly by women, housecleaning jobs mostly by the sweeper's caste, gardening services, laundering and dying, and general manual jobs). The preparation of low-cost food stuffs such as candies, bakery items, and confectionary items *(halwais)*, as well as the roasting of cereals, popcorn, peanuts, and the like, were also established as family operations in the settlement to meet internal and external needs in the adjacent planned sector. One large group of young settlers from the urban areas of Punjab and Haryana began selling bicycle rickshaws and two-seater scooter cabs to meet a certain demand for individualized, affordable transportation in the city. As Madhu Sarin pointed out,[9] the "nonplan locations" in the city contained about 54 percent of the city's commercial and service establishments, operated mostly by the residents of the settlements. In this respect, the colony we examined was no exception with its busy shopping bazaar and several scattered workplaces.

Another essential development in the settlement was the growth of a rather profitable but labor-intensive dairy operation on the southern periphery of the main settlement, carried on by several migrants (numbering around sixty households) coming from a rural marginal farmers' class as well as by a group of the traditional dairy cattle keepers' caste (originally from Mathura). For generations they accompanied, along with their milch cattle, the movements of large British-Indian army units throughout the north and northwest of Pakistan and into the towns and cities in India and finally to Chandigarh. Their residences with large courtyards for stalls and shelters for their milch cattle and storage facilities occupied almost one-third of the settlement's area. With a ready and large market in the adjacent planned sectors, at a time when bottled milk supplies were not fully established and people had a strong preference for fresh milk dispensed in their presence, the need for such enterprises in close proximity to Chandigarh was quite strong.

More recently, low-level public service and office-related jobs were opening up for the younger and somewhat better educated in-migrants, who became clerks, watchmen, postal workers, health workers, laboratory attendants and assistants, and so forth. The settlement also served as a low-rent dormitory for several poor young men from backward areas who had entered one of Chandigarh's higher educational institutions. Thus the settlement at the time of the survey was being rapidly transformed into a community of "low-income consolidators"[10] with an increased family orientation (95 percent of the settlers were married and living with families), upgraded housing, and a broad economic and cultural base. The cultural milieu of the settlement was highlighted by a fairly well-built Guardwara (a Sikh temple) and a Hindu temple, both of which provided a venue for numerous shared religious festivities and celebrations, drawing their participants and audience not only from the population within but also from the adjacent planned sections.[11] Moreover, the residents acquired from the administration two elementary schools in frugal buildings but with high enrollment.

Residents' Perception of Environment and Future

The settlers, irrespective of their source area, caste, and occupational background, overwhelmingly expressed a strong positive feeling for their settlement, the city, and their role in it. More than 96 percent had no plans to move to another city or back to their source area. Even the Tamil Nadu migrants, though still employed in construction jobs, particularly in the city's roadbuilding and maintenance operations at relatively low wages, were not willing to admit that they were either socially or economically dissatisfied. Most settlers felt uneasy at the suggestion of being moved again at some future date to a low-income housing estate; over the years they had established their roots in the area and had invested a fair share of their savings in improving and upgrading their housing. Most would prefer a sort of permanent status for the settlement within some planned framework, an arrangement which would involve environmental improvements, limited layout planning and redevelopment, and upgrading of the basic urban amenities and services.

Conclusions

In this examination of the Chandigarh labor colony, which is no more, it is abundantly clear that it evolved over at least seventeen years. It was

not an unauthorized or illegal settlement of landgrabbers. It was an officially allotted "resettlement" colony for those who were forced to start
their lives as squatters, because although they were needed in the city's
labor force, no residential space was allocated for them in the official
plan. If the planners continued to view this colony as a temporary or
transitional arrangement, the settlers' perception was quite different. It
had provided them sites on which to build their homes, which they tried
to improve as time passed. It was a part of the city to them. It had developed into a peaceful community with a strong family base, replicating
aspects of their rural social and physical environment, and it played several critical roles in the city's economy. In this community the deprived
segments of society found a narrow path for upward movement in the
socioeconomic ranks in face of formidable hurdles through their consistent effort and determination. Physically, no doubt, it presented a contrast to the developed planned sectors. With an absolute minimum of
municipal amenities and services, these frugal structures stood in stark
contrast to the residential developments of and for the materially and
socially better endowed planned sectors. Yet the settlers were just as satisfied as the better-off, because these were their homes in a cohesive and
economically viable community.

From the preceding discussion, we can safely conclude that squatting
is not a consequence of the malignant action of a large number of economically redundant or marginal rural in-migrants or invaders. Such a
view might, in some cases, be applicable to a small proportion of squatters in some locations in the exploding, overurbanized, large and old
cities, as might be the case in some parts of Delhi.[12] In Chandigarh,
however, it was not a symptom of a disease; it was rather a consequence
of a failure in the planning process and attitudes, which resulted in
static land use planning influenced by Western practices, excessively
rigid, antiseptic, and idealistic.[13]

There is no easy and humane way to cut off and reverse the process of
migration—not only because the intensity of push factors in the rural
depressed areas cannot significantly be reduced in the near future, but
also because the urban economy in an energy- and capital-restrained
developing country has several important segments that are highly
dependent on these in-migrants. Most urban poor, as this study as well
as several others brings out,[14] are not, by any logic, residual, unproduc-
tive, or superfluous.

The planners of Chandigarh would affirm that they did find a solution—first, by accommodating these squatters in resettlement colonies
that were intended as transitional from the very beginning; second, in
1975–1976, when the political climate permitted demolition of squatter
areas, these dwellers in the transitional settlements were settled in a

housing development at a fairly high public cost in a fringe village planned specifically for them, thus releasing the land for some of its originally designated purposes.

Many of us would be tempted to accept this logic. On the basis of our study, however, it would be reasonable to question these premises on two grounds. First, by no means was this particular colony over the two decades of its existence, except for the first few years, looked upon as transitional by its dwellers. Two decades, even one decade, would be too long a period to hold onto the perception of transition. Second, if the purpose was to release the land for preferred uses in line with the master plan, that purpose has so far not been served. Even in 1984, a few scattered huts, possibly those of new squatters, and a dozen structures and enclosures of milch cattle owners still stood there along with the two places of worship amidst rubble—rubble that represented several hundred thousands of rupees of savings invested by hundreds of hardworking citizens. As for their resettlement, a topic that needs further investigation, some have expressed misgivings about the satisfaction levels of the affected people.[15]

The solution lies in establishing migrant colonies right from the start in every city affected significantly by in-migration. What we require is a new approach to migrants by providing for migrant colonies and not squatter colonies on predetermined sites with basic civic amenities matched to the needs of migrants. In cases where we have failed to do so, particularly in new towns, we might adopt a more humane, selective approach of "conservative surgery"—but not destroying totally what has been built and improved over a long period of time. On the basis of scientific case studies, we might determine what still can be saved and preserved, coupled with environmental improvement programs, an approach that would be less expensive in human and financial terms.

NOTES

1. David Drakakis-Smith, *Urbanization, Housing and the Development Process* (New York: St. Martin's Press, 1980), pp. 42, 66–67.

2. R. K. Majumdar, *Urbanizing Poor: A Sociological Study of Low-Income Migrant Communities in the Metropolitan City of Delhi* (New Delhi: Lancer's Publishers, 1983), pp. 1–2.

3. Jagmohan, *Islands of Truth* (New Delhi: Vikas Publishers, 1978), pp. 20–25; Jagmohan, *The Challenge of Our Cities* (New Delhi: Vikas Publishers, 1984), pp. 11–12, 31–32.

4. Oscar Lewis, *Five Families: Mexican Case Studies in the Culture of Poverty* (New York: Basic Books, 1959).

5. W. Mangin, "Latin American Squatter Settlements," *Latin American*

Research Review 2 (1967): 65–68; W. Mangin, "Latin American Squatter Settlement: A Problem and a Solution," in D. B. Heath (ed.), *Contemporary Cultures and Societies of Latin America* (New York: Random House, 1974), pp. 355–357; E. Leacock, (ed.), *Culture and Poverty* (New York: Simon & Schuster, 1971); Majumdar, *Urbanizing Poor.*

6. Norma Evenson, "Chandigarh: Monumental Sculpture," in E. W. Eldredge (ed.), *World Capitals* (Garden City, N.Y.: Anchor Doubleday, 1975), pp. 391–429.

7. Census of India, 1971.

8. Ibid.

9. Madhu Sarin, "Planning and the Urban Poor: The Chandigarh Experience," Ph.D. dissertation, Development Planning Unit, University of London, 1975; Madhu Sarin, *The Chandigarh Experience: The Urban Poor and Urban Planning* (Ahmadabad: New Order Book Company, 1982).

10. John Turner, "Housing Priorities, Settlement Pattern and Urban Development in Modernizing Countries," in *Journal of the American Institute of Planners* 34 (6) (1968): 354–363.

11. As a resident of an adjacent planned sector during 1959–1962, I can attest to their drawing power.

12. Jagmohan, *Islands of Truth.*

13. D. J. Dwyer, "Attitudes Towards Spontaneous Settlements in the Third World," in D. J. Dwyer (ed.), *The City in the Third World* (New York: Barnes and Noble, 1974), pp. 208–209.

14. Johannes F. Linn, *Cities in the Developing World: Policies for Their Equitable and Efficient Growth* (New York: Oxford University Press, 1983), pp. 37, 40; Collin Rosser, *Urbanization in India* (New York: Ford Foundation, International Urbanization Survey, 1973), pp. 40–41.

15. Sarin, "Planning and the Urban Poor"; Sarin, *The Chandigarh Experience.*

19. Land Tax Policy to Control Urban Land Speculation in the Republic of Korea

Yong Hyo Cho and Young Sup Kim

THE industrialization of the economy of the Republic of Korea (Korea hereafter) during the past two decades is a remarkable success story in economic development. The economic change from subsistence farming to industrial manufacturing has also brought about a profound change in the nation's settlement pattern. Indeed, the transition of Korea from a village society to an urban society in such a short span of time may be unparalleled elsewhere.

To undergo such a rapid change in the economy and social structure is not without its price. One cost clearly includes the impact of development on the real estate market, particularly land. Price escalation, monopolistic ownership, and speculation have become a chronic problem of the real estate market. Real estate speculation, a notorious source of windfall profit making, is a potential threat to the stability and progress in the nation's social, economic, and political systems. The government has repeatedly attempted to control real estate speculation, but all efforts, thus far, have been utterly ineffective.

Policy Implications of Land Speculation

Land price escalation, land speculation, and the concentration of land-ownership in the hands of a limited number of people disrupt the economic and social order of the nation and reduce the country's capacity to manage its most critical resource. Korea is a country small in land area and high in population density. Currently, more than 60 percent of the nation's population is urban and the urban population is projected to approach 80 percent by the year 2000. The nation as a whole is likely to become one "urban state" in the near future, if it is not one already. Land speculation is a major obstacle to developing a national land policy that satisfies both short-term needs and long-term development objectives.

The causes underlying land price inflation and land speculation include economic development, urban development, and population growth, all of which drive up the demand for the limited supply of land. When demand for land vastly exceeds the supply, land investment promises windfall profits for landowners. Windfall profits generate artificial demands, and the artificial demands accelerate the inflation of land prices. Thus speculative land investment assures that the wealthy individuals and corporations will become wealthier.

As land speculation remains pervasive and becomes a way of life, its adverse effects are diverse and serious. Some of these effects are:

1. Land speculation is, in a social sense, nonproductive investment because it does not produce more land.

2. It takes away capital needed for industrial and other business investment, thus hindering productive economic development.

3. It demoralizes the society and destroys the spirit for honest work.

4. It is unfair for speculators to privatize the profits created by social and economic changes, thus accentuating the inequality in income distribution.

5. Inflated land prices caused by speculation also raise prices for other commodities by increasing their production cost.

The Korean government, political leaders, and the public all realize that real estate speculation must be eradicated because of the social and economic problems it creates. It is also clear, however, that the real estate speculation problem is as complex as it is serious. Its effects are not always one-sided. A case in point is the role of real estate speculation in the rise of new corporations. Many corporations have depended on the windfall profits from real estate speculation to maintain their initial viability and subsequent expansion. Nevertheless, it is no longer justifiable for mature or maturing corporations to continue to rely on speculative gains from real estate deals. They must compete and grow by employing advanced technology and sophisticated management practices.

Trends of Land Price Inflation

In the process of industrial and urban development, land prices have increased at explosive rates as land has changed hands in quick succession. Some of the less expensive land, such as agricultural and forest lands in the rapidly growing urban and industrial regions, increased in price from less than W10,000 per *pyong* in 1960 to more than W2 million in the 1980s.[1] Unbelievable as it may seem, this is not an uncommon experience.

Table 19.1 gives trend data for land price increases during a ten-year period from 1974 to 1983. The average rate of land price increase in large cities was 823 percent, while that for dry farmlands was 1184 percent. The average rate of increase for all types of land was 559.39 percent for the entire nation, 628.28 percent for the medium and small-size cities, and 396.44 percent for rural areas. The inflation of land price, particularly in urban areas, was far in excess of the wholesale price index, which increased by 359.7 percent during the same period.

Corporate participation in the real estate market has grown, thus manifesting the intent of the corporate sector to ride with the continuous real estate price inflation. The increasing number of corporations paying capital gains tax on lands held for nonbusiness purposes is an indicator of this tendency. Some 187 corporations had to pay capital gains tax on corporate-owned land for nonbusiness purposes in 1976 and the number grew to 660 in 1979—a 353 percent increase in a three-year period.

Land Tax Policy and Its Effects on Land Speculation

Korea's Land Tax System

Land tax policy is believed to be an effective instrument for government to control the timing of land development, to improve the efficiency of land use, and to limit the concentration of landownership. In a society where private property and a free-enterprise, market-based economic system enjoy constitutional protection, tax policy is particularly significant in controlling speculative economic behavior.

Taxation is effective in controlling land speculation when it is designed to absorb the portion of increased value of land resulting from broad social change such as industrialization and urbanization, thus rendering landholding not particularly profitable. To the extent that the tax system allows the profits expected from land investment to exceed the profits expected from other investments such as industry and bank deposits, the prospect for speculation is great. The propensity to speculate in land tends to depend on the extent of the margin of the excess profit that land investment is expected to bring over other types of investment.

Other nations, particularly the Western industrial nations, have experienced land speculation and land price inflation in the process of industrial and urban growth. They have devised tax measures to counter such problems, and some of the tax measures considered effec-

Table 19.1.   Trend of Land Price Changes in Seoul: 1974-1983

Location	1974	1975	1976	1977	1978	1979
Nationwide						
Average	100	126.99	160.76	214.69	319.84	373.02
Dry farm	100	126.76	161.36	226.37	360.48	415.67
Wet farm	100	125.32	157.82	207.62	298.85	328.70
Housing lot	100	124.70	153.29	200.50	319.08	378.15
Forest land	100	128.75	167.64	221.02	295.24	350.27
Large cities						
Average	100	121.87	147.51	216.35	387.44	472.53
Dry farm	100	126.87	153.55	242.74	488.04	638.51
Wet farm	100	124.19	151.46	218.21	396.59	485.99
Housing lot	100	118.73	136.69	194.98	327.24	395.40
Forest land	100	121.36	152.96	229.65	359.73	510.35
Medium-small Cities						
Average	100	125.84	161.85	217.93	346.04	396.18
Dry farm	100	122.70	158.66	225.95	386.62	441.25
Wet farm	100	122.05	157.02	211.91	324.37	354.79
Housing lot	100	122.52	151.92	200.90	357.35	414.81
Forest land	100	122.83	162.77	210.45	280.00	311.39
Rural areas						
Average	100	125.92	156.68	196.98	255.46	287.29
Dry farm	100	125.84	156.82	199.46	278.32	305.82
Wet farm	100	123.54	149.70	183.07	207.24	217.97
Housing lot	100	124.93	153.76	196.95	275.20	329.11
Forest land	100	129.15	166.65	208.85	263.78	305.45

Source: Ministry of Construction, The 1983 Land Price Change Rates, 1983.

tive include site value taxation (also known as land value taxation or land tax), graded tax (which taxes land at a higher rate than buildings), vacant land tax, land value increment tax, and capital gains tax. Scholarly research has often dealt with the effect of taxes on the timing of land development, land price, and the efficiency of land use. The research findings of the tax effects on land price, for example, tend to conclude that there is an inverse relationship between the tax level imposed on land and the movement of land prices.[2]

The Korean land tax system currently in effect utilizes nearly all of the tax concepts developed and applied in the Western nations. There are nine categories of taxes levied on real estate. Four of them—capital gains tax on properties owned by individuals, capital gains tax on land owned by corporations for nonbusiness purposes, inheritance tax, and

1980	1981	1982	1983
416.59	447.88	472.06	559.39
433.29	453.39	506.69	580.65
347.21	372.77	394.39	464.59
435.21	470.16	496.49	599.26
389.29	412.61	432.00	402.42
552.95	592.26	625.43	823.69
766.47	838.59	895.61	1,184.00
561.71	632.88	670.22	920.21
462.50	491.50	519.52	684.72
604.56	680.80	709.39	914.40
453.11	492.21	531.09	628.28
503.91	539.94	575.04	677.97
385.02	411.86	440.69	527.07
482.26	528.17	576.23	580.53
340.97	364.94	395.96	469.61
310.82	332.95	349.60	396.44
323.07	342.78	357.18	400.40
227.02	243.18	257.04	296.63
369.06	400.54	421.37	472.35
339.39	357.68	373.42	426.82

gift tax—are national taxes. The rest—property tax, registration tax, acquisition tax, city planning tax, and urban facilities tax—are local taxes. Only three of the nine taxes (the property tax, city planning tax, and urban facilities tax) are regular taxes levied and collected annually; the others are applied when taxable activity occurs such as property sales and inheritance. Further, the city planning tax and urban facilities taxes are not universal but are applied only to those properties affected by the service financed by the given tax revenues.

The taxes that can exert the most positive influence on controlling land price and speculation are the property tax and the capital gains taxes on properties owned by individuals and those owned by corporations for nonbusiness purposes. These three taxes are intended to serve as policy instruments to absorb part or all of the increased value of a

property as tax revenues, thus discouraging ownership of land for speculative purposes. Nevertheless, tax policies and other policy measures
have not succeeded in controlling speculative manipulation of land and
other properties.

Recently a new tax measure is reportedly under consideration by the
government and the political parties. This is a comprehensive property
tax with a progressive rate structure.[3] There are approximately 31 million parcels of land and 6 million units of buildings in Korea today, and
the new approach seeks to apply a steeply graduated tax rate to the total
property holdings owned by each individual and corporation.

The proposal put forth by the Democratic Korea Party (the major
opposition party before the February 1985 parliamentary election)
argues for a ceiling on total landownership allowable for individuals and
corporations. The portion exceeding the limits should be taxed at a prohibitive rate, thus resulting in the nationalization of excess land in the
form of tax payment in kind.[4] The reform measure under consideration
by the government and the Democratic Justice Party (the ruling party)
seems to espouse the concept of a landownership ceiling and graduated
comprehensive property tax system to control speculative landholding
and to reduce the concentration of landownership.[5] This graduated
comprehensive property tax system is a radical concept without prece-
dent in Korea or elsewhere. It is too early to tell what the actual legislative proposal will be like, if and when the idea reaches that stage. But it
is clear that a systematic study must precede the formulation of a legislative proposal in view of the complexity of the problem. Here we will
review the two principal taxes on land and real estate—the property tax
and the capital gains tax—in order to assess their effects on land speculation.

Property Tax

Some of the distinct characteristics of Korea's property tax system are
the application of differential tax rates to land and buildings and a further differentiation in the tax rates according to the use, size, and value
of taxable property. More important, a system of graduated tax rates is
applied to the property tax.

Land is classified into six categories for property tax purposes: (1)
residential parcels; (2) land used for golf courses, villas, and expensive
recreation facilities; (3) vacant land and corporate-owned land for nonbusiness purposes; (4) land used for primary-sector economic activities
such as farmland (for dry as well as wet farming), forest land, orchard,
and pasture; (5) large-city plant sites; and (6) all others. Tax rates vary
among the six different categories of land as follows.

Residential parcels are taxed at a progressive rate according to lot size: lots of less than 100 *pyongs*, 3/1,000; 100–200 *pyongs*, 5/1,000; 200–300 *pyongs*, 10/1,000; 300–500 *pyongs*, 30/1,000; more than 500 *pyongs*, 50/1,000.

Land used for golf courses, villas, and expensive recreation facilities is taxed at a uniform rate of 50/1,000.

The tax rates for vacant land and corporate-owned land for nonbusiness purposes progress with the duration of landholding: land held under three years, 50/1,000; three to five years, 70/1,000; five to seven years, 80/1,000; seven to ten years, 90/1,000; over ten years, 100/1,000.

Dry and wet farms, orchards, forest land, and pastures are taxed at a uniform rate of 1/1,000.

Large-city plant sites are taxed at a uniform rate of 60/1,000.

Other lands are taxed at a rate of 3/1,000.

Property Tax Effects on Land Speculation. Why has the property tax failed to have a decisive effect on controlling land speculation? The answer can be found in the extent of anticipated profits from landholding taken away in the form of taxation. The property tax is part of the carrying cost of holding land. The larger the proportion of the anticipated profits eroded by the carrying cost, the smaller the margin of the anticipated profits and the less the desire to own and hold land for economic gain. As the desire to hold land diminishes due to the prospect of declining profit, landowners who want to sell their land will increase and the supply of land will grow. In the event that a land tax triggers this effect, those who have real needs for land will replace speculative investors and land prices will decline and stabilize at a level which can be supported by a speculation-free land market.

For the property tax to create a stable land price and a speculation-free land market, three conditions appear necessary: The land tax should be high enough to disallow windfall profits; assessment of land value for tax purposes should be fair and fully reflect the current market value; and tax administration should be effective enough to close all possible loopholes for tax evasion. We turn now to these three aspects of the current property tax system.

Tax Rates. Tax rates may be evaluated on the basis of two criteria. One is the effective tax rate in relation to the price trend of the land; the other is a comparison with the experience of other countries.

The nominal tax rates for various classes of land do not show levels of tax rates because they are applied to the assessed value of the land, not the market value. To calculate the effective tax rates, the relation of the assessed value to the market value must be known. Table 19.2 shows the average assessed value and average market value of lands in selected areas of Seoul. The average assessed value ranges from 23.3 percent to 45.0 percent of the market value. The data presented in Table 19.2 are spotty, but they do tell us that there is a sharp variance in the relationship between the two sets of values depending on the locational difference within the city.

If we make a highly conservative assumption based on the data in Table 19.2—that the assessed value may average 40 percent of the market value—the effective tax rates decline by three-fifths of the nominal rates. The effective tax rates based on this assumption will range from 1.2/1,000 for a parcel under 100 *pyongs* to 20.0/1,000 for a parcel over 500 *pyongs*. The effective tax rates for land used for luxurious purposes range from 20/1,000 for land held under three years to 40/1,000 for land held over ten years. The effective tax rates for other categories of land can be calculated similarly.

If property taxes are administered as stipulated, the effective tax rates would range from 0.04 percent for farmland to 4 percent for the largest category of residential parcels, land for luxury use, and corporate-owned lands for nonbusiness purposes. As shown in Table 19.1, the average increase in the value of all categories of lands during the ten-year period from 1974 to 1983 in large cities was 823.69 percent, or a 82.4 percent annual increase on average. If the maximum land tax is only 4 percent of the land value, the property tax burden does not make even the slightest dent in expected profits due to price escalation. This relationship between the estimated effective tax rates and the price trend of land clearly explains why the property tax has not been effective in curbing land speculation.

It is clearly arguable whether the property tax burden on urban land in Korea can be compared with those in other countries. Though a precise comparison may not be possible, a comparison of the effective tax rates and the share of property tax collection in GNP may tell what kind of burden is placed on property through taxation in various countries.

Table 19.2. Assessed Value and Market Value of Selected Land Parcels in Seoul (W1000 per Pyong)

Location	(A) Assessed Value	(B) Market Value	(%) A/B
I	140	400-600	35.0-23.3
II	350	1,500	23.3
III	180	400	45.0

Source: Korea Research Institute for Human Settlements, Data Files, 1984.

The property tax rates of American cities may not be a fair comparison, but the data are conveniently available. The median of the average effective tax rates on FHA-financed single-family homes (building and land) in fifty SMSAs in the United States grew from 1.42 percent in 1958, 1.71 percent in 1962, 1.95 percent in 1966, to 2.13 percent in 1971. Moreover, the average effective property tax rates in 1971 exceeded 3 percent in three SMSAs (3.21 percent in Boston, 3.08 percent in Philadelphia, and 3.52 percent in Milwaukee). In contrast, two SMSAs showed a rate of below 1.0 percent (0.98 percent in Birmingham and 0.48 percent in New Orleans).[6]

In the case of Korea, an estimate based on fragments of available information shows that the effective tax rates on land ranged from 0.04 to 4 percent depending on the class, size, and use of the land and the length of its holding. The U.S. data show that the SMSA average of the effective tax rates for single-family homes (FHA-financed) ranged from 0.48 percent to 3.52 percent. These data are not quite comparable, but the property tax rates in the American urban areas seem to be generally higher than those in Korea.

This comparison becomes more meaningful when the trend of price change is taken into consideration. Data representing the general trend of real estate price changes are not available for the United States. The best data that can be assembled are the approximate market value of all parcels of real estate as estimated by the U.S. Bureau of the Census for selected SMSAs for the years 1976 and 1981. The price change rates are available for thirty-five SMSAs and range from a decline of 23.3 percent in the Buffalo SMSA to an increase of 163.56 percent in the Baton Rouge SMSA.[7] The change rates of the thirty-five SMSAs averaged a 75.49 percent increase during the five-year period and a 15.1 percent increase per year. The Korean land value increase in large cities averaged 82.4 percent a year during the ten-year period from 1974 to 1983 compared with a 15.1 percent increase per year from 1976 to 1981 in the thirty-five selected SMSAs. The land value in large Korean cities increased nearly six times as fast as that in American SMSAs, while the effective tax rates tended to be higher in American SMSAs than that in large Korean cities.

The revenues from property taxes as a percentage of GNP for Korea, Japan, and Taiwan are presented in Table 19.3. The property tax share of GNP in Korea is only 0.36 percent, while those in Japan and Taiwan are 1.20 percent and 2.56 percent, respectively. The available evidence compels us to conclude that the property tax burden on land in Korea is lower than in the United States, Japan, and Taiwan.

Assessing Property Value for Tax Purposes. The assessment of property value for tax purposes is a matter of ongoing controversy in the United

Table 19.3.   Property Tax Revenues in Comparison with GNP: Republic of
              Korea, Japan, and Taiwan, 1981

	Korea (in W100 million)	Japan (in billion yen)	Taiwan (in million NT$)	
Property tax revenues	1,527	3,053	43,457	(20,060)
GNP	423,971	253,811	1,694,482	
%	0.36	1.20	2.56	(1.18)

Note: Figures in parentheses exclude revenue from the land value
increment tax.

Sources: Bank of Korea, The National Income of Korea, 1982; Ministry of
Home Affairs, Korea, Statistical Yearbook of Local Taxes, 1983; Bureau
of Statistics, Japan, Statistical Yearbook of Japan, 1983; Office of
Statistics, Ministry of Finance, People's Republic of China,
Statistical Yearbook of Finance, 1981.

States. Nevertheless, a realistic assessment with acceptable precision is
indispensable if property tax and capital gains taxes on lands owned by
individuals or by corporations for nonbusiness purposes are to maintain
their fairness and effectiveness. As demonstrated by the data shown in
Table 19.2, the assessment/market value ratio depends on locations
within the same city. In a society where land price is changing rapidly
and the change rate is highly dependent on location, to maintain a consistency in the assessment/market value ratio among different parcels of
real estate in different locations is indeed difficult if not impossible. This
difficulty in maintaining the consistency of assessment further weakens
the already low tax rates as a policy instrument to counter escalating
land prices and land speculation.

Administrative Effects. For a tax system to have its full effect, the stipu-
lations governing tax exemption or tax reduction must be precisely
defined. Further, tax assessment and tax collection must be carried out
systematically and with precision. The available evidence leads us to
believe that property tax administration in Korea suffers from lax
implementation. The case in point is the vacant land tax. It has been
reported that some 90 percent of the taxable vacant land receives tax-
exempt status. Vacant land is a serious source of land speculation.[8]
When the relatively low tax rate is coupled with prevalent tax exemption, it is not surprising that land speculation has been going on
unchecked despite its recognition as a serious problem by all parties
concerned including the government, political parties, and the general
public.

Capital Gains Tax

There are two types of capital gains tax levied on lands: tax on land owned by individuals and tax on corporate-owned land for nonbusiness purposes. Capital gains tax on land is designed to absorb a substantial portion of the profits resulting from value appreciation as tax revenue when the land is sold. A capital gains tax certainly promises a chilling effect on speculative investment in land, provided that its rates are high enough and its implementation is strict.

Tax Rates. The rate structure of capital gains tax on land and other real estate owned by individuals is different in a number of ways. When the property is sold after two years or more, the capital gains tax rate is 30 percent for low-priced housing (or low-income family homes) and 40 percent for other properties, but 50 percent if they are sold in less than two years. For those properties sold without registration of the sales transaction, the rate is 75 percent.

The capital gains tax rate on corporate-owned land for nonbusiness purposes is considerably lower than that for real estate owned by individuals. The tax rate is only 25 percent, but when the sales transaction is not registered the rate is 35 percent. This capital gains tax rate becomes meaningful when the definition of taxable capital gains is understood. The relationship between the capital gains tax rate and taxable capital gains is similar to the property tax rate and its relationship to the assessed value of taxable property. Taxable capital gains are defined as follows:

$$\text{Taxable capital gains} = \text{transfer price} - (\text{acquisition price} + \text{improvement cost} + \text{special exemption} + \text{W1.5 million})$$

Transfer price is defined as the assessed value for property tax purposes as determined by the Ministry of Home Affairs. For those properties in which transfers occurred in areas declared to be speculation control areas by the National Tax Administration, however, standard market value is used as the transfer price. In either case, the actual sale price is not used as the transfer price. By special exemption is meant the annual inflation allowance, 15 percent a year through 1983 and 5 percent a year beginning in 1983. The acquisition price is the standard market price at the time of purchase; the actual purchase price is used only in those cases where presidential decree requires it.

Tax Effects on Transfer Profits. How effective would the capital gains tax be in absorbing profits from capital gains into the public treasury?

Would that effect be substantial enough to discourage speculative investment? Let us use a hypothetical case. Assuming that a piece of property is purchased at W10 million and sold at W30 million three years later, what would be the net profit to the investor?

Transfer price = W12 million (40% of sale price)

Acquisition price = W4 million (40% of purchase price)[9]

Capital gains exemption = W1.5 million

Special exemption = W600,000 (5% per year)

Improvement cost = W280,000 (7% of acquisition price)

Thus

Taxable capital gains = W12 million – (W4 million + W1.5 million + W0.6 million + W0.28 million)
= W5.62 million

Finally,

Capital gains tax = W5.62 million × 40/100
= W2.548 million

If we base this computation on the actual purchase and sale prices, the result will give us a more realistic effect of the tax on the profit margin of the property transferred. The actual difference between the purchase and sale price is W20 million. When the capital gains tax as calculated above is deducted from the gross capital gains, the actual profit is W17.752 million. This is a 177 percent profit after capital gains in three years. In view of the lower tax rate, a capital gains tax on corporate-owned land for nonbusiness purposes is less likely to suppress the likelihood of windfall profits from corporate land speculation.

Administrative Effects. Another important issue related to the capital gains tax is administrative effectiveness in identifying all the taxable capital gains resulting from property transactions. Data are not readily available for a conclusive assessment of the administrative effectiveness of the capital gains tax. The best data we could locate clearly indicate that the enforcement of capital gains tax is pitifully limited.

Table 19.4 shows the number of taxable property units on which were

Table 19.4.   Number of Land Parcels and Housing and Building Units Levied
               Acquisition Tax in Comparison to Those Levied Capital Gains,
               Inheritance, and Gift Taxes: 1979-1982

	1979	1980	1981	1982
No. of units levied acquisition tax (A)	1,332,304	1,264,499	1,146,917	1,295,341
No. of units levied capital gains, inheritance, and gift taxes (B)	30,842	65,552	127,618	226,086
B/A (%)	2.31	5.21	11.13	17.45

Sources: Ministry of Home Affairs, Yearbook of Local Tax Administration,
appropriate years; National Tax Administration, Statistical Yearbook of
National Taxation, appropriate years.

levied the acquisition tax in row 1. The number of combined taxable incidents for capital gains tax, inheritance tax, and gift tax is shown in row 2.[10] The number of acquisition tax incidents is approximately equal to the number of property transfers. If a capital gains tax is paid on all capital gains from the transferred properties, the number of cases for the two tax incidents should be identical or similar. However, even when the number of inheritance and gift tax incidents are combined with the number of capital gains tax incidents, the latter is only a fraction of the number of acquisition tax incidents—namely 2.31 percent in 1979, 5.21 percent in 1980, 11.13 percent in 1981, and 17.45 percent in 1982—but the trend of improvement is encouraging and significant. Another anomaly found in the capital gains tax is that it is often paid by the buyers instead of the sellers, thus forward-shifting the tax. The Korea Research Institute for Human Settlements' survey of real estate agents in 1984 reveals that in more than 30 percent of the cases, capital gains tax is paid by buyers.[11] This phenomenon is an eloquent statement about the prospect of windfall profits expected from land speculation in particular and real estate speculation in general.

Land Tax Systems in Other Countries

The problem of land speculation is not a common one in every country. Even in a country where land speculation is a serious problem, the problem is usually confined to certain locations. Therefore, examples of land tax policy to control land speculation and land price inflation are not plentiful. Tax policies are used for different purposes by different countries—to expedite land development, to retard land development, to improve the efficiency of land use, or to reduce the concentration of landownership, not just to control speculative investment and price inflation alone.

The taxes most often used to affect the land market or land price include site value taxation (also called land value taxation or land tax), vacant land tax, land value increment tax, and capital gains tax. In principle, site value taxation is only on land, not the improvements on the land.[12] Presently no country is using a pure form of site value taxation. The system in use taxes both land and buildings, but land is taxed more heavily. The vacant land tax, which is designed to speed up the development of land and to enhance the efficiency of land use, levies a heavier tax on vacant than developed land. The land value increment tax is levied on the realized value increment when the land is sold, or it is levied on the accrued value increment periodically while the land is still held by one owner. The capital gains tax is levied on the positive difference between the sale price and purchase price with allowance for appropriate deductions.

Some combination of these taxes has been used at one time or another by various countries including Taiwan and the United States. In fact, Taiwan's experience closely parallels that of Korea in many ways: rapid economic development and urbanization, limited land space, high density of population, and the resultant land speculation and concentration of landownership.[13] To deal with these problems, the Statute of Equalization of Urban Land Rights was adopted in 1954 and modified through subsequent amendments in 1968 and 1977. The basic land tax system established by this statute includes land value tax (LVT), vacant land tax (VLT), and land value increment tax (LVIT). Taiwan's tax system is based on the principle that the existing value of the land at the time of acquisition belongs to the owner, but the value accrued due to social and economic development belongs to the public.

Taiwan's land value tax combines the concepts of ordinary property tax and capital gains tax on accrued value increment and applies a graduated tax rate. A graduated tax rate is applied to the value in excess of the progressive starting value (PSV) ranging from 1.5 to 7 percent. The PSV is defined as the average value of 700 square meters of land in each taxing district. Thus the PSV varies from district to district. Two exceptions are made in the land value tax—for lands preserved for public facilities development, which are taxed at 1 percent, and owner-occupied housing lots not exceeding 300 square meters, which are uniformly taxed at 0.5 percent.

The assessed value for the land value tax is based on the value reported by the landowner. However, the government establishes the standard land value every three years. When the owner-reported value is less than 80 percent of the standard land value established by the government, the government reserves the right to purchase the land at the value reported by the owner.

The vacant land tax is levied on undeveloped land where road, water, sewer, and electricity are available and on land in which the value of buildings is less than 10 percent of the land value. The vacant land tax is a surtax added to the land value tax and ranges from 200 to 500 percent of the land value tax. Usually the minimum 200 percent surtax is levied and collected rather than the maximum 500 percent surtax. Thus the vacant land tax ranges from three to six times as high as the land value tax. Since the maximum for the land value tax is 7 percent of the assessed taxable value, the vacant land tax can range from 21 to 42 percent of the assessed value of the vacant land. Considering that assessed value is almost equal to the market value, Taiwan's vacant land tax is truly prohibitive.[14]

The land value increment tax is paid by the seller of the land, and taxable value is determined by subtracting the purchasing price and inflation adjustment cost (development cost is an allowable deduction) from the sale price.[15] A progressive tax rate is applied to this taxable increment value as follows: if taxable increment value is less than 100 percent, a tax rate of 40 percent; 100–200 percent, 50 percent; more than 200 percent, 60 percent.

What about the tax effects? The evidence is not readily available as to the effects of this tax system on land speculation and land price stabilization on Taiwan. Some changes attributed to the tax effects show that 28 percent of land owned by large landowners was sold, the number of absentee landlords was reduced by 59 percent, the number of urban land-owning households increased by 14 percent, the average per household landholding increased by 12 percent, and the land area for urban construction use increased by nearly 700 percent in the decade following implementation of the urban land reform program.[16]

Approaches to Land Tax Reform

South Korea's present land tax system has few conceptual defects, but the tax rates and the assessment level of property values are too low to have a decisive effect on curbing speculation. A reform of the land tax system in order to enhance its speculation-controlling effect can be approached in two ways. First, the current system can be strengthened by correcting its weaknesses. Second, the current system can be replaced by an entirely new system. Here we will consider both approaches. The first is concerned with marginal adjustments to the present system such as tax rate hikes, realistic assessment (assessment of property value at the current market value), restricting tax exemptions, and closing tax loopholes. A new approach, one utilizing comprehensive and progressive property tax systems, will also be discussed.

Marginal Adjustments to the Present System

Tax Rate Increases. Property tax and both forms of capital gains tax need a drastic increase in rates. The property tax rates should be raised to the level at which the carrying cost (tax cost) would nearly eliminate the prospect of possible profits. How high should the tax rates be raised? The extent of the rate increase must be closely related to the rate of price increase. Although it would be imprudent to suggest a specific rate increase without the benefit of further research and additional information, it would not be unreasonable to set the minimum at a 300 percent increase.

A sudden 300 percent increase may be considered ill-advised. Rather, the increase may be spread over three or six-year periods. This step-by-step increase can be considered an experimental approach. After doubling the tax rates at the first round, for example, its effect on land price and land speculation should be evaluated. If this tax increase is inadequate in controlling land speculation, the second-round increase may be implemented. In the event that the second-round tax increase succeeds in curbing speculation, the third-round increase may be postponed indefinitely until needed.[17]

Capital gains taxes on land owned by individuals as well as land owned by corporations for nonbusiness purposes must be directly related to the actual gross profit realized. The tax rates should ensure that the net profit from the land transaction should not exceed the profit levels expected from bank certificate of deposits or the average dividends from industrial investment. In short, the opportunity for windfall profits from land transactions should be eliminated by the capital gains tax.

Assessment for Taxable Value. No less important than tax rates is the assessed value of the taxable property. In a society where land value changes rapidly, it is difficult to capture the current value in tax assessment. For taxes on land to have their intended effects, the taxable assessed value must represent the current market value at the time of tax levy.

Tax Loopholes. For general property tax as well as capital gains taxes, those properties eligible for tax exemption or tax reduction must be strictly defined and kept at the absolute minimum. Properties owned and sold by religious organizations, welfare organizations, and cultural and educational institutions should not be allowed to become a hotbed of tax evasion by abusing the privilege of tax exemption unless the properties are directly utilized in their missions as stipulated by a constitution and appropriate statutes.

Comprehensive Progressive Property Tax: An Alternative?

Recently the concept of a comprehensive progressive property tax has been hailed in Korea's mass media as a possible cure for the problems of land speculation, land price escalation, and concentration of land-ownership in the hands of a few. This approach bases property tax rates on the total amount of all properties owned by each taxpayer and applies a progressive tax rate, so that the larger the landholding, the higher the tax rate.

The comprehensive progressive tax for property seems to be encouraged by two events. First, computerization of land and property records has just become possible in Korea, thus identifying the owner of all properties for compilation of consolidated information. Second, a personal income tax system taxing the aggregate income of each taxpayer has been implemented successfully with the assistance of computerized tax information. The comprehensive progressive property tax is a revolutionary concept and a creative idea with no known precedents. As far as the concept itself is concerned, the comprehensive progressive property tax, designed properly and administered effectively, would be a powerful policy tool to control speculation and disperse landownership. However, the real effect of the tax system based on this concept will be determined by the specific provisions of the tax legislation and by competence and thoroughness in its administration.

A progressive property tax system is much more complex and technically difficult to design and implement than a progressive income tax system. Income will be the same in terms of value unit whatever the income's source. Income from all sources can be aggregated to determine one's tax obligation. But the method of aggregating properties for progressive taxation is not that simple. How can one add up different parcels of land, different units of housing, and multiple units of other types of properties for taxation? First, should the land and buildings be aggregated separately? Second, in the case of land, should the size of land or the value of land be the basis of tax rate differentiation? Other vexing questions certainly abound.

Since the computerization of land and property records will be the data base for the comprehensive progressive tax system, the quality of the data computerized will determine the quality of the tax system. The variables selected for inclusion and their accuracy and timeliness will determine the quality of the data.

Should the comprehensive property tax be a national or a local tax? If it becomes a local tax, how should the tax revenue collected from each taxpayer be distributed among the different local tax jurisdictions in which the taxpayer's properties are located? If the comprehensive property tax is made a national tax, how should the revenue loss of the localities be compensated? These are all complex and politically sensitive questions that defy easy resolution.

Structuring the progressive tax rate is another difficult problem. What should be the baseline and the ceiling of the progressive rate? What should serve as the criteria to determine the progressivity of the rate structure? Should there be a standard exemption? If so, what should be the criteria on which the standard exemption is to be based and at what level? How should the different types of properties be treated in relation to the tax rate? When a person owns a million dollars worth of property, the property may be all land, all buildings, or a mix of many different types such as farmland, vacant land, and housing lots. Should the rate structure be differentiated according to the pattern of aggregate property or not? All these questions point to the fact that the comprehensive property tax system may be a technical nightmare to design if it is to be just and effective. The complexity of the tax system will also compound the difficulty of its effective implementation and management.

The closer one looks at this tax reform, the more complex and problematic it appears, but this tax system promises enormous potential as an antispeculation policy instrument. Before a decision is made as to whether a comprehensive property tax system is to be adopted or not, careful research must be undertaken to answer all the questions raised here and more.

Conclusion

The effectiveness of a land tax system to control land speculation cannot be judged by the concepts underlying the tax system alone. After all, Korea's tax system is based on a set of sound principles. The tax system fails to create the desired effect due to a low tax rate, unrealistic assessment, tax loopholes, and weak tax administration. An effort to correct these technical and operational deficiencies certainly merits a try before attempting to replace the present system with a new one like the comprehensive progressive property tax system under consideration.

However powerful a tax system may be as a policy instrument to control economic behavior, including land speculation, a tax policy alone is not a panacea. An opportunity for alternative safe and productive investment must exist. A long-range plan for public ownership of land and specific programs to implement such a plan must be established, and a funding system such as a trust fund can be set up with tax revenue from speculation control taxes. Before it becomes too late, the land of the nation must be rescued from the speculative manipulation of profiteers and a system in which the public interest can govern the use (including permanent preservation of some of the nation's land) must be established on a firm foundation.

NOTES

1. 1,222 *pyongs* are equivalent to 1 acre.
2. Roger S. Smith, "Land Prices and Tax Policy: A Study of Fiscal Impacts," *American Journal of Economics and Sociology* 37 (1) (January 1978): 51–59.
3. *Chosen Daily,* 31 July 1984, p. 1.
4. *Dong-A Daily,* 17 July 1984, p. 1.
5. *Chosen Daily,* 28 July 1984, p. 1.
6. ACIR, *Financing Schools and Property Tax Relief—A State Responsibility* (Washington, D.C.: U.S. Government Printing Office, 1973), table A-2 (p. 135).
7. U.S. Bureau of the Census, *Taxable Property Values and Assessment–Sales Price Ratios: 1982 Census of Governments* (Washington, D.C.: U.S. Government Printing Office, 1984), table 21 (pp. 118–221).
8. *Chosen Daily,* 31 July 1984, p. 1.
9. Assessment/market value ratio is assumed to be 40 percent, based on the assessment data in selected areas of Seoul.
10. The data in Table 19.4 tell us that the actual level of capital gains tax enforcement realized is lower than the level shown in row 3. The exact level is unascertainable due to the inseparability of the cases of capital gains tax incidence from the inheritance and gift tax incidences.
11. Korea Research Institute for Human Settlements, unpublished survey data, 1984.
12. Site value taxation is based on the single-tax principle, originally advocated by Henry George.
13. The literature on Taiwan's land tax is extensive. See, for example, Sein Lin, "Urban Land Reform: The Case of Taiwan," *International Journal of Public Administration* 6 (3) (1984): 331–344; C. Howell Harris, "Land Taxation in Taiwan: Selected Aspects," in Roy W. Bahl (ed.), *The Taxation of Urban Property in Less Developed Countries* (Madison: University of Wisconsin Press, 1979), pp. 191–206.
14. The highest estimated tax rate on land in Korea is approximately 4 percent of the market value of the land. Taiwan's vacant land tax is five to ten times as high as Korea's.

15. The land value increment tax is levied on the accrued value for land which has not undergone market transaction. The tax is levied every ten years in Taiwan according to W. S. King, "Urban Land Policy and Land Taxation of the Republic of China," in A. M. Woodruff and J. R. Brown (eds.), *Land for the Cities of Asia* (Hartford: University of Hartford, 1971), pp. 261–263.

16. See Lin, "Urban Land Reform," pp. 341–343.

17. When the tax rate is tripled, its effect on low-income homeowners will become unbearably oppressive. To avoid such a predicament, the basic distinction of an owner-occupied home for tax exemption or reduction may be established at an appropriate level.

20. The Influence of Foreign Direct Investment on Spatial Concentration

ROLAND J. FUCHS AND ERNESTO M. PERNIA

THE spatial concentration of development in one or two major cities in developing countries has been a concern among scholars and governments for some time. This concern relates to the efficiency and equity objectives of development policy.[1] It has been argued that equity should not continually be sacrificed for efficiency and that some accommodation between the two should be found to achieve national spatial integration and growth. An additional concern relates to the integrity of the environment and quality of life, which have also become prominent goals in recent development plans and which are seen as threatened by the growth of the very large metropolis.

Previous research and policy thrusts have focused largely on the internal dynamics of urbanization and spatial development; in other words, a closed economy has usually been assumed. Increasing transnational economic, sociopolitical, and cultural relations, however, facilitated by increased sophistication of transportation and communications, now make an introspective study of national spatial development less satisfactory. This is a criticism that has been raised especially in the world-system/dependency theories of development[2] and by geographers concerned with the spatial effects of the internationalization of national economies who have begun to examine the links between the global economy and urban or regional change.[3]

In this chapter we consider a major external economic force—namely, foreign direct investment—in relation to national spatial development. Specifically we examine Japanese direct investments in East and Southeast Asian countries in terms of their contribution to the spatial concentration of population and economic activity in these countries.

Adapted, by permission of the East–West Center, from *Urbanization and Urban Policies in Pacific Asia,* edited by Roland J. Fuchs, Gavin W. Jones, and Ernesto M. Pernia (Boulder and London: Westview Press, 1987), pp. 88–111.

Prior Empirical Research

Empirical research examining the relationships between external economic forces and national spatial development, including urbanization patterns, is still sparse. In one of the few cross-national studies concerned with spatial impacts, Koo and Timberlake investigated the relationship between various measures of dependency (including direct foreign investment) and urbanization patterns (including degree of primacy, rates of urbanization, and overurbanization).[4] They conclude that "external economic dependency seems to have no significant short-run effects on urbanization patterns of developing countries," at least in the direction suggested by dependency theories.[5] As part of the effort for this research, we also experimented with regression analyses on international cross-sectional data. After using different specifications and functional forms, we found no significant relationship between urbanization and foreign direct investment. This finding is consistent with an earlier result of Chenery and Syrquin using a similar procedure and variables.[6]

In contrast to the limited number of cross-sectional studies, there has been considerable empirical study of the impact of foreign investment or multinational corporations on the spatial organization of individual *developed* nations, including study of the geography of Japanese investments in the United Kingdom[7] and Australia.[8] These studies suggest that foreign investors have generally preferred to invest in the economic core regions of developed countries, following domestic investors as a matter of risk avoidance, unless political influences, including economic incentives, make peripheral locations more attractive or, in the special case of investment in a neighboring country, adjoining border regions may have appeal. Such studies also provide evidence that there may be national differences in preferences—a German preference for small towns, for example, an American preference for regional centers, and a general preference to continue investing in subnational areas pioneered by earlier firms of the same nation.[9] Edgington shows that Japanese investment in Australia, focused on Sydney and Melbourne, is more concentrated than domestic investment and, in the case of Sydney, has contributed measurably to its incorporation in the emerging world system of cities.[10]

Because of limitations of theory and a lack of data, the literature concerning the subnational patterns of multinational investments within developing countries is still sparse.[11] Abumere,[12] studying such investments in Nigeria, finds that they differ from indigenous investments: They are more concentrated, more attracted by amenities and basic infrastructure, and prefer areas known from the corporation's previous distribution network. Little appears to have been published on the spatial impact of foreign investment in Asia with the exception of Forbes' studies of Indonesia[13] and recent studies of the regional impact of the internationalization of financial and product services.[14]

Approach and Data

As a preliminary investigation into the relationship between external economic forces and national spatial development in Asia, this chapter examines the spatial patterns of Japanese direct investments cross-nationally and within six Pacific Asian countries: Taiwan, South Korea, Malaysia, the Philippines, Thailand, and Indonesia. Commonly referred to as NICs (newly industrializing countries) and near-NICs, these countries exhibit varied patterns of spatial and urban development (Table 20.1). All of them, however, have enunciated policies of regional development and dispersal from the metropolitan capital city. All have already been hosts to substantial Japanese capital and are likely to absorb much more in the future.

A modified core/periphery framework is used in the analysis, which involves the following types of locations: metropolitan center, remainder of metropolitan area, metropolitan periphery, regional centers, and rural periphery. The first two elements form the usual metropolitan definition of the older central city or cities plus recently added cities or towns. The metropolitan periphery refers to areas outside but relatively close to the metropolitan capital region (within 100–150 kilometers). Regional centers are the designated urban centers in outlying regions

Table 20.1. Background Economic and Urbanization Statistics for Selected Southeast and East Asian Countries

Country	GNP Per Capita (US$) 1980	Urbanization Level (%) 1960	Urbanization Level (%) 1980	Percentage of Urban Population in Largest City 1960	Percentage of Urban Population in Largest City 1980
Indonesia	430	14.6	22.2	20	23
Thailand	670	12.5	17.0	65	69
Philippines	690	30.3	37.4	27	30
South Korea	1,520	27.7	56.9	35	41
Malaysia	1,620	25.2	29.4	19	27
Taiwan	2,097	58.0	77.0	18	19

Sources: World Bank, World Development Report, 1982, annex tables 1 and 2 for GNP per capita; for Taiwan, Taiwan Statistical Data Book, 1982; urbanization levels from United Nations, "Estimates and Projections of Urban, Rural and City Populations, 1950-2025," 1985.

(provinces) according to national development plans. The rural periphery is the catchall for all other places.

Using this framework, we analyzed data on Japanese-owned firms to examine:

1. The subnational spatial pattern of Japanese investments in Pacific Asia, including the degree to which firms, employees, and capital are concentrated in the core regions of each nation
2. Temporal changes in the location of Japanese investments
3. The relation between location and industry sector
4. The relation between location and firm size and capital intensity
5. The relation between location and investment objectives
6. The relation between location and market orientation

As its data source the study employs responses to questionnaires distributed by the *Oriental Economist* to leading listed and unlisted Japanese corporations.[15] In the six nations involved, the survey covered 893 firms with 342,000 employees. The information provided includes year of establishment, size of capital investment, number of employees, industry type, location, and investment objectives.[16]

The study is thus primarily an exploratory empirical contribution to the understanding of the impact of foreign investment on the space economy of selected nations in Pacific Asia. Using Western-language literature and data on direct foreign investment originating in Japan, the largest overseas investor in Asia, we examine through an inductive approach the spatial patterns of these investments within the core/periphery framework and the structural characteristics that may explain location. Our study is directed ultimately toward such policy-related questions as whether or not Japanese investments are unduly concentrated in core or metropolitan areas (and thus contributing to "unbalanced" urban growth) and whether or not special locational controls are required for Japanese, and by extension other foreign investors. These issues are of more than passing interest because of the strong concern voiced by Asian governments regarding their urban population distributions, the failure of existing policies, and a growing tendency to place the blame for unbalanced urban growth on foreign investors and more specifically multinational corporations.[17]

Japan's Direct Foreign Investments

Growth and Characteristics

Japanese investments overseas before and during the Pacific War, heavily concentrated in Asia, especially in the former Japanese colonies of

Manchukuo, Formosa, and Korea,[18] were either destroyed or liqui-
dated in the war and its aftermath. Throughout the 1950s Japan was
necessarily concerned with domestic reconstruction and dependent
upon Western nations for technology and capital. Full employment was
achieved about 1960, but until the mid-1960s wage rates remained low
and the yen weak. Japan's overseas investments therefore remained
limited until the late 1960s, when they grew rapidly as a result of various convergent factors: a growing trade surplus, a relaxation of government restrictions on overseas investments, the increased value of the
yen, an abundance of managerial resources, growing shortages of
domestic labor and natural resources, and growing protectionism in
markets located in both developed and developing countries.[19] Also
important were government policies designed to restructure domestic
industry in Japan by exporting senile and environmentally damaging
industries.[20]

Throughout the 1970s Japanese foreign direct investment grew at a
more rapid rate than that of other source nations. Approximately half of
the total Japanese overseas investment occurred in the late 1970s and
early 1980s. Despite the spectacular growth during this period, on a
global basis Japan until recently accounted for only 7 percent of the outstanding foreign direct investment by leading industrial countries,
ranking behind the United States (42 percent) and the United Kingdom
(9 percent) and standing approximately on a par with West Germany
and Switzerland.[21]

The sharp rise in the value of the yen from 1985 to 1986 is expected to
lead to another surge in Japanese overseas investment from US$120 bil-
lion at the end of 1985 to an estimated US$556 billion in 1995.[22] While
much of the investment will take the form of portfolio investment, foreign direct investment is anticipated to expand dramatically as Japanese
business is forced to expand abroad in order to supply local markets,
third countries, or components and finished goods to Japan. Much of
this investment will occur in the countries of East Asia because of their
proximity and similar industrial structures, but restrictions in Taiwan
and South Korea may channel additional investments to Hong Kong
and the ASEAN countries.

The structural and other characteristics of Japanese overseas investments have been studied by a number of analysts who have noted significant differences between Japanese investments and those of other
source nations.[23] These differences include a broader sectoral spread for
Japanese investments with a greater emphasis on extractive industries,
service, and trade and less emphasis on manufacturing than commonly
found in the case of other major source nations; a preference for joint
ventures; and the high proportion of investment accounted for by small
and medium-size Japanese firms, many organized by *soga shosha*, the

uniquely Japanese general trading companies.[24] Unlike their U.S. and German competitors, Japanese investors tended initially to concentrate in labor-intensive industries or those with a standard technology, thus employing comparative advantage. There later appeared a shift from labor-intensive consumer goods, such as textiles, electrical appliances, and transport equipment assembly, to more capital-intensive industries such as chemicals, food processing, and machinery.[25] But recently overseas direct investment has been dominated by investment in the non-manufacturing sector, including finance and insurance.[26] Japan's experience thus appears sufficiently unique to question the applicability of the general theoretical frameworks employed to explain the behavior of Western multinational corporations: industrial organization approaches, the product-cycle approach, and the factor endowment approach.[27]

Structural Patterns

In contrast to investment by other source nations, Japanese overseas investment has also been distinguished by the high proportion going to developing countries (some 56.5 percent, twice the U.S. proportion) and the significant portion (29.0 percent) going to Asia (Table 20.2).[28] Of the total number of employees in Japanese overseas subsidiaries— 770,000 in March 1978—416,000 were employed in Asia. Japan has become the largest direct investor in South Korea, Thailand, Malaysia, and Indonesia and the second largest in Hong Kong, the Philippines, and Singapore.

Japan's increasing dominance of Asia in investment and trade reinforces Taylor and Thrift's contention that the world economy is being rearranged into a "set of more regionally based zones of production dependent on a dominant regional power."[29] The overall Japanese domination of foreign investment in Asia, and the spatial distribution of Japanese investments within Asia, also seem in accord with recent attempts to explain spatial patterns of geoinvestment on the basis of distance, market size, and political factors.[30]

A more detailed explanation of the extent, timing, and nature of investment in individual nations requires reference to other factors, however.[31] Initially, in the 1960s, Taiwan was the most popular country for Japanese manufacturing investment because of the prior colonial relationship, sociocultural similarities between the two countries, geographical proximity, and abundant cheap labor. Favorable government legislation and the opening of the Kaohsiung export zone were further inducements. Although South Korea is even closer to Japan and also had prior colonial ties with Japan, investments there initially lagged because

Table 20.2.   Japanese Overseas Investment: 1951-1981

Region	Value (US$ millions)	% of Total
Asia	13,068	29.0
Indonesia	6,858	15.1
Hong Kong	1,424	3.1
South Korea	1,209	2.7
Singapore	1,202	2.6
Philippines	687	1.5
Malaysia	581	1.5
Thailand	427	0.9
Taiwan	424	0.9
Brunei	100	0.2
Others	154	0.3
North America	12,295	27.1
Latin America	7,349	16.2
Europe	5,270	11.6
Oceania	2,949	6.5
Near and Middle East	2,355	5.2
Africa	2,018	4.4
Total	45,303	100.0

Source: F. Marsh, Japanese Overseas Investment (London: Economist Intelligence Unit, 1983).

of strained political relations but grew rapidly with the return of normal political relations in 1965, the adoption of favorable government policies, and the opening of the Masan export processing zone in 1970.

Investment in both Taiwan and South Korea temporarily slowed after the 1970 announcement of Chou En-lai's "four principles" which made the prohibition of investment in Taiwan and South Korea a condition for trade with the PRC. Investments elsewhere in Asia increased rapidly, however, especially in the ASEAN nations.[32] In Thailand growing anti-Japanese sentiments during the early to mid-1970s temporarily reduced the tempo of Japanese investments, but at the same time Indonesia and Malaysia began to attract increasing investment both in resource development ventures and in manufacturing. Indonesia now ranks second only to the United States as a home for Japanese investment; the giant Asahan hydropower and aluminum refinery project is the single largest investment. Japan's entrance into the Philippines was more recent than in Indonesia and Malaysia, despite both resource and labor attractions, because of earlier anti-Japanese sentiments and restrictive government policies. Investments in China and the USSR, despite their proximity, have been impeded by institutional and political reasons.[33]

Table 20.3. Worldwide and Asian Distribution of the Value of Japan's
Overseas Manufacturing Investments by Industry

Industry	Worldwide (%)	Asia (%)	Asia's Share in Each Industry (%)
Food	5.5	4.3	29.4
Textiles	22.2	38.3	65.5
Timber and pulp	10.2	5.9	22.0
Chemicals	15.3	7.0	17.4
Ferrous and nonferrous metals	15.3	8.7	21.6
Nonelectrical machinery	7.4	4.2	21.8
Electrical appliances and machinery	10.3	13.6	50.2
Transport equipment	6.4	6.1	36.5
Sundries	7.3	11.6	60.7
Total[a]	100.0	100.0	

Source: Lawrence G. Franko, The Threat of Japanese Multinationals—How the West Can Respond (Chichester, U.K.: John Wiley and Sons, 1983), p. 66.

[a]Subject to rounding errors.

Although the structure of Japanese investments varies considerably from country to country, it is still possible to make some generalizations. On the whole, Japan's investments in Asia are more heavily oriented to natural resource extraction and manufacturing and less so to commerce and services than in other world regions. Investments in Asian manufacturing have concentrated in labor-intensive sectors; more than half of the manufacturing investments have been in textiles and electrical appliances (see Table 20.3).

Consequences

While the extent, characteristics, and causes of Japanese direct investment in Asia are generally agreed upon, the consequences for most countries—in balance of payments, national income, technology transfer, employment generation, skill transfer, impact on local entrepreneurs, and so forth—remain a matter of dispute despite a considerable body of research on these topics.[34] The spatial implications of Japanese investment in Asia similarly remain in dispute, but in this case the reason is that they are yet to be studied.

Spatial Patterns

On the whole, Japanese direct investments tend to be highly concentrated in the metropolitan capitals of Asian countries (Figure 20.1)

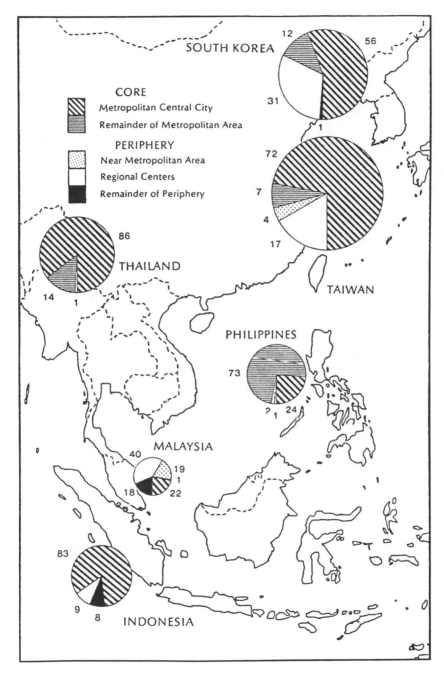

Figure 20.1. Location of Employees in Japanese Firms in Asian Nations (by Percentage)

thereby contributing to core/periphery differentiation. This is true whether investments are measured in terms of number of firms, employment, or capital, although the concentration of capital seems most pronounced. Metropolitan concentration of capital ranges from a high of nearly 100 percent in Thailand to about 62 percent in Malaysia; in terms of firms and employment, the range is from 99 percent in Thailand to around 30 percent in Malaysia.

The degree of metropolitan concentration of Japanese investments is apparently associated with the level of economic development. If the six countries are split into NICs (Taiwan, South Korea, and Malaysia) and near-NICs (Philippines, Thailand, and Indonesia), it is evident that metropolitan concentration is lower in the former than in the latter group of countries.

It is also interesting, but probably not surprising, that the subnational spatial patterns of Japanese investment in Pacific Asia are somewhat associated with the degree of urban primacy (percentage of urban population in the metropolitan area) in these countries (see Table 20.1). Thus Thailand, which has the highest urban primacy, has virtually all Japanese investments located in the Bangkok metropolis, while Malaysia and Taiwan, whose metropolitan centers are far less primate, have a substantial part of investments as measured by firms and employment dispersed, particularly to their regional centers. South Korea, despite the primacy of Seoul, also exhibits a relatively high proportion of Japanese investments in its regional centers. What distinguishes Malaysia from both Taiwan and South Korea is that even its rural periphery has some share of foreign investments. To a lesser degree the same can be said of Indonesia vis-à-vis the Philippines and Thailand.

The subnational patterns of Japanese investment within Asian countries thus appear to follow to some extent existing spatial patterns of economic activity and population.[35] These patterns in turn have been affected by both spatial and sectoral policies. It is by now well documented that development policy in both Taiwan and Malaysia paid considerable attention to rural and regional development at an early stage, thus avoiding or shortening the phase of excessive urban primacy, even as these countries were industrializing rapidly.[36] For instance, Taiwan and Malaysia appear to have minimized the implicit biases for spatial concentration of macroeconomic growth, industrial, and trade policies by early on adopting explicit policy instruments to promote rural off-farm employment, as well as labor-intensive and resource-based industries. On the other hand, South Korea's phenomenal industrialization was accompanied by unbalanced urbanization because its rural development thrust came relatively late.[37] The Philippines, Thailand, and to a lesser degree Indonesia appear to have followed the concentrated industrialization–urbanization pattern of South Korea, rather than the less concentrated pattern of Taiwan or Malaysia.[38]

Temporal Shifts in Subnational Location

Despite considerable variation on a nation-by-nation basis, it seems clear that Japanese foreign direct investment has generally been concentrated in national core regions as represented by the primary metropolitan area. But an additional question may be posed as to the stability of this pattern over time. Based on the core/periphery model, and the neoclassical economic equilibrating mechanism upon which it rests, one can hypothesize that over time the proportion of Japanese firms located in the core will decline: Improved information available to foreign investors, as well as growing congestion and other agglomeration diseconomies in the core region, accompanied by improvements in peripheral area infrastructure, should lead to a growing proportion of foreign (as well as domestic) firms locating in peripheral regions.

To test this hypothesis, the location of Japanese firms established since 1972 was compared with those established in 1950–1972. (Approximately half of the Japanese firms for which dates of establishment are provided were established since 1972.) As shown in Table 20.4, for Asia generally the location pattern of those firms established since 1972 is virtually the same as for those established earlier. From these results one would conclude that overall there has been no shift away from the core regions on the part of Japanese investors and that forces conducive to dispersal, such as improved information or growing agglomeration diseconomies, may still be too weak to overcome the attractions of the core, at least for Japanese investors.

It can also be argued, however, that aggregating the results of all six nations, in various stages of development, is inappropriate. Depending on their stage of development, some nations—the less developed—should still be experiencing polarization while others more economically advanced should be experiencing polarization reversal. Examination of the temporal patterns on a national basis indicates that four of the nations (South Korea, Thailand, Malaysia, and the Philippines) exhibit no significant shift in location of later as opposed to earlier investment. Indonesia, however, still in an early stage of development and with the lowest per capita income, demonstrates a significant shift toward *increased* polarization in the Jakarta region while Taiwan, which enjoys the highest per capita income of the six nations, reveals a significant shift toward *dispersal* outside the Taipei metropolitan area. The disag-

Table 20.4. Location of Japanese Firms in Pacific Asia by Year of Investment

Period	Total	Metropolitan Core City	Remainder of Metropolitan Area	Near Metropolitan Area	Regional Centers	Remainder of Periphery
1950-1972	420	256	57	26	67	14
	(100)[a]	(61)	(14)	(6)	(16)	(3)
1973-1981	460	280	56	23	81	20
	(100)	(61)	(12)	(5)	(18)	(4)
Total	880	536	113	49	148	34
	(100)	(61)	(13)	(5)	(17)	(4)

Note: Chi-square statistic = 1.81; this is significant at the 0.80 level with 4 degrees of freedom.

Source: Computed from Oriental Economist, 1978-1980.

[a]Percentages are given in parentheses.

gregated analyses thus suggest that Japanese investments may follow a more general pattern of polarization and polarization reversal linked to per capita income levels.[39]

Relation Between Location and Industry Sector

As part of the analysis, the relationship between location and industry sector was examined. Location theory suggests, and numerous empirical studies confirm, that tertiary-sector activities, especially producer services, will be most concentrated in the larger metropolitan centers or core economic regions while primary, resource-based activities (agriculture, forestry, fishing, mining) will be found largely in the rural periphery. Secondary manufacturing and processing activities ordinarily are found over a considerable portion of the settlement hierarchy and are relatively most important in intermediate-size cities—a reflection of the fact that sectoral efficiency depends on location both within the space economy and within the settlement hierarchy.[40] Japanese investments apparently follow the anticipated pattern only in part (Table 20.5): Investments in the tertiary sector (wholesale, retail, financial) are overwhelmingly (97 percent) found in the core regions; manufacturing activities, while concentrated in the core (76 percent), are more widely distributed. Primary activities, surprisingly, are shown as heavily concentrated in the core—leading one to suspect the use of a metropolitan area office address for resource activities actually located in the periphery.[41]

When the individual types of manufacturing activity, which account for over 88 percent of all employees covered in the survey, are examined, there are again considerable differences in location pattern by industry type. While the majority of manufacturing categories show a decided concentration in the core region, fabricated metals (by far the largest single employer), textiles, wood and "other" manufacturing have above average representation in regional centers, and food, wood, and paper industries—as one would expect—are more heavily represented in the rural periphery than are other industries. The net result is to confirm that location is indeed related to industry sector or type, although not always in the manner anticipated.

Relation Between Location and Firm Size and Capital Intensity

Yet another factor that may explain the location of Japanese firms is the scale of operations. It can be hypothesized that enterprises operating on a large scale, as measured by size of labor force per unit, are more likely to locate in the primary metropolitan area, which can offer the largest

Table 20.5. Employees of Japanese Firms by Sector and Location

Sector	Total	Metropolitan Core City	Remainder of Metropolitan Area	Near Metropolitan Area	Regional Centers	Remainder of Periphery
Primary	11,537	3,701	7,445	70	115	206
	(100)[a]	(32)	(65)	(1)	(1)	(2)
Secondary	302,521	194,984	35,682	10,502	52,821	8,532
	(100)	(64)	(12)	(3)	(17)	(3)
Tertiary	28,454	15,029	12,463	191	753	16
	(100)	(53)	(44)	(1)	(3)	(0)
Total	342,512	213,714	55,590	10,763	53,689	8,756
	(100)	(62)	(16)	(3)	(16)	(3)

Source: Computed from Oriental Economist, 1978-1980.

[a]Percentages are given in parentheses.

Table 20.6. Number of Employees per Japanese Firm

	Core		Periphery		
Country	Metropolitan Core City	Remainder of Metropolitan Area	Near Metropolitan Area	Regional Centers	Remainder of Periphery
Indonesia	79	10	—	299	284
South Korea	457	371	80	384	458
Malaysia	122	330	146	373	220
Philippines	249	682	278	147	—
Taiwan	873	511	363	388	89
Thailand	292	214	—	133	—
Total	395	471	206	368	243
	409			313	

Source: Compiled from Oriental Economist, 1978-1980.

labor market with the greatest array of labor skills. Such large-scale enterprises should favor locations within the metropolitan area but outside the central city, where land costs are highest.

Although the parent Japanese overseas firms are often small or medium in size compared to the multinational corporations of other countries, the individual plants they have established in Asia are not necessarily small—in fact, in size they average 385 workers (Table 20 6). Although there is some national variation, core region establishments with an overall average size of 409 workers are substantially larger than establishments in the periphery, which average 313 workers. Metropolitan locations outside the central city have the largest work forces, averaging 471 workers.

Regarding capital intensity, it seems clear that investments in the metropolitan area have a higher ratio of capital to labor than to investments elsewhere in the periphery. Capital intensity of Japanese investments in all metropolitan areas is above the national average whereas in the other locations, with the exception of the metropolitan periphery, it is by and large below the national average.

Relation Between Location and Investment Objectives

Another possible explanation of variation in location of Japanese firms is that of differences in investment objectives. Queried about their objective in investing overseas, 334 firms indicated a primary interest in achieving cost reductions through utilization of low-cost labor; 241 firms indicated their primary objective was to take advantage of tariff protection or other government incentives; 104 firms were primarily attracted by raw materials and natural resources (Table 20.7). Location in the core or periphery is not independent of these investment objectives. Chi-square analysis indicates a significant association (0.001 level): Firms primarily interested in raw materials and natural resources are disproportionately represented in the rural periphery; firms seeking cost reduction and low-cost labor are found more frequently than expected in regional centers; those firms especially attracted by tariff protection and other forms of government incentives are especially attracted to the core region.[42]

Relation Between Location and Market Orientation

Of the 464 Japanese firms expressing their market orientation, the majority—some 280—were primarily oriented to the domestic market whereas 81 had their primary market in Japan and 103 in third countries. A chi-square analysis reveals there is a significant (at the 0.001 level) association between location and market orientation (Table 20.8). Firms with a local market orientation are substantially overrepresented in the core and underrepresented in the periphery. Firms with a primary orientation to exports, however, whether to Japan or their countries, are relatively overrepresented in the periphery, especially in regional centers.

Conclusions and Policy Implications

The analysis detailed above may be summarized as follows. Overseas Japanese firms in the Pacific Asian nations of Indonesia, South Korea, Malaysia, the Philippines, Taiwan, and Thailand have chosen on the whole to locate in the core region of these nations; some three-fourths of the firms and their employees are located in the primary metropolitan area.

There is, however, considerable variation in location patterns from nation to nation; Japanese firms are highly concentrated in the core or metropolitan regions of the Philippines, Thailand, and Indonesia but more dispersed in Taiwan, South Korea, and especially Malaysia. Japanese investments apparently reflect national patterns of economic activity and population distribution and the level of development, with a greater dispersal in NICs than in the near-NICs.

For the six nations overall there has been no shift over the years from a location preference for the core to the periphery; recent investments have nearly the same location pattern as earlier investments. If the pat-

Table 20.7. Objectives of Overseas Japanese Firms by Location

Objective	Total	Metropolitan Core City	Remainder of Metropolitan Area	Near Metropolitan Area	Regional Centers	Remainder of Periphery
Access to raw materials and natural resources	104 (100)[a]	53 (51)	8 (8)	5 (5)	19 (18)	19 (18)
Use of labor and cost reduction	334 (100)	173 (52)	37 (11)	24 (7)	92 (28)	8 (2)
Take advantage of government incentives and tariff protection	241 (100)	134 (56)	30 (13)	20 (8)	44 (18)	13 (5)
Total	679 (100)	360 (53)	75 (11)	49 (7)	155 (23)	40 (6)

Note: Chi-square statistic = 43.93; this is significant at the 0.001 level with 8 degrees of freedom.

Source: Compiled and computed from Oriental Economist, 1978-1980.

[a]Percentages are given in parentheses.

Table 20.8. Market Orientation of Japanese Firms by Location

Market Orientation	Total	Metropolitan Core City	Remainder of Metropolitan Area	Near Metropolitan Area	Regional Centers	Remainder of Periphery
Domestic	280 (100)a	174 (62)	41 (15)	20 (7)	35 (12)	10 (4)
Japan	81 (100)	35 (43)	8 (10)	6 (7)	26 (32)	6 (7)
Third countries	103 (100)	56 (54)	7 (7)	10 (10)	25 (24)	5 (5)
Total	464 (100)	265 (57)	56 (12)	36 (8)	86 (18)	21 (5)

Note: Chi-square statistic = 26.40; this is significant at the 0.001 level with 8 degrees of freedom.

Source: Compiled and computed from Oriental Economist, 1978-1980.

aPercentages are given in parentheses.

terns are examined country by country, however, Indonesia exhibits a significant trend toward increased concentration in Jakarta, while Taiwan exhibits a significant shift toward dispersal outside the Taipei area. As postulated in the core/periphery model, location preference may reflect the host country's stage of development.

Finally, the locations of Japanese firms have been shown to be significantly associated with the firm's characteristics:

1. Type of economic activity plays a role in location: Service-oriented activities are disproportionately located in the core while certain raw material processing activities are more frequently found in the periphery. Manufacturing is most widely distributed, and its location varies by type of manufacturing.

2. Enterprises in the core are of larger scale, and more capital-intensive, than those in the periphery.

3. Firms seeking access to raw materials are disproportionately located in the periphery; firms seeking low-cost labor tend to concentrate in regional centers; and firms taking advantage of tariff protection are found mostly in the primary metropolitan center.

4. Japanese firms producing for the local market are relatively more concentrated in the primary metropolitan area; those producing primarily for export markets tend to locate in the periphery.

The study was intended primarily as an empirical contribution to our knowledge of the spatial impact of foreign investment in Pacific Asia. The study's theoretical and policy implications are circumscribed by the restriction to Japanese investments, limitations of the data, and the general nature of the analysis. In regard to the implications for spatial development theory, although the finding of an overall concentration of Japanese investments in metropolitan or core regions is compatible with world-system/dependency views, the broad set of findings support the more traditional models of polarized growth, polarization reversal, and location theory. It appears that Japanese investments per se (and probably other foreign investments for that matter) do not exert a systematic and independent bias toward the metropolitan region. They seem to reflect instead the country's level of economic development, the existing patterns of economic activity, population, and infrastructure,[43] and the type and characteristics of the industries involved, including investment objectives and market orientation.

In regard to policy, the findings thus provide no support for the proposition that foreign investors require special *spatial* restrictions or controls. Until there is evidence that foreign investors, including Japanese investors, differ markedly in locational behavior from their indigenous counterparts, such restrictions would seem unwarranted. If spatial measures designed to prevent regional or settlement imbalances can be justified at all, they should be applied equally to indigenous and foreign firms.

In those cases where policy intervention does seem warranted, indirect sectoral measures may be preferable to explicit spatial measures. In view of the relation between economic structure and location shown in our study, sectoral policies designed to affect the composition of the economy—industry types, factor orientation, or market orientation—should have strong spatial effects. For example, sectoral policies favoring raw material processing, labor-intensive, or export-oriented industries should contribute to dispersal outside the core. In the current economic climate, such sectoral policies should also meet with more favor on the part of governments and lending institutions than would explicit spatial policies.

In discussing the need for spatial policies directed to foreign investments in Pacific Asia, one should also keep in perspective the current role of foreign direct investment (FDI) in the total picture of investment and employment. Despite the spectacular growth of FDI and especially Japanese investment in Pacific Asia in recent decades, and the commanding shares of ownership achieved in selected industries in individual countries, FDI still forms overall only a very small proportion of gross domestic investment flows (Table 20.9). In the years 1977–1981

Table 20.9. Share of Foreign Direct Investment
in Gross Domestic Investment

Country	1969-1971	1972-1976	1977-1981
Hong Kong	4.3	6.9	7.9
South Korea	0.8	2.3	1.5
Taiwan	1.3	0.5	0.8
Indonesia	6.0	11.4	5.7
Malaysia	3.4[a]	4.5	2.5
Philippines	1.8	2.7	1.9
Singapore	2.2	3.7	11.0
Thailand	0.6[b]	0.8	1.6
All countries[c]	2.1	8.1	2.8

Source: Hal Hill and B. Johns, "The Role of Direct Foreign
Investment in Developing Countries." Unpublished
paper (Canberra: Australian National University,
1984).

[a] 1971 only.

[b] 1970 and 1971 only.

[c] Weighted average.

the proportion ranged from less than 1.0 percent in the case of Taiwan to 5.7 percent in Indonesia. The total employment of Japanese firms in all of Asia was only 416,000 in 1978. In South Korea, in the same year, firms with any degree of foreign investment at all accounted for only 2.3 percent of total employment and 9.5 percent of manufacturing employment, a significant but hardly a dominant role.[44] Obviously whatever problems South Korea and other Asian nations may have with the spatial distribution of their economies and employment are still primarily the result of the location decisions of indigenous, not foreign, investors and lie beyond solution by policies forged to control foreign investment alone.[45]

NOTES

1. H. W. Richardson, *City Size and National Spatial Strategies in Developing Countries*, Staff Working Paper no. 52 (Washington, D.C.: World Bank, 1977).
2. I. Wallerstein, *The Capitalist World Economy* (London: Cambridge University Press, 1979).
3. See T. G. McGee, "Circuits and Networks of Capital: The Internationalization of the World Economy and National Urbanization," paper presented at the Conference on Urban Growth and Economic Development in the Pacific Region, Taipei, 1984; John Friedmann, *Regional Development Policy: A Case Study of Venezuela* (Cambridge: MIT Press, 1966); Michael Taylor and Nigel Thrift, *The Geography of Multinationals* (London and Canberra: Croom Helm, 1982); and Michael Taylor and Nigel Thrift (eds.), *Multinationals and the Restructuring of the World Economy: The Geography of Multinationals*, vol. 2 (London: Croom Helm, 1986).
4. Hagen Koo and Michael Timberlake, "External Dependency and Urbanization Patterns in the Third World: A Cross-National Survey" (n.d.).
5. Ibid., p. 17.
6. Hollis B. Chenery and Moises Syrquin, *Patterns of Development, 1950–1970* (London: Oxford University Press for the World Bank, 1975).
7. Peter Dicken, "Japanese Manufacturing Investment in the United Kingdom: A Flood or Mere Trickle?" *Area* 15 (4) (1983): 273–284.
8. D. W. Edgington, "Some Urban and Regional Consequences of Japanese Transnational Activity in Australia," *Environment and Planning*, Series A, vol. 16 (1984): 1021–1040.
9. A. Blackbourn, "The Impact of Multinational Corporations on the Spatial Organization of Developed Nations: A Review," in M. Taylor and N. Thrift (eds.), *The Geography of Multinationals* (London: Croom Helm, 1982), pp. 147–157.
10. Edgington, "Consequences."
11. Nigel Thrift, "The Internationalization of Producer Services and the Integration of the Pacific Basin Property Market," in M. Taylor and N. Thrift

(eds.), *Multinationals and the Restructuring of the World Economy* (London: Croom Helm, 1986), pp. 142–192.

12. S. I. Abumere, "Multinationals and Industrialization in Nigeria," in M. Taylor and N. Thrift (eds.), *The Geography of Multinationals* (London: Croom Helm, 1982), pp. 158–177.

13. Dean Forbes, "Energy Imperialism and a New International Division of Resources: The Case of Indonesia," *Tijdschrift voor Economische en Sociale Geografie* 73 (2) (1982): 94–108; Dean Forbes, "Spatial Aspects of Third World Multinational Corporations' Direct Investment in Indonesia," in M. Taylor and N. Thrift (eds.), *Multinationals and the Restructuring of the World Economy* (London: Croom Helm, 1986), pp. 105–141.

14. Masahiro Fujita and Kenichi Ishigaki, "The Internalization of Japanese Commercial Banking," in M. Taylor and N. Thrift (eds.), *Multinationals and the Restructuring of the World Economy* (London: Croom Helm, 1986), pp. 193–227.

15. *Oriental Economist,* Japan's Overseas Investments: Philippines, December 1978, pp. 24–32; Thailand, January 1979, pp. 49–60; Malaysia, February 1979, pp. 30–38; Republic of Korea, May 1979, pp. 33–43; Taiwan, May 1980, pp. 38–45, June 1980, pp. 42–45; Indonesia, July 1980, pp. 49–54, August 1980, pp. 44–49.

16. According to the *Oriental Economist* (December 1978), p. 24: "The survey is primarily based on questionnaires sent to and returned from leading Japanese corporations, both listed and unlisted on the nation's stock exchanges, as well as telephone calls and other methods of inquiry. The survey is as of May 1978, and mostly covers companies listed on the stock exchanges in Tokyo, Osaka, and Nagoya. Unlisted companies also are covered in case they have joint investments with listed companies."

17. Roland J. Fuchs, *Population Distribution Policies in Asia and the Pacific: Current Status and Future Prospects,* Paper 83 (Honolulu: East–West Population Institute, 1983).

18. Charles A. Fisher, "The Expansion of Japan: A Study in Oriental Geopolitics: Part II, The Greater East Asia Co-prosperity Sphere," *Geographical Journal* 115 (January–June 1950): 179–193.

19. See Kiyoshi Kojima, *Direct Foreign Investment: A Japanese Model of Multinational Business Operations* (New York: Praeger, 1978); Kiyoshi Kojima, "Japanese Direct Foreign Investment in Asian Developing Countries," mimeo, 1980; Sueo Sekiguchi, *Japanese Direct Foreign Investment* (London: Macmillan, 1979); Ippei Yamazawa, Koji Taniguchi, and Akira Hirata, "Trade and Industrial Adjustment in Pacific Asian Countries," *Developing Countries* 21 (4) (December 1983): 281–312; Seiji Naya and Chung Hoon Lee, "Trade and Investment Patterns in the Asian NIC's," mimeo, 1983.

20. Terutomo Ozawa, *Multinationalism, Japanese Style: The Political Economy of Outward Dependency* (Princeton, N.J.: Princeton University Press, 1979).

21. Felicity Marsh, *Japanese Overseas Investment: The New Challenge,* Special Report 142 (London: Economist Intelligence Unit Limited, 1983).

22. Nigel Holloway and others, "Direct Investment: Japan's Portfolio," *Far Eastern Economic Review* 133 (36) (4 September 1986): 59–66.

23. Kojima, "Japanese Direct Foreign Investment."

24. Toshikazu Nakase, "Some Characteristics of Japanese-Type Multinational Enterprises Today," *Capital and Class* 13 (1981): 61–98.

25. Kojima, *Direct Foreign Investment.*

26. *Wall Street Journal*, "Foreign Investment Rises by Japanese Companies," 29 August 1986, p. 21.

27. Ozawa, *Multinationalism*, pp. 42–75.

28. Kojima, "Japanese Direct Foreign Investment."

29. Taylor and Thrift, *Geography of Multinationals.*

30. Grant I. Thrall, "Geoinvestment: The Interdependence Between Space, Market Size and Political Turmoil and Attracting Foreign Direct Investment," paper presented at annual meeting of the Association of American Geographers, 1984.

31. Ozawa, *Multinationalism;* Marsh, *New Challenge.*

32. M. Ikema, "Japan's Economic Relations with ASEAN," in R. Garnaut (ed.), *ASEAN in a Changing Pacific and World Economy* (Canberra: ANU Press, 1980), pp. 453–473.

33. Japan has been surprisingly slow to invest in the People's Republic of China; the nineteen joint ventures with the PRC as of 1985 had a total value of only $80 million. This has been ascribed to problems of infrastructure and institutional problems, including the bureaucracy, labor relations, and capital repatriation. Investments in the USSR have been impeded by similar reasons as well as territorial disputes regarding the Kurile Islands; nevertheless existing joint ventures and Japanese-supplied capital equipment appear to have been associated with accelerated urban growth in the Soviet cities affected.

34. Economist Intelligence Unit, "What Is the Case Against Multinationals?" *Multinational Business,* April 1975, pp. 1–12; C. W. Lindsey and E. M. Valencia, "Foreign Direct Investment in the Philippines," *Survey of Philippine Development Research,* vol. 2 (Manila: Philippine Institute for Development Studies, 1982); Gunter Krumme, "Review of the *Geography of Multinationals,*" *Professional Geographer* 35 (1983): 519–520.

35. But the exact degree of correspondence remains to be determined. Also requiring study is comparison of Japanese and indigenous investments controlled for industry sector, scale, and so on. A key question, beyond the scope of this study, is whether Japanese investments are more or less concentrated than comparable indigenous investments.

36. Paul K. C. Liu, "Factors and Policies Contributing to Urbanization and Labor Mobility in Taiwan," *Industry of Free China* (May 1983): 1–20; Tan Siew Ee and Lai Yew Wah, "Internal Migration in Peninsular Malaysia: Patterns, Determinants, and Implications," draft paper for CAMS, August 1984.

37. Song-Ung Kim, "An Analysis of Social Forces Underlying Migration Patterns in Korea," draft paper for CAMS, May 1984; P. W. Kuznets, "Employment Absorption in South Korea: 1970–1980," paper prepared for the CAMS conference on Major Issues in Manpower and Development Policies, Manila, 15–18 December 1984.

38. Medhi Krongkaew and P. Tongudai, "The Growth of Bangkok: The Economics of Unbalanced Urbanization and Development," Discussion Paper Series, no. 90, Faculty of Economics, Thammasat University, May 1984;

Ernesto M. Pernia, "Migration, Development and Employment in East and Southeast Asia," ILO Labor and Population Team for Asia and the Pacific, Bangkok, October 1984.

39. William Alonso, "Five Bell Shapes in Development," *Papers of the Regional Science Association* 45 (1980): 5–16; H. Richardson, "Polarization Reversal in Developing Countries," *Papers of the Regional Science Association* 45 (1980): 67–85.

40. F. Lo and K. Salih, "Growth Poles and Regional Policy in Open Dualistic Economies: Western Theory and Asian Reality," in F. Lo and K. Salih (eds.), *Growth Pole Strategy and Regional Development Policy* (Oxford: Pergamon, 1978), pp. 243–269.

41. If this is the case, the data exaggerate the degree of metropolitan concentration of Japanese direct investment. This would further weaken the case for spatial policies regulating foreign investment.

42. Since government policies attract a disproportionate number of firms to the primary metropolitan area, this suggests ironically that the net effect of existing government policies, including tariffs, is to contravene stated spatial policy goals.

43. Of course in some cases it can be argued that these are the result of prior colonial or other forms of dependent relations.

44. R. Lueddle-Neurath, "State Intervention and Foreign Direct Investment in South Korea," *IDS Sussex Bulletin* 15 (2) (April 1984): 18–25.

45. Unless foreign investments guide the location of domestic investments, the reverse is more likely to be true.

Index

MOL
GOM
ZAIA.

COLMACK..

BAIDÀ.

M O Y E

Oba fl.

Siber

KITAIA LACVS.

E N.

CAS

SAC

GAIA.

K I

A

R I.

TVRK

BO

SHA
MAR
GHAN.

TASKENT.

GH Kyrm na

AR

Vrgeme

Cante

Cosm

Taskent

Shaysure

Oughs fl.

Ghudou

Acsou

KIR

Mare

Bophar

...rithis

...an pissima

Corasan parua, à Rege Persico adiuuantibus Tar taris 1558. expugnata fuit

Carakol

Mesheut

Korshy

Indeghen

GES.

Corasam magna

MHOGOL

SIA

Balgh

Parapomisi montes

400	480	560	640	720	800
300	360	420	480	540	600
100	120	140	160	180	200

OCT 17 '72

RUSSIA UNDER WESTERN EYES
1517 - 1825

Front endpapers 1 and
Anthony Jenkinson's ma
Russia 1562: Russia. From
Abraham Ortelius *Orbis
Terrarum*, Antwerp 1570.

For Margaret, Jane and Serena

RUSSIA
UNDER
WESTERN
EYES
1517-1825

Edited with an introduction by Anthony Cross

St. Martin's Press New York

Acknowledgement

I would like to record my thanks to Mr and Mrs Paul Elek
for the initial suggestion to prepare this volume and for their
continuing support and active assistance in gathering together
the necessary texts and illustrative materials; also to Miss
Moira Johnston and Mr Julian Hall for their invaluable
editorial efforts on my behalf.

AFFILIATED PUBLISHERS: Macmillan & Company, Limited,
London—also at Bombay, Calcutta, Madras and Melbourne—
The Macmillan Company of Canada, Limited, Toronto

CONTENTS

List of illustrations

Table I

THE RULERS OF RUSSIA

From Rurik up to the Romanovs

Chronological history only

a) The Princes of Kiev

Rurik   862–79

Oleg   879–912

Igor   913–45

Olga   945–61

Svyatoslav   962–72

Yaropolk   973–80

Vladimir (The Saint)   980–1015

Svyatopolk   1015–19

Yaroslav   1036–54

Vladimir Monomakh   1113–25

b) The Grand Princes and Tsars of Muscovy

Ivan I (Kalita)   1325–41

Simeon   1341–53

Ivan II   1353–59

Demetrius (Dmitry Donskoy)   1359–89

Basil I   1389–1425

Basil II   1425–62

Ivan III (The Great)   1462–1505

Basil III   1505–33

Ivan IV (The Terrible)   1533–84

Theodore I   1584–98

Boris Godunov   1598–1605

Theodore II (Son of Boris)   1605

False Demetrius   1605–6

Basil IV (Shuisky)   1606–10

Vladyslav (Tsar-elect)   1610–13

Time of Troubles

Table II

THE ROMANOV DYNASTY

From Michael to Nicholas I

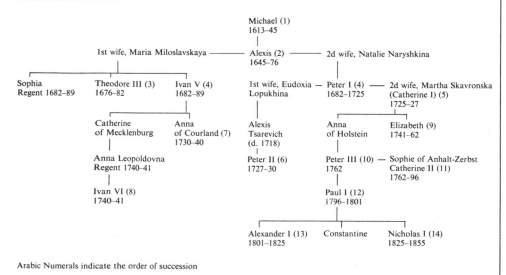

Arabic Numerals indicate the order of succession

INTRODUCTION

1

Forasmuch as it is meete and necessary for all those that minde to
take in hande the travell into farre or strange countreys, to endevour
themselves not onely to understande the orders, commodities, and
fruitfulnesse thereof, but also to applie them to the setting foorth of
the same whereby it may incourage others to the like travaile; therefore
have I nowe thought good to make a brief rehearsal of this my travaile
in Russia and Moscovia, and other countreys thereunto adjoyning.

It is with such commendable intentions that Richard Chancellor
opens the account of his voyage to the lands of the tsars of
Muscovy, an altogether unexpected and momentous outcome
of the otherwise unfortunate expedition, led by Sir Hugh
Willoughby, to discover a new trade-route by sea along the
northern coasts of Europe and Asia to China (see p. 60).
Chancellor's voyage, begun in 1553 when Edward VI was still
on the English throne, initiated that intense period of Anglo-
Russian mercantile and diplomatic relations which is associated
predominantly with the reigns of Elizabeth I of England and
Ivan IV ('the Terrible'). It also gave rise to a body of English
writing on sixteenth-century Russia, unmatched in its detail
and volume, carefully collected by Richard Hakluyt in his
*Principall Navigations, Voiages, and Discoveries of the English
Nation* (1589 and 1598). It is 'to the lasting honor of our nation'
that Hakluyt records 'all their long and dangerous voyages for
the advancement of traffique by river and land to all parts of
the huge and wide Empire of Russia'; reviewing the same
English achievement in his *Brief History of Muscovia,* compiled
almost a century later (1682) 'from the writings of several eye-
witnesses', the more sober Milton concludes that 'the discovery
of Russia by the northern Ocean, made first, of any nation that
we know, by English men, might have seem'd an enterprise
almost heroik; if any higher end than the excessive love of
Gain and Traffick, had animated the design. Nevertheless that
in regard that many things not unprofitable to the knowledge
of Nature, and other Observations are hereby come to light,
as good events ofttimes arise from evil occasions, it will not be
the worst labour to relate briefly the beginning and prosecution
of this adventurous Voiage; untill it became a last a familiar
Passage.' The English contribution to making the 'adventurous
Voiage' to Russia by any route a 'familiar Passage' was con-

siderable and, in its way, unique, although it is but part of the general picture of European penetration into Russia over the centuries. Perhaps on a psychological level, however, the transition from the strange to the familiar was never completed, despite the ever-increasing flow of European travellers to Russia and their readiness to commit to paper with ever-increasing prolixity their impressions and observations. In recent times, describing Russia as 'a riddle wrapped in a mystery inside an enigma', Winston Churchill gave his own characteristic expression to a feeling often consciously cultivated and perpetuated in written accounts over four centuries.

2

The selections which form the present anthology are all taken from works written over a period of three centuries, beginning with the reign of Basil III (1505-33) and ending with the death of Alexander I in 1825 and the famous Decembrist uprising which ensued. During this period the state of Muscovy, consolidating its position and expanding its boundaries in the sixteenth century, eventually emerged as the great empire of Russia in the eighteenth and early nineteenth centuries, an undeniably mighty and influential world power. It is therefore necessary at the outset to describe the changing territorial limits over the centuries of this always vast country and to outline briefly certain major historical events.

The six centuries from the close of the ninth century to the end of the fifteenth, which form the prehistory to the period covered by the present work, saw momentous changes in the fortunes and shape of Russia. Towards the end of the ninth century a single Kievan state emerged under the rule of the founder of the Varangian dynasty, Rurik (862-79), but it was Prince Vladimir's introduction of Christianity in 989, combined with the unceasing struggle against the nomadic tribes to the south and east, which gave Kievan Russia its sense of identity and unity. By the middle of the eleventh century this state had reached its apogee, stretching its boundaries from the Carpathians in the south-west to the Urals in the east and reaching the Baltic beyond Novgorod in the north-west. Although the Kievan period is sometimes seen as enduring until the Tartar invasion in the thirteenth-century, internecine strife among rival principalities weakened Kiev's power, which was transferred to the north-east, to Suzdal and Vladimir, whose prince, Andrey Bogolyubsky, was to sack Kiev in 1169. Some years before that date, in 1147, occurs the first mention of Moscow in the chronicles, of what R. J. Kerner has called 'this insignificant *ostrog* [outpost] built in the first half of the twelfth century on an insignificant river by an insignificant

1 The cathedral of St Sophia at Kiev as it appeared in the twelfth century. A reconstruction by F. Suddaby.

princeling'. It was to grow steadily through the following centuries–despite being razed in 1237–to become a great capital, a would-be 'third Rome'.

Between the period of Kievan decline and Muscovite ascendancy lay over two hundred and fifty years of Tartar oppression, which disrupted the cultural and social development of the land. The impressive cultural achievements of Kievan Russia were lost, its strongly developing ties and contacts with the western world were broken. When western

2 View of the port of Riga. The towns of Riga and Revel (now Tallin) were founded in 1201 and 1219 respectively and became important Hanseatic ports on the Baltic. They were taken by Peter the Great and became a strategic part of the Russian empire.

eyes again focussed on Russia in the sixteenth century, it was a 'rude and barbarous kingdom' which they saw, a land and people whose customs, religion and government they perceived as strange, unenlightened and anachronistic. The Tartar invasion of 1237-42 devastated the country, particularly the towns. One after another Ryazan, Moscow, Vladimir, Suzdal, Rostov, Chernigov, Kiev and Galich were sacked and their inhabitants massacred or enslaved. Although by the beginning of the fifteenth century the population of Russia, or more properly, East Russia, is put at ten million as compared with an estimated population of seven and a half million in 1200, it is striking testimony to the ruthlessness of Tartar attention to the towns that the urban population had suffered a decrease from fifteen to five per cent of the total. The populous city of Kiev, for an awesome example, was reduced to a mere two hundred households after the massacre of 1240. The Tartar invasion had lasting economic, political and social repercussions; it also led to far-reaching territorial divisions. The Tartars exercised their control principally over the southern and eastern parts of the land, but the inevitably weakened western and north-western areas lay open to incursions from a strong and ambitious Lithuania, as well as from Sweden. Lithuania gradually expanded eastwards until by the opening of the fifteenth century it controlled most of West Russia with boundaries running from the Baltic down to the Black Sea: it absorbed Smolensk and Kiev, controlled the territory between the estuaries of the Dniester and Dnieper on the Black Sea littoral, and bordered and threatened the lands of Moscow along the Ugra River. Yet soon after the middle of the century its decline had been so sharp that it was incorporated into the kingdom of Poland. This was in the event a merging which created an even greater gulf between the eastern and western lands of Russia; by the time the south-western provinces were re-united with Muscovy in the seventeenth century they had long been exposed to Polish influences, particularly in matters of religion and language, and Little Russia, or the Ukraine, as the region was now called, possessed a sense of difference and distinction which it has never lost.

Before returning to the particular fortunes of Moscow it is essential to speak of Novgorod, the great trading city of north-west Russia, whose ultimate fate is closely linked with the establishment of Muscovite power. The home in the ninth century of the so-called Ilmensky Slavs, inhabiting the region around Lake Ilmen, which was linked by the River Volkhov to Lake Ladoga in the north and gave rise to the Lovat and other rivers to the south, Novgorod occupied a position on the main Baltic-Black Sea waterway which allowed it to grow into the most famous and important merchant town in Russia. During the decline of the Kievan state, Novgorod gained in strength, having freed itself from Kiev as early as the eleventh

16

century. By the twelfth century it commanded a vast empire stretching to the Arctic Sea and the Urals and had a strategically important, if tenuous, outlet to the Baltic on the Gulf of Finland. Almost unique among the great towns of Russia, it escaped Tartar depredations and supported a population of some 400,000. It continued its profitable trade with Europe through membership of the Hanseatic League, using overland routes as well as the Hansa ports of Revel and Riga. Into the fifteenth century close relations with Moscow were maintained out of political and economic necessity, but Moscow's expansionist designs led to an inevitable confrontation (later in the century). Attacked in 1456 and heavily defeated in 1471, Novgorod was finally reduced to complete submission and dependence in 1478.

Moscow's reduction of Novgorod coincided in time with the final lifting of the 'Tartar yoke'. Moscow now reigned supreme and unchallenged; in the last decades of the fifteenth century it made territorial acquisitions which made Ivan III ruler of one of Europe's largest, if not yet most influential, states. The early princes of Moscow had with no little cunning manipulated to their own advantage their subservience to the Tartar overlords; they became the tribute-collectors for the Tartars, replenishing their own treasury at the same time, as the nickname of the first of the Ivans (Kalita = 'money-bag') eloquently reveals. They even helped to quell anti-Tartar uprisings. Significant support for their authority came with the establishment of the metropolitan see in Moscow in the early fourteenth century, when the Princes, in imitation of the head of the church, added the words 'and of all Russia' to their list of titles. Soon they were to use the title of 'Tsar' (Caesar), and the Muscovy tsars' insistent demand for the enumeration of all the imposing array of their titles was to be recorded by many foreign visitors in the sixteenth century. The real expansion and power of Muscovy came in the fifteenth and sixteenth centuries in the reigns of Ivan III ('the Great'), Basil III and Ivan IV ('the Terrible'). It was precisely during this period that attempts were made to fashion a fitting capital for the new Russia; the Moscow Kremlin was rebuilt and new churches and palaces, often from the designs of Italian architects, began to appear. During the sixteenth century, from which our first extracts from foreign accounts are taken, Muscovy was ceaselessly striving to extend its borders, but with comparatively limited success. A secure outlet to the Baltic was not achieved nor was access to the Black Sea; by way of compensation, however, Ivan the Terrible overran the Khanate of Kazan and took the city in 1552, soon following this with the capture of Astrakhan, which gave him control of the Volga and the north-western shores of the Caspian Sea. Significant expansion did occur in the east, beyond the Urals, where Cossack bands under Yermak penetrated into Siberia in 1582. New settlements, soon to be considerable towns were springing up both in the Volga territories and in Siberia: Orel (1564), Voronezh (1586), Ufa (1586), Tobolsk (1587).

Russian colonization in Siberia proceeded rapidly throughout the late sixteenth and seventeenth centuries reaching the eastern seaboard as early as 1639. Again the dates of the establishment of now famous towns and cities graphically chart the Russian advance: Tomsk (1604) on the Tom River

3 Tobolsk, founded in 1587 on the confluence of the Tobol and Irtysh rivers. From Ysbrant Ides' *Travels*, London 1706.

beyond the Ob, Yeniseisk (1619) and Krasnoyarsk (1628) on the Yenisey, Yakutsk (1632) on the Lena, Verkhoyansk (1638) on the Yana, Irkutsk (1652) on the Angara near Lake Baykal, Okhotsk (1649) on the Sea of Okhotsk and Bolsheretsk (1704) near the tip of Kamchatka. Of greater importance for contemporary Russians, however, were the gains in south-west Russia in the second half of the seventeenth century. This meant the recovery of both recently and long-lost territories, for Russia had suffered a disastrous setback in its triumphant progress with the advent of the Time of Troubles after the death of Boris Godunov in 1605. Disruption, chaos and famine came to the country as rival factions fought for the throne and foreign powers took the opportunity to invade the country: the Swedes seized Novgorod and the north-western provinces, while the Poles took Smolensk and Moscow itself. Only with the establishment of the Romanov dynasty in 1613 by the election of Tsar Michael (1613-45) was a semblance of internal order restored, and then only at the cost of ratifying considerable Polish and Swedish gains. During the reign of Michael's successor, Alexis, the territories in White Russia and the Ukraine were regained with the help of the Ukrainian Hetman,

18

Bogdan Khmelnitsky, but not until the eighteenth century did Peter the Great succeed in restoring to Russia its vital outlet on the Baltic.

The actual territorial expansion of Russia in the reign of Peter seems relatively insignificant when seen on a map of the period: an area to the west and north of Novgorod, a narrow strip of land along the southern and western shores of the Caspian, the peninsula of Kamchatka. But it represented a

wide and untroubled landmass, stretching from the Baltic to the Pacific, a thrust southwards into the Ottoman empire; it indicated the crushing of Swedish and Polish power in the west, the imminence of further confrontation with the Turks. It was the emergence of the Russian colossus as a threat to, and a power in, Europe, if not as a European power. If Europeans continued to call Peter 'the tsar of Muscovy', he, forcibly westernizing his country, styled himself 'Emperor of Russia' (*Imperator*). His 'Great' successor, Catherine, in the second half of the eighteenth century had her own plans for Russian aggrandisement, inevitably and clearly directed to the south and south-west. Russia shared in the gradual dismemberment of an enfeebled Poland in 1772, 1793 and 1795, which gave it some 185,000 square miles of Polish territory, although much of it had belonged to the old Kievan state. Other land from

4 The great port of Odessa was founded by Catherine II in 1794 on the north shore of the Black Sea, between the mouths of the Dnester and the Bug. Within a hundred years it became the third largest city in Russia.

which Russia had been separated for many centuries came at last into its possession, when Catherine's generals took the Black Sea steppes and the Crimea. In the same way that Peter hastened to proclaim his new rights to the Baltic by the founding of St Petersburg in 1703, Catherine was determined to exploit the trading and military advantages of the Black Sea, creating the port of Odessa in 1794 on its north shore and developing Sevastopol, which became from 1804 the headquarters of the southern fleet and closed to commercial traffic. The reign of Alexander I, which covered the first quarter of the nineteenth century, brought under Russian control further important areas in the shape of the Grand Duchy of Finland (1815), Napoleon's Grand Duchy of Poland (1812), Bessarabia (1812), which brought Russia up to the borders of the Austrian Empire, and the whole of Georgia (by 1810), to which were added other parts of the Caucasus by 1825. Such was the vast empire at the end of the period covered by our travellers' accounts and perhaps it might be added by way of a postscript that by this time the seemingly insatiable Russia had crossed into a whole new continent: Russian fur-traders were well-established in Alaska and pushed down into northern California, where they built in 1812 Fort Ross (possessions finally ceded to the United States only by 1867).

3

Such were the changing contours, the fluctuating boundaries of the Russian empire between the tenth and early nineteenth centuries; it is in such a context that western knowledge of this land may be explored.

Vladimir's Christianization of his country, a step prepared four decades earlier by the baptism of Princess Olga by the Patriarch of Byzantium, brought the young Russian state under increasing foreign influences. The first stone churches, including the Cathedral of Saint Sophia in Kiev, were built after the Greek model and with the assistance of Byzantine architects; the first icons were painted and the chronicles begun. Trade began to develop not only with Byzantium but with Europe, and German merchants arrived in the city. The Tartar invasion disrupted the cultural ties between Russia and the West but trade increased significantly through the thirteenth and fourteenth centuries. The east-west caravan routes in the south were now mainly through Tartar-held territories and linked with the important sea traffic on the Sea of Azov, and the adjoining coasts. Italian merchants in particular brought prosperity to the Black Sea ports and it is from Italian pens in the fifteenth century that some of the first interesting accounts of Russia come. The Venetian nobleman, Giosofat Barbaro, spent sixteen years in the Crimea in the first half of the century and journeyed to the East and through southern Russia; he was later followed by Ambrosio Contarini, the Venetian ambassador to the Persian court, who passed through Moscow at the end of 1476 and left a description of the 'tall, lean and handsome' Ivan III. Ivan's reign brought to Russia the first foreign architects and craftsmen since Kievan days, and Contarini met several of his countrymen engaged in changing the face of Moscow and undertook to recruit more. Under Ivan III, 'the gatherer of the Russian lands', who had married Zoë, a niece of the last Byzantine Emperor, and thereby, in his own eyes at least, had inherited the glory that was Byzantium's before its sack by the Turks in 1453, 'the third Rome' received the first buildings worthy of its pretensions in the shape of Fioraventi's Uspenskiy Cathedral (consecrated in 1479), Ruffo's and Solari's Granitovaya (or 'Faceted') Palace (completed 1491) and the impressive stone walls, ramparts and towers of the Kremlin. Thus already by the end of the fifteenth century Muscovy was ready to use western expertise and throughout the following century foreigners of very varied skills came to Russia, long before Peter the Great opened the flood-gates. But paradoxically Russia and Europe during the same period were not engaged in a lively commercial traffic nor did diplomatic contacts flourish. Muscovy's growing isolation from Europe was underlined dramatically by Ivan III's expulsion of the Hanseatic League from Novgorod in 1494 after centuries of prosperous and important commerce and it was not until the arrival of the English over half a century later that Russian trade with the West recovered. In terms of literature, however, the Hanseats contributed nothing and in this respect differed greatly from their English successors. The Anglo-Russian contacts from 1553 until after the turn of the century are perhaps the best-known and best-researched chapter in the story of Russia's general relations with the West, although Russians might argue that preceding England's so-called discovery of Russia there came Russia's discovery of England with the visit to London in 1524 of a Russian boyar. At all events, English penetration into Russia by the northern sea route and down from the port of Archangel (a route already used in reverse by Russian merchants trading with Denmark) was, as we have already seen, preceded by commerce and contacts through more traditional routes. Equally, ante-dating English accounts in general and the first great English work on Russia in particular, a book appeared in Vienna in 1549 which occupies a unique place in foreign literature on Russia.

Rerum Moscoviticarum Commentarii was the product of two visits to Russia made by Sigismund von Herberstein, in 1517 as ambassador from the Emperor Maximilian I, and in 1526 from King Ferdinard I; it was to appear in numerous editions and translations and was widely influential in shaping western

5 Baron Sigmund von Herberstein in Russian dress, from his *Rerum Moscoviticarum Commentarii*, Vienna 1566.

21

views of Russia. Herberstein possessed virtues which were often conspicuously absent in subsequent travellers and visitors who attempted to write on Russia: his comparatively unprejudiced eye; his interest in all aspects of Russia, economic, geographic, military, political, religious, social; his scholarship which led him to make use of little-known manuscript sources; and not least, his knowledge of the Russian language, which facilitated contact with the Russians themselves. The respect in which Herberstein's work was held is shown by the tribute contained in the last of three colourfully critical verse epistles on Russian mores (the first is reproduced in the anthology, on p. 70) by George Turberville, secretary to Thomas Randolph, the English ambassador in Russia in 1568: '–if thou list to know the Russes well,/To Sigismundus booke repaire, who all the trueth can tell.'

Herberstein's visits to Moscow coincided with an important development in the city encouraged by Tsar Basil III; near the Kremlin the first 'German Quarter', or Nemetskaya Sloboda was growing. There steadily increasing numbers of foreigners were making their homes and creating a township, the cleanliness and order of which was to arouse wonder and admiration in all but the most xenophobic of Russians. Peter the Great might have concurred with the Croat, Yuriy

6 Moscow. A view of the Kremlin at the end of the eighteenth century. Water colour by Giacomo Quarenghi.

Krizhanich when he wrote in the seventeenth century: 'Let us not imitate too much the curious and painstaking cleanliness of the Germans, who so often wash the floors of their houses, and where a guest may not spit or spew on to the floor. And if by chance he does so, straightway a servant wipes it up. Such men, in their voluptuousness and carnal cleanliness, attempt to make a heaven out of a mere earthly home.' But this would be a question of personal habits, and he certainly would not have followed him in condemning the technical and military achievement about which he learned so much as a boy in the German Quarter. Peter's marked preference for, and wooing of foreigners who were able to contribute to the advancement of his country as he conceived it, were the extreme example of the Russian tsars' readiness to exploit Western expertise. Under Ivan the Terrible the German Quarter grew and flourished, housing a multitude of architects, craftsmen, engineers, gunsmiths, doctors, merchants and military men, Germans, English, Scots, Italians, Dutch, Scandinavians. The German Emperor Charles V was prevailed upon by Ivan to allow the active recruitment of specialists, the enlisting of the service of 'doctors, masters of all the free arts, metal-workers, master-miners, goldsmiths, carpenters, stone-masons and particularly such as are skilled in the building of fine churches,

7 The new Foreign Quarter in Moscow as it appeared in 1661. The old quarter was demolished in 1643 on the orders of the xenophobic Patriarch, and the new established as a suburb to the east of the city. From the 1827 St Petersburg edition of drawings from the journal of Baron von Mayerberg.

master bridge-builders, paper manufacturers and physicians with a view to visiting the Russian Grand Duke without further ado or permission, and of agreeing to work for him.' Soon, after the unexpected but heaven-sent arrival of the English, Ivan was addressing similar requests to Elizabeth and was handsomely rewarded both by the quality of the goods and of the men English vessels were to bring to Kholmogory on the White Sea.

Much of the early English writing on Russia is terse and factual, designed to inform the officers of the Muscovy Company. Chancellor's account is, nonetheless, the first English eye-witness account of Russia with its succinct description of Moscow ('The Mosco it selfe is great: I take the whole towne to bee greater than London with the suburbes: but it is very rude, and standeth without all order . . .') and a series of intelligent observations of an economic and geographic nature (see p. 60). Chancellor, not surprisingly, knew no Russian, but it was not long before some of the Company's agents made progress in the language and Christopher Burrough, whose father Stephen and uncle William went with Chancellor on the first momentous voyage, has claims to be considered the 'first English slavist' for the knowledge he had gained by the 1580s. Another Englishman with a good knowledge of Russian who spent many years in Russia, performing with varying degrees of notoriety and success numerous commercial and diplomatic functions, was Sir Jerome Horsey, who left extensive, if often unreliable memoirs, which were published only in 1856. It was also Horsey who contributed much, according to his own estimate, to the outstanding English work of the period on Russia, Giles Fletcher's *Of the Russe Commonwealth* (first published in 1591), which has been termed 'in many ways, the summary of the English experience in Muscovy.' Fletcher was only briefly in Russia (less than a year between 1588 and 1589) but his work is an invaluable historical document, a thorough and systematic analysis of the resources and potential of the Muscovite state.

Throughout the sixteenth and seventeenth centuries the most detailed and generally trustworthy account of Russia came from diplomats or from members of their retinue. Veritable peaks of the literature are provided by Herberstein and Fletcher, who was Elizabeth's special ambassador, and in the seven-

24

teenth century by Adam Olearius, who accompanied the
Holstein embassy on two occasions between 1633 and 1639,
and Johann Korb, secretary to the Austrian legation at the
court of Peter the Great in 1698-9. These are flanked by
numerous other accounts which vary in scope and intent, from
brief diplomatic communiqués to longer, more impressionistic
relations designed for wider· audiences. English-language
examples are the accounts of the ambassadors Sir Thomas

Randolph and Sir Jerome Bowles, which are found in Hakluyt,
the description of the *Voiage and Entertainment in Rushia* of
Sir Thomas Smith in 1604, which was completed by the
dramatist George Wilkins, and 'A Relation' of the embassy
of the Earl of Carlisle in 1663 from the pen of Guy Miège, a
Swiss attendant. Among other interesting issues from English
diplomatic embassies was *A Voiage of Ambassad Undertaken
by the Right Honorable Sir Dudlie Digges* in the year 1618;
its author, the famed botanist John Tradescant, studied and
described the flora and fauna of north Russia and was to
cultivate on his return the *Rosa Moscovita,* which he had found
on an island in the delta of the Dvina. Digge's chaplain,
Richard James, also recorded at length his observations in
Russia but the manuscript has been lost. His transcript of
Russian songs from the Time of Troubles has, however,
survived and represents a unique contemporary document,
anticipating by over a century the first Russian written record.

In the sixteenth and seventeenth centuries there was a
handful of books, out of an admittedly far from impressive
overall total, which achieved the stature of key-works, or

8 Adam Olearius. From the French edition of his travels, published Amsterdam 1727.

9 Portrait of the rebel leader Yemelyan Pugachev. Painted in oils over part of an official portrait of Catherine the Great, it was finished in September 1773 probably by a dissenter icon painter in Pugachev's army.

primary sources, but few if any books thereafter were accorded such distinction. Olearius's account, first published in 1647, was for seventeenth-century Europe what Herberstein's had been for the previous century. (Fletcher's book suffered, as we shall see, a curious and chequered publishing history, which to some extent impeded its influence.) The publication record of Olearius's work in the first fifty years is remarkable: nine German editions, five French, three Dutch, two English and one Italian – and more were to follow in the eighteenth century. Olearius provided, particularly in his revised and considerably enlarged edition of 1647, a work exceeding all its predecessors in both length and comprehensiveness. Like Herberstein and Fletcher, Olearius was a scholar, meticulous and conscientious in his detail and description. His account is however continually enlivened and enhanced by his love of illustrative anecdote, his shafts of humour and his ironic observation. Willy nilly, he reveals his prejudices and provenance, his sense of intellectual and cultural superiority in his negative pen-pictures of Russian habits and practices. Among Olearius's companions was Paul Fleming, the famous German poet, many of whose poems found their way into Olearius's text. Fleming, like his English poet-predecessor Turberville, vividly portrayed Russian vices, but understandably only the poem which he devoted to the beauty of the city of Moscow found a Russian translator, the eighteenth-century poet A. P. Sumarokov.

Korb's account of his stay in Russia, published in Vienna in 1700, differs in scope and form from the works discussed earlier; he provides a series of concluding essays on Peter, the revolt of the Streltsy, Russian characteristics, military resources, etc., but the major part of his book is in diary form, a day-to-day account of the two years he spent in Moscow during the tsar's absence abroad and after his return. The major interest lies in the description of the bloody suppression of the Streltsy uprising, in which Peter himself participated, and its impact is all the greater for the alternation of everyday events, diplomatic procedures, wild carousals and horrendous brutalities. It is in order to catch this aspect of Korb's work that a fortnight's entries from February, 1699 is given on p. 133, rather than an edited extract on the execution alone.

Korb's work brings us to the threshold of a new era with the return of the young Peter from Holland and England, intent on bringing Russia in line with the European countries he had seen, but the description of his ruthless intolerance of any opposition provides a fitting coda to the preceding centuries of savagery and bloodshed, caught in the accounts of Ivan the Terrible, the Time of Troubles with the murder of the False Demetrius and the massacre of the Poles, the rising of Stenka Razin and his subsequent execution. Obviously, the adoption of western dress, the cutting off of beards, the issuing of well-intentioned decrees, the change of name from Muscovy to Russia, do not signal the end of old habits, oppression and misery. Indeed the period of our anthology ends with the tragedy of the Decembrists and embraces a series of earlier upheavals, reprisals and suppressions, concealed perhaps more easily behind the voluminous petticoats of the eighteenth-century empresses.

Before we leave the seventeenth century one further account deserves mention. In 1671 there appeared anonymously in London *The Present State of Russia*, a work which was in fact written by Samuel Collins. For nine years, between 1660 and 1669, Collins had been physician to Tsar Alexis, a position which British doctors had enjoyed since the time of Ivan the Terrible (Standish, Robert Jacob, Mark Ridley, Arthur Dee, the alchemist) and continued to occupy with some interruptions, up to the reign of Alexander I (the most famous of them was probably John Rogerson, the 'health inspector' of Catherine's lovers). An Italian visitor to Moscow at the beginning of Alexis's reign, M. Joly, writes of one of Collins's predecessors, 'of the English doctor who was the Tsar's chief physician and well experienced in his art and was given as his privilege the care of people of quality', although 'fearing for my well-being at the hands of this quack, I ordered my servant to tell him that I was sleeping'. A century and a half later, in the reign of Paul I, Edward Clarke describes how 'persons calling themselves English Physicians are found in almost every town' and adds: 'sometimes they have served in apothecaries' shops in London and Edinburgh; but generally they are Scots apothecaries who are men of Professional Skill and acknowledged Superiority.' Whatever the medical abilities of Collins and his colleagues might have been, they undoubtedly were on intimate footing with the tsars and in a position to observe life around them, particularly of the court. Collins's contemporary editor (the book was published in 1671, the year following Collins's death) believed the doctor 'made a farther discovery of the Russ affairs than any Stranger has been capacitated to do before or since', and if the book does not justify its blurb, its merit is nonetheless considerable. In a work of small compass, Collins dwells on all the already canonized topics: religion (including icons), marriage rites, the tsar's powers, his revenues, the commercial prospects (he is particularly disturbed by Dutch privileges), the appearance of Moscow, the characteristics of the people–and adds a few of his own: the preparation of caviar, species of mushrooms, Russian music. He is a lively raconteur, preferring the anecdote to the objective discussion, and in general is intent on justifying his view that 'the Russians are a People who differ from all other Nations of the world, in most of their Actions'.

Collins, the foreign doctor in Russian employ, exemplifies a species of author somewhat different from those we have already considered. Hitherto the authors (with the conspicuous exception of Horsey) had been in Russia for comparatively short periods, engaged on specific diplomatic or commercial missions. But, as we have noted, the numbers of foreign professional men contracting to work in Russia were steadily growing and some of them were beginning to write their memoirs and impressions. The foreign soldier of fortune is as familiar a figure as the foreign physician, and obviously numerically far more common; the Russian tsars were as anxious to enlist military experts as they were to attract more 'peaceful' craftsmen. Ivan the Terrible paid particular attention to the development of his foundry and the production of cannon; his siege of Kazan owed its success to the trenchworks and siege towers of his foreign engineers. Foreign soldiers were members of his *oprichnina* (his own specially created state within the state) and one of them, the Westphalian Heinrich von Staden, has left a highly interesting account, which has only recently become available in English. From the reign of Boris Godunov we have *L'Estat de l'empire de Russie* by Captain Jean Margeret, who served there between 1601 and 1606 and again in 1611. But perhaps the most famous and long-serving of these men was General Patrick Gordon who came to Russia in the reign of Tsar Alexis and remained until his death in 1699. His extensive memoirs have never been published in their entirety and the extracts which were published in 1859 are almost certainly not the most interesting in a Russian context. Gordon, one of the most trusted supporters of the young Peter and instrumental in suppressing the Streltsy

10 The official unveiling of Falconet's statue of Peter the Great, the Bronze Horseman, in St Petersburg in 1782.

uprising, stands at the head of a long and illustrious line of Scots who are encountered in all walks of Russian life and service in the eighteenth century.

Peter the Great, the convinced westernizer, was himself the major focus of western interest in Russia; it was he who caught the public imagination, gave birth to the greatest anecdotal literature to surround any modern ruler, and won the accolades of philosophers and poets (Fontenelle, Aaron Hill, James Thomson). His Russia was not yet a country to attract the tourist, but his legend was being created in the descriptions given by men brought to Russia not by curiosity alone. It was soon to be sustained and expanded in the numerous histories of his reign, compiled by authors who were not eye-witnesses of the events or even acquainted at first hand with the country, such as Defoe, Mottley, Banks, Mauvillon and Voltaire. The last of these was author of *Histoire de l'empire de Russie sous Pierre le Grand* (1759) characterized by Coxe later in the century as 'the work from which most foreign nations have formed their ideas of Russia; which many French and English authors have servilely copied until it is considered as a standard book, to which we may refer as to the most unquestionable authority'.

The 'Great Embassy', which left Moscow on 10 March 1697 and included Peter the Great not at its head but in its ranks as the seaman Peter Mikhailov, was an immense exercise in inspection, assimilation and recruitment; the two hundred and seventy members of the expedition were ordered to study all aspects of western technical achievement and to persuade European masters to enter Russian service. It is estimated that some nine hundred Europeans accepted the offer and of those who subsequently left accounts of their experiences pre-eminent is Captain John Perry, whose *State of Russia under the Present Czar* (1716) became popular and influential in forming western opinion of the 'new' Russia. Perry describes his personal tribulations as a hydraulic engineer and canal builder, and the deep-seated hostility of the Russians towards foreign 'barbarians' and 'heretics' (the Russian patriarch described General Gordon in such terms in 1688 and pro-phesied, quite wrongly, that Russia would never gain victories under foreign leaders), but at the same time evinces deep sympathy for the tsar and the reforms he was attempting to introduce. The image of Peter which foreign eye-witness accounts projected was in accord with the views of the Russian Westernizers in the nineteenth century and obviously had little of the negative content which their opponents, the Slavophiles, were to exploit. Perry spoke of the approval for the tsar's reforms 'amongst the more knowing and better sort of people', and John Bell, a Scots doctor who spent many years in Russia later in Peter's reign, wrote of 'the unbounded genius of this great and active prince who spares no expense and overlooks nothing' of advantage to Russia; even Korb, despite casting doubt by his description of the execution of the Streltsy on the rightness, if not the efficacy, of the means, approved of the tsar's objectives. Europeans, convinced of the backwardness and barbarism of the country, could not withhold their admiration of Peter at first or second hand; Thomson, welcoming Russia's progress towards enlightenment, eulogized the tsar as:

Immortal Peter! First of monarchs! He
His stubborn country tamed, – her rocks, her fens
Her floods, her seas, her ill-submitting sons;
And while the fierce barbarian he subdued,
To more exalted soul he raised the man.

Peter's Europeans included not only such men as Perry who were lured to Russia but others who were the spoils of war and whose talents were immediately utilized. There were many precedents from earlier reigns, but Peter's captured Swedes seem to have made a particular contribution. Bell records his meeting with Swedish prisoners of war in Siberia, who were teaching languages to local inhabitants and cultivating the arts and sciences. One of them, P. J. von Strahlenberg, a Swedish officer captured at Poltava, used his long years in Siberia to produce a pioneering work of major importance, his *Das nord– und ostliche Theil von Europa und Asia, in so weit solches das gantze russische Reich mit Sibirien und der grossen Tartarey in sich begeiffet* (Stockholm, 1730), which went through German, English, French and Spanish editions by the end of the century; it was the fore-runner of works of a geographical and ethno-graphical nature to be produced under Catherine the Great by a whole series of imported German professors, including Georgi, Guldenstaedt, Gmelin and Pallas.

Of all Peter's projects to utilize western expertise the found-ing and development of the city of St Petersburg, or Sankt Piterburkh to give it its first title which reveals Peter's Dutch sympathies, was the one which was to draw Europeans like a magnet. In May, 1703, Peter laid the first stone of what was to become the Peter and Paul Fortress and gradually over the years the bleak uninviting spot in the delta of the river Neva was to be transformed into a great capital city. Built by slave labour and the skill of foreign engineers and architects, starting with Domenico Tressini, Petersburg began slowly to show its first palaces and major houses—fifteen by 1704, one hundred and fifty by 1709; in 1712 Peter declared the city the imperial capital. One of the first detailed descriptions of the city comes from Friedrich Weber, an Hanoverian in the English Embassy from 1714, who records how, 'when I arrived there, I was surprised to find instead of a regular city, as I expected, a Heap of Villages linked together, like some Plantation in the West Indies,' yet adds 'however at present

Petersbourg may with reason be looked upon as a Wonder of the World, considering its Palaces, sixty odd thousand Houses, and the short time that was employed in the building of it' (see p. 155). In 1739, Count Francesco Algarotti, describing the city as Peter's 'great window lately opened in the north, thro' which Russia looks into Europe' (see p. 183), coined the phrase which Pushkin was to popularize, with due acknowledgement, in his epic of the city, *The Bronze Horseman*. The phrase became equally meaningful in reverse: Petersburg became the entrance to Russia for visitors from the West, the 'Palmyra of the North' which began to attract the attentions of the tourist.

The figure of the Englishman on the Grand Tour is a familiar one in the eighteenth century and the route which took him to France, Switzerland, Italy, perhaps to Germany and Greece, in search of monuments of European civilization and scenic beauties becomes easily predictable. There were tourists, however, who had followed the familiar paths and were eager to sample the offerings of more distant and challenging lands. Towards the end of the eighteenth century there had emerged the concept of the 'Northern Tour' (the title seems to have been first used, with reference to Russia, on the recently discovered manuscript of the Oxford don, John Parkinson, who was in Russia in 1792-4), including Scandinavia, Russia, Poland and Germany, which provided a new and exciting alternative. Perhaps the most noted chronicler of the new tour is William Coxe, who accompanied George, Lord Herbert, to Russia in 1778 and weaved his immediate impressions into a vast canvas of historical and guide-book material; but the first tourist of the new breed, who was at the same time his own memoirist, was none other than Sir Francis Dashwood, the founder and guiding spirit of the notorious Hell-Fire Club. In keeping with Dashwood's later reputation Horace Walpole circulated stories of how Sir Francis disguised as Charles XII of Sweden seduced the Empress Anna, although the incident which seems to have given rise to it was connected with the English resident, Charles Whitworth, and the Empress Catherine I. At all events, Dashwood himself makes no allusion to the alleged events in the diary of his visit to St Petersburg in 1733, in which he gives a succinct description of buildings, dignitaries and the organization of the army. He spent nineteen days in the capital before sailing for home, reflecting that, 'I am very well contented with my journey, and think it very much worth any curious man's while going to See, and to stay there three weeks or a month, but after once curiosity is Satisfied, I think one could amuse oneself better, in more Southern Climates.' Other tourists, whose Tours and Travels, *Reisen* and *Voyages* began to appear increasingly in European bookshops in the second half of the century, were much more adventuresome than Dashwood in their exploration of Russia and not only

11 The Alexander Nevskiy Monastery, founded in 1710 and built by M. Zemtsov, stood at the head of the Nevskiy Prospekt, some three miles from the Admiralty. Lithograph by Karl Petrovich Beggrov (1799–1875).

described at length their impressions of St Petersburg and Moscow and of the townships on the road that joined them, but also penetrated into Siberia, the Crimea and eventually the Caucasus. Parkinson's account, for instance, is of a truly remarkable journey through all these territories; Lady Elizabeth Craven and Mrs Marie Guthrie visited the Crimea in the later years of Catherine's reign; Edward Daniel Clarke travelled the same route under Paul. The reign of Alexander brought a veritable flood of travellers spilling into areas both old and fresh in the literature of travel: Captain John Cochrane performed a journey on foot across Russia and Siberia to the Pacific and is soon followed on a similar route by James Holman, not on foot but 'while suffering from total blindness'; the Frenchman Jean Reuilly, and the Englishwoman Mary Holderness, explored the Crimea, which was visited by Robert Lyall, who also describes in great detail his further travels in the Caucasus, as do the Scot, Robert Ker Porter, and the German lady, Fredericka von Freygan. There existed in many languages considerably earlier works on Siberia, the Crimea and other far-flung reaches of the Russian empire but they were written in a totally different spirit and circumstances and did not pretend to the minute, although often erroneous detail found in the travel books of the late eighteenth and early nineteenth centuries. Even at this period the eyes of the majority of travellers were directed solely to St Petersburg and Moscow

32

and their accounts exploit with vastly varying degrees of insight and understanding the contrasts between the cities, the social classes, backwardness and progress, the quaint and the familiar.

Towards the end of the eighteenth century women appear increasingly on the scene as tourists and authors of travel accounts (Elizabeth Craven, Marie Guthrie, Fredericka von Freygan, Mary Holderness), but their works are antedated by books from other women who were brought to Russia through marriage and necessity and it seems singularly appropriate that the first accounts should appear almost at the beginning of a virtual century of Empresses. The first to be published was *A Voyage to Russia* by Elizabeth Justice, the governess to an English merchant's children in St Petersburg; her brief account gives us *en passant* entertaining snippets about Russian life and customs but reveals much more about the prejudices and tribulations of poor Mrs Justice herself, who thought Russia a barbaric place and whiled away the hours, reading *The Spectator*. Of a different station and a much more informed and lively nature was the wife of the English Resident, Mrs Rondeau, who lived in Russia between 1728 and 1739, and who recounts much of historical interest in her gossipy letters to a woman friend (see p. 178). The delightful and informative letters of the Wilmot sisters Martha and Catherine, who were guests of the renowned Princess Dashkova between 1803 and 1808, are, however, the outstanding contribution from women resident in Russia, although they belong already to the nineteenth century and were not in fact published until 1934. From the reign of Alexander dated the most famous account of Russia by a woman visitor—attributable in no small measure to her already established fame and reputation: Mme de Staël, at daggers drawn with Napoleon, found naturally much to commend in Russia and lionized its emperor (see p. 299).

The mention of the name of Mme de Staël raises the question of the French in Russia before the Napoleonic invasion and the extent of their writing on the country. Up to the beginning of the eighteenth century contacts between France and Russia were insignificant and France was little concerned about possible trade and political alliances with a distant and barbaric land. The bibliographies of travel literature indicate a corresponding paucity of French-language materials; the dominant languages and nations are German, English, Dutch, Italian and Swedish. Accounts in French are found, by Margeret and Joly (an Italian) in the seventeenth century for instance, but Frenchmen penetrated but rarely into Russia, and then only briefly. Indeed, Tsar Alexis made it plain that the French were far from welcome in his domains and forbade their employment under severe penalties; it was, however, more an indication of Louis XIV's blissful ignorance of Russian affairs and actions rather than a calculated snub to Alexis, when *le roi*

12 Count Francesco Algarotti.
From *Opere Scelte di
Francesco Algarotti,* Vol I,
Milan 1823.

soleil addressed a letter in 1657 to the tsar's long-deceased father. Almost a century was to pass before changes in political allegiances brought the French into favour in Russia under the third of the eighteenth century's empresses, Elizabeth, and allowed them to dictate social and cultural fashions. However, even under the German-dominated Anna the signs and future direction of French influences were obvious. Algarotti, arriving in St Petersburg in the summer of 1739, noted: 'As to France, there is very little direct trade between these two nations, and nothing is more uncommon than to see a French ship in these seas, which however does not prevent there being an incredible quantity of French commodities in Russia. France draws from hence, by means of her wines, her rich stuffs, her laces, her snuff-boxes, her millinary wares, and other glittering gew-gaws, which serve to feed the luxury of the Czarian Court, all the gold that the English leave at Petersburg'; he believes that 'it would be difficult to determine whether this ostentation is the effect of the government of women, who are naturally fond of shew and dress, rather than the consequence of the administration of foreigners' but at all events the nobles 'who are obliged now to spend, every year, a great part of their income in laces and cloaths, used formerly, by the Sovereign's command, to build a ship.' French, scarcely known in Russia before this time, soon became the new *lingua franca* and gallomania such a distinguishing mark of the Russian nobility that native writers, sharpening their wits and their idiom on French models, resorted to easy parody in the satirical journals and comedies which flourished under Catherine. La Messelière who accompanied the French ambassador in 1757 spoke of Elizabeth's courtiers speaking French 'comme à Paris' and went on to note with disapproval the presence throughout the Russian Empire of 'a swarm of French of every complexion, the majority of whom, having been in trouble with the police in Paris, have come to infest the northern regions' (see p. 193). La Messelière's visit came a decade after Louis XV's assiduous wooing of Elizabeth away from the English in general and their ambassador, Sir Charles Hanbury Williams, in particular, had been crowned with success, allegedly by a stratagem which was the subject of some of the most famous anecdotes of the century, though indeed reminiscent of the alleged escapades of Whitworth-Dashwood. The Chevalier d'Éon, entrusted to act as direct intermediary between Louis and the empress, was introduced to Elizabeth as Mlle de Beaumont and was immediately appointed her 'lectrice intime et particulière', an office which gave free access to the empress's quarters at any time of day or night; the empress, the Chevalier tells us in one of the few passages in his memoirs said to be in his own words (but really his editor's), lost no time in attempting to seduce the young man, who saved his honour with considerable difficulty but managed to keep her affection over a long period during which he visited Russia on three occasions. Éon's memoirs contain few remarks of a general nature on Russia, but his part in effecting a Franco-Russian reconciliation and alliance in 1756 aided the penetration of the French into Russia, which led inevitably to a significant increase in French written accounts. La Messelière was perhaps the first to record his (very favourable) impressions of Russia at any length, but it was in the following reign that a dazzling array of French diplomats, writers and philosophers hurried to the court of the Great Catherine, dubbed by Casanova (a visitor in 1765) 'the monarch in petticoats', a formula which Pushkin a generation later emended to a 'Tartuffe in petticoats and a crown'. In 1762 the young Bernardin de Saint Pierre came to present Catherine with a project for setting up a Utopian colony on the shores of the Arai Sea, but returned dissatisfied to France, where he wrote at a later date his rather negative *Observations sur la Russie*. Voltaire relied on his correspondence to inform him of Russian affairs, but two other *philosophes,* Diderot and Grimm, arrived in St Petersburg in 1773, at the same time as Levesque, who was later in the century to produce almost the first large-scale and widely influential history of Russia in a European language. On the diplomatic scene, the comte de Ségur was particularly prominent and his extensive memoirs of his stay in Russia present a lively picture of court intrigue in a polished and urbane manner. Ségur accompanied Catherine on her triumphant journey to the Crimea in 1787 to inspect her newly acquired territories, although it is his friend, the Prince de Ligne, whose letters provide its most revealing commentary (p. 232).

The important contribution to European knowledge of Russia which ambassadors and members of their retinues made during the period up to the reign of Peter the Great has been already emphasized; in the eighteenth century the pattern of diplomatic life in Russia changed, as did the nature of the writings emanating from this source. Intercourse with European nations increased on all fronts, not least the diplomatic: on Peter's accession Russia had no ambassadors abroad; by the end of his reign there was a Russian representative at almost every European court. The foreign diplomat in Russia was gradually accorded more freedom of movement, enjoyed a comparatively more gracious court and social life, was able to intrigue and persuade, but almost invariably he was restricted by an ignorance of the Russian language and an absence of the scholarly interests which had distinguished some of his predecessors. Diplomats, nevertheless, continued to produce work of a general nature on Russia; Charles Whitworth, the British ambassador extraordinary, wrote *An Account of Russia as it was in the year 1710*, perhaps more interesting as a product of the Strawberry Hill press than for the profundity of its contents; and Sir George Macartney, visiting St Petersburg to negotiate the renewal of the Anglo-Russian commercial treaty of 1734, compiled a more ambitious and perceptive *Account of Russia,* MDCCLXVII. In general, ambassadors and residents confined themselves to dispatches and reports of a naturally restricted nature which are of greater interest for the student of diplomatic history than for increasing western understanding of Russia.

The eighteenth and early nineteenth centuries witnessed an immense increase in the sheer weight of material on Russia published in European languages and the number of editions and translations of often mediocre and compilatory works testifies to the interest, if not to the discrimination of the European public. The diplomat, the soldier of fortune, the physician, the foreign specialist all continue to appear as authors; their ranks are swelled with tourists of all Sternian varieties, merchants, semi-professional explorers, adventurers of the Casanova-Cagliostro mould, visionaries and would-be reformers. A new and rich source of writings on Russia in the early nineteenth century was provided by missionaries of the British and Foreign Bible Society, exemplified in the present anthology by Robert Pinkerton on p. 321. The foreigners who have left records of their stay in Russia obviously represent but a tiny fraction of those spread throughout the reaches of the empire: St Petersburg, where a Foreign Quarter sprang up immediately after the founding of the city, had representatives of numerous foreign merchant houses, scores of foreign architects, craftsmen and artists, academicians and scientists; Moscow had its foreign colonies, which were also found in Siberian towns and in the South.

4

The Russians have always been attentive to foreign writings about their country and particularly sensitive to adverse criticism. Often such works are far better known there than in the countries where they were originally published. During the nineteenth century especially, careful Russian translations and detailed commentaries were prepared of almost all foreign works of note and interest. The reasons are to be sought in part in the lack of written records by the Russians themselves during the early period, in the almost complete absence of historical research and writing in Russia until late in the eighteenth century and the consequent reliance on the more scholarly of early travellers to supply information about customs, events and people. The first great Russian historian, N. M. Karamzin, writing in the opening decades of the nineteenth century, was well acquainted with, for instance, the work of Herberstein, Fletcher, Horsey and Olearius, which he evaluated in a series of essays around 1802 and subsequently used in his own history. Russian interest in works on Russia dating from much later periods was sustained, however, right through the nineteenth century and into the twentieth, as S. R. Mintslov's bibliography, *Review of Notes, Diaries, Memoirs, Letters and Travels Relating to the History of Russia and Printed in Russian* (1911-12), clearly demonstrates. Yet because of the mixture of academic curiosity and national pride which informed Russian interest, Russica, as writings on Russia are often termed, have undergone a somewhat chequered history.

Curiously enough, the first chapter was occasioned not by the Russians themselves but by the English merchants of the Muscovy Company who were alarmed at the content of Fletcher's *Of the Russe Commonwealth* and petitioned with success that unless all copies of the original edition of 1591 were called in, the book would 'turn the Companie to some great displeasure with the Russe Emperour.' Whether in fact Theodore I was acquainted with the book is not known, but when in 1848 a Russian scholar attempted to publish his translation of the work, the Minister of National Enlightenment, S. S. Uvarov, informed Nicholas I of the book's venomous attack on the autocracy and the church and the journal in which the translation appeared was confiscated and new pages substituted. Of the eighteenth-century rulers, Peter I and Catherine II were particularly anxious that their 'greatness' should not be minimized in western eyes by scurrilous revelations. Peter took strong exception to Korb's harrowing description of the execution of the Streltsy and of his own sadistic participation and instructed his agents in Europe to do all they could to buy up copies and suppress the book. Catherine faced two similar predicaments early in her reign. Claude Carloman de Rulhière, member of the French Academy and a friend of Jean-Jacques Rousseau whose views on the Russian autocracy he shared, wrote his *Anecdotes sur la révolution de Russie en l'année 1762*, which was circulated in manuscript in 1763, but only published in 1797, after Catherine's death, through the combined efforts of Catherine's well-wishers, Voltaire, Diderot and Mme Geoffrin. The French astronomer, Jean Chappe d'Auteroche, who travelled through Russia to Siberia in 1761-2 to observe the passing of Venus over the sun, succeeded, however, in publishing soon afterwards his *Voyage en Sibérie* with its damning criticisms of Russian customs and government; Catherine herself, in the guise of a 'Lover of Truth', was moved to write a rebuttal, entitled *L'Antidote,* which was successful in persuading subsequent European travellers such as Coxe, Andrew Swinton and William Thomson to polemicize with Chappe d'Auteroche, whose account, nonetheless, adorned with the engravings of Le Prince, continued to be popular and influential with

European readers. In the reign of Alexander I, Robert Lyall wrote his monumental *Character of the Russians, and a Detailed History of Moscow* (1823), which he dedicated to the Emperor: Russian reaction to his damning moral characterization of the Russian people was immediate and revealing. The Russian Vice-Consul in London wrote a letter to *The Times*, protesting about the unauthorized dedication, and soon English newspapers were carrying reports of an Imperial decree, according to which 'no foreign writer shall be authorised to dedicate any work to his Majesty, without having previously solicited permission from the Minister for Foreign Affairs, through the Russian Ambassador resident in the country in which the author resides. This prohibition has been caused by the inconceivable audacity of an Englishman, who has, with great effrontery, dedicated to his Majesty a book, written against his government, and the entire Russian nation.' This was followed by general denunciations of English travellers and the expulsion of 'a Blind spy [Holman], a Methodistical one, and a Quaker'.

The Russians never possessed the strong faith in their country's cultural and social traditions, the general sense of superiority which distinguished the English and the French in particular and seemingly immunized them against foreign opinion; they could not enjoy an equal partnership in the European heritage which their tsars decreed should also be theirs and which with changes of emphases and periods of ill-concealed but understandable xenophobia they attempted to assimilate. At the same time foreigners who went to Russia were often blinded by their prejudices and prevented by their uncritical acceptance of oft-repeated travellers' tales from being just in their verdict on the country. Horace's dictum – 'caelum, non animam mutant, qui trans mare currunt' – seems a truism, measured against most of the travellers to Russia, who exemplify both Cowper's view of, 'How much a dunce that has been sent to roam,/Excels a dunce that has been left at home' (a felicitous Russian eighteenth-century variant likens the Paris-bound Russian squireen to a piglet who returned a perfect swine) and that which contends that travel broadens the (prepared and receptive) mind.

Foreigners' accounts not only served the public at large; they became the necessary reading for all would-be travellers and inevitably dictated certain procedures, canonized certain topics for discussion, certain towns and areas to be visited. Plagiarism among travel writers was rampant, but not always appreciated by contemporary audiences, who seemed to take the similarity between accounts as consolidating evidence of their notions of Russia and its people. Perhaps the outstanding example of undetected plagiarism on a massive scale was Pierre-Nicholas Chantreau's *Voyage philosophique, politique et littéraire, fait en Russie dans les années 1788 et 1789,* which

38

was translated into English and German in the year of its publication (1794) and received generally sympathetic reviews – despite the fact that Chantreau had already published a three-volume account of his travels through Great Britain for precisely the same period and that his Russian materials were compiled entirely from such existing and well known sources as Manstein, Levesque, Leclerc and Coxe. Few writers were conscientious in registering their sources, as Lyall's later protest in a specific case makes clear: 'though in different languages, and though the arrangement be different, we cannot but remark, the almost verbal coincidence of the account of the burning of Moscow, in *Lettres sur l'incendie de Moscou, par l'abbé Surrugues* and that in *James's Journal.*' Some travellers would refer readers to other writers for detailed accounts of particular places and many were fond of polemicizing with predecessors' opinions, but on the whole writers plundered each other wholesale and over a surprisingly long period perpetuated obvious errors and fallacies. Travel literature on Russia abounds in a series of myths which would seem to place the country alongside Africa and the New World as repositories of God's most curious creations. Some of these were connected with linguistic misunderstandings: the Samoyeds were long thought to be cannibals (the word was split into the two components 'self' and 'eater' by analogy with the true Russian word for cannibal, '*lyudoyed*' or 'people-eater') and the *baranets* (*Lycopodium selago*) was known as 'the vegetable lamb', which growing as a plant consumed everything within reach and then died of starvation. Far into the eighteenth century travellers (Bell, Chappe d'Auteroche) thought the story sufficiently widely accepted to write against this myth cultivated by 'grave German authors'. The *rosomakha* (*Gulo borealis*), which Bell saw during his travels and described accurately as of the size of a badger, enjoyed legendary fame for its alleged 'self-service midwifery': Milton wrote of the female, 'which bringeth forth by passing through some narrow place, as between two Stakes, and so presseth her Womb to a disburthening.'

In view of the obvious signs that Russia itself encouraged European influences (if not in all their implications), it would be somewhat unexpected to find a European in Russia during our period who believed that the West could not bring untold benefits to a backward and barbaric land – and it is essentially in such terms, and not as uniquely different, that all visitors from Herberstein through to Clarke and beyond described Russia. Such a view might be accompanied by the belief that the Russians were nevertheless not equal to the challenge, as when, for example, Richard Ford wrote to the Russophile George Borrow in 1841: 'People regard them as barbarians, and what is more, uninteresting barbarians – Scythians in Paris-cut coats.' On the other hand, writers such as Chappe

39

d'Auteroche, Coxe and Clarke, although commenting on the often misplaced energies of the Russians for slavish imitation, believed that imitation was a necessary part of the catching-up process in which Russia was involved by historical accident and its forcible removal from the major European development by the Tartar invasion. Clarke suggested that 'the resemblance to Asiatic customs and manners, perceptible in Moscow and Petersburg, will probably decrease, in proportion to the intercourse of the Russians with other parts of Europe' and his words are interesting for their implicit acceptance of Russia as a European nation with an unfortunate Asiatic admixture. Visitors to Russia were always ready to exploit contrasts in their descriptions. Early commentators were inclined to make the contrast in terms of the differences between Muscovy and the West, when describing the Russian classes, religion, tsarist opulence and government; with the age of Peter the Great these contrasts continued to be made but ceded pride of place to those found *within* the country – between Asiatic Moscow and western St Petersburg, between the westernized gentry of the capitals and the oppressed and unenlightened masses. Travellers were obsessed with the problem: was Russia European?, and in face of the ever-expanding territories of the Russian empire often aspired to geographical precision in their demarcation of east and west. The Urals

13 The Bazaar at Nerchinsk. British Museum, *Des Peuples de la Russie*, C. Rechberg.

gained particular prominence in such deliberations and Captain John Cochrane in 1820 makes much of 'standing with one foot in Asia and the other in Europe, surrounded on all sides by lofty mountains'. Once on the eastern side, he believes he finds the inhabitants 'much more civil, more hospitable, and more cleanly dressed'.

In general the Russian people received negative characterizations in foreigners' accounts over the centuries: given the

14 A Samoyed sledge, an engraving from Ysbrant Ides' *Travels*, London 1706.

premise that Russia was barbaric, it followed that the masses would be the most obvious illustration of backwardness in their homes, dress, manners and customs. Foreigners dwelt with often ill-concealed relish on the bestial nature of the Russian 'boor' – they described his ill-treatment of his women, his superstitions and misplaced religious fervour, his vices, particularly sodomy (Hakluyt discreetly removed a passage on this subject from one of Tuberville's epistles), and his inordinate love of drinking. This last characteristic is encountered in most accounts from the sixteenth century to the nineteenth. Jenkinson describes how 'after that sevennight fast is past, then they return to their old intemperance of drinking, for they are notable tosspots'; Olearius graphically depicts their carousing, and it is perhaps only in the eighteenth century that travellers suggest that Russians were far from unique in their addiction. Swinton notes that 'a drunken Dane is proverbial; but this may be applied, with equal justice, to all nations of the Danish stock, the English, the Scots, the Norwegians, and Swedes', although this might be balanced against the line from the old Russian chronicles – 'Russia's joy is found in drink and we cannot do without it' – which suggests that it was no mere fabrication of foreigners. As the eighteenth century moved towards its end, travellers, influenced by the Rousseauist notion of the particular strengths and attractions of primitive and backward peoples, began to note with approval the kindness and hospitality of the Russian peasants. Mme de Staël, in accents characteristic of her age, enthused over the Ukrainian

41

peasants and their dances, noting that their 'indolence and vivacity are indicative of reverie and passion, two elements of character which civilization has yet neither formed nor subdued' (see p. 304).

The delights of folk song and dance were small compensation for the lack of a vital and sophisticated culture. In a famous phrase Mme de Staël declared that 'In Russia there are a few gentlemen concerned with literature' and pointed to the lack of a strong middle class. She suggested that 'poetry, eloquence, literature are not yet found in Russia; wealth, power and courage are the principal objects for pride and ambition'; it is a diagnosis of the obstacles to the social respectability of the man of letters with which many contemporary Russian authors would have agreed, but at the same time it illustrated a general European ignorance of what Russia had already achieved in the arts. Milton voiced the prevalent European view of pre-Petrine Russians who 'have no learning nor will suffer it to be among them' and early visitors had little interest in discovering evidence to the contrary. The one form of Russian art with which visitors seemed to come into contact was the icon – and this they dismissed as primitive, unenlightened daubing, a fitting reflection of a misguided church and clergy. It was once again only from the reign of Catherine the Great that foreigners were prepared to speak of Russian interest in true enlightenment and point to the advances made under the 'present August Patroness', although Chappe d'Auteroche looked to Montesquieu's climate theory to explain why so much endeavour should meet with so little success. Macartney, although protesting that 'a writer could scarcely be thought serious who professed to treat of the arts and sciences of an empire in which there is no university, at least none which resembled the seminaries of that appelation thro' the rest of Europe,' provided the first brief account in English of Russian attainments in the arts and sciences, which included a eulogy of the Russian language and its suitability for poetry as well as of its two most eminent practitioners, the 'very extraordinary geniuses', Lomonosov and Sumarokov. These two names begin to appear in a number of books towards the end of the century and it is in the works of Levesque and Leclerc in France, of Coxe in England and of a number of russified or resident Germans such as Bachmeister, Storch and Richter that the first detailed surveys of Russian culture, past and contemporary, are given.

The obstacles to a rich cultural life were to be found not merely in the climate, but also in the form of government, as Chappe d'Auteroche was quick to add. The British in particular were wont to point out the evil effects of the autocracy on all aspects of Russian life, on the nobility as well as on the peasantry. Richardson, one of the most perceptive writers on the question in the eighteenth century, insisted that 'most of

15 A Kaluga merchant.

42

the defects which appear in their national character are in consequence of the despotism of the Russian government'. It was a despotism which western Europeans almost inevitably described as oriental and the contemplation of which caused British visitors, one after the other, to utter 'O fortunatos nimium, sua si bona norint, Britannos!'

This antipathy towards the system of government was almost invariably accompanied from earliest times by a lack of sympathy and understanding for the Russian Orthodox Church. It was seen as working hand-in-hand with the autocracy to prevent the spread of true enlightenment, to be a misguided, misinformed, even barbaric off-shoot of the True Church. Visitors tended to content themselves with impatient criticism of its ritual and satirical portraits of its priests. Macartney voiced the widely-held conviction that the Eastern Church had given the Russian people 'the greatest degree of superstition and bigotry, the lowest notions of the duties of morality, and the most idolatrous ideas of the adoration of the Deity imaginable'.

5

The anthology which follows is made up of selections from the works of fifty-four authors writing over a period of three hundred years. The disposition of the material is chronological, with a somewhat arbitrary division into the sixteenth century, the seventeenth century, the reigns of Peter the Great, Anna and Elizabeth, Catherine the Great, Paul and Alexander I. No attempt has been made to produce a close-knit narrative either thematically or historically; the selections form at best a mosaic of foreigners' impressions and observations on a wide range of subjects, some firmly anchored at a specific historical moment, others with pretensions at generalization and 'eternal truth': the resulting picture is not complete, in the same way that none of the individual accounts, however systematically and comprehensively planned, is complete. Throughout the anthology there occur pen-pictures of Russian autocrats (Ivan the Terrible, Peter, Anna, Elizabeth, Catherine and Alexander) and descriptions of a number of historical events, both of major and minor significance (the murder of the False Demetrius, the rebellion and execution of Stenka Razin and of the Streltsy, the triumphal entry of Peter into Moscow after his victory at Nöteborg, Catherine's journey to the Crimea, Napoleon's entry into Moscow and the burning of the city, the Petersburg flood of 1824 and the Decembrist uprising); these are woven into a context of wide-ranging commentaries on the characteristics and mores of the Russian people, bureaucratic procedures, customs, traditions, and festivals, court life, religion, serfdom, government. At the

16 A maiden from the Moksha tribe, one of the two ethnic groups which constitute the Mordvinian people.

17 A Kaluga maiden.

43

same time there appear more static descriptive pieces of towns and cities, lakes and rivers, mountains and countryside, far-flung provinces of the empire and the people who inhabit them. Again, the picture is selective and impressionistic; designed to suggest rather than cover all the infinite variety of Russian life and land.

The authors of the accounts represent the majority of the countries of Europe and America which had contacts with Russia in the early period: the U.S.A., England, France, Germany, Holland, Italy, Sweden, as well as many of the types of foreigners encountered in Russia over the period: diplomats, merchants, doctors, soldiers, artists, tourists, coming from varied backgrounds and in Russia for varying lengths of time and under varying circumstances, not always of their own making. Extracts from many of the most famous accounts are included, for it is a fame which is in general justified and based on the writer's gifts as an observer and/or stylist; yet many of the selections are taken both from works and writers who are little-known and little-read, often unjustly. In two cases, the extracts have appeared previously only in a scholarly journal; in a further case (Baroness Dimsdale), a selection is made from a manuscript diary, which was obviously not produced for publication.

Although the arrangement is chronological, many of the subjects treated under one specific century or reign are not simply of importance to that time alone; in some cases, the subjects, be they deliberations on manners or descriptions of cities, are taken up again at a later date to afford some idea of the change, or lack of change, in the viewer and the viewed; yet again, space dictates a single extract to illustrate a topic, which could well be parallelled from other sources published before and after. The distribution of material reflects to some degree the gradual increase and diversity in written accounts over the period. Although substantial selections are given from the sixteenth and seventeenth century, the main weight is on the eighteenth century and early nineteenth.

From the sixteenth century onwards visitors travelled beyond Moscow to the east and to the south, but it is only towards the end of the eighteenth century that the more substantial accounts appear; although extracts on Siberia, for instance, are given from the end of the seventeenth century and again in the eighteenth, it is from the age of Alexander when the Crimea and the Caucasus became great tourist attractions, that the bulk of the material on outlying areas is given.

As the feeling for nature was encouraged throughout Europe in the eighteenth century, finding expression physically in the cult of the English garden and intellectually in the vogue for *poésie descriptive,* travellers began to exult over the beauties of landscape and the majesty of mountains. By the end of the eighteenth century even travellers to Russia affected in their writings the modes of the Age of Feeling, describing as Gothic the churches of Byzantine design, recording their melancholy emotions as they viewed the ruins of old Novgorod or the burnt-out shell of Moscow. They began to introduce the words 'romantic' and 'picturesque' into their descriptions of St Petersburg and Moscow, and even more, of the Crimea and the Caucasus. It is indeed appropriate that the visual impact of the Caucasus should have been given its exotically romantic expression in the descriptions of a painter, Robert Ker Porter, whose mountainscapes are inevitably peopled with the banditti of Salvator Rosa. The reviewers of the *Edinburgh Review,* whose tastes were satisfied much better by the critical broadsides of Clarke than by what they termed 'the ranting' of Porter, nevertheless said of his earlier book on Russia that, 'We really think a person who has never been at St Petersburgh, will rise, from Mr Porter's description, with a much more lively idea of the exterior of that magnificent capital than if he perused all the other accounts of it put together.'

However precise or evocative the descriptions visitors have left of Russian characters, customs, cities and landscapes, however great their appeal to the mind's and imagination's eye, they lack the true visual dimension. It was a typically sentimentalist gesture to throw down the pen and regret that it could not rival the brush; Porter was fortunate: he possessed both an ability to describe with his pen and a talent to depict

18 The women of Valdai had the reputation of being dangerous sirens intent on seducing the weak-willed traveller. From *La Russie, ou Moeurs, Usages et Costumes des habitants . . . de cet Empire.* M. Breton, Paris 1813.

with the brush, when words (if only occasionally) failed him. The plates which adorn his books on Russia, however badly executed by his engraver, are an important adjunct to his narrative, a painter's record of what he saw. They form part of the enormous quantity of paintings and engravings of Russia which appear during the first quarter of the nineteenth century; not only did most of the travel books contain series of engravings of cities, buildings and typical scenes, but whole collections devoted to recording the different nationalities of the Russian empire, churches, palaces, cities and towns appeared. Such were John Atkinson's and James Walker's *A Picturesque Representation of the Manners, Customs, and Amusements of the Russians in one hundred coloured plates* (1803-4), Frederic Shoberl's *Russia* (1815, 72 coloured engravings), Mornay's *A Picture of St Petersburg* (1815). Similar collections appeared in the eighteenth century, including J. B. Le Prince's *Divers ajustements et usages de Russie.* As in the case of travel narratives there was a good deal of plagiarism among artists and engravers, who often looked to each other's work rather than focussing on the scene before them. Equally, the reproduction of what they saw was influenced by their own schooling and allegiances (Le Prince was a pupil of Boucher's for example) and by their prejudices. In this connection it is interesting to record the remarks of A. Olenin, the President of the Russian Academy of Fine Arts, in a letter to Porter, although he is specifically speaking of other than Russian subjects: 'In conclusion, I repeat, draw only what you see! Correct nothing; and preserve in your copies, the true character of the originals. Do not give to Persian figures a French *tournure,* like Chardin; nor a Dutch, like Van Bruyn; nor a German, or rather Danish, like Niebuhr; nor an English grace, like some of your countrymen . . .'

Porter, like Walker and Atkinson before him, belonged to the number of English painters who were invited to Russia under Catherine and Alexander: others were Edward Miles, Christina Robertson and George Dawe, the addressee, incidentally, of a Pushkin poem. They produced portraits of the Imperial family, nobles, generals, and in so doing followed in the steps of a whole line of European painters, headed by the Italians in the reign of Elizabeth. But it was perhaps the artists of a more transient kind who produced the best pictorial record of Russia through the centuries. One of the great attractions of the early editions of the works of Herberstein, Olearius, Korb and Le Brun lies in their magnificent engravings. Olearius, for instance, was not only a talented author but an accomplished artist. Mayerberg, who was in Russia in 1661, was accompanied by an artist whose wonderful collection of line drawings, principally of the small settlements and towns between the Polish frontier and Moscow did not appear in early editions but may be appreciated in the magnificent album produced in St Petersburg in 1827.

It is from such rich sources that a second, pictorial anthology has been selected, providing on occasions an integral part of the anthology of texts, at others, standing independently or providing a connecting link. However, works by native Russian masters have been included in the way that extracts from Russian written accounts are not, for many of the outstanding Russian painters and engravers learned their trade in the studios

of foreign masters in Russia and abroad: Levitsky with Lagrenais in St Petersburg, and Rokotov with Claude Lorrain, while the engraver Skorodumov, whose work illustrates the account of Archdeacon Coxe, studied for many years in London.

It is hoped that this volume will provide the modern European reader with something of the flavour and impact of Russia which foreigners attempted to convey to their contemporaries during the early important centuries of intercourse with that great empire.

19 The Iberian monastery on an island in the lake at Valdai was founded in the late seventeenth century by Patriarch Nikon (1605–81). The legend of the love-sick monk who nightly swam across the lake to his Valdai siren and was drowned during a storm is recounted in A. N. Radishchev's famous *Journey from Petersburg to Moscow* (1790). From the 1827 St Petersburg edition of drawings from the journal of Baron von Mayerberg.

A note on editions

The extracts from original English accounts are taken from early editions, which are frequently also the only edition. This applies equally to many of the translations, although English versions sometimes appeared for the first time long after the publication of the foreign-language originals. However, in the case of the selections from Olearius, the recent excellent translation by Samuel Baron was used in preference to the old seventeenth-century version by John Davies. In addition, the piece from La Messelière appears for the first time in English translation. For permission to reproduce extracts our thanks are due to Professor Samuel Baron and Stanford University Press (Olearius), Professor S. Konovalov and the Clarendon Press, Oxford (Fabritius and Hebdon) and Baron Dimsdale (Baroness Dimsdale).

The spelling of Russian personal and place names has been standardized for the sake of consistency.

THE SIXTEENTH CENTURY

The Reception of Foreign Ambassadors

Ambassadors to Russia throughout the sixteenth century were involved in complex and protracted matters of protocol, designed to emphasize the eminence and majesty of the Russian ruler. Sigismund von Herberstein describes the stratagems to which foreign ambassadors when they were not utterly depressed and frustrated by such procedures, would resort to assert their own dignity and disconcert Russian officials.

When a person going to Russia as ambassador approaches the frontiers of that country, he dispatches a messenger to the nearest city, to intimate to the governor of such city, that he is about to enter the territory of the prince as ambassador from such and such a sovereign. Upon which the governor makes careful inquiry not only as to the prince by whom he is sent, but also as to the condition and dignity of the ambassador himself, and with what retinue he comes; and having informed himself upon these points, he sends some one with a company to receive and escort the ambassador, taking into consideration the dignity of the prince by whom the ambassador is sent, and the rank of the ambassador himself. At the same time also he signifies to the grand-duke whence and from whom the ambassador comes. The person dispatched by the governor to meet the ambassador in the same manner sends one of his people in advance to intimate to him that a great man is coming, who intends receiving him at a certain place, which he specifies. They use the expression 'great man', because it is given to all persons of superior rank, for that is the title which they bestow upon every powerful or noble personage, or baron, or other illustrious or distinguished man. But at the point of meeting the said delegate is so jealous of giving place, that in winter time he orders the snow to be swept away wherever it may lie, so that the ambassador may pass, but he himself will not give way on the public beaten road. This further custom also they observe at the meeting: they send a messenger to the ambassador to desire him to alight from his horse or carriage, and if the latter should excuse himself on the plea of weariness or sickness,

49

the servant makes answer, that the message of his master is not allowed either to be delivered or heard, unless the parties are standing. The delegate takes watchful heed not to alight first from his horse or carriage, lest by so doing he should seem to derogate from his master's dignity, and will not himself alight till he has first seen the ambassador dismount from his horse.

In my first embassy, I told the person who came to meet me from Moscow, that I was.weary with travelling, and that we could transact our business on horseback: but for the reason I have mentioned, he did not think fit to go through the ceremony in this fashion. The interpreters and the rest had already alighted, and advised me to do the same; to which I replied, 'That as soon as the Russian alighted, I would alight'. The fact was, that when I found they laid so much stress upon the matter, I was equally unwilling to fail in my duty to my own master, or to compromise his dignity. But as he refused to descend first, and as this question of pride was causing some little delay, in order to put a stop to the business I moved my foot from the stirrup as if I were about to alight, and the delegate seeing this, immediately dismounted; I, however, got down from my horse very slowly, which made him greatly vexed that he had been cheated by me.

After this, he approached me, and with uncovered head, said, 'The Captain N., of the province, etc., representative of the great lord Basil, by the grace of God, king and lord of all Russia, and grand-duke, etc. (repeating the names of the chief principalities), hath ordered me to inform thee, that having understood thou wert come as ambassador of so great a prince to our great master, he hath sent us to meet thee, and to conduct thee to him (repeating the title of the prince and governor). He also desired us to inquire whether you had ridden well?' (for this is their fashion in receiving you, to inquire, have you travelled well). The delegate then holds out his right hand to the ambassador; but after this, he no more takes the lead in showing respect, unless he sees the ambassador also uncover his head. After this, perhaps actuated by the duty of courtesy, he of his own accord presses upon the ambassador the inquiry as to whether he has travelled in comfort; he finally gives a signal with his hand, as much as to say, 'mount, and proceed'. When all have mounted their horses, or entered the carriages, he remains together with his people in the same spot, nor does he give place even to the ambassador, but follows a long way behind, and is particularly careful that no one shall go backward or ride behind him. As the ambassador proceeds, he soon begins to make inquiries, first as to the name of the ambassador and each of his servants, then as to the names of his parents, and from what province such an one comes, what language such an one knows, and what is his condition in life, and whether he is the servant of any

prince, or a relative or kinsman of the ambassador, or whether he had ever been before in that province; all which points are immediately reported by letter to the grand-duke. After the ambassador has proceeded a little distance, a man meets him saying, that he has an order from the governor to provide him with everything that he requires.

The consequence was, that after leaving Dubrovno, a little town of Lithuania, situated on the Dnieper, and having that day accomplished eight [German] miles, when we reached the frontiers of Russia, we had to pass the night in the open air. We threw a bridge across a little river which had over-flowed its banks, so as to enable ourselves when midnight was passed to proceed, in order to reach Smolensk; for the city of Smolensk is only twelve German miles distant from the frontier or entrance into the principality of Russia. On the morrow, when we had advanced nearly one German mile, we were entertained with every mark of distinction; but after proceeding half a mile further, we found that we had patiently to pass the night in a place appointed for us in the open air. Having again made an advance of two miles on the following day, a spot was again allotted to us for passing the night,

20 The Tsar Alexis Mikhaylovich receiving a foreign embassy. On the far left and right of the Tsar stand four Stolniki or Chamberlains, who carried silver axes and wore gold chains around their bodies. Next to them is the Marshal of the Realm, Prince Dolgoruky, who is offering the Tsar's hand to be kissed, and to the right of the Tsar stands the Keeper of the Exchequer, Prince Vorotynsky. From Erich Palmquist, 1674.

51

where we were sumptuously and gaily received by our attendant.

But on the following day, which was Palm Sunday, although we had ordered our servants to make no stoppages whatever, but to proceed straight on to Smolensk with our luggage; yet, after advancing two German miles, we found that they had been detained in a place allotted to them for passing the night. When they found that we were proceeding further, they begged us at least to take dinner there, to which request we were obliged to yield, for on that day our conductor had also invited some of his master's ambassadors, the Prince Ivan Yaroslavsky, and Simeon Trofimov, his secretary, who were returning from the emperor with us on their road from Spain.

I, who knew the reason of their detaining us so long in these deserts (for they had sent on a messenger from Smolensk to the grand-duke announcing our arrival, and waited for an answer as to whether they should conduct us to the fortress or not), wished to put their intentions to the test, and started on my road towards Smolensk. When the other caterers observed this, they immediately ran to our conductor to inform him of our departure, and soon returned and besought us, mingling even threats with their prayers, that we would remain. But while they were running backwards and forwards, and as we had nearly reached the third station for passing the night, my caterer said, 'What art thou doing, Sigismund? why, in pursuance of thine own will, dost thou venture to advance in a strange country against the command of its sovereign?' To which I replied: 'I am not accustomed to live in woods like the wild beasts, but under shelter and amongst men. The ambassadors of your sovereign have passed through my master's kingdom at their own pleasure, and have been conducted through cities, towns, and villages; let the same privilege be granted to me. Nor, indeed, is it the command of your master; nor do I see any cause or necessity for such delay.' They afterwards said that they intended to make a little digression from the main road, giving as a reason that night was already drawing on; and that, moreover, it was by no means expedient to enter the fortress at a late hour. We, however, despising the arguments which they advanced, bent our steps direct to Smolensk, where we were received at a distance from the fortress in such narrow sheds, that we could not have led our horses in without first breaking down the doors. On the following day, we again sailed along the Dnieper, and passed the night upon that river, nearly opposite the fortress. The lieutenant-governor at length sent his people to receive us, and honoured us with almost a quintuple quantity of drink,—namely, Malmsey and Greek wines,—and also with different kinds of mead, bread, and various dishes of meat.

We remained ten days in Smolensk awaiting the reply of the grand-duke; two nobles came from the grand-duke to

52

take charge of us, and to conduct us to Moscow, but on entering either of our houses, dressed as they were, in suitable apparel, they by no means thought of uncovering their heads, and considered that it was our place to do so first; but this we neglected to do. When, however, the message of each prince had, in its turn, to be delivered and received, at the mention of the prince's name we made our obeisance. In the same manner, however, as our arrival at Smolensk had been delayed through our detention at various places, so were we also detained longer than was seemly in that city. But to prevent our being too seriously offended by the extension of the delay, and that they themselves might not seem in any way to slight our wish, they came to us more than once to say that we should depart tomorrow morning; we consequently rapidly prepared ourselves for departure in the morning, and waited in readiness the whole of the day. At length in the evening they came with a considerable amount of ceremony; but the reply was, that they could by no means start on that day. A promise, however, was again given, as before, that they would enter on the journey in the morning; but a similar delay occurred, for with difficulty we made our departure on the third day after, and the whole of that day we were kept fasting.

Sigismund von Herberstein, *Notes Upon Russia* (London 1881)

Moscow

Sigismund von Herberstein provides a precise description of Moscow as it was at the beginning of the sixteenth century–'a city of wood', dominated by the Kremlin and its churches.

The city of Moscow then, the capital and metropolis of Russia, together with the province itself, and the river which flows by it, have but one and the same name, and in the vernacular language of the people are called Moskva. Which of the three gave its name to the other two is uncertain; but it is likely that the name was derived from the river. For although the city itself was not formerly the capital of the nation, yet it is evident that the name of Muscovites was not unknown to the ancients. The river Moskva, moreover, has its source in the province of Tver, nearly seventy versts above Mozhaisk (a verst is nearly the length of an Italian mile), not far from a place called Oleshko, and measuring thence a distance of ninety versts, flows down to the city of Moscow, and having received

21 Red Square, the Kremlin and the shopping arcades in Moscow towards the end of Alexander I's reign. By A. Cadolle, Paris 1825.

some streams into itself, flows eastward into the river Oka. It begins, however, to be navigable six miles above Mozhaisk, at which place materials for building houses and other purposes are placed on rafts and brought down to Moscow. Below the city the merchandize, etc., imported by foreigners,

is brought up in ships. The navigation is, however, slow and difficult, on account of the numerous turnings and windings with which the river is indented, especially between Moscow and the city of Kolomna, situated on the bank of the river about three miles from its mouth, where, by its many long windings, it increases the length of the passage by two hundred and seventy versts. The river is not very abundant in fish, for indeed, with the exception of mean and common sorts, it has none at all. The province of Moscow also is not over extensive or fertile, for the sandy soil which covers it and which kills the corn with the least excess of dryness or moisture, is a very great obstacle to fertility. To this must be added the immoderate and excessive inclemency of the atmosphere, for as the severity of the winter overpowers the heat of the sun, the seed which is sown cannot in some places reach maturity. For the cold is sometimes so intense there, that in the same manner as with us in summer time the earth splits into clefts with too much heat, so with them it does so from the extreme cold, and water thrown into the air, or saliva spit from the mouth, freezes before it reaches the ground. We ourselves, when we arrived there in the year 1526, saw some boughs of fruit-bearing trees that had entirely perished with the rigour of the preceding winter, which had been so severe that year, that many couriers (whom they call *gontsy*) were found frozen in their carriages. There were some men driving cattle tied together with ropes from the neighbouring districts to Moscow, who, overpowered by the excessive cold, perished together with the cattle. Several itinerants also, who were accustomed to wander about the country with bears taught to dance, were found dead in the roads. The bears also, stimulated by hunger, left the woods and ran about hither and thither through the neighbouring villages and rushed into the houses, while the rustic multitude, terrified at their aspect and strength, fled and perished miserably out of doors with the cold. This excess of cold is sometimes equalled by the too great heat, as in A.D. 1525, when nearly everything that had been sown was burnt up by the immoderate heat of the sun; and such a want of provision followed that drought, that what could previously be bought for three dengs, would afterwards cost twenty or thirty. A great many districts, and woods, and corn-fields, were seen burnt up by the excessive heat. The smoke of this so filled the country, that the eyes of those who walked out were severely injured by it; and besides the smoke, a certain darkness supervened, which blinded many.

It is evident from the trunks of large trees which still exist, that the whole country was not long since very woody; but although the husbandmen give care and labour to the culti-vation of trees, all except such as grow in the fields are brought hither from the neighbouring provinces. There is abundance of corn and common vegetables, but none of the sweeter kinds of cherries or nuts (except filberts) are found in the whole country. They have indeed the fruits of other trees, but they are insipid. They cultivate melons with particular care and industry. They put earth mixed with manure into beds of a good depth, and set the seed in them, by which plan it is equally protected against immoderate cold or heat; for if the heat should happen to be too great, they prevent it from suffocating the seed by making little spiral chinks in the earth, which has been thus mixed with manure, while in excessively cold weather the warmth of the manure itself affords protection to the buried seed.

There is no honey in the province of Moscow, nor is there any game, except hares. Their cattle are much smaller than ours, but not without horns, as a certain person has written, for I have seen there oxen, cows, goats, and rams, all horned. The city of Moscow has a very eastward position among the other cities of the north, which we easily perceived in our journey thither; for when we left Vienna, we proceeded direct to Cracow, and thence travelled nearly a hundred German miles northward; at length the road turning eastward, we reached Moscow, situated, if not in Asia, at any rate on the very extreme confines of Europe, where it joins Asia, of which circumstance I shall say more hereafter in my description of the Don.

The city itself is built of wood, and tolerably large, and at a distance appears larger than it really is, for the gardens and spacious court-yards in every house make a great addition to the size of the city, which is again greatly increased by the houses of smiths and other artificers who employ fires. These houses extend in a long row at the end of the city, interspersed with fields and meadows. Moreover, not far from the city, are some small houses, and the other side of the river some villas, where, a few years ago, the Prince Basil built a new city for his courtiers, called Nali (which in their language means 'pour in'), because other Russians were forbidden to drink mead and beer, except on a few days in the year, and the privilege of drinking was granted by the prince to these alone; and for this reason they separated themselves from intercourse with the rest of the inhabitants to prevent their being corrupted by their mode of living. Not far from the city are some monasteries, which alone appear like a great city to persons looking from a distance. Moreover, in consequence of the great extent of the city, it is confined by no settled boundary, nor has it any useful defences in the shape of walls, fosses, or ramparts. The streets are, however, blocked up in some places by beams thrown across them, and are guarded by watchmen placed there at early nightfall, so that no one is allowed access by that way after a stated hour; and any who are taken after that by the watchmen are either beaten, stripped, or thrown into prison, unless they happen to be persons of distinction or respectability: and even these are generally accompanied home by the watchmen. Such watches are generally set wherever there is an open entrance to the city, for the Moskva flows by one side of the city, and the river Yauza, which flows into it under the city itself, has such steep banks, that it scarcely admits of being forded. In this latter river many mills have been erected for the public use of the city, which seems to be mainly defended by these rivers; with the exception of a few stone houses, churches, and monasteries, it is entirely a city of wood. The number of houses which it is said to contain is scarcely credible. For they say, that six years before my arrival at Moscow, the houses were counted by an order of the prince, and that the number

22 The palace at Kolomenskoye near Moscow where Peter the Great was born. Water colour by Giacomo Quarenghi.

exceeded 41,500. This city is so broad and spacious, and so very dirty, that bridges have been constructed here and there in the highways and streets and in the other more distinguished parts. There is a fortress in it built of burnt tiles, which on one side is washed by the Moskva and on the other by the River Neglinnaya. The Neglinnaya flows from certain marshes, but is so blocked up before the city around the upper part of the fortress, that it comes out like stagnant water, and running down thence, it fills the moats of the fortress, in which are some mills, and at length, as I have said, is joined by the Moskva under the fortress itself. The fortress is so large, that it not only contains the very extensive and magnificently built stone palace of the prince, but the metropolitan bishop, the brothers of the prince, the peers, and a great many others, have spacious houses of wood within it. Besides these, it contains many churches, so that from its size it might itself almost be taken for a city. This fortress was at first surrounded only by oaks, and up to the time of the Grand Duke Ivan Danilovich was small and mean in appearance. It was he, who, by the persuasion of Peter the metropolitan, first transferred the imperial residence to this place. Peter had originally selected that place from love of one Alexis, who was buried there, and who is said to have been famous for miracles; and after his death, being buried in this place, miracles were

likewise done at his tomb, so that the place itself acquired such a celebrity, from a certain notion of its sacredness and religious character, that all the princes who succeeded Ivan thought that the seat of empire ought to be held there. For on the death of Ivan, his son of the same name retained his seat there; and after him, Demetrius; and after Demetrius, that Basil, who married the daughter of Witovt, and left behind him Basil the Blind. Of him was born Ivan, the father of that prince, at whose court I was ambassador, and who first surrounded the fortress with a wall; and his descendants, nearly thirty years after, have brought the work to completion. The ramparts and battlements of this fortress, as well as the prince's palace, were built of brick, in the Italian style, by Italians, whom the prince had sent for from Italy with the offer of large remuneration. There are also, as I have said, many churches in it, nearly all of wood, except the two

59

handsomest, which are built of brick. One of these is conse-crated to the Blessed Virgin, the other to St. Michael. In the church of the Blessed Virgin are buried the bodies of the two archbishops who were the cause of the prince's transferring thither the seat of empire and the metropolis; and principally on that account they have been enrolled among the number of the saints. The other church is used as a burial-place for the princes. There were also many churches, being built of stone, at the time that I was there.

The climate of the country is so wholesome, that, from the sources of the Don, especially northwards, and a great way towards the east, no plague has raged there in the memory of man. They sometimes, however, have a disorder of the bowels and head, not unlike the plague, which they call 'the heat': those who are seized with it die in a few days. That disorder was very prevalent when I was at Moscow, and took off one of my servants; but from the people being accustomed to live in so wholesome a climate, if the plague at any time be raging in Novgorod, Smolensk, or Pskov, from fear of contagion they exclude from their own country any people who come thence to them.

The people of Moscow are more cunning and deceitful than all others, their honour being especially slack in business contracts, – of which fact they themselves are by no means ignorant, for whenever they traffick with foreigners, they pretend, in order to attain greater credit, that they are not men of Moscow, but strangers.

Sigismund von Herberstein, *Notes Upon Russia* (London 1881)

First English Impressions of Muscovy

Richard Chancellor's account is of interest as the first written by an Englishman. He gives a brief description of the country between Kholmogory on the White Sea and Moscow, and in more detail records his reception by Ivan IV in 1553.

Russia is very plentifull both of land and people, and also wealthy for such commodities as they have. They be very great fishers for Salmons and small Coddes: they have much oyle which wee call treine oyle, the most whereof is made by a river called Dvina. They make it in other places, but not so much as there. They have also a great trade in seething of salte water. To the North parte of that countrey are the places where they have their Furres, as Sables, marterns, greese

Bevers, Foxes white, blacke, and redde, Minkes, Ermines, Miniver, and Harts. There are also a fishes teeth, which fish is called a Morzh. The takers thereof dwell in a place called Pustozersk, which bring them upon Hartes to Lampozhniya to sell, and from Lampozhniya carie them to a place called Kholmogory, where the hie market is holden on Saint Nicholas day. To the West of Kholmogory there is a place called Gratanowe, in our language Novgorod, where much fine flaxe and Hempe groweth, and also much waxe and honie. The Dutch marchants have a Staplehouse there. There is also great store of hides, and at a place called Pskov: and thereabout is great store of Flaxe, Hempe, Waxe, Honie; and that towne is from Kholmogory 120. miles,

There is a place called Vologda; the commodities whereof are Tallowe, Waxe, and Flaxe: but not so great plenty as is in Novgorod. From Vologda to Kholmogory there runneth a river called Dvina, and from thence it falleth into the sea. Kholmogory serveth Novgorod, Vologda and the Moscow with all the countrey thereabout with salte and saltfish. From Vologda to Yaroslavl is two hundred miles: which towne is very great. The commodities thereof are hides, and tallowe, and corne in great plenty, and some Waxe, but not so plentifull as in other places.

Moscow is from Yaroslavl two hundreth miles. The countrey betwixt them is very wel replenished with small Villages, which are so well filled with people, that it is wonder to see them: the ground is well stored with corne which they carie to the citie of Moscow in such abundance that it is wonder to see it. You shall meete in a morning seven or eight hundred sleds comming or going thither, that carrie corne, and some carie fish. You shall have some that carie corne to Moscow, and some that fetch corne from thence, that at the least dwell a thousand miles off; and all their cariage is on sleds. Those which come so farre dwell in the North partes of the Dukes dominions, where the cold will suffer no corne to grow, it is so extreme. They bring thither fishes, furres, and beastes skinnes. In those partes they have but small store of cattell.

Moscow it selfe is great: I take the whole towne to bee greater then London with the suburbes: but it is very rude, and standeth without all order. Their houses are all of timber very dangerous for fire. There is a faire Castle, the walles whereof are of bricke, and very high: they say they are eighteene foote thicke, but I doe not beleeve it, it doth not so seeme, notwithstanding I doe not certainely know it: for no stranger may come to viewe it. The one side is ditched, and on the other side runneth a river called Moskva which runneth into Tartarie and so into the sea called Mare Caspium: and on the North side there is a base towne, the which hath also a bricke wall about it, and so it joyneth with the Castle wall. The Emperour lieth in the castle, wherein are nine fayre

Churches, and therin are religious men. Also there is a Metropolitane with divers Bishops. I will not stande in description of their buildinges nor of the strength thereof because we have better in all points in England. They be well furnished with ordinance of all sortes.

The Emperours or Dukes house neither in building nor in the outward shew, nor yet within the house is so sumptuous as I have seene. It is very lowe built in eight square, much like the olde building of England, with small windowes, and so in other poynts.

Now to declare my comming before his Majestie: After I had remained twelve daies, the Secretary which hath the hearing of strangers did send for me, advertising me that the Dukes pleasure was to have me to come before his Ma. with the kings my masters letters: whereof I was right glad, and so I gave mine attendance. And when the Duke was in his place appointed, the interpretour came for me into the utter chamber, where sate one hundred or moe gentlemen, all in cloth of golde very sumptuous, and from thence I came into the Counsaile chamber, where sate the Duke himselfe with his nobles, which were a faire company: they sate round about the chamber on high, yet so that he himselfe sate much higher then any of his nobles in a chaire gilt, and in a long garment of beaten golde, with an emperial crowne upon his head, and a staffe of Cristall and golde in his right hand, and his other hand halfe leaning on his chaire. The Chancelour stoode up with the Secretary before the Duke. After my dutie done and my letter delivered, he bade me welcome, & enquired of me the health of the King my master, and I answered that he was in good health at my departure from his court, and that my trust was that he was now in the same. Upon the which he bade me to dinner. The chancelour presented my present unto his Grace bareheaded (for before they were all covered) and when his Grace had received my letter, I was required to depart: for I had charge not to speake to the Duke, but when he spake to me. So I departed unto the Secretaries chamber, where I remayned two houres, and then I was sent for agayne unto another palace which is called the golden palace, but I saw no cause why it should be so called; for I have seene many fayrer then it in all poynts: and so I came into the hall, which was small and not great as is the Kings Majesties of England, and the table was covered with a tablecloth; and the Marshall sate at the ende of the table with a little white rod in his hand, which boorde was full of vessell of golde: and on the other side of the hall did stand a faire cupborde of plate. From thence I came into the dining chamber, where the Duke himselfe sate at his table without cloth of estate, in a gowne of silver, with a crowne emperiall upon his head, he sate in a chaire somewhat hie: There sate none neare him by a great way. There were long tables set round about the chamber, which were full set with such as the Duke had at dinner: they were all in white. Also the places where the tables stoode were higher by two steppes then the rest of the house. In the middest of the chamber stoode a table or cupboard to set plate on; which stoode full of cuppes of golde: and amongst all the rest there stoode foure marveilous great pottes or crudences as they call them, of golde and silver: I thinke they were a good yarde and a halfe hie. By the cupborde stoode two gentlemen with napkins on their shoulders, and in their handes each of them had a cuppe of gold set with pearles and precious stones, which were the Dukes owne drinking cups. when he was disposed, he drunke them off at a draught. And for his service at meate it came in without order, yet it was very rich service, for all were served in gold, not onely he himselfe, but also all the rest of us, and it was very massie: the cups also were of golde and very massie. The number that dined there that day was two hundred persons, and all were served in golden vessell. The gentlemen that waited were all in cloth of gold, and they served him with their caps on their heads. Before the service came in, the Duke sent to every man a great shiver of bread, and the bearer called the party so sent to by his name aloude, and sayd, Ivan Vasilevich Emperour of Russia and great Duke of Moscovia doth reward thee with bread: then must all men stand up, and doe at all times when those wordes are spoken. And then last of all he giveth the Marshall bread, whereof he eateth before the Dukes Grace, and so doth reverence and departeth. Then commeth the Dukes service of the Swannes all in pieces, and every one in a severall dish: the which the Duke sendeth as he did the bread, and the bearer sayth the same wordes as he sayd before. And as I sayd before, the service of his meate is in no order, but commeth in dish by dish: and then after that the Duke sendeth drinke, with the like saying as before is tolde. Also before dinner hee changed his crowne, and in dinner time two crownes; so that I saw three severall crownes upon his head in one day. And thus when his service was all come in he gave to every one of his gentlemen waiters meate with his owne hand, & so likewise drinke. His intent thereby is, as I have heard, that every man shall know perfectly his servants. Thus when dinner is done he calleth his nobles before him name by name, that it is wonder to heare howe he could name them, having so many as he hath. Thus when dinner was done I departed to my lodging, which was an hower within night. I will leave this, and speake no more of him nor his houshold: but I will some-what declare of his land and people, with their nature and power in the wars. This Duke is Lord and Emperour of many countreis, & his power is marveilous great. For he is able to bring into the field two or three hundred thousand men: he never goeth into the field himselfe with under two hundred thousand men: And when he goeth himselfe he furnisheth his borders all with men of warre, which are no small number. He leaveth on the borders of Livonia fortie thousand men, and upon the borders of Lithuania 60 thousand men, and towarde the Nogay Tartars sixtie thousand, which is wonder to heare of: yet doeth hee never take to his warres neither husbandman nor marchant. All his men are horsemen: he useth no footmen, but such as goe with the ordinance and labourers, which are thirtie thousand. The horsemen are all archers, with such bowes as the Turkes have, and they ride short as doe the Turkes. Their armour is a coate of plate, with a skull on their heads. Some of their coates are covered with velvet or cloth of gold: their desire is to be sumptuous in the field, and especially the nobles and gentlemen: as I have heard their trimming is very costly, and partly I have seene it, or else I would scarcely have beleeved it: but the Duke himselfe is richly attired above all measure: his pavilion is covered either with cloth of gold or silver, and so set with stones that it is wonderfull to see it. I have seene the Kings Majesties of England and the French Kings pavilions, which are fayre, yet not like unto his. And when they bee sent into farre or strange countreys, or that strangers come to them, they be very gorgious. Els the Duke himselfe goeth but meanly in apparell: and when he goeth betwixt one place and another hee is but reasonably apparelled over other times. In the while that I was in Moscow the Duke sent two ambassadours to the King of Poland, which had at the lest five hundred horses; their sumptuousnes was above measure, not onely in themselves, but also in their horses, as velvet, cloth of golde, and cloth of silver set with pearles and not scant. What shall I farther say? I never heard of nor saw men so sumptuous: but it is no dayly guise, for when they have not occasion, as I sayd before, all their doing is but meane.

Richard Chancellor, *The Booke of the Great and Mighty Emperor of Russia* (London 1811)

Russian Religious Festivals

An early description (1558), attributed to Robert Best, of the Blessing of the Waters and the Easter rites, observed and described by many subsequent visitors.

On Christmas day we were all willed to dine with the Emperors Majestie, where for bread, meat and drinke, we were served as at other times before: but for goodly and rich plate, we never saw the like or so much before. There dined that day in the Emperors presence above 500 strangers, and two hundred Russes, and all they were served in vessels of gold, and that as much as could stand one by another upon the tables. Besides this there were foure cupbords garnished with goodly plate both of gold & silver. Among the which there were 12 barrels of silver, conteining above 12 gallons a piece, and at each end of every barrell were 6 hoopes of fine gold: this dinner continued about sixe houres.

Every yeare upon the 12 day they use to blesse or sanctifie the river Moskva, which runneth through the citie of Moscow, after this maner.

First, they make a square hole in the ice about 3 fadoms large every way, which is trimmed about the sides & edges with white boords. Then about 9 of the clocke they come out of the church with procession towards the river in this wise.

First and foremost there goe certaine young men with waxe tapers burning, and one carying a great lanterne: then follow certain banners, then the crosse, then the images of our Lady, of S. Nicholas, and of other Saints, which images men carie upon their shoulders: after the images follow certaine priests to the number of 100 or more: after them the Metropolitane who is led betweene two priests, and after the Metropolitan came the Emperour with his crowne upon his head, and after his majestie all his noble men orderly. Thus they followed the procession unto the water, & when they came unto the hole that was made, the priests set themselves in order round about it. And at one side of the same poole there was a scaffold of boords made, upon which stood a faire chaire in which the Metropolitan was set, but the Emperours majestie stood upon the ice.

After this the priests began to sing, to blesse and to scnse, and did their service, and so by that time that they had done, the water was holy, which being sanctified, the Metropolitane tooke a little thereof in his hands, and cast it on the Emperour, likewise upon certain of the Dukes, & then they returned againe to the church with the priests that sate about the water: but that preasse that there was about the water when the Emperour was gone, was wonderful to behold, for there came above 5000 pots to be filled of that water: for that Moscovite which hath no part of that water, thinks himselfe unhappy.

And very many went naked into the water, both men and women and children: after the prease was a little gone, the Emperours Jennets and horses were brought to drinke of the same water, and likewise many other men brought their horses thither to drinke, and by that means they make their horses as holy as themselves.

All these ceremonies being ended, we went to the Emperour to dinner, where we were served in vessels of silver, and in all other points as we had bene beforetime.

The Russes begin their Lent alwaies 8 weekes before Easter:

the first weeke they eate egs, milke, cheese & butter, and make great cheare with pancakes and such other things, one friend visiting another, & from the same Sunday until our Shrofe-sunday there are but few Russes sober, but they are drunke day by day, and it is accompted for no reproach or shame among them.

The next weeke being our first weeke of Lent, or our clensing weeke, beginning our Shrofesunday, they make and

23 A Winter Scene on the River Moskva, looking towards the Stone Bridge. By A. Cadolle, Paris 1825.

keepe a great fast. It is reported, and the people do verily beleeve that the Metropolitan neither eateth nor drinketh any manner of thing for the space of seven dayes, and they say that there are many religious men which doe the like.

The Emperors Majestie eateth but one morsel of bread, and drinketh but one draught of drinke once in the day during that weeke, and all men that are of any reputation come not out of their houses during that time, so that the streetes are almost void of company, saving a few poore folkes which wander to and fro. The other six weekes they keepe as we do ours, but not one of them will eate either butter, cheese, egs or milke.

On Palme sunday they have a very solemne procession in this manner following.

First, they have a tree of a good bignesse which is made fast upon two sleds, as though it were growing there, and it is hanged with apples, raisins, figs and dates, and with many other fruits abundantly. In the midst of ye same tree stand 5 boyes in white vestures, which sing in the tree before the procession: after this there followed certaine yong men with waxe tapers in their hands burning, & a great lanterne that al the light should not go out: after them followed two with long banners, & sixe with round plates set upon long staves: the plates were of copper very ful of holes and thin: then followed 6 carying painted images upon their shoulders, after the images followed certaine priests of the number of 100 or more, with goodly vestures, wherof 10 or 12 are of white damaske, set and imbrodered round about with faire and orient pearles, as great as pease, and among them certaine Sapphires and other stones. After them followed the one halfe of the Emperours noble men: then commeth the Emperors majestie and the Metropolitane, after this manner.

First, there is a horse covered with white linnen cloth down to ye ground, his eares being made long with the same cloth like to an asses ears. Upon this horse the Metropolitane sitteth sidelong like a woman: in his lappe lieth a faire booke, with a crucifix of Goldsmiths worke upon the cover, which he holdeth fast with his left hand, and in his right hand he hath a crosse of gold, with which crosse he ceaseth not to blesse the people as he rideth.

There are to the number of 30 men which spread abroad their garments before the horse, and as soone as the horse is past over any of them, they take them up againe and run before, and spred them againe, so that the horse doth always go on some of them. They which spred the garments are all priests sonnes, and for their labours the Emperour giveth unto them new garments.

One of the Emperors noble men leadeth the horse by the head, but the Emperour himselfe going on foote leadeth the horse by the ende of the reine of his bridle with one of his hands, and in the other of his hands he had a branch of a Palme tree: after this followed the rest of the Emperours Noble men and Gentlemen, with a great number of other people. In this order they went from one church to another within the castle, about the distance of two flights shot: and so returned againe to the Emperours Church, where they made an end of their service. Which being done, the Emperours majestie and certaine of his noble men went to the Metropolitane his house to dinner, where of delicate fishes and good drinks there was no lacke.

The rest of this weeke untill Easter day they kept very solemnely, continuing in their houses for the most part, and upon Munday or Thursday the Emperour doth alwayes use to receive the Sacrament, and so doe most of his nobles.

Upon good Friday they continue all the day in contem-

plation and prayers, and they use every yere on good Friday
to let loose a prisoner in the stead of Barrabas. The night
following they go to the Church where they sleepe untill the
next morning, & at Easter they have the resurrection, & after
every of the Lents they eat flesh the next weeke following,
Friday, Saturday and all.

They have an order at Easter which they alwaies observe,
and that is this: every yere against Easter to die or colour red
with Brazell a great number of egs, of which every man and
woman giveth one unto the priest of their Parish upon Easter
day in the morning. And moreover the common people use

to carie in their hands one of their red egs, not onely upon Easter day, but also three or foure dayes after, and gentlemen and gentlewomen have egs gilded which they cary in like maner. They use it as they say for a great love, and in token of the resurrection, whereof they rejoyce. For when two friends meete during the Easter holy dayes, they come & take one another by the hand: the one of them sayth, the Lord or Christ is risen, the other answereth, it is so of a truth, and then they kisse and exchange their egs both men and women, continuing in kissing 4 dayes together.

The 12 of Aprill being Tuesday in the Easter weeke, master

Jenkinson and master Graie, and certayne other of us English men dined with the Emperor, where we were served as we had bin before time. And after diner the Emperours majestie gave unto master Jenkinson and unto M. Gray, and so orderly unto every one of us a cup of Mead, according to his accustomed maner which when every man had received and given thanks, M. Jenkinson stepped into the midst of the chamber before the Emperours majestie, and gave thankes to his highnesse for his goodnesse unto him extended, desiring his grace to licence him to depart, and in like maner did Master Gray. His majestie did not onely licence them to depart, but also graunted unto master Jenkinson his letters under his great seale, unto all princes through whose dominions master Jenkinson should have occasion to passe, that he might the sooner and quietlier passe by meanes thereof. Which being granted, master Jenkinson and Gray lowly submitted themselves, thanking his majestie. So the Emperour gave unto either of them a cuppe of mead to drinke, and willed them to depart at their pleasure in Gods peace.

[Robert Best], *The Voyage, wherein Osep Napea, the Muscovite Ambassadour Returned Home* . . . (London 1811)

'A people passing rude, to vices vile inclinde'

George Turberville paints with Elizabethan gusto a consistently damning picture of Russian moral turpitude, in his epistle 'to his especiall friend Master Edward Dancie'.

My Dancie deare, when I recount within my brest,
My London friends, and wonted mates, and thee above the rest:
I feele a thousand fits of deepe and deadly woe,
To thinke that I from land to sea, from blisse to bale did go.
I left my native soile, full like a retchlesse man,
And unacquainted of the coast, among the Russes ran:
A people passing rude, to vices vile inclinde,
Folke fit to be of Bacchus traine, so quaffing is their kinde.
Drinke is their whole desire, the pot is all their pride,
The sobrest head doth once a day stand needfull of a guide.
If he to banket bid his friends, he will not shrinke
On them at dinner to bestow a douzen kindes of drinke:
Such licour as they have, and as the countrey gives,

70

25 Cover of the Slavonic Bible 1581. Library of Pembroke College, Cambridge.

But chiefly two, one called Kvas, whereby the Muzhik lives.
Small ware and waterlike, but somewhat tart in taste,
The rest is Mead of honie made, wherewith their lips they baste.
And if he goe unto his neighbour as a guest,
He cares for litle meate, if so his drinke be of the best.
Perhaps the muzhik hath a gay and gallant wife
To serve his beastly lust, yet he will lead a bowgard's life.
The monster more desires a boy within his bed
Than any wench, such filthy sinne ensues a drunken head.
The woman to repay her drowsie husband's dettes
From stinking stove unto her mate to bawdy banquets gets.
No wonder though they use such vile and beastly trade,

71

Sith with the hatchet and the hand, their chiefest gods be made.
Their Idoles have their hearts, on God they never call,
Unlesse it be (Nichola Bough) that hangs against the wall.
The house that hath no god, or painted Saint within,
Is not to be resorted to, that roofe is full of sinne.
Besides their private gods, in open places stand
Their crosses unto which they crooche, and blesse themselves
with hand.
Devoutly downe they ducke, with forehead to the ground,
Was never more deceit in ragges, and greasie garments found.
Almost the meanest man in all the countrey rides,
The woman eke, against our use, her trotting horse bestrides.
In sundry colours they both men and women goe,
In buskins all, that money have on buskins to bestoe.
Ech woman hanging hath a ring within her eare,
Which all of ancient use, and some of very pride doe weare.
Their gate is very brave, their countenance wise and sadde,
And yet they follow fleshly lustes, their trade of living badde.
It is no shame at all accompted to defile
Anothers bedde, they make no care their follies to concile,
Is not the meanest man in all the land but hee,
To buy her painted colours doeth allow his wife a fee,
Wherewith she decks her selfe, and dies her tawnie skinne,
She pranks and paints her smoakie face, both brow, lip, cheeke,
& chinne.
Yea those that honest are, if any such there bee
Within the land, doe use the like: a man may plainely see
Upon some womens cheekes the painting how it lies,
In plaister sort, for that too thicke her face the harlot dies.
But such as skilfull are, and cunning Dames indeede,
By dayly practise doe it well, yea sure they doe exceede.
They lay their colours so, as he that is full wise,
May easily be deceiv'd therein, if he doe trust his eyes.
I not a little muse, what madnesse makes them paint
Their faces, waying how they keepe the stoove by meere
constraint.
For seldome when, unlesse on Church or marriage day
A man shall see the Dames abroade, that are of best aray.
The Russie meanes to reape the profit of her pride,
And so he mewes her to be sure, she lye by no mans side.
Thus much, friend Dancie, I did meane to write to thee,
To let thee weete in Russia land, what men and women bee.
Hereafter I perhaps of other things will write
To thee, and other of my friends, which I shall see with sight:
And other stuffe besides, which true report shall tell,
Meane while I ende my loving lines, and bid thee now farewell.

George Turberville, *Tragicall Tales* (London 1587)

72

Ivan the Terrible

Jerome Horsey came into contact with Ivan on more occasions than possibly any other foreign visitor. His description of the Tsar includes the relation of incidents not always supported by the historical facts but in keeping with the legends which grew around his name; at the same time Horsey does attempt to show the achievements of Ivan's reign and certain more positive sides to his character.

This Emperor lived in great danger and fear of treasons and his makinge awaye, which he daily discovered; and spent much tyme in the examinacion, torteringe, execution and putting to death, such noble captains and officers that wear found practisers against him. Knyaz Ivan Kurakin beinge found dronck, as was pretended, in Wenden, a fast town in Livonia, when King Stephen besiged it, beinge voyevoda therof, was stripped naked, laied in a cartt, whipped thorow the marcket with six whips of wyer, which cutt [his] backe, belly, and bowells to death. Another, as I remember, [cald] Ivan Obrossimov, a master of his hors, was hanged on a gibbett naked by the heels [heyre of his head]; the skinne and flesh of his body from topp to toe cutt of, and minst with knives into small gobbetts, by fower palachi; the one, wearied with his longe carvinge, thrust his kniff somwhatt farr into his bowells, the sonner to dispatch him, was presentlye had to another place of execution and that hand cutt of; [which being] not well seard, [he] died the next daye. Many other wear knocked in the heads, cast into the pools and lakes near Sloboda, their flaesh and carcasses fead upon by such huge overgrowen pieks, carps, and other fishes, so fatt as any other [anything but fatt] could hardly be deserned upon them. That was the valey compared to Gehenna or Tophett, wher the fathles Egipcians did sacraefice their children to the hiddeus divills. Knyaz Boris Tulupov, a great favorett of that tyme, [being] discovered to be a treason worcker [traytor] against the emperor, and confederatt with the discontented nobillitie, was drawen upon a longe sharpe made stake, soped to enter [so made as that it was thrust into] his fundament thorrow his bodye, which came owt at his naeck; upon which he languished in horable paine for fifteen howres alive, and spake unto his mother, the Duches, brought to behold that wofull sight. And she, a goodly matronlye weoman, upon like displeasure, geaven to 100 gunners, whoe defiled her to deathe one after the other; her bodye, swollen and lieinge naked in the place, comanded his huntsmen to bringe their hongrie hounds to eat and devouer her flesh and bones, dragged everiewher; [the Emperour at the sight saying], 'such as I favour I have honored, and such as be treytors will I have thus done unto.' The frends of the Dukes fortuns and servants of his favours lamentablie

73

mourninge at this disaster and sudden chainge. I could innumerat many and much more that have felt the like severite and crueltie of this emperors heavy hand of displeasur, but I forbare to trouble the modest eyrs and Christian pacience of such as shall read it.

This Emperors delight, hands and hart being thus imbrued in bloud, makinge his chieff exercise to device and put in execucion new torments, tortors and deaths, upon such as he toke displeasur against and had in most jelousye, those especiallie of his nobillitie of best creditt and most beloved of his subiects, he countenancinge the most desperatt captaines, souldiers and deceyed sortt, to offront them and breed fection; wherby indeed their grew such faections and jelousy, as they durst not trust one another to ruinat and displace him, as they wear willinge to doe; all which he perceaved, and knew that his estate and case for saffetie grew everie daye more desperat and in dainger than other, and, trowbled much how to shun and escape the same, was verie inquisitive with one Eleazar Bomelius, as you have haerd, sometymes a cosninge impostur, Doctor of phizicke in England, a rare matimatician [magicion], and of others, what years Quen Elizabeth was of; what likely of success yer might be, if he should be a shutter unto her for himself. And though he was much dishartned, not only for that he had two wiffes livinge, and that many Kings and great princis that had ben shuters to her majesty and could not prevalle, yet he magnified himself, his person, his wisdome, greatnes and riches, above all other princes; would give the asaye, and presently puts that Emporis, his last wiff, into a nunrie, to live ther as dead to the world. And, as you have formerly read, having it in his thoughts longe beforr to make England, in case of extremitie, his saffest refuge; built and prepared many goodlie barcks, large bargies or boats at Vologda, and drawen and brought his most richest treasur thether to be imbarqued in the same, to pass down the river Dvina, and so into England by the English shipps, upon a sudden, leavinge his eldest sonn, Tsarevich Ivan, to govern and pacifie his so troubled estate . . .

This Emperowr, Ivan Vasilevich, reigned above sixty years. He conquered Polotsk, Smolensk, and many other great towns and castells, 700 miells southweast from the cittie of Moscow, into the countries of Lithuania, belonginge to the crown of Poland. He conquered also as much and as many towns and castells eastward Livonia, and other dominions of the kinge of Sweden and Poland: he conquered the kingdom of Kazan and the kingdom of Astrakhan, and all the regions and great people of the Nogay and Circassian Tartars, and many other of that kinde, inhabitinge above two thowsand miells of each side that famous river of Volga, sowthward eaven to the Mare Caspian Sea. He freed himself from the servill tribute and homage that he and his predicessors did yearly paie and

26 Ivan IV (the Terrible
painted on wood.

perform to the great Scythian Emperowr, the Khan or Krym
Tartai, not without some yearly charge for defence of their
yearly incurcions. He conquered the kingdom of Siberia, and
all those ajacent countries northwardes above 1500 miells: so
that he hath mightely inlarged his country and kingdoms
everie waye; so peopled and inhabited as great trade and
trafficque is mainteyned with all nacions for the severall
commodities each countrie yeldes; wherby his customs and
crown revenews ar not only increased, but those towns and
provinces richly mainteyned. So spacious and large is now
the dominions of this empeir as it can hardly be haeld within
one regiment, but to be devided againe into severall kingdoms
and principallites, and yet under one compleat monarcicall
soveraintie, and then to over mightie for all his neighbor princis.
This did he ayme at, was in good hope and waye to make it
feacable. But the boundles ambicion and wisdom of man
semed but follishnes to the preventinge pleasur and power of
the Almightie, as the sequaell declareth. This Emperowr
reduced the ambiguities and uncertanties of their lawes and
pleadinges into a most perspicuous and plain forme of a
written lawe, for everie man universall to understand and
plead his own cause without any advocat, and to challenge
upon a great mult to the crown judgment without delaye. This
Emperowr established and published one universall confession

75

of faith, doctrine and discipline of church, consonant to the three symbollic, as they terme it, or orthadoxall creedes, most agreable to the apostollicall order used in the primitive church, alowed in the opinion of the best and aunctiest fathers, Athanasius and others, in thier Nicene, best and most aproved counsalls. He and his aunchestors acknowledginge thier originall and fundamentall lawes of religion of Christian belieff to be grownded upon the Greek church, derivinge their antiquitie from their apostell [St. Andrew] and patron St. [Nicholas]; which church, since, by reason of their dissentinge and dissapacion in late ages, have fallen and erred from the essenciall points, both in substance of doctrin and ceremonie.

Whereupon, this Emperower hath aquitted this sea of Moscow from the societie, and consequently of the oblacions and sinodalls heretofore contrabuted to the necessitie of that church; and by the haelp of the Trinitie hath inspired the hollow hart of the patriarch Ερεμ[ιας] to resigne over the patriarcship of Constantinople [or Sio] to the μεττραπολετταυ sea of Moscow, to save that charge. The Emperowr utterly denies and disclaimes the doctrine of the pope; holds it of all Christian churches to be the most erronus; goes together with his ambicion, both grownded upon invencion, to maintain an herachie never allowed him; marvelinge that any prince Christian will yeld him any supraemacie or seculer authoritie. All which, and largely more, did he cause his metropolitans, archbishops and bishops, archimandrites and hegumens, to declare and deliver to his nunciat [Pater Antonio] Possevino, the great Jesuit, at the church dore of Prechista, articulated in the cittie of Moscow. This Emperowr hath built in his tyme above 40 faire stone churches, richly bedaect and adorned within, and the turrets all gilt with fine pure gold. He hath built above 60 monnasteries and nunries; indowed them with bells and ornaments, and maintenance, to praie for his sowlle.

He built a goodly stepell of hewen stoen in the inner castell of Moscow, called Bolshaya Kolokolnya, with 30 great swaet soundinge bells in it, which serves to all those cathedrall and goodly churches standing round about it, ringinge all together every faestivall daye, which ar many, and verie dolsomlye at everie midnights praiers.

One deed of charitie I maie not omytte, one memorable act, to shutt up his devocion with. In anno 1575 a great famine followed the pestilence of the better sortt of people. The towns, streets and waies swarmed with the rogs, idell beggers and counterfeit crippells; no riddence could be made of them in the time of scarsetie. Proclamacion was made they should resortt to receav the Emperors great almes upon such a day at Sloboda. Owt of som thowsands that came, 700 of the most villest and counterfeits wear all knockt in the heads and cast into the great lake, for the fish to receav their doll ther: the rest most febliest wear disperst to monnestaries and hospitalls to be relived. This Emperowr, among many other such like acts, did build in his tyme 155 castells, in all parts of kyngdoms, planted them with ordinance and garrisons. He built 300 towns in wast places and wildernesses, called yamy, of a miell and two in lenght; geave every inhabitant a proporcion of land to kepe so many spedie horsses for his use as occasion requiers. He built a goodly, stronge and spacious stone wall about the Moscow, planted and placed ordinance and officers to maintaine his garrisons.

Thus much to conclude with this Emperor Ivan Vasilevich. He was a goodlie man of person and presence, wæll favored, high forehead, shrill voice; a right Scythian; full of readie wisdom, cruell, bloudye, merciles; his own experience mannaged by direction both his state and commonwælth affares. Was sumptuously intomed in Michael Archangel church, where he, though garded daye and night, remaincs a fearfull spectacle to the memorie of such as pass by or heer his name spoken of, [who] ar contented to cross and bless themselves from his resurrection againe, etc.

Jerome Horsey, *A Relacion or Memorial Abstracted owt of Sir Jerom Horsey His Travels* (London 1856)

'Of the Private Behaviour and Qualitie of the Russe People'

Although reiterating certain unfavourable observations made by Turberville, Giles Fletcher is consciously more sympathetic in his characterization of the Russian peasant and seeks the causes of his backwardness in the deliberate policies of a despotic government.

The private behaviour and qualitie of the *Russe* people, may partly be understood by that which hath beene said concerning the publique state and usage of the countrie. As touching the naturall habite of their bodies, they are for the most parte of a large sise, and of very fleshly bodies: accounting it a grace to bee somewhat grosse and burley, and therefore they nourish and spread their beardes, to have them long and broad. But for the most part they are very unweldy & unactive withall. Which may bee thought to come partly of the climate, and the numbnes which they get by the cold in winter, and partly of their diet that standeth most of rootes, onions, garlike, cabbage, and such like things that breed grosse humors, which they use to eate alone, and with their other meates.

Their diet is rather much, then curious. At their meales they beginne commonly with a *charka* or small cuppe of Aqua vitae, (which they call *Russe* wine) and then drinke not till towardes the ende of their meales, taking it in largely, and all together, with kissing one another, at every pledge. And therefore after dinner there is no talking with them, but every man goeth to his bench to take his afternoones sleepe, which is as ordinary with them as their nightes reste. When they exceede, and have varietie of dishes, the first are their baked meates (for roste meates they use little) and then their broathes, or pottage. To drinke drunke, is an ordinary matter with them every day in the weeke. Their common drinke is *Mead*, the poorer sort use water, and thinne drinke called *kvas*, which is nothing els (as wee say) but water turned out of his wittes, with a little branne meashed with it.

This diet would breede in them many diseases, but that they use bathstoves, or hote houses in steede of all Phisicke, commonly twise or thrise every weeke. All the winter time, and almost the whole Sommer, they heat there *pechi*, which are made lyke the *Germane* bathstoaves, and their *Potlads* like ovens, that so warme the house, that a straunger at the first shall hardly like of it. These two extremities, specially in the winter of heat within their houses, and of extreame colde without, together with their diet, maketh them of a darke, and sallow complexion, their skinnes beyng tanned and parched both with colde and with heate: specially the women, that for the greater parte are of farre worse complexions, then the men. Whereof the cause I take to bee their keeping within the hote houses, and busying themselves about the heating, and using of their bathstoves, and *pechi*.

The *Russe* because that hee is used to both these extremities of heat and of cold, can beare them both a great deale more patiently, then straungers can doo. You shal see them sometimes (to season their bodies) come out of their bathstoves all on a froth, and fuming as hote almost as a pigge at a spitte, and presently to leape into the river starke naked, or to powre colde water all over their bodies, and that in the coldest of all the winter time. The women to mende the bad hue of their skinnes, use to paint their faces with white and redde colours, so visibly, that every man may perceyve it. Which is made no matter, because it is common, and liked well by their husbandes: who make their wives and daughters an ordinarie allowance to buy them colours to paint their faces withall, and delight themselves much to see them of fowle women to become such faire images. This parcheth the skinne, and helpeth to deforme them when their painting is of.

They apparell themselves after the Greeke manner. The Noblemans attire is on this fashion. First a *tafya* or little night cappe on his head, that covereth little more then his crowne, commonlie verie riche wrought of silke and gold thread, & set with pearle & pretious stone. His head he keepeth shaven close to the very skin, except he be in some displeasure with

78

the Emperour. Then hee suffereth his haire to growe and hang
downe upon his shoulders, covering his face as ugly and
deformedly as he can. Over the *tafya* he weareth a wide cap
of black Foxe (which they account for the best furre) with a
Tiara or long bonnet put within it, standing up like a *Persian*
or *Babilonian* hat. About his neck (which is seene al bare) is a
coller set with pearle and pretious stone, about three of foure
fingers broad. Next over his shirt (which is curiously wrought,
because he strippeth himselfe into it in the Sommer time,
while he is within the house) is a *zipun*, or light garment of
silke, made downe to the knees, buttoned before: & then a
kaftan or a close coat buttoned, and girt to him with a *Persian*
girdle, whereat he hanges his knives and spoone. This commonly
is of cloth of gold, and hangeth downe as low as his ankles.
Over that he weareth a lose garment of some rich silke, furred
and faced about with some gold lace, called a *feryaz*. An other
over that of chamlet, or like stuffe called an *okhaben,* sleeved
& hanging low, and the cape commonly brooched and set all
with perle. When hee goeth abroad; he casteth over all these
(which are but sleight though they seeme to be many) an other

27 The Uspenskiy, or Great
Bell of the Moscow Kremlin,
weighing about 70 tons and
dating from the seventeenth
century. It is not to be
confused with the Tsar-Bell,
cast in 1735 and cracked
during a fire two years later,
which now stands at the foot
of the Bell Tower of Ivan
the Great. From J. G. Korb,
Vienna 1700.

garment called an *odnoryadka*, like to the *okhaben*, save that
it is made without a coller for the neck. And this is commonly
of fine cloth, or Camels haire. His buskins (which he weareth
in stead of hose, with linnen solles under them in steed of
boot hose) are made of a *Persian* leather called *saffian*,
embroidered with pearle. His upper stockes commonly are of
cloth of gold. When he goeth abroad. he mounteth on horse-
backe, though it be but to the next doore: which is the manner
also of the *boyars*, or Gentlemen.

The *Boyarskiy* or Gentlemans attire is of the same fashion,
but differeth in stuffe: and yet he will have his *kaftan* or under-
coat sometimes of cloth of gold, the rest of cloth, or silke.

The Noble woman (called *zhena boyarskaya*) weareth on
hir head, first a caull of some soft silke (which is commonly
redde) and over it a fruntlet, called *ubrus* of white colour. Over
that hir cap (made after the coife fashion of cloth of gold)
called *shapka zemskaya*, edged with some riche furre, and set
with perle and stone. Though they have of late begonne to
disdaine embrodering with pearle about their cappes, because
the *dyaki,* and some Marchants wives have taken up the
fashion. In their eares they weare earerings (which they call
sergi) of two inches or more compasse, the matter of gold set
with Rubies, or Saphires, or some like pretious stone. In
Sommer they goe often with kerchieffes of fine white lawne,
or Cambricke, fastned under the chinne, with two long tassels
pendent. The kerchiefe spotted and set thicke with rich pearle.
When they ride or goe abroad in raynie weather, they weare
white hattes with coloured bands (called *shlyapa zemskaya*).
About their necks they were collers of three or foure fingers
broad, set with riche pearle and pretious stone. Their upper
garment is a loose gowne called *opashen* commonly of skarlet,
with wide loose sleeves, hanging downe to the ground buttened
before with great gold buttons, or at least silver and guilt nigh
as bigge as a walnut. Which hath hanging over it fastned under
the cappe, a large broad cape of some riche furre, that hangeth
downe almost to the middles of their backes. Next under the
opashen or upper garment, they weare another called a *letnik*
that is made close before with great wide sleeves, the cuffe or
half sleeve up to the elbowes, commonly of cloth of golde:
and under that a *feryaz zemskaya*, which hangeth loose
buttoned throughout to the very foote. On the hand wrests
they weare very faire braselets, about two fingers broad of
pearle and pretious stone. They go all in buskins of white,
yellow, blew, or some other coloured leather, embrodered
with pearle. This is the attire of the Noblewoman of *Russia,*
when shee maketh the best shew of hir selfe. The Gentle
womans apparell may differ in the stuffe, but is all one for the
making or fashion.

As for the poore *muzhik* and his wife they go poorely cladde.
The man with his *odnoryadka,* or loose gowne to the small of

the legge, tyed together with a lace before, of course white or blew cloth, with some *Shuba* or long wastcoat of furre, or of sheepskinne under it, and his furred cappe, and buskins. The poorer sort of them have their *odnoryadka*, or upper garment, made of Kowes haire. This is their winter habite. In the sommer time, commonly they weare nothing but their shirts on their backes, and buskins on their legges. The woman goeth in a redde or blew gowne, when she maketh the best shew, and with some warme *shuba* of furre under it in the winter time. But in the Sommer, nothing but her two skirts (for so they call them) one over the other, whether they be within doores, or without. On their heades, they weare caps of some coloured stuffe, many of velvet, or of cloth of golde: but for the most part kerchiefes. Without earings of silver or some other mettall, and her crosse about her necke, you shal see no *Russe* woman, be shee wife, or maide.

As touching their behaviour, and quality otherwise, they are of reasonable capacities, if they had those means that some other nations have to traine up their wittes in good nurture, and learning. Which they might borrowe of the *Polonians,* and other their neighbours, but that they refuse it of a very self pride, as accounting their owne fashions to be far the best. Partly also (as I said before) for that their manner of bringing up (voide of all good learning, and civill behaviour) is thought by their governours most agreable to that State, and their manner of government. Which the people would hardly beare, if they were once civilled, & brought to more understanding of God, and good policie. This causeth the Emperours to keep out al meanes of making it better, and to be very warie for excluding of all peregrinitie, that might alter their fashions. Which were lesse to bee disliked, if it set not a print into the very mindes of his people, For as themselves are verie hardlie and cruellie dealte withall by their chiefe Magistrates, and other superiours, so are they as cruell one against an other, specially over their inferriours, and such as are under them. So that the basest & wretchedest *krestyanin* (as they call him) that stoupeth and croucheth like a dogge to the Gentleman, and licketh up the dust that lieth at his feete, is an intollerable tyrant, where he hath the advantage. By this meanes the whole Countrie is filled with rapine, and murder. They make no account of the life of a man. You shall have a man robbed sometimes in the very streats of their townes, if hee goe late in the evening: and yet no man to come forth out of his doores to rescue him, though hee heare him crie out. I will not speake of the straungenesse of the murders, and other cruelties committed among them, that would scarsly bee beleeved to bee done among men, specially such as professe themselves Christians.

The number of their vagrant and begging poore is almost infinite: that are so pinched with famine and extreame neede, as that they begge after a violent and desperate manner, with *give mee and cut mee, give mee and kill mee,* and such like phrases. Whereby it may bee gheassed, what they are towardes straungers, that are so unnaturall and cruell towardes their owne. And yet it may bee doubted whither is the greater, the crueltie or intemperancie that is used in that countrie. I will not speake of it, because it is so foule and not to bee named. The whole countrie overfloweth with all sinne of that kinde. And no marveile, as having no lawe to restraine whoredomes, adulteries, and like uncleannesse of life.

As for the truth of his word, the *Russe* for the most part maketh small regard of it, so he may gaine by a lie, and breache of his promise. And it may be saide truely (as they know best that have traded most with them) that from the great to the small (except some fewe that will scarcely be founde) the *Russe* neither beleeveth any thing that an other man speaketh, nor speaketh any thing himselfe worthie to be beleeved. These qualities make them very odious to all their neighbours, specially to the *Tartars*, that account themselves to be honest and just, in comparison of the *Russe*. It is supposed by some that doe well consider of the state of both countries, that the offence they take at the *Russe* government, and their maner of behaviour, hath beene a great cause to keepe the *Tartar* still Heathenish, and to mislike (as he doeth) of the Christian profession.

Giles Fletcher, *Of the Russe Common Wealth* (London 1591)

THE SEVENTEENTH CENTURY

The Death of the False Demetrius

With the death of Theodore, the son of Ivan the Terrible, in 1598, the so-called Rurik dynasty ended in Russia. His younger brother, Demetrius, had been murdered in 1591, allegedly on the orders of Boris Godunov, who was elected to the Russian throne after Theodore and whose reign lasting until 1605 ushered in the epoch of Russian history which is known as 'the Time of Troubles'. When Godunov died suddenly in 1605 his authority was already challenged by an army led by an adventurer who claimed to be the murdered Demetrius. With Polish support the False Demetrius, as he is called, seized the Russian throne but reigned less than a year before he was overthrown and murdered by a mob led by the boyar Basil Shuisky in May 1606. A vivid account of the last days of the Pretender is provided by an eye-witness, an unknown Dutch merchant residing in Moscow. The original text was lost and there survives only the English version which was produced almost immediately in Moscow by an English employee of the Dutch Company, William Russell.

On Wednesday, a day whereon Russians eate no flesh, all was verie silent, and still, as also the Thursday following, and by reason the Emperor had a little inckling of what was a brewing amongst the Russians, having alwaies his eare, and eye here-upon, he advised all the Polonians to stand upon their guard, commanding all those of his owne guard, that they should repaire to the Castle, with their harquebuzes charged, bullet in mouth, the match light, and in truth, there was to the number of 15000 Muscovites, which were now in readiness, to effect their enterprise: but by reason that the Polonians kept good watch, and shot off many Harqusbazadors in hearing, making a great rutte with their kettle drummes, the Russians durst attempt nothing: that present night, which might have served the other well, for an admonition, and fore-fight: as also they might clearly perceive, that the joy of this marriage sodainely ceased, and that all the time passed away, in an uncouth and dead silence, and the Friday after, there was none that would sell them any powder, or other warlike munition.

In the meane while, the young Empresse passed the time merrily amongst her damoselles, in measures, daunces, and masking, intending to have come the Sonday following, in a gallant mummerie to find out the Emperour, when he should be at a banquet, with the Great Lords and to present them yet further, with some new recreations, but all this was interrupted: for the Russians now plotted, to put in execution a designe, which long time before they had resolved upon: which was, the same Satterday, being the 17. of May, according to the old stile, about seaven by our clockes in the morning. For this conspiracie to kill the Emperour, was proiected before the Voyevoda comming into the countrie, with his daughter, they bethinking themselves long before, to entrap all the Polonians, which should then be there present, with their armes, and also because by the same meane, they would recover at that instant, all the treasure which has bin sent out of the countrie, to the said Voyevoda, his daughter, and thus this tragedie began.

On the same day, most terribly, the Boyars, with their servants being mounted on horse backe, with harnesse, and coates of male on their backes, having lances in their handes, iavelines, and darts, bowes, and arrowes, cymitars, and all other kind of armes, the common people running up and downe, with their steele mases, stockes, and cymitars in their hands, the number of them being so great, as it seemed, that the Myridons swarmed as thicke as haile stones, all the world ranne hastily towards the Castle, crying no other thing, along the streets as they went, but, to the murder, to the fire, kill, kill, making one another beleeve, that the Polonians massacred the Boyars within the Castle, though verie few of them were lodged within the same: but this was done to no other end, but the more to fleth the rakehell vulger, against the poore Polonians.

28 The False Demetrius. From D. A. Rovinsky, *Materialij,* 1884–91.

This uproare was so sodaine, that divers Russians, apparelled after the Polonian fashion, were slayne amiddst the presse, and incontinently, they belayed the Innes, and lodgings of all the Polonian Gentlemen, so as no bodie could either come forth, or assist one another, with their armes.

They ranne in thousands towardes the Castle, where no resistance was made against them, by the Princes Archers, who were all Russians, and held correspondencie with the rest.

And evill fortune went so hard on this miserable Princes side, that where as he was wont to have every day, an 100 halberdiers, in a corps de guard, there was not now 30, no, not so much as one Captaine to be seene, and yet if they had beene there all togither, and performed their best, in defending of themselves, it had been nothing against so great a multitude of people, but the slaughter, and butchery had been so much the greater, besides the evident danger, whereto wee Dutch Merchants, and of all other strange nations should have runne into.

The Russians therefore, cryed out to them of the guard, (so few of them as there were) that they should lay aside their armes, to come and ioyne with them, and take their part, and then they should have no hurt at all, the which they presently did, and willingly yeelded themselves with their armes laid aside.

The Russians then ranne up towardes the great Hall, with great presse, the above named Peter Basmanov going before them, who was a very faithfull friend of the Emperours, and who, heretofore had a servant, who many times spake very evillie of the Emperour, and defamed him amongst the common people; the same was he, who sodainely stroke his old master, in such a sort, that he died.

The great troupe then ranne with like haste, thorow the chambers, and even to the Emperours owne lodging, who hearing this tumult, leapt out of his bed, putting on his night gowne, and demaunding what the matter was: whereupon one of his household Russes answered, that he knew nothing, and that it might be they cryed out for some fire.

No, villainous traytor as thou art, (said the Emperour) it is not for fire they thus crie out, but there must needes be some other matter in it, for all the belles, as well as the Cittie, as of the Castle doe ring alarum.

Ah (saide he further) doe you think you have to do with an other Boris and so hee made himselfe ready, tucking up his shirt sleeves very high, and calling for his two edged Curtleare, which they were wont to carry before him, to lay about him, within on all sides, but he who had it in keeping, could not finde it: and when he sawe the enemies troupe to presse forward, to flie upon him, hee requested his Halberdiers which were before the gate, that they woulde not thus yeelde him into the Boyars handes, shutting the door himselfe, and so retiring within some other more inward chambers, even to the stuffe where he was wont to bathe himselfe, whither he was presently pursued by his enemies, so that hee leaped downe out of a window, falling a marvellous height, uppon the pavement: for his lodging was in the toppe of the Castle, so as it was a great wonder, that he broke not his armes, and legs, or that he was not crushed all in pieces.

One of his Halberdiers, called Farstenberg, came presently downe the staires, and found him yet alive, but all his breast was bruised, so as he did nothing, but vomite bloud, and his head was also all to be crushed and bloudy.

The said Halberdier, with others helpe, carried him up againe into his chamber, where he was alittle refreshed with waters and other comfortative drugges, while hee came alittle againe unto himselfe, and then the Boyars had much talke with him, and interrogated with him upon some points, but it could never yet be well knowne, what passed betwert them. And to the end that the Halberdier might divulge nothing of such matters as had passed betwirt them they presently killed him; and afterwards they slew their Prince, with many cuttes and thrusts, and so they drew out his body, throwing it downe from aloft with a cord fastened about his privities, and thus hacked, dragged it towards the market place like a dogge or

85

some other vile carrion, leaving thus his stript and naked dead body, to the view of all the world, upon a plancher or stage erected on high, till the forth day after, and under him the body of his friend Peter Basmanov.

There went every day thither great numbers of men and women, to see this hideous sight, and they put an ugly vilard upon the Emperours belly, which they had found amongest the Empresses spoyls, and in his mouth the flute, with a kind of little bagpipe, under the arme with a peece of money of the valew of halfe a Pater, giving to understand by this, that for the peece of money hee gave them a hunts up, or fit of an old song.

The popular sort in the meane while, forbare not to runne headlong up and downe the Castle, and into the Polonians lodgings, killing divers of them, and pilling of their houses, ransacking them in such sorte as they had not a shirt left to putte on their bodies.

The Musitions defended themselves a good while, and five or six of them escaped, but the rest to the number of about twenty persons, were all hewen in peeces.

The Lord Voyevoda's house, by reason it was environed with good walles, and had also a good guard within, was saved: the gates were well baricadoed without, to the end that no man might go out or fly away. I leave every man now to imagine, how this poore Princesse with all her Ladies and Damosels, were discomforted in their hearts: for she was presently robbed and spoyled of all her riches, iewells, mooveables, apparell; and even the cowches, and beds whereon she reposed, were taken away from under her: as also all the Lords and Polonian Gentlemen were robbed of all the iewels and presents that had before beene given them. True it is, that they within the towne defended themselves very valiantly in their Innes, but in the end they were driven to yeelde, and leave the boote to the others.

The Lorde of Vitebsk onely saved himselfe, and his traine, and killed many Russes, though they had planted the canon against his house, and at last seeing himselfe hardly beset, he hung out a white cloth, in signe that hee determined to have yeelded, causing presently a number of duckats to be scattered before his chamber doore.

The Russians ranne thicke and threefolde to annoint their fingers herewith, but his people issued out sodainely upon them, and so flashing and hewing on every side, they slue above an hundred Russes, and made an open way for themselves to goe out, when in the meane while, divers Boyars of the Castle came, who tooke the said Lord into their protection, and drive out all the common people, so that in the end, all this allarum was appeased . . .

Anon, *The Reporte of a Bloudie and Terrible Massacre in the Citty of Mosco* (London 1607)

The Rising against the Poles by the Muscovites under Prince Pozharsky

Shuisky reigned uneasily for four years up to 1610; threatened himself by a second False Demetrius, he was obliged to call for help from Charles IX of Sweden, an act which led the King of Poland, Sigismund III, to declare war on Russia. Shuisky was deposed, a Polish garrison occupied Moscow and Sigismund's son, Vladyslav, was proclaimed tsar. A national uprising soon followed, led by the Novgorodian Kuzma Minin and Prince Pozharsky. For twenty-two months the Kremlin was in a state of seige before the Poles were finally starved into submission. A British eye-witness records the final events of these times which led up to the election in 1613 of Michael, the first of the Romanovs.

All things had such lamentable issue, in this terrible daies worke, and the peoples crie was so dreadfull, the alarum bell ringing continually, and there being no end of slaughter, that I was in great anguish of mind, especially when I sawe, that they sacked the next house to my lodging, where the Lord Peter Basmanov dwelled, looking every minute, for no better a bargaine than the rest: but in the end, I took courage, and mounting on horse back, I brake through the presse, being accompanied with three of my servants, committing my selfe to Gods protection, and I went to find out one of the Lords and Boyars, to obtaine from them a safe conduct for feare of being massacred in mine owne house, the number of them was so great, whome I mette with their cymitars all bloudie, in so fearefull a manner, that I was many times exceedingly affrighted, and thought to have forsaken my way, which had beene my apparent death.

But God was so gratious to me, that I mette in the streetes two Marshalles, which were officers of Justice in the Citie, who left me one of their men, for my guide, and guard, with whome I returned to my lodging, but one of my servants remayned, and went with them, who procured me further six others of their men, to withstand them in the Justices name if the multitude should have gone about to force my house.

I can never be sufficiently thankfull to God, for preserving me in this so evident and manifest a danger.

And so this alarum continued, from morning till evening, but the night following, there was such a deepe silence over all this great Citie, as though there had not beene one living soule therein.

The Innes of the Polonian Lords, were invironed round about and kept with a good guard, and all their armes taken from them.

If this nation had kept good centinell, and held themselves in armes, and good order, or but set fire to some parts of the Citie, when the alarum began, it had beene the horriblest slaughter, and the greatest effusion of bloud that ever was heard of: for there was a great number of them, and they were well horsed, and had good armes, and there, the houses are all of woode: but God had this hand herein, so that of the two, the lesse calamitie happened: for the Polonians have no goodnesse in them, but are full out as villanous, and bad as the Russians.

The furie being thus pacified by the Emperours brother, being assisted by the principall Lords, and Boyars, they assembled togither about the election of another Emperour, and so they ioyntly elected for they Prince, the Lord Basil Shuisky, and this election was made, on the 20 of May. Amongst the Dukes of this countrie, he is one of the most auncient, and of the auncientest, and most renowned familie, of all the Boyars: God give him a long and happie life, and make him to governe well and iustlie.

The 29 of May, Demetrius his body, was disinterned, and drawne out of the Citie, it being there burnt, and consumed to ashes, and the multitude said, they would have it thus preformed: alleadging, how it was to prevent the charmes of that dead Enchaunter.

For the same night after he was slaine, there was such a great, and wonderfull frost, that all the corne of the fields was spoyled, and as divers verie old men also affirmed, in their life time, they never heard of the like, in so forward a season of the Spring. All their fruites, and gardens were spoyled, and the leaves of the trees in the forrests, were so withered, as it was to be feared, that this would cause a great dearth of all things throughout the whole Countrie: all corne grew presently double, above the ordinarie prise, but the night after his bodie was burnt, it was yet a far greater frost, so that these barbarous, and infidell people beleeve, that in his life time, he was a great Nigromancer, but they should rathe have ascribed it, to the great enormitie of their owne grievous sinnes. The Nobility and flattering Clergie forthwith proceed in electing *Vladislav*, the King of *Poland's* eldest son, for their Emperour; who thereupon sent one *Panne Zoltiewski* with 10000 Horse, to take and keep possession for him: upon whose arrival into the Imperial City of *Moscow,* the Citizens made some opposition; but were soon appeased by the Lords of the Councel. The Polish General thereupon gained a greater strength into the City, which caused several tumults; the Lords thereupon caused all the Citizens to be disarmed, but one hatchet left to every three houses to cleave their wood: which act did mightily enrage the Citizens against the Lords and Polonians.

Zoltiewski well weighing the power of the Citizens, and weakness of his Army to keep possession of so vast a City, did thereupon administer an Oath of Loyalty to all his Souldiery, commanding them on the sixth day of the then-month of *May,* every one at one of the clock in the morning to fire their lodgings, and not to spare man, woman, nor childe: which was done accordingly, and above 130000 persons massacred, besides those that were burnt in their beds and houses.

Thus the buildings of that famous City (said then to be 26 miles in compass) were all turned into ashes in one day, except the three stone-walls environing each other at a very great distance, and the Emperours Palace, with some Monasteries, and other buildings of stone: but the fourth wall, which environed all the rest, together with the suburbs without that wall, reaching above three miles in length, were all burned; the wall being all of massie timber, and earth.

But the unsavoury fruit of this their bloody Tragedie, was by the just hand of heaven returned into their own bosomes: for, the Country forthwith raised two mighty Armies under the conduct of the Lord *Trubetskoy* and the Lord *Pozharsky*, who beseiged the Polonians in the City, close on every side, for the space of two yeers; and, through extreme famine, enforced the Polonians to yeeld up that famous Metropolitan City, and therewith the Prince of *Poland's* right to the Empire of *Russia:* so as of 35000 valiant men, there returned not twenty persons into *Poland*. Those few hundreds that yeelded up the City, coming once to plenty of victuals, died with meat in their mouthes, through meer weakness, having not tasted a bit of bread in six months before. In which Seige, a loaf of bread sometimes was sold for a thousand Rubles, which is 500.1 sterling.

29 The first of the Romanovs, Michael, was elected Tsar in February 1613. From Olearius' *Travels*, Amsterdam 1727.

During the time of this cruel Siege, wherein I continued 22 months, being lodged in the Imperial Palace, several objects of misery presented themselves to my sight and observation, from the besieged; as the eating of the flesh of horses, dogs, cats, and all sorts of leather, boyled in ditch-water; which served in stead of Tripes. But that which took most impression of grief upon my spirits, was, to see many Russian Ladies nobly descended, and brave young Gentlewomen, who not long before scorned that the moist earth should have touched the soles of their feet, were now become miserable, constrained to go bare-footed, and for food to prostrate themselves to every mean persons disposal; yea, when they were discarded by some, I have seen them with tears in their eyes profer their service to others, and all for a miserable livelihood: which, then called to my remembrance this old saying, *Pride must have a fall:* and, *Hunger will break stonewalls.*

But after the famine grew very great, and all women, children, and aged persons turned out of the City, to the Russians, (who received them very courteously, very much condoling their miserable conditions) there followed a very great judgement of God upon the Polonians, (obstinacie and hardness of heart) who all bound themselves by Oath, and receiving the Sacrament upon it, not to yeeld up the City to the Russians, so long as there was a man of them alive: which brought them to that extremity, that they by casting lots (who should die next, to maintain the rest alive) did devour one another, from 3000 to 4000 persons. And at the surrender of the City, divers Commanders of the Russian Army seizing upon sundry large chests, conceiving them to be full of treasure, having them broken up, found in them nothing but the bodies of men slain for food to the living.

Upon the regaining of this Imperial City in 1612, forthwith followed the free election of *Michael Fedorovich*.

J. F., *A Brief Historical Relation of the Empire of Russia* (London 1654)

Russian Mores

The first extracts from Adam Olearius's famous and influential work continue that unfavourable portrayal of the habits of the Russian people, of their apparent distaste for the fruits of enlightenment, which is found in most sixteenth century works and in works contemporary to Olearius's, such as Collins and Milton.

1

When you observe the spirit, the mores, and the way of life of the Russians, you are bound to number them among the barbarians. Although they preen themselves on their connection with the Greeks, they have adopted neither their language nor their art. Indeed, they have little in common with the Greeks, of whom it was said in ancient times that they alone were intelligent and discerning, and the rest, the non-Greeks, were barbarians. For the Russians do not love the liberal arts and the lofty sciences, much less occupy themselves with them. And yet it has been said: 'Good instruction in the arts refines the customs and makes them secure against barbarization.' Thus they remain untutored and uncouth.

Although they know nothing of them, most Russians express crude and senseless opinions about the elevated natural sciences and arts, when they meet foreigners who do possess such knowledge. Thus, for example, they regard astronomy and astrology as witchcraft. They consider it unnatural for anyone to know and foretell eclipses of the sun and moon, and the movements of the stars. Therefore, when we were returning from Persia, and it became known in Moscow that the Grand Prince had invited me to become his astronomer, some began to say, 'A sorcerer in the suite of the Holstein embassy who can tell the future from the stars will soon be back in Moscow.' I learned that people were already hostile to me, and this, among other reasons, led me to decline the invitation. Moreover, the Muscovites were perhaps not interested in having me as an astronomer, but wished to keep me in the country because they learned that I had charted and mapped the Volga River and the Persian provinces through which we passed. When later, in 1643, my most gracious Prince again sent me to Moscow, once for amusement I placed a glass lens over a little hole in the wall of a dark room and began to draw in bright colors what was in the street opposite the window. The chancellor, who came in on me just then, crossed himself and said, 'This is truly sorcery, especially since the horses and people are going along upside down.'

Although they admire and value physicians and their art, nevertheless they will not employ the means of learning better cures that are generally resorted to in Germany and other countries, such as the dissection of human corpses and the study of skeletons. To everything of the kind they are extremely hostile. Some years ago an experienced barber, a Dutchman of jovial disposition, named Quirinus, was in the Tsar's service. He had a human skeleton hanging on the wall above a table in his room. Once he was sitting before the table playing the lute, as was his habit, when the streltsy who then always guarded the foreign quarter came toward the sound of the music and looked in through the doorway. When they saw the bones hanging on the wall, they were frightened, and especially since they saw the skeleton stir. Accordingly, they left and let it be known that the German barber had a skeleton hanging on his wall, that moved when he played the lute. The rumour reached the Grand Prince and the Patriarch, who sent others with instructions to look into the matter attentively. These people not only confirmed the testimony already given, but added that the corpse danced on the wall to the sound of the lute.

Very astonished at this, the Russians took counsel and decided that the barber must surely be a sorcerer; he and his skeleton would therefore have to be consigned to the flames. When Quirinus learned that such a dreadful end was being planned for him, he sent a leading German merchant who enjoyed the favor of the magnates to Prince Ivan Borisovich Cherkassky, to give a veracious report and frustrate the design. The merchant said to the boyar: 'The barber certainly ought not to be accused of sorcery on account of the skeleton, for in Germany the best doctors and barbers use them. Then, if some living person breaks a leg or is wounded in some part of the body or other, it is easier to know how to go about curing him. The bones moved because the wind blew in through the open window and not because the lute was played.' After this the sentence was rescinded. However, Quirinus had

30 (*overleaf*) Olearius's map of mid-seventeenth-century Moscow. The capital letters refer to *A* the Kremlin, *B* Kitaygorod (Chinatown), *C* Belyygorod (the white town), and *E* the Streltsy quarter.

91

MOSCOU,
Capitale de la Moscovie
suivant Olearius.

...uand il va benir l'eau . | o. Cimetiere des Allomands .

93

to leave the country, and the skeleton was dragged out beyond the Moscow River and burned.

Later on they proposed to work a similar tragedy on a German painter named Johann Deterson. Four years ago, when a great fire broke out in Moscow, the streltsy came to tear down the neighbouring houses to extinguish it. In so doing, they came upon an old skull in the painter's house, and would have cast it and the painter both into the fire, had not some of those present declared that German painters customarily used skulls to draw from.

2

The Russians are in general a very quarrelsome people who assail each other like dogs, with fierce, harsh words. Again and again on the streets one sees such quarrels; the old women shout with such fury that he who is unaccustomed to it expects them at any moment to seize each other's hair. They very rarely come to blows, however; but when they do, they strike with their fists, beating one another with all their might on the sides and genitals. No one has ever seen Russians challenge one another to an exchange of sabre blows or bullets, as Germans and other Europeans do. Still, there are cases when the foremost magnates, and even princes, fiercely lash at one another with knouts, while mounted on horses. We heard reliable testimony of this, and we ourselves saw two noblemen so engaged at the entry of the Turkish ambassador.

When their indignation flares and they use swear words, they do not resort to imprecations involving the sacraments—as unfortunately is often the case with us—consigning to the devil, abusing as a scoundrel, etc. Instead they use many vile and loathsome words, which, if the historical record did not demand it, I should not impart to chaste ears. They have nothing on their tongue more often than 'son of a whore,' 'son of a bitch,' 'cur,' 'I fuck your mother,' to which they add 'into the grave,' and similar scandalous speech. Not only adults and old people behave thus, but also little children who do not yet know the name of God, or father, or mother, already have on their lips 'fuck you,' and say it as well to their parents as their parents to them.

Recently, by a public order, this foul and shameful swearing and abuse was severely and strictly forbidden, upon pain of knouting. Certain secretly appointed people were sent to mix with the crowd on the streets and in the markets and, with the help of streltsy and executioners assigned to them, were to seize swearers and punish them on the spot by beating, as an object of public disgust. This habitual and deeply rooted swearing demanded more surveillance than could be provided, however, and caused the observers, judges, and executioners such an intolerable burden of work that they tired of spying out and punishing that which they themselves could not refrain from, and gave it up as a bad job.

However, so that swearing, abuse, and dishonour might not be leveled indiscriminately at the notables and commoners alike, the authorities ordered that anyone, Russian or foreign, who strikes or otherwise dishonours a notable or his wife, or one of the Grand Prince's aides, must pay a very heavy fine, which they call 'paying for dishonouring'. The amount of the *beschestye* varies according to the quality, office, or title of the person dishonored and is called *oklad*. In accordance with a special census, everyone is assigned a particular oklad. Depending upon his ancestry and worth, a boyar who has been reviled is paid 2,000, 1,500, or 1,000 thalers, or less. An official of the Tsar is awarded the amount of his annual salary. Thus, for example, since a physician earns 600 thalers (not counting his additional weekly allowance), a calumniator, on being sentenced by the court, must pay him that amount. If the physician's wife and children are insulted, the wife must be paid double, each daughter 1,800 thalers, and each son 600 thalers. If, further, the slanderer also abuses his victim's parents, grandfathers, and grandmothers – as often happens when some frivolous rascal is in a rage – he is obliged to pay equally for dishonouring them, even though they may be long since dead. If it is impossible for the offender to pay what is due with all the money or property he possesses, then he himself is sent to the house of the injured party, who may do with him as he pleases. Accordingly, offenders are often held as serfs, or are ordered publicly knouted . . .

One should not seek great courtesy and good manners among the Russians, for neither is much in evidence. After a meal, they do not refrain, in the presence and hearing of all, from releasing what nature produces, fore and aft. Since they eat a great deal of garlic and onion, it is rather trying to be in their company. Perhaps against their will, these good people fart and belch noisily – as indeed they did intermittently during the secret audiences with us.

Just as they are ignorant of the praiseworthy sciences, they are little interested in memorable events or the history of their fathers and forefathers, and they care little to find out the qualities of foreign peoples. One hears nothing of these subjects in their gatherings. I am not speaking here, however, of the carouses of the great boyars. Most of their conversation is directed to the side of things toward which their nature and base way of life incline: they speak of debauchery, of vile depravity, of lasciviousness, and of immoral conduct committed by themselves and by others. They tell all sorts of shameless fables, and he who can relate the coarsest obscenities

95

and indecencies, accompanied by the most wanton mimicry, is accounted the best companion and is the most sought after. Their dances have the same character, often including voluptuous movements of the body. They say that roving comedians bare their backsides, and I know not what else. The Danish ambassador [Ulfeldt] was entertained by such shameless dances when he was there. He tells in his *Hodoeporicon* of seeing Russian women assume strange poses and make strange signs at the windows of their houses.

So given are they to the lusts of the flesh and fornication that some are addicted to the vile depravity we call sodomy; and not only with boys (as Curtius [*De Rebus Gestis*] tells) but also with men and horses. Such antics provide matter for conversation at their carouses. People caught in such obscene acts are not severely punished. Tavern musicians often sing of such loathsome things, too, in the open streets, while some show them to young people in puppet shows. Their dancing-bear impresarios have comedians with them, who, among other things, arrange farces employing puppets. These comedians tie a blanket around their bodies and spread it above their heads, thus creating a portable theatre or stage with which they can run about the streets, and on top of which they can give puppet shows.

'They have divested themselves of every trace of shame and restraint,' says Jakob [Ulfeldt]. In Moscow we ourselves several times saw men and women come out of public baths to cool off, and, as naked as God created them, approach us and call obscenely in broken German to our young people. Idleness strongly prompts them to this kind of dissolute behaviour. Daily you can see hundreds of idlers standing about or strolling in the market place or in the Kremlin. And they are more addicted to drunkenness than any nation in the world. Hieronymus [St Jerome] said, 'A stomach filled with wine craves immediate sexual satisfaction.' After drinking wine to excess they are like unbridled animals, following wherever their passions lead. I recall in this connection what the Grand Prince's interpreter told me at Great Novgorod: 'Every year there is a great pilgrimage to Novgorod. At that time a tavern keeper, for a consideration given the Metropolitan, is permitted to set up several tents around the tavern; beginning at daybreak, the pilgrim brothers and sisters, as well as the local people, gather to toss off several cups of vodka before the service of worship. Many of them stay all day and drown their pilgrim devotion in wine. On one such day it happened that a drunken woman came out of the tavern, collapsed in the street nearby, and fell asleep. Another drunken Russian came by, and seeing the partly exposed woman lying there, was inflamed with passion, and lay down with her to quench it, caring not that it was broad daylight and on a well-peopled street. He remained lying by her and fell asleep there. Many youngsters

31 A group of itinerant entertainers: a puppeteer, bear-master and musicians. From the Hamburg edition of Olearius, 1696.

32 Scenes of drunkenness, such as Olearius frequently witnessed during his travels through Russia. From the Hamburg edition, 1696.

gathered in a circle around this bestial pair and laughed and joked about them for a long time, until an old man came up and threw a robe over them to cover their shame.'

The vice of drunkenness is prevalent among this people in all classes, both secular and ecclesiastical, high and low, men and women, young and old. To see them lying here and there in the streets, wallowing in filth, is so common that no notice is taken of it. If a coachman comes across any such drunken swine whom he knows, he throws them aboard his wagon and takes them home, where he is paid for the trip. None of them any-where, anytime, or under any circumstance lets pass an oppor-tunity to have a draught or a drinking bout. They drink mainly vodka, and at get-togethers, or when one person visits another, respect is rendered by serving one or two 'cups of wine.' that is, vodka. The common people, slaves, and peasants are so faithful to the custom that if one of them receives a third cup and a fourth, or even more, from the hand of a gentleman, he continues to drink up, believing that he dare not refuse, until he falls to the ground—and sometimes the soul is given up with the draught. We met with such situations while we were there, for our people were very generous and obliging to the Russians. Not only the common people, I affirm, but also the leading lords—even the Tsar's Grand Ambassadors, who are bound to uphold the honour of their sovereign in foreign countries—are without restraint when strong drink is offered them. If something they rather like is put before them, they pour it out like water, until they begin to behave like people robbed of reason, and finally must be picked up as though they were dead. A case of this sort involving the Grand Ambassador sent to His Majesty King Charles IX of Sweden occurred in 1608. He became so intoxicated by the strongest vodka—even though he had been warned of its fiery power—that on the day he was to have been brought to an audience he was found dead in bed.

While we were there, taverns and pothouses were everywhere, and anyone who cared to could go in and sit and drink his fill. The common people would bring all their earnings into the tavern and sit there until, having emptied their purses, they gave away their clothing, and even their nightshirts, to the keeper, and then went home as naked as they had come into the world. When, in 1643, I stopped at the Lübeck house in Novgorod, I saw such besotted and naked brethren come out of the nearby tavern, some bareheaded, some barefooted, and others only in their nightshirts. One of them had drunk away his cloak and emerged from the tavern in his nightshirt; when he met a friend who was on his way to the same tavern, he went in again. Several hours later he came out without his nightshirt, wearing only a pair of underdrawers. I had him called to ask what had become of his nightshirt, who had stolen it? He answered, with the customary 'Fuck your mother,' that it was the tavern keeper, and that the drawers might as well go where the cloak and nightshirt had gone. With that, he returned to the tavern, and later came out entirely naked. Taking a handful of dog fennel that grew near the tavern, he held it over his private parts, and went home singing gaily.

It is true that recently these public taverns, some of which belonged to the Tsar and some to the boyars, have been abolished, because they drew people away from work and gave them an opportunity to drink up their earnings. Now one can no longer buy two or three kopeks worth of vodka. Instead, His Tsarist Majesty ordered that each town have one *kruzhechnyy dvor,* which sells vodka only by the jug or tankard. The people who are appointed managers of these establishments have taken a special oath, and they annually supply an unbelievable sum of money to His Tsarist Majesty's treasury. However, daily drunkenness has hardly diminished as a result of this measure, for several neighbors pool their funds to buy a tankard or more, and do not disperse until they have emptied it to the dregs. Some of them also buy up large quantities and secretly sell it by the cup. It is true that now fewer people are seen naked, although the number of drunkards wandering about and wallowing in the gutters is not much reduced.

Women do not consider it disgraceful to themselves to get intoxicated and collapse along with the men. From my inn in Narva, the Niehoff House, I saw an amusing spectacle. Several women came with their husbands to a carouse, sat with them, and drank amply. When the men had got drunk, they wanted to go home. The women demurred, and though their ears were boxed, nevertheless, they declined to get up. When at last the men fell to the ground and went to sleep, the women sat astride them and continued toasting one another with vodka until they, too, became dead drunk. Our host in Narva, Jakob von Köllen, related that just such a comedy took place at his wedding. After they got drunk, the men struck their wives for the pleasure of it, and then proceeded to tipple with them again. Finally the women, sitting astride their sleeping husbands, drank to each other until they toppled over alongside them and slept. One may easily imagine the peril to honour and modesty, and its frequent ruin, under such conditions of life.

Adam Olearius, *The Travels of Olearius in Seventeenth-Century Russia* (Stanford 1967)

The Tsar and his Powers

Adam Olearius, who travelled to Russia one hundred years after Herberstein, between 1633 and 1639, is careful to point out the changes which have occurred since the sixteenth century in the extent and use of the Tsar's powers.

The Russian system of government, is what the political thinkers call 'a dominating and despotic monarchy.' After he inherits the crown, the Tsar, or Grand Prince, alone rules the whole country; all his subjects, the noblemen and princes as well as the common people, townsmen, and peasants, are his serfs and slaves, whom he treats as the master of the house does his servants. This mode of rule is very like that which Aristotle describes in the following words: 'There is also another kind of monarchy, found in the kingdoms of some of the barbarian

33 Olearius's engraving shows on the left a shoe-maker's shop and on the right Russian coins from the reigns of Ivan the Terrible, the False Demetrius, Michael Fedorovich and Alexis Mikhaylovich, Amsterdam 1727.

peoples, which stands closest of all to tyranny.' If one keeps in mind the basic distinction between a legitimate and a tyrannical order, that the first subserves the welfare of the subjects and the second the personal wants of the sovereign, then the Russian government must be considered closely related to tyranny.

In addressing the Tsar the magnates must unashamedly not only write their names in the diminutive form, but also call themselves slaves, and they are treated as such. Formerly the gosti and magnates who were supposed to turn out at public audiences in sumptuous dress, were beaten on the bare back with the knout, like slaves, if they failed to appear without good reason. Now, however, they get off with a two- or three-day confinement in prison, depending upon [the influence of] their patrons and intercessors at court.

They call the Grand Prince, their ruler, 'Tsar' or 'His Tsarist Majesty,' and some trace the title's origin to the word Caesar. Like the Holy Roman Emperor, he has an imperial coat of arms and a seal depicting a two-headed eagle with its wings hanging downward. Formerly one crown was shown above the eagle's head, but now there are three, to represent, in addition to the Russian realm, the two Tartar kingdoms of Astrakhan and Kazan. On the eagle's breast hangs a shield showing a horseman plunging a spear into a dragon. This eagle was first introduced by the tyrant Ivan Vasilevich, for his glorification, for he prided himself on being descended

100

from the Roman emperors. The Tsar's interpreters and some of the German merchants call him 'Emperor.' However, since the Russians also call King David 'Tsar,' the word is much closer in meaning to king. Perhaps it derives from the Hebrew *zarah*, which means balsam, or a scented oil (as is evident from the First Book of Moses, Chapter 37, and Jeremiah, Chapter 51), and connotes the anointed, because in ancient times the kings were anointed.

The Russians exalt their Tsar very highly, pronouncing his name with the greatest reverence at assemblies, and they fear him exceedingly, even more than God. One may say of them, too, what [the Persian poet] Saadi said of the king's timid servant in *The Rose Garden:* 'If you honoured and feared God as the king / You would appear before us as an angel incarnate.' Beginning very early, they teach their children to speak of His Tsarist Majesty as of God, and to consider him equally lofty. Thus they often say, 'God and the Grand Prince [alone] know that.' The same idea is expressed in others of their bywords: they speak of appearing before the Grand Prince as 'seeing his bright eyes.' To demonstrate their great humility and sense of duty, they say that everything they have belongs not so much to them as to God and the Grand Prince. They came to use such expressions partly in consequence of the violent acts perpetrated by the tyrant Ivan Vasilevich and partly because they and their property indeed are in that condition. So that they might remain tranquil in slavery and terror, they are forbidden, on pain of corporal punishment, to travel out of the country on their own initiative [for they might then] tell [their countrymen] of the free institutions that exist in foreign lands. Likewise, no merchant may cross the border and carry on trade abroad without the Tsar's permission.

Ten years ago, through the special favour of the Grand Prince, the old German translator Hans Helmes (who died at the age of 97) was allowed to send his son, who had been born in Moscow, to a German university to study medicine; [the son was expected] afterwards to serve the Tsar. He was so successful that he obtained the medical degree with great honor, and at Oxford University in England was considered almost a marvel. But once having escaped from Muscovite slavery, he had no wish to return. Later the Novgorod merchant Petr Miklyayev, an intelligent and knowledgeable man who was ambassador to our country a year ago and who then asked me to instruct his son in Latin and German, was unable to obtain permission [for his son to leave] from either the Patriarch or the Grand Prince.

Although they possess the same power, the most recent grand princes have not emulated the former tyrants, who violently assaulted their subjects and their subjects' property. Yet some [of our contemporaries] hold to the contrary view, perhaps basing themselves on old writers such as Herberstein,

Jovius, Guagnino, etc., who depicted the Russians' miserable condition under the tyrants' iron sceptre. In general, a great deal is written about the Russians which no longer applies, undoubtedly because of general changes in time, regime, and people. The present Grand Prince is a very pious ruler who, like his father, does not wish a single one of his peasants to be impoverished. If one of them, whether a boyar's serf or his own, is stricken by misfortune as a result of a bad harvest or some other untoward occurrence, the prikaz to whose jurisdiction he is subject gives him assistance and, in general, keeps an eye on his activity so that he may recover, pay his debt, and fulfill his obligations to the authorities. And if someone is sent in disgrace to Siberia for having abused His Majesty or for some other serious offence – which seldom happens nowadays – even this disfavour is mitigated by providing the exile with a tolerable livelihood, in keeping with his personal condition and worth. Magnates are given money, scribes positions in the chancelleries of Siberian cities; streltsy and soldiers are given places as soldiers, which yield an annual salary and a decent living. The most oppressive aspect for most of them is that they are banished from His Majesty's countenance and deprived of the right to see his bright eyes. Moreover, there have been instances in which such disgrace worked a great advantage, namely when the exiles' professions or trades were more fruitfully pursued [in Siberia] than in Moscow; some prospered so well that, if they had their wives and children with them, they did not wish to return to Moscow even when released.

The Tsar is understandably concerned about his majesty and quality, and enjoys the rights of majesty as other monarchs and absolute rulers do. He is not subject to the law and may, as he desires and deems fit, publish and establish laws and orders. These are accepted and fulfilled by all, whatever their station, without any contradiction and as obediently as if they had been given out by God himself. As Chytraeus justly remarks (*Saxonia*, Book I), the Russians imagine that the Grand Prince does everything according to the will of God. To signify the infallible truth and justice of his actions, they have a proverb: 'One may not alter the word of God and the Tsar, but must obey it without fail.'

The Grand Prince appoints and removes officials, and even expels and executes them as he pleases. Thus they have precisely the same customs that, according to the prophet Daniel, prevailed in the reign of Nebuchadnezzar, who slew, had beaten, elevated, or humbled whomsoever he wished. In all the provinces and cities, the Grand Prince appoints the voyevody, namestniki, and administrators, who, with the clerks and dyaki, or scribes, are supposed to hold court and dispense justice. The decisions they hand down the [Grand Prince's] court considers just, and there is no appeal from their verdict to the court. In the administration of the provinces and

102

34 The Patriarch and the Tsar during the Feast of the Trinity at the *lobnoye mesto* in front of St Basil's in Moscow. From the German edition of Olearius, 1656. The cathedral of Basil the Blessed was built on Red Square between 1555 and 1560 to commemorate the capture of Kazan. Legend has it that Tsar Ivan the Terrible had the eyes of the architects put out so that they should never again create a church as beautiful.

towns the Tsar follows the system that Kleobul, in Barclajus's work, praises and commends to the King of Sicily, that is, he does not leave a voyevoda or chief official in one place for more than two or three years unless there is a compelling reason. This practice is followed, on the one hand, so that a locality may not be subjected too long to an unjust administration, and, on the other, so that the namestnik may not become too friendly with the inhabitants and be tempted to neglect his duty.

The Grand Prince alone has the right to declare war on foreign nations and may conduct it as he sees fit. He does consult with the boyars and counsellors about this, but in the manner of Xerxes, the Persian Emperor, who assembled the Asian princes not so much to secure their advice on the proposed war with the Greeks as to personally declare his will to the princes and prove that he was a monarch. He said then that he had, in truth, assembled them in order that he not do everything at his own discretion, but at the same time they were to understand that their business was more a matter of listening than of advising.

The Grand Prince also distributes titles and honours, making princes of those who have rendered services to him or to the country, or whom, in general, he considers worthy of his favor.

Some grand princes who heard that in Germany a monarch may confer doctors' degrees have imitated that right, too. Some of them, as already pointed out, have given such titles to their physicians, and some even to their barbers.

The Tsar coins his own money of pure silver, and sometimes of gold, in four cities of the realm: Moscow, Novgorod, Tver, and Pskov. The coins are as small as Danish sechslings, smaller than the German pfennig; some of them are round and some oblong. On one side there is usually shown a horseman plunging a spear into a rampant dragon (they say that this was earlier the coat of arms of Novgorod alone); on the other side, the name of the Grand Prince and the city where the money was coined are inscribed in Russian letters. This kind of coin is called a denga or kopek, and each is equal in worth to a Dutch stuiver or, almost, a Meissen groschen or a Holstein schilling. There are 50 of them to a reichsthaler. They have still smaller coins, half-kopeks and quarter-kopeks, which they call polushkas and moskovkas. They are difficult to use in commerce, for they are so small that they easily slip between the fingers. Therefore, the Russians have acquired the habit of putting as many as 50 kopeks in their mouths when they are occupied in examining or measuring some good, and continuing to talk and bargain unhindered, so that an observer cannot notice. One may say that the Russians transform the mouth into a pocket. In business dealings they count by altyns, grivnas, and rubles, even though these coins do not exist as such. They reckon them in terms of certain numbers of kopeks, thus: three kopeks equal one altyn, ten a grivna, and 100 a ruble. They also use our reichsthalers, which they call efimki (from the work Joachimsthaler), and gladly exchange them for 50 kopeks apiece. Then they trade them to the mint and gain on the transaction, since a ruble or 100 kopeks weighs one-half a loth less than two reichsthalers. Gold coins are not much in evidence. The Grand Prince orders them struck only for distribution to the soldiers to celebrate a victory over an enemy or for other special occasions.

Adam Olearius, *The Travels of Olearius in Seventeenth-Century Russia* (Stanford 1967)

Forms of Corporal Punishment

Olearius provides a comprehensive catalogue of the various forms of torture and chastisement employed in the seventeenth century, including the most notorious of them all – the knout.

They use various horrible methods of torture to force out the truth. One of them involves tying the hands behind the back, drawing them up high, and hanging a heavy beam on the feet. The executioner jumps on the beam, thus severely stretching the limbs of the offender from one another. Besides, beneath the victim they set a fire, the heat of which torments the feet, and the smoke the face. Sometimes they shear a bald place on top of the head and allow cold water to fall on it a drop at a time. This is said to be an unbearable torture. Depending on the nature of the case, some may, in addition, be beaten with the knout, after which a red-hot iron is applied to their wounds.

If a case of brawling is being tried, usually the one who struck first is considered guilty, and he who first brings a complaint is considered in the right. One who commits a murder not in self-defence (they consider the opposite justified), but with premeditation, is thrown into prison, where he must repent under severe conditions for six weeks. Then he is given communion and decapitated.

If someone is accused of robbery and convicted, he is put to torture all the same [to determine] if he has stolen something besides. If he admits nothing more, and this is the first offence, he is beaten with the knout all along the road from the Kremlin to the great square. Here the executioner cuts off one of his ears, and he is put into a dungeon for two years. If he is caught a second time, then, in the manner described above, he has the other ear cut off and is installed in his previous lodging, where he remains until other birds of the kind are found, whereupon they are all sent together to Siberia. However, no one pays with his life for robbery, unless a murder is committed along with it. If, under torture, the thief names those to whom he sold stolen goods, the buyers are brought to court and ordered to make restoration to the complainant. They call such payment *vyt,* and on its account many are constrained against purchasing suspicious things.

Cases involving debts and debtors are more numerous than any other kind. He who will not or cannot pay is obliged to sit locked up in the house of a servant of the court, just as in cases of arrest and detention among us. If the debt is not paid in the period of grace allowed, the debtor, no matter who he may be, Russian or foreigner, man or woman, merchant or artisan, priest, monk, or nun, is placed in the debtors' prison. Every day he is brought to an open place before the chancellery and is beaten on the shinbones for a whole hour with a supple stick

105

of about a small finger's thickness, which frequently causes the victim to shriek aloud with pain. However, if the beater has received a bribe or a present, he beats lightly and amiss. Some also place heavy sheet-metal or long wooden strips in their boots, so that these will absorb the blows. After having borne these torments and humiliations, the debtor either is returned to prison or must furnish guarantors [to promise] that he will appear on the following day to be beaten again. They call this form of punishment *stavit na pravezh*. If the debtor is entirely without means to pay, he becomes the slave of the creditor and must serve him.

Other common punishments inflicted upon criminals include slitting the nostrils, beating with cudgels, and beating with the knout on the bare back. A person's nostrils are slit if he has used snuff. We had occasion to see several who had been punished in this manner. Every master may use a cudgel on his servants or anyone over whom he has the least authority. A criminal must take off his cloak and other clothes, down to his nightshirt, and then lie down with his stomach to the ground. Two people then sit astride him, one on his head, the other on his legs, and he is beaten on the back with a supple rod. The spectacle produced resembles that of a furrier flaying a hide. This kind of punishment was often resorted to among the Russians who accompanied us on our journey.

In our opinion, beating with the knout is a barbaric punishment. On September 24, 1634, I saw this form of punishment inflicted upon eight men and a woman, who, in violation of the Grand Prince's order, had sold tobacco and vodka. Before the chancellery called the Novaya Chetvert, they had to bare their bodies down to the waist. Then each in turn was obliged to place his stomach to the back of one of the executioner's servants, while holding him around the neck. The legs of the offender were bound together, and a special person held them down with a rope, so that the one being punished could move neither up nor down. The executioner retired a good three paces behind the offender and flailed as hard as he could with a long thick knout, making the blood gush forth freely after each stroke. To the end of this knout were attached three thongs made of hard, tanned elk hide, each the length of a finger, which cut like knives. (In this manner some persons whose crimes were great were beaten to death.) A servant of the court stood by and read from a paper the number of strokes each was to receive. When the prescribed number had been fulfilled, he cried, *Polno!*, that is, 'Enough!' Each was given from 20 to 26 strokes, and the woman 16, after which she fell unconscious. Their backs retained not so much as a finger's thickness of skin intact. They looked like animals whose skin had been flayed. After this, each of the tobacco sellers had a paper of tobacco hung around his neck, and the traders in vodka a bottle. They were joined by twos, the arms of a pair bound together, and

35 Forms of punishment and torture. Palmquist 1674. A debtor is beaten across the shins with a stick each day until he pays his debts or becomes his creditor's slave.

36 Constant dripping of ice-cold water on the prisoner's head.

37 The batogi or canes—a common form of punishment against all classes of society.

driven, with lashes, out of the city and then back to the Kremlin.

It is said that the friends of some of the whipped apply warm, freshly cut lamb's skin to the lacerated back to help it heal. Formerly, those subjected to such punishment were afterward treated as well as anyone else; others spoke, ate, and drank with them as they pleased. Now, however, these people are considered somewhat disgraced.

The Russians, in the course of time, are in many respects changing for the better because they imitate the Germans a good deal and have been influenced by them in the matter of

38 Administering the knout. The victim's hands and legs are held rigid and a stroke of the whip is given for each of the crimes read out, whilst a priest stands by with spiritual comfort. Palmquist 1674.

glory and shame. For example, they formerly did not consider the office of executioner as infamous and dishonourable as they do now. Now no honest or notable person has friendly relations with someone who has been whipped unless false witness was given against him, or unless he was wrongly punished because of the judge's enmity toward him. In the latter case, he is more pitied than shunned, and to prove his innocence good people fearlessly have traffic with him.

Honest people nowadays avoid the company of knouters and executioners. Although the latter may take up other business or trades, they are loath to do so, since executioners receive large income. For each punishment they receive money not only from the authorities but also from the criminals (if they have money, and he is not too hard on them). Besides they sell vodka—secretly of course—to the arrested persons, of whom there are many every day, and thus acquire a goodly sum each year. For this reason, some purchase these offices with gifts. However, the resale of these offices is now forbidden. When there is a shortage of such people and it is necessary to carry out a large number of executions, the butchers' guild is obliged to assign several executioners from its ranks.

Adam Olearius, *The Travels of Olearius in Seventeenth-Century Russia* (Stanford 1967)

Inconveniences of Travel

Travellers, both Russian and foreign, always devoted much time and space to complaints about the state of Russian roads, the lack of amenities in the post-houses, and the shortage of fresh horses. In the spring the roads were almost impassable, pitted with holes and axle-deep in mud, although in winter, Russia's Macadam, as the poet Vyazemsky dubbed it, travel was often swift, dangerous, but exhilarating for a time. Guy Miège, accompanying the Earl of Carlisle's embassy, describes their journey down to Moscow in the winter of 1663.

The weather was so sharp, and the frost so violent, when Mr. Godbolt (the Master of the Horse) departed with my Lord's coach and horses from Vologda, that notwithstanding our provision of furs, we thought we should never have been able to overcome it. But this extremity continued not above five or six days, the Heavens had reserved more mild and propitious weather for his Excellencies departure, so that it thawed till the very day we arrived at Yaroslavl; but it began then to reassume its former fierceness, as by very sensible convictions we found afterwards. We marched as well night as day, every one in his sledge at his full length. And, because the upper parts of us were more exposed to the injuries of the aire, we took a particular care of covering our selves, and to stop all the chinks the cold might possibly come in at. We had every one of us (besides our furs) his bottle of strong water, which we drunk off now and then as an excellent preservative of heat. The kitchin went still before with the Russ harbingers, which the Pristavs sent away to take up our Lodgings in good time, and to get such meat dressed as they had along with them, and having dispatched these away, they advanced to the next place some three or four hours before the Ambassador. The Pristav's equipage made the whole journey on horse-back; true it is they were well mounted and warmly clad, yet in my judgment their manner of travailing was very much disagreable with the Season. The waggoners or drivers condition was lamentable too, who as the other had no other covering than the sky, but they had this advantage that they could warm themselves as they ran by their Sledges sides, besides a certain dexterity they had got in begging strong waters, which they would do so frequently, it was a hard matter to prevent them by offering it. Moreover we had three relaies or stages by the way, viz. at Yaroslavl, at Pereslavl, and at Troitza, where some of us changed both their horses and sledges; others whom his Excellence had furnished with sledges from Vologda, provided themselves with fresh horses only, so that each of us had four several waggoners or drivers by the way.

The greatest inconvenience I found in our whole voyage was in our lodging; for besides that the accommodation of inns is not known in that country, there are very few towns

39 The shipyards outside Archangel, which was founded in 1584 at the mouth of the Dvina on the White Sea, and was Russia's only seaport until the founding of St Petersburg. From Cornelius Le Brun's *Travels into Muscovy*.

40 The winter travelling sledge of a high-born lady. Palmquist 1674.

upon the road that are capable of receiving an Ambassador. So that his Excellence had never good quarters, but at Yaroslavl, at a Moscovite's house which was newly built, and there we stayed near four compleat days to refresh our selves, most of us lying in sheets, which we had scarce done any where but there in our whole Voyage. Our usual lodgings were cabbins, or little cottages of wood, one story high, black all over with smoak, so that to dissipate the stinks which are occasioned by the same, and the sweltring heat of their skins, which would be otherwise intollerable, we were forced to keep the windows continually open. But the greatest trouble we had in these lodgings, or *izby* (as they call them) was when they heated their stoves, for having no chimneys they make their fires within side of the chambers, and the smoak having no passage but at the windows into the streets, it is scarce possible to subsist one moment in that condition.

And hence it was also we were so ill accommodated with diet: for, besides that we almost alwayes eat in a scramble,

110

mutton, beef, or hens, which were rosted in their furnaces, was commonly our fare. They having no other invention for the dressing their meat, & we doing it ordinarily in hast, it fell out often our meat was but half dressed, insomuch that some rather chose to eat their meat that had been frozen in the way, provided it had been better dressed. This it was that in the beginning of this relation gave me occasion to say, that amongst the utensils of the kitchin that the Ambassador brought from England, a chimney would not have been superfluous in several places. However as we were well lodged at Yaroslavl, so our entertainment was very splendid, the Governour of the town shewing so much generosity, that he would spare no cost in regaling the Ambassador and his train. There was an English Merchant there, that treated his Excel-

41 A kibitka for winter travel, described as 'a very long, wide cradle, on which the passenger lies down on a feather bed or mattress'. In Breton's *La Russie, ou moeurs, usages et costumes des habitants . . . de cet Empire*, Paris 1813.

lence very nobly, Nesterov entertained him twice also in his Voyage, and amongst the rest at Pereslavl, where we had the diversion of musique, though in an *izba* all blackned with smoak.

Furthermore, in the condition where in we travailed, it was no easie matter for us to divert our selves being every one in his sledg by himself as in another world, marching as well night as day amidst the snow, and in the Violence of the winter, which to us seemed very bitter, though to the Moscovites it appeared very Favourable; our employment for the most part was sleeping, the solitude, the warmth of our furrs, and the agreeable motion of our sledges inviting us thereunto; so that the greatest part of us did nothing almost but sleep all the Voyage. And for this reason when we came near any town or village, the Ambassador gave order that the trumpets should sound, to give advertisement to his train.

[Guy Miège], *A Relation of Three Embassies* (London 1669)

Russian Marriages

Consistent with his view that 'their marriages are not very solemn', Samuel Collins gives a typically humorous and lively description of Russian marriage ceremonies and allied customs.

Their Marriages are not very solemn; a few attend the bride about three a clock in the afternoon, and at their coming out of the church, the *ponomar*, or clerk, strews hops upon the bride, and wishes her children as thick as hops; another with a sheep-skin coat turn'd outward meets her, and prays she may have as many children as there are hairs on his coat.

The bridegroom is led home by young fellows, and the bride (being cover'd all over) by an old woman, and the Pope marches before with his cross. They sit a while down at table with bread and salt before them, but eat nothing; in the mean time a quire of boys and girls standing aloft, sing Epithalamiums, or nuptial Songs, so bedawb'd with scum of bawdry and obscenity, that it would make Aretines ears glow to hear them. After this they are conducted by the Pope and old-women to a room, where she advises the bride to be debonair and buxom, and exhorts the bridegroom to bestow due benevolence, and here they are shut up for two hours; the old woman in the interim attends for the tokens of virginity, which having gotten, she goes triumphantly, and demands Albricias of the parents, first tying up the bride's hair which before hung

42 The marriage of a Tsar. After J. B. Le Prince.

over her ears. The married couple must have no earth over their heads (a ceremony strictly observed, as if mortality then ought not to be the object of their meditations) for you must know all warm rooms are covered with earth half a yard thick to keep in the heat.

The bridegroom has a whip in one boot, and a jewel or some money in the other, he bids the bride pull them off, if she happens upon the jewel, he counts her lucky, and bestows it upon her; but if she lights upon the boot with the whip in it, she is reckon'd amongst the unfortunate, and gets a bride-lash for her pains, which is but the earnest-penny of her future entertainment. The Russians discipline to their wives is very rigid and severe, more inhumane in times past then at present. Yet three or four years ago a merchant beat his wife as long as he was able, with a whip two inches about, and then caused to put on a smock dipt in brandy three or four times distilled, which he set on fire, and so the poor creature perished miserably in the flames: certainly this person was a monster, not a man, born of a tygress, not a woman, and in no wise deserved the epithete of good or wise. For the heathens themselves condemn such unchristian villany.

And yet what is more strange, none prosecuted her death; for in this case they have no penal law for killing of a wife or slave, if it happen upon correction; but it is a strange chastisement to kill, seeing the design hereof was never intended to end people, but to mend them. Some of these barbarians will

43 Squabbles at a peasant wedding. Drawing by Le Prince 1767.

tye up their wives by the hair of the head, and whip them stark naked. But this severity is not commonly used, unless it be for adultery or drunkenness: and I perceive it begins to be left off, or at least the parents endeavour to prevent it, by their cautious contracting their daughters; for in their jointures they oblige their husbands to find them with clothes suitable to their quality, to feed them with good wholesom meat and drink, to use them kindly without whipping, striking or kicking them, many more terms and tautologies they use; not unlike the Common Laws of England. Upon forfeiture they put this in execution, which is determin'd in one court, but not without bribery, as all other suites are. I wish the English had more of the former (I mean their expedition) and less of the latter, *viz.* their corruption. Seldom a wedding passes without some witch-craft (if people of quality marry) chiefly acted as 'tis thought by nuns, whose prime devotion tends that way. I saw a fellow coming out of the bride-chamber, tearing his hair as though he had been mad, and being demanded the reason why he did so, he cry'd out: I am undone: I am be-witch'd. The remedy they use, is to address themselves to a white witch, who for money will unravel the charm, and untie the codpiece-point, which was this young man's case; it seems some old woman had tyed up his codpiece-point. The ecclesiastical law commands their abstinence from venery three days a week, *viz.* Monday, Wednesday, Friday. After coition they must bath before they enter the church. A man that marries a second wife is debar'd the church, but not the church-porch: if a third the Communion. If a man thinks his wife barren he will perswade her to turn nun, that he may try another; if she refuses he will cudgel her into a monastery. If the Empress had not brought a second *tsarevich* or Prince, born June 2nd. 1661. after four girls together, 'tis thought she would have been sent to her devotions. His Imperial Majesty intending to marry, had divers young ladies brought before him, at last he liked one (which they say is very beautiful still) but his chief confessor had a mind to perswade him to another, who had an younger sister, so when this fair Lady was brought, they found his Majesty's inclinations so strong for her, as they fear'd she would get the crown, and indeed so she did; it being a ceremony, upon his liking, to tye the crown upon her head, but the plot was so laid, that the women should tye up her hair so hard as to put her into a swoon, which they did, crying out she had the falling-sickness: upon this her Father was accused of treason for proposing his daughter, whip't, and sent with disgrace into Siberia, where he died. The maid remains still a virgin, and never had any fit since. The Emperor being conscious of the wrong he had done her, allows her a very great pension. The King's father in law, Eliah the son of Daniel, dares not say the Empress is his daughter, nor dare any of her kindred own themselves to be so; nor dare Ivan Pavlovich

Martyshka say he is his uncle. None are suffer'd to see the tsarevich; but at fifteen years old he is exposed to publick view, though not seen by any before, but his chief tutor, and some family-servants: only relations may see young children among the Russians, for they will seldom permit any strangers to look upon them, for fear they should cast some ill aspect upon them.

Their children are commonly strong and hardy, they give

them suck not above a month or two at the most; after which they feed them with a horn, or silver cup made horn-wise, with a dryed cow's-dug tied to the small end, through which they suck. At two years old they observe their fasts, which are severe: they have four in a year, and in Lent, upon Wednesdays, Fridays and Saturdays, they eat no fish, but feed on cabbage and cucumbers, and course rye bread, and drink *kvas*, which is a liquor one degree below our small beer.

They will not drink after a man that eats flesh. If a medicine has *Cor. cervi, ungul. Al.* or *pil. lepor.* in it, they will not take it, though to save their lives, so precise are they in observing their fasts. Their pennance commonly is so many bowings, and knockings of their heads before an image, and some-

44 Celebration of a marriage. An oil painting of 1777 by the Russian artist M. I. Shibanov.

115

times to eat nothing but bread and salt and cucumbers, and to drink water for a season. That which is *pogano* (or unclean) may not be eaten at any time; as horse-flesh, mares-milk, asses-milk, hares, squirrels, coneys, elks: *Theriaca* or treacle, is *pogano*, because it has viper's flesh in it. *Castorium*, musk and civet are not to be used internally amongst them. Sugar-candy, and loaf-sugar are *skoromno*, or prohibited in fasting-dayes; a knife that has cut flesh is *skoromno* for a *sutki*, or twenty four hours. 'Tis good policy, as it happens, that they are so strict, else the flesh in the country would soon be destroyed; for the Russian boors being perfect slaves, are careless of more than what serves from hand to mouth; and as for the surplus, the lord or his steward takes it away.

Samuel Collins, *The Present State of Russia* (London 1671)

Russian Icons

Samuel Collins, like Olearius and many later visitors, has little appreciation for icon painting, which seemed a fitting reflection of an unenlightened and bigoted church.

Their imagery is very pitiful painting, flat and ugly, after the Greek manner; I asking why they made their Gods so deformed, they answered me, they were not proud. When a picture is worn out, they bring it into the God-market, where laying it down, they chuse out a new one, and deposite money for the exchange (for they must not be said to buy it) if the money be not enough the God-maker shoves it back, and then the *Devoto* adds more, till the other be satisfied.

An obliterate image they put into the river, and crossing themselves, bid it *prosti*, i.e. Farewell Brother. And if any of their brethren meets with Jove, he turns into Neptune, and they crossing themselves, cry, *prosti, brat*, God be with you Brother. In time of fire they arrive above all things to save their images: but if they escape not the conflagration they must not be said to be burnt, but gone up. If a church be burn'd, they say it is ascended, they must not say burn'd. These are their pretty ridiculous distinctions, 'tis wonder they do not, with Anaxagoras, affirm snow to be black.

Sometimes they will hold their Gods to the fire, trusting they can help them, if they will. A fellow thinking to have staid the fire by that means, held his St Nicholas so long, that he had like to have been burnt himself, and seeing he did him no good, he threw him into the midst of the fire, with this curse. *Nu, chort. i.e.* The Devil take thee. They bestow jewels upon them of a great value. This year a woman, who had formerly

45 One of the most famous Russian icons, the Holy Trinity by Andrey Rublev, between 1422 and 1427, painted on wood, Tretyakov Gallery, Moscow. Western travellers such as Collins and Clarke showed no appreciation of Russian icon painting which reached its height in the work of Rublev and his school in the fifteenth century.

116

adorn'd her St Nicholas with some pearl, being necessitated, came to the church and pray'd St Nicholas to lend her some of his jewels, for she was at present in great want, the dumb brute not speaking anything to the contrary, she (thinking silence gave consent) made bold to take a ruby or two off him: but the Pope spying her, complains to the Justice, who commanded both her hands to be cut off, which was done three months since.

117

In their private houses they do ordinarily give and take, as they thrive in their business; for if they have any great losses, they will come home and rob St Nicholas to his shirt. Heresy among the Russes is punished with fire. The heretick goes up to the top of a little house and so jumps in, and upon him they throw straw and *luchiny,* which are dry splinters of fir-wood, these being fir'd soon soffocate him. *Satis sapere severa est hac animadversio.*

46 St Nicholas, sixteenth century. Ikon-Museum, Recklinghausen.

47 St George, Novgorod, sixteenth century. Ikon-Museum, Recklinghausen.

The fryars and nuns are not so strict as in the Roman Church. The fryars are great traders in malt, hops, a sort of corn, horses, cattle, and whatsoever else may but enrich them. The nuns go abroad, some begging, others visiting the great ladies, where they get a fox before they return home. These are fine Votaresses indeed!

Now that I am discoursing of the Russian Church, it will not be amiss to relate a sad tragical story, which was acted in the time of our English resident, who it seems had a monkey famous amongst the Muscovites to this day, for he would take money in his mouth, and go into the market, and shew it to the costard-mongers, who in kindness would give him nuts and apples; many such apish pranks he was wont to play. But we come now to the catastrophe of his mirth. Being not content to act a merry part in *Foro,* he begins *ludere cum Sacres,* and goes into a church hard by the English house, where he crept in and tumbled down their Gods. The priest amaz'd to see what was done, crosses himself a thousand times, and sets their God-ships in their places again, exorcises the foul fiend, taking his horse-tail dipt in holy water, he dashes the doors and windows; that this devil might not re-enter. But for all this, one morning early Pug came in at a window, and began with St Nicholas and the rest of the Gods and Goddesses in order, as they stood in his way; down he throws Dagon and the wares of Rimnon as zealously as if he had been bred up in new England, and ever and anon he grinn'd in the Pope's face, who standing arm'd with a cross and holy water, therewith besprinkled Pug, who (hating it as bad as the devil,) fled home.

Presently the Pope goes to the Patriarch, and complains most bitterly against a *nicheynyy* (or Stranger) living in the English house, for throwing down many of their Gods, breaking their lamps, pulling off their jewels and chains of pearl wherewith they were adorn'd, and lastly for prophaning the holy place. Hereupon an order was sent to search and examine the embassador's house; all his retinue was brought forth. No, it was none of them, but a little *nicheynyy*; so the young children were brought out, and by chance the monkey came jumping in with the children: O that is the *nicheynyy*, quoth the Pope, apprehend him, which was done accordingly, and the Patriarch finding out the folly, was asham'd, and sent away the Priest with disgrace for a fool. But however, poor Pug (to pacifie the angry Gods) was deliver'd over to the secular power, who chastised him so severely that he dyed upon it. Now chronology would be enquir'd into, whether Ben Johnson's Zeal of the Land, or countrey man of Banbury, who in a fanatick fury destroy'd the gingerbread-idols in Bartholomew Fair, for which he suffer'd persecution, and was put into the stocks: or this American reformer, who threw down the Russian Ginger-bread (for if you saw their images, you would take them for no better than guilded ginger-bread) I say whether of these two is the proto-monkey, martyr, and ought to have precedency in their canonization. But I leave the determination of this nicety to those who are profess'd criticks, and well versed in controversie.

Samuel Collins, *The Present State of Russia* (London 1671)

Account of the Razin Rebellion

The Rebellion led by the Cossack Stenka Razin in the years 1667-71 is one of the most famous events in early Russian history, celebrated in folk song and witnessed by a number of foreigners. The account of Ludvig Fabritius (1648-1729), a soldier of fortune of Dutch parentage who served in Russia between 1660 and 1677, has only recently been brought to the attention of historians. Fabritius was captured by the rebels in 1670 and the story of his imprisonment and escape contains much valuable and fresh information.

Then Stenka with his company started off upstream, rowing as far as Tsaritsyn, whence it took him only one day's journey to Panshin, a small town situated on the Don. Here he began straightaway quietly gathering the common people around him, giving them money, and promises of great riches if they would be loyal to him and help to exterminate the treacherous boyars.

This lasted the whole winter, until by about spring he had assembled 4,000 to 5,000 men. With these he came to Tsaritsyn and demanded the immediate surrender of the fortress; the rabble soon achieved their purpose, and although the governor tried to take refuge in a tower, he soon had to give himself up as he was deserted by one and all. Stenka immediately had the wretched governor hanged; and all the goods they found belonging to the Tsar and his officers as well as to the merchants were confiscated and distributed among the rabble.

Stenka now began once more to make preparations. Since the plains are not cultivated, the people have to bring their corn from Nizhniy-Novgorod and Kazan down the Volga in big boats known as *nasady*, and everything destined for Astrakhan has first to pass Tsaritsyn. Stenka Razin duly noted this, and occupied the whole of the Volga, so that nothing could get through to Astrakhan. Here he captured a few hundred merchants with their valuable goods, taking possession of all kinds of fine linen, silks, striped silk material, sables, soft leather, ducats, talers, and many thousands of rubles in Russian money, and merchandise of every description – these men used to do much trade with the Persians, the Bokharans, the Uzbeks, and the Tartars.

In the meantime four regiments of *streltsy* were dispatched from Moscow to subdue these brigands. They arrived with their big boats and as they were not used to the water, were easily beaten. Here Stenka Razin gained possession of a large amount of ammunition and artillery-pieces and everything else he required. While the above-mentioned *streltsy* were sent from Moscow, about 5,000 men were ordered up from Astrakhan by water and by land to capture Stenka Razin. As soon as he had finished with the former, he took up a good position, and, being in possession of reliable information regarding our forces, he left Tsaritsyn and came to meet us half way at Chernyy Yar, confronting us before we had suspected his presence or received any information about him. We stopped at Chernyy Yar for a few days and sent out scouts by water and by land, but were unable to obtain any definite information. On 10 July [*sic*: June] a council of war was held at which it was decided to advance and seek out Stenka. The next morning, at 8 o'clock, our look-outs on the water came

48 Stenka Razin's sacrifice of a captured Tartar princess to the water god in 1660. Versions of the tale exist in the accounts of Ludvig Fabritius, and Johann Struys who records Razin's alleged words of sacrifice: 'Thou art a Noble River, and out of thee have I had so much Gold, Silver and many things of Value, thou art the sole Father and Mother of Fortune and Advancement, I, unthankful man that I am, have never offered thee any thing; well now, I am resolved to manifest my gratitude'. From *Voyages and Travels of John Struys.*

hurriedly and raised the alarm as the Cossacks were following at their heels. We got out of our boats and took up battle positions. General Knyaz Semen Ivanovich Lvov went through the ranks and reminded all the men to do their duty and to remember the oath they had taken to His Majesty the Tsar, to fight like honest soldiers against these irresponsible rebels, whereupon they all unanimously shouted: 'Yes, we will give our lives for His Majesty the Tsar, and will fight to the last drop of our blood.'

In the meantime Stenka prepared for battle and deployed on a wide front; to all those who had no rifle he gave a long pole, burnt a little at one end, and with a rag or small hook attached. They presented a strange sight on the plain from afar, and the common soldiers imagined that, since there were so many flags and standards, there must be a host of people. They [the common soldiers] held a consultation and at once decided that this was the chance for which they had been waiting so long, and with all their flags and drums they ran over to the enemy. They began kissing and embracing one another and swore with life and limb to stand together and to exterminate the treacherous boyars, to throw off the yoke of slavery, and to become free men.

The general looked at the officers and the officers at the general, and no one knew what to do; one said this, and another that, until finally it was decided that they and the general should get into the boats and withdraw to Astrakhan. But the rascally *streltsy* of Chernyy Yar stood on the walls and towers, turning their weapons on us and opened fire; some of them ran out of the fortress and cut us off from the boats, so that we had no means of escape. In the meantime those curs of ours who had gone over to the Cossacks came up from behind. We numbered about eighty men, officers, noblemen, and clerks. Murder at once began. Then, however, Stenka Razin ordered that no more officers were to be killed, saying that there must be a few good men among them who should be pardoned, whilst those others who had not lived in amity with their men should be condemned to well-deserved punishment by the Ataman and his *Krug*. A *Krug* is a meeting convened by the order of the Ataman, at which the Cossacks stand in a circle with the standard in the centre; the Ataman then takes his place beside his best officers, to whom he divulges his wishes, ordering them to make these known to the common brothers and to hear their opinion on the matter; if the proposals of the Ataman please the commoners, they all shout together, 'Lyubo, lyubo'.

A *Krug* was accordingly called and Stenka asked through his chiefs how the general and his officers had treated the soldiers under their command. Thereupon the unscrupulous curs, *streltsy* as well as soldiers, unanimously called out that there was not one of them who deserved to remain alive, and they all asked that their father Stepan Timofeyevich Razin should order them to be cut down. This was granted with the exception of General Knyaz Semen Ivanovich Lvov, whose life was specially spared by Stenka himself. The officers were now brought in order of rank out of the tower, into which they had been thrown bound hand and foot the previous day, their ropes were cut and they were led outside the gate. When all the bloodthirsty curs had lined up, each was eager to deal his former superior the first blow, one with the sword, another with the lance, another with the scimitar, and others again with martels, so that as soon as an officer was pushed into the ring, the curs immediately killed him with their many wounds; indeed, some were cut to pieces and straightaway thrown into the Volga. My stepfather, Paul Rudolf Beem, and Lt. Col. Wundrum and many other officers, senior and junior, were cut down before my eyes.

My own time had not yet come: this I could tell by the wonderful way in which God rescued me, for as I – half-dead – now awaited the final blow, my [former] orderly, a young soldier, came and took me by my bound arms and tried to take me down the hill. As I was already half-dead, I did not move and did not know what to do, but he came back and took me by the arms and led me, bound as I was, through the throng of curs, down the hill into the boat and immediately cut my arms free, saying that I should rest in peace here and that he would be responsible for me and do his best to save my life. Since there were no scissors handy with which to cut my long hair – detested by the villains – he took a small bread knife and cut off my hair (this tickled rather). In the meantime the fellow spoke kindly to me and told me to be of good cheer. My clothes, made of taffeta after [our] local custom, he took off, as they would have given me away as a foreigner, and gave me. a rough coat made of coarse sacking, removing my whole attire – coat, shirt, cloak, trousers, and everything. Then my guardian angel told me not to leave the boat, and left me. He returned in the evening and brought me a piece of bread which I enjoyed since I had had nothing to eat for two days.

The following day all our possessions were looted and gathered together under the main flag, so that both our bloodthirsty curs and the Cossacks got their share. The murderers who had so long thirsted after blood, and yet had still not slaked their thirst, now demanded spirits and beer – which led to the Tsar's cellar being opened and everything drained. When nothing was left the villains took counsel as to what their next move should be: whether they should press on to the north into the country or first make quite sure of Astrakhan. It was decided to adopt the latter course because once sure of Astrakhan they would be free to turn their backs on it and could then proceed unhindered all the way up the Volga to Kazan. In Kazan the populace was already on their side and at their approach intended to do away with the governor and all the officers. We then broke camp.

Ludvig Fabritius, *Account of the Razin Rebellion* (*Oxford Slavonic Papers, 10,* 1955)

The Execution of Razin

Thomas Hebdon, an English merchant in Moscow, wrote his graphic account of Razin's execution on the very day it took place from the words of an eye-witness.

Nova Sloboda, ye 6th of June 1671.
Richard Daniell.

Sir, my last to you was of the 30th past, in answere to yours of the 11th ditto; these are only to give you notice that on Fryday last, the great Rebell Razin was brought in, in manner thus: a guard of about 300 soldiers on foote marcht before him with flying cullers, and lighted match but the mussell of there musketts downwards beehind him about the same number and in the same manner only but 6 cullers; then about him were a Partye of the Cossacks that took him, the cheife (by name Kornela Yakolovich) riding just before with his cullers, and all the rest likewise on horseback about 50 or 60, Razin himself placed upon a scaffold under a gallows standing with a chaine about his neck & soe thrown over the gallows with a halter hanging by it, then another chaine from his middle and fastened to each post of the gallowes where unto his hands were likewise fastened (upon his feete haveing only stockings); he was alsoe fettered; then on the scaffold was fastened another chain which was about his brothers necke, and beeinge shackled had followed on foote; the scaffold being drawn with 3 horses, beetween 9 and 10 aclocke in the forenoon hee was brought in and presently put to the pine, where the [sic] had about 30 stripes, beesides the tryall of the fire; but what confession hee made is not yett certainely known, severall reports there is, to tedious to relate, but the same day hee was condemned to suffer the next day, and preparation accordingly made for his execution, which after a long expectation, was put off till the Tewsday following; yesterday he was againe pined but not much; and to-day hee was brought to the place of execution where after a long scrowle read of all his Roguerry from the yeare 1663 to his being taken sentence of death was pronounced against him, and soe presently brought to the blocke which was in the open place beefore the castle, and there hee had his armes, his leggs, and then his head cut off which were presently sett up upon 5 poles, the trunke of his body left upon the earth to bee eaten by the doggs—a fitt death for such a villaine. His brother stood by till execution was done and was then carryed backe to the pine where he was againe pined and then returned to prison; what will be his sentence as yett not known, though as many poles were provided for him as for his brother. This is the certaintye for the present—what may further come forth wee must waite a little tyme, and as occasion serves I shall advise you. Soe take leave and rest,

Yours to serve you,
Thomas Hebdon

Thomas Hebdon, *Letter on Razin's Execution* (*Oxford Slavonic Papers, 12*, 1965)

49 Stenka Razin brought to Moscow for execution in June 1671. The accuracy of the engraving, which appeared in *A Relation Concerning the Particulars of the Rebellion Lately Raised in Muscovy by Stenko Razin* (London 1672), is confirmed by the description in Thomas Hebdon's letter.

THE REIGN OF PETER
THE GREAT

Peoples beyond the Urals

Ysbrant Ides, a Dutchman in Russian service, was sent by Peter the Great as his ambassador to China in 1692. Although Ides was by no means the first foreigner to travel eastwards from Moscow through Siberia, his description of the country and of the peoples he encountered are among the most detailed and interesting. The first extract is devoted to the Siberian Tartars, the first tribe he encountered on entering 'Asia'; the second concerns the Ostyaks, a people inhabiting the territories around the River Ob in Western Siberia.

Having thus got out of Europe, entred Asia, and come to the Asiatick River Chusovaya, we found it far less agreeable than the beautiful Kama; which is an extraordinary fine river, blessed with all sorts of fish, and from Solikamsk to this place adorned with populous banks, which incessantly present to our view, very fine large villages and towns, several very expensive salt-works, fertile corn grounds, fruitful lands, large fields beautified with all sorts of flowers, woods, &c. all very well worth seeing and extraordinary pleasant. But tho' the banks of the Chusovaya, which falls westward into the Kama, are not less beautiful charming and fruitful, yet we found our passing this river very tedious: For by reason of the high water we made but a very small progress in several days, being obliged to be towed along with a line; however, at last, after twelve days, and a tiresome tugging against the stream, we came too, and touched at a pleasant shoar on the 25th of May, amongst the first Siberian Tartars, called Voguls. I must acknowledge that the lands indifferently well peopled on this River, deserve really to be reckoned amongst the most charming in the world. And when in the mornings or evenings I stepped on shoar to divert my self, and went forwards towards the hills, I every where found the most beautiful flowers and plants, which emitted a most agreeable fragrant scent, and all sorts of great and small wild beasts running about in great quantities. But the Vogul Tartars to which this river led us, are stupid heathens, which made me desirous to pry more narrowly into their religion, manner of living, and other circumstances: and for this end I went on shoar and lodged a night amongst them.

They are naturally strong, and have large heads. Their

whole religious worship consists in making an offering according to their custom once each year: when they go in crouds into the woods, and kill one of each species of beasts, of all which they prefer the horse and tyger as best; they flea off the skins, hang up the carcass on a tree, and fall prostrate to the earth, and in their way, pray to it; after which they eat the flesh together, and return home; which done they are free from the trouble of praying for a year. What need of praying

50 Tobolsk, an important Siberian fish and fur-trading town at the confluence of the Irtysh and Tobol rivers. Engraving by Le Prince.

any oftner than once a year, say they? They are not able to give any the least account of the original or import of their faith, but only say that their forefathers did so, and they follow their example.

I asked them concerning their knowledge of God; whether they did not believe that there was a God and Lord in Heaven above, that had created, and did at present preserve and govern all things, and also gave rain and fair weather? To which they replied; We may very well believe that, for we see, that the Sun and Moon, those two bright lights which we worship, and the stars also, are in Heaven, and that there is one which rules them. They would not in the least hear of the Devil, as not knowing him, since he never appeared, or revealed himself to them. They acknowledge a Resurrection of the dead, but are ignorant what sort of reward to expect, whether corporal or not. When any of them die, they bury the carcass under ground without any grave-stone, and be it man or woman, all his or her best apparel and ornaments, besides some money, according to the ability of the deceased, are buried with the corps; to the end, that, pursuant to their opinion, he may have some cloaths on, and something to spend at the time of the Resurrection. They cry over the dead corps in a dismal manner, and the husband is obliged to continue a widower a whole year after the death of his wife. If a dog dies, that in hunting or any other way has been serviceable to them, they erect in honour of him, a small wooden hutt, on four heaps or props of earth: In which they lay the dead dog, and suffer him to continue there as long as the hutt lasts. They take as many wives as they can keep, and when any of these is pregnant, and near her delivery, she is obliged to retire into a hutt in a wood, erected for that purpose, where she is delivered, and the husband and she are not permitted to come near each other for the space of two months after.

When a man desires to marry, he is obliged to buy the bride of her father. They have very few marriage ceremonies besides inviting and treating the nearest relations: after which the bridegroom goes to bed to the bride without any ceremony. They have no priests, nor do they marry any nearer than the fourth degree of consanguinity. Amongst other discourse I admonished them, that it was time to acknowledge Christ the saviour of the whole world, and turn to him; which would secure their not only temporal, but eternal welfare. To this they answered; as for what concerns temporals, we daily see vast numbers of poor wretched Russians, that can hardly get a piece of dry bread, and yet nevertheless some of them believe in Christ: and as for the eternal things they would accommodate themselves; then they farther declared that they would live and die in the opinion of their forefathers, whether right or wrong. The habits of men and women as well as theirs and

51 A Tartar household. From C. Rechberg, *Des Peuples de la Russie*.

127

their children's shape are expressed by the annexed cut, which shews that they are indeed neither extravagant nor ridiculous.

Their dwellings are quadrangular wooden rooms, like those of the Russian peasants; only instead of ovens they use hearths, on which they burn wood, and dress their victuals. The smoak-hole which is in the roof, is covered with ice, as soon as the wood is burnt to a coal, which keeps the warmth in the room, and the light strikes through the bright and clear

52 The Voguls or Siberian Tartars. An illustration from the edition of 1706.

53 The Ostyaks or Khanty, who inhabited western Siberia. An illustration from the edition of 1706.

ice. They have no chairs, but instead of them a broad bench round the room, about an ell high, and two ells broad, on which they sit like the Persians, with their leggs across under them, and sleep on them at night. They live upon what their bow and arrows furnishes them with. Their chiefest game is that of Elks, whole herds of which are found here; these they cut in pieces, and hang in the air round their houses to dry; if it happen to rain upon them, and they begin to stink abominably, they dry them again, and eat them as a delicacy. They eat neither cocks, hens, nor hoggs. They have a pleasant way of catching wild beasts, for they place a sort of great bow in the woods, fastning a string to 'em, to which they fix some corn, or other bait, leaving only a place for the game to enter, so that the Elk, or any other beast that comes in there, cannot pass by without touching this snare; and when the bow lets fly, the arrows enter the fore part of the body, and he presently falls down. They also dig great pits in the woods, which they cover with reeds and grass, so that if any beast comes thither he is sure to fall in and is taken. These Tartars live in their villages all along the river Chusovaya to the castle of Utka, and are under the protection of his Tsarish Majesty, to whom they pay tribute, and live in security and peace. The extent of land which they inhabit reaches about 800 German miles in the north part of Siberia, nay, which is yet farther, to the North Samoyeds.

128

Having passed several miles up the Ob, part of which we sailed, and towed the rest with a line, on the 13th of August we passed by the mouth of the Vagay, which riseth originally out of the Truganian Mountains: This is a large river, its water is brown, and its course is extended north-north-west into the Ob, on this side of Narym, at which city we arrived on the 24th of the same month. It is situate on the side of the river in a fine country, and is provided with a fortress or castle, and an indifferent strong garrison of Cossacks. All the country around this city abounds with crosse and red foxes, beavers, ermines, sables, &c.

The banks of the Ob to this place are inhabited by a people called Ostyaks; which worship terrestrial gods, but acknowledge that according to nature, there must be a Lord in Heaven, that governs all; nevertheless they don't pay any worship at all to him, but have their own gods made of wood and earth, in several humane shapes. Some of the richest amongst them dress these deities in silken cloaths, made after the fashion of those of the Russian women. All of them have these idols placed in their hutts, which are made of barks of trees, sewed together with harts guts. On one side of the god hangs a bunch of humane and horse hair, and next that a wooden vessel, with milk pap, with which they daily supply their gods, and thrust it into their mouths with a spoon made for that purpose; but by reason the idols cannot swallow this their milk diet, it runs out again at both sides of their mouth, down their whole bodies, in such a filthy manner as is sufficient to disgust one from eating of that diet. When this nice god is to be worshipped or prayed to, his adorers stand bolt upright and toss their head up and down, without bending their back in the least; besides which they chirrup or whistle through the lips as we do when we call a dog.

They call their gods Saitan, and might indeed very well say Satan. Once several Ostyaks came on board the ship in which I was, to sell us fish, and one of my servants had a Nurenberg-bear in clockwork, which when wound up drummed and turned his head backward and forwards, continually moving his eyes, till the work was down. Our people set the bear at play a little: and as soon as ever the Ostyaks saw it, all of them performed to it their customary religious worship, and danced excessively to the honour of the bear, nodding their heads, and whistling at a great rate. They represented our bear for a right Saitan, crying out, What are our Saitans which we make? If we had such a Saitan, we would hang him all over with sables and black fox skins. They also asked whether this clock-work was to be sold; but I ordered it out of their sight, to avoid administring any occasion to idolatry.

As for what farther concerns these heathens, they have as

129

many wives as they can maintain, and marry their near relations without any scruple. If a relation dies, they cry incessantly for several days, covering their heads, and sitting on their knees in their hutts, and will not suffer themselves to be seen; but they carry the corps on poles to the ground to be buried. They are a poor people, and live very miserable in sorry hutts. They might indeed live well, since all parts near the Ob abound with great quantities of rich furrs; besides that there's extraordinary good fishing in that river, in which are very fine sturgeons, jacks, &c. insomuch that twenty great sturgeons may be bought of them for three penny-worth of tobacco; but they are so horrid lazy, that they don't desire to get any more than will barely suffice them annually for the winter: for when they travel they eat mostly fish, especially when they are on the water fishing, for then they live on nothing else. They are all of a middle stature, most of them yellowish or red haired; and their faces and noses disagreably broad; they are weak and unable to labour hard, not at all enclined to wars, and utterly uncapable of military exercises. Bows and arrows are their weapons, with which they shoot wild beasts, tho' not much addicted to this neither. Their cloaths consist of sturgeon and other fish skins, and they wear neither linnen nor woollen; their shoes and stockens are fastned together, and they wear a short coat with a cape, which in case of rain they pull over their heads. Their shoes are also made of fish-skins, and are sowed fast to their stockens, but not closely, so that their feet must necessarily be always wet. When they are upon the water, notwithstanding the thinness of their cloathing they will bear extraordinary great cold; for if it be but a common winter they are no better clad than above-mentioned; but if the winter prove hard, those who are thus clad are necessitated to put another coat of the same sort of fish-skins over that; and they express this severe weather amongst one another, by saying, Do you like the winter that forces one to wear two coats of skins? They sometimes go a hunting in the winter with a single coat only, and their breasts bare, depending upon warming themselves quickly with sliding and running over the ice in their schaites or sliding shoes; but if, as it several times happens, they are overtaken by an extraordinary severe frost, and it seems utterly improbable to escape it or save their lives, (so incredibly hard does it sometimes freeze on the Ob) they with utmost hast throw off their fish-skin coat, and fling themselves into the deep snow and willingly freeze to death; the reason why they pull off their coat is only that they may die the sooner, and with less pain.

The women's cloaths are almost like the men's; the men's greatest diversion is bear-hunting, to which sport they gather together in crouds, armed with no other weapon than a sharp iron like a large knife, fixed to a stick, about a fathom long. As soon as they have put up a bear, they run at him with these short spears, and having killed him they cut off his head, stick it upon a tree, run round it, and pay the profounded respect to it: After which they run to the dead body with repeated cries, asking the bear as follows, Who killed you? the Russians they answer themselves. Who cut off your head? A Russian Ax. Who cut up your belly? A knife which a Russian made. And more such like follies are they guilty of. In a word the Russians bear all the blame, and they are intirely innocent of the murther of the bear.

They have a sort of petty princes amongst them, one of which is called *Knyazka,* or Prince *Kurza Muganak,* whose authority extends over some hundreds of hutts, and he lays on and collects the tribute which they are obliged to pay to the Voyevody of his Tsarish Majesty. This potentate came with all his princely family and servants on board me, paid his compliment, and brought me a parcel of fresh fish as a present; which I requited by presenting him with some brandy and tobacco, with which he went on shoar very well contented; but returned immediately and invited me to his princely palace. I being very curious to see this great lord in his sumptuous place of residence, went thither, tho' I had no great appetite to his entertainment. Coming on shoar, the introductory ceremonies were not very particular. He acted the master of the ceremonies himself, and without much ado brought me to his magnificent apartment, which like the other hutts of the Ostyaks, was composed of only barks of trees very slightly sewed together. I found here four of his wives, two old and two young: one of the young ones had a red cloath coat on; and was set off with all sorts of glass corals about her neck and her middle, and in the curls of her hair, which hung down on both sides of her head in two rows; she had also in her ears great thread-wrought rings, with long strings of the same coral hanging at them. Each of these princesses presented me with a barrel made of birch-bark sewed together, and full of dry fish; but the youngest gave me a barrel of sturgeon fat, which was as yellow as gold. After I had received these presents, I caused them to be treated with brandy and tobacco, which is a great delicacy amongst them. In this whole princely building, I saw no other furniture than some cradles and chests made of barks of trees sewed together, in which the bed-cloaths lay, being of planed wood shavings, and yet almost as soft as feathers. These cradles stand at one end of the hutt, to avoid the fire, which is kindled in the middle, and the children lye naked in them. I also saw a copper kettle there, and some other kettles composed of barks of trees sewed together, in which they boil their victuals on coals, for in the flame they cannot do it.

To smoke tobacco (to which all both men and women are very much addicted) instead of pipes they use a stone kettle, in which they stick a pipe made for that purpose, and at two or three drawings after they have taken some water in their mouths, can suck out a whole pipe; and they swallow the smoak, after which they fall down and lye insensible, like dead men with distorted eyes, both hands and feet trembling for about half an hour. They foam at mouth, so that they fall into a sort of epilepsie: and we could not observe where the smoak vented it self, and in this manner several of them are lost. For as they are upon the water travelling, or sitting by the fire, some of these violent smokers fall into the water and are drowned, or into the fire and are burned; but some after they have sucked in the smoak let it out at their throats again, and these are in a better condition than the other; tho' some weaker constitutions are sometimes suffocated even thus with the smoak which they let into their bodies.

It is further observable that they are very angry, if any of their relations, tho' long dead, are named or mentioned. They are utterly unacquainted with all things before their own life time, and do not pretend to give any relation of them: nor can they either write or read: and tho' they are very fond of bread, they never trouble themselves with the tillage of land, or culture of gardens.

They have neither temples nor priests. Their shipping or boats on the outside are barks of trees sewed together, and the inside ribbs of very thin wood; they are two or three fathom long, and but an ell broad. And yet they can secure themselves in them in great storms, till they get on shoar. In winter time these Ostyaks live intirely under ground, there being no other entrance to their caves, but a hole left open on the surface of the earth to let out the smoak. If as is frequent a great snow falls, it often happens that as according to their custom they lye asleep naked round the fire, part of their body which lies a little distant from the fire, is two or three fingers thick covered with snow; when they perceive themselves cold they turn about to the fire, and bestow the best place on the cold part of their body a little while, and so take no more notice of it, being a very hardy people.

When an Ostyak is jealous of one of his wives with another man, he cuts some hair off the under part of a bear's skin, which he carries to the man whom he suspects: if he be innocent he then accepts it, but if he be guilty, they believe he dare not venture to touch it, but acknowledges the truth, and then amicably makes up the business with the husband, and the wife is sold. But if any should presume to be so rash, as to take the hair, tho' he was guilty, they tell us they are assured, that the bear's skin from whence that hair was cut off, will again become a living bear, which after the expiration of three days, will appear in the wood, and tear the perjured wretch to pieces who was not affraid fraudulently to receive his hair in order to deny the truth. On this occasion they invoke bows, arrows, axes, and knives, and firmly believe that

132

if the guilty take any of these he shall certainly be killed by
those individual instruments which he accepts, within the
space of a few days: which is not only averred by themselves,
but also unanimously backed by the Russians, who live all
round those parts. But enough of these Ostyaks. The shoar of
the river Ob on which they live, is all untilled land from the
sea to the River Tom, by reason of the extream cold; so that
no corn, fruit, or honey is here produced; there being only a
few nuts which grow on the cedar trees.

Ysbrant Ides, *Three Years Travels from Moscow over-land to China*
(London 1706)

Two Weeks in February 1699

Peter the Great's 'Great Embassy' to Western Europe was cut short by
news of a further rebellion among the Streltsy, who were intent on
bringing Peter's half-sister, the former Regent Sophia, to the throne.
Peter's revenge was savage and merciless. Here it is recorded in the
diary of Johann Korb, an Austrian diplomat.

February 1.—The Imperial Lord Envoy acquitted himself
of a duty of punctilio by visiting the Brandenburgh Lord
Envoy in state.

A Tsar's entertainment given to the Brandenburgher. He
was more honoured than the Pole or the Dane, for the table
was laid with fifty dishes and twenty-four jars of drinkables—
a token to the others how much less they are liked.

2.—To-day Bacchus consecrated with solemn Epicurean
rites, to wit with feasting, the house which the Tsar lately gave
to his favourite Menshikov. Last week thirty Streltsy came here
from the camp at Azov to inspect the state of Moscow, and to
see how they might bring their treasonable designs to bear
according to their desires. But indications of their impious
designs being conveyed to the Tsar, all were seized, and
underwent for the first time the atrocious torture of the rack.
the Tsar questioning them.

3.—The Brandenburgh Envoy, reciprocating the customary
civilities, visited the Imperial Lord Envoy, with the whole of
his magnificent train for greater state.

While the thirty Streltsy above mentioned are undergoing
torture here, again 500 Streltsy more have revolted in the
neighbourhood of Moscow.

4.—For the fresh rebels new racks were made ready. Every
Boyar is an inquisitor; to torture the guilty was deemed a
token of remarkable loyalty. The officials of a certain Envoy,
whose curiosity for sight-seeing had led them to Preobrazhen-

133

skoye, had inspected various prisons of the criminals, hastening whithersoever more atrocious howls betokened a tragedy of greater anguish. Already they had passed with horror through three, when howls more appalling and groans more horrible than they had yet heard stimulated them to examine what cruelty was going on in a fourth house. But hardly had they set foot within it than they were about withdrawing again, being startled at the sight of the Tsar and the Boyars. Naryshkin,

54 Standards of the fourteen regiments of Streltsy, from Erich Palmquist 1674.

Romadonovsky, and Tikhon Nikitovich were the chief persons. As they were about retiring Naryshkin addressed them, inquiring who they were, and whence and why they had come there. They felt sore at being caught by foreigners in the performance of that office. He then ordered an interpreter to tell them to go to Romadonovsky's house, for that the Prince had something to say to them. When they refused, the Tsar's commands were added, with the threat, that if they would not obey, their contempt should not go unpunished. Nothing dismayed by this threat, trusting in their freedom, they replied still more confidently to those who were giving these orders, that they listened to commands from no person whatsoever—that if the Prince had anything to say to them, he was not ignorant what Envoy's household they were, and that at his residence all could be better settled. As they were going off, one of the military officers followed them to drag them by violence to the place the Boyars had ordered, and did not hesitate to lay hands upon a horse at full gallop, to stop him; but the party of the officials was stronger both in courage and numbers; they dashed aside by main force his attempt to stop them, and reached safe shelter. Perhaps for penalty of their rash curiosity, they would have been forced to exhibit themselves before the Boyars in the same capacity as they had detected them.

5.—Placards were put up in the city that those who meant to enlist in the army might withhold, except serfs of the Boyars, or others that were liable in virtue of other bonds to their lords.

An accomplice of the rebellion was undergoing the penal question. While he was being tied to the rack, his lamentations gave rise to a hope that the truth might be pressed from him by torments; but the event was quite the contrary, for as soon as his body began to be stretched with the rope, besides the horrible crackling of his members which were being torn from their natural sockets, he remained mute, even when twenty strokes of the knout were superadded, as if the accumulation of his pain were too great to afflict the senses. All believed that the man must be crushed with excess of calamity to such a degree, that he must have lost the power of moaning and speech. So he was loosed from the infamous rack and rope, and then asked whether he knew the persons present. To the astonishment of all, he enumerated the names of every one of them. But when they put a fresh question about the treason, once more he became utterly dumb, and did not break silence during a whole quarter of an hour, while he was roasted at a fire by the Tsar's command. The Tsar, tired at last of this exceedingly wicked stubbornness of the traitor, furiously raised the stick which he happened to have in his hand, and thrust it violently into his jaws—clenched in obstinate silence—to break them open, and make him give tongue and speak. And these words, too, that fell from the raging man: 'Confess, beast, confess!' loudly proclaimed how great was his wrath.

About eleven at night, Prince Galitsyn summoned the Brandenburgh Envoy to his presence, alleging that he had business of great importance to treat of with him. I don't know where the Muscovites found out this custom of preferring to treat of their affairs in fear and trembling at night, rather than avail themselves of the daylight. Perhaps it is because a Sovereign—whom absolute power renders more feared than revered—is suspicious of frequent meetings between the magnates and foreigners.

6.—The first conference of the Brandenburgh Envoy with the High President of the Ambassadorial Chancery, Leo Kirilovich Naryshkin, took place.

7.—Dr. Zoppot began to practise anatomy in the presence of the Tsar and a great number of Boyars, who, to their disgust, were coerced by the Tsar's commands.

One of the rebels under examination had made a dagger to kill himself, but strength failed him to complete his crime; still the wound was such that, if neglected, it would lead to death. It was the Sovereign's interest that the man should not

135

escape examination and torture by a premature death; so he commanded that every diligence should be employed by the physicians to heal his wound. Nay, he had the heart to be present, and to solace the criminal-patient when the medicines were being prepared, in order that the doctors might be more attentive to do everything faithfully for the best to effect a cure on account of his presence.

8, 9.—Mr. Adam Weyd splendidly entertained the Tsar, the Boyars, the Foreign Representatives, and a great many other officials, at a sumptuous banquet. The Tsar, however, was wrapped in deep thought, and his features bore rather the impress of sadness than gaiety.

10.—The nobility summoned by the recent mandates came in to learn what commands they were to receive. To those who had offered their services for the army it was intimated that they could not be incorporated in the troops. It seems monstrous that the news of peace that have come are a cause of public sorrow, even to those that were sighing so ardently for peace up to the present, and they are adverse to it, at least in outward appearance, in order not to give offence.

11.—The Tsar when, to his discontent, he heard of his armistice for two years, as there was nothing else to be done, had publication made by ukaz placarded in the public places that there would be no military expedition that year, and that those who had come on summons for that purpose might go home again. Of the eighty German colonels he had resolved to discharge forty, that the expense might be reserved for times when there would be more need for it, and that fifty Russian colonels might retain their functions without pay.

Fresh treason broke out in Siberia: six hundred horsemen of those they call the Tartar horde raised dangerous troubles, and with horrible robberies, rapine, and spoils, infested and upset everything. Public placards were put up inviting all the populace to come to Preobrazhenskoye, in order that they might see what penalties followed upon the treason of the Streltsy. In divers places there was an execution of criminals: many lost their heads, a hundred others their ears and noses; some were branded with the mark of an eagle upon the face by way of a sign of ignominy.

12.—A certain foreigner, distinguished by an office which is held sacred among the nations, looking for comforts that are not compatible with the rigours of a northern climate, drank an immoderate quantity of wine, and in order to try and cool the heat of his body with the freezing air, drove round all the streets of the city in an open carriage, and did not return home until he had, by striking and banging against things, shattered the carriage so that it was no longer capable of bearing its burden and driver. He attributes it to his good luck that he was not caught by the Muscovite night-rovers, or massacred utterly, especially as the main delight of the

Muscovite populace is to rob and run riot against the Germans. We had a splendid proof of this to-day. One of our messengers that knows the Muscovite language fell in with a Russian, who was furiously vomiting forth a quantity of foul speeches against the Germans. 'Ye German dogs!' he was saying, 'you have been robbing long enough at your ease, but the day is at hand when you shall suffer and pay the penalty.' The messenger,

55 The imperial emblem of Peter I, with the two-headed Byzantine eagle and showing the provinces under his rule. An illustration from the Vienna edition of 1700.

56 The mass execution of the Streltsy by hanging and beheading. An illustration from the Vienna edition of 1700.

in order to have another witness to this contumelious language, called a soldier, and at last ordered the rascal to be dragged off in custody; but, by command of the Imperial Lord Envoy, the fellow was left to the discretion of the soldiers, who stripped him naked and loaded him with a sound fustigation.

138

13.—A direful day is this, and one that ought truly to be
marked with a black token, for it beheld the execution of two
hundred men, all whose heads were cut off with the axe. In a
very wide space, close to the Kremlin, beams were stretched
for the criminals to lay their heads upon. I measured the length

myself in paces—it was two beams in breadth. His Majesty the Tsar, along with a certain Alexander, in whose society he takes great delight, came thither in an open carriage, and crossing the funeral area, entered a place near at hand, where thirty that were found guilty of this nefarious conspiracy expiated their crime with death. Meanwhile the dismal crowd of criminals had filled up the space above described, and the Tsar had come back in order that the men should be punished in his presence who cogitated such a crime with impious counsels against him when absent. A scribe, mounting upon a bench that was brought by soldiers, proclaimed, in several places, the sentence framed against the rebels, that the enormity of the fault and the justice of the punishment about being inflicted, might be the better known to the multitude round about. When he ceased the executioner began the tragedy; there was a kind of order among the unfortunate wretches; they all followed one another in turn, without any sadness on their features, or any horror of their imminent death. Yet I do not want to refer that contempt of death to greatness of soul. I rather think that the infamy of their atrocious guilt, and the cruel remembrance of the tortures with which they were daily butchered, had brought them to that contempt of life and self. A wife and children followed one of them up to the very beam, with great and frightful wailing. As this man was on the point of lying down, he gave his gloves and linen—all that he had left—to his wife and the sorrowful group of his beloved offspring, by way of last farewell. Another, to whose turn it came to kiss the fatal beam, complained that he was forced to go innocent to death; and the Tsar, who was not farther than one step away from him, answered him: 'Die, wretch! If thou be innocent, the guilt of thy blood will be mine.' Besides the Tsar and the above-named Alexander, some others of the principal Muscovites were there. The Tsar told one of them to take the axe himself; and when he would excuse himself, saying that he had not sufficient courage for that office, he was deemed worthy of being told he was an ass. When the execution was over, it pleased the Tsar's Majesty to sup at General Gordon's; but he showed no sign of cheerfulness, insisting to several upon the obstinancy and stubbornness of the criminals. He detailed with indignant words to General Gordon and the Muscovite magnates present, that one of the condemned was so insolent that he dared, just as he was about lying down upon the beam, to address the Tsar with these words: 'Make way, my lord, it is for me to lie here.' Out of 150, only three confessed themselves guilty of the crime and treason, and begged pardon of the Tsar's Majesty there present, for which they were held worthy of their Sovereign's clemency, were freed from the penalty of death, and obtained pardon for their delict. But for next day a fresh scene of execution was being decked; and the Tsar invited General Gordon to it, telling him that he wished to execute the criminals by a new mode, unknown to his people, to wit, with the sword instead of the axe. Moreover, the often-mentioned Alexander showed that evening, riding in an open carriage through all the thoroughfares of the city, by the exceedingly frequent flourishing of a naked sword how sanguinary a tragedy he expected next day.

Before it was quite dark, a certain Russian and eighteen accomplices of his were arrested and imprisoned for rapine committed.

14.—A selection of officers took place at General Sheyn's, in Preobrazhenskoye,–but at the Yauza 150 rebels were dragged to execution. The Tsar is said to have cut off 84 rebel heads with the sword, Boyar Pleshcheyev holding up each criminal in such a manner by the hair as to render the blow more certain. Three swords were prepared for this use: one, while it was being brandished, flew in pieces and missed its stroke. The Cossacks who had mixed themselves up with this revolt were quartered and set upon the ignominious stake, as a terror and example of punishment to those whose restless spirit might henceforward, perhaps, tempt them to flagitious daring. Five more, guilty of more insolent counsel, had their hands and feet first cut off, and then were beheaded.

The Tsar's Postmaster has had Wednesday announced as the day for bringing letters to the post–for it was previously Saturday.

Johann Korb, *Diary of an Austrian Secretary of Legation at the Court of Czar Peter the Great* (London 1863)

Peter the Great

Although a witness of Peter's excesses, Johann Korb was fulsome in his praise of the Tsar's aims and of the benefit which would inevitably come to backward Russia.

Those brilliant gifts of nature and of soul which have spread his fame throughout almost every realm of the earth, pointed him out from his infancy for kingly power and sovereign sway. A well set stature, well proportioned limbs, the vivacity of his youth, and an address beyond his years, so conciliated the affections and good will of his subjects, on account of their expectations of his natural qualifications, that he was openly preferred by the contending suffrages of numbers of people to his brother Ivan Alekseyevich, who was called to the throne of his progenitors by that pre-eminence of primogeniture which is held sacred by the nations. Ever self-reliant, he con-

57 In 1699 Peter had a fleet of some eighty ships under construction in the yards at Voronezh which were soon to sail down the Don to the sea of Azov and Kerch. From the Vienna edition of 1700.

temns death and danger, the apprehension of which terrifies others. Often he has gone quite alone to traitors and conspirators against his life, and either from their reflection on the greatness of their crime, or dread and remorse for their divulged treason alone he has made them quail by his Majestic presence; and, lest this creeping and dangerous pest should spread, he has delivered them up to chains and prison. In 1694 he sailed out of the port of Archangel, into the North Sea, beyond Kola. A storm arose and drove the ships upon the most perilous rocks. The seamen were already crying out in despair; the Boyars, who had accompanied their sovereign, had betaken themselves to their prayers and their devotion of making thousands of crossings–no doubt in terror at the contemplation of such an awful shipwreck. Alone, amidst the fury of the wild sea, the fearless Tsar took the helm with a most cheerful countenance, restored courage to their despairing souls, and, until the sea subsided, found an asylum for life and limb on that very rock upon which, in rough weather, many vessels had been a prey to the foaming brine.

A few years ago, before his two years' tour, he told his magnates, at Sheremetev's, at whose house he was dining, to what Saint, under God's providence, he ascribed his happy

142

escape from that tempest, 'When,' said he, 'I was sailing to the Solovetskiy Monastery from Archangel, with several of you, I was, as you know, in danger of shipwreck. How great was the horror of death and the dread of what seemed certain destruction that beset your minds, I forbear to record. Now we have escaped that danger, we have got through our peril, but I hope you will think with me, that it is but right to do what I swore to do, and fulfil the vow I made to heaven. I then proffered a vow to God and to my holy patron, the Apostle Peter, that I would go to Rome to pray at his tomb, less out of anxiety for my own safety than for all yours. Tell me, Boris

58 Peter the Great by Sir Godfrey Kneller, painted for William III during the Tsar's visit to London in 1698.

59 The stone for the bronze statue of Peter the Great being brought to St Petersburg, 20 March 1770.

Petrovich,' thus he addressed Sheremetev, 'what are the country and the towns like? As you have been in those parts you must be able to tell all about them.' Sheremetev praised the amenity and beauty of the country, and the Tsar subjoined: 'Some of you shall come with me when I am going there; when the Turk has been humbled, I will acquit myself of my vow.' His late most serene mother tried to discourage him from this project, and through her the Russians suggested many figments against the Apostolic See. His answer to her was: 'If you had not been my mother I could hardly restrain myself. My veneration for that name pleads your excuse for what you have dared to speak. But know that death is the penalty that awaits whosoever henceforward shall presume to blame my intention or resist it.' And to Rome assuredly he

would have gone in performance of his vow, had not such pressing dangers summoned him back to Moscow, on the breaking out of a revolt in his realm.

With what spirit, too, he laboured to introduce into Muscovy those polite arts that had for ages been proscribed there, may be easily gathered from his having sent into various countries of Europe,—into Germany, Italy, England, and Holland,—the more talented children of his principal subjects, in order that they might learn, by intercourse, the wisdom and arts of the most polished nations, and on their return be ornaments of Muscovy, and in their turn excite their juniors to the like deserts. He made known his reasons for this plan, some years ago, to his Boyars, explaining its utility to them. They all commended the monarch's prudence, but insinuated that such immense good, however desirable it might be, was unattainable. That the genius of the Muscovites was unsuited to such pursuits; that the money expended on it would be wasted in vain; and that he would fatigue himself and his subjects with profitless labour. The Tsar was indignant at these sayings, which were only worthy of the profound ignorance of those that gave utterance to them. For they liked their benighted darkness, and nothing but shame at their own deformity was capable of drawing them into the light. 'Are we then born less blest than other nations.' the Tsar continued, 'that the divinity should have infused inept minds into our bodies? Have we not hands? Have we not eyes? Have we not the same habit of body that suffices foreign nations for their internal culture? Why have we alone degenerate and rude souls? Why should we alone be left out as unworthy of the glory of human science? By Hercules! we have the same minds; we can do like other folk if we only will it. For nature has given to all mankind the same groundwork and seed of virtues; we are all born to all those things; when the stimulus is applied, all those properties of the soul that have been, as it were, sleeping, shall be awakened.' The greatest things may be expected from such a Prince. Let the Muscovites congratulate themselves on the treasure they possess in him, for they are now really fortunate. He chose his wife in the family of Lapukhin, and she bore him a son named Alexis Petrovich, a youth splendidly gifted and adorned with ingenuous virtues, on whom rest the hopes of his father, and the fortunes and tranquillity of Muscovy.

Johann Korb, *Diary of an Austrian Secretary of Legation at the Court of Czar Peter the Great* (London 1863)

60 Cornelius Le Brun, frontispiece to his book *Travels into Muscovy,* London, 1737. After a painting by Kneller, engraved by Valek.

The Entry into Moscow of Peter the Great after his Victory at Nöteborg

After his return from Europe in the summer of 1698 Peter decided to start war with Sweden for possession of the Baltic provinces. After signing a peace treaty with Turkey in 1700, under which Azov was ceded to the Russians, Peter moved against the Swedes and besieged the Swedish town of Narva on the Gulf of Finland, but was routed by Charles XII. Peter immediately began to re-organize his armies and launched them in a campaign which gave him the whole of Ingria by 1704 and led eventually to his famous victory at Poltava in the Ukraine in 1709. The storming of the fortress of Nöteborg in 1702, which he was to rename Schüsselburg, was the first of his victories and made possible the founding of the city of St Petersburg in the following year. Cornelius Le Brun was a Dutch painter in Moscow at the time of Peter's victory and provides a detailed description of Moscow's welcome for its triumphant Tsar.

On the twentieth [September 1702], news arrived that Nöteborg had been taken by his Majesty's forces, and that the city had surrendered on certain terms and conditions, after it had sustained three vigorous attacks, and on the twenty-third Te Deum was sung upon the occasion . . .

News came, in the beginning of December, that the Tsar was arrived at a place called Pskov, which is about fourscore and ten versts from Moscow; from thence he came to Solnikov, a country seat belonging to Prince Lofrëilis, his uncle, thirty versts only from this capital; from thence to Nikolskoye, at the mansion-house of Prince Michael Cherkassky, Governor of Siberia, which is but seven versts from Moscow.

At that time every thing was in readiness for his Tsarian Majesty's triumphal entry; and most of the foreign merchants had received orders to furnish themselves with a greater number of horses than usual; with an attendant, drest in the German fashion, to conduct the artillery, that had been taken from the Swedes. The foreign ministers, our resident, and the English Consul, accompanied by several merchants, set out the next day, in order to pay their compliments to the Tsar at Nikolskoye, and returned the next morning, which was the fourth of December, and the day appointed for this Monarch to make his entry. For this purpose several triumphal arches had been prepared before-hand made of wood, and erected in the street of Myasnets; the first in the Red-Wall, over-against the Greek monastery, which is situate near the printing-house, and the house of the Marshal Sheremetev; the second in the White-Wall, near the Admiralty-Office, about four hundred paces from the former. The streets and the fields were crowded with spectators to see this pompous procession; and for my own part, I crossed the streets, and went out of town to see the first of it. When I came, I perceived there was a halt, that things might be put in order, and that the Tsar himself was personally employed in the regulation; and as I was on foot, I approached him in order to pay him my congratulations on the occasion; and his happy return. He thanked me, and favoured me with his friendly embraces, and seemed to be pleased that I was still resident in his dominions. He then took

61 The Russian victory over the Swedes at Hangöudd, 27 July 1714.

me by the hand, and told me, that he had some ship's colours to shew me, and that I should have free liberty to draw whatever I pleased. Whilst I was taking a draught, a certain Russian nobleman, with several servants in his retinue, came, and took the paper from me, and called to a German officer to know what I was doing; but when he was informed that I was at work by the Tsar's own order, he returned it me again, and I finished my design, which I could never have done, had not I been favoured with his Majesty's special licence.

This public entry was made in the following order. In the first place came the regiment of guards, which consisted of eight hundred men, under the command of Colonel de Ridder, by birth a German. One half of this body were drest in scarlet, after the German manner; and the other in Russian habits; because there had not been time sufficient to finish their new cloaths. The Swedish prisoners, as well such as were soldiers, as others who were peasants, walked between two, three a-breast; and were divided into seven several bands, each consisting of about fourscore, or fourscore and four persons, making in the whole, about five hundred and eighty men, between three companies of soldiers. After these came two fine sumpter-horses, and a company of grenadiers, drest in green, lined with scarlet, after the German mode, with this exception only, that they had bear-skin caps on, instead of hats; these were the first grenadier-guards; and after them came six halberdiers, five hautboys, and six officers. Then came the Royal regiment of Preobrazhenskoye, consisting of four hundred men, all new-cloathed after the German fashion; in green, lined with scarlet, and white laced hats; with the Tsar himself, and Prince Alexander at the head of them, who were preceded by nine German flutes, and some fine led horses. This regiment was followed by a party of that belonging to Semenovskoye, his Majesty's guards also, all cloathed in blue, lined with scarlet; and after them came the colours which had been taken from the Swedes. First, two standards, followed by a large flag, which had been displayed upon the castle of Nöteborg, carried by four soldiers; next came six ships-colours, and twenty-five ensigns, blue, green, yellow, and red. Each carried by two soldiers. Most of these ensigns had two golden lions and a crown painted over their heads. After these came forty pieces of cannon; some drawn by four, some by six horses, all of a colour; four great mortars, and fifteen brass field-pieces; some larger than the other; then came another mortar-piece; and after that came several very long and heavy brass cannon; some drawn by six, and others by eight horses. After these came a large chest of kitchen utensils, ten sledges with fire-arms, three drums, and another sledge with smith's tools, and a large pair of bellows. Then came the officers who had been taken prisoners, amounting in the whole, to the number of forty; each of whom walked between two soldiers; and after them came several sledges with such other prisoners as were either sick or wounded. When these were passed by, a small band of Russian soldiers closed the procession. It was about one in the afternoon when they first entered into the city; and after they had passed Tver Gates, which stands to the northward, they marched up to the first triumphal arch, and the regiment of guards went through. Here his Tsarian Majesty halted for a full quarter of an hour, in order, not only to refresh himself, but to receive the congratulations of his clergy. As in this place, the street was pretty broad, the triumphal structure was composed of three arches; that in the middle was a large one, and the two on each side were considerably smaller: all which were so covered with tapestry, pictures, figures, and devices, that none of the wood-work could be discerned. At the top was a balcony, where were planted eight young musicians, two and two, very richly drest. The middle arch was crowned with an eagle, and a great variety of trophies.

62 The Barber cuts the Dissenter's Beard. A pro-Petrine popular print, depicting one of the Tsar's moves to Europeanize Russia.

149

And all the houses, within sight of it, were hung with carpets, tapestry, and pictures; all the balconies were full of streamers; and in some, which were very near the arches, were planted a large band of musicians, with all sorts of instruments, which, being accompanied by a very good organ, made a very polite concert. The streets were strewed with green boughs, and other things of the like colour, in which were planted a great number of the nobility. The Princess, his Tsarian Majesty's sister, the Tsarina, and the Princesses her daughters, attended by a great number of Russian and foreign ladies, were planted at some small distance, in the house of Yakov Vasilevich Fedorov, in order to see the procession.

After the Tsar had saluted the Princess, he advanced on towards the second arch, which was decorated in as elegant a manner as the first; and having marched through the city, in the same order, he went out at the gate of Myasnets, and proceeded towards the Sloboda, which is principally inhabited by the Germans; where, when he was arrived, the Dutch resident made him an offer of some of the best wine he had; but his Majesty chose a glass of beer, which I had the honour to deliver into his own hand. As the glass was somewhat large, he drank only some part of it, and moved forwards to Preobrazhenskoye; as night, however, came upon him before his departure from the Sloboda, he mounted his horse; and then the show was over. Notwithstanding the multitude of spectators on this joyful occasion, I did not hear that any fatal consequences attended it; every thing was conducted with the utmost decency and decorum, and every one seemed pleased, since there was no mischief done (as we hinted before) in any of the streets, notwithstanding there were numberless scaffolds erected all along for the reception of the spectators.

Cornelius le Brun, *Travels into Muscovey* (London 1759)

Peter's Social Reforms

Captain John Perry, an accomplished hydraulic engineer, served fourteen not particularly contented years under Peter (up to 1712), but was a fervent admirer of the Tsar and opponent of the reactionary factions working to subvert his policies. The extract describes Peter's attempt to westernize the clothes and habits of the Russian people.

It had been the manner of the Russes, like the Patriarchs of old, to wear long beards hanging down upon their bosoms, which they comb'd out with pride, and kept smooth and fine, without one hair to be diminished; they wore even the upperlip of that length, that if they drank at any time, their beard dipp'd into the cup, so that they were obliged to wipe it when they had done, altho' they wore the hair of their head cut short at the same time; it being the custom only for the popes or priests, to wear the hair of their heads hanging down upon their backs for distinction sake. The Tsar therefore to reform this foolish custom, and to make them look like other Europeans, ordered a tax to be laid, on all gentlemen, merchants, and others of his subjects (excepting the priests and common peasants, or slaves) that they should each of them pay 100 rubles per annum, for the wearing of their beards, and that even the common people should pay a kopek at the entrance of the gates of any of the towns or cities of Russia, where a person should be deputed at the gate to receive it as often as they had occasion to pass. This was look'd upon to be little less than a sin in the Tsar, a breach of their religion, and held to be a great grievance for some time, as more particularly by being brought in by the strangers. But the women liking their husbands and sweet-hearts the better, they are now for the most part pretty well reconciled to this practice.

It is most certain, that the Russes had a kind of religious respect and veneration for their beards; and so much the more, because they differed herein from strangers, which was back'd by the humours of the priests, alledging that the holy men of old had worn their beards according to the model of the picture of their saints, and which nothing but the absolute authority of the Tsar, and the terror of having them (in a merry humour) pull'd out by the roots, or sometimes taken so rough off, that some of the skin went with them, could ever have prevailed with the Russes to have parted with their beards. On this occasion there were letters drop'd about the streets, sealed and directed to his Tsarish Majesty, which charged him with tyranny and heathenism, for forcing them to part with their beards.

63 An eighteenth-century Boyar.

About this time the Tsar came down to Voronezh, where I was then on service, and a great many of my men that had worn their beards all their lives, were now obliged to part with them, amongst which, one of the first that I met with just coming from the hands of the barber, was an old Russ carpenter that had been with me at Kamyshinka, who was a very good workman with his hatchet, and whom I always had a friendship for. I jested a little with him on this occasion, telling him that he was become a young man, and asked him what he had done with his beard? Upon which he put his hand in his bosom and pull'd it out, and shew'd it to me; farther telling me, that when he came home, he would lay it up to have it put in his coffin and buried along with him, that he might be able to give an account of it to St. Nicholas, when he came to the other world; and that all his brothers (meaning his fellow-workmen who had been shaved that day) had taken the same care.

As to their cloaths, the general habit which the Russes used to wear, was a long vestment hanging down to the middle of the small of their legs, and was gathered and laid in pleats upon their hips, little differing from the habit of women's petticoats.

The Tsar therefore resolving to have this habit changed, first gave orders, that all his Boyars and people whatsoever, that came near his Court, and that were in his pay, should, upon penalty of falling under his displeasure, according to their several abilities, equip themselves with handsome cloaths made after the English fashion, and to appear with gold and silver trimming, those that could afford it. And next he commanded, that a pattern of cloaths of the English fashion should be hung up at all the gates of the city of Moscow, and that publication should be made, that all persons (excepting the common peasants who brought goods and provisions into the city) should make their cloaths according to the said patterns; and that whosoever should disobey the said orders, and should be found passing any of the gates of the city in their long habits, should either pay 2 *grivni* (which is 20 pence) or be obliged to kneel down at the gates of the city, and to have their coats cut off just even with the ground, so much as it was longer than to touch the ground when they kneeled down, of which there were many hundreds of coats that were cut accordingly; and being done with a good humour, it occasioned mirth among the people, and soon broke the custom of their wearing long coats, especially in places near Moscow, and those other towns wherever the Tsar came.

The woman also, but more particularly the ladies about court, were ordered to reform the fashion of their cloaths too, according to the English manner, and that which so much the more and sooner reconciled them to it, was this: it had been always the custom of Russia, at all entertainments, for the women not to be admitted into the sight or conversation with men; the very houses of all men of any quality or fashion, were built with an entrance for the women a-part, and they used to be kept separate in an apartment by themselves; only it was sometimes the custom for the master of the house, upon the arrival of any guest whom he had a mind to honour, to bring out his wife the back way from her apartment, attended with the company of her maids, to be saluted, and to present a dram of brandy round to the whole company; which being done, they used to retire back to their own apartment, and were to be seen no more. But the Tsar being not only willing to introduce the English habits, but to make them more particularly pleasing to the Russ ladies, made an order, that from thenceforward, at all weddings, and at other publick entertainments, the women as well as the men, should be invited, but in an English fashion dress; and that they should be entertained in the same room with the men, like as he had seen in foreign countries; and that the evenings should be concluded with musick and dancing, at which he himself often used to be present with most of the nobility and ladies about court. And there was no wedding of any distinction, especially amongst the foreigners, but the Tsar had notice of it, and he himself would honour it with his presence, and very often gave a present to the bride, suitable to the extraordinary expence that such entertainments cost them, especially when married to the officers that were newly come into the countrey. At these entertainments, the Russ ladies soon reconciled themselves to the English Dress, which they found rendred them more agreeable.

There was another thing also which the women very well liked in these regulations of the Tsar. It had been the custom of Russia, in case of marriages, that the match used always to be made up between the parents on each side, without any previous meeting, consent or liking of one another, tho' they marry very young in that countrey, sometimes when neither the bride nor the bridegroom are thirteen years of age, and therefore supposed not to be fit judges for themselves. The bridegroom on this occasion was not to see nor to speak to the bride but once before the day that the nuptials was to be performed; at which meeting, the friends on both sides were to come together at the bride's father's house, and then the bride was to be brought out between her maids into the room where the bridegroom was; and after a short complement being made, she was to present the bridegroom with a dram of brandy, or other liquor, in token of her consent and good liking of his person. And afterwards all care was to be taken that she was not to see the bridegroom again until the day of marriage; and then she was to be carried with a veil all over her face, which was not to be uncover'd till she came into the church. And thus this blind bargain was made.

But the Tsar taking into his consideration this unacceptable way of joining young people together without their own approbation, which might in a very great measure be reckon'd to be the occasion of that discord and little love which is shewn to one another afterwards, it being a thing common in Russia to beat their wives in a most barbarous manner, very often so inhumanly that they die with the blows; and yet they do not suffer for the murther, being a thing interpreted by the law to be done by way of correction, and therefore not culpable. The wives on the other hand being thus many times made desperate, murther their husbands in revenge for the ill usage they receive; on which occasion there is a law made, that when they murther their husbands, they are set alive in the ground, standing upright, with the earth fill'd about them, and only their heads left just above the earth, and a watch set over them, that they shall not be relieved till they are starved to death; which is a common sight in that countrey, and I have known them live sometimes seven or eight days in this posture.

153

These sad prospects made the Tsar in much pity to his people, take away the occasion of these cruelties as much as possible; and [the forced marriages being supposed to be one cause thereof, made an order that no young couple should be marry'd together, without their own free liking and consent; and that all persons should be admitted to visit and see each other at least six weeks before they were married together.] This new order is so well approved of, and so very pleasing to the young people, that they begin to think much better of foreigners, and to have a better liking of such other new customs as the Tsar has introduced, than they ever did before, especially amongst the more knowing and better sort of people.

It had been a very pompous custom among all the great Boyars, to retain in their service, as a piece of state and grandeur, a great number of useless servants or attendants, which when they went any where abroad in the streets of Moscow, some went before them bare-headed, and others follow'd after in a long train, in all sorts of dresses and colours; and when their Boyars or Lords went either on horseback, or in a coach or sled in Moscow, it was a piece of grandeur to ride softly, though in the coldest weather, that these people might keep pace with them on foot; and the great Boyars' ladies also used to have the like numerous attendance.

But the Tsar, who always rides swift, had set them another pattern, for he went only with a few servants on horseback, cloath'd in a handsome uniform livery; his courtiers did the same; and commanded the example to be follow'd among all the Boyars and persons of distinction; and that the same might be the more effectual, the Tsar, soon after he came from his travels, [order'd a list to be taken of all the loose attendants that hung about these Boyars' houses, and order'd them to be sent into the Army.] This went very much against the grain, and great interest and intercession was made, and sums of money given for many of them to be excus'd, especially such of these

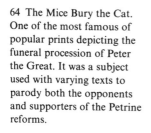

64 The Mice Bury the Cat. One of the most famous of popular prints depicting the funeral procession of Peter the Great. It was a subject used with varying texts to parody both the opponents and supporters of the Petrine reforms.

attendants as were really gentlemen, and waited on these lords only in expectation of preferment; but however, the Tsar's orders were to be obey'd, and there was a draught made of several thousands of the unnecessary or supernumerary attendants, and sent to serve in the army.

John Perry, *The State of Russia Under the Present Czar* (London 1716)

Manners and Masquerades

F. C. Weber, an Hanoverian, worked as a secretary in the English Embassy in St Petersburg for six years during the latter half of Peter's reign. His book, originally published in Dutch, is a valuable and reliable source of information on many aspects of life at the time. The extracts which follow provide *a.* an amusing description of his first encounter with Russian social etiquette; *b.* an account of the famous mock-wedding of Peter's jester Zotov, which is followed by *c.* a description of the real, tragicomic marriage of two dwarfs. The last extract is the general preface to what was the first detailed account of the buildings of St Petersburg.

.a

On the 23d of February [1714] the Tsar set out on his return to Petersburg. When I arrived there, I was surprized to find instead of a regular city, as I expected, a heap of villages linked together, like some plantation in the West Indies. However at present Petersburg may with reason be looked upon as a wonder of the world, considering its magnificent palaces, sixty odd thousand houses, and the short time that was employed in the building of it.

I was hardly arrived in this new residence when Admiral Apraksin gave a magnificent entertainment to the whole Court, and by his Tsarish Majesty's Order, caused me also to be invited. This was the day on which I entered upon my apprenticeship, and paid pretty dear for my first instructions. Being come to the door of the hall, I acquainted the commanding officer who I was, but instead of being admitted, I had foul language returned to me, and they kept me out by putting their halbards across the door. I alledged the abovesaid invitation and my character, but this had so little effect that with the greatest rudeness they turned me down stairs. I forthwith applyed to a friend, who acquainted the Court with the rude usage I had met with; soon after which the said officer came to me to conduct me in, begging my excuse for what had passed. On this occasion a certain minister gave me the following lesson, that seeing the Russians knew nothing as yet from whence I came, I ran a great hazard of exposing my self to the like treatment for the future, unless I changed my plain though clean dress, and appeared all trimmed over with gold and silver, and with a couple of footmen walking before me, and bawling out, *Clear the Way*. I had no time to conn over this important lesson, and to reflect on that rude method of teaching people; for I was soon made sensible that I had a great many things more to learn. After having gulped

65 View of the Taurida Palace from the other side of the River, near the Bezborodko estate (1799), unknown artist, engraved by G. L. Lory.

down at dinner a dozen of bumpers of Hungary wine, I received from the hands of the Vice-Tsar Romadonovsky (who is since dead) a full quart of brandy, and being forced to empty it in two draughts, I soon lost my senses, though I had the comfort to observe that the rest of the guests lying already asleep on the floor, were in no condition to make reflexions on my little skill in drinking.

The following morning I had the honour to meet an Ambassador of a Khan of the Calmucs at the Chancery Office for Foreign Affairs, a man of a frightful and fierce aspect; his head was shaved all over, except a lock of hair which hung from the crown down to the neck, according to the custom of that nation. He delivered to the Great Chancellor on the part of his master, who is the Tsar's Vassal, a roll of paper, throwing himself down to the ground, and muttering for a long while something between his teeth, which complement being interpreted to the Great Chancellor by a Jew, he had this short answer, that it was very well. This ceremony being over the Ambassador resumed his fierce air, and made but short replies to the questions we took the liberty to ask him. However we learnt so much from some Russians, that he had brought from the Khan for the Tsar, a saddle made all of iron and very artificially wrought, and from the Khan's wife for the Tsarina several pieces of silk with figs and other fruits of their country.

Having left this dirty company, I went according to the

66 Kalmucs wrestling. From C. Rechberg, *Des Peuples de la Russie.*

custom in all polite countries to pay my respects to the chief nobility of the Russian Court, in order to get acquainted with them. It is to be observed that it is not the custom in Russia to send in word of one's coming, and that for this reason it is very difficult to see their great men. This was more than I knew, and therefore being gone to pay a visit to a certain Boyar, none of his servants would acquaint his master with it, so that I was obliged to wait in the court yard half starved with cold, till his Lordship came out. Having made my complements to him, he asked me whether I had any thing else to say; upon my answering in the negative, he dismissed me with this reply: *I have nothing to say to you neither.* Though this behaviour would not easily go down with me, yet I ventured to go a second time to visit another Russian. But as soon as he heard me mentioning my own country, he cut me short and flatly told me; *I know nothing of that Country, you may go and apply to those to whom you are directed.* This put an end to my desire of making visits, and I firmly resolved never to go any more to any Russian without being desired, except to the Ministers with whom I had business, who indeed shewed me all imaginable civility. A week after I met those impolite courtiers at Court, and as they had observed his Tsarish Majesty discoursing with me for a considerable while, and treating me with a great deal of favour, besides that he had given particular orders to Admiral Apraksin to see me well entertained, they now both came up to me, and in a very mean and abject manner asked my pardon for their fault, almost falling down to the ground, and very liberally offering me all their brandy to oblige me.

b

Preparations having been made by the whole Court during three months for a great masquerade, the same was at length kept on the 27th and 28th of January. I will relate the main particulars, the world never having heard, for ought I know, of the like before. The occasion of this masquerade was a wedding. One Zotov, who had been the Tsar's writing-master in his Majesty's younger years, was in the 70th year of his age advanced to be his jester, or merrymaking privy-counsellor, and afterwards mock-Patriarch. Moreover for humour sake he was raised to the dignity of a Prince, and at length declared Pope. Invested with those imaginary characters, and being now in the 84th year of his age, the Tsar married him to a buxom widow of thirty four, and the nuptials of this extra-ordinary couple were solemnized by the court in masks, or mock-shew. The company consisted of about four hundred persons of both sexes. Every four persons had their proper dress and peculiar musical instruments, so that they repre-sented a hundred different sorts of habits and musick, particu-larly of the Asiatick nations. The four persons appointed to invite the guests, were the greatest stammerers that could be found in all Russia. Old decrepit men who were not able to walk or stand, had been picked out to serve for bridesmen, stewards, and waiters. There were four running footmen, the most unweildy fellows, who had been troubled with the gout most of their life-time, and were so fat and bulky that they wanted others to lead them. The mock-Tsar of Moscow, who represented King David in his dress, instead of a harp had a lyre covered with a bearskin, to play upon. He being the chief of the company, was carried on a sort of Pageant placed on a sled, to the four corners of which were tied as many bears, which being prickt with goads by fellows purposely appointed for it, made such a frightful roaring as well suited the confused and horrible dinn raised by the disagreeing instruments of the rest of the company. The Tsar himself was dressed like a boor of *Friedland,* and skilfully beat a drum in company with three Generals. In this manner, bells ringing everywhere, the ill-matched couple were attended by the masks to the altar of the great church, where they were joined in matrimony by a priest a hundred years old, who had lost his eyesight and memory, to supply which defect a pair of spectacles were put on his nose, two candles held before his eyes, and the words sounded into his ears, which he was to pronounce. From church the procession went to the Tsar's Palace where the diversions lasted some days. Many strange adventures and comical accidents happened on their riding on sleds through the streets, too long to be related here. Thus much may suffice to shew, that the Tsar among all the heavy cares of government knows how to set apart some days for the relaxation of his mind, and how ingenious he is in the contrivance of those diversions.

c (June 1709)

That month a woman dwarf was brought to bed, and added a new member to the society or species of those diminutives of mankind, whom they take particular care in Russia to propagate by marrying them together, so that there is scarcely a man of quality but keeps a man or woman dwarf for his lady. In the year 1710. the Tsar was pleased to add to the solemnities of the nuptials between Princess Anna, his niece, and the late Duke of Courland Frederick William, the diversion of a wedding of a couple of dwarfs, which humour I think deserves a place in this account of the Russian Court, though it happened before the time of my arrival there. The solemnity of the principal marriage of the illustrious couple being performed on the 11th of November, N. S. the 13th of the same month was appointed for celebrating the dwarf-wedding. The day before, two dwarfs of well proportioned shape and finely dressed drove about in a little chaise with three wheels, drawn by a good horse adorned with ribbons of divers colours, to invite the guests, two of the waiters appointed for the wedding riding before on horse-back, likewise well trimmed, after the way of the country. On the day appointed in·the morning bride and bridegroom were married in the Church of the Fortress according to the Russian rites. A very little dwarf marched at the head of the procession, as being the Marshal, that is to say, the conductor and master of the ceremony, carrying a staff on which hung a large tassel of ribbons, the distinguishing sign of his office. He was followed by the bride and the bridegroom neatly dressed. Then came the Tsar attended by his Ministers, Princes, Boyars, Officers and others;

next marched all the dwarfs of both sexes in couples. They were in all seventy two, some in the service of the Tsar, the Tsarina Dowager, the Prince and Princess Menshikov, and other persons of distinction, but others had been sent for from all parts of Russia howsoever remote. The procession was closed by a vast number of spectators. At the church the couple took their place in the midst of the company: the priest asking the bridegroom, whether he would take his bride to

67 A street masquerade in Moscow in 1722.

be his wife, he answered with a loud voice, addressing himself to his beloved: *You and no other*. The bride being asked whether she had not made any promise of marriage to another than her bridegroom, she answered: *That would be very pretty, indeed*. However when the main question came to be asked, whether she would have the bridegroom for her husband, she uttered her *Yes* with such a low voice as could hardly be heard, which occasioned a good deal of laugh to the company. The Tsar in token of his favour, was pleased to hold the garland over the bride's head, according to the Russian custom. The ceremony being over, the company went by water to the Prince Menshikov's palace. Dinner was prepared in a spacious hall, where two days before the Tsar had entertained the guests invited to the solemnity of the Duke's marriage. Several small tables were placed in the middle of the hall for the new-

married couple, and the rest of the dwarfs, who were all splendidly dressed after the German fashion. The bride and bridegroom sate each at a separate table under small canopies of silk. Over the bride and her two bridemaids that sate over-against her, hung three garlands of laurel; there hung also one over the bridegroom's head. Between the two bridesmaids sate a little carver who in acknowledgment for his trouble was presented by them with a cocade, which favour he returned to each in a kiss. This little company were attended by one Marshal, and eight Deputies, or Under-Marshals, all dwarfs, who wore each a cocade of lace and ribbons on the right arm in token of their office, in the management of which they acted with so much dexterity, mirth, and noise, as afforded a great deal of diversion to their superiors. On one side sate the Tsar, the Duke of Courland, the several Russian and foreign

68 The wedding of the dwarfs arranged by Peter the Great in 1710 to accompany the ceremony between Princess Anna and the Duke of Courland.

Ministers, the Generals; on the other the Dutchess of Courland, the Princesses her sisters, and the principal ladies of the Russian Court; then the several Princes, Boyars, and Officers Russians as well as Germans. They were placed along narrow tables which went around the four sides of the hall, sitting with their backs to the wall, in order to have a full view of the sporting dwarfs in the middle of the room. The first health was proposed by the little Marshall, who with his eight Deputies stept before the Tsar's table, holding in one hand their staffs, and in the other the glasses, and after having made a bow to the ground, they emptied them under the sound of the musick which was in the next room. Some small pieces had been mounted behind the house to be fired on each health, but this was countermanded by reason of Prince Menshikov's youngest son being then a dying, who actually expired the same day. After dinner the dwarfs began to dance after the

162

Russian way, which lasted till eleven at night. It is easy to imagine how much the Tsar and the rest of the company were delighted at the comical capers, strange grimaces and odd postures of that medley of pigmies, most of whom were of a size, the mere sight of which was enough to provoke laughter. One had a high bunch on the back, and very short legs; another was remarkable by a monstrous big belly; a third came waddling along on a little pair of crooked legs like a badger; a fourth had a head of a prodigious size; some had wry mouths and long ears, little pig-eyes, and chub-cheeks, and many such other comical figures more. When these diversions were ended, the new married couple were carried to the Tsar's house, and bedded in his own bedchamber.

d

The Founding of St Petersburg

I am now going to relate many particulars not yet mentioned, of a city which may be called a wonder of the world, was it only in consideration of the few years that have been employed in the raising of it.

His Tsarish Majesty from his younger years shewed a particular inclination for shipping and sea-affairs. At Moscow he was always navigating and making use of sails on the rivers there, as far as the situation of that country would admit. But when fortune seconded his arms so far that in the years 1702. he took Nöteborg (now called Schüsselburg) and the year following Nie-Schanta (or Schantz-ter-Nie) a trading town in Ingria, having observed that about a German mile further down, the River Neva (Nie) forms several islands, the conveniency of that situation inspired him with thoughts of building a town there, in order to get footing in the Baltic. His army was thereupon ordered to encamp there, so that the infantry stood on the territory of Finland, or properly Karelia, and the cavalry on that on Ingria. A small fort was raised on the place where at that time only stood two poor fishermens huts, but where now stands Petersburg. The Tsar himself went with some sloops to view the river down to the main sea, and send other vessels to examine and sound the coasts on all sides. As they spied several Swedish ships cruising in the sea, a detachment of about one thousand men were ordered for the island Retusari, or Rutzari, (on which now lies Kronschlot) where they took post. The Swedes endeavouring to dislodge the Russians again by continually firing upon them from one of their ships, the Russians retired and hid themselves behind a great quantity of large stones lying on the shore; which made the Swedes believe that they had quite retired to the other shore of the island, under the cover of the bushes and made off in some vessels; upon this supposition the Swedes landed with

163

the design of maintaining so advantagious a post, but they were so warmly received by the Russians, that they were obliged to retire to their ships with the loss of some of their men, and to put to sea again. After this rencounter the Tsar maintained the possession of that island, and afterwards made a harbour there and built a fort upon it, with a pretty large borough, which is now famous under the name of Kronschlot, of which mention shall be made more at large hereafter.

69 Peter the Great founding the city of St Petersburg in the spring of 1703.

70 View of the 'Twelve Colleges' (now the University of Leningrad) designed by D. Trezzini (1722–42) and part of the Gostinyy Dvor. Engraving by Ye. G. Vnukov after a painting by M. Makhayev (1753).

The Tsar being more and more pleased with the situation of the neighbouring country, which actually is one of the most agreeable that is to be found in those parts, resolved not only to build a fortress on the River Neva, as he designed at first, but also to make his chief dock there for building large men of war. The river being very deep near the place where the fort or citadel stands at present, viz. fourteen or fifteen fathoms, or ninety foot, and the neighbouring territory round about being all morass, which makes the place inaccessible, the Tsar pitched upon the several islands formed by the river, in this manner that the fortress should be built on the small island and the town partly on the other islands, partly on the continent.

This resolution was no sooner taken, but orders were forthwith issued, that next spring a great number of men, Russians, Tartars, Cossacks, Calmucs, Finlandish and Ingrian peasants, should be at the place to execute the Tsar's design. Accordingly in the beginning of May 1703 many thousands of workmen, raised from all the corners of the vast Russian Empire, some of them coming journies of 200 to 300 German miles, made a beginning of the works on the new fortress. There were neither sufficient provisions for subsisting such a number of men, nor care taken to furnish them with the necessary tools, as pick-axes, spades, shovels, wheel-barrows, planks and the like, they even had not so much as houses or huts; notwithstanding which the work went on with such expedition, that it was surprizing to see the fortress raised within less than five

71 A view of the old winter palace at the canal joining the Moyka Canal and the Neva. An engraving by Ye. Vinogradov from a drawing by M. Makhayev (1753).

165

166

months' time, though the earth which is very scarce thereabouts, was for the greater part carried by the labourers in the skirts of their clothes, and in bags made of rags and old mats, the use of wheel-barrows being then unknown to them. It is computed that there perished on this occasion very nigh one hundred thousand souls, for in those places made desolate by the war, no provisions could be had even for ready money, and as the usual supplies carried by the Lake Ladoga were frequently retarded by contrary winds, those people often were in the utmost misery. This fortress was afterwards from time to time inlarged, and in the year 1704 a crown-work added to it, as also some redoubts (which however are said to be now in a decaying condition) the whole being projected and directed by the Tsar himself.

At the same time that they were going on with the fortress, the city also by degrees began to be built, and to this end numbers of people both of the nobility and the trading part of the nation were ordered to come from Russia to settle at Petersburg and to build houses there, all which was executed with such forwardness, that in a short time the place swarmed with inhabitants. The Boyars and others of the nobility brought along with them numerous retinues and many

72 Oranienbaum, built on the Gulf of Finland facing Kronstadt, was the country palace of Peter the Great's favourite Menshikov, and was built for him in 1714 by the German architect, G. Schädel. The palace was rebuilt at the end of the century by the Italian A. Rinaldi in the neo-classical style shown by this contemporary engraving. Née, after Lespinasse.

73 The church of St Peter and St Paul, St Petersburg. Lithograph of 1822 by Karl Petrovich Beggrov (1799–1875).

servants. The merchants and shop-keepers found their account at this new place, where every thing was excessive dear. Many Swedes, Finlanders, and Livonians, not being able to subsist in their towns and villages, which were ruined and many of them destroyed by fire, and not knowing where else to go, were obliged by necessity, to mingle with the greater number of people. All sorts of artificers, mechanicks, and seamen with their families were drawn to Petersburg, in order to encourage shipping and settle a commerce by sea. Many labourers being Russians, Tartars, and Calmucs, having served the time prefixed by their sovereign, and being unwilling to return so far home, engaged with the Boyars who were building houses every day, and got sufficient work to get their bread by; some thousands of them even built houses for themselves, and

74 The Celebrations in St Petersburg in May 1803 to mark the centenary of the founding of the city by Peter the Great. 1804 by an unknown artist, engraved by G. L. Lory.

settled at Petersburg, the rather because every body was allowed to build on what place he liked. All those circumstances together very much contributed to the sudden peopling of Petersburg, which now hardly yields to any in Germany as to the number of houses and inhabitants: for there are reckoned at this time sixty odd thousand houses in that city, among which however, it must be owned, are many poor and small ones, which in two hours time may be taken to pieces and put up again in another place, which is particularly the case in the Tartarian Sloboda, in the German Sloboda southwest of the dock, and in the Finlandish Scheren, about the Finlandish and Roman Catholick churches.

F. C. Weber, *The Present State of Russia* (London 1722)

Lake Baykal

John Bell travelled extensively through Russia over a period stretching from the reign of Peter to almost the end of that of Anna. His description of his crossing of Lake Baykal in 1720 is precise and detailed in its topographical information and gives the reader a vivid sense of the immensity of the lake and the dangers confronting those who sailed across it.

The 15th of May, the weather being very hot, we did not set out till after dinner, when we left Irkutsk, accompanied by the commandant and some other officers of the place. We rode along the north bank of the river, through pleasant woods, and some open fields, till we came, about midnight, to a few fisherman's huts, where we halted for a few hours, and repeated our journey early next morning.

At noon, we arrived at a small chapel, dedicated to St Nicholas, where travellers usually pay their devotions, and pray for a prosperous passage over the lake. About this religious house there are a few fishermen's huts. Two monks constantly attend, to put people in mind of their duty, and receive a small gratuity from the passengers.

Here we found our boats waiting for us below the falls of the Angara. From hence you can see the lake, bursting out betwixt two high rocks, and tumbling down over huge stones, that lie quite cross the river, which I reckon to be about an English mile broad. The whole channel of the river is covered with these rocks, from the mouth of the lake down to the Chapel of St Nicholas, about the distance of an English mile. There is no passage for the smallest boats, except along the east shore, thro' a narrow strait, between the rocks and the land. In the most shallow places, there is about five or six feet water, and breadth all the way sufficient for any single vessel. But if, by stress of weather, or any other accident, a boat should have the misfortune to miss this opening, and be thrown upon the rocks, she must immediately be dashed to pieces, and the whole crew inevitably perish. The waters, dashing upon the stones, make a noise like the roaring of the sea, so that people near them can scarce hear one another speak. I cannot express the awfulness with which one is struck, at the sight of such astonishing scenes of nature as appear round this place, and which, I believe, are not to be equalled in the known world. The pilots and sailors who navigate the lake speak of it with much reverence, calling it the Holy Sea, and the mountains about it the Holy Mountains; and are highly displeased with any person who speaks of it with disrespect, or calls it a lake. They tell a story of a certain pilot who always gave it that appellation, but was severely punished for his contempt. Being on a voyage in autumn, he and his crew were tossed from side to side of the lake, till they were half starved, and in great danger of perishing. Necessity, at last, forced this hardy mariner to comply with the prevailing custom, and pray to the Holy Sea and Mountains to have compassion on him in such distress. His prayers were effectual, and he arrived safe to land; but was observed, ever after, to speak of the sea with the greatest respect.

The afternoon was spent in adjusting the tackle, and preparing the barks for being drawn up the strong narrow current.

The 17th, the wind being contrary, and blowing pretty fresh, the pilots would not venture out. I, and three more of our company, took this opportunity of walking up to the top of the mountains, where we had a full view of the sea, and the land to the south, on the other side of it, and also to the west, as far as it extends. The land on the south side of the lake rises gradually, till it terminates in hills mostly covered with wood; but, on the western shore, there are very high mountains, several whereof are overspread with deep snow, which we could easily discern, though at a great distance.

The Baykal Sea, opposite to the mouth of the Selenga, is reckoned about fifty English miles broad, though it is much broader in some other places, and about three hundred miles in length. It is wholly fresh water, and is supplied by the Selenga, and many other rivers, from the south, and by the higher Angara from the east. The course of the sea is from south-west to north-east, and has very few shelves or rocks. There is only one large island, near the middle of it, called Olkhon. It is bounded on the north by a ridge of high rocks, which run from one end of it to the other. The only opening by which it discharges itself is that into the Angara, which, though it is a natural passage, appears as if cut through the rocks by art. In my opinion, one cannot imagine a more beautiful prospect of nature, than is seen from the top of these mountains, which may easily be perceived from the short and imperfect sketch I have drawn of it. The woods on the summit of the rocks are short, and thinly scattered; but, on their declivity towards the north, and in the valleys, the trees become gradually both taller and larger. There is abundance of game and wild beasts in these woods, particularly the wild boar, which was the first of that species we found in this country; a certain sign of a temperate climate; for these animals cannot endure the excessive cold in more northerly parts. The hunting of these animals being a dangerous kind of sport, we carefully avoided their haunts. In the evening, we returned to our barks at the chapel of St Nicholas.

The Baykal is abundantly furnished with various kinds of excellent fish, particularly sturgeon, and a fish called *omul*, in shape and taste resembling a herring, but broader and larger. The sea produces also great numbers of seals, whose skins are preferred in quality to those of seals caught in salt-

75 A view of the town of Yakutsk on the west bank of the river Lena showing the curious rock columns. Engraving by Née after Lespinasse.

water. I am of opinion, that both the seals and fish in the Baykal came originally from the Northern Ocean, as the communication between them is open, tho' the distance be very great.

The seals are generally caught in winter, by strong nets hung under the ice. The method they use is, to cut many holes in the ice, at certain distances from one another, so that the fishermen can, with long poles, stretch their nets from one hole to another, and thus continue them to any distance. The seals, not being able to bear long confinement under the ice, for want of air, seek these holes for relief, and thus entangle themselves in the nets. These creatures, indeed, commonly make many holes for themselves, at the setting in of the frost.

172

In this manner they catch, not only seals, but fish of all kinds, in winter.

The 18th, the wind being favourable, we put off from St Nicholas's. As we had workmen enough, we left part of them on board, to assist the pilot, by setting poles, while the rest were employed on shore, in towing the barks against a strong current. In about the space of three hours we got clear of the current, and all hands came on board. We were now quite becalmed, and obliged to take to our oars. We rowed along shore to the eastward till about noon, when we had an easy breeze, which soon carried us two thirds over the sea, under our main-sail. The wind now chopped about to the east, and blew so fresh, that we could not make the river Selenga, which was the port where we intended to land. As these barks cannot turn to windward, we were drove about ten miles to the westward of the Posolskiy monastery, which stands about six miles to the westward of the Selenga, in a pleasant and fruitful plain, furnishing an extensive view in all directions; where, endeavouring to get to land at any rate, we steered into a bay, in which we fancied we saw the shore covered with cockle-shells or white sand. On a nearer approach, our mistake appeared. For what seemed shells or sand, at a distance, was only great and small cakes of ice, beating with the waves against the main body of the ice, which lay firm, and covered the whole bay. Our people, on distinguishing the ice, immediately struck sail, and were in no small confusion. But Mr Izmaylov ordered the sail to be again set, and to steer directly for the ice. In the mean time, all hands were employed in hanging boards about the bow of the vessel, to prevent the cutting of the planks, and in setting poles to push off the large cakes. At last we came among the ice, which made a terrible rattling at first; but the farther we advanced, the easier our bark lay, till we came to the main body of the ice, where she remained as unmoved as if she had been in a mill-pond, though it still continued to blow hard. We now quitted the ship, and walked about upon the ice, which was yet strong enough to carry horses. By this time the sun was set, which prevented our design of going ashore, for the distance was at least five English miles; and there was a great gap in the ice near the place where we lay.

About midnight the wind turned westerly, and, at break of day, we left our station, and sailed to the eastward, and, about noon, entered the river Selenga, where we found our other three barks. They having been two or three miles before us the preceding night, had time enough to reach anchoring ground, and, by this means, escaped the ice, so little expected at this season of the year. We ourselves, before entering the bay, had sounded, in order to discover whether we could come to an anchor; but no bottom could be found, tho' we joined several lead-lines together, amounting to about one hundred and fifty fathoms.

John Bell, *Travels from St Petersburg in Russia to Diverse Parts of Asia* (London 1764)

174

THE REIGNS OF ANNA
AND ELIZABETH

A Prisoner in Moscow

An Italian soldier-of-fortune involved in somewhat Kafkaesque
misunderstanding with the Russian authorities, Francesco Locatelli
was hardly prepared to be just or objective in his appraisal of Russians.
The description of his arrival and imprisonment in Moscow in 1733
conveys that sense of helpless frustration felt by many foreigners
before—and since.

From Cheboksary, we went to Nizhniy Novgorod, and from
thence to Moscow, where we arrived the 23d of November.
You will imagine, without doubt, that at my arrival in the
metropolis of so vast an empire, the face of things must
necessarily be changed, with regard to me: that I met with
another kind of men, and especially a Governour of better
understanding, and more just and human, than the Governour
of Kazan; and consequently, that I was soon discharged from
my confinement, or, at least, treated in a manner more
becoming my quality. If these be your thoughts, Sir, you are
greatly mistaken. A Muscovite is the same every where, and
you will find them, at Moscow, just such as you have seen them
at Kazan. Imagine the inhabitants of this great city, to be a
new colony of Laplanders, Samoyeds, and Ostyaks, who are
accounted the most stupid nations of the north, and then you
may form, at least, some idea of the character of the people,
who dwell in this capital. Do not, however, suppose this
parallel just in every part of it. The Muscovites are infinitely
beneath all these other nations: They are more barbarous,
more irrational and less human. The evidences I shall give
you of this, in the sequel, will put it beyond all doubt . . .

My last gave you an account of my arrival at Moscow. I was
first carried to the house of a baker, till the serjeant and one
of the soldiers went to give an account of my being there. The
soldier who was left, instead of following his orders, to have a
watchful eye over me, laid himself down upon an oven, and
slept most profoundly. You must know, in Muscovy, the
houses of the meaner sort of people, consist generally of one
large room only, which serves them for chamber, kitchen, and
every other occasion. In this room you find an oven, in which

175

they bake their bread, meat, and almost all their eatables, so that it is kept very hot all the year round. The top of it is covered with a great number of boards, which form a sort of square scaffold; upon which the whole family almost continually lives, as well in summer as winter. I have sometimes happened to lay my hand upon it, but found it so hot, that I was soon obliged to take it away. Some natural philosophers of your acquaintance, who have made so many curious experiments concerning Salamanders, did not perhaps know, that so peculiar a species of them was to be found in Muscovy. It is to be supposed, that if they had made this discovery, they would have allowed those animals the property given them, by the most early of the ancients, of living in fire. Pray assure those Gentlemen, that the Salamanders in Muscovy, not only pass almost all their time, but eat, sleep and perform every office of life, in that element.

Nothing would have been more easy, than for me to have escaped, while my Salamander was asleep on the oven; and could I have forseen what was to ensue, I assure you, I should not have neglected the opportunity. In a city so full of strangers as Moscow is, I might easily have been concealed in the crowd, and have freed my self from the pursuit of my enemies: But I was so far from having the least thought of it, that I looked upon all that had happened to me till then, as a farce, which would end with my arrival at Petersburg. The first scene which was opened at Moscow, was humorous enough, but that which followed was as tragical: but you shall be judge of them.

As soon as the serjeant returned, I was conveyed to Kremlin the residence of the Tsars, I was not uneasy that the first scene was opened in a place, where such tragical pieces have been represented. This building consists of several enormous piles, heaped upon one another, without any order. I was carried into a large hall, which they call the Palace or Civil Court, but is one of the most filthy places in the world. I there found a great number of clerks, busied in dispatching a crowd of people, who were round about them. My coming in put an immediate stop to their labour, and the eyes of every one were turned upon me. As the Muscovites are sworn enemies to the rest of mankind, the sight of a foreign prisoner was a diversion to them, and the hall was soon frequented in a more than ordinary manner.

I was committed to the care of an officer, a corporal and six old soldiers. One of them stood always before me, with his sword drawn, but he had not the most terrifying countenance. At length, they brought some of my goods, but I saw neither my sword nor my trunk. They shewed me one corner of the hall, which was destined for my prison: but I had no sooner begun to prepare my lodging, than a person appeared at the gate, to inform my guard that I had a pair of scissars about me. They immediately set about to visit a little bag, into which I had put such things as were most necessary on my journey, and upon my opposing them, they called the officer, who told me he had orders to visit every thing I had. I then opened the bag my self, and in a moment they seized the scissars, which they found there. I endeavoured to convince them, that I could not do without them, that I should make no ill use of them, and that they need not fear my making my self a eunuch with them. None of these arguments had any effect, so I was obliged to give way to force. By good fortune, I had another pair of scissars which escaped their notice. I had, likewise, a large fork, which, upon occasion, would have done the service of a dagger; for the least terrifying weapons are more than sufficient to affright a Muscovite.

So excellent a beginning gave me room to judge what I had to expect in the sequel; I, therefore, endeavoured to make my self easy under the state I was in. My greatest mortification was to see my self exposed as a sight to crowds of people, who were continually flocking into the hall. I should have been very glad of an interpreter; but all the application I made for that end was in vain, nor could I, with all my entreaties, prevail upon them to let me have a barber. Dinner-time approaching, I made signs for something to eat, and was answered, in the same manner, that I must open my purse. After long waiting, and seeing nothing appear, I was obliged to be content with a morsel of bread, and some scraps which I had yet left in my hamper. While I was at dinner, they asked me for the key of my trunk, which they had not thought fit to entrust to my care. I thought it something strange, that they should ransack my trunk out of my sight; however, I gave them the key, tho with reluctance. At supper-time, I was obliged to have recourse to my pocket, and upon this occasion I found, that stewards at Moscow, are greater thieves than those of Kazan. You will not need to ask me what sort of a bed I had, I believe, I have already told you, that they lye on benches, in Muscovy. I was so happy to have sheets, and coverlets, of my own, which did me good service: but what a surprize appeared in my guard, when they saw me making my bed! They could not conceive what I was going to do with those bed-cloaths.

You see, Sir, I keep my word with you: it was your command, that I should inform you of the most minute circumstances, and you have no cause to complain on that score. Since then you have a taste that way, you shall know some particulars of what happened the next day. I was disturbed, very early, at my toilet, by the same troop of clerks, I mentioned above, and a great number of other people, whom curiosity or business had drawn together, in the hall. I continued exposed as a sight to these crowds, who could not forbear fixing their eyes upon me. At length, I began to think of making advantage of this concourse of people. When I saw any one come in, who had a good appearance, or who seemed to be an officer or foreigner, I immediately accosted him speaking in Italian, French or Latin: but it was all in vain, I did not find one who could understand me. My guard, in the mean time, offended at the freedom I took, pretended to impose silence upon me; but I gave them to understand, by signs, that they must cut out my tongue, if they would debar me the use of it. Two Poles coming in, I addressed my self to them in Latin, and they began to answer me, but their mouths were soon stopped. Their silence did not, however, hinder me from asking them, if it was customary, in Muscovy, to treat prisoners as the most abject slaves? If it was usual to let them perish for hunger, by denying them an interpreter? And, finally, if, since Peter the Great, had obliged the Muscovites to cut off their beards, there was no such thing as a barber established in that city?

Francesco Locatelli, *Lettres Moscovites: or, Muscovian Letters* (London 1736)

A Russian Funeral

The wife of the British Resident in St Petersburg, Mrs, later Lady, Rondeau is informative about many social events at the courts of Anna in the 1730s. Here she describes the funeral of the youngest daughter of Peter the Great's favourite, Menshikov.

I am going to give you the history of a Russ burial, as I have already done of a christening and a wedding. The only one I have seen was of the youngest daughter of prince Menshikov, who was recalled from banishment, with her brother, by the present empress, and by her married to count Gustavus Biron, youngest brother to the duke of Courland. She died in child-bed, and was buried with great pomp. After the company had sat some time, they all went into the room to the corpse. The coffin was open: she was dressed in an undress, as she died in that condition (otherwise, as they told me, she would have been full dressed) in a night gown of silver tissue, tied with pink ribbon; on her head a fine laced mob, and a coronet, as princess of the Roman empire; round her forehead was tied a ribbon, embroidered with her name and age; in her left arm lay the child, who died a few minutes after its birth, dressed in silver tissue; in her right hand was a roll of paper, which was a certificate from her confessor to St Peter. When all the company were ranged in the room, her servants came to take their leave of her; the inferiors first: they all kissed her hand, and the child, asked her pardon for any crime they had committed, and made the most terrible noise imaginable,

178

rather howling than crying. After that, her acquaintance took their leave, with this difference, that they kissed her face, and made a hideous noise, though not so bad as the others. Then came her relations, the most distant ones first; when her brother came, I really thought he would have pulled her out of the coffin. But the most moving scene was the husband, who had begged to be excused this dismal ceremony, but his brother thought he ought to comply with the Russ custom, lest, as he was a foreigner, it should be deemed a slight. He was brought from his own apartment by two gentlemen, as supporters, and they were really, in this case, more for use than shew. He had true sorrow painted in his face, but silent sorrow. When he came to the door of the room where the corpse lay, he stopped and asked for some hartshorn; which when he had drank, and seemed to have armed himself, he advanced to the side of the coffin, and there fainted; when he was carried out of the room and recovered, the corpse was carried down and placed in an open chariot; a great train of coaches followed, and, as a general officer's-wife, a party of guards. She was carried to St Alexander's monastery to be buried, and though the coffin-lid was put on as the corpse passed the streets, it was taken off again when it came into the chapel, and the same ceremony of leave was taken over again, except by the husband, who was carried home in a second fainting fit, the moment the coffin was uncovered. The rest of the ceremony was much like the Roman-Catholics. When the corpse was buried, all the company returned to the house, to a grand dinner, which had more an air of rejoicing, than mourning, as everybody seemed to have forgot their sorrow; but stop a malicious smile I fancy you have, for the husband did not appear, and is, I believe, truly concerned, as he had a great fondness for her, which always appeared in all his behaviour to her in her lifetime, a more convincing sign of sincerity than howling at her death.

[Lady Jane Rondeau], *Letters from a Lady who Resided some Years in Russia* (London 1775)

Fishing for Sturgeon and the Preparation of Caviar

John Cook, a Scottish doctor, arrived in St Petersburg in 1735 and served in Russia until 1751, during which period his travels took him principally to the South and Astrakhan. The excerpt which follows describes the techniques of fishing for the sturgeon and of preparing the delicacy which the European inevitably associates with Russia.

76 The city of Astrakhan, a thriving port on the Volga at the Caspian Sea. It was originally the capital of the Astrakhan khans until its capture by Ivan the Terrible. From *Voyages and Travels of John Struys.*

With lines and hooks baited they take the sturgeon, and all other fish less in magnitude; but very seldom can they take the beluga in this manner; wherefore they make use of a strong rope, 1, 2, or 300 ells long, and, at the distance of every two ells or less, from one end of the rope to the other, they fix large barbed hooks, but not baited, with their sharp points standing upwards, looking over each side of the rope. The rope thus prepared they place across the river, letting it down to the bottom, with the points of the hooks above the rope, and fix a buoy to each end of it. The beluga, which is chiefly taken in this manner, loves to swim near the sandy bottom of the river, and he swims ordinarily very rapidly; therefore, whether he is swimming with or against the stream, he has a great chance of being hooked in the belly, because the points of the hooks look to each side of the rope. If the grip is but small, he breaks

180

off; but the greatest number of the largest beluga are thus taken. When the fisher misses his buoys at the places he put them in, he is certain that a fish has been there, and so sails about till he finds them, and then coils up the rope very carefully into the boat. If the fish is not spent, he may draw the boat and rope after him for a long while; but at last, being quite exhausted, the fishers gently draw him near the boat, and, before he touch it, they strike him on the head with an iron hammer, but have the rope ready to let go, if they should miss the proper place, for he will swim a great way, and, if they do not give him rope enough, he would easily draw the boat, tho' large, under water. Thus to the fisher it is very troublesome and dangerous to take a beluga, though, to a spectator, it affords very agreeable diversion.

The nets which are used in the Volga are both strong, long, and deep: they are from 50 to 100 fathoms long. In summer they place the net so as to make the figure of half a circle, out of their boats, and bring the ropes fixed to both ends of the net ashore, at a great distance the one end from the other; then, having a great number of men, they pull till they get near the bank, when they row their boats within the net, and, with their barbed irons, they strike the larger fish, and take them into their boats; but it requires much patience and great toil. Lastly, they draw out the net with an incredible number of different fish. If a strong old beluga happens to be amongst them, he frequently breaks the net, gets away, and lets many prisoners escape; so that the fisher is never glad to see a large beluga in the net. In the winter season they cannot use such large nets, but I have seen them use nets of betwixt 30 and 50 fathoms long; and the way they do is this: they cut a large square hole through the ice on the side of the river, for extracting the net; then, opposite to that square hole, they cut another at a just distance, so that a straight line drawn betwixt these two holes forms a diameter to a large circle, which they afterwards form with a number of holes cut thro' the ice, at such a distance one from the other, that they can reach with a long pole. Having now made all their holes, they introduce into the middle hole, far in the river or lake, two poles, for the greater expedition, and shove one forward on each side, from one hole to the other, till they meet at the first made square hole at the shore. A rope having been made fast to the end of each pole, serves to conduct the net regularly, so as to form a circle, which, with the assistance of many men, they draw out of the square hole.

In this manner, I once, near Astrakhan, saw an incredible number of different fish taken by a number of men. They catch smaller fish as big as carp, pike, or salmon, with a barbed harping iron, made fast to a long pole, (which the Scots call lister,) as we do, particularly in the time of high water, when the fish play among the grass; but there are few if any red salmon in the Volga. As every one knows how fish are taken with bait, I shall say nothing of it further, than that I have seen a beluga thus taken in the winter season, which was so ponderous, that, the fishermen assured me, it would be, though fixed upon sledges, a large load for two good horses to draw on the ice.

The Russians prepare caviar almost from every kind of fish: thus, I have frequently, at the best tables in that empire, eaten

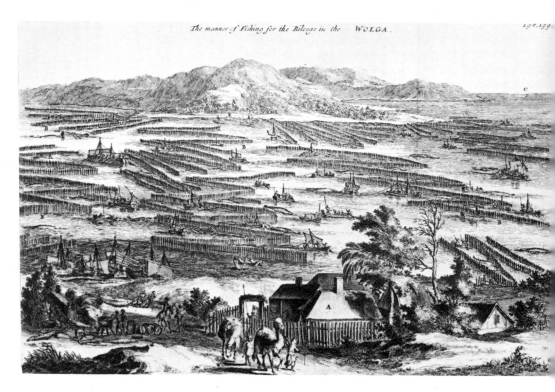

The manner of Fishing for the Bilooge in the WOLGA.

77 Fishing for the Beluga sturgeon on the Volga. Letter *A* in the engraving denotes the two watch houses on either side of the river; *B,* the arrangement of sticks used to catch the fish; *C,* the mouth of the river at the Caspian Sea. A seventeenth-century engraving from *Voyages and Travels of John Struys.*

fresh caviar from pike. The Russians have three different ways of preparing caviar: the first is the simplest and best, and is truly but a part of the other two operations. Caviar is the spawn or *ova* of the female fish. That prepared for keeping, and for the Russian and foreign market, is extracted chiefly from the beluga and sturgeon; that of the stirlet is, I imagine, all consumed at home, being extremely delicious food. The only art used in the first preparation, is, carefully to clear the *ova* from their membranes and filaments, which they do by shaking and washing them; then, under a shade, they place them upon a sieve or board, so that the superfluous moisture may drain off. This fresh caviar is sold at Astrakhan at about three pence per 12 ounce. The second method of preparing it is, first to cleanse it, as has been said, and cask it up well salted, which is fit either for foreign or Russian markets. The third way is, to prepare as formerly, and, when well salted, they

182

put it into a press to squeeze out much of the moisture; this is called pressed caviar; but I do not think it good, for it loses much of the delicious taste of that prepared the second way. I imagine no part of any fish, at least which I have tasted, is comparable to the fresh caviar. The fishermen have stages well aired, though the rays of the sun cannot penetrate the roof, where they cut open their large fish, and either sun-dry them, or salt them, and then pack them up for the market. The smaller fish, being cut open, and the guts taken out, are so perfectly sun-dried, that, upon the banks of the river, they build them up into stacks, and let them stand exposed to the open air till they are shipped off. In this manner they prepare the carp. I have known 100 carp bought from the net for a ruble. In London, their tongues preserved alone, I doubt not, would bring to the fishmonger ten times that value. I have frequently bought a live sturgeon at Astrakhan for three pence, and so the rest. One is always sure of fish upon the Volga. The fishers never would take money from me, but gave gratis, for me and the people with me, as much as we could eat, and some to carry along with us; and if I gave them a glassful of spirits, they expressed great satisfaction. I had almost forgot to acquaint the reader, that the largest, fullest, and best tasted cray-fish I ever met with, are to be found on the banks of the Volga; and, for a penny, one may get as many as six men can eat. In half an hour, a man accustomed to catch them, may get a basket full, or as many as he can conveniently bring home.

John Cook, *Voyages and Travels through the Russian Empire* (London 1770)

Impressions of St Petersburg (1739)

In this letter to Lord Hervey, Count Francesco Algarotti, the close friend of Voltaire, describes his impressions of the city as it was at the end of the reign of Anna and records his sense of disappointment that it was not more imposing than he found it.

Petersburg, June 30th, 1739

I have not a greater pleasure, my lord, than that of writing to you; and accordingly I enjoy it as often as possible. I am at length going to give you some account of this new city, of this great window lately opened in the north, thro' which Russia looks into Europe. We arrived at Petersburg, a few days ago, after having spent two at Kronschlot, at admiral Gordon's: We left there our frigate, which, drawing eleven feet of water,

78 The fortress of Kronshlot, a detail from D. Trezzini's design for the development of Vasilyevskiy Island in St Petersburg, in the sketch map by I. B. Homann (1716).

79 A panorama of the Neva with the Admiralty and the shipyards on the left. After a drawing by M. Makhayev, 1753.

could not have sailed up beyond Peterhoff; and we came here in a bark as handsome as it is well decorated, which the admiral lent us.

Seven months of the year one travels upon the Neva in barks, and the other five months in sledges. The Tsar had one of these in the shape of a wherry. When the wind was east or west, he went and came upon the ice with sails, carrying in that manner his orders from Petersburg to Kronschlot, and from Kronschlot to Petersburg. He guided his sledge with a pole pointed with iron, like to those which are used upon mount Cenis. By this means he had the pleasure of sailing even upon land.

But the greatest satisfaction he ever felt in his life, was when he sailed up the Neva in triumph, after having beat the Swedish fleet at Hangöudd, in 1714; leading in his train the admiral prisoner, with a great part of his ships. He then really beheld the completion of his works. A nation which, but a few years before, had not so much as a single sloop in the Baltic, was become sovereign of that sea; and Peter Mikhailov, formerly a carpenter in one of the docks of Amsterdam, merited, by this important victory, to be promoted to the rank of vice-admiral of all the Russias: a farce full of instruction, said a thinking man, and which should have been acted in the presence of all the kings of the earth.

This triumphal way, this sacred way of the Neva, is not however adorned with either arches or temples: from Kronschlot to Petersburg, it is flanked with a forest on the right hand and

on the left. In it are neither majestic oaks, tufted elms, nor ever-green laurels; but the most wretched generation of trees that ever the sun shone upon. They are a kind of poplar, quite different from those into which the sisters of Phaeton were transformed, and which shade the borders of the Po.

We listened in vain to hear the melodious song of birds, with which the Tsar had endeavoured to people these wild and gloomy woods. In vain did he cause numerous colonies of them to be transported thither from the southern provinces of the empire; they all perished in a short time, without even trying to leave some of their posterity.

After having sailed some hours in the midst of this hideous and silent wood; behold, the river turns at once, and the scene changing in an instant, as at an opera, we see before us the imperial city. On either shore, sumptuous edifices grouped together; turrets with gilded spires rising every here and there like pyramids; ships, which, by their masts and floating streamers, mark the separation of the streets, and distinguish the several quarters; such was the brilliant sight which struck our eyes: we were told, here is the Admiralty, there is the Arsenal, here the Citadel, yonder is the Academy, on that side the Tsarina's winter palace. On our landing, Mr Craamer, an

80 Peter's palace at Peterhof on the Gulf of Finland was begun by Leblond but finished by the great Italian architect Rastrelli. The engraving shows the famous cascade which was designed by Leblond.

English Merchant, equally polite and well acquainted with the affairs of Russia, came to receive us, and it is at his house that we are lodged. Soon after, we had a visit from Mr Rondeau, who has been many years resident of your nation at this Court.

When we were in Petersburg, we no longer found it so superb as it had seemed to us from a distance; whether it be that the gloominess of the forest had ceased to embellish the perspective, or that travellers resemble sportsmen and lovers, I will not pretend to determine. However, the situation of a city built upon the borders of a great river, and formed of different islands, which give room for a variety of points of view and effects of optic, cannot but be fine. When one recollects the huts of Revel, and of the other cities and towns in these countries, it is impossible not to be content with the houses and buildings of Petersburg: but the ground upon which it is founded is low and marshy, the immense forest, in the middle of which it stands, is frightful, the materials of which it is built are not worth much, and the plans of the buildings are not those of an Inigo Jones, or a Palladio.

There reigns in this capital a kind of bastard architecture, which partakes of the Italian, the French, and the Dutch: this last is, however, the most prevalent, and it is no wonder.

The Tsar's first studies were in Holland, and it was at Saardam that this new Prometheus took the fire with which he animated his nation. It seems likewise to have been solely in remembrance of Holland, that he planted rows of trees along the streets, and intersected them with canals, which certainly are not of the same use here as at Amsterdam and Utrecht.

The Tsar obliged the Boyars and Grandees of the Empire to leave Moscow, in the neighbourhood of which their estates were, and to settle where the court removed to. The palaces of most of them are upon the banks of the Neva, and it is easy to see that they were built out of obedience rather than choice. Their walls are all cracked, quite out of perpendicular, and ready to fall. It has been wittily enough said, that ruins make themselves in other places, but that they were built at Petersburg. Accordingly, it is necessary every moment, in this new capital, to repair the foundations of the buildings, and its inhabitants build incessantly; as well for this reason, as on account of the inability of the ground and of the bad quality of the materials. If therefore we are to call happy those *quorum iam moenia surgunt*; how completely so must be the Russians, who have the pleasure to see their houses raised anew more than once in their lives.

Count Francesco Algarotti, *Letters to Lord Hervey and the Marquis Scipio Maffei Containing the State of the Russian Empire* (London 1769)

The Empress Anna and her Court

Christoph von Manstein was in Russian service from the reign of Peter II to that of Elizabeth. He was among those who persuaded Anna to reject the 'conditions' proposed by the Supreme Privy Council and assert her own autocratic powers. As a German he enjoyed particular favour throughout a reign notorious for the power invested in the Empress's German advisers, Biron, Osterman and Münnich. Chiefly concerned with military campaigns, Manstein nevertheless gives a detailed description of the Empress, her Court and particularly of her predilection for buffoonery and comic ceremonies such as practised by Peter the Great.

The empress's usual manner of life was very regular. She was always up before eight in the morning. At nine, she began business with her secretary and ministers. At noon, she dined in her chamber with the Biron family. It was only on great occasions that she dined in public. When that happened, she was placed on a throne under a canopy, with the two princesses, Elizabeth the present empress and Anna of Mecklenburgh.

On these occasions the Grand-chamberlain waited on her at table. There was commonly also a great table in the same hall, for the noblemen and ladies of the empire, the clergy, and the foreign ministers. But in the last years of the empress's life, she did not any longer dine in public, and the foreign ministers were entertained by count Osterman.

In summer, the empress took a good deal of exercise in walking; and in winter in playing billiards. She made a light supper and went regularly to bed, between eleven and twelve.

The court used to pass the best part of the fine season at a villa, which Peter I had built at about seven leagues distance from Petersburg, called Peterhoff. It is one of the pleasantest situations that can be imagined. It stands on the sea-side; and from it you may, on the left, see Kronstadt and the whole fleet; on the right, there is a prospect of Petersburg; and opposite are the coasts of Finland. There is a spacious garden, and a magnificent *jet-d'eau,* but the house is no great matter; the apartments are extremely small and low. The rest of the summer, the empress resided at her summer palace at Petersburg, which is far from being a successful building. It stands on the banks of the Neva: the garden to it is large, and well kept up. The Princess Anna caused a new house to be set about, the old one being almost in ruins, but she did not live to finish it. It was reserved for the Empress Elizabeth to see the last hand put to it, and to place there the furniture which was in the house of marshal Munich at the time of his arrest.

There used to be deep play at court: many made their fortunes by it, and yet more were ruined. I have myself very often seen as much as 20,000 rubles lost in one sitting at quinze or pharaoh. The empress did not care for play; if she did play, it was only to lose. She then held the bank; and none were allowed to punt but those to whom she called. Any person that won was immediately paid; but as they played with counters, she never received the money from those who lost.

She was fond of public entertainments and music; and sent to Italy for all that was necessary for those objects. Comedies, which were acted both in Italian and in German, pleased her extremely; because they generally end with some one getting a beating. In 1736, the first opera was played at Petersburg, and although very well executed, was less relished than comedy and the Italian interludes.

In the time of Peter I and in the following reigns, drinking had been much practised at court; but it was not so in the time of Anna, who could not bear to see any one drunk. There was nobody but Prince Kurakin who had free permission to drink as much as he pleased. But that so excellent a custom might not be entirely lost, the 29th of January (Old Style), being the day of the empress's accession to the throne, was consecrated to Bacchus. On that day every courtier was obliged to toss off

a great bumper of Hungary wine, with one knee on the ground, in the presence of her majesty. This reminds me of another singular ceremony. On the eve of the great festivals, the courtiers and officers of the guards had the honour of paying their compliments to her majesty, and of kissing her hand; her majesty thereupon presenting each with a glass of wine on a salver.

There is another old Russian custom that, when a married man receives a visit, and his wife is present, he is bound to request those who come to see him to give her a kiss. The visitors beg the husband to set them an example, and the lady's lips are forthwith saluted by the whole company all round. The mistress of the house is, also, obliged to offer her own visitors something to drink. In the morning it is generally *eau-de-vie,* in the afternoon wine and all kinds of other beverages, which are taken even to excess. If any of the party decline on the first solicitation, the lady redoubles her entreaties, and if she cannot succeed otherwise, even throws herself at her guest's feet, to make him swallow his glass of wine or brandy.

Court jesters were formerly much in vogue. It was an ancient custom in Russia for every one in easy circumstances to keep at least one buffoon. Of course the court was well provided with them, and it is only since the regency of the princess Anna, that they have been entirely done away with; for the present empress could not bear them. As for the first Peter, he had quite a passion for them, and often kept as many as a dozen, or even more.

The empress Anna had six: La Costa, Pedrillo, a prince Galitsyn, a prince Volkonsky, Apraksin, and Balakirev. The

190

names will sufficiently indicate that these four last were chosen from among the most ancient families of the Russian nobility. Volkonsky is the brother-in-law of count Bestuzhev, at this time chancellor of the empire. His special duty was to take care of the empress's pet greyhound.

The way in which this princess amused herself with these gentry was extraordinary. Sometimes she made them dress up in a line along the wall; when one of the number would trip up the heels of the others, and make them come plump upon the floor. Sometimes in tussling they got to pulling each other's hair, and fighting till the blood flowed, while her majesty with the whole court looked on in raptures, exploding with laughter at the spectacle. Balakirev, who disliked practical jokes of the kind, one day would not let himself be tripped up, forgetting that a Russian sovereign does not know what the meaning is of listening to an excuse. La Costa was a Portuguese Jew, who had already served Peter I in the same capacity. That monarch gave him the title of king of the Samoyeds. Pedrillo was an Italian, who had come to Petersburg to play the violin in the orchestra of the theatre, but finding that he had a talent for buffoonery, he changed his trade, and made so good a thing of the new one, that in nine years he realised more than 20,000 roubles. Like a wise man, he left the country with his money. The way in which he made the first 10,000 roubles was the following. It is a custom in Russia to pay a visit to a lady who has been confined, and to make her a present in money; if a person of quality, the least sum must be a ducat; and in acknowledgment of the compliment, the fair recipient's lips are saluted by the donor. The duke of Courland told Pedrillo one day by way of a joke that he was married to a she-goat. The jack-pudding replied, with a profound bow, that it was true; that his wife was just about to lie in, and that when the happy event occurred, he would take the liberty to ask her majesty, with the whole court, to come and see her; and that he trusted he should receive on the occasion presents enough to enable him to give a good education to his family. The court thought the joke excellent. On the day fixed, Pedrillo was put in a bed on the stage of the theatre with a she-goat by his side; the curtains were drawn for the whole world to have a view of the pair, and the empress, first of all making her own present, fixed the sum which each of the members of the court was to give to the interesting mother.

In order to distinguish Pedrillo and La Costa from the other jesters, her majesty instituted an order in their favour, which she called the order of St Benedetto, and invested them with it. The decoration consisted of a miniature cross of St Alexander, hung by a red riband from the button-hole.

The prince Galitsyn, although of one of the first houses of the empire, was forced to become a court-jester. Though above forty years of age, and even having a son serving in the army, of the rank of lieutenant, he was made this, and at the same time page of the court, by way of punishment for having in his travels embraced the Catholic religion. His first wife being dead, the empress told him he ought to marry again, and that she would be at the expense of the wedding. He accepted the proposal; and, pitching upon a girl in low life, acquainted the empress with his choice, and claimed her promise. The empress, in giving this entertainment, had a mind, while amusing herself, to give at the same time an idea of her power, by showing how many different races of inhabitants there were in her vast dominions. Accordingly, she caused orders to be dispatched to the governors of the provinces to send up to Petersburg several persons of both sexes. These being arrived, were now dressed at the expense of the court, each in the habit of his respective country.

Monsieur de Valinsky, a cabinet minister, was appointed manager of the arrangements for this wedding, and winter, the end of the year 1739, was the season chosen for the celebration of it. The empress, to make it the more completely extraordinary, had a house built wholly of ice: it consisted of two chambers, in which every article of furniture, [even the bedplace on which the new-married couple were to lie,] was of ice. There were four small cannons and two mortars made of the same matter. The cannon were fired several times, [with half an ounce of powder in each,] without bursting; [and little wooden grenades were thrown out of the mortars, without their being damaged.]

On the wedding-day, when the feast was to be celebrated, all the guests were assembled in the courtyard of M. de Valinsky: thence the procession set out, and passed in front of the imperial palace, and through the principal streets of the town. There was a great train, consisting of more than 300 persons. The new-married couple were placed at the head of all upon an elephant, shut up in a great cage. The guests, two and two, were in sledges, drawn by all kinds of beasts, as reindeer, dogs, oxen, goats, hogs, &c. Some were mounted on camels. After the procession had gone the round prescribed to it, it was brought into the duke of Courland's riding-house, [where a flooring of planks had been laid for the purpose, and] where there was a dinner prepared on several tables. Each guest was treated according to the manner of the cookery in his own country. After the repast, there was a ball; each nation had its own music, and danced in the fashion of its own country. When the ball was over, the bridegroom and bride were conducted into the house of ice, where they were put into a dismally cold bed, with guards posted at the door, that they might not get out before morning.

Christoph von Manstein, *Contemporary Memoirs of Russia* (London 1856)

Elizabeth's Reception of the French Ambassador

A striking aspect of foreign literature on Russia in the eighteenth century is the lack of works dating from the reign of Elizabeth, although the St Petersburg of this period with its magnificent new buildings and its richer and gayer social life offered much to attract the foreign visitor. Apart from diplomatic dispatches, the main English work was Jonas Hanway's lengthy account, which is very informative on trading prospects through Russia to Persia, but deals only sketchily with St Petersburg and Moscow. La Messelière's book, *Journey to Petersburg,* is almost unique for the period. It arose from his visit to the Russian Court with the French Ambassador in 1757 and his account of their cordial reception by the Empress is in keeping with the generally sympathetic tone of the whole work. It includes an interestingly pejorative characterization of the sort of Frenchman who was finding his way to Russia at this period. (cf. Macartney's words in a later extract).

82 Portrait of the Empress Elizabeth of Russia by Louis Tolque.

The moment she was informed of our arrival, the Empress set aside all custom, and advanced the time of giving audience to our ambassador. On no account does she ever leave Tsarskoye Selo during the appointed time of her stay; yet she speedily commanded that all should be made ready at her summer palace, and on the third day after our arrival, which was St Peter's day, she admitted us to her court, amid all the brilliance and magnificence of the Empire. All the lords and ladies were present, thronging the rooms of the palace, glittering in array and jewellery. The high officers of the crown came to the bottom of the steps to receive M. le Marquis de l'Hôpital. Chancellor Bestuzhev alone, for reasons already mentioned, had an attack of diplomatic colic; Count Vorontsov, the Vice-Chancellor, took his place. The beauty and sumptuousness of the rooms are much to be wondered at, but even they were second to the pleasing effect of four hundred ladies, most of them very beautiful and very richly arrayed, lining the edges of the room. This cause for admiration soon gave way to another; sudden darkness, created by blinds descending in unison, was as soon remedied by the light of twelve hundred candles, reflected in looking-glasses on every side. The Grand Duke and Grand Duchess arrived with their retinue, and the Ambassador was immediately presented to them; he embraced the Grand Duke and kissed the Grand Duchess's hand; he himself then presented us to their Imperial Highnesses, and we had the honour of kissing the hand of the Princess, and made to kiss the Prince's, but he kissed us on the face, which was far beyond the dictates of etiquette, but was probably on the Empress's orders and against the will of the Grand Duke, who is very devoted to the Anglo-Prussian faction. After the ceremony, an orchestra of eighty instruments struck up, and

83 Silver coronation medal (1742) of Elizabeth of Russia.

84 The Prison at Kholmogory, where the family of the infant Tsar Ivan VI (1740–64) was held for some thirty years after the Tsar and the regent, his mother Anna Leopoldovna, were deposed by Elizabeth in 1741. After the murder of Ivan VI, his parents Anton and Anna Ulrich and their remaining children lived in constant terror of attempts on their lives. Only in 1780, in the reign of Catherine the Great, were they released and allowed to go to Denmark and set up court at Horsens in Jutland (where they are now buried). The prison, near Kholmogory, the town on the Northern Dvina which is famous for its original associations with the English explorers of the sixteenth century, was sketched by the Ulrich's elder daughter, Catherine Antonovna (d. 1807).

the Grand Duke and the Grand Duchess led the dance; the former with the Countess Shuvalova and the Grand Duchess with M. de l'Hôpital. In the middle of these first minuets we heard a heavy yet somewhat majestic sound, and a sudden opening of double doors showed us a dazzling throne, whence the Empress attended by her officers made her entrance into the ballroom. Everybody stood still and silence fell, allowing the Empress's voice to be heard. After making three inclinations of her head to right and left, she addressed the French Ambassador in a tone of majesty mingled with grace and gentleness: 'Here you are at last, M. l'Ambassadeur, and I am able to hear news of the King your master from your own lips, and to tell you of all my feelings for him and of my affection for France.' The Ambassador made a very fine speech and presented his letters of credit, after which he kissed the Empress's hand and presented us each by name, to be admitted to the same honour. The next moment the Ladies and Lords attended us in the most obliging manner, speaking French as it is spoken in Paris, and we were immediately led into the dance with permission to choose whom we would. The room being very large, as many as twenty minuets were danced at a time, a remarkable sight, and very pleasing to the eye; there were not many quadrilles, except for a few polonaises and English country dances; the ball lasted until eleven o'clock, at which time the Master of the Household came to announce to her Majesty that supper was ready. We passed into another room, very large and ornate, lit by nine hundred candles, and adorned with a table laid for four hundred. From a gallery overlooking this room, came a concert, both instrumental and vocal, which lasted all through the meal; there were dishes of every nation and also waiters, French, Russian, German and Italian, each asking the guests from his country what they desired. The Empress prepared with her own hands some strawberries with cream from her dairy, and sent them specially to M. de l'Hôpital and the Frenchmen who were with him. The Grand Duke drank to us by name, a favour he had never before vouchsafed to anyone. While we were enjoying this welcome, great was the rage of the English Ambassador, who was sulking at home, with all his supporters. The festivities lasted till three in the morning. The Empress returned to Tsarskoye Selo to complete her customary stay there.

During her absence, we occupied ourselves in paying our respects where they were due and in making necessary acquaintances. We were assailed by a swarm of French of every complexion, the majority of whom, having been in trouble with the police in Paris, have come to infest the northern regions. We were surprised and grieved to find at the houses of many great lords, deserters, bankrupts, libertines and many women of the same sort, who thanks to the

194

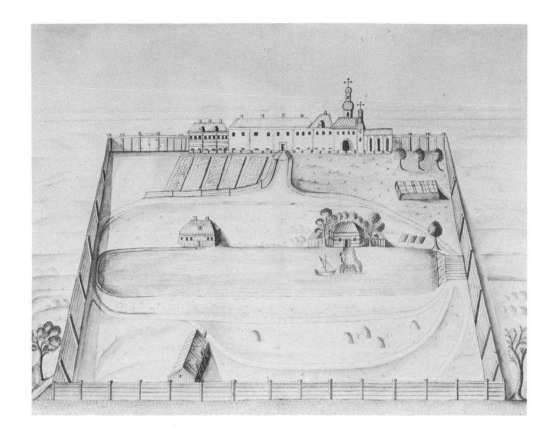

current prejudice in favour of the French, were entrusted
with the upbringing of children of the highest birth. This
scum of our land must have spread as far as China; I have
found them to be everywhere. The Ambassador thought that
it was a matter of decency to make an offer to the Russian
Ministry to have their conduct investigated, and to sort them
out, in order to send the most dubious characters back by sea
to where they belonged. This suggestion, being accepted,
produced a considerable emigration, which doubtless lost
itself in the wastes of Tartary. The Russian nation seemed to
feel gratitude for this action, so just and so honourable to our
country. The Empress heard of it with satisfaction, and made
fun of those who had been deceived by these scoundrels.

La Messelière, *Voyage à Pétersbourg ou Nouveaux Mémoires sur la
Russie* (Paris 1803)

195

THE REIGN OF CATHERINE THE GREAT

Russian Baths

Chappe d'Auteroche's book, *Journey to Siberia*, infuriated Catherine; both the Comte de Ségur and the Prince de Ligne record her continued annoyance as late as 1787. Despite, or possibly because of her opposition, the book was extremely popular. One of the most impressive set-pieces is his description of a Russian bath, which was accompanied by Le Prince's engraving, which is reproduced here. Russian bathing habits never failed to attract the attention of European visitors and to exercise their descriptive talents–even if the truth was distorted as Coxe pointed out with reference to the passage in d'Auteroche's work.

I rose very early in the morning on the 31st instant, in order to go into the bath, which I had been desired to do the evening before. As soon as I was up, they came and told me the baths were ready, as well as the sledge on which I was to go. I wrapped myself up in my fur night-gown, took my servant with me, and was conducted to the baths; the cold was so sharp, that I hastened across a small antichamber to a door, which I opened, thinking it led to the baths. There came out immediately such a suffocating volley of smoke, that I ran back again to the door as fast as possible, imagining the bath was on fire. Observing the Russians were as much disconcerted at my going back as I was at the circumstance, and at their astonishment, I asked my servant the reason of it: he told me, those were the baths, and that I was to undress and go into them. A Russian then opened the door again, and went in with his clothes on. I found this smoke was nothing more than the vapour rising from the baths, which formed an exceeding thick mist, and presently became snow from the extreme cold. The great heat however I found in these baths, did not agree with the notion I had that they were only to be used for cleanliness. I knew not they were intended for sweating, till I had asked several other questions, and being satisfied with the state of my health, was going away immediately, if my servant had not stopped me, and acquainted me that the baths had been all night preparing, and that the people of the house would be very much disappointed, if I should decline going into them. Prompted by these reasons, and by my own curiosity, I resolved to bathe; I therefore had the door opened, and bore at once all the heat. I undressed quickly, and found myself in a small square room, so much heated by a stove that I was instantly in a profuse sweat. On one side of the stove there was a kind of wooden bedstead, raised about four feet; there were some steps to get up to it: the atmosphere is exceedingly heated towards the upper part of the apartment, on account of the lightness of the particles of heat, while the floor keeps much cooler, so that these steps are contrived to prepare gradually for the

85 The baths at Serebenskoye on the outskirts of Moscow. Painting by de la Barthe, 1796.

degree of heat one is to experience on the bed. Being unacquainted with these circumstances, and in a great hurry to get out of the bath, I went immediately and placed myself in the highest part of the room.

Here the floor had got such a degree of heat, that I could scarcely bear the pain I felt in the soles of my feet, and could not have staid here, if they had not thrown some cold water upon the spot, which evaporated almost instantaneously. I took my thermometer in with me, which in a few minutes rose to sixty degrees. This prodigious heat presently seized my head, and made me very sick. My servant, who pretended to be much used to these baths, advised me to sit down, assuring me this giddiness would soon go off; but having taken his advice, I felt such acute pain that I thought I was sitting on a plate of red hot iron. I had not time to consider what gave me this pain, nor to find the steps, but fell in an instant at the foot of the bed, my thermometer breaking to pieces with

197

the fall. The heat being much less on this flooring, I lay there at first without daring to stir, and ordered the door and the little windows to be opened directly. There was a tub of water and some basons near me; I had one of them filled, and sat down in it, while with the other I made them throw water all over me. Being a little recovered, I thought of nothing but getting out as fast as I could, yet did not dare stand up-right, because I should then have been in the hottest part of

86 Le Prince's famous picture of the Russian bath.

the atmosphere. Attempting therefore to put on my clothes with my body bent, while I was wet, and in too great a hurry, I found them too little for me, and the more eager I was, the less able was I to get them on. Overpowered with all these difficulties, I threw myself into the antichamber almost naked, where again the extreme cold prevented me from staying to dress, so that I wrapped myself up in my fur night-gown, ran to my carriage, dragging some of my clothes after me, and ordered them to drive home as fast as possible, where I went to bed immediately. The mistress of the house was afraid, from the condition I came back in, and from my re-turning so soon, that some accident had happened to me: she came directly to see me, I removed her fears, and desired I might

198

be permitted to take some rest, as that was the only medicine I wanted: she left me, and returned soon after with a bason of tea, which she offered me. Observing that I did not care to accept of it, she gave me to understand by the Russian serjeant, who began to know a little of French, that I had not stayed long enough at the baths to have been sufficiently sweated; and that it was necessary I should drink the tea to promote perspiration.

Although it was by no means my intention to be sweated, yet she persisted in offering me the tea with so much kindness, that I took it; but as she promised to bring me another bason in a few minutes, I rose as soon as she left me. My serjeant had stayed at the baths, but not finding him returned in half an hour, I was going to inquire after him, taking it for granted some accident had befallen him. He came in just as I was sending a man away for him; he threw himself directly on his bed without saying a word, at last he told me, after I had made him several questions, that he had been taken ill at the baths, and would have persuaded me that he was so ill, it was impossible he should get over it. As he was used to these baths, I judged that his indisposition might arise from some unwholesome vapours, and as a change of air is the quickest and most efficacious remedy in such cases; I therefore had all the windows opened, giving orders that he should be kept quiet; and in two hours after he was perfectly recovered.

This first trial put me so much out of conceit with the Russian baths, that I would not venture into them again during my five months stay at Tobolsk, although I was frequently importuned on this point. However my curiosity was so much raised by what I learned in this town, and through the rest of my journey, of the advantages of these baths, and the method of using them, that I tried again at Yekaterinburg, on my return from Tobolsk; but the heat was too much for me to bear. Yet as I was unwilling to leave the country without being convinced by my own experience of what had been reported to me concerning these baths, I went into them again at a private house in St Petersburg, two months before I set out for France.

These baths are in use all over Russia; every inhabitant of this vast tract of land, from the sovereign to the meanest subject, bathes twice a week, and in the same manner. Every individual, even of the smallest fortune, has a private bath in his own house, in which the father, mother, and children sometimes bathe all together. The lower sort of people go to the public baths, of which there is generally one for the men, and another for the woman; they are separated from each other by wooden partitions; but as they come out of the baths quite naked, the two sexes are seen by each other in this condition, and often converse together in this posture upon indifferent subjects; they afterwards throw themselves promiscuously into the water, or among the snow. In poor and lonely hamlets, the two sexes are oftentimes all together in the same bath. At the salt-houses in Solikamsk I saw some men bathing, who came to the door now and then to cool themselves, and stood there quite naked, talking with women, who were most of them employed in bringing salt provisions, brandy, or kvas, to the workmen. The baths of the rich differ only from those of the poor people in being more clean; the bathing room is

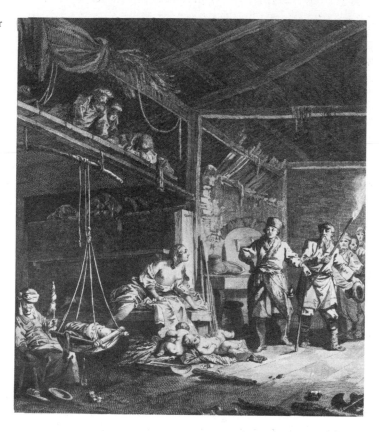

87 A night visit to an *izba* or peasant hut, by Le Prince.

generally all wood; it contains a stove, some tubs full of water, and a kind of amphitheatre, with several steps leading up to it. There are two openings to the stove like those that are in common ovens; by the lower opening the wood is put into the stove, the other contains a heap of stones supported by iron bars; these stones are always red hot, from the heat of the fire kept up in the stove; the use of them will appear hereafter. On going into the bath a person provides himself with a bundle of twigs, a small pail of seven or eight inches in diameter, filled with water, and places himself on the first or second step. Although the heat is less here than in any other part, yet it soon throws him into a sweat, the pail of water is then emptied over his head, some little time after a second, and then a third. He then mounts a little higher, where the same process is repeated, and at last he gets up to the amphitheatre, where the greatest heat is felt. He stays here one quarter, or about half an hour, and in this space of time warm water is frequently poured on his body. A man, who stands before the stove, throws now and then some water on the red hot stones: volleys of steam immediately rush out of the stove with a noise; these ascend to the ceiling, and fall down again on the amphitheatre, in a kind of cloud, carrying a burning heat along with it. At this time the twigs are used, after they have been made very soft, by holding them in the steam as it comes out of the stove; the man who is bathing then lies down on the amphitheatre, and the person next to him whips him with the twigs, expecting he will return the good office: but in many baths women are employed for this purpose. While the leaves remain on the twigs, a considerable quantity of the steam is collected by a turn of the hand; this steam acts the more powerfully, as the pores are very open; and that these burning vapours are briskly driven in by the twigs, which are continually applied to all the parts of the body.

In the private baths I used, I felt such a suffocating heat on my face, when the clouds of steam were collected by the twigs, that I could not have supported it, had it lasted any time. Being willing to ascertain the degree of heat brought on by this process, I had it repeated on the thermometer, which however did not rise more than three degrees higher than it was before.

After having been flogged, water was thrown on me, and I was rubbed with soap; a person then taking hold of the twigs at both ends, rubbed me down so violently, that he was soon in as profuse a sweat as myself. Water was again poured on my body, and on the stones, and they were preparing to flog me again; but the twigs having lost their leaves, I sprang up so suddenly at the first stroke, that I pushed the operator down the stairs on the floor; and determined not to be flogged or rubbed any longer. In a few minutes my skin was all as red as scarlet. I could not bear to stay on the amphitheatre, but had my thermometer carried there, which rose to fifty degrees, while it stood at five and forty in the place where I was: I got out of these baths as soon as I could.

The Russians stay in them sometimes above two hours, and go through all the aforementioned operations several times: most of them rub their body besides with onions, in order to sweat more profusely; they get out of these baths all in a sweat, and immediately throw themselves and roll in the snow in the most severe seasons, passing thus almost in the same instant from a heat of fifty or sixty degrees, to a cold of more than twenty degrees, without feeling any inconvenience.

People of the first rank in Russia go to bed on coming out

of the baths, and rest for some time. It is a received opinion that the baths are more beneficial to the common people, who pass immediately from this intense heat to the extreme cold, than to those, who go to bed after them.

All the Russians, in general, are much addicted to the scurvy; the languid and inactive life they lead, being shut up in their stoves all the winter, makes them very full of humors, and they perspire very little. These baths seem therefore to be absolutely necessary for them, as they might be liable to a great number of diseases if they did not use them. They produce a great fermentation in the blood and humors, and bring on plentiful discharges of perspiration. The extreme cold drives the humors back from the skin, and restores the equilibrium again. Whether these conclusions are just or not, it is an undoubted fact, that these baths are very salutary in Russia: they would certainly be very useful in Europe also for a variety of disorders, especially for rheumatic complaints. Distempers of this kind are hardly known in Russia, and many foreigners have been radically cured of them by the use of these baths.

Jean Chappe d'Auteroche, *Journey into Siberia* (London 1770)

The Russian Nobility

As a young man of twenty-seven, George Macartney was entrusted with the important task of re-negotiating a trade agreement with Russia and during the two years he spent in the Russian capital (1765-7) he was eminently successful and gained the esteem and affection of Catherine and the influential Count Panin. His book was published in the year following his return from Russia and is one of the most lucid surveys of the state of Russia and its people to appear in English in the eighteenth century. His magnificent description of the Russian nobility reveals his great gifts as a stylist, and powers of analysis; his criticism of the gentry's vices, the inordinate imitativeness of things foreign, the arbitrary authority and lack of true learning, is consonant with the attacks made by Russian writers in the journals and plays of the time.

The common people, the merchants, and the clergy having now past in review, the nobility demand our next attention: we should naturally suppose this order to be superior to the others in sentiment, in knowledge and in behaviour; and yet, either so depraved are their dispositions, or so perverted their judgments, that we may safely say, the nobility derive few advantages from birth or education, which claim the respect of others, or are of use to themselves: in their hearts, mean profligacy and vulgar weakness, too often triumph over genius

and honor, without which, birth loses its dignity and fortune has no value.

Conscious and jealous of the superior civilization of foreign nations, sensible of, yet unwilling or unable to correct the errors of their own, they endeavour to conceal their disadvantages under the affectation of despising the stranger, and under the practice of mortifying him. But these are principally exerted against those whom they are jealous of, or those whom they envy for their eminence of talents and superiority of genius: for the humbler foreigner, who has pliancy or bareness enough to submit to their pride, to flatter their vanity, or minister to their pleasures, is certain of securing their favour, of acquiring a confidence and enjoying an influence, which wisdom or virtue could never have obtained. Of this we see innumerable instances in these crowds of French adventurers, who daily resort here, and are received into most families with open arms, as secretaries, librarians, readers, preceptors and parasites; tho' the greatest part of these gentry are equally impudent and illiterate, vagabonds from indigence, or fugitives for crimes.

The Russian gentlemen are certainly the least informed of all others in Europe; the chief point of their instruction is a knowledge of modern languages, particularly, the French and German; both which they usually speak with very great facility, tho' incapable of writing either with precision or propriety. Those who can afford the expence, and indeed many who cannot afford it, complete their education by a tour to France; where ignorant and unprincipled as they are, they catch at every thing that feeds the fancy or inflames the

88 View of the Stroganov estate on Vasilyevskiy Island. Unknown artist, 1805, engraved by G. L. Lory.

203

passions; there they find ample fuel for both; they greedily devour all that is set before them without selection, and lose their delicacy of taste in enormity of appetite: to Frenchmen they become despicable Russians, to Russians despicable Frenchmen, to others equal objects of pity and contempt. So seldom do they derive advantage from those circumstances which form and accomplish the gentleman of other countries, that instead of solid instruction or real improvement, they rarely acquire more than personal affectation and mental distortion, and after all their travels return home far inferior, in the virtues of a good citizen, to those who have never traveled at all.

89 Sir George, later Earl Macartney.

Their natural parts are tolerably good, but they universally want the discriminating faculty; whence they fall into the most absurd imitations of foreign life and manners, and abandoning the common sense of nature, adopt fashions and customs totally contrary to their climate and troublesome to themselves. Tho' freezing under the 60th degree of northern latitude, they build their houses like the airy palaces of Florence and Sienna; in France it is the etiquette of fashion to begin the spring season at Easter, and to mark it by dress, the imitative Russian does the same, and flings off his winter garments whilst the earth is covered with snow, and himself shivering with cold. It is the peculiar privelege of the noblesse at Paris to have Swiss porters at the gates of their hotels. At Petersburg a Russ gentleman of any fashion must have a Swiss also, or some tall fellow with a laced belt and hanger, which it seems are the indispensable accoutrements of a Parisian janitor. It would be an endless task to recite the follies and absurdities of this kind, which they every day fall into, but these few examples, will I presume, appear sufficient.

This ridiculous imitation of foreign, and particularly of French manners, is attended with the most serious consequences, and with innumerable ill effects: it not only divests them of all national character, but prevents them from aspiring to the praise of all national virtue; it represses their native energy of mind and extinguishes every spark of original genius. Nothing was ever more just than Rousseau's censure of Peter the first's conduct; that monarch, instead of improving his subjects as Russians, endeavoured totally to change and convert them into Germans and Frenchmen; but his attempts were unsuccessful; he could not make them what he wished to make them, he spoiled them in the experiment, and left them worse than they were before. His successors have continued the same process, but their projects have been equally ineffectual to the people, and unprofitable to the state.

The Russian nobility from this error of their late princes, have contracted that unfortunate bias which will not suffer their nature to shoot upright: warped by imitation of alien manners without selection, they too often appear vain, petulant, light, inconsequent, indiscreet, envious and suspicious, faithless in their engagements, traitors to one another, incapable of true friendship, and insensible to all the nobler movements of the soul: luxurious and effeminate, listless and indisposed. Tho' in a northern climate they have an Asiatic aversion to all corporal activity and manly exercise, and scarce form an idea of either, beyond the smooth velocity of a sledge, or the measured paces of a managed horse; they have no passion for the sports of the field: hunting, shooting and fishing, as practised with us, they are utterly strangers to. Avoiding every recreation attended with exertion and fatigue: they prefer the more indolent amusements of chess, cards or billiards, in all which they are usually extraordinary proficients: few of them employ their leisure in polishing their minds: insensible to the charms of conversation and the refinements of literature, they loiter and sleep away life and wake but to the calls of sensuality and the grosser pleasures.

Those who serve in the army or in the navy seldom arrive at any extraordinary excellence in either profession, and seem in general as unambitious as undeserving of military fame. They are looked upon as very moderate proficients by all foreign officers; and if sometimes they seem to perform their duty with the spirit of a soldier, they are rather actuated by the principle of mere obedience and the dread of punishment, than inspired by the nobler motives and generous impulse of magnanimity and true valour.

The nobility, in common with the inferior classes, are remarkable for filial piety; but this their so much boasted duty to parents seems to proceed more from principles of dependence and slavery, than from unmixed affection or well founded gratitude; for every father, in the little sphere of his family, is as despotic as the sovereign, in his larger dominion. But this virtue, whether real or pretended, is the principal one which they practise; they have not, nor do they affect to have, that abhorrence of vice and dishonesty, which prevails among other nations: insomuch, that many persons retain their employments, nay, judicial employments, tho' notorious for the most infamous frauds and cruel extortions; for, excepting a few and those in the highest offices, the rest of the nation, tho' in the morn of greatness have all the corruptions incident to a declining state, instead of the sterner virtues which raise an empire to meridian glory.

The abject court and adulation, which they pay to minions, ministers and men in power, are intolerably offensive to every mind, that feels for freedom and independence: to an Englishman they are particularly disgusting: chiefly attentive to their own fortunes, and the immediate gratification of personal vanity, the Russian nobility are regardless of publick virtue, and improvident of posterity; preferring the smile of a courtier, or the hollow patronage of a favourite to the rational pleasures of equal society, and to the happiness of conscious virtue. Their fondness for external honors makes a striking part of their character; there are few of them who would not sacrifice the most solid advantage to the superficial decorations of a ribband or a title; so much attached and accustomed are they to these ornaments, that a foreigner, however great his merit, is but little respected, who does not wear such marks of distinction.

From hence a rigid observer might be led to pronounce them a nation of inconsistence, contradiction and paradox, uniting in themselves the most opposite extremes; hating the stranger, they copy him; affecting originality, they are the slaves of imitation; magnificent and slovenly; irreligous, yet superstitious; at once proud and abject, rapacious and prodigal, equally incapable of being reformed by lenity, or corrected by punishment. The severity of the Empress Anna's reign wrought but little change in their character; nor has the gentleness of subsequent administrations produced any considerable alteration. Perhaps a mistake in the means rendered their labors ineffectual, but certainly the perfect civilization of this class, would be a more difficult task than that of the peasants; for being advanced thus far, the obstinacy and conceit, that usually attend half knowledge, may prevent them from advancing farther. And yet when we reflect on the barbarism of our own and of other countries a few centuries past, we may be induced to form more favourable conjectures of a nation who are far from being destitute of radical virtues. A docile and humane peasantry, such as I have already described them may under better laws be molded into a better people. Farther instructions may wear out their inveterate superstition. A nobility not deficient in natural abilities, must at length feel their errors and misconduct, and acquire that good sense, which will point out the means of amendment. Their present absurd, ridiculous, motley manners are such as must ever arise where foppery is ingrafted on ignorance, and ignorance grows presumptuous from sudden elevation. Another generation may melt these extremes into a more consistent mass. The Russians may one day become what we now are, and notwithstanding our present boasted superiority, we may possibly relapse into that barbarism from which they are endeavouring to emerge . . .

Many ingenious men have amused themselves devising hypotheses, and forming conjectures, why the Russians should have so long continued in barbarism; why, tho' emerging from it for a century past, they still continue the least virtuous, and least ingenious nation in Europe. Some have ascribed it to the climate, whilst many think it owing to the manner of education, and others attribute it to the form of government.

The first of these causes seems to be of less force than the others; for the Swede who lives under the same parallel, certainly bears no resemblance to the Russian. But laying aside the physical cause, let us examine for a moment the moral ones, which seem to have more weight: we have seen that the people continue barbarous, the clergy ignorant, and that the nobleman is but half civilized; that the two first can scarcely be said to have any education at all, whilst the latter had better have none than that which he has; as it is neither calculated to make him useful to society, nor happy and virtuous in himself.

We shall prove, in the following pages, that the government has always been despotic, is still despotic, and likely long to continue so: if then, the form of government can be supposed to influence, or rather create the mental qualities and temper of the people, the Russians must remain unaltered, as long as the form of government continues the same.

Despotism can never long flourish, except in a barbarous nation, but to despotism Russia owes her greatness and dominion; so that if ever the monarchy becomes more limited, she will lose her power and strength, in proportion as she advances in moral virtue and civil improvement.

It will therefore, always be the interest, as it has ever been the practice, of the sovereign to hold the scale of civilization in his own hand, to check every improvement where it might clash with his authority, and encourage it only when subservient to his grandeur and glory.

I am sensible that the various projects of the present Empress may seem to contradict what I have said above; but the fact is, that most of her projects are impracticable; and therefore my assertion loses nothing of its weight. Besides, should the least inconvenience arise from the execution of them, the Empress, than whom no sovereign was ever more jealous or tenacious of *her* authority, can suppress them with a nod, or overthrow them with a breath.

Tho' the form of government certainly is, and will always be, the principal cause of the want of virtue and genius in this country, as making the motives of one, and the rewards of both, depend upon accident and caprice: yet, there are many others, the examination of which might prove a source of very ingenious investigation to the curious enquirer. I must, however, confess that my own consideration of these points has never been attended with any great degree of demonstration, or conviction to myself. In moral and political, as well as in metaphysical and theological researches, there is nearly the same incertitude; and tho' we may amuse ourselves with the speculation of second causes, we must still remain ignorant of the first: we are bewildered in our pursuit, and at the moment we think the case within our reach, it mocks our eagerness and vanishes from our view.

Sir George Macartney, *An Account of Russia* MDCCLVII (London 1768)

The Slavery of the Russian Peasants

In 1768 William Richardson, later to become a distinguished Professor of Humanity at the University of Glasgow, accompanied Charles, Lord Cathcart, who had been appointed Ambassador Extraordinary to the Court of Catherine, to Russia in his capacity as tutor to his Lordship's children. His letter on the hapless state of the Russian serfs is among the most perceptive analyses in contemporary European literature.

Dear Sir,

I will endeavour, in so far as my own observation extends, and in so far as I may depend on the information I have received from others, to satisfy your enquiries concerning the political situation, and national character, of the Russians. On this subject I shall lay the facts and observations before you in the order in which they occur; and with such occasional incidents or anecdotes, as may tend to illustrate any general remark. Nor will I trouble you with any apology for a method, if it may be termed method, so very desultory. In truth, I want leisure, and, perhaps, many other requisites, for composing a formal treatise. I will therefore console myself, and endeavour to satisfy you, by observing, that, for the purposes of mere amusement, the arrangement I have chosen is perhaps as proper as any other. I have also to premise, that if any thing severe shall happen to escape me concerning the form of the Russian government, it can only be concerning the *form*, and without any view to the present administration. I believe sincerely that no despot, or, if you like the term better, no absolute monarch, ever ruled with more prudence, or studied the welfare of his people with more rectitude of intention, than the present Empress of Russia. Yet it is impossible for a native of Britain, giving an account of this country to an Englishman, not to express such feelings and reflections, as a comparison between the British government, and that of other nations, must naturally suggest.

The peasants in Russia, that is to say, the greatest part of the subjects of this empire, are in a state of abject slavery; and are reckoned the property of the nobles to whom they belong, as much as their dogs and horses. Indeed, the wealth of a great man in Russia is not computed by the extent of land he possesses, or by the quantity of grain he can bring to market, but by the number of his slaves. Those belonging to Prince Shcherbatov, and constituting his fortune, are said to be no less in number than a hundred and twenty-seven thousand.

Every slave pays about a ruble yearly to his owner; and if he be in the way of making money, the tribute he pays is augmented. In general, every Russian nobleman allots to the peasants that belong to him, a certain portion of land to be

90 Yemelyan Pugachev, the Cossack leader of the popular rebellion which threatened Catherine's Russia in the years 1773–75. Pugachev was executed in Moscow in January 1775.

cultivated by them, the produce of which, excepting what suffices for their own maintenance, is paid to the proprietor. Sometimes those slaves practise trades, or engage in traffic; and all such persons pay a much greater sum yearly to their owners, than is done by the labourer of the ground. In fact, a Russian peasant has no property; every thing he possesses, even the miserable raiment that shelters him from the cold, may be seized by his master as his own. A carpenter, being known to have made some money, was commanded by the rapacious steward of a rapacious Knyaz, to give two hundred rubles to his owner. The man obeyed, and brought the money in copper. 'I must have it in silver,' said the steward. The slave, denying that he had so much, was instantly scourged till he promised to fulfil the demand. He brought the silver, and the covetous superior retained both the silver and copper. You will easily conceive, that men in this situation, if they are ever enabled to improve their fortunes, will conceal their wealth, and assume an external appearance of indigence and misery.

The owner has also the power of selling his slave, or of hiring his labour to other persons; and, it happens sometimes, that a Knyaz, or Boyar, shall give a slave to a neighbouring Boyar in exchange for a dog or a horse. The owner may also inflict on his slaves whatever punishment he pleases, and for any sort of offence. It is against law, indeed, to put any of them to death; yet it happens, sometimes, that a poor slave dies of the wounds he receives from a passionate and unrelenting superior. I have heard, that not long ago a lady at Moscow, the sister of Marischal S———, was convicted of having put to death upwards of seventy slaves, by scourging, and by inflicting upon them other barbarous punishments. It was a matter of amusement with her to contrive such modes of punishment as were whimsical and unusual. Such enormity, however, notwithstanding her rank, and the great power which the nobility have over their slaves, was not to pass with impunity. She was tried, was found guilty, and condemned to stand in the market-place, with a label on her breast declaring her crime, and to be shut up in a dungeon. But she, who had felt no reluctance in making her fellow-creatures suffer the most inhuman torments, and had even amused herself with the variety of their sufferings, had such a sense of her rank, and such lively feelings of her own disgrace, that pride, shame, and resentment deprived her of her reason. In truth, both the crime and the punishment seem to me strongly marked with the characters of barbarity.

As a Russian peasant has no property, can enjoy none of the fruits of his own labour more than is sufficient to preserve his existence, and can transmit nothing to his children but the inheritance of wretched bondage, he thinks of nothing beyond the present. You are not, of consequence, to expect among them much industry and exertion. Exposed to corporal punishment, and put on the footing of irrational animals, how can they possess that spirit and elevation of sentiment which distinguish the natives of a free state? Treated with so much inhumanity, how can they be humane! I am confident, that most of the defects which appear in their national character, are in consequence of the despotism of the Russian government.

I mentioned that the revenue of a Russian nobleman arises from those lands which are cultivated by his slaves; and sometimes in their being employed in other occupations than tillage. They often come from distant provinces, and are either employed as domestic slaves, mechanics, or as day-labourers, at Moscow, Petersburg, and other cities. In these cases they must have certificates and a written permit, specifying their names, owners, and the time they are allowed to be absent. When they come to any great town, with a view of remaining there, and engaging themselves in any work, the person who employs them must lodge their certificates with the master of the police in the place where they are about to reside. After remaining their allotted time, they must return to their former owners, and must be accountable to them for every thing they have earned. To these practices the Empress alludes in the following passages, in her instructions to the deputies assembled for making laws: 'It seems too, that the method of exacting their revenues, invented by the lords, diminishes both the inhabitants, and the spirit of agriculture, in Russia. Almost all the villages are heavily taxed. The lords, who seldom or never reside in their villages, lay an impost on every head, of one, two, and even five rubles, without the least regard to the means by which their peasants may be able to raise this money. It is highly necessary that the law should prescribe a rule to the lords, for a more judicious method of raising their revenues; and oblige them to levy such a tax as tends least to separate the peasant from his house and family: this would be the means by which agriculture would become more extensive, and population more increased in the empire. Even now, some husbandmen do not see their houses for fifteen years together, and yet pay the tax annually to their respective lords; which they procure in towns at a vast distance from their families, and wander over the whole empire for that purpose.'

Another hardship to which the Russian peasants are exposed, is, that they are obliged to marry whatsoever persons, or at what time their superiors please. Every slave who is a father, pays a certain tax to his owner for each of his children; and the owner is therefore solicitous that a new progeny be raised as soon as possible. Marriages of this sort must produce little happiness; neither husband nor wife are very studious of conjugal fidelity: hence the lower classes are as profligate as can possibly be conceived; and, in such circumstances, we cannot expect that they will have much care of their children.

The condition of those peasants who are immediate slaves of the crown, is reckoned less wretched than the condition of those who belong to the nobility; and they are of three kinds: The first are those who, having either secretly, or by the favour of a humane superior, been able to procure as much money as may enable them to purchase their freedom, have also the good luck to live under a superior who is equitable enough to free them for the sum they offer. Such persons, and their children, are ever after immediate slaves of the crown. On the same footing are all priests and their children; though the dependance of the inferior upon the superior clergy, is sometimes as grievous as the most painful bondage. Soldiers also, and their children; and this class includes the whole body of the nobility, are immediate slaves of the crown.

O fortunatos nimium, sua si bona norint, Britannos!

Adieu.

William Richardson, *Anecdotes of the Russian Empire* (London 1784)

'A Very Singular Entertainment'

William Coxe describes with obvious astonishment a vast party given by a successful Russian 'businessman', which ended in the tragic death by freezing of many of the inebriated revellers.

On the 6th of December we were witness to a very singular entertainment given to the public by a Russian, who had acquired a large fortune by farming, during four years only, the right of vending spirituous liquors. Upon surrendering his contract, he gave, as a proof of his gratitude to the lower class of people, by whom he had enriched himself, a feast near the garden of the summer-palace, which was announced by hand-bills distributed throughout the city. As strangers, desirous of observing the national manners, we did not fail to be present at this carousal, which commenced at two o'clock in the

91 William Coxe. Drawing by J. Jackson after Sir W. Beechey.

212

afternoon. Upon our first arrival, we examined the preparations. A large semicircular table was covered with all kinds of provision, piled in different shapes, and in the greatest profusion: Large slices of bread and caviare, dried sturgeon, carp, and other fish, were ranged to a great height, in the form of pent-houses and pyramids, and garnished with craw-fish, onions, and pickles. In different parts of the grounds were rows of casks full of spirituous liquors, and still larger vessels of wine, beer, and kvas. Among the decorations I observed the representation of an immense whale in pasteboard, covered with cloth and gold and silver brocade, and filled in the inside with bread, dried fish, and other provisions.

All sorts of games and diversions were exhibited for the amusement of the populace. At the extremity of the grounds was a large square of ice well swept for the scaters; near which were two machines like the swinging vehicles at Bartholomew Fair. One of these machines consisted of two cross-beams fixed

92 'The Genuine Russian Mountains'. Lithograph by Arnout, according to the drawings of Sauerweid. 'They build on the frozen surface of the Neva two timber works, between 40 and 50 feet in height, and from 800 to 900 feet apart, inclining one toward the other, lest the sledges that descend should meet. Every slope is soon metamorphosed into a mountain of ice, occasioned by the torrents of water/thereon, or by pieces of ice which are placed/poured one after another the whole length of the course. The sledge descends with a frightful rapidity, and continues with the same velocity to run over the level space between the two theatres. This exercise is the principal amusement of the Russians during the winter.'

213

horizontally to a pole in the center by means of a pivot: from the ends of the beams hung four sledges, in which the people seated themselves, and were turned round with great velocity; the other had four wooden horses suspended from the beams, and the riders were whirled round in the like manner as their rivals in the sledges. Beyond these were two ice-hills, similar to those which I have described on a former occasion, and for the same diversion. Two poles, above twenty feet in height,

93 View of the city of Novgorod in the late eighteenth century.

were also erected, with colours flying; and at the top of each was placed a piece of money, as a prize for those who could swarm up and seize it. The poles, being rubbed with oil, soon froze in this severe climate: many and tedious where the attempts of the various competitors in this slippery ascent to fame. The scene was lively and gay; for above 40,000 persons of both sexes were assembled on the occasion. Having thus far satisfied our curiosity, we found our way, not without great difficulty, through the crowd to a pavilion in the garden; where the master of the feast and several of the nobility were assembled; and were regaled with a cold collation, and various sorts of wine.

It had been preconcerted, that, upon the firing of a rocket, the people were to drink a glass of spirituous liquor; and, upon the discharge of a second, to begin the repast. But the impatience of the populace anticipated the necessity of the second signal; and the whole multitude was soon and at once in motion. The whale was the chief object of contention: within the space of a few minutes he was entirely divested of his gaudy trap-

214

pings, which became the spoils of his successful invaders. They had no sooner flead off his drapery, and secured the fragments of rich brocade; than they rent him into a thousand pieces, in order to seize the provisions with which his inside was stored. The remaining people, who were too numerous to be all engaged in contending about the whale, were employed in uncovering the pent-houses, and pulling down the pyramids; in conveying with one hand provender to their mouths, and with the other to their pockets. Others crowded round the casks and hogsheads; and with great wooden ladles lapped incessantly wine, beer, and spirits. The confusion and riot, which soon succeeded, is better conceived than described; and we thought it expedient to retire. The evening was closed with a superb illumination of the gardens, and magnificent fire-works.

But the consequences of this feast were indeed dreadful. The cold had suddenly increased with such violence, that Fahrenheit's thermometer, which at mid-day stood only at 4, sunk towards the close of the evening to 15 below freezing point; consequently many intoxicated persons were frozen to death; not a few fell a sacrifice to drunken quarrels; and others were robbed and murdered in the more retired parts of the city, as they were returning late to their homes. From a comparison of the various reports, we had reason to conclude, that at least 400 persons lost their lives upon this melancholy occasion.

William Coxe, *Travels into Poland, Russia, Sweden and Denmark* (London 1784)

Novgorod

As Moscow reached the zenith of its power, the great city of Novgorod declined. Many eighteenth-century travellers shared William Coxe's historical melancholy as they viewed the vestiges of its former splendour.

At Bronnitsy we crossed the Msta upon a raft composed of seven or eight trees rudely joined together, and which scarcely afforded room for the carriage and two horses. We then continued our route, through a level country, to the banks of the Volkhovets, or little Volkhov, which we passed in a ferry; and, after mounting a gentle rise, descended into the open marshy plain of pasture, which reaches, without interruption, to the walls of Novgorod: that place, at a small distance, exhibited a most magnificent appearance; and, if we might judge from the great number of churches and convents, which on every side presented themselves to our view, announced

216

94 Plan of Novgorod which stands on the river Volkhov. From Palmquist 1672.

217

our approach to a considerable city; but upon our entrance our expectations were by no means realized.

No place ever filled me with more melancholy ideas of fallen grandeur, than the town of Novgorod. It is one of the most antient cities in Russia; and was formerly called *Great* Novgorod, to distinguish it from other Russian towns of a similar appellation.

The present town is surrounded by a rampart of earth, with a range of old towers at regular distances, forming a circumference of scarcely a mile and an half; and even this inconsiderable circle includes much open space, and many houses which are not inhabited. As Novgorod was built after the manner of the antient towns of this country, in the Asiatic style; this rampart, like that of the Zemlyannoy gorod at Moscow, probably enclosed several interior circles: without it was a vast extensive suburb, which reached to the distance of six miles, and included within its circuit all the convents and churches, the antient ducal palace and other structures; that now make a splendid, but solitary appearance, as they lie scattered in the adjacent plain.

Novgorod stretches on both sides of the Volkhov, a beautiful river of considerable depth and rapidity, and somewhat broader than the Thames at Windsor. This river separates the town into two divisions; the Trading Part, and the Quarter of St Sophia, which are united by means of a bridge, partly wooden and partly brick.

The first division, or the Trading Part, is, excepting the governor's house, only a rude cluster of wooden habitations, and in no other respect distinguished from the common villages than by a vast number of brick churches and convents, which stand melancholy monuments of its former magnificence. In all parts I was struck with these remains of ruined grandeur; while half-cultivated fields enclosed within high palisadoes, and large spaces covered with nettles, attested its present desolate condition. Towards its extremity a brick edifice, and several detached structures of the same materials, erected at the empress's expence, for a manufacture of ropes and sails, exhibited a most splendid figure when contrasted with the surrounding wooden hovels in the town.

The opposite division, denominated the Quarter of St Sophia, derives its appellation from the cathedral of that name; and comprehends the fortress or Kremlin, erected for the purpose of curbing the inhabitants, and of preventing the frequent insurrections occasioned by the rising spirit of oppressed liberty. It is of an irregularly oval form, and surrounded by an high brick wall, strengthened with round and square towers: the wall is similar to that which encloses the Kremlin at Moscow; and was built in 1490 by the Italian architect Solarius of Milan, at the order of Ivan Vasilevich I soon after his conquest of Novgorod. The fortress contains the cathedral of St Sophia; the old archiepiscopal mansion with its stair-case on the outside; part of a new palace which was not yet finished; a few other brick buildings; but the remaining space is a waste, overspread with weeds and nettles, and covered with ruins.

William Coxe, *Travels into Poland, Russia, Sweden and Denmark* (London 1784)

Catherine at Tsarskoye Selo

In 1781 Elizabeth Dimsdale accompanied her husband Thomas, whom Catherine had made a Baron in 1768, to the Imperial Summer residence at Tsarskoye Selo, where he was to inoculate the young Grand Dukes, Alexander and Constantine. Baroness Dimsdale recorded her visit in a diary which was not intended for publication. The extract below, although obviously not revised or polished, nevertheless contains, alongside descriptions of a guide-book nature, intimate details of the life of the Royal family. The description of Catherine in the park with the greyhounds which Baron Dimsdale had previously given her recalls the famous painting by Borovikovsky (reproduced opposite), which was in turn the model for Pushkin's description of Catherine in his novel, *The Captain's Daughter*.

The next month (September) was fixed for the innoculation for the two Dukes at Tsarskoye Selo, Empress said I might accompany him, she lives in retirement there, her public court days are in St Petersburg. I understood our household was to be kept at St Petersburg, nothing was omitted, the same officer came every morning and gave the housekeeper fifty ruble and said the Baron was not to pay anything, he was told to come every day. All our letters came and went free of postage.

August 27th I accompanied the Baron to Tsarskoye Selo, Palace magnificent and built by Empress Elizabeth, many exterior ornaments, and pillars, wooden statues support the cornices, roof painted and gilded, and green paint makes it gay.

We had rooms under the regal apartments, the best in the Palace except for the Empress and Grand Duke's. Mr Bush from England visited me and asked me to dine with him, he knew the Baron was dining with the Empress. He is the Empress's gardener. Dr Rogerson came in and said to me, 'I hear you and I dine together at Mr Bush's.' At dinner a running footman in green and silver came in and said if not inconvenient, Sir James Harris and the Imperial Minister were coming to dine, we had a good English dinner. Mrs Bush and four daughters are agreeable people. I had a favour of being introduced in a private manner, which was more agreeable to me. Madam Naryshkina presented me to the Empress. I kissed her hand and she my cheek. Fine looking woman, not tall, fine expression, blue eyes and a sweet sensible look, a handsome person in her fifty-fourth year. The Grand Duke and Duchess passed through and spoke to me, I had not been introduced to them, I could not before being presented to the Empress; she went out and the community followed into a

95 In 1768 Catherine was inoculated against smallpox by Thomas Dimsdale and was applauded by the senate for 'saving others to the danger of herself'. These two contemporary popular prints are urging the empress' subjects to follow her worthy example.

96 (*overleaf*) The layout of the gardens at Tsarskoye Selo (now Pushkin) designed by the imperial gardener, the Englishman Joseph Bush (c. 1790).

large room for a concert. The Duke is a little man, not handsome, the Duchess was gracious, they asked me to play cards, I declined. She is taller than I am, handsome, about 22 years. The two princes Alexander Pavlovich, 12th December 1781, aged 4 years. Constantine Pavlovich, April 27th aged 3 years. They are beautiful and sensible and clever. Empress allows 30,000 rubles a year for their clothes. We went for a walk with them in the garden, two English women who have charge of them are sisters, Mrs Guslar and Mrs Nichols, both civil.

Empress ordered them to call them by their christian names only, as pride would come fast enough without encouraging it. I went into the children's apartments, clever old lady Madam Benkendorff showed me the toys, really beyond anything that can be imagined for expense. They had a silver boat and two men in it which wound up and went on the water for some time, some gold, I am sure cost £2000. The Empress was continually giving them some. Empress is very fond of them and cannot refuse them anything, nothing pleases them like soldiers and exercising. Each of them would have a regiment, twenty four boys, two in turn to guard their apartments. Prince Alexander know all the uniforms of the Empress's services, as much as the officers. He stopped a soldier in the garden and asked sensible questions and where his Captain was? He turned to Mrs Guslar and said, 'He is a poor man, give him some money.' Empress's orders were Mrs Guslar was always to have it and give it when the boys said so. Each have their apartments and footmen in laced liveries and a coach and six. One room in the Palace is inlaid with amber a present from the late King of Prussia. Only three were finished before I came away, one in Chinese taste, fine China jars, one Turkish manner, very grand. At the end a room inlaid with pit red and green, it dazzled one's eyes. Lyons room tapistry in it made there. These particulars were sent to me as they were not finished.

Plastering, gilding, painting and glasses	10,000	Rubles
Tapestry £10,000 equal to	50,000	,,
2 Ovens or fireplaces, solid silver doors	10,000	,,
Floor inlaid with Mother of Pearl	11,000	,,
Brass mouldings, cornice etc gilt	32,000	,,
Window and frames for Tapestry	1,500	,,
36 chairs carved and gilt made in Paris at £200 per chair	36,000	,,
36 chairs made in St Petersburg at £100 per chair	18,000	,,
Tables and 3 brass doors figured with lapis lazuli	15,000	,,
Mans labour for working the lapis lazuli	17,000	,,
Sterling £40,250	201,250	,,

The lapis lazuli was found in Siberia, the weight used was one hundred Poods. A Pood is equal to 36 lbs. 3600 lbs used. Dimensions of the room 36 ft. × 32½ ft. Height 28 ft. 12 plate glasses 13 ft. long × 4½ ft. wide. Windows are 7 ft. in length. They open with hinges. Gardens are laid like English ones, paths and woods, a piece of water near the centre with an island, has a building in it, it was frequented when flying

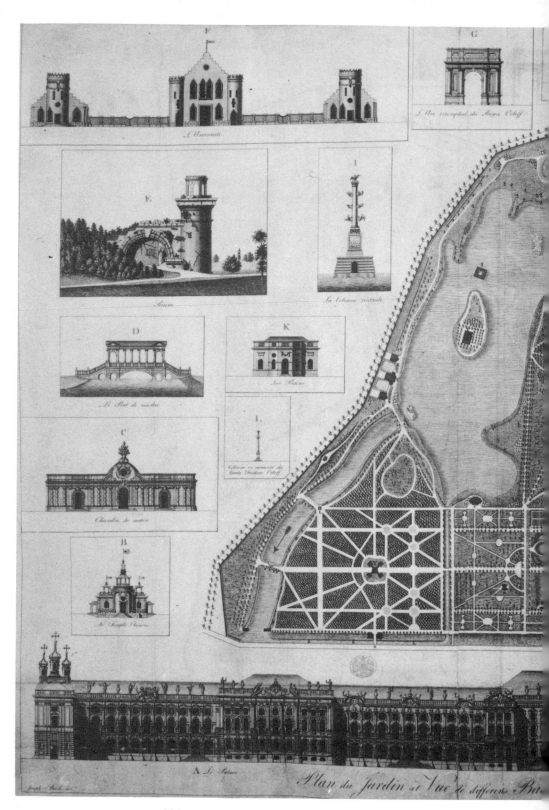

F

L'Amarante

G

L'Arc triomphal du Prince Orloff

E

Ruine

I

La Colonne rostrale

D

Le Pont de marbre

K

Les Bains

L

Colonne en mémoire du Comte Orloff

C

Chambre de nation

B

Le Temple Chinois

A Le Palais

Joseph Bach del.

Plan du Jardin et Vue de differens Bat...

222

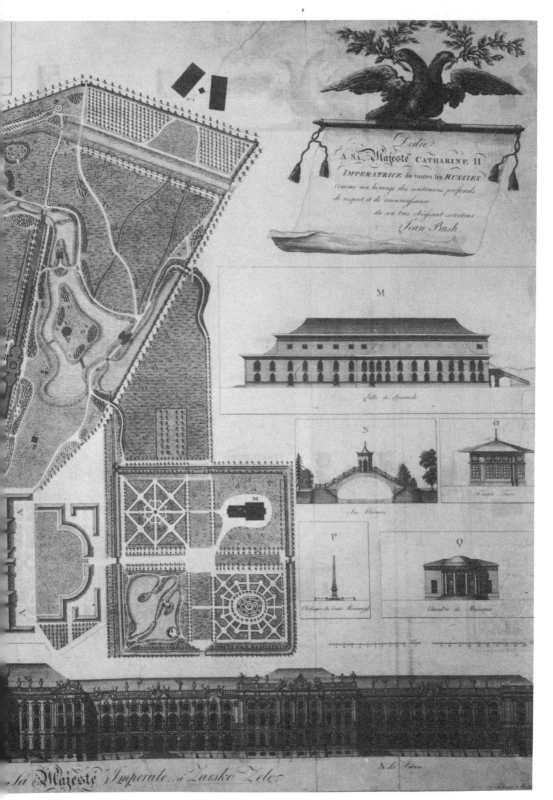

mountains came in fashion, they were all destroyed except one which I saw go off.

Empress often amused herself, she went in one and the car got off the groove, it might have entailed a nasty accident, they go with such speed.

Prince Orlov is strong. He guided it with his leg, the exertion strained his leg, he was lame for some time after. Mr Bush said after this they were destroyed. Empress Elizabeth had these mountains made, she was fond of it. The highest remains 30 ft. perpendicular, next mountain five or six feet lower to allow friction and resistance, the slides are wood about a furlong and a half long. It is used in winter and summer, the carriage was on castors, the more people in it the quicker it went. The horses worked a machine to take the company up again. Upon the mount two very high swings are placed and a chaise to hold one person and two or three wooden horses so constructed anyone can ride round the mound, wheels underneath are worked by a horse with great swiftness.

Another part of the garden was a Hermitage and a sopha, I and the Princes and the English women sat on it, we were immediately drawn into an apartment. A room with large bow windows each made a room, a table in the middle which would dine ten people and four small tables round it, and four dumb waiters plates with silver rims and something of the slate kind in the middle of them and a pensil fixed to each plate, you wrote on the plate what was ordered, then pulled another string

97, 98 Two designs by the Scottish architect Charles Cameron (1740–1812) for features in the imperial palace at Tsarskoye Selo.

97 Elevation of a doorway wall.

98 Elevation of a door wall. Agate study, Agate pavilion.

99 The Hermitage Pavilion in Tsarskoye Selo. Built 1743–54 by architects A. V. Vlasov, S. I. Cherakinsky, B. B. Rastrelli. Engraving by A. Grekov after a drawing by M. Makhayev.

225

and the plate sunk down and returned again with the order, dishes the same. The Empress neglects it, occasionally she dines if a foreigner is with her. Empress Elizabeth liked dining here. No servant was admitted for pulling the string of the bell and writing on the plate answered the purpose.

The Admiralty is near, boats etc are kept there, it overlooks water and lofty pillar to the memory of Count Alexis Orlov who gained a naval victory at Chesme. There are buildings in the garden to different people who distinguished themselves. A Triumphal Arch to the memory of Prince Orlov for his repairing to Moscow to quell the insurrections of the people at the time of the plague in 1775, people who died from the Plague 1771, 56,772 persons: 1772, 3,692: 1773, 7,295: 1774, 7,527: 1775, 6,559: 81,845 persons. A number of persons equally great died in Moscow.

There are two bridges in the garden, one Turkish and one Chinese. Turkish built of marble. A rope is tied from one side to the other starting on one bridge, they are alike, and pulling the rope, I gently crossed over. This motion brought the other bridge from the other side, so there is always a bridge ready to convey you. In the garden there is a Pyramid cost no less than £2000, under it was a large hollow dome with a door,

100 Catherine the Great with her greyhound in the gardens of Tsarskoye Selo. After V. L. Borovikovsky.

we were in the garden one day and opened it, crept in it was large enough to hold the Baron. This mausoleum was the deposit two Italian greyhounds which the Baron presented to the Empress. It was the fashion for the Courts to keep one. She informed the Baron that Tom the dog, and his wife had been very prolific and ran more of their kind than Abraham. Empress was in the garden with the two greyhounds and she wished him to attend her. She is often in the garden a little after 6 a.m., walks in leather shows and several dogs. She goes in at nine, while she is finishing dressing, papers are read to her. She had two hairdressers and always wore a large bonnet, on particular days her head was drest low with two side curls, piece of gauze pinned on the top, the shape of a cap. In the summer she lives on a leather mattress, a handkerchief for nightcap, Russian women are partial to Handkerchiefs, it is the old Russian headdress; middling people and servants wear them now when drest, they pin it on a large piece of pasteboard. Russian ladies of the 1st rank wear only a handkerchief on their heads like a turban. Gentlemen of Court used to wear plain clothes but now they vie with each other in rich clothes and spend a lot of money.

Baroness Elizabeth Dimsdale, *Diary* 1781 (Unpublished)

Crimean Cameos

Lady Elizabeth Craven was the first of the new breed of lady tourists to venture beyond the capitals and take delight in the 'picturesqueness' of the southern provinces. She records her impressions in a series of letters to her future husband, the Margrave of Anspach; the letter which follows is a typical example of her lively but superficial manner.

April, 1786

Yesterday I went to see the source of the river, it lies in the recess of a rock, which is placed between many others that line the steep sides of a valley; a Major Ribas, a very lively handsome officer of the Chasseurs, has drawn it for me. I rode a white horse of the general's, a very quiet creature, but awkward, not being used to a sidesaddle.

I never saw a scene so lively as this visit – there were near forty people on horseback – the variety of dresses and colours upon the green carpet was gay and picturesque. We continued going up hill to the source, till we perceived the rocks, but the sides of them were so steep that we were all obliged to dismount and scramble down as we could; this spring does not present itself like the Vaucluse, majestic and terrible, but pretty and romantic – and might be copied in a park where huge fragments of stone could be had. As we returned, I got off and walked beside the soldiers' houses, and went into some; they are placed in a line of the declivity of the down, as they descend to the General's house – all things were very neat and orderly. The old Cossack chief had looked with the greatest astonishment at my riding, and when I jumped down from my horse on returning home, he kissed the edge of my petticoat, and said

101 A view of the source of the river Karasou in the Crimea, drawn by a Major Ribas in April 1786 for Lady Elizabeth Craven. From *A Journey through the Crimea to Constantinople,* 1789.

102 Map showing the route taken by Catherine II on her journey to the Crimea in 1787; from Count Ségur's *Memoires,* Vol III.

something in his language which I did not comprehend, but the general told me he had paid me the highest compliment imaginable, viz. I was worthy of being a Cossack.

In the evening I went in a carriage with the governor and general to Karasubazar – and on the road saw a mock battle between the Cossacks. As I was not apprised before-hand, I confess the beginning of it astonished me very much. I saw the Cossack guard on each side the carriage spring from their stirrups, with their feet on the saddle and gallop away thus with a loud shriek. The General smiled at my astonished looks – and told me the Cossack Chief had ordered an entertainment for me – and desired me to get out and stand on the rising part of the down, facing that where a troop of Cossacks was posted – which I saw advancing with a slow pace – a detached Cossack of the adverse party approached the troop, and

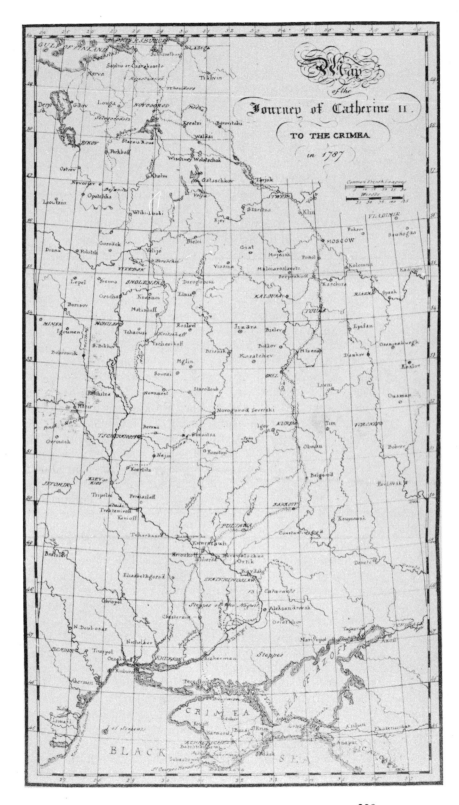

Map

of the

Journey of Catherine II.

TO THE CRIMEA

in 1787

turning round sought his scattered companions, who were in search like him of the little army—they approached, but not in a squadron, some on the left, some on the right, some before, some behind the troop—a shriek—a pistol fired, were the signals of battle—the troop was obliged to divide in order to face an enemy that attacked it on all sides. The greatest scene of hurry and agility ensued; one had seized his enemy, pulled him off his horse, and was upon the point of stripping him, when one of the prisoner's party came up, laid him to the ground, remounted his companion, and rode off with the horse of the first victor. Some flung themselves off their horses to tear their foe to the ground—alternately they pursued or were pursuing, their pikes, their pistols, their hangers all were made use of— and when the parties were completely engaged together, it was difficult to see all the adroit manœuvres that passed.

I was much entertained and pleased—and desired the Cossack Chief might have my best thanks—I arrived at the town, and was led to the Kadis' house, where his wife received me, and no male creature was suffered to come into the room, except the interpreter and a young Russian nobleman only twelve years of age. This woman had a kind of turban on, with some indifferent diamonds and pearls upon it. Her nails were dyed scarlet, her face painted white and red, the veins blue; she appeared to me to be a little shrivelled woman of near sixty, but I was told she was not above fifty. She had a kind of robe and vest on, and her girdle was a handkerchief embroidered with gold and a variety of colours. She made me a sign to sit down; and my gloves seeming to excite much uneasiness in her I took them off—upon which she drew near, smiled, took one of my hands between her's, and winked and nodded as a sign of approbation—but she felt my arm up beyond the elbow, half way up my shoulder, winking and nodding—I began to wonder where this extraordinary examination would end—which it did there. Coffee was brought, and after that rose-leaves made into sweatmeats—both of which the interpreter obliged me to taste. The sweetmeats are introduced last, and among the Orientals they are a signal that the visit must end. Our conversation by the interpreter was not very entertaining. She asked if I had a child, and told me what I have been told so often before, though I confess not by women, that would be unnecessary to repeat it. A Tartar house is a very slight building of one story only—no chair, table, or piece of furniture in wood to be seen—large cushions are ranged round the room, on which we sat or reclined—but what is extremely convenient, I observed more than double the space of the room behind the wainscot, which drew back in most places, so that in a small room, where it appears there is nothing but the cushions—every necessary is to be found. As the visit was at an end, I curtsied and she bowed. In the court-yard there was a dancer, a woman accompanied in her gestures by a boy, but it was impossible to see them either with pleasure or propriety; she never lifted her feet off the ground but once in four minutes, and then only one foot at a time, and every part of her person danced except her feet. I went to a Mosque, where several pious Mussulmen were going round in a circle in the midst of the building, groaning and flinging their heads almost to the ground and then up again, a constant motion which with the moving round one

103 A Tartar Horse Race. From C. Rechberg, *Des Peuples de la Russie*.

way soon puts them into a kind of torture, under which they fall to the ground; and then are dragged into recesses in the Mosque, made on purpose to receive these holy men, who sacrifice so many hours, and their persons to idle pain, in order to prove their devotion to Mahomet. They frequently pronounced Allah.

In one of the recesses I saw a man lying, that I was told had been there without eating or drinking forty hours; which abstinence is another pious act, and if their courage is excessive, and Allah can inspire them with strength enough, they endeavour in getting out of the dark and damp hole where they lay for many hours, to join in the circle, and begin to move, but in this attempt they generally fall senseless to the ground, and are carried home to recover their strength. This kind of mummery inspires the people with a great reverence and esteem for those who practise it. I returned home as much disgusted with this nonsense as I was displeased with the dirt of the town. The Mosque was shabby on the outside and gloomy within, notwithstanding many lamps in it. The Minaret, which we should call a steeple, and all the other Minarets I saw in the town, are uncommonly light, being very high and narrow. A man stands at the top and calls to prayers, instead of tolling bells as we do, at particular hours–and makes a noise to the full as agreeable.

The chief traffic of this town is the leather which we call Morocco, of various colours, yellow, red, green, and blue – it is to be had very cheap, and is like sattin. The innumerable sheep with which these plains are covered furnish much leather, which is a cheap commodity, as well as the most beautiful and costly pelisses. The sheep are all spotted. The lamb-skins are beautiful, and they kill the ewes to have the lamb-skins before the birth; these have small spots, and are smooth like the lightest and finest sattins. As many of these little animals must be skinned to make the lining of one coat, it is no wonder this is one of the most sumptuous presents the Empress can make to an ambassador. I wish I was rich enough to send you a pelisse made of these skins.

I remain dear Sir,
Your affectionate sister,
E. C.

Lady Elizabeth Craven, *A Journey through the Crimea to Constantinople* (London 1789)

With Catherine in the Crimea

In 1787 Catherine set out to inspect her newly-acquired territories in the Crimea, accompanied by a retinue which included the Comte de Ségur and the Prince de Ligne. Potemkin's efforts to impress the Empress with the flourishing state of the country and well-being of its inhabitants led to the famous stratagem of the 'Potemkin villages', a combination of movable scenery and well-dressed peasant actors. The Prince de Ligne discusses the rumours and attempts to explain Catherine's position.

Tula

Alas! here we are on our way back. Do you know that I was on the point of loving you in Asia, and of writing to you from Azov? A cursèd prudence of doctors and ministers (in neither of whom does the empress believe) prevented our leaving Europe–if what we have lately seen can be called

232

Europe, for it resembles it little enough. I know it is not the fashion to believe travellers, or courtiers, or any good told of Russia. Even those Russians who are vexed at not having come with us pretend that we are deceived, and deceiving. They have already spread about the ridiculous story that cardboard villages were set up along the line of our route for hundreds of miles; that the vessels and cannons were painted images, the cavalry horseless, and so forth.

104 Mud baths in the Crimea.

For the last two months I have been throwing money out of window; this has happened to me before, but never in precisely the present way. I have already distributed, it may be, millions, and this is how it is done. Beside me, in the carriage, is a great green bag, like the one you will put your prayer-books in when you become devout. This bag is filled with imperials–coins of four ducats. The inhabitants of the villages and those from ten, fifteen, and twenty leagues round line our route to see the empress, and this is how they see her. A good quarter of an hour before she passes, they lie down flat on their stomachs and do not rise for a quarter of an hour after we have passed. 'T is on their backs and on their heads kissing the earth that I shower a rain of gold while passing at full gallop, and this usually happens ten times a day; my hands are soiled with my beneficence. I have become the grand-almoner of all the Russias. He of France throws money also through his window, but it is his own.

I know very well what is trickery: for example, the empress, who cannot rush about on foot as we do, is made to believe that certain towns for which she has given money are finished; whereas they are often towns without streets, streets without houses, and houses without roofs, doors, or windows. Nothing is shown to the empress but shops that are well-built of stone,

233

colonnades of the palaces of governors-general, to forty-two of which she has presented silver services of a hundred covers. In the capitals of the provinces they often give us balls and suppers for two hundred persons. The furs and gold chains of the wives of the merchants, and the sort of grenadier-caps the people wear adorned with pearls show wealth. The costumes of the gentlemen and ladies in these vast halls are a fine sight. The provinces of the East wear brown and gold and silver; the others red and sky-blue.

In this place is one of the finest manufactories of arms that can be seen anywhere; besides this, they work in steel nearly as well as they do in England. I am loaded with presents that I do not know what to do with. The empress buys everything, to give away and at the same time to encourage manufacture. I have a stool, an umbrella, a table, a cane, a damascened dressing-case; all of which are very useful to me, as you may suppose, and very convenient to carry about.

'See,' says the empress to me sometimes, pointing to fields in the governments of Kharkov and Kursk as well cultivated as in England, with a population almost as numerous, 'see how the Abbé Chappe never *saw* anything through the wooden windows of his carriage, closed on account of cold; and how wrong he was in saying that there were "nothing but deserts in Russia." I will not warrant that some village seigneur, abusing his power (which might happen any where), may not have produced, whip in hand, the cries of joy to drown the cries of misery. But as soon as such seigneurs are complained of to the governors of the provinces, they are punished; and certainly the hurrahs we have heard along our route were shouted heartily and with very smiling faces.'

As I have quitted the empress from time to time and made various trips, I have seen many things that the Russians themselves do not know: superb establishments in process of building, manufactories, villages well built, streets laid out in lines, surrounded by trees, and watered by brooks. All that I tell you is true; because, in the first place, I never tell lies except to women who are not like you; and next, because no one here reads my letters. Besides, we never flatter people whom we see from six in the morning till ten at night; on the contrary, one is sometimes out of temper with them in a carriage . . . I remember one day we were talking of courage, and the empress said to me: 'If I had been a man I should have been killed before I was a captain.' I answered, 'I think not, Madame, for I still live.' I noticed that after taking some time to understand what I meant, she laughed softly to herself on perceiving that I had corrected her for thinking herself more brave than I and so many others. Another time I was disputing with her very seriously about the Court of France; and as she seemed to be putting faith in certain pamphlets that were being circulated in foreign countries, I said to her

105 Women of Yaroslavl and a female gardener from Tula. Travellers noted that in Tula the so-called 'Sheffield' of Russia, women were frequently employed in 'occupations which are generally considered as belonging to the more robust sex'. From *La Russie, ou Moeurs, Usages et Costumes des habitants . . . de cet Empire*. M. Breton, Paris 1813.

234

almost sharply: 'Madame, they lie at the North about the West, and at the West about the North; we should no more believe the sedan-bearers of Versailles than your izvozchiki in Petersburg.'

We look upon the rest of our journey as a trifle; unhappily, we have only four hundred leagues more to do. We have required throughout six hundred horses for each relay. All the carriages are filled with peaches and oranges; our valets are drunk with champagne, and I am dying with hunger, for everything is cold and detestable at the empress's table. She never sits there long, and if she has anything agreeable or useful to say she does it so slowly that nothing is hot except the water we drink. One of the charms of this country is that the summers are more scorching than they are in Provence. In the Crimea I came near suffocating from the fumes of the brazier one breathes. Another charm of the country is that we get no news of your little Europe from any of you. I do not believe my letters reach you; and I shall receive none from you if, as I hope, war will be declared one of these days with the good Mahometans. I am in haste to fight, my dear marquise, that I may see you all the sooner; meantime I adore you as a divinity without seeing you.

Prince Charles de Ligne, *Memoirs, Letters and Miscellaneous Papers* (London 1899)

The Kamchadals

Jean de Lesseps, who had accompanied the French explorer La Pérouse as far as Kamchatka, left the ships in 1787 and proceeded with dispatches by land through Siberia to St Petersburg and thence to Paris. He has left a particularly detailed account of life and conditions in Kamchatka, stressing the often unfortunate effects which the Russian colonizers had on the natives.

There are three sorts of inhabitants, the natives or Kamchadals, the Russians and Cossacks, and the descendants from inter-marriages.

The indigenes, that is, those whose blood is unmixed, are few in number; the small pox has carried off three fourths of them, and the few that are left are dispersed through the different ostrogs of the peninsula; in Bolsheretsk it would be difficult to find more than one or two.

The true Kamchadals are in general below the common height; their shape is round and squat, their eyes small and sunk, their cheeks prominent, their nose flat, their hair black, they have scarcely any beard, and their complexion is a little

235

106 The route of Lesseps through the peninsula of Kamchatka.

tawny. The complexion and features of the women are very nearly the same; from this representation, it will be supposed they are not very seducing objects.

The character of the Kamchadals is mild and hospitable; they are neither knaves, nor robbers; they have indeed so little penetration, that nothing is more easy than to deceive them, as we have seen in the advantage that is taken of their propensity to intoxication. They live together in the utmost harmony, and the more so, it would seem, on account of the

236

ROUTE of

M. de Lesseps

——— Consul of France. ———

in the PENINSULA *of*

KAMTSCHATKA,

and along the GULF *of* PENGINA,

from the Port of S.t Peter & S.t Paul *as far as* Yamsk.

Russian Wersts, 10½ to a Degree.

100   200   300

smallness of their number. This unanimity disposes them to
assist one another in their labours, which is no small proof
of their zeal to oblige, if we consider the natural and extreme
slothfulness of their disposition. An active life would be
insupportable to them; and the greatest happiness, in their
estimation, next to that of getting drunk, is to have nothing
to do, and to live for ever in tranquil indolence. This is carried
so far with these people, as frequently to make them neglect
the means of providing the indispensable necessaries of life;

237

and whole families are often reduced to all the severities of famine, because they would not take the pains of providing in summer a reserve of fish, without which they are unable to live. If they neglect in this manner the preservation of their existence, it is not to be supposed that they are more attentive to the article of cleanliness; it displays itself neither in their persons, nor their habitations; and they may justly be reproached for being addicted to the contrary extreme. Notwithstanding this carelessness, and other natural defects, it must be regretted that their number is not more considerable; as, from what I have seen, and what has been confirmed to me by different persons, if we would be sure of finding sentiments of honour and humanity in this country, it is necessary to seek for them among the true Kamchadals; they have not yet bartered their rude virtues for the polished vices of the Europeans sent to civilize them.

It was at Bolsheretsk that I began to perceive the effects of their influence. I saw the trace of European manners, less in the mixture of blood, in the conformation of features, and the idiom of the inhabitants, than in their inclinations and mode of life, which did not always discover any very considerable fund of virtue. This striking difference between the inhabitants and the indigenes, springs, in my opinion, from the difficulties which lie in the road to civilization, and I will assign my reasons.

Bolsheretsk, not long ago, was the chief place of Kamchatka, particularly as the governors had thought proper to establish their residence there. The chiefs and their suites introduced European knowledge and manners: these, it is known, generally become adulterated in transmission, according to the distance from the source. Meanwhile it is to be presumed that the Russian government was careful, as far as it was possible, to confide its authority and the execution of its orders, only to officers of acknowledged merit, if I may judge from those who are at present employed; and it is therefore to be supposed that these officers, in the places of their residence, were so many examples of the virtues, the acquirements, and all the estimable qualities of civilized nations. But unfortunately the lessons which they gave, were not always so efficacious as might have been expected; either because being only sketches, they were not sufficiently felt, or rather, not being imbibed in all their purity, they made but momentary or perhaps vicious impressions on the mind.

These reformers found not the same zeal either in the Cossacks who composed the garrison, or in the merchants and other Russian emigrants who settled in the peninsula. The disposition to licenciousness, and the desire of gain, which the first conquerors of a country almost always bring with them, and the continual development of these qualities, by the facility with which the natives may be duped, contributed to check the progress of reform. The fatal infection was still more diffusely spread by intermarriages, while the seed of the social virtues, which had been attempted to be sown, scarcely found a reception.

The consequence has been, that the natives, or true Kamchadals, have preserved almost universally their ignorant simplicity and uncultivated manners; and that a part of the rest of the inhabitants, Russians and mixed breed, who have settled themselves in the ostrogs where the governors reside,

107 Kamchadals, inhabitants of the easternmost part of Siberia which came under Russian control by the end of the seventeenth century. From *La Russie, ou Moeurs, Usages et Costumes des habitants . . . de cet Empire.* M. Breton, Paris 1813.

still retain indeed a faint shade of European manners, but not of such as are most pure. We have already had a proof of this in what has been said of their commercial principles, and my conviction has been rendered stronger during my abode at Bolsheretsk, by a closer study of the inhabitants, who, this faint shade excepted, differ little from the indigenes.

M. Kozlov, and those who accompanied him, in imitation of his example, frequently give entertainments or balls to the ladies of this ostrog, who accept such invitations with equal alacrity and joy. I had an opportunity of seeing that what I had been told was true; that these women, the Kamchadals as well as the Russians, have a strong propensity to pleasure; their eagerness indeed is so great, that they are unable to conceal it. The precosity of the girls is astonishing, and seems not at all to be affected by the coldness of the climate.

With respect to the women of Bolsheretsk, who were present at these assemblies, and who were chiefly either of mixed blood or of Russian parents, their figures in general did not appear disagreeable, and I perceived some who might be considered as handsome: but the freshness of youth is not of long duration; from child-bearing, or the painful labours to which they are subjected, it fades away almost in the flower of their age. Their disposition is extremely cheerful; a little, perhaps, at the expence of decency. They endeavour to amuse the company by every thing which their gaiety and playfulness can furnish. They are fond of singing, and their voice is pleasant and agreeable; it is only to be wished that their music had less

108 The interior of a *Yurta*, the dwelling of the Kamchadals and other nomadic Asiatic tribes. A detailed description is found in Lesseps' work on Kamchatka. From *La Russie, ou Moeurs, Usages et Costumes des habitants . . . de cet Empire*. M. Breton, Paris 1813.

resemblance to their soil, and approached nearer to our own. They speak both the Russian and Kamchadal languages, but they all preserve the accent of the latter idiom. I little expected to see in this part of the world Polish dances, and still less country dances in the English taste; but what was my surprise to find that they had even an idea of the minuet! Whether my abode for twenty six months upon the sea, had rendered me less fastidious, or that the recollections they revived facinated my eyes, these dances appeared to be executed with tolerable precision, and more grace than I could have imagined. The dancers of whom we speak, have so much vanity as to hold in contempt the songs and dances of the natives. The toilet of the women on these occasions is an object of no trivial attention. They deck themselves out in all their allurements, and whatever is most costly. These ceremonious and ball dresses are principally of silks; and in the article of commerce we have already seen that they must be expensive. I shall finish this account with a remark that I had occasion to make, both in these assemblies and in those of the Kamchadals; it is, that the majority of husbands, Russians as well as natives, are not susceptible to jealousy; they voluntarily shut their eyes upon the conduct of their wives, and are as docile as possible upon this chapter.

The entertainments and assemblies of the native Kamchadals, at which I was also present, offered a spectacle equally entitled to notice for its singularity. I know not which struck me most, the song or the dance. The dance appeared to me to be that of savages. It consisted in making regular movements, or rather unpleasant and difficult distortions, and in uttering at the same time a forced and gutteral sound, like a continued hiccough, to mark the time of the air sung by the assembly, the words of which are frequently void of sense, even in Kamchadal . . .

In their dances they are fond of imitating the different animals they pursue, such as the partridge and others, but principally the bear. They represent its sluggish and stupid gait, its different feelings and situations; as the young ones about their dam; the amourous sports of the male with the female; and lastly, its agitation when pursued. They must have a perfect knowledge of this animal, and have made it their particular study, for they represent all its motions as exactly, I believe, as it is possible. I asked the Russians, who were greater connoisseurs than myself, having been oftener present at the taking of these animals, whether their pantomime ballets were well executed; and they assured me that the dancers were the best in the country, and that the cries, gait, and various attitudes of the bear, were as accurate as life. Meanwhile, without offence to the amateurs, these dances are, in my opinion, not less fatiguing to the spectators than to the performers. It is a real

240

pain to see them distort their hips, dislocate every limb, and wear out their lungs, to express the excess of pleasure which they take in these strange balls, which, I repeat it, resemble the absurd diversions of savages: the Kamchadals may indeed, in many respects, be considered as of that rank.

Jean de Lesseps, *Travels in Kamtschatka, during the Years 1787 and 1788* (London 1790)

The Shaman

Jean de Lesseps was very unimpressed by the Russian Orthodox priests he saw, and showed sympathetic understanding of the important role the Shaman, or tribal witch doctor, played in the lives of the native peoples, although he viewed their ceremonies with obvious distaste.

All the Kamchadals of this village, men and women, are shamans, or believers in the witchcraft of these pretended sorcerers. They dread to an excess the popes or Russian priests, for whom they entertain the most inveterate hatred. They do all they can to avoid meeting them. This is sometimes impossible, and in that case, when they find them at hand they act the hypocrite, and make their escape the first opportunity that offers. I attribute this fear to the ardent zeal which these priests have doubtless shown for the extirpation of idolatry, and which the Kamchadals consider as persecution. They accordingly look upon them as their greatest enemies. Perhaps they have reason to believe, that in wishing to convert them, the overthrow of their idols was not the only thing these missionaries had in view. These popes probably set them no example of the virtues upon which they declaim. It is suspected that their object is the acquisition of wealth, rather than of proselytes, and the gratification of their inordinate propensity to drunkenness. It is not therefore to be wondered at that the inhabitants retain their ancient errors. They pay a secret homage to their god Kutka, and place in him so entire a confidence, that they address their prayers exclusively to him when they are desirous of obtaining any boon, or of engaging in any enterprise. When they go to the chace, they abstain from washing themselves, and are careful not to make the sign of the cross: they invoke their Kutka, and the first animal they catch is immediately sacrificed to him. After this act of devotion they conceive that their chace will be successful; on the contrary, if they were to cross themselves, they would despair of catching any thing. It is also a part of their superstition to consecrate to Kutka their new-born children, who, the moment they have left their cradle, are destined to become

109 A Kamchadal *shaman.*

shamans. The veneration of the inhabitants of this village for sorcecerers can scarcely be conceived; it approaches to insanity, and is really to be pitied; for the extravagant and wild absurdities by which these magicians keep alive the credulity of their compatriots, excites our indignation rather than our laughter. At present they do not profess their art openly, or give the same splendour they once did to their necromancy. They no longer decorate their garments with mystic rings and other symbolic figures of metal, that jingled together upon the slightest motion of their body. In like manner they have abandoned the kind of kettle, which they used to strike with a sort of musical intonation in their pretended enchantments, and with which they announced their approach. In short, they have forsaken all their magic instruments. The following are the ceremonies they observe in their assemblies, which they are careful to hold in secret, though not the less frequently on that account. Conceive of a circle of spectators, stupidly rapt in attention and ranged round the magician, male or female, for as I have before observed, the women are equally initiated into the mysteries. All at once he begins to sing, or to utter shrill sounds without either measure or signification. The docile assembly strike in with him, and the concert becomes a medley of harsh and insupportable discords. By degrees the shaman is warmed, and he begins to dance to the confused accents of his auditory, who become hoarse and exhausted from the violence of their exertions. As the prophetic spirit is excited in the minister of their Kutka, the animation of the dance increases. Like the Pythian on the tripos, he rolls his ghastly and haggard eyes; all his motions are convulsive; his mouth is drawn awry, his limbs stiffened, and every distortion and grimace is put in practice by him, to the great admiration of his disciples. Having acted these buffooneries for some time, he suddenly stops, as if inspired, and becomes now as composed as he was before agitated. It is the sacred collectedness of a man full of the god that governs him, and who is about to speak by his voice. Surprised and trembling, the assembly is instantly mute, in expectation of the marvels that are to be revealed. The self-created prophet then utters at different intervals, broken sentences, words without meaning, and what ever nonsense comes into the head of the impostor; and this is invariably considered as the effect of inspiration. His jargon is accompanied either with a torrent of tears or loud bursts of laughter, according to the complexion of the tidings he has to announce; and the expression and gesture of the orator vary in conformity to his feelings. I was furnished with this account by persons entitled to credit, and who had contrived to be present at these absurd revelations.

Jean de Lesseps, *Travels in Kamtschatka, during the Years 1787 and 1788* (London 1790)

Summer Entertainments

Andrew Swinton, an English tourist who was in Russia for just over two years (between 1788 and 1791) gives a series of lively pen-pictures of Russian traditional customs. The extract which follows is a description of a summer entertainment provided by Count Stroganov at his home in St Petersburg. Swinton often describes the same sort of scenes as Coxe encountered some years earlier, although the idyllic nature of his summer scene contrasts sharply with the winter tragedy described earlier by Coxe.

The Russians take as much delight in the firing of guns, as they do in ringing of bells. Artillery, in summer, makes a part of rural entertainments. I was yesterday at one of the summer carnivals given by the nobility to the public. Count Stroganov's villa and gardens are pleasantly situated, on one of the islands at the mouth of the Neva, and bordering on this river. Here were collected a very great concourse of people of all ranks. In the front gallery of the Count's house were a chosen band of vocal and instrumental performers: the first consisted chiefly of boys and girls. As we walked in the forests adjoining to the house, we were serenaded with favourite Russian airs. Dukes, Generals, Admirals, Traders, and Boors, mixed together. The tents, erected among the trees, received those guests, who conceived, with Sancho Pancha, that eating and drinking is the best part of all earthly enjoyments. I could see

110 St Petersburg: the summer garden, with its famous ornamental fence designed by Yu. Feldten and P. Yegorov (1770–84).

243

a select company of Germans, snugly seated; their ears attentive to the music – their eyes to some slices of ham, which the Master of the hotel was cutting for them.

Under a wooden pavillion, open at the sides, those who chuse to exercise their limbs, had a room railed in for dancing, and a band of musicians. Here the ladies of easy virtue, and the virtuous maiden, dressed in her Sunday gown, tripped about, to the great entertainment of the titled spectators. Few

111 Troitskiy Bridge (now the Kirovskiy), St Petersburg. Lithograph by Karl Petrovich Beggrov (1799–1875). Royal Library, Stockholm.

join in this assembly besides the lower ranks; but the outside of the rail was crouded with ladies and gentlemen of the first distinction.

A sky-rocket gave notice that the fireworks were begun. The assembly broke up: the fiddlers and the dancers crouded together through the woods, to the open area before Count Stroganov's villa. A very entertaining Greenwich Park scene, too, was exhibited, when Beaux and Belles, amidst a display of various fireworks, endeavoured, in tumultuous throngs, to escape the falling fire-balls. The Count's windows and galleries accommodated his visitors of quality, among whom were distributed the good things of this life. The Count has a great property, in iron mines, from which he derives a liberal income, and which he spends with equal liberality. This evening's amusement concluded with a general discharge of the cannon from a battery upon the banks of the Neva.

The company now filed off towards Petersburg, some in coaches, others in troikas, which convey half a dozen or a dozen people. The forest echoed with the sound of wheels and songs. Several Russians had devoted the day to Bacchus, and were singing his praises, with all the strength they had remaining. Their drunken songs are sung in a different strain from their sober ditties, though the words and air may be the same.

244

In the former, you hear a continued roar, for some moments, or minutes, as their breath may hold out; silence then succeeds for the same length of time, until they have recovered breath. When a drunken Russian has finished his first stanza and his breath, he rests his head upon his shoulders, gaping for a fresh supply of æther: he recovers gradually, as from a fainting fit, and joins again the grand chorus of his friends. He who first recovers wind begins, and the rest instantly accompany him,

112 A summer promenade by the banks of the Neva. Lithograph by Karl Petrovich Beggrov (1799–1875).

113 The Naryshkin estate in St Petersburg. Andrew Swinton was present at a summer festival there in 1791.

with what breath they have gathered. Many fall off from the troika before the journey is ended; but the song is not interrupted by these trifling accidents: there is always one or two in their seats, who keep the music alive: the driver stops the carriage, until his prostrate brothers replace themselves, but continues his song. Even the unfortunate, while they lie upon their back in the road, do not cease to perform their tasks in the concert.

In the Summer evenings, when the weather is calm, the citizens of Petersburg delight in sailing upon the Neva in their pleasure boats. The boats of the nobility are very elegantly ornamented. The company are seated in the stern, under a canopy of silk, or other stuff, and have with them musicians, or frequently the party themselves perform upon different instruments. The rowers are all chosen among such of their servants as have the best voices, and either sing in concert with the instruments, or without them. When they have rowed the boat against the stream, beating time to their songs with the oars, they allow her to drive with the current, fixing their oars in a horizontal position from the boat's sides; and the rowers collect in a circle. It is at this period they exert their vocal powers, and make such exquisite harmony, as to draw the inhabitants to the galleries of their houses upon the river's banks, and the foot passengers to the water's edge, to listen to the music; and many follow the boat, to enjoy their native tunes. The vocal and instrumental parts are generally performed alternately, and among the former is always one, who, with a whistle, or, by blowing upon his fingers, makes a very shrill noise, accompanying the music at intervals. When the concert is ended, the audience upon the streets go away, repeating the songs, and echoing them into every quarter of the city. Perhaps another boat, conveying another concert approaches, and arrests the auditors of the first melodies.

These concerts often continue to ten and eleven o'clock at night, and when still silence reigns upon the face of the waters, it is beyond the power of description to convey any idea of the pleasing effect they have upon the mind.

Thus we spend the flowery months in Russia, notwithstanding war's alarms.

Andrew Swinton, *Travels into Norway, Denmark and Russia*
(London 1792)

Petersburg High Society

There had been immense changes and reforms in Russian social life between the age of Peter and that of Catherine, but it was difficult for the visitor who was familiar with European court life not to feel a sense of condescension and superiority on his first contacts with Russia. This is well illustrated in the following passage referring to 1790 by an unknown English author, described in the foreword to his work as 'an accomplished gentleman'.

The Russians have certainly not what the French call *l'esprit de société;* they come together as often as they can, but when they are together, they are neither at ease themselves, nor do they make others so: they sit at the four corners of the room, and, if you speak to them, never utter a word but Yes or No. The women crowd together; and, if some unfortunate young man goes to sit down by one of them, instead of turning to him to speak, she very calmly gets up from her chair, and sets herself down at the further end of the room, as if she were afraid of being bit. At first this shocked me very much; but as I found it was in vain to persevere, I leave them all to themselves, and walk about with an air of *insouciance,* which is the *ton du pays.* In any other country this would totally destroy all society, but here it is a thing of course, and is not so much felt, as they generally dance six nights out of seven. The Court

114 A Petersburg street scene. Lithograph by Karl Petrovich Beggrov (1799–1875).

is the thermometer of the town; and the people are well or ill received in society, in proportion as they are well or ill received at Court: you can have no idea how much this influences the behaviour of the first people, and how ridiculous it appears to a stranger. I live in hopes that Prince P——n [Potemkin] will come here before I go away: all those who appear of great consequence now, shrink into nothing, and scarcely dare sit down in his presence, without his permission;

115 F. Ya. Alekseyev: A view of Rinaldi's marble palace from the Peter and Paul fortress, St Petersburg, 1794.

he certainly is the most powerful subject in Europe, and one of the most singular of men. When I came here, the Court had not received any news from him, for near six weeks: at last a courier arrived: away flew the news to the Empress and the Privy Council, who waited with violent impatience for an account of some important victory; when, behold! the courier had been despatched to bespeak an *eel-pye* at a famous pastrycook's, and as soon as it was ready, set out again for the army, with the eel-pye carefully packed up. It is said that P——n will be here next month, but I much doubt it; he is at Jassy with a prodigious retinue – several of the prettiest women of the Court, married to officers who serve under him in the army, with all the best singers, best actors, and best musicians which are to be had.

There is a Countess W——a [Vorontsova] here, and is all

248

impatience to see him again: she is a Russian, but married to a Pole, a cousin of Countess Julie Potocka's. She is going to be brought to bed, which is an interesting piece of intelligence to you, but it will cost me a ducat; as it is the fashion here, when you pay a caudle visit to a lady, to present her with a new ducat. I think it the strangest custom imaginable, but certainly a very convenient one, as it defrays the expenses of the cradle. Two days ago I saw the great beauty of the Russian empire, Countess Dol——i [Dolgorukaya]; her husband serves under Potemkin, and, like a dutiful wife, she followed him to the army. She returned four days ago, and supped at the Imperial Ambassador's: she certainly eclipses all the Russian women I have hitherto seen. You recollect, in Cox's Travels, a description of the ice-hills on the Neva; the Ambassador had one made in his *room,* for the amusement of his company; understand that it was built with boards, and rendered slippery by means of soap and water. We all climbed up to the top, then sat in little sledges, and slided down with great velocity. Here it is positively necessary to have some such invention, to supply the place of conversation: besides, it is the fashion of the Court. The Empress never gave so many entertainments as she has done this winter. Not a week passes but there is a *fête* at the Hermitage; sometimes a masquerade, sometimes an opera, sometimes both opera and masquerade; and then, *pour pis-aller,* they play at blindman's-buff, hide and seek, hot cockles, and other innocent pastimes of the kind. In London, you say, nothing is thought of but Faro. Hazard is now the favourite game here. The Russians had no idea of the game till about six weeks ago, when two Englishmen took it into their heads to teach them: now they are all so fond of it, that as soon as the dice-box is heard, away fly men, women, and children; rich and poor all crowd round the table; dancing is given up; the old women sit down to supper with the few unfortunate beaux who have no money to lose, and the rest of the company keep shaking their elbows till four o'clock in the morning. I in my poverty never thought of playing.

Anon, *Letters from the Continent* (London 1812)

Catherine in the Last Years of Her Reign

F. C. P. Masson gives a well-observed and detailed physical description of the elderly Catherine and then moves to a discussion of her character as reflected in her policies and actions.

Though nearly seventy years of age, Catherine still retained some remains of beauty. Her hair was always dressed in the old style of simplicity, and with peculiar neatness, and no head ever became a crown better than hers. She was of the middle stature, and corpulent. Few women, however, with her corpulence, would have attained the graceful and dignified carriage for which she was remarked. In private, the good-humour and confidence with which she inspired all about her seemed to keep up an unceasing scene of youth, playfulness, and gaiety. Her charming conversation and familiar manners placed all those who were admitted to her dressing-room, or assisted at her toilet, perfectly at ease; but the moment she had put on her gloves to make her appearance in the neighbouring apartments, she assumed a very different countenance and deportment. From an agreeable and facetious woman she appeared all at once the reserved and majestic Empress. Whoever had seen her there for the first time would have found her not below the idea he had previously formed, and would have said, 'This is, indeed, the Semiramis of the North!' The maxim, *Præsentia minuit famam,* could no more be applied to her than to Frederick the Great. I saw her once or twice a week for ten years, and every time with renewed admiration. My eagerness to examine her person caused me repeatedly to neglect prostrating myself before her with the crowd; but the homage I paid by gazing at her was surely more flattering. She walked slowly and with short steps, her majestic forehead unclouded, her look tranquil, and her eyes often cast on the ground. Her mode of saluting was by a slight inclination of the body, yet not without grace; but the smile she assumed vanished with the occasion. If, upon the introduction of a stranger, she presented her hand to him to kiss, she demeaned herself with great courtesy, and commonly addressed a few words to him upon the subject of his travels and his visit; but all the harmony of her countenance was instantly discomposed, and you forgot for a moment the great Catherine, to reflect on the infirmities of an old woman, as, on opening her mouth, it was apparent that she had no teeth. Her voice, too, was hoarse and broken, and her speech inarticulate. The lower part of her face was rather large and coarse; her gray eyes, though clear and penetrating, evinced something of hypocrisy; and a certain wrinkle at the base of the nose indicated a character somewhat sinister. The celebrated Lampi had lately

116 A portrait of Catherine the Great by Battista Lampi to which Masson refers in his description of the Empress.

painted a striking likeness of her, though extremely flattering. Catherine, however, remarking that he had not entirely omitted that unfortunate wrinkle, the evil genius of her face, was greatly dissatisfied, and said that Lampi had made her too serious and too wicked. He must accordingly retouch and spoil the picture, which appeared now like the portrait of a young nymph, though the throne, the sceptre, the crown, and some other attributes sufficiently indicate that it is the picture of an empress. In other respects the performance well deserves the attention of the amateur, as also does a portrait of the present Empress by the same hand.

With respect to the government of Catherine, it was as mild and moderate within the immediate circle of her influence as it was arbitrary and terrible at a distance. Whoever, directly or indirectly, enjoyed the protection of the favourite, exercised, wherever he was situated, the most undisguised tyranny. He insulted his superiors, trampled on his inferiors, and violated justice, order, and the *ukazes,* with impunity.

It is to the policy first, and next to the weakness of Catherine, that the relaxed and disorganised state of her internal government must, in part, be attributed; though the principal cause will be found in the depraved manners and character of the nation. How was a woman to effect that which the active discipline of the cane and the sanguinary axe of Peter I were inadequate to accomplish? The usurper of a throne, which she was desirous to retain, she was under the necessity of treating her accomplices with kindness. A stranger in the Empire over which she reigned, she sought to remove everything discordant, everything heterogeneous, and to become one with the nation, by adopting and even flattering its tastes and its prejudices. She often knew how to reward, but never how to punish; and it was solely by suffering her power to be abused that she succeeded in preserving it.

She had two passions, which never left her but with her last breath – the love of man, which degenerated into licentiousness; and the love of glory, which sank into vanity. By the first of these passions she was never so far governed as to become a Messalina, but she often disgraced both her rank and her sex; by the second she was led to undertake many laudable projects, which were seldom completed, and to engage in unjust wars, from which she derived at least that kind of fame which never fails to accompany success.

The generosity of Catherine, the splendour of her reign, the magnificence of her Court, her institutions, her monuments, her wars, were precisely to Russia what the age of Louis XIV was to Europe; but, considered individually, Catherine was greater than this prince. The French formed the glory of Louis; Catherine formed that of the Russians. She had not, like him, the advantage of reigning over a polished people; nor was she surrounded from infancy by great and accomplished characters. She had subtle ambassadors, not unskilled in the diplomatic art, and some fortunate generals; but Rumyantsev, Panin, and Potemkin excepted, she could not boast a single man of genius; for the wit, cunning and dexterity of certain of her ministers, the ferocious valour of a Suvorov, the ductile capacity of a Repnin, the favour of a Zubov, the readiness of a Bezborodko, and the assiduity of a Nicholas Saltykov, are not worthy of being mentioned as exceptions. It was not that Russia did not produce men of merit; but Catherine feared such men, and they kept at a distance from her. We may conclude, therefore, that all her measures were her own, and particularly all the good she did.

Let not the misfortunes and abuses of her reign give to the private character of this Princess too dark and repulsive a shade! She appeared to be thoroughly humane and generous, as all who approached her experienced. All who were admitted to her intimacy were delighted with the good-natured sallies of her wit. All who lived with her were happy. Her manners were gay and licentious; but she still preserved an exterior decorum, and even her favourites always treated her with respect. Her love never excited disgust, nor her familiarity contempt. She might be deceived, won, seduced, but she would never suffer herself to be governed. Her active and regular life, her moderation, firmness, fortitude, and even sobriety, are moral qualities which it would be highly unjust to ascribe to hypocrisy. How great might she not have been, had her heart been as well governed as her mind! She reigned over the Russians less despotically than over herself; she was never hurried away by anger, never a prey to dejection, and never indulged in transports of immoderate joy. Caprice, ill-humour, and peevishness formed no part of her character, and were never perceived in her conduct. I will not decide whether she were truly great, but she was certainly beloved.

[F. C. P. Masson], *Memoirs of Catherine II and the Court of St Petersburg* (London 1904)

117 Catherine in her boudoir. From Masson's Memoirs.

253

THE REIGN OF PAUL

The Vagaries of Paul

F. C. P. Masson served ten years under Catherine and his obvious sympathy for her is in marked contrast to his antipathy for her son, the Emperor Paul I, who succeeded her in 1796. Masson was in fact expelled from Russia by Paul. He gives a scathing portrayal of Paul, his notorious fondness for Prussian military manoeuvres, the maniacal nature of his decrees on dress.

These measures were extended to all the officers of the army, and those on the staff as generals were equally obliged to join their regiments or resign, because these staffs were abolished. By this impolitic step he pretended to commence a reform and gain the army. But what soon showed that Paul, in becoming emperor, by no means renounced the military trifles which had alone occupied his time as Grand Duke, was his devoting all his attention, from the morning of his ascending the throne, to the frivolous changes which he wished to introduce into the dress and exercise of the soldiers. For a moment the palace had the appearance of a place taken by assault by foreign troops, – those who began to mount guard there differing so much in dress and style from those who had been seen there the day before. He went down into the court, where he was manœuvring his soldiers three or four hours, to teach them to mount guard after his fashion, and establish his *wacht-parade* (guard-parade), which became the most important institution and central point of his government. Every day since he had dedicated the same time to it, however cold it might be. There, in a plain deep green uniform, great boots and a large hat, he spends his mornings in exercising his guards; there he gives his orders, receives reports, publishes his favours, rewards and punishments; and there every officer must be presented to him, surrounded by his sons and aides-de-camp, stamping his heels on the pavement to keep himself warm, his bald head bare, his nose cocked up, one hand behind his back, and with the other raising and falling his cane in due time and crying, *raz, dva; raz, dva* (one, two; one, two). He prides himself in braving a cold of fifteen or twenty degrees of Réaumur without furs. After this none of the officers dared any longer appear in pelisses, and the old generals, tormented with coughs, gout,

254

and rheumatism, were obliged to form a circle round Paul, dressed like himself.

After the first impressions which his accession caused in the heart of Paul, punishments and disgraces succeeded, with the same rapidity and profusion with which he had lavished his favours. Several experienced the two extremes in a few days. It is true that most of these punishments at first appeared just; but then it must be allowed that Paul could scarcely strike

118 F. Ya. Alekseyev. View of Paul I's palace in St Petersburg, the Saint Michael Castle (now the Palace of Engineers). Water colour and Indian ink.

any but the guilty, so corrupt had been all who were about the throne.

Notwithstanding the assurances he had given Zubov, one of the first orders that followed was to seal up his office and that of Markov, and to turn their officers and secretaries out of Court with disgrace. One Chersky, master of requests and reporter to the senate, who publicly sold justice to the highest bidder, was at first gratified with an order of knighthood, and obtained some lands, which he said the late Empress had promised him a few days before her decease. Next morning he was dismissed from his offices. This respect of Paul to the pretended will of his mother, and his care to enrich a rascal before discarding him, were strangely admired. Surely he ought rather to have brought to trial this despoiler of the widow and orphan, and made him an example to satisfy public justice.

Samoylov, the attorney-general, whom likewise he had honourably confirmed in his office, with a present of four thousand peasants, amounting in value to more than twenty thousand rubles a year, was displaced a few days after, put under arrest, and his secretary was sent to the fortress. Thus was everything reformed, except Bezborodko, Nicholas Saltykov, and Arkharov.

This wavering and uncertain conduct, which characterised the first steps of Paul, clearly proves that his favours were the effects of policy, and the disgraces that followed them were to be ascribed to passion rather than to justice. But what confounded all who had admired him was to see him, at the moment when he entered such an intricate labyrinth of business and abuses (the importance of which to the State should have occupied him at least some days), applying the

119 Paul I, perhaps by Schukin, or contemporary copy (oil), wearing the blue ribbon and star of St Andrew, the cross of St John of Jerusalem (of which he was Grand Master) and the cross of St Anne in diamonds.

very morning of his accession, with the same eagerness, to the most trifling details of military service. The shape of a hat, the colour of a feather, the altitude of a grenadier's cap, boots, spatterdashes, cockades, queues and sword-belts, became the affairs of State that absorbed his astonishing activity. He was surrounded by patterns of accoutrements and uniforms of all kinds. The greatest proof of zeal and merit any one could give him, during the first days of his reign, was to appear before him in the new uniform he had introduced. An officer who

256

could give his tailor a hundred rubles to have a dress of the new fashion made in a few hours, and appear in it the next morning in the *wacht-parade,* was almost certain of obtaining some post, or, at least, a cross. Several had no other merit, and employed no other means to gain the good graces of their new Emperor.

Another whim, which caused no little surprise, was the imperial prohibition of wearing round hats, or, rather, the

sudden order of taking them away or tearing them to pieces on the heads of those who appeared in them. This occasioned some disgraceful scenes in the streets, and particularly near the palace. The Cossacks and soldiers of the police fell on the passengers to uncover their heads, and beat those who, not knowing the reason, attempted to defend themselves. An English merchant, going through the streets in a sledge, was thus stopped and his hat snatched off. Supposing it to be a robbery, he leaped out of his sledge, knocked down the soldier, and called the guard. Instead of the guard arrived an officer, who overpowered and bound him; but as they were carrying him before the police, he was fortunate enough to meet the coach of the English minister, who was going to Court, and claimed his protection. Sir Charles Whitworth made his complaint to the Emperor, who, conjecturing that a round hat might be the national dress of the English, as it is of the Swedes, said that his order had been misconceived, and he would explain himself more fully to Arkharov. The next day it was published in the streets and houses, that strangers who were not in the Emperor's service, or naturalised, were not

120 View of the Royal palace of Gatchina, where Paul lived up to his accession. Unknown artist, 1805, engraved by G. L. Lory.

257

comprised in the prohibition. Round hats were now no longer pulled off, but they who were met with this unlucky head-dress were conducted to the police to ascertain their country. If they were found to be Russians, they were sent for soldiers; and woe to a Frenchman who had been met with in this dress, for he would have been condemned as a Jacobin. It was reported to Paul that the *chargé d'affaires* of the King of Sardinia, indulging himself in raillery at this singular proscription of round hats, said that such trifles had often been on the point of occasioning seditions in Italy. The *chargé d'affaires* received orders, through Arkharov, to quit the city in twenty-four hours. Thanks to the distance and situation of the King of Sardinia, he could not demand an explanation of such an insult; otherwise round hats might have become the motive of a war between two monarchs.

A regulation equally incomprehensible was the sudden prohibition of harnessing horses after the Russian mode. A fortnight was allowed for procuring harness in the German fashion, after the expiration of which the police were enjoined to cut the traces of every carriage, the horses of which were harnessed in the ancient manner. Almost as soon as it was made public, several persons dared not venture abroad, still less appear in their carriages near the palace, for fear of being insulted. The saddlers, availing themselves of the occasion, asked as far as three hundred roubles for a plain harness for a pair of horses. To dress the *izvozchiki*, or Russian coachmen, in the German fashion, was attended with another inconvenience. Most of them would neither part with their long beards, their kaftans, nor their round hats; still less would they tie a false tail for their short hair, which produced the most ridiculous scenes and figures in the world. At length the Emperor had the vexation to be obliged to change his rigorous order into a simple invitation to his subjects gradually to adopt the German fashion of dress, if they wished to merit his favour.

Another reform with respect to carriages; the great number of splendid equipages that swarmed in the streets of St Petersburg disappeared in an instant. The officers, even the generals, came to the parade on foot, or in little sledges, which also was not without its dangers.

It was anciently a point of etiquette for every person who met a Russian autocrat, his wife, or son, to stop his horse or coach, alight, and prostrate himself in the snow, or in the mud. This barbarous homage, difficult to be paid in a large city, where carriages pass in great numbers and always on the gallop, had been completely abolished under the reign of the polished Catherine. One of the first cares of Paul was to re-establish it in all its rigour. A general officer, who passed on without his coachman's observing the Emperor riding by on horseback, was stopped and immediately put under arrest.

The same unpleasant circumstance occurred to several others, so that nothing was so much dreaded, either on foot or in a carriage, as the meeting of the Emperor. Instances have even happened where the fault and its punishment have been attended with consequences so serious as must induce a benevolent monarch to abolish so troublesome an etiquette.

The ceremony established within the palace became equally strict, and equally dreaded. Woe betide him who, when permitted to kiss the hand of Paul, did not make the floor resound by striking it with his knee as loud as a soldier with the butt-end of his firelock. It was requisite, too, that the salute of the lips on his hand should be heard, to certify the reality of the kiss, as well as of the genuflection. Prince George Galitsyn, the chamberlain, was put under arrest on the spot by his Muscovitish Majesty himself, for having made the bow and kissed the hand too negligently.

Another of Paul's first regulations was a strict injunction to all tradesmen to efface from the front of their shops the French word *magazin,* and substitute the Russian word *lavka* (shop); assigning as a reason that the Emperor alone could have magazines of wood, flour, corn, etc.; while a tradesman ought not to be above his condition, but to stick to his shop.

To report all the ordinances of similar weight and importance that succeeded each other in the course of one week, I must descend into particulars too tedious. What can be said, what can be hoped, of a man who, succeeding Catherine, could consider the regulating such things as the most urgent? Frequently these new and important regulations contradicted or frustrated one another, and what was ordained one day was often obliged to be modified or annulled the next. In a word, we may say that Paul, when he wrapped himself in the imperial mantle, let the Grand Duke peep out; that he thought to govern a vast empire as he had governed his Pavlovsk; his capital, like his house; and thirty millions of men of all ranks and all nations, like a score of lackeys.

[F. C. P. Masson], *Memoirs of Catherine II and the Court of St Petersburg* (London 1904)

The Russian Easter

Edward Clarke was one of the most critical and trenchant observers of the Russian scene. Although he would have been harsh in his descriptions of Russia at any period, the capricious and arbitrary rule of Paul allowed his satirical gifts full rein. His magnificent description of the Easter religious ceremonies is punctuated continually with comic observations and satirical cameos.

121 Edward Daniel Clarke painted by Opie. Frontispiece to *Travels in Various Countries of Europe, Asia and Africa.*

The people of Moscow celebrate the *Pâque* with a degree of pomp and festivity unknown to the rest of Europe. The most splendid pageants of Rome do not equal the costliness and splendour of the Russian Church. Neither could Venice, in the midst of her Carnival, ever rival, in debauchery and superstition, in licentiousness and parade, what passes during this season in Moscow.

It should first be mentioned, there are no people who observe Lent with more scrupulous and excessive rigour than the Russians. Travelling the road from Petersburg to Moscow, if at any time, in poor cottages, where the peasants appeared starving, we offered them a part of our dinner, they would shudder at the sight of it, and cast it to the dogs; dashing out of their children's hands, as an abomination, any food given to them; and removing every particle that might be left, entirely from their sight. In drinking tea with a Cossack, he not only refused to have milk in his cup, but would not use a spoon that had been in the tea offered him with milk, although wiped carefully in a napkin, until it had passed through scalding water. The same privation takes place among the higher ranks; but, in proportion as this rigour has been observed, so much the more excessive is the degree of gluttony and relaxation, when the important intelligence that 'Christ is risen' has issued from the mouth of the archbishop. During Easter they run into every kind of excess, rolling about drunk the whole week; as if rioting, debauchery, extravagance, gambling, drinking, and fornication, were as much a religious observance as starving had been before; and that the same superstition which kept them fasting during Lent, had afterwards instigated them to the most beastly excesses.

Even their religious customs are perfectly adapted to their climate and manners. Nothing can be contrived with more ingenious policy to suit the habits of the Russians. When Lent fasting begins, their stock of frozen provisions is either exhausted, or unfit for use; and the interval that takes place allows sufficient time for procuring, killing, and storing, the fresh provisions of the Spring. The night before the famous ceremony of the Resurrection, all the markets and shops of Moscow are seen filled with flesh, butter, eggs, poultry, pigs, and every kind of food. The crowd of purchasers is immense. You hardly meet a foot-passenger who has not his hands, nay his arms, filled with provisions; or a single *drozhki* that is not ready to break down beneath their weight.

The first ceremony which took place, previous to all this feasting, was that of the *Pâque fleuries,* or Palm Sunday. On the eve of this day the inhabitants of Moscow resort, in carriages, on horseback, or on foot, to the Kremlin, for the purchase of palm-branches, to place before their icons, and to decorate the sacred pictures in the streets, or elsewhere. It is

one of the gayest promenades of the year. The Governor, attended by the *Maître de Police,* the Commandant, and a train of nobility, go in procession, mounted on fine horses. The streets are lined with spectators; and cavalry are stationed on each side, to preserve order. Arriving in the Kremlin, a vast assembly, bearing artificial bouquets and boughs, are seen moving here and there, forming the novel and striking spectacle of a gay and moving forest. The boughs consist of artificial flowers, with fruit. Beautiful representations of oranges and lemons in wax are sold for a few kopeks each, and offer a proof of the surprising ingenuity of this people in the arts of imitation. Upon this occasion, every person who visits the Kremlin, and would be thought a true Christian, purchases one or more of the boughs called Palm-branches; and, in returning, the streets are crowded with *drozhki,* and all kinds of vehicles, filled with devotees, holding in their hands one or more palm-branches, according to the degree of their piety, or the number of *Bogi* in their houses.

The description often given of the splendour of the equipages

122 Podnovinskiy suburb of Moscow during the Easter Carnival, by Gabriel Lory the Elder after Gerard de la Barthe.

in Moscow but ill agrees with their appearance during Lent. A stranger, who arrives with his head full of notions of Asiatic pomp and Eastern magnificence, would be surprised to find narrow streets, execrably paved, covered with mud or dust; wretched-looking houses on each side; carriages drawn, it is true, by six horses, but such cattle! blind, lame, old, out of condition, of all sizes and all colours, connected by rotten ropes and old cords, full of knots and splices; on the leaders,

262

123 F. Ya. Alekseyev:
Moscow, cathedral square in
the Kremlin. Oil painting
(c. 1800).

and on the box, figures that seem to have escaped the galleys;
behind, a lousy, ragged lackey, or perhaps two, with countenances exciting more pity than derision; and the carriage itself
like the worst of the night-coaches in London. But this external
wretchedness, as far as it concerns the equipages of the nobles,
admits of some explanation. The fact is, that a dirty tattered
livery, a rotten harness, bad horses, and a shabby vehicle,
constitute one part of the privation of the season. On Easter

263

Monday the most gaudy but fantastic splendour fills every street in the city.

The second grand ceremony of this season takes place on Thursday before Easter, at noon, when the archbishop is said to wash the feet of the Apostles. This we also witnessed. The priests appeared in their most gorgeous apparel. Twelve monks, designed to represent the twelve Apostles, were placed in a semicircle before the archbishop. The ceremony was performed in the cathedral, which was crowded with spectators. The archbishop, performing all and much more than is related of our Saviour in the thirteenth chapter of St John, took off his robes, girded up his loins with a towel, and proceeded to wash the feet of all the monks, until he came to the representative of Peter, who rose and stood up; and the same interlocution passed, between him and the archbishop, which is recorded to have taken place between our Saviour and the apostle.

The third, and most magnificent ceremony of all, is celebrated two hours after midnight, in the morning of Easter Sunday. It is called the Ceremony of the Resurrection, and certainly exceeds every thing of the kind at Rome; not even excepting the Papal benediction, during the holy week.

At midnight, the great bell of the cathedral tolled. Its vibrations seemed to be the rolling of distant thunder; and they were instantly accompanied by the noise of all the bells in Moscow. Every inhabitant was stirring, and the rattling of carriages in the streets was greater than at noon-day. The whole city was in a blaze; lights were seen in all the windows, and innumerable torches in the streets. The tower of the cathedral was illuminated from its foundation to its cross. The same ceremony takes place in all the churches; and, what is truly surprising, considering their number, they are all equally crowded.

We hastened to the cathedral: it was filled with a prodigious assembly, consisting of all ranks of both sexes, bearing lighted wax tapers, to be afterwards heaped as vows upon the different shrines. The walls, the ceilings, and every part of this building, are covered by the pictures of Saints and Martyrs. In the moment of our arrival, the doors were shut; and on the outside appeared Plato, the archbishop, preceded by banners and torches, and followed by all his train of priests, with crucifixes and censers, who were making three times, in procession, the tour of the cathedral; chaunting with loud voices; and glittering in sumptuous vestments, bespangled with gold, silver, and precious stones. The snow had not melted so rapidly within the Kremlin as in the streets of the city: this magnificent procession was therefore constrained to move upon planks, over the deep mud which surrounded the cathedral. After completing the third circuit, they all halted opposite the great doors, which were still closed; the archbishop, with a censer, then scattered incense against the doors, and over the priests.

Suddenly, these doors were opened, and the effect was magnificent beyond description. The immense throng of spectators within, bearing innumerable tapers, formed two lines, through which the archbishop entered, advancing with his train to a throne near the centre. The profusion of lights in all parts of the cathedral, and, among others, of the enormous chandelier in the centre, the richness of the dresses, and the vastness of the assembly, filled us with astonishment. Having joined the suite of the archbishop, we accompanied the procession, and passed even to the throne: here the police-officers permitted us to stand, among the priests, near an embroidered stool of satin placed for the archbishop. The loud chorus, which burst forth at the entrance to the church, continued as the procession moved towards the throne, and after the archbishop had taken his seat; when my attention was for a moment called off, by seeing one of the Russians earnestly crossing himself with his right hand, while his left was employed in picking my companion's pocket of his handkerchief.

Soon after, the archbishop descended, and went all round the cathedral; first offering incense to the priests, and then to the people as he passed along. When he had returned to his seat, the priests, two by two, performed the same ceremony, beginning with the archbishop, who rose and made obeisance, with a lighted taper in his hand. From the moment the church doors were opened, the spectators had continued bowing their heads and crossing themselves; insomuch, that some of the people seemed really exhausted, by the constant motion of the head and hands.

We had now leisure to examine the dresses and figures of the priests, which were certainly the most striking we had ever seen. Their long dark hair, without powder, fell down, in ringlets, or straight and thick, far over their rich robes and shoulders. Their dark thick beards, also, entirely covered their breasts. Upon the heads of the archbishop and bishops were high caps, covered with gems, and adorned by miniature paintings, set in jewels, of the Crucifixion, the Virgin, and the Saints. Their robes of various-coloured satin were of the most costly embroidery; and even upon these were miniature pictures set with precious stones. Such, according to the consecrated record of antient days, was the appearance of the high-priests of old; of Aaron and of his sons; holy men, standing by the tabernacle of the congregation, in fine raiments, the workmanship of 'Bezaleel, the son of Uri, the son of Hur, of the tribe of Judah.' It is said there is a convent in Moscow where women are entirely employed in working dresses for the priests.

After two hours had been spent in various ceremonies, the archbishop advanced, holding forth a cross, which all the people crowded to embrace, squeezing each other nearly to suffocation. As soon, however, as their eagerness had been

265

somewhat satisfied, he retired to the sacristy, under a pretence of seeking for the body of Christ; where putting on a plain purple robe, he again advanced, exclaiming three times, in a very loud voice, 'Christ is risen!'

The most remarkable part of the solemnity now followed. The archbishop, descending into the body of the church, concluded the whole ceremony by crawling round the pavement on his hands and knees, kissing the consecrated pictures, whether on the pillars, the walls, the altars, or the tombs; the priests and all the people imitating his example. Sepulchres were opened, and the mummied bodies of incorruptible saints exhibited: all of these underwent the same general kissing.

Thus was Easter proclaimed: and riot and debauchery instantly broke loose. The inn where we lodged became a *Pandæmonium*. Drinking, dancing, and singing, continued through the night and day. But, in the midst of all these excesses, quarrels hardly ever took place. The wild, rude riot of a Russian populace is full of humanity. Few disputes are heard; no blows are given; no lives endangered, but by drinking. No meetings take place, of any kind, without repeating the expressions of peace and joy, Khristos voskrese! Christ is risen!–to which the answer always is the same, Vo istinu voskrese! He is risen indeed!

On Easter Monday begins the presentation of the Paschal eggs: lovers to their mistresses, relatives to each other, servants to their masters, all bring ornamented eggs. Every offering at this season is called a Paschal egg. The meanest pauper in the street, presenting an egg, and repeating the words Khristos voskrese, may demand a salute even of the Empress. All business is laid aside; the upper ranks are engaged in visiting, balls, dinners, suppers, masquerades; while boors fill the air with their songs, or roll intoxicated about the streets. Servants appear in new and tawdry liveries, and carriages in the most sumptuous decoration.

Edward Clarke, *Travels in Various Countries of Europe, Asia and Africa* (London 1810)

Impressions of Moscow

Edward Clarke was much given to exploiting contrasts in his pen-pictures of Russia, and Moscow proved a highly suitable subject. It was for him the confrontation of Asia and Europe, poverty and wealth, impressive churches and palaces and filthy hovels.

The rising towers and spires of Moscow greeted our eyes six versts before we reached the city. The country around it is flat and open; and the town, spreading over an immense district, equals, by its majestic appearance, that of Rome, when viewed at an equal distance. As we approached the barrier of Moscow, we beheld, on the left, the large palace of Petrovskiy, built of brick. It wears an appearance of great magnificence, though the style of architecture is cumbrous and heavy. It was erected for the accommodation of the Russian Sovereigns, during their visits to Moscow; the inhabitants of which city pretend that none of them durst take up a lodging within its walls, being kept much more in awe of their subjects than they are at Petersburg. It is said the Empress Catherine used to call Moscow her little haughty republic. This palace is about four versts from the city.

Arriving at the barrier, we were some time detained during the examination of our passports. This entrance to the city, like most of the others, is a gate with two columns, one on each side, surmounted by eagles. On the left is the guard-house. Within this gate a number of slaves were employed, removing the mud from the streets, which had been caused by the melting of the snow. Peasants with their *kibitki,* in great numbers, were leaving the town. Into these vehicles the slaves amused themselves by heaping as much of the mud as they could collect, unperceived by the drivers, who sat in front. The officer appointed to superintend their labour chanced to arrive and detect them in their filthy work, and we hoped he would instantly have prohibited such an insult from being offered to the poor men. His conduct, however, only served to afford another trait of the national character. Instead of preventing any further attack upon the *kibitki,* he seemed highly entertained by the ingenuity of the contrivance; and, to encourage the sport, ordered every peasant to halt, and to hold his horse, while they filled his *kibitka* with the mud and ordure of the streets; covering with it the provisions of the poor peasants, and whatever else their *kibitka* might contain, with which they were going peaceably to their wives and families. At last, to complete their scandalous oppression, they compelled each peasant, as he passed, to sit down in his *kibitka,* and then they covered him also with the black and stinking mud. At this unexampled instance of cruelty and insult, some of the peasants, more spirited than the rest ventured to murmur. Instantly, blows, with a heavy cudgel, on the head and shoulders, silenced the poor wretches' complaints. Before this began, the two sentinels at the gate had stopped every *kibitka,* as it passed, with a very different motive. First, a loud and menacing tone of voice seemed to indicate some order of Government; but it was quickly silenced, and became a whisper, in consequence of a small piece of money being slipped into their hands by the peasants; when they passed on without further notice. If the practice continues, the post of sentinel at a Russian barrier must be more profitable than

124 *Budochniki* or sentry policemen in the cities. The box was known as a *budka*.

that of a staff-officer in the service. We were witness to upwards of fifty extorted contributions of this nature, in the course of half an hour, when the plunder ended as has been described.

A miserable whiskered figure on horseback, intended for a dragoon, was now appointed to conduct us to the Commandant's; and here our *podorozhnaya,* together with our other passports, underwent a second examination. The snow was by this time entirely melted; and the sledge upon which our

125 A view of Moscow from the Kremlin heights overlooking the Moskva River, from the painting made by de la Barthe in 1797.

carriage moved was dragged over the stones by six horses, with so much difficulty, that at last the drivers gave it up, and declared the carriage would break, or the horses drop, if we compelled them to advance. The dragoon said we must take every thing, exactly as we arrived, to the Commandant's; and proceed sitting in the carriage. At the same time he threatened the peasants with a flagellation; and giving one of them a blow over his loins, bade him halt at his peril. Another effort was of course made, and the sledge flew to pieces. It was highly amusing to observe the dilemma into which the dragoon was now thrown; as it was not probable either his menaces or his blows would again put the carriage in motion. A *drozkhi* was procured, on which we were ordered to sit; and thus we proceeded to the Commandant. From the Commandant we were next ordered to the Intendant of the Police: and all this did not save us from the visits and the insolence of two or three idle officers, lounging about as spies, who entered our apartments, examined every thing we had, and asked a

268

number of frivolous and impertinent questions, with a view to extort money. Some of them found their way even into our bed-rooms, when we were absent, and gave our servant sufficient employment to prevent them from indulging a strong national tendency to pilfer; a species of larceny which actually took place afterwards, committed by persons much their superiors in rank.

The accommodations for travellers are beyond description

bad, both in Petersburg and in Moscow. In the latter, nothing but necessity would render them sufferable. Three rubles a day are demanded for a single room, or rather a kennel, in which an Englishman would blush to keep his dogs. The dirt on the floor may be removed only with an iron hoe, or a shovel. These places are entirely destitute of beds. They consist of bare walls, with two or three old stuffed chairs, ragged, rickety, and full of vermin. The walls themselves are still more disgusting, as the Russians cover them with the most abominable filth . . .

We arrived at the season of the year in which this city is most interesting to strangers. Moscow is in everything extra-ordinary; as well in disappointing expectation, as in surpassing it; in causing wonder and derision, pleasure and regret. Let the Reader be conducted back again to the gate by which we entered, and thence through the streets. Numerous spires, glittering with gold, amidst burnished domes and painted

126 View of the Troitso-Sergeyevskiy Monastery from the Convent of Bethany, the residence of the Metropolitan of Moscow, Plato. Plato was much visited and esteemed by English visitors. By Daniel Lafond after Gerard de la Barthe. Gottfried Keller-Stiftung, Kunstmuseum, Bern.

palaces, appear in the midst of an open plain, for several versts before you reach this gate. Having passed, you look about, and wonder what is become of the city, or where you are; and are ready to ask, once more, How far is it to Moscow? They will tell you, 'This is Moscow!' and you behold nothing but a wide and scattered suburb, huts, gardens, pig-sties, brick walls, churches, dunghills, palaces, timber-yards, warehouses, and a refuse, as it were, of materials sufficient to stock an empire with miserable towns and miserable villages. One

127 View of the bridge over the Yauza and the home of a Mr Shapkin.

might imagine all the States of Europe and Asia had sent a building, by way of representative to Moscow: and under this impression the eye is presented with deputies from all countries, holding congress: timber-huts from regions beyond the Arctic; plastered palaces from Sweden and Denmark, not white-washed since their arrival; painted walls from the Tirol; mosques from Constantinople; Tartar temples from Bucharia; pagodas, pavilions, and virandas, from China; cabarets from Spain; dungeons, prisons, and public offices, from France;

architectural ruins from Rome; terraces and trellisses from Naples; and warehouses from Wapping.

Having heard accounts of its immense population, you wander through deserted streets. Passing suddenly towards the quarter where the shops are situate, you might walk upon the heads of thousands. The daily throng is there so immense, that, unable to force a passage through it, or assign any motive that might convene such a multitude, you ask the cause, and are told that it is always the same. Nor is the costume less various than the aspect of the buildings: Greeks, Turks, Tartars, Cossacks, Chinese, Muscovites, English, French, Italians, Poles, Germans, all parade in the habits of their respective countries.

We were in a Russian inn; a complete epitome of the city itself. The next room to ours was filled by an ambassador, and his suite, from Persia. In a chamber beyond the Persians, lodged a party of Kirgisians; a people yet unknown, and any of whom might be exhibited in a cage, as some newly-discovered species. They had bald heads, covered by conical embroidered caps, and wore sheep-skins. Beyond the Kirgisians lodged a nidus of Bucharians, wild as the asses of Numidia. All these were ambassadors from their different districts, extremely jealous of each other, who had been to Petersburg, to treat of commerce, peace, and war. The doors of all our chambers opened into one gloomy passage; so that sometimes we all encountered, and formed a curious masquerade. The Kirgisians and Bucharians were best at arm's length; but the worthy old Persian, whose name was Orazai, often exchanged visits with us. He brought us presents, according to the custom of his country; and was much pleased with an English pocket-knife we had given him, with which he said he should shave his head. At his devotions, he stood silent for an hour together, on two small carpets, bare-footed, with his face towards Mecca; holding, as he said, intellectual converse with Mohammed.

Orazai came from Cherkey, near Derbent, on the western shore of the Caspian. He had with him his nephew, and a Cossack interpreter from Mount Caucasus. His beard and whiskers were long and grey, though his eye-brows and eyes were black. On his head he wore a large cap of fine black wool. His dress was a jacket of silk, over which was thrown a large loose robe of the same materials, edged with gold. His feet were covered with yellow Morocco slippers, which were without soles, and fitted like gloves. All his suite joined in prayer, morning and evening; but the old man continued his devotions long after he had dismissed his attendants. Their poignards were of such excellent steel, that our English swords were absolutely cut by them. Imitations of these poignards are sold in Moscow, but of worse materials than the swords from England. When they sit, which they generally do during the whole day, they have their feet bare. Orazai was very desirous that we should visit Persia. Taking out a reed, and holding it in his left hand, he began to write from right to left, putting down our names, and noting the information we gave him of England. Afterwards he wrote his own name, in fair Persian characters, and gave it to us, as a memorial by which to recognise us if we ever should visit Persia.

Upon the journey, they both purchased and sold slaves. He offered an Indian negro, who acted as his cook, for twelve

hundred roubles. An amusing embarrassment took place whenever a little dog belonging to us found his way into the ambassador's room. The Persians immediately drew up their feet, and hastily caught up all their clothes, retiring as far back as possible upon their couches. They told us, that if a dog touch even the skirt of their clothing, they are thereby defiled, and cannot say their prayers without changing every thing, and undergoing complete purification. His slaves sometimes played the balalaika, or guitar with two strings. The airs were very lively and not unlike our English hornpipe. The ambassador's nephew obliged us by exhibiting a Persian dance; which seemed to consist of keeping the feet close together, hardly ever lifting them from the ground, and moving slowly, to quick measure, round the room. They drink healths as we do; and eat with their fingers, like the Arabs, all out of one dish,

128 De la Barthe: Pashkov's elaborate mansion in Moscow, designed by V. I. Bazhenov. It became the home of the Rumyantsev Museum in the nineteenth century and after the Revolution became part of the Lenin State Library.

129 Russian nationalities: the inhabitants of the lands of the Tsars. From C. Rechberg, *Des Peuples de la Russie*.

which is generally of boiled rice. If they eat meat, it is rarely any other than mutton, stewed into soup. The young man drank of the Russian beverage called *hydromel,* a kind of mead; and sometimes, but rarely, he smoked tobacco. The ambassador never used a pipe; which surprised us, as the custom is almost universal in the East. Their kindness to their slaves was that of parents to children: the old man appearing, like another Abraham, the common father of all his attendants. The dress of their interpreter, a Cossack of the Volga, was very rich. It consisted of a jacket of purple cloth lined with silk, and a silk waistcoat, both without buttons; a rich shawl round his waist; large trowsers of scarlet cloth; and a magnificent sabre.

Ambassadors of other more Oriental hordes drove into the court-yard of the inn, from Petersburg. The Emperor had presented each of them with a *barouche*. Nothing could be more ludrcrous than was their appearance. Out of respect to the sovereign, they had maintained a painful struggle to pre-serve a sitting posture in the carriage, but cross-legged, like Turks. The snow having melted, they had been jolted in this posture over the trunks of trees, which form a timber causeway between Petersburg and Moscow; so that, when taken from their fine new carriages, they could hardly move, and made the most pitiable grimaces imaginable. A few days after their arrival at Moscow, they ordered all their carriages to be sold, for whatever sum any person would offer.

Edward Clarke, *Travels in Various Countries of Europe, Asia and Africa* (London 1810)

THE REIGN OF ALEXANDER I

Theatres in St Petersburg

Sir John Carr visited St Petersburg as part of his 'Northern Tour' early in the reign of Alexander I. He was a sympathetic and enthusiastic observer, delighting in the city's architectural splendours and the outward, colourful manifestations of Russian life. His description of Russian theatrical life contains much interesting detail and amusing comparisons of English and Russian dramatic tastes.

Soon after our arrival, we visited the Grand Imperial Theatre, or Opera House, called the Stone-Theatre, which stands in a large open place, nearly in front of the Marine Garrison, formerly the New Goal, and the Nicholas Canal. At four angles, in this spacious area, are four pavilions of iron, supported by pillars of the same metal, resting upon a circular basement of granite, within which, in winter, large fir fires are constructed, the wind being kept off by vast circular moveable shutters of iron, for warming and screening the servants of those who visit the theatre in the winter. Previous to the erection of these sheds, many of those unfortunate persons were frozen to death. The government, attentive to the lives of the people, has interdicted performances at the opera, when the frost is unusually severe. The front is a noble portico, supported by doric pillars; the interior is about the size of Covent-Garden, of an oval shape, and splendidly but rather heavily decorated. The lower tier of boxes project from the sides, at the back of which are pilasters, adorned with appropriate decorations, richly gilded, above which are three rows of boxes, supported by corinthian pillars, each of which, as well as those below, contain nine persons. Nothing less than the whole box can be taken. It frequently happens that servants stand behind their masters or mistresses in the boxes, during the performance, and present a curious motly appearance. The Imperial box is in the centre of the first tier, projecting a little, is small, and very plainly decorated. The pit has seven or eight rows of seats with backs to them, in which a commodious portion of space for each spectator is marked of by little plates of brass, numbered upon the top of the back seat; this part is called the *fauteuils*. Such is the order observed here, and in every theatre on the continent, that however popular the piece, a spectator may, during any part of the performance, reach his seat, in this part of the theatre, without any difficulty. Behind, but not boarded off, is the pit and the parterre. The price of admission to the boxes and *fauteuils* are two silver rubles, little more than five shillings. There are no galleries. The massy girandoles, one of which is placed at every pilaster, are never illuminated but when the Imperial family are present, on which occasion only, a magnificent circle of

130 The Kamennyy (Stone) or Bolshoy (Large) theatre in St Petersburg, built in 1783. The engraving shows the four iron pavilions, described by Carr, which afforded warmth and shelter for coachmen. By an unknown artist, 1800, engraved by G. L. Lory.

large patent lamps is used, descending from the centre of the roof; at other times its place is supplied by one of smaller dimensions, when the obscurity which prevails induces the ladies generally to appear in an undress. Although this gloom before the curtain is said to be advantageous to the effect of scenery, yet the eye is saddened, as it runs its circuit in vain for forms adorned with graceful drapery, the glittering gem, the nodding plume, and looks of adorned beauty, that give fresh brilliance to the gay galaxy of light. This theatre is furnished with a great number of doors and passages, reservoirs of water, and an engine in case of fire, and with concealed flues and stoves, to give it summer warmth in winter. It is always strongly guarded by a detachment from the guards, as well as by the police officers, who preserve the most admirable order among the carriages and servants. It is not an ungratifying sight, after the opera, to pause at the doors and see with what uncommon skill and velocity the carriages, each drawn by four horses, drive up to the grand entrance under the portico, receive their company, and gallop off at full speed; pockets are very rarely picked, and accidents seldom happen.

Owing to the size and quantity of decorations, and the spacious arrangements of the boxes, I should not think the theatre could contain more than twelve hundred persons. Its receipts have never yet exceeded one thousand six hundred and eighty rubles, or two hundred and forty pounds. How different from a London theatre, which, on a crowded night,

when a Siddons or a Litchfield delight their audience, is lined with faces, and the very walls appear to breathe!

The first opera I saw was Blue Beard, performed by Italian performers, the subject of which varied but little from the representation of it in England, except that the last wife of Blue Beard has a lover, who in the concluding act lays the sanguinary tyrant breathless with his sword. The catastrophe was finely worked up, and drew from the Russians successions of enthusiastic acclamation. Do these sentiments of tenderness, these noble notions of retributive justice, denote an immutable barbarism? The processions were in the first style of magnificence, the dresses and ornaments were very costly, and it is not unusual to introduce, on these occasions, one thousand men, selected from the guards for the expression of their faces and symmetry of their figures, to swell the scene of pomp. The orchestra was very full, and combined the first-rate powers of music. The scenes were handsome and well managed. A room was formed of entire sides, and well

131 Catherine's Hermitage Theatre, built by Quarenghi between 1783 and 1785, with the bridge which connects it to the Winter Palace.

277

furnished; and a garden was displayed with all its characteristics. The Emperor contributes very munificently to the support of this theatre; and as all the machinists and workmen are his slaves, they are all under admirable discipline. The introduction of a tree into a study, or fringing the top of a forest with a rich cieling, scenic blunders which frequently occur on the English stage, would hazard the backs of the Russian scene shifters. This theatre has a very beautiful set of scenes, which

132 F. Ya. Aleksevev. View of the Stock Exchange and the Admiralty from the Peter and Paul Fortress (1810).

is never displayed but on nights when the Imperial Family honour it with their presence. The silence and decorum of the audience cannot but impress the mind of any one, who has witnessed the boisterous clamours of an English audience. The curtain ascends at six o'clock precisely. No after-piece, as with us, only now and then a ballet, succeeds the opera, which

278

is generally concluded by nine o'clock, when the company go to the Summer Gardens, drive about the city, or proceed to card and supper parties.

This theatre is as much dedicated to the Russian muses, as to those of more genial climates. In this respect Catherine II pursued the same plan of domestic policy, so widely adopted by Gustavus III but the plan since her demise has never been encouraged by the higher circles. A Russ play has the same

effect upon fashion in Russia, as George Barnwell has upon the same class in England. Although in the former there are some inimitable performers, as in the hero of the latter, one of the most perfect and affecting imitations of nature, in that walk of the drama, ever exhibited upon any stage, is displayed by Mr Charles Kemble.

279

I went one evening, in company with my amiable and gallant friend, Captain Elphinstone, to see a Russ opera, called 'The School for Jealousy': it is not much esteemed. As it proceeded Captain E. explained it to me: the sentiments were frequently coarse, sometimes very obscene; the actors, who were Russians, appeared to perform with great ability; the heroine of the piece was represented by a very pretty and interesting girl, who was taken from the hospital of foundlings: she manifested grace, and a bewitching *naiveté,* and played and sung most sweetly. I am sorry I have forgotten her name; she is the principal Russ actress, and is a very great favourite. In the course of the play, to my astonishment, was introduced a scene of the inside of the mad-house at Petersburg, in which, amongst a number of horrible grotesque figures, a mad periwig-maker threw a handful of hair-powder into the face of a frantic girl, who ran raving about the stage with dishevelled locks, which excited strong risibility amongst the audience. I was so disgusted at the spectacle, and the applause, that I wished it had not happened; but as it did, I record it. Although an English audience has been delighted at a dance of under-takers, laughed at the feats of skeletons in pantomimes, and in Hamlet has expressed great mirth at seeing a buffoon grave-digger roll human skulls upon the stage, and beat them about with his spade, it could not endure a sight in which those objects, whom pity and every tender feeling have consecrated, are brought forward with ridicule. But let it be remembered that madness is less frequent in Russia than in milder regions; and hence the people, for they are very far from being strangers to feelings which would do honour to the most civilized of the human race, are less acquainted with, and consequently less affected by its appearance; and when it is thus wantonly displayed upon the stage, it appears under the mask of buffoonery. The government would do well to suppress this and every similar exhibition, calculated only to imbrute a civilized mind, and postpone the refinement of a rude one.

I was much more pleased with the Russ opera of the Nymph of the Dnieper, which is so popular and attractive, that it never fails to fill the seats of fashion. It is chiefly intended to display the ancient costume and music of Russia. The story is very simple: a prince has sworn eternal constancy to a nymph, who is violently attached to him; his father, a powerful king, wishes him to marry a princess of an ancient house; the prince consents, but the nuptials are always interrupted by the stratagems of the jealous nymph, who appears in various disguises. The first scene was singularly beautiful: it displayed a river and its banks, and nymphs swimming; the manner in which they rose upon the water was admirably natural; the music of the ancient Russ airs, in which the celebrated Kazachok is introduced, were exquisite; the scenery was very fine, and displayed a number of pantomimic changes.

280

The Russian noblemen are fond of the drama; almost every country mansion has a private theatre. Those of the nobility, who, from disgust to the court, or some other cause, confine their residence to Moscow and the adjacent country, live in the voluptuous magnificence of eastern satraps: after dinner they frequently retire to a vast rotunda, and sip their coffee, during a battle of dogs, wild bears, and wolves; from thence they go to their private theatres, where great dramatic skill is frequently displayed by their slaves, who perform, and who also furnish the orchestra. These people are tutored by French players, who are very liberally paid by their employers.

Sir John Carr, *A Northern Summer* (London 1805)

Winter Scene on the Neva

Receiving a personal invitation from Alexander I to paint a series of large paintings on the accomplishments of Peter the Great, Robert Ker Porter left for Russia in 1805 and remained until 1807. His book is based on a series of letters he sent to his sisters in England and captures vividly his delight in the picturesque aspects of Russian life. Here he depicts with typical panache and bold strokes a winter scene on the Neva.

St Petersburg, October, 1805

How changed is the face of nature since last I addressed you! all is frozen; and covered with the chilling snows of winter. If the city astonished me when under the glowing tints of an autumnal atmosphere, how much more striking does its

133 Cutting blocks of ice on the Neva. From J. A. Atkinson and J. Walker, *A Picturesque Representation of the Manners, Customs and Amusements of the Russians*, London 1812.

present pale silvery light make it appear!

Now *indeed this is Russia!* every sensation, every perception, confirms the conviction. The natives have suddenly changed their woollen kaftans, for the greasy and unseemly skins of sheep. The freezing power which has turned every inanimate object into ice, seems to have thawed their hearts and their faculties: they sing, they laugh, they wrestle; tumbling about like great bears amongst the furrows of the surrounding snow.

134 Skaters on the Neva, from a painting by Ye. Karneyev. In C. Rechberg, *Des Peuples de la Russie.*

In fact, this season, so prolonged with them, seems more congenial with their natures than their short but vivid summer.

This year the bosom of the Neva was encrusted with ice at an unusually early period: it took place on the 14th of the present month: but in the September of 1715 it was shut up by a frost so intense as to become in a few hours safe for carriages of the heaviest burthen. Soon after the commencement of the present winter the bridge of boats (which communicates with that part of the city built on an island called Vasilevskiy Ostrov), was allowed to swing to the opposite side of the river, in order to permit vast sheets of congealed water to pass forward into the gulph. After an early frost followed by a temporary thaw, these masses find their way down the

282

Neva; they come from the interior, the lake Ladoga, &c. and proceed with frightful velocity. Sometimes a quick frost arrests these accumulations, and renders them in one night safe for conveyances of every description. Frequently the ice thus collected does not finally dissolve till the expiration of the ensuing May. In that charming month, I am told summer re-appears with the suddenness of enchantment; and every thing around seems rather like the instantaneous mechanism of an English pantomime, than the regular action of the season.

Far different is the scene at present! Where are now the expanded waters of the Neva? The gay gondolas and painted yachts? The myriads of vessels and boats continually passing and repassing? All have disappeared: one bleak extended snowy plain generalizes the views: and scarcely a trace is left to convey an idea that a river ever glided through the heart of this imperial city. The roofs of the palaces, public buildings, and private houses, are shrouded in the same pale garb. But no objects are so strangely beautiful as the trees which grow in several divisions of this metropolis; when divested of their leaves, the repeated coats of snow thickening on their branches, form them into the appearance of white coral encrusted with a brilliant daimond dust. Even the beards of men and horses are white and glittering with this *northern ornament*.

Cold to the Russians, seems to be what heat is to the torpid animal; for Petersburg at this moment presents a prospect of much greater bustle and activity than during the warmer months. The additional multitudes, spread in busy swarms throughout every quarter, are inconceivable: sledges, carriages, and other *traineau* vehicles, cross and pass each other with incredible velocity. The sensation excited in the eye by the swift, transitory movement of so many objects upon the unbroken glare of the snow, is painful and blinding: and you might as well determine to fix your sight upon a particular ant (at the demolition of its little world), as on one of these figures when beholding them from a height. From the fortress tower for instance; where I have just been beholding a scene as extraordinary to an English eye, as it is undescribable and amusing.

You will naturally expect a description of the sledge, a prominent feature in a Russian view. It is a machine on which not only the persons of the people are transported from place to place with unparalleled speed, but likewise the product of other nations is passed many thousand versts into the interior. The sledge is precisely a pair of colossal skates joined together. On these (according to the taste of the owner) is erected the most agreeable and convenient carriage which either his purse may afford or his situation claim. The sledges of the humbler order are solely formed of logs of wood bound together with ropes into the before-mentioned shape: on this is an even surface of plank or matting, for the accommodation of themselves or loads. You will see a Russian pair in one of these conveyances, amongst my pencil memorandums. The sledges which succeed the drozhki (the St Petersburg hackney-coach), are generally very neat, yet always gaudy, being decorated with red, green, gold and silver, with strange carved work and uncouth whirligigs of iron. Their interior is well bespread with *damp* hay, for the benefit of the hirer, in order to keep his feet *warm*. It is so difficult to describe the precise *cut* of these

135 A highly stylized picture of the *izvozchik*, or coach-man, waiting for custom at a street corner. From *A Picture of St Petersburg,* drawing by Mornay.

vehicles, that I must again refer you to the more accurate delineation in my sketch-book.

The sledge carriage of a prince, or a nobleman, is uncommonly handsome. All its appointments are magnificent; and never out of harmony. In it we behold the genuine uncontaminated taste of the country: no bad imitations of German or English coach-work are here attempted; all is characteristic; and a picturesque effect, peculiarly its own, is produced by the vehicle itself, its furs, its horses, their trappings, and the streaming beards of the charioteers. The nobleman's sledge is built exactly on the same principle with those of inferior people; only differing in the width of the body, which is made to hold two persons. It is warmly lined with rich furs; and to prevent the lower extremities of the occupier from being cold, has an apron (like those of our curricles) formed of green or crimson velvet, bordered with gold lace. On a step behind, stand the servants with appropriate holders. This place is often filled by gentlemen when accompanying ladies on a sledging party.

The horses attached to this conveyance are the pride of the opulent. Their beauty and value are more considered than the sledge itself. The excess of vanity amongst the young officers and nobility here, consists in driving about two animals whose exquisite elegance of form, and playfulness of action, attract the attention of every passenger. The form of these horses is slight and Arabic, possessing the grace of an Italian greyhound with a peculiar lightness and looseness of pace. One only, is placed in the shafts which never alters its pace from a rapid trot: the other is widely traced by its side; and is taught to pace, curvet, and prance, in the most perfect taste of a finished manège. Their tails and manes are always of an enormous length; a beauty so admired by the Russians that twenty horses out of thirty have false ones. Indeed this custom is so prevalent, that frequently the most rascally Rosinante and pigmy Fin-galloway have long artificial appendages, richly clothed with knots of dirt, hanging as low as the ground.

But to return to the sledge horses. The harness of these creatures is curiously picturesque, being studded with polished brass or silver, hundreds of tassels, intermixed with embossed leather and scarlet cloth. These strange ornaments give the trappings an air of eastern barbaric splendour, perfectly consonant with the animal's shape. However, as every carriage in Russia (even should it be built in the excess of the British mode), is drawn by horses thus romantically caparisoned, the union is sometimes monstrous: and I have often felt the contradiction so forcibly, as to remind me of an absurd sight I once saw at home. It was an Indian chief in a London assembly. He was decorated with chains, shells, and tyger's teeth, while all the spruce, powdered beaux around him were in the extreme of European costume.

The passion of the Russians for rapid motion, has produced the sport called a sledge-race. A regular course for that purpose is kept always smooth, and railed off upon the Neva. Crowds assemble there to witness the wonderful velocity with which this race is performed. The species of horse used on this occasion is an animal whose swiftest pace is a peculiar sort of trot. No race is ever run quicker. Indeed the rapidity of this is incredible, being not at all inferior to that of a gallop. The sledge-horses never step out in the usual way, but are taught to lift up both legs on the same side, which gives their motion a singular appearance. By this habit the action of the horse's body is doubled, and their speed consequently increased twofold. I do not yet know whether regular matches are made; or whether the spirit of sport produces bets, &c. I did not perceive any symptoms of this species of gambling, nor did I investigate that *important* question; contenting myself with surveying the

285

tout ensemble merely as a picture of rude magnificence.

The surrounding winter scenery; the picturesque sledges and their fine horses; the scattered groupes of the observing multitude; the superb dresses of the nobility, their fur cloaks, caps, and equipages, adorned with coloured velvets and gold; with ten thousand other touches of exquisite nature, finished the scene, and made it seem like an Olympic game from the glowing pencil of Rembrandt.

Robert Ker Porter, *Travelling Sketches in Russia and Sweden* (London 1809)

A Post-House

Travellers were often delayed for long periods at posting-stations, awaiting teams of fresh horses, and were obliged to while away their time in buildings such as Robert Ker Porter describes, and were frustrated by the lack of amenities offered. Porter's sketch is also interesting for his unflattering portrayal of the Russian priest he encountered there.

136 A Russian tradesman. From Sir Robert Ker Porter, *Travelling Sketches in Russia,* Vol I, 1809.

We now hoped to proceed quietly to Moscow; but alas! we had not gone very far before the barouche-sledge shewed symptoms of disunion again; and at the village of Klin our servants had the extraordinary pleasure of another *summer-set* in the *snow*. While our plague was refitting, I left the management to the hero who had so well acquitted himself during the last affair, and entered the post-house. By way of amusing my almost exhausted patience, as the apartment was rather curious, I made a sketch of the scene within. These dwellings being all alike, my drawing will present you with the image of their form and inhabitants; but my pen, reluctant to be idle in your service, insists upon bringing before your *mind's-senses,* its dirt, effluvia, and varieties of wretchedness. As the poet recommends *pomp* to *take physic,* perhaps it may not be less salutory now and then to give the delicacy of British organs a similar regimen! So, without further apology. I shall, notwithstanding my 'damnable faces, begin!'

One room is the habitation of all the inmates. Here they eat, sleep, and perform all the functions of life. One quarter of it is occupied by a large stove or pech', flat at the top; on which many of them take their nocturnal rest; and during the day loll over its baking warmth, for hours, by threes and fours together, in a huddle, not more decent than disgusting. Beneath, is an excavation like an oven, used for the double duty of cooking their victuals, and heating the dwelling to the desired temperature. The apartment I am describing, rendered

286

insufferably stifling by the stove, the breaths, and other fumigations, contained the post-master, his wife, his mother, his wife's mother, an infant, and two men, apparently attached to the post department, as they wore green uniforms. There were others besides, who being rather withdrawn in a dark corner, we could not distinctly observe.

When we entered, the top of the oven was occupied by the three women and child, almost all in a state of nature. The

137 Village near Klin. From J. T. James *Travels and Views,* 3rd edition. 'This view affords an idea of a Russian village in the wealthier parts of the country; being situate on the grand road from Petersburg to Moscow, at a distance of about forty versts from the latter. The log houses of the peasants here appear more shapely without and more roomy within, and the church, with its green cupolas, forms no inelegant object in the scene. The bearded men are seen, as usual, sleeping on the ground; the children playing at *babki,* that is, pelting from a certain distance at knuckle-bones disposed in pairs; the women working their coloured lace. This village is the property of Count Stroganov. Here were placed, for some time at least, the advanced posts of the French army during their occupation of Moscow, in 1812; General Witzingerode being posted at Klin, which is but a few versts distant.'

youngest was extremely pretty, and seemed, though a mother. not more than fifteen. This is nothing surprizing; as the warmth of these stoves act upon the human constitution as hot-houses do upon exotics. A bed with dirty curtains filled one corner of the room; a few benches and a table, completed the furniture. The walls were not quite so barren, being covered with uncouth prints and innumerable daubings. In one spot was placed a picture or effigy of our Saviour and the Virgin, decorated with silver plates, stamped most curiously. From the ceiling was suspended a lamp, which during certain holy-days is kept continually burning. Having finished my sketch, we left this cyclopean den, not only to look into the state of our carriages, but to breath a little fresh air, as its heat and stench became so pestiferous that we felt ourselves compelled to make our escape, or resign ourselves to suffocation. As we opened the door, the steam issued with us like smoke from the crater of a volcano.

While we stood by the repairing barouche, a priest came forth from the house we had quitted. He was a young, healthy, and good-looking man, with long and beautiful hair divided on his forehead, and flowing gracefully on each shoulder, in the style of Raphael's head. He addressed us in his native tongue, but finding us ignorant in that point, changed his eloquence to the Latin language; and now being understood, he poured forth with such vehemence and inconsistency that we soon discovered he had been paying his devotions to a certain heathen deity, from whom he had received a most *spirited* afflatus; so much so, that he seemed to forget both himself and the dignity of his profession. Indeed he pestered us so adhesively that we were glad to shake him off, even by darting back into the apartment of the post-master. He followed us in, proceeding as most men do who *take an enemy into their mouth to steal away their senses*; and after a most tormenting half hour, he at last said something in his native tongue,

138 'A travelling Russian boor.' From Sir Robert Ker Porter, *Travelling Sketches in Russia,* Vol I, 1809.

139 A Russian post house. From Sir Robert Ker Porter, *Travelling Sketches in Russia,* Vol I, 1809.

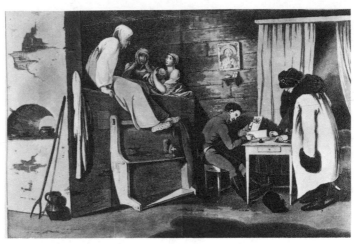

unintelligible to us, but so level to the understanding of the rest, that the females made their escape as if a shot had fallen amongst them. Our host seemed extremely angry; and, I suppose, intimated to the ecclesiastic that he desired his absence; for he turned round with a sullen reluctance, and proceeding towards the door, cast his eye on the painted effigy of our Saviour and his Mother. He stopped suddenly, and with the greatest reverence crossed himself several times, and then left the place.

I cannot say the example of this pastor was very edifying to his flock, it being now one of their most sacred fasts in the Greek calendar, when it is infamous amongst the Russians not to abstain from all strong liquors. This man was a secular priest; and, I am told that many of the lower rank of that order are rather free in their modes of life. Not so with those of higher dignity: they are celebrated for qualifications quite the contrary; for purity of heart and sanctity of manners.

Robert Ker Porter, *Travelling Sketches in Russia and Sweden* (London 1809)

288

Visit to a Cotton Mill

John Quincy Adams was the first recognized United States Minister in Russia, between 1809 and 1814. His memoirs are a diary account of his life in the Russian capital, full of interesting information on Russians and foreigners, diplomatic affairs, social engagements, national customs and ceremonies. The description of a visit to a cotton mill near St Petersburg in April 1810 is unusual in its detail and subject. It is illuminating on the role of the foreign technical experts in Russia and also on the conditions under which the unfortunate young workers existed.

At ten this morning I called at the office of Mr Grootten, who accompanied me to the Aleksandrovskiy manufactory, of which he is the superintendent–a manufactory for spinning cotton yarn, under the patronage of the Empress-mother.

The buildings are about seven versts, or five miles, from the city, on the banks of the Neva, beyond the Monastery of St Alexander Nevskiy. The establishment is under the direction of a Mr Wilson, an Englishman. There are four or five hundred carding, spinning, and winding machines, which are kept at work by three steam-engines, variously constructed, according to the recent improvements upon that great mechanical invention. There is also connected with the establishment a manufactory of cotton stockings; where they also wove silk stockings while the silk was to be procured. The needles, cards, and much of the machinery are made within the manufactory. The labor is executed by about five hundred

140 Launderesses. From *La Russie, ou Moeurs, Usages et Costumes des habitants . . . de cet Empire*. M. Breton, Paris 1813.

foundling children, nearly an equal number of both sexes, and most of whom are taken, at the age of eight, nine, or ten years, from the foundling hospitals of St Petersburg and of Moscow. They remain here, the boys until twenty-one, and the girls until twenty-five years, unless sooner married. They then have liberty to quit the establishment, or to remain connected with it, at their option. They have apartments accommodated for the married couples, of which there are now about twenty-five, and they are increasing. The institution having existed not more than twelve years, it has only been within four or five years that the marriages began to take place. Of the earliest, almost all the children died, and even now a small proportion of those that are born are likely to live. This mortality is attributed to the ignorance of the parents. But the confinement of the chambers allowed to the families, their extreme poverty, the want of cleanliness, and the almost pestilential air which I found in them, sufficiently accounted in my mind for the fact.

In two of the family apartments I saw Russian cradles, which are a sort of hammock suspended by four small cords from the end of an elastic pole, fastened by the other end near the head of the bed. It hangs about four feet from the floor, and the mother can reach her hand to the pole to rock the cradle from her bed, by bending the pole at pleasure. It is a very clumsy contrivance, and the child must be always in danger of falling to the floor, an accident which four times in five must prove fatal.

The working foundlings themselves look for the most part wretchedly, and very unwholesome. Of two hundred and forty girls from ten to twenty-five years of age, I scarcely saw one that could be called handsome, and very few not positively ugly. When we arrived, they were just going to dinner – the girls in a long room, with tables on the two sides, and a passage-

141 Portrait of Quincey Adams.

142 A popular game, known as babki, a kind of skittles played with knuckle-bones. From J. A. Atkinson and J. Walker, *A Picturesque Representation of the Manners, Customs and Amusements of the Russians*, 1812.

way between them. The girls were all standing between the bench and the table, with their faces towards the little image of the Virgin hanging at the wall, at the other end of the hall, and chanting grace before meat. At the farthest end the floor of the room was raised a step higher, and a separate small table was placed, at which about twenty of the girls took their seats. Their fare was the same as at the other tables. But to be seated there is an honorary distinction for particular industry and good

conduct. The dining-hall of the boys is of the same form and dimensions, a story higher. But there were not more than nine or ten at their table of distinction. The plates and dishes of the girls were of wood, those of the boys pewter. Their dinner was a thin turnip soup, and a dish of boiled buckwheat, of the consistency of hasty-pudding; their bread rye, and their drink kvas. They are served at tables by invalids belonging to the establishment, and who have no other duty. They have school-rooms, where, at certain hours of leisure and on Sunday mornings, they are taught to read, write, and cipher. They attend public work at a church in the neighbourhood, the priest of which gives them also occasional religious instruction at the buildings of the institution. The girls all sleep in one long bed-chamber, where there are four rows of beds the whole length of the room, and in several recesses there are four rows

143 A cloth-merchant's shop. Engraving of 1792 after a drawing by Le Prince.

291

more. The appearance was neat, the bedding all clean; but the air was not good. That of the boys' bed-chambers, which were in two or three stages of a large square hall, with inside staircases to the second and third stages, was much worse—almost insupportable. Mr Wilson told us it had not been ventilated the whole winter. By the regulations they must all be in bed before ten at night, and rise at six in the morning. Their task of work is twelve hours a day, and for any extra work which they choose to do they are paid.

The girls and boys are kept very carefully separate, and although marriages between them are encouraged, yet Mr Grootten says not a single *accident* has happened. Is this owing to constitutional coldness, to the continence of hard labor and penurious subsistence, or to the perfection of subserviency secured by their mode of breeding and education? Perhaps to all the causes, combined with the climate and the rigor of the regulations.

The machinery has been very expensive, and before the introduction of the steam-engines, which is only four or five years, it was kept at work also at great expense. French and German projectors devised a number of water-wheels, which, after the waste of much time and money, were found utterly useless. Then came a Mr Gascoigne, an Englishman, of great mechanical genius, the inventor of the sort of great guns now called carronades, but which from him were in the first instance called Gasconades. Some unsuccessful speculative inventions had impaired his fortune in England, and he had come to Russia, where he was employed at the head of a manufactory of iron some one hundred and fifty or two hundred versts from St Petersburg, when the direction of this institution was also put into his hands. He introduced horse-mills to work the machines—a great improvement upon the former processes, but which still left the establishment so expensive that they could not vie with the cheapness of the English manufacturers. Mr Gascoigne had one-third of the profits from the sales, and accumulated a great fortune, of which he died possessed a few years since. He had introduced Mr Wilson as his assistant in the direction, and since his death Mr Wilson has his place; but without his emoluments. He has introduced the steam-engines, which have much reduced the expense of the works, and since the war with England, followed by the prohibiting of English goods, this manufacture is in a flourishing condition. But Mr Wilson has no pay—nothing but occasional presents; leaving him in a state of anxiety and suspense with regard to his future prospects—and the order of St Vladimir, which he received last year from the Emperor as a mark of his favour. There are twelve different kinds of machines used in the process of carding and spinning the yarn. But three or four of them are employed in effecting the modification of the cotton, which might be accomplished by one, and Mr Wilson has invented a

292

machine for that purpose, which is now just beginning to work. There is also much of the labor still done by the hand which might be done by machinery; particularly the wiring of the leather for the carding-machines. I mentioned to Mr Wilson the American invention for this purpose, of which he told me he had heard before. They have also here various small machines for making up the yarn into packages for sending away. The reels wind off seven threads of a given length, which are fastened together and form the first combination of the prepared article. A number of these gatherings, according to the fineness of the yarn, forms a skein. The skein is weighed, and according to the number of skeins to a pound is numbered from twelve to twenty. The skeins of the same numbers are weighed in parcels of ten pounds, and from the scales are put into a hollow squared steel press, in which they are screwed down into as small a compass as the hand of the workman can press them; then they are taken out in a cube apparently solid, and made into packages of brown paper tied up with twine. These are deposited upon shelves in the place where they are made up, for ten days together–after which the ten days' work is all removed at a time to the warehouse of the manufactory, ready to be taken away by the traders from Moscow and other parts of the country, who purchase it by wholesale and take it here at the manufactory. Very little of it is taken at St Petersburg. Besides the cotton, they also spin some coarse thread from flax – a material to which Mr Grootten wishes that the whole manufactory were confined; because the flax is the produce of the country itself. After spending about four hours in going over the different parts of this establishment, I returned with Mr Grootten to the city, and left him at his house.

John Quincy Adams, *Memoirs* (Philadelphia 1874)

The Circassians

The Caucasus and Georgia were to become a favourite setting for works by the Russian Romantics, their equivalent to the exotic Orient dear to their European counterparts. Julius von Klaproth, Aulic Councillor to Alexander I, gives a detailed account of the customs of the Circassians, or Cherkassians, as he called them, the people who were made famous in Pushkin's *Prisoner in the Caucasus.*

The Kabardian has a haughty and martial air, commonly possesses great physical strength, is tall in stature, and has expressive features. He is a most scrupulous observer of the laws of hospitality; and when he had taken any person under his protection or received him as his guest, the latter may repose implicit confidence in him, and trust his life in his hands: never will he betray or deliver him up to his enemies. Should these prepare to carry him off by force, the wife of the host gives the guest some milk from her own breast to drink, after which he is regarded as her legitimate son, and his new brethren are bound to defend him against his enemies at the peril of their

144 Circassians dancing. From C. Rechberg, *Des Peuples de la Russie.*

lives, and to revenge his blood. This revenge of blood, in every respect similar to the practice of the Arabs, is called by the Cherkessians *Ili'luassa,* or Price of Blood, and by the Tartars *Kangleh,* from *Kan,* blood. It is universal throughout the Caucasus, and is the usual occasion of the feuds of the inhabitants. Their implacable enmity to the Russians partly originates in the same cause; for the revenge of blood is transmitted from father to son, and involves the whole family of him who roused it into action by the first murder.

As no nation carries the pride of birth to such a height as the Cherkessians, so there are no instances of unequal marriages among them. The prince invariably takes to wife the daughter of a prince; and his illegitimate children can never obtain their father's title and prerogatives, unless they marry a legitimate princess, by which they become princes of the third class. As the Abasses were formerly subject to the Cherkessians, their princes are considered equal to Kabardian

294

usdens only, and can obtain in marriagé females of no higher rank than the daughters of such usdens; while the latter, on the other hand, marry the daughters of Abassian princes.

The price given for a bride (in Tartar *Kalim*) by princes may be valued at about 2000 rubles in silver. The person to whom the education of a young prince is intrusted likewise marries him, and, in association with the other usdens, pays the *kalim* in muskets, sabres, horses, horned cattle, and sheep; and the father of the bride makes an optional present of a few vassals to his new son-in-law.

When a new-married man finds that his bride is not a virgin, he immediately sends her back to her family, and the kalim is returned to him. The woman is either sold or put to death by her relatives. If a wife commits adultery, her husband has her head shaved, slits her ears, cuts off the sleeves of her garments, and sends her home on horseback to her parents, who in this case also either sell or dispatch her. Certain death awaits the adulterer at the hands of the injured husband or his friends.

They have two kinds of divorce. Either the husband parts from his wife in the presence of witnesses, giving up the kalim to her parents, and then she is at liberty to contract a second marriage; or he merely commands her to go from him, in which case he has a right to take her back again at the expiration of a year. Should he not do so in two years, the wife's father or her relations go to him and complete the actual separation, after which she may marry a second husband.

A husband cannot publicly visit his wife in the day-time without being deemed guilty of a breach of decorum. Common people, however, live together with their wives, especially when they are grown old.

As soon as a prince becomes the father of a child, he celebrates the event with extraordinary festivities. If it be a boy, he consigns him on the third day to the care of one of his usdens, who commonly vie with one another for the honour of bringing him up. A nurse is then provided for the boy; she gives him a name; and it is not till his third or fourth year that he is circumcised, for which operation the mulla is presented with a horse. The father never sees his son till his marriage, and hence results the utmost indifference between the nearest relations. A prince reddens with indignation when he is asked concerning the health of his wife and children, makes no reply, and commonly turns his back on the inquirer in contempt.

The sons of the usdens remain under the paternal roof till they are three or four years old, and are then committed to a preceptor, who needs not be of the same rank. The parents pay him nothing either for his trouble or for the board and clothing of their child. On the other hand, when his ward is grown up, he receives as long as he remains with him the best part of the booty which he makes in predatory excursions or in war.

The Kabardians formerly did not marry till they were thirty or forty years old; but now they enter into the married state between the ages of fifteen and twenty-five, and females between the twelfth and sixteenth year. A girl who continues single beyond the age of seventeen scarcely ever meets with a husband.

The foster-father seeks a wife for his ward; and if the inclinations of the female whom he selects are not pre-engaged, and there is no prior suitor for her hand, he causes her to be carried off by stealth. Should there be two rivals, they either fight themselves for the bride, or their friends fight for them, and strive to kill the opponent. The surviving lover then obtains the lady.

When the father dies, the mother superintends the domestic concerns, and the property continues undivided. At her death the wife of the eldest son generally supplies her place; but if the brothers determine to divide the inheritance, she makes the allotment, taking care to assign the largest portion to the eldest and the least to the younger brother. Illegitimate children have no claim upon the patrimony, but are commonly supported by the family.

The dead are deposited in graves lined with boards, in such a manner that the face may be turned towards Mecca. In case of death, the women set up a dismal howling, and formerly even the male mourners beat themselves about the head with horsewhips, to express their grief. Some time ago they used to bury all the effects of the deceased along with him, but now they give him nothing but his usual dress. The Cherkessians wear black mourning a whole year; but never for those who fall in battle with the Russians, because they believe that the spirits of such persons go straightway into paradise. At funerals the Mulla reads some passages from the Koran, for which he is amply remunerated, and is commonly presented with one of the best horses of the deceased.

According to the present laws of the Cherkessians, theft, if committed upon a prince, is punished by the forfeiture of nine times the value of what has been stolen, and a slave. Thus the thief who steals a horse is obliged to give nine other horses and a vassal. He who robs an usden must return what he has taken, and forfeits thirty oxen besides. According to the regulations made by Lieutenant-general Gudovich, offences of this kind, committed against the Russians, were to be punished in the same manner; but this law has scarcely ever been enforced.

The Cherkessian language is totally different from every other, and is spoken in purity in the Great and Little Kabarda and by the tribe of Belsen on the Laba; while the other Cherkessian tribes beyond the Kuban, between that river and the Black Sea, employ dialects deviating more or less from the genuine standard. It contains a great number of hissing and harsh lingua-palatic consonants, which render the pronunciation almost impossible for a foreigner. I took particular pains to collect words and phrases in it, which shall be given at the conclusion of the second volume.

They have no books or manuscripts in their native language; but in writing they commonly employ the Tartar, which is understood all over the Caucasus.

The Cherkessians upon the whole may be termed a handsome nation; and the men in particular are distinguished by the elegance of their shape, which they use all possible means to preserve and improve. Their stature does not exceed the middle size; but they are extremely muscular, though not corpulent. The shoulders and breast are broad, but the waist is always extremely small. They have in general brown hair and eyes, rather long faces, and thin straight noses. Their women are by far the most beautiful of any in the whole Caucasus; but I should observe that the common notion, that the Turkish seraglios are chiefly supplied with them, is totally unfounded; for the Cherkessians very rarely sell people of their own country to the Turks, but only captive slaves. Most of the handsome females sent to Turkey come from Imerethi and Mingrelia; on the other hand the slave-trade carried on by the Cherkessians is almost exclusively confined to the male sex. The young unmarried Cherkessian females compress their breasts with a close leather jacket, in such a manner that they are scarcely perceptible; and mothers, on the contrary, suffer them to be stretched to such a degree by their infants in suckling, that they soon become pendulous. For the rest, the fair sex among the Cherkessians is by no means under such restraint as among the other Asiatics.

The dress of the men resembles that of the Kumück Tartars, but it is lighter, made of better materials, and in general richer. The shirt *(Yana)* is either of white linen, or, agreeably to the Georgian fashion, of fine red taffety, and buttons at the bosom. Over this they wear a silk waistcoat, which is generally embroidered, and above that a short jacket (in Cherkessian *Ziéh,* in Tartar *Chekmen*), which scarcely reaches half way down the back, and buttons very close over the belly. On either side it is provided with a small embroidered pocket, having several divisions for cartridges. The men crop the hair of the head quite short, leaving only a lock of the length of a finger hanging down from the crown, which is called *Haidar.* The Tartars and Kists, on the contrary, shave the whole of the head. The Cherkessians formerly shaved the beard, leaving mustaches only, but now many suffer the whole to grow. Both sexes remove the hair from the privities, partly by cutting it off, partly by eradicating it, and partly by means of a caustic ointment composed of unslaked lime and orpiment. On the head they wear a small wadded and embroidered cap in the shape of a half melon. Their feet are commonly small; and they appear in neat red boots with very high heels, which makes

145 A look-out post for surveillance of the Circassian tribesmen in the Kuban. From Clarke's *Travels in Various Countries of Europe, Asia and Africa*. Engraved by Joseph Skelton from a drawing by Clarke himself.

them appear much taller than they really are.

A Cherkessian never goes abroad unarmed, at least not without his sabre and a dagger in his girdle, and his coarse felt-cloak (in Cherkessian *Dshako,* in Tartar *Jamatsche,* in Armenian *Japindshi,*) thrown over his shoulders. When completely equipped he has also, besides a musket and pistols, a coat of mail (*Affeh*), a small helmet (*Kip'ha*), or a larger one (*Tasch*), gauntlets (*Aschteld*), and brassets (*Abchumbuch*). When these people ride out in state, or pay visits, they are provided moreover with bow, quiver, and arrows; but they are strangers to the use of the shield. Their coats of mail are in general very costly, and there are said to be some of such excellent quality, that if they are laid upon a calf, and a loaded pistol is discharged at them, the ball produces no other effect than to make the animal stagger a little. Under this cuirass they wear, in war, a wadded coat, which helps by its elasticity to repel bullets the more effectually. Their best armour they procure from Kuba in Daghestan; but it is said to be manufactured of excellent quality in the country of Abkhaziya, contiguous to the Black Sea. The Cossacks however have learned the art, even when riding ever so swiftly, of raising the cuirass with the point of the pike, and transfixing the wearer. Their arms in general are of superior quality, but extremely dear; for the value of the whole equipage of a prince is estimated at 2000 rubles in silver. One of their chief employments consists in cleaning their arms, and keeping them in order; and in truth they are always in the brightest and best possible condition. The first thing they do in the morning is to gird on their sabre and poniard, and to see whether the rest of their arms have suffered any injury from the damp night-air. In their excursions their saddle serves them for a pillow, the piece of felt laid underneath it for a bed, and their felt-cloak for a covering. In bad weather they also construct a small tent with the felt, which is supported by branches of trees. Their other

298

weapons they procure partly from the Turks, and partly from Georgia; but many ancient Venetian and Genoese sabres and pistols, which are very highly prized, are still to be met with among them. Flints are rare, and they now receive most of them from the Russians. Like almost all the Caucasians, they manufacture their gunpowder (*Gin*) themselves. Saltpetre (*Gin-chusch,* or *Gin-schuch,* that is, powder-salt) is said to be found partly in a natural state in the mountains, and they make the rest by the application of ley to the soil of their sheep-folds. There are very few handicraftsmen among them, and of these only smiths, some of whom work in iron, and the others in silver; the former make scarcely any thing else than daggers, sickles, and bits for bridles, and the latter than arms or armour. The wife performs the part of tailor to her family, and the husband makes all the household furniture and utensils, in which there is no metal. For cooking they commonly use large copper pots, and these are brought from Georgia.

Their houses are of the very same construction as those of the Kumücks, being formed of plaited osiers, and plastered both within and without. They differ however from the others, in being covered with straw, because the clay in the country of the Cherkessians is not sufficiently tenacious. From forty to fifty houses generally form a circle, which is called a village (in Cherkessian *Kuadshe,* in Tartar *Kaback*), into the area of which the cattle are driven at night, and where the defenceless people are secured in case of attack. Without the circle, at the distance of about twenty paces, are erected huts, which serve for privies. The hedges are formed, like the houses, of plaited oziers. In winter sheds are run up near the rivers and meadow-grounds; these are called *Khutora,* or *Kutan,* and are used as sheep-folds. The utmost cleanliness prevails in all their buildings, as well as in their dress and cookery.

Julius von Klaproth, *Travels in the Caucasus and Georgia* (London 1814)

Alexander I

Mme de Staël came to Russia in 1811 prepared to pay homage to its ruler, who symbolized for her opposition to the hated Napoleon. Eulogizing Alexander she remained fully conscious of the great deficiencies in Russian government.

I had at last the pleasure of seeing that monarch, equally absolute by law and custom, and so moderate from his own disposition. The empress Elizabeth, to whom I was at first presented, appeared to me the tutelary angel of Russia. Her manners are extremely reserved, but what she says is full of life, and it is from the focus of all generous ideas that her sentiments and opinions have derived strength and warmth. While I listened to her, I was affected by something inexpressible, which did not proceed from her grandeur, but from the harmony of her soul; so long was it since I had known an instance of concord between power and virtue. As I was conversing with the empress, the door opened, and the emperor Alexander did me the honor to come and talk to me. What first struck me in

146 Alexander I by George Dawe, painter to the Tsar, c. 1825.

147 Elizabeth, Empress of Russia, by George Dawe, painted after the death of the Tsar on 1 December 1825.

him was such an expression of goodness and dignity, that the two qualities appear inseparable, and in him to form only one. I was also very much affected with the noble simplicity with which he entered upon the great interests of Europe, almost among the first words he addressed to me. I have always regarded, as a proof of mediocrity, that apprehension of treating serious questions, with which the best part of the sovereigns of Europe have been inspired; they are afraid to pronounce a word to which any real meaning can be attached. The emperor Alexander, on the contrary, conversed with me as statesmen in England would have done, who place their strength in themselves, and not in the barriers with which they are surrounded. The emperor Alexander, whom Napoleon has endeavoured to misrepresent, is a man of remarkable understanding and information, and I do not believe that in the whole extent of his empire he could find a minister better versed than himself in all that belongs to the judgment and direction of public affairs. He did not disguise from me his regret for the admiration to which he had surrendered himself in his intercourse with Napoleon. His grandfather had, in the same way, entertained a great enthusiasm for Frederic II. In these sort of illusions, produced by an extraordinary character, there is always a generous motive, whatever may be the errors

that result from it. The emperor Alexander, however, described with great sagacity the effect produced upon him by these conversations with Bonaparte, in which he said the most opposite things, as if one must be astonished at each, without thinking of their being contradictory. He related to me also the lessons *à la Machiavel* which Napoleon had thought proper to give him: 'You see,' said he, 'I am careful to keep my ministers and generals at variance among themselves, in order that each may reveal to me the faults of the other; I keep up around me a continual jealousy by the manner I treat those who are about me: one day one thinks himself the favorite, the next day another, so that no one is ever certain of my favor.' What a vulgar and vicious theory! And will there never arise a man superior to this man, who will demonstrate its inutility? That which is wanting to the sacred cause of morality, is, that it should contribute in a very striking manner to great success in this world; he who feels all the dignity of this cause will sacrifice with pleasure every success: but it is still necessary to teach those presumptuous persons who imagine they discover depth of thinking in the vices of the soul, that if in immorality there is

148 The Winter Palace by Gerard de la Barthe, engraved by M. G. Lory 1804.

301

sometimes wit, in virtue there is genius. In obtaining the conviction of the good faith of the emperor Alexander, in his relations with Napoleon, I was at the same time persuaded that he would not imitate the example of the unfortunate sovereigns of Germany, and would sign no peace with him who is equally the enemy of people and kings. A noble soul cannot be twice deceived by the same person. Alexander gives and withdraws his confidence with the greatest reflection. His youth and personal advantages have alone, at the beginning of his reign, made him be suspected of levity; but he is serious, even as much so as a man may be who has known misfortune. Alexander expressed to me his regret at not being a great captain: I replied to this noble modesty, that a sovereign was much more rare than a general, and that the support of the public feelings of his people, by his example, was achieving the greatest victory, and the first of the kind which had ever been gained. The emperor talked to me with enthusiasm of his nation, and of all that it was capable of becoming. He expressed to me the desire, which all the world knows him to entertain, of ameliorating the state of the peasants still subject to slavery. 'Sire,' said I to him, 'your character is a constitution for your empire, and your conscience is the guarantee of it.' Were that even the case,' replied he, 'I should only be a fortunate accident.' Noble words! the first of the kind, I believe, which an absolute monarch ever pronounced! How many virtues it requires, in a despot, properly to estimate despotism! and how many virtues also, never to abuse it, when the nation which he governs is almost astonished at such signal moderation.

At Petersburg especially, the great nobility have less liberality in their principles than the emperor himself. Accustomed to be the absolute masters of their peasants, they wish the monarch, in his turn, to be omnipotent, for the purpose of maintaining the hierarchy of despotism. The state of citizens does not yet exist in Russia; it begins however to be forming; the sons of the clergy, those of the merchants, and some peasants who have obtained of their lords the liberty of becoming artists, may be considered as a third order in the state. The Russian nobility besides bears no resemblance to that of Germany or France; a man becomes noble in Russia, as soon as he obtains rank in the army. No doubt the great families, such as the Naryshkins, the Dolgorukys, the Galitsyns, &c. will always hold the first rank in the empire; but it is not less true that the advantages of the aristocracy belong to men, whom the monarch's pleasure has made noble in a day; and the whole ambition of the citizens is in consequence to have their sons made officers, in order that they may belong to the privileged class. The result of this is, that young men's education is finished at fifteen years of age; they are hurried into the army as soon as possible, and everything else is neglected. This is not the time certainly to blame an order of things, which has produced so noble a

302

resistance; were tranquility restored it might be truly said, that under civil considerations, there are great deficiences in the internal administration of Russia. Energy and grandeur exist in the nation; but order and knowledge are still frequently wanting, both in the government, and in the private conduct of individuals. Peter I by making Russia European, certainly bestowed upon her great advantages; but these advantages he more than counter-balanced by the establishment of a despotism prepared by his father, and consolidated by him; Catherine II on the contrary tempered the use of absolute power, of which she was not the author. If the political state of Europe should ever be restored to peace: in other words if one man were no longer the dispenser of evil to the world, we should see Alexander solely occupied with the improvement of his country, and in attempting to establish laws which would guarantee to it that happiness, of which the duration is as yet only secured for the life of its present ruler.

Madame de Staël, *Ten Years' Exile* (London 1821)

The Character of the Russians

Mme de Staël's, appreciation of the character of the Russian people is sympathetic but balanced and perceptive.

I was always advancing nearer to Moscow, but nothing yet indicated the approach to a capital. The wooden villages were equally distant from each other, we saw no greater movement upon the immense plains which are called high roads; you heard no more noise; the country houses were not more numerous: there is so much space in Russia that every thing is lost in it, even the chateaux, even the population. You might suppose you were travelling through a country from which the people had just taken their departure. The absence of birds adds to this silence; cattle also are rare, or at least they are placed at a great distance from the road. Extent makes every thing disappear, except extent itself, like certain ideas in metaphysics, of which the mind can never get rid, when it has once seized them.

On the eve of my arrival at Moscow, I stopped in the evening of a very hot day, in a pleasant meadow: the female peasants, in picturesque dresses, according to the custom of the country, were returning from their labour, singing those airs of the Ukraine, the words of which, in praise of love and liberty, breathe a sort of melancholy approaching to regret. I requested them to dance, and they consented. I know nothing more graceful than these dances of the country, which have all the originality which nature gives to the fine arts; a certain modest voluptuousness was remarkable in them; the Indian bayadères should have something analogous to that mixture of indolence and vivacity which forms the charm of the Russian dance. This indolence and vivacity are indicative of reverie and passion, two elements of character which civilization has yet neither formed nor subdued. I was struck with the mild gaiety of these

149 The construction of a wooden hut, or *Izba*. From *La Russie, ou Moeurs, Usages et Costumes des habitants . . . de cet Empire.* M. Breton, Paris 1813.

female peasants, as I had been, in different degrees, with that of the greater part of the common people with whom I had come in contact in Russia. I can readily believe that they are terrible when their passions are provoked; and as they have no education, they know not how to curb their violence. As another result of this ignorance, they have few principles of morality, and theft is very frequent in Russia as well as hospitality; they give as they take, according as their imagination is acted upon by cunning or generosity, both of which excite the admiration of this people. In this mode of life there is a little resemblance to savages; but it strikes me that at present there are no European nations who have much vigor but those who are what is called barbarous, in other words, unenlightened, or those who are free: but the nations which have only acquired from civilization an indifference for this or that yoke, provided their own fire-side is not disturbed: those nations, which have only learned from civilization the art of explaining power and of reasoning servitude, are made to be vanquished. I frequently imagine to myself what may now be the situation of the places which I have seen so tranquil, of those amiable young girls, of those long bearded peasants, who followed so peaceably the lot which providence had traced for them; they have perished or fled, for not one of them entered into the service of the victor.

A thing worthy of remark, is the extent to which public spirit is displayed in Russia. The reputation of invincible which

304

their multiplied successes have given to this nation, the natural pride of the nobility, the devotedness inherent in the character of the people, the profound influence of religion, the hatred of foreigners, which Peter I endeavoured to destroy in order to enlighten and civilize his country, but which is not less settled in the blood of the Russians, and is occasionally roused, all these causes combined make them a most energetic people. Some bad anecdotes of the preceding reigns, some Russians who have contracted debts with the Parisian shopkeepers, and some *bon-mots* of Diderot, have put it into the heads of the French, that Russia consisted only of a corrupt court, military chamberlains, and a people of slaves. This is a great mistake. This nation it is true requires a long examination to know it thoroughly, but in the circumstances in which I observed it, every thing was salient, and a country can never be seen to greater advantage than at a period of misfortune and courage. It cannot be too often repeated, this nation is composed of the most striking contrasts. Perhaps the mixture of European civilization and of Asiatic character is the cause.

150 A Russian peasant girl. From J. A. Atkinson and J. Walker, *A Picturesque Representation of the Manners, Customs and Amusements of the Russians*, 1812.

The manner of the Russians is so obliging, that you might imagine yourself, the very first day, intimate with them, and probably at the end of ten years you would not be so. The silence of a Russian is altogether extraordinary; this silence is solely occasioned by what he takes a deep interest in. In other respects, they talk as much as you will; but their conversation teaches you nothing but their politeness; it betrays neither their feelings nor opinions. They have been frequently compared to the French, in my opinion with the least justice in the world. The flexibility of their organs makes imitation in all things a matter of ease to them; they are English, French, or German in their manners, according to circumstances; but they never cease to be Russians, that is to say uniting impetuosity and reserve, more capable of passion than friendship, more bold than delicate, more devout than virtuous, more brave than chivalrous, and so violent in their desires that nothing can stop them, when their gratification is in question. They are much more hospitable than the French; but society does not with them, as with us, consist of a circle of clever people of both sexes, who take pleasure in talking together. They meet, as we go to a fête to see a great deal of company, to have fruits and rare productions from Asia or Europe; to hear music, to play; in short to receive vivid emotions from external objects, rather than from the heart or understanding, both of which they reserve for actions and not for company. Besides, as they are in general very ignorant, they find very little pleasure in serious conversation, and do not at all pique themselves on shining by the wit they can exhibit in it. Poetry, eloquence and literature are not yet to be found in Russia; luxury, power, and courage are the principal objects of pride and ambition; all other methods of acquiring distinction appear as yet effeminate and vain to this nation.

But the people are slaves, it will be said: what character therefore can they be supposed to have? It is not certainly necessary for me to say that all enlightened people wish to see the Russian people freed from this state, and probably no one wishes it more strongly than the Emperor Alexander: but the Russian slavery has no resemblance in its effects to that of which we form the idea in the West; it is not as under the feudal

151 A Russian village. From J. A. Atkinson and J. Walker, *A Picturesque Representation of the Manners, Customs and Amusements of the Russians*, 1812.

system, victors who have imposed severe laws on the vanquished; the ties which connect the grandees with the people resemble rather what was called a family of slaves among the ancients, than the state of serfs among the moderns. There is no middling class in Russia, which is a great drawback on the progress of literature and the arts; for it is generally in that class that knowledge is developed: but the want of any intermedium between the nobility and the people creates a greater affection between them both. The distance between the two classes appears greater, because there are no steps between these two extremities, which in fact border very nearly on each other, not being separated by a middling class. This is a state of social organization quite unfavorable to the knowledge of the higher classes, but not so to the happiness of the lower. Besides, where there is no representative government, that is to say, in countries where the sovereign still promulgates the law which he is to execute, men are frequently more degraded by the very sacrifice of their reason and character, than they are in this vast empire, in which a few simple ideas of religion and country serve to lead the great mass under the guidance of a few heads. The immense extent of the Russian empire also prevents the despotism of the great from pressing heavily in detail upon the people: and finally, above all, the religious and military spirit is so predominant in the nation, that allowance may be made for a great many errors, in favor of those two great sources of noble actions. A person of fine intellect said, that Russia resembled the plays of Shakspeare, in which all that is not faulty is sublime, and all that is not sublime is faulty; an observation of remarkable justice. But in the great crisis in which Russia was placed when I passed through it, it was impossible not to admire the energetic resistance, and resignation to sacrifices exhibited by that nation; and one could not almost dare, at the contemplation of such virtues, to allow one's self even to notice what at other times one would have censured.

Madame de Staël, *Ten Years' Exile* (London 1821)

The Perils of Winter Travel in the Caucasus

Travelling through the passes of the Caucasus was a harrowing experience at any season. Mme Fredericka von Freygan's understandable concern for her own and her children's safety during a journey undertaken not only in winter but during a blizzard does not, however, prevent her from responding to the magnificence of the scenery.

Koshauri, seventeen versts from Kobi
23d Nov. 1811

We are providentially arrived in safety; but what a journey have we just performed! It was infinitely more dangerous than represented: any one, indeed, may believe in miracles, who arrives safe at Koshauri, through a snow-storm, like that we had all the way. I am so sensible of the great mercy vouchsafed us, that I every now and then embrace my children, while I offer up thanksgivings for their preservation; but there still remains for us the descent of this awful mountain.

So overpowered am I with the fatigue of body and mind, that I must defer, until to-morrow the detail of its adventures.

24th Nov.

Precisely at seven o'clock yesterday morning, I seated myself in my basket, with the children in my lap. It is to be sure the most inconvenient vehicle that ever was used. I was obliged to sit in a stooping posture, with knees bent, and scarcely able to hold my children; having at the same time to defend them from the cold. To complete the awkwardness of this machine, it was hardly ever balanced properly, although placed upon a

307

sledge. My husband and the four Ossetinians were continually employed in propping it, and were frequently plunged to their shoulders in the snow, during the laborious march. We proceeded slowly, our horses and oxen sinking every now and then in the drift; for our path was only of the width the bat horses made it by their track. We marched on in mournful silence, which was interrupted only by the whistling of the wind, or the cries of my children.

152, 153 Two views of the Terek. From Madame Freygang's *Letters*.

Upon leaving Kobi, we entered a valley of some breadth, which, as we advanced, became narrower, leading into a pass, where huge masses of snow appeared to hang from the lofty crags; as if the slightest breath would precipitate them and overwhelm us. It sometimes happens that an avalanche falling into the Terek, will stop its course, so as to cause the water to overflow, for a time, a considerable extent of country. We halted for a few minutes at some chalybeate springs, of which the Ossetinians drank very eagerly, plunging their heads into the water, to recruit their strength; we also partook of this restorative, and then went on.

As we ascended, we approached the Bi-gora, which is seldom free from storms during winter. On this mountain a hut has been built by an Ossetinian family, who devote themselves to the assistance of unfortunate travellers, and shelter such as cannot otherwise escape the dangers of the road. We found some poor creatures who had taken refuge there ten days before, and dared not yet proceed.

When we got near the Bi-gora, even Major Kasibek had his fears; the winds whistled round us, seeming as if they had broken loose to dispute our passage: suddenly a drifting snow darkened the air, rendering respiration difficult. We were all seized with panic, and the Major, in great anxiety, was about to conduct us hastily to the Ossetinian hut: the storm, however, abated, and we were enabled to go on; after having paid this tribute of our fears to the horrific spirit of the mountain.

The day was now more than half spent, and we never thought of eating or drinking; for every moment was of importance, and each step we took seemed as so much danger past. All this while I had a difficulty even of respiration, so uncomfortable was I in the basket; my husband, moreover, wet to the skin and nigh fainting from fatigue. After mounting for a long time. we got a view of the summit of Krestovaya gora, and of the cross erected upon it. It is usual to leave at the foot of this cross some pieces of money, which deposit is respected even by the robbers; and travellers are accustomed to return thanks at the spot for having been permitted to reach it. My devotions were most fervent.

The prospect displayed from these heights is magnificent; but a view of the long descent from the Krestovaya, and the ascent of the Gud-gora, soon recall one's fears. I no longer admired the Terek, which seemed like a silver band at the base of these precipices; nor could I dwell with pleasure upon the villages grouped along its banks: my eyes were fixed upon our advanced guard, who, already at the bottom of the Krestovaya, were proceeding to scale the perilous Gud-gora; and we had to follow them. We descended the Krestovaya gora with greatest caution, for in a considerable extent of the road was a precipice, at the distance of a step on the left of our path. I shuddered as our advanced guard appeared again; they looked as if suspended from the top of the Gud-gora. and as about to fall into the dreadful abyss beneath them. We in our turn arrived at the pass, which is cut through the side of the mountain; it is in summer wide enough, but was now reduced by the snow to five feet at most. Upon our right was the brink of a frightful chasm; on the left large masses of snow hung threatening over us. Some of our party crossed themselves at times; others cried out; while some would shrink back with alarm: for my part, I endeavoured with closed eyes to fortify myself in prayer. Our prudent leader, Major Kasibek, ordered profound silence, cautioning the party that the least noise might occasion the fall of an avalanche.

We had already performed half our journey, and were beginning to feel some joy, at seeing ourselves so near the top of the hill, when we discovered a regiment of infantry within a few yards of us; it had just descended the Gud-gora. I cannot to this hour comprehend how the troops could pass without precipitating us down the hill: they were obliged to make a new path upon the mountain's side, where the snow lay more than six feet deep. The danger of both parties, and the absolute necessity of an effort, succeeded in effecting what seemed to me impossible. No sooner had we escaped this peril, than we were menaced by another. An unruly horse, among the followers of the regiment, pressed upon my basket, which losing its balance leaned towards the precipice. I still tremble at the thoughts of it, and owe the preservation of myself and children to my husband; who, being close to the vehicle, succeeded by a strength of desperation in supporting it.

I felt great relief upon arriving at the summit of the Gud-gora, and got out of my basket to breathe for a moment at my ease; but, casting a look behind me, sickened at sight of the danger to which we had been exposed. Still we had four versts more to the end of our stage; by a path that was very narrow, upon account of the snow, yet otherwise free from risk. We arrived here at eight in the evening, quite exhausted with fatigue and hunger, and chilled with the wet and cold; which, at this late season, is excessive upon the Koshauri mountain.

Our dwelling is again comfortless: the windows are not glazed, and the room has no stove; but any one who had survived ten days at Kobi, may pass one night at Koshauri without complaining. I have given you a faithful account of our journey yesterday; we were thirteen hours in travelling the seventeen versts, and I leave you to judge how tedious the time appeared, in the midst of so much danger and distress. The old lady, our companion, fell upon her knees, as soon as she got out of her basket; and remained more than a quarter of an hour in that posture, returning thanks for her preservation. Her son, in a similar position by her side, completed this picture of pious gratitude.

We are about to descend the hill of Koshauri, upon our way to Pasanauri; it is a journey of twenty versts, and not without risk. We hope to meet the promised calêche; for my poor children, as well as myself, are in equal need of being released from our uncomfortable basket. The signal for marching has been given. We are to go directly.

[Fredericka von Freygan], *Letters from the Caucasus and Georgia* (London 1823)

310

The Burning of Moscow

After the inconclusive battle at Borodino the Russian forces retreated towards Moscow, which the Russian Commander-in-Chief, Kutuzov, decided to yield to Napoleon. The French Emperor entered the old Russian capital on 14 September 1812, and took up residence in the Kremlin. Two days later, however, fires were started throughout the city and Napoleon was forced to withdraw to the Petrovskiy Palace outside Moscow. The events of these days are described in the detailed account of Napoleon's quartermaster, General de Ségur.

Napoleon did not enter Moscow till after dark. He stopped in one of the first houses of the Dorogomilov suburb. There he appointed Marshal Mortier governor of that capital. 'Above all,' said he to him, 'no pillage! For this you shall be answerable to me with your life. Defend Moscow against all, whether friend or foe.'

That night was a gloomy one: sinister reports followed one upon the heels of another. Some Frenchmen, resident in the country, and even a Russian officer of police, came to denounce the conflagration. He gave all the particulars of the preparations for it. The Emperor, alarmed by these accounts, strove in vain to get some rest. He called every moment, and had the fatal tidings repeated to him. He nevertheless entrenched himself in his incredulity, till, about two in the morning, he was informed that the fire had actually broken out.

It was at the exchange, in the centre of the city, in its richest quarter. He instantly issued orders upon orders. As soon as it was light he himself hastened to the spot, and threatened the young guard and Mortier. The Marshal pointed out to him houses covered with iron; they were closely shut up, as yet untouched and uninjured without, and yet a black smoke was already issuing from them. Napoleon pensively entered the Kremlin.

At the sight of this half Gothic and half modern palace of the Ruriks and Romanovs, of their throne still standing, of the cross of the great Ivan, and of the finest part of the city, which is overlooked by the Kremlin, and which the flames, as yet confined to the bazaar, seemed disposed to spare, his former hopes revived. His ambition was flattered by this conquest. 'At length then,' he exclaimed, 'I am in Moscow, in the ancient palace of the Tsars, in the Kremlin!' He examined every part of it with pride, curiosity, and gratification.

He required a statement of the resources afforded by the city; and in this brief moment given to hope, he sent proposals of peace to the Emperor Alexander. A superior officer of the enemy's had just been found in the great hospital; he was charged with the delivery of this letter. It was by the baleful light of the flames of the bazaar that Napoleon finished it, and the Russian departed. He was to be the bearer of the news of this disaster to his sovereign, whose only answer was this conflagration.

Day-light favoured the efforts of the Duke of Treviso; he subdued the fire. The incendiaries kept themselves concealed. Doubts were entertained of their existence. At length, strict injunctions being issued, order restored, and alarm suspended, each took possession of a commodious house, or sumptuous

154 A view of Borodino, scene of the famous battle in 1812.

palace, under the idea of there finding comforts that had been dearly purchased by long and excessive privations.

Two officers had taken up their quarters in one of the buildings of the Kremlin. The view hence embraced the north and west of the city. About midnight they were awakened by an extraordinary light. They looked and beheld palaces filled with flames, which at first merely illuminated, but presently consumed the elegant and noble structures. They observed that the north wind drove these flames directly towards the Kremlin, and became alarmed for the safety of that fortress, in which the flower of the army and its commander reposed. They were apprehensive also for the surrounding houses, where our soldiers, attendants and horses, weary and exhausted, were doubtless buried in profound sleep. Sparks and burning fragments were already flying over the roofs of the Kremlin, when the wind, shifting from north to west, blew them in another direction.

One of these officers, relieved from apprehension respecting his corps, then composed himself to sleep again, exclaiming, 'Let others look to it now; 'tis no affair of ours.' For such was the unconcern produced by the multiplicity of events and misfortunes, and such the selfishness arising from excessive suffering and fatigue, that they left to each only just strength and feeling sufficient for his personal service and preservation.

It was not long before fresh and vivid lights again awoke them. They beheld other flames rising precisely in the new direction which the wind had taken towards the Kremlin, and they cursed French imprudence and want of discipline, to which they imputed this disaster. But three times did the wind thus change from north to west, and three times did these hostile fires, as if obstinately bent on the destruction of the imperial quarters, appear eager to follow this new direction.

At this sight a strong suspicion seized their minds. Can the Muscovites, aware of our rash and thoughtless negligence, have conceived the hope of burning with Moscow our soldiers, heavy with wine, fatigue and sleep; or rather, have they dared to imagine that they should involve Napoleon in this catastrophe; that the loss of such a man would be fully equivalent to that of their capital; that it was a result sufficiently important to justify the sacrifice of all Moscow to obtain it; that perhaps Heaven, in order to grant them so signal a victory, had decreed so great a sacrifice; and lastly, that so immense a colossus required a not less immense funeral pile?

Whether this was their plan we cannot tell, but nothing less than the Emperor's good fortune was required to prevent its being realized. In fact, not only did the Kremlin contain, unknown to us, a magazine of gunpowder; but that very night, the guards, asleep and carelessly posted, suffered a whole park of artillery to enter and draw up under the windows of Napoleon.

It was at this moment that the furious flames were driven from all quarters and with the greatest violence towards the Kremlin; for the wind, attracted no doubt by this vast combustion, increased every moment in strength. The flower of the army and the Emperor would have been lost, if but one of the brands that flew over our heads had alighted on one of the caissons. Thus upon each of the sparks that were for several hours floating in the air, depended the fate of the whole army.

At length the day, a gloomy day, appeared: it came to add itself to the horrors of the scene, and to deprive it of its brilliancy. Many of the officers sought refuge in the halls of the palace. The chiefs, and Mortier himself, overcome by the fire, with which, for thirty-six hours, they had been contending, there dropped down from fatigue and despair.

They said nothing, and we accused ourselves. Most imagined

that want of discipline in our troops and intoxication had begun the disaster, and that the high wind had completed it. We viewed ourselves with a sort of disgust. The cry of horror that all Europe would not fail to set up affrighted us. Filled with consternation by so tremendous a catastrophe, we accosted each other with downcast looks: it sullied our glory; it deprived us of the fruit of it; it threatened our present and our future existence; we were now but an army of criminals,

155 The great fire of Moscow which began shortly after Napoleon entered the Kremlin on 14 September 1812. Drawing by John Vedramini.

whom Heaven and the civilized world would severely judge. From these overwhelming thoughts and paroxysms of rage against the incendiaries, we were roused only by an eagerness to obtain intelligence; and all the accounts began to accuse the Russians alone of this disaster.

In fact, officers arrived from all quarters, and they all agreed. The very first night, that between the 14th and 15th, a fire-balloon had settled on the palace of Prince Trubetskoy, and consumed it: this was a signal. Fire had been immediately set to the Exchange: Russian police soldiers had been seen stirring it up with tarred lances. Here, howitzer shells, perfidiously placed, had discharged themselves in the stoves of several houses, and wounded the military who crowded round them. Retiring to other quarters which were still standing, they sought fresh retreats; but when on the point of entering houses closely shut up and uninhabited, they had heard faint explosions within; these were succeeded by a light smoke, which immediately became thick and black, then reddish, and lastly the colour of fire, and presently the whole edifice was involved in flames.

All had seen hideous-looking men, covered with rags, and women resembling furies, wandering among these flames, and completing a frightful image of the infernal regions. These

314

wretches, intoxicated with wine and the success of their crimes, were no longer at the pains to conceal themselves: they proceeded in triumph through the blazing streets; they were caught, armed with torches, assiduously striving to spread the conflagration: it was necessary to strike down their hands with sabres to oblige them to loose their hold. It was said that these banditti had been released from prison by the Russian generals for the purpose of burning Moscow; and that in fact

so grand, so extreme a resolution could have been adopted only by patriotism and executed only by guilt.

Orders were immediately issued to shoot all the incendiaries on the spot. The army was on foot. The old guard, which exclusively occupied one part of the Kremlin, was under arms: the baggage, and the horses ready loaded, filled the courts; we were struck dumb with astonishment, fatigue and disappointment, on witnessing the destruction of such excellent quarters. Though masters of Moscow, we were forced to go and bivouac without provisions beyond its gates.

While our troops were yet struggling with the conflagration, and the army was disputing their prey with the flames, Napoleon, whose sleep none had dared to disturb during the night, was awoke by the two-fold light of day and of the fire. His first feeling was that of irritation, and he would have

156 The Petrovskiy Palace outside Moscow, to which Napoleon retreated when the fires began in the city in 1812.

commanded the devouring element; but he soon paused and yielded to impossibility. Surprised that when he had struck at the heart of an empire, he should find there any other sentiment than submission and terror, he felt himself vanquished and surpassed in determination.

This conquest, for which he had sacrificed every thing, was like a phantom which he had pursued, and which at the moment when he imagined he had grasped it, vanished in a

157 The Battle of Berezina. 20 November 1812. Painted English handkerchief.

mingled mass of smoke and flame. He was then seized with extreme agitation; he seemed to be consumed by the fires which surrounded him. He rose every moment, paced to and fro, and again sat down abruptly. He traversed his apartments with quick steps: his sudden and vehement gestures betrayed painful uneasiness: he quitted, resumed, and again quitted, an urgent occupation, to hasten to the windows and watch the progress of the conflagration. Short and incoherent exclamations burst from his labouring bosom. 'What a tremendous spectacle!–It is their own work!–So many palaces!–What extraordinary resolution!–What men!–These are Scythians indeed!'

Between the fire and him there was an extensive vacant space, then the Moskva and its two quays; and yet the panes of the windows against which he leaned were already burning to the touch, and the constant exertions of sweepers, placed on the iron roofs of the palace, were not sufficient to keep them clear of the numerous flakes of fire which alighted upon them.

316

At this moment a rumour was spread that the Kremlin was undermined: this was confirmed, it was said, by Russians, and by written documents. Some of the attendants were beside themselves with fear; while the military awaited unmoved what the orders of the Emperor and fate should decree; and to this alarm the Emperor replied only by a smile of incredulity.

But he still walked convulsively; he stopped at every window, and beheld the terrible, the victorious element furiously consuming his brilliant conquest; seizing all the bridges, all the avenues to his fortress, inclosing and as it were besieging him in it; spreading every moment among the neighbouring houses; and, reducing him within narrower and narrower limits, confining him at length to the site of the Kremlin alone.

We already breathed nothing but smoke and ashes. Night approached and was about to add darkness to our dangers: the equinoxial gales, in alliance with the Russians, increased in violence. The King of Naples and Prince Eugene hastened to the spot: in company with the Prince of Neufchâtel they made their way to the Emperor, and urged him by their intreaties, their gestures, and on their knees, and insisted on removing him from this scene of desolation. All was in vain.

Napoleon, in possession of the palace of the Tsars, was bent on not yielding that conquest even to the conflagration, when all at once the shout of 'The Kremlin is on fire!' passed from mouth to mouth, and roused us from the contemplative stupor with which we had been seized. The Emperor went out to reconnoitre the danger. Twice had the fire communicated to the building in which he was, and twice had it been extinguished; but the tower of the arsenal was still burning. A soldier of the police had been found in it. He was brought, and Napoleon caused him to be interrogated in his presence. This man was the incendiary: he had executed his commission at the signal given by his chief. It was evident that every thing was devoted to destruction, the ancient and sacred Kremlin itself not excepted.

The gestures of the Emperor betokened disdain and vexation: the wretch was hurried into the first court, where the enraged grenadiers dispatched him with their bayonets.

This incident decided Napoleon. He hastily descended the northern staircase, famous for the massacre of the Streltsy, and desired to be guided out of the city, to the distance of a league on the road to Petersburg, towards the imperial palace of Petrovskiy.

Count Philip de Ségur, *History of the Expedition to Russia Undertaken by the Emperor Napoleon in the Year 1812* (London 1825)

Moscow after the Fire of 1812

It was estimated that less than two and a half thousand of Moscow's nine thousand houses survived the great fire, in which most of the churches were either razed or damaged. R. Johnston visited the city two years after the fire and described the melancholy scene.

Moscow, September, 1814

The toils and fatigues of a long journey were now to have some repose; the long looked for object of our cares and wishes was approaching, and the spires of Moscow soon hailed our gladdened sight. When the weary pilgrim with tired limbs comes in view of the turrets of Medina, he stops at the distant fonts of the city, and his zeal and strength are awakened. In like manner did we, at view of this holy city, feel refreshed and restored. We forgot our toils, our sufferings, and our cares; and a full and fresh tide of enthusiasm carried us along.

And here we must pause: before us stood the ancient and once proud seat of the mighty Tsars; the once grand emporium of the North, where the fates of kings and nations were so proudly wielded; where despotism had so long reared its crest; where vice had so long held her court; and where the tides of wealth and luxury were for ages rolling in as to a common centre. Here was to be seen every thing costly and magnificent; the grand mart of European and Asiatic splendour, the pride and envy of the northern world.

This is the spot we now gazed on; what a change! lowly and prostrate it now lies, its crumbling towers, falling into decay, its proud banners torn from their burning walls, and scattering their shivered fragments to the hollow winds—its temples torn —its gates demolished—its houses ransacked—its streets laid waste. One sad and sorrowful picture of desolation is thrown around: wherever the traveller turns his wearied eye it is still the same; he will yet see the dæmon of ruin stalking abroad in all the majesty of devastation, and treading on those mouldering piles, where perched the proud eagle of the north; he will still see the sorrowing inhabitant sighing over the ruins of his roofless dwelling, and clinging to the yet warm ashes of those sacred shrines, where so lately he had invoked his fathers and his saints.

Here indeed was a melancholy picture; on every side we turned our eye, fresh objects of dilapidated splendour presented themselves; fresh scenes of falling greatness were strewed around, and as we gazed on the crumbling heap, we needed not memory to give outline; we needed not fancy to give colouring,—the picture was complete.

And who can look on this sorrowing group without one sad, one solitary sigh? Who can muffle himself up in his cold-blooded *philosophy,* and look on with unconcern? Can his eye be as unmoved as the ruin on which it is gazing; cannot the wreck of fallen greatness shadow it with a cloud; cannot the wail of his fellow-man dim it with a tear? Happy, ye few, if such there be! your feelings may be envied, but ye have them not of nature!

The appearance of the city from the point at which we now were, is not equal to that from the opposite country; however, the innumerable spires and domes glittering in the horizon powerfully arrest and astonish the beholder. The extensive plain surrounding this part of the suburbs occupies nearly ten thousand acres, uncovered either by trees or houses: at a distance it is bounded by forests of birch. Here the army of Napoleon Bonaparte spread themselves, as a lawless band of ruffians, sharing the spoils of this devoted city. To this spot were conveyed every thing that could be snatched from the all-devouring flames; and even the helpless mothers and infants came to beg a covering to their nakedness, but who, as might be expected, were refused at the point of the bayonet. About two miles from the gate we passed the palace of Petrovskiy, embellished by Peter the Great, and which he used as his favourite residence when at Moscow. It is a huge gothic brick building, encompassed by a circular wall, with regular bastions. One great and vast feature of desolation surrounds it; the vestiges of war are strewed around its multilated walls. Here Napoleon fixed his head quarters, when he found the Kremlin no longer a place of security against the raging flames; and here he became the dupe of his own credulity, and brought on himself that contempt and disgrace, which his unwarrantable pretensions so justly merited. From this palace he issued those empty decrees, which trumpeted forth falsehood in all its unblushing colours, while his dastardly soul shrunk with fear and meanness from the dangers which surrounded him.

Crossing the first barriers of the city, a small dry ditch, we entered the Sloboda or suburbs, and reached the gate of the second division, where we were received by the guard, who strictly examined our passports, and escorted us to the police, where we left them, and entered our names. Here money was as necessary to afford an entry into the town, without delay and vexation, as at the other capital. The entrance to the city exhibits a general scene of ruin, and appears, from those parts of the houses now standing, to have consisted of brick and wooden houses, huddled together without any order or neatness. At present nothing more excites the appearance of wretchedness and filth; as we proceeded, the streets began to assume a more regular form, with the remains of large and splendid edifices divided from each other by mean hovels and gardens; churches of the most singular and gothic forms, with numerous gilded spires and domes, crowd on each other;

319

it is almost impossible by any description to convey a correct idea of this singular appearance. All that ingenuity and religious enthusiasm could suggest, have been here executed, exhibiting more the laboured effects of rude show and expense, than elegance or utility. At the termination of the street by which we entered the city, we ascended a gentle elevation, and approached a lofty and massive wall, which appeared as the bulwark of an interior city. This is partly supported by an earthen mound, with a broad open space, through which a muddy puddle runs, called the Neglinnaya river. To the right of this wall another immediately appears, more massive, and on a situation more elevated, and crowded with gilded spires and domes. This is the bulwark of the Kremlin, and the central part of the city . . .

Many of the churches were injured, some almost destroyed, but the greater number of them escaped the dreadful effects of the conflagration of the city. From being entirely built of brick, with little or no wooden work connected with them, they could not be so easily destroyed, as the wooden houses, or those churches partly built of wood. The whole city appears as one group of spires, cupolas or domes. From being painted in light colours or gilded, their appearance is remarkably shewy. If the spires had been loftier, the effect would have been inexpressibly grand. From the present state of the churches, the appearance of the town is but little altered. At a distance, Moscow must present nearly the same form that it did before the conflagration. But what a sad and melancholy difference is seen when passing along the streets; scarcely a house is seen that escaped the all-devouring flames, except a small portion of the buildings in the division of the Belyy gorod. The walls of the houses are still standing, and in tolerable preservation; from this the original form of the city might be imagined, but all that singular contrast of wooden huts and mean hovels are completely destroyed. The blank places are therefore the greater, and more numerous. The walls of the houses now remaining shew them to have been of a most extensive and superb form. Every other house seems to have been a stately palace in size and structure; but now only broken walls, roofless houses, and gaping windows, remain in solitary and deserted grandeur.

All the houses seem to have been stuccoed and washed with different colours; the roofs were either of wood, or iron, or tin, and generally painted green. Almost every house is surrounded with endless tiers of pillars and piazzas. No view can be so truly diversified, nor more astonishing and wonderful than that of this city. To admire Moscow it should be viewed from a distance; from thence the churches, with their numerous glittering domes and painted spires, seem to cloud the horizon.

The appearance of the city from the Kremlin is truly fascinating. Hundreds, nay thousands of spires and cupolas, varying in size, form, and colours, and grouped in the most picturesque and irregular manner, strike the eye with admiration and delight: added to this, the solemn and constant tones of the ponderous bells, echoing through the vaulted canopy of heaven, like the distant thunder!

Robert Johnston, *Travels through Parts of the Russian Empire* (London 1815)

Russian Religious Sects

Robert Pinkerton is perhaps the best known of the missionaries of the British and Foreign Bible Society working in Russia in the reign of Alexander. Of a considerable literature produced by such men as Swan, Henderson, Paterson and Venning, his book was the only one to reach a wide audience: he writes not only of the affairs of the Society but of more general topics – the state of enlightenment, social problems and gives a whole chapter on Russian proverbs and sayings. The extract which follows, however, treats of a visit he made in 1816 to one of the best-known of Russian religious sects, the Dukhobortsy.

During the last stage before reaching Yelizavetograd, the frost set in; and being drenched from travelling the whole day exposed to the rain, we were in a pitiable condition on entering that town. It was a great favour that we obtained a warm room, in an inn kept by a German; where we lost no time in

158 Russian orthodox monks. From J. A. Atkinson and J. Walker, *A Picturesque Representation of the Manners, Customs and Amusements of the Russians*, 1812.

exchanging our frozen wet clothes for dry ones.

Yelizavetograd has a considerable fortress attached to it; and, independent of the military, the inhabitants are about 3000, most of them Raskolniki, or Dissenters from the National Church. The severe persecutions to which the different sects of Raskolniki have been subjected, have caused them, like the Protestants of France, to take refuge in the most southern provinces and borders of the empire, and especially among the Poles, Little Russians, and Don Cossacks; where they enjoy greater freedom than in the interior; and whence, in the time of persecution, they can more easily escape to a foreign land. Yet, notwithstanding all the severities of the civil and ecclesiastical powers—which however, so far as I have been able to learn, never amounted to capital punishment, (though exile, stripes, confiscation of property, imprisonment, &c. &c. have all been employed,) they still abound in almost every province. Their morality is generally of a higher standard than that of the common Russians; and many of the most wealthy and eminent merchants of Moscow and St Petersburg belong to the Dissenters . . .

In 1816, after having visited the tribe of Nogay Tartars that wander with their flocks and herds about the extensive steppes of Little Tartary, on the Sea of Azov, and having made preparations for supplying the villages of German colonists, recently settled there, with the Holy Scriptures, I purposed, on my way towards the Crimea, to see the Dukhobortsy who live on the River Molochnaya and one the Sea of Azov.

On approaching the first of their villages, on the Molochnaya, I met with a female, and inquired of her where the chief person of the place resided. The answer she gave me was, 'Among us, no one is greater than another'. The next person I met was a shepherd attending his flock, an old man with grey hair. I made my driver stop, and beckoned to the man to draw near. This he did; and uncovering his head, he leaned over his staff and replied to my inquiries. I asked him if he could read: he replied, 'Yes; I can read the word of life.' From this I naturally thought that he was able to read the Bible, and offered him a Tract on the Bible Society. He refused, however, to accept it; saying, that he could not read our books, but only the book of life which he had learnt by heart; in other words, that he could repeat the principal doctrinal and moral Articles of the sect. And when I touched upon some of the Articles, as given in my work on the Greek Church, he repeated them distinctly: in others of them his memory failed him.

I stopped in a second village, and without ceremony entered one of the best-looking houses, requesting a glass of water: this a young man readily handed to me. After a little talk with him, I discovered that I was in the Chancery, or place where the civil affairs of the sect are transacted. I told him distinctly what my object was in visiting them, and begged him to introduce me to some of their seniors. All this seemed rather suspicious to him; yet he sent for one of the Elders, who had been in Petersburg as a deputy to the Government, and who soon after, with several of his brethren, made his appearance. After a little talk about Senator Hoblitz, and other gentlemen who had shewn them kindness during their stay in Petersburg, they seemed in some degree to lay aside their reserve, and replied more freely to my inquiries. I took out my volume on the Greek Church, and read to the assembly the passages which I had written concerning the Dukhobortsy; and I had the satisfaction of hearing them distinctly state their principles in the very terms there given. As soon as I began any paragraph by translating a few words, they generally gave the remainder exactly as stated in the book. The two Prayers they repeated verbatim. One passage only was found to require explanation—that of their having all things in common. This was their practice when they came to the Molochnava: but now every family has its own private property, cattle, fields, &c. &c. Still they have fields of corn, gardens, and flocks which belong to the whole community, and the revenues of which are applied for the common benefit of the society. This is also the custom of the Mennonites, who live near them, and of other German colonists; a custom, in their case, independent of religious considerations.

This extraordinary sect (the Dukhobortsy) is settled in eight villages, and consists of about 2500 souls. I saw an individual of them who had been sixteen years exiled to Siberia, for conscience sake. He spoke with great feeling, when contrasting his former sufferings with his present prosperous circumstances. He was a fine-looking, middle-aged man, and was returning on horseback from viewing his corn-fields and flocks, country like, without his coat. They have been collected from every part of the empire, and are entirely separated from the Greek Church: indeed it was the object of Government, in colonizing them here, to put it out of their power to make any more proselytes to their peculiar opinions. Their neat and clean dress, comfortable-looking huts, and industrious habits, their numerous flocks, and extensive and well-cultivated fields, widely distinguish them from the common Russian peasantry.

Their neighbours the Mennonites, and other German colonists, speak well of their morals; but all complain of the reserve and shyness of their character. No doubt they have been taught this by the severe persecutions to which they have for ages been exposed, and out of which they can scarcely yet believe themselves delivered. Their neighbours seem to know but little of their religious tenets. The Mennonites say they are a peaceable and industrious people, but accuse them of hypocrisy: hence, say they, when some of their members were convicted of drunkenness, they denied the fact, and maintained that their members were *all holy*. Very few among them appear to be capable of reading; yet their members seem to have had the doctrines of the sect instilled into them by oral instruction. These lessons are committed to memory. They have no schools for their children; nor did I see a book of any kind among them. I recommended to them the Bible, and offered to supply them with it; but they refused to accept any copies, saying, 'That what was in the Bible was in them also!' I told them that some of their neighbours suspected them of immoral habits, because in speaking of females and children they did not use the common expressions of 'My wife,' 'My child,' &c., but 'My sister,' 'Our child,' &c. This insinuation they indignantly repelled, exclaiming–'Are we then beasts?' 'But,' continued they, 'we are accustomed to every kind of false accusation.'

Their whole aspect, and manner of intercourse with strangers, indicate a degree of shyness and distrust which is quite extraordinary; hence, also, their evasive answers to all direct inquiries respecting their sect. Some of them, however, ventured to speak with me freely, and with warmth, against the use of images in worship. Their assemblies for religious purposes are held in the open air, or in private dwellings, according as the weather suits. They say their doctrines are as old as the world; and they either would not, or could not, give me any particulars of the rise of the sect in Russia. It was, doubtless, the heavy burden of superstitious ceremonies in the services of the Greek Church which drove the founders of this sect to reject all ceremony, and external ordinances of every kind. Many, of this sect, I fear, are Deists.

But we need not wonder at these indications of fear and distrust; for at the very time I visited them, as I afterwards learned, intrigues were on foot in order to ruin them, under the twofold accusation of their harbouring deserters, and making proselytes.

Robert Pinkerton, *Russia* (London 1833)

Crossing the Dnieper

William Macmichael, an Oxford doctor, travelled south from Moscow after an extended stay in the city. His description of the hazardous winter crossing of the Dnieper by the ferry is graphic and full of interesting detail (the attitude to the Jews, etc.).

Dec. 22 [1817].—A considerable fall of snow during the night, which we passed at Nezhin, enabled us to proceed somewhat more smoothly in the morning for the distance of a few versts; but we soon again had to contend with mud, water, and deep holes, from which we were extricated with great toil, and did not, in consequence, reach Kozolets, till late in the evening. Through a deep forest of pine trees that extends hence to the banks of the Dnieper, we passed with great rapidity; and, in the morning, at five o'clock, entered the cottage of a Malo-Russian, distinguished by an air of comfort, ease, and comparative opulence, far above the wretchedness of the huts where we had usually stopped, since our departure from Moscow. Nor is this superiority confined to their habitations alone, but distinguishes in a remarkable manner the inhabitants of Little Russia, who resemble Tartars in their appearance, and wear only mustachios instead of the bushy beard of the more northern boor. A little before mid-day, our *kibitki* halted on the left bank of the Borysthenes in the midst of at least 100 peasants, the accumulated crowd of the three or four preceding days. The thaw of the last twenty-four hours had broken up the thin crust of ice, with which the surface of the river had been previously covered, and rendered its passage again practicable.

The boat which was to ferry us across was seen on the other side of the river, slowly making towards us; and the prospect of our speedily reaching the wished-for shore was not very cheering, when we looked upon the numerous claimants around us, and, measured by the eye, the breadth of the stream, amounting to at least the third of a mile. The hopeless nature of the affair, and the exercise of patience which the peasants had already endured, seemed to have reconciled them to their situation; their horses were taken from their sledges, and they had formed a sort of temporary encampment. Men, women, and children, composed the crowd, habited in various dresses, of the most grotesque description, and calculated in different ways to resist the severity of the climate. Some of the peasants were clothed in wigs, with long pendent ears, not unlike the grave coiffure of a judge; others, again, had large brown serge cloaks, with cowls closely drawn over their faces like so many capuchins; while the girls, who wore long tails of their own hair plaited, had their heads enveloped in numerous folds of linen, in the manner of a turban. Huge gloves without fingers, enormously heavy boots, and girdles round their waists, into which their whips were thrust and hanging from behind, completed the accoutrement of the men, whose appearance was rendered still more picturesque by the white and stiffened hair of their beards. At length the boat arrived, and, as the right of embarking seemed to be regulated more by the expected amount of remuneration than by any vague notions of priority of claim, we were lucky enough to be allowed to go on board. The vessel was not a large one, but they contrived to wedge three *kibitki*, twelve horses, and as many men, into its small capacity. In the bustle of the moment, a Jew had managed to embark along with us, and had secreted himself behind one of the carriages; but he was detected in his hiding-place, and, for some reason or other, by no means apparent, was kicked out of the boat without the least ceremony. He made no resistance, and his tame acquiescence shewed that he either thought he deserved this usage, to which by habit he was probably accustomed, or that he dared not resent the ill-treatment. Perhaps, he had no business on this side the Dnieper, for though the Hebrew population of Kiev is considerable, there are very few Jews in Russia; and if they are generally served in this manner, they have a still stronger motive than the superior sagacity and cunning of the native Russ, to induce them to prefer a residence in Poland.

When this ejection was effected, and the party which had usurped the boat was left in quiet possession, we attempted to push off and quit the shore. But this was not the affair of a moment, for we were bound motionless, and fairly caught and entangled in the great masses of ice that had drifted down, and were accumulated on the margin of the river. Greeted by the shoutings of the discontented peasants on shore, the efforts of our boatmen, who, with long poles, endeavoured to push away the frozen impediments, (for which purpose they sometimes even ventured several yards on the surface of the loose ice,) were, for a long time, unavailing; but their strength and patience were ultimately successful, and we then got into tolerably clear water. We rowed up the middle of the stream for a considerable distance, constantly beset by large floating masses of ice, and landed under the high banks upon which the town of Kiev is built, amongst women employed in beating and treading linen with their half-frozen and livid bare feet, by the sides of holes made in the ice.

William Macmichael, *Journey from Moscow to Constantinople* (London 1819)

Plague Quarantine

J. Johnson, a British soldier returning from India to England in 1817, travelled through the southern regions of Russia as far as Kiev. He describes in detail the conditions he encountered in one of the numerous quarantine posts which were set up in the South to guard central Russia from the ravages of the plague.

The quarantine at Sredniy Yegarlik consists of many separate small buildings forming squares for the accommodation of travellers; the whole encompassed by palisades and a ditch. The barriers, and I believe the adjacent heights, are guarded by Cossacks. The regulations of this place are, as far as I could ascertain, as follows, in a description of what took place with regard to ourselves.

On our arrival at the barrier, we were delayed some time, and were then desired to send in all the papers or passes we possessed, which we prepared to do. A carrier dressed in greasy black clothes advanced with all due solemnity to the barrier, and seizing the papers with a pair of long tongs, disappeared with them. After this we were kept waiting in the carriage somewhat more than an hour. An officer and a soldier then advanced and opened the barrier, the soldier leading the carriage in the first instance to a fumigating room. Here we were met by several persons, and required to give in our things, which were to be kept twenty-four hours; therefore a change of clean clothes had to undergo fumigation immediately in order that we might put them on when we had been duly purified.

Our baggage and boxes were all taken into this confined room, where every thing was unpacked and opened. We were told that all articles of iron or leather, as pistols and swords, as also tin canisters of tea and sugar, would not be smoked; all our clothes, linen, and other apparel were taken out and hung on cords; all paper-packets, even such as contained specimens of minerals, were opened, and the contents, as well as other objects of curiosity, were jumbled together and the papers exposed. All sealed letters were pricked through with an iron instrument preparatory to their exposure to vapour. Any trinkets, cash, or paper currency that we might have, we were desired to take with us to another place. We left all our things, after selecting a change of linen, and some bedding for the night, which were taken to be purified by smoke and gas.

We then got into the kibitka and were taken to another house, and shown into an apartment in which were stoves and iron gratings placed at about the height of a table, on which we were desired to place every bit of paper bound round our trinkets, &c. On another table of wood was placed a wooden bowl, containing what appeared to be a mixture of vinegar, salt, and water, in which we were enjoined to put all our cash, either silver or gold, and afterwards to wash in this liquid the outside of each of our trinkets separately; Captain Salter's watch, with hair-chain, my compass and chain, seals, keys, rings of whatever stones, and other similar articles were subjected to this process; not a single thing would they allow us to exempt from it. Every minute article of our property was either washed or fumigated; every packet, even one containing a small portion of Dr. James's powder was opened, and the papers removed to the grate, as were also the paper currency, and every bag of leather or other material. After this exposure of all our minute articles over the grate, which occupied more than an hour, our clean smoked clothes were brought in and deposited on a bench: we were informed that we could not be allowed to touch them until we were quite naked, and we were told to undress even while people were in the room. Having taken off all but our shirts we desired them to leave us, which they did, warning us on no account to touch the clean clothes until we were naked. At this time the physician came in and examined our armpits, groins, the glandular parts of the neck, and in short all the parts of the body in which the plague displays itself. He gave us a black and filthy-looking sponge saturated with vinegar to pass over each of those parts separately, and then left us, hearing us previously declare that we were in health and had not the plague.

We then put off our apparel and dressed ourselves in the clean fumigated clothes. Vessels were brought containing the usual ingredients for the production of gas, which being mixed up, the vapour was passed under all the papers, lying on the grate, and we retired into another apartment to avoid its effects. In half an hour we were allowed to return and collect our trinkets, papers, &c. and then proceeded to a small separate habitation that had been allotted for our residence. During the above-mentioned process, a heavy storm had come on which drenched the carriage and wet many of our things which were spread on the cords, &c. in the fumigating room, the roof of which, though made of a double layer of bark, was in such bad repair as to admit the rain in streams.

The hovel to which we were removed, and in which we were to pass the ensuing seven days, had its floor about three and a half feet below the level of the ground, being one half of its height. The small openings of the windows at the ground level were almost obscured by rank weeds which grew all round the place, reaching to the eaves of the roof. The storm of rain had wetted the floor and the benches within. On entering we found that the place swarmed with fleas, mosquitoes and mice. The walls and beams were actually blackened with flies, which rested on every thing that was laid down even for a moment. There were fixed bed-places or tressels on which we laid our leather-covered bedding; but as we had not provided ourselves

328

with any sheets or light covering, we were unable to sleep during the whole night, and it was out of the question to place our beds in the open air, as the ground was covered with high weeds and was then wet with rain.

At the time of our arrival no provisions could be procured but lean and bad mutton, a bit of which was roasted by a fire of wet wood, and some very bad, sour, brown bread was brought us to eat with it. In the evening we made some tea,

159 The *telega*, or cart used for haulage in the summer and early autumn months. From J. A. Atkinson and J. Walker, *A Picturesque Representation of the Manners, Customs and Amusements of the Russians*, 1812.

which was all the sustenance that we had found palatable since the preceding day: we passed a miserable night. At day-break I walked out and found the fresh air quite reviving to my exhausted spirits; but through loss of sleep the sensation of fatigue was greater than on my arrival. At nine the next morning, when we had passed twenty-four hours in this place, our baggage was given to us, and I took out the letter which I received from General Yermolov, for the Hetman Platov, who has this district under his command. I requested that a Cossack might be sent with it and with another from ourselves.

Information was brought to us that we must pay eighteen rubles thirty kopeks, to send a messenger post in a kibitka; and that our letter, unsealed, must be fumigated. This was accordingly done, and two ten-ruble assignats were given to the officer who came to receive them.

Of him I enquired if there were not Cossacks at every post between this place and the residence of the Hetman, and why a single horseman could not be sent with the letters, adding that in fact the duty was General Platov's, and that without General Yermolov's letter I should not have written to him. To all this he merely answered that a messenger in a kibitka would go the fastest; I replied that I was certain there would be a loss of more time in changing horses at the post-houses, nearly half an hour at each post, and that not more than one third of that time would be required for a change of Cossacks; but that he ought to know best, and I begged he would act accordingly.

I also enquired concerning the letter-post, and was informed that letters left this place every Saturday: this was Monday.

As Captain Salter found himself feverish, I requested that people might be sent to clear the weeds from the space around the house, for which labour we would pay them. It was promised that this request should be attended to. Meantime we began to be aware of another annoyance: the oven or fire-place for cooking was within the room; and though it was doubtless serviceable in preventing miasmata, it produced intolerable heat which continued all night.

The water at this place stinks, and is very unwholesome to drink, as it invariably produces diarrhœa on all strangers who use it. The name of the place is derived from the bad odour of its water.

Another circumstance which appears to me of serious import, is, that all travellers from Georgia and every other place, are made to perform quarantine *promiscuously* with those from the Kabarda, or Circassia, where it is believed that the plague continually exists. These men are allowed to bring with them wool and woollen-cloths, and hundreds of thousands of skins of sheep, goats, hares, foxes, &c. &c. which are exposed to the air under sheds, in a situation near which people are passing indiscriminately all day long.

Even prisoners brought in irons from those districts, the Kabarda or Circassia, are kept with other travellers, and sleep under the same roofs with them. For these reasons, the fact appears to be, that although it is very certain that we should have gone through Russia without carrying the plague with us if we had never entered the quarantine, we were here exposed to great danger of taking the infection and carrying it with us from hence.

That gold, silver, and copper coin, and even paper money, should be duly purified, is a proper regulation which should be scrupulously attended to, because those articles pass through inumerable hands, and are thus liable to infection; but the annoyance of unpacking all trinkets, (which foreign travellers keep safely locked up, and which are not so likely to change their owners) and of washing them in the filthy brine, is surely needless, whilst the boots, belts, and other articles of leather or iron belonging to people of the country who may have actually had intercourse with persons infected by the plague, are left unpurified.

There is another grievance which requires to be abolished. There are double keys to all the padlocks placed on the doors of the fumigating rooms, one of which keys the quarantine

330

servants reserve, and can thus enter the rooms where a traveller's property is deposited when they please, though they pretend to deliver the sole key of the room to him, and thus relieve him from all apprehension. We witnessed a proof of this custom of keeping double keys. A Monsieur Jervais, a French wine-merchant, who had accompanied us from Tiflis, had received the key of the room in which his effects were deposited for fumigation; it was opened by the servants in our presence with another key. He warned them at the time of the serious consequences which must ensue if he reported this act of theirs to the government, and they appeared to be sensible of the propriety of his remarks.

The room in which our effects were placed for fumigation was immediately adjoining that which contained the property of M. Jervais, consisting of bales of shawls, chintzes and other merchandise, which the officers of this quarantine had obliged him to open out; although in order to obviate any occasion for this trouble the bales had been closed and sealed, at the quarantine near Tiflis. The officers alleged that they knew not of the quarantine to which he adverted, and denied that any authority existed there for sealing up merchandise. M. Jervais would be in consequence liable to undergo a much longer detention than he expected, as all goods fresh imported must remain in quarantine a whole fortnight. Hence it appears, that in these establishments a great deal is left to the discretion of the officers; and this seems a defect in the regulations, for which a remedy should be speedily provided.

No care whatever is taken to preserve cleanliness in the hovels, or rooms of accommodation. On the contrary, every thing detrimental to the health of the persons confined in them is tolerated. The bread and water are bad, the wine worse; the air is impregnated by the effluvia of stagnant ditch-water in trenches choked up with rank weeds, which, as we have already observed, nearly close up the small apertures of the room, fifteen inches by twelve, which are called windows.

Within the precincts of the quarantine there are no artisans; not a carpenter, tailor, or shoemaker; not even a washer-woman. The linen that has been soiled by the gas-process cannot be made clean at this place.

To each hovel there is, I believe, a Cossack or servant appointed to fetch in wood and water, which are gratuitously allowed. He who attended upon us was in himself a nuisance that no one who could avoid it would endure under the same roof. His kvas stood fermenting in the door-way, attracting myriads of flies to blacken the adjoining walls. His couch was a bench in the passage covered with sheepskin cloaks and felts, in which were vermin of every kind. In his person he was loathsome and disgusting; his pale face and his extremities were swelled, and he appeared to be labouring under a salivation which was then subsiding; his dress and habits were

160 Feodosiya, a city in the
Crimea. An ancient Greek
colony, it became a noted
Genoese trading town under
the name of Kaffa. It was
eventually ceded to Russia in
1774. From Mary Holder-
ness, *A Journey from Riga to
the Crimea.*

161 A panoramic view of the
city of Bakhchisaray in the
Crimea, famed for its palace
and gardens built by the
Crimean Khans in the
seventeenth century. The
harem and the so-called
'Fountain of Tears' are
immortalized in Pushkin's
poem 'The Fountain of
Bakhchisaray' (1823). From
Peter Simon Pallas and
Berner Kningen, *Auf einer
Reise in die Sulichen
Provinzen*, Leipzig, 1779.

so filthy, that it was really disgusting to allow him to bring any
article of subsistence; but he alone was permitted to go out,
and he knew where every thing that we wanted was to be
procured.

For ladies who are detained at this place on their return
home, a regulation is made, by which the wife of the attending
surgeon examines them. This is done in a manner equally
indelicate with that in which the surgeon himself examined us,
as already described. The apartments for ladies of course are
distinct, and females alone are suffered to attend on them.
The lower classes of Russians, however, have very little more
sense of decency than savages; we saw numbers of them
running about the rivers at Mozdok, and at work in the boats
or on shore, entirely naked.

It is not unlikely that the habit of smoking all day long
greatly tends to prevent the ill effects of the noxious air in
which the Russians habitually sleep. This habit every stranger
may not be disposed to adopt; but there is another more
unequivocally salubrious, which any one confined from one
to six weeks in succession at a quarantine, should be no means
forego. This is the exercise of walking to and fro in the open
air, which should be practised as much as possible; for it is a
well ascertained fact, that all persons who suddenly rest from
the fatigues of travelling, become after the lapse of a few days
of quiet, extremely predisposed to fever and to bilious complaints. When the place to which they are confined is low,
damp, and exposed to the miasmata of rank and putrescent
vegetation, they can with difficulty prevent the attacks of
fevers and agues, particularly in autumn, when the atmosphere
is alternately hot and humid.

John Johnston, *Journey from India to England* (London 1818)

Colonizing 'New Russia'

Mary Holderness's 'New Russia' is the area bordering the Black Sea
including the Crimea, long desired by the Russians but only coming
into their possession during the reign of Catherine the Great. Miss
Holderness spent a period of four years (1816-20) in the village of
Karagoss and her account is the most detailed and 'scientific' among
early works in English.

New Russia comprehends the governments of Taurida,
Yekaterinoslav, and Kherson: extending eastward, it includes
the district of Yekaterinodar in Asia; and to the west, we may
comprise within its boundaries, Bessarabia, and such part of
Moldavia as is now subject to Russia.

The whole of the government of the Taurida, with the exception of the Crimea, is one united mass of colonization. Of course, in point of numbers, the Russians rank first, and occupy by far the greatest part of this vast space, which, previously to its conquest from the Tartars, was a flat and fertile waste of interminable extent of pasture land, over which the Nomadic nation of Nogay Tartars wandered with their flocks and herds. It is now colonized by, 1st Little Russians; 2nd, Great Russians; 3rd, Nogay Tartars; 4th, Greeks; 5th, Germans; 6th Armenians; and, 7th, Bulgarians. The two latter are comparatively few in number to the others.

The boundary line of colonization might be extended to the Danube, including Bessarabia and Moldavia, which assuredly form a most material part of this immense colony, which is twice as large as Great Britain, and its soil certainly thrice as fertile as that of England in general; so much of which requires artificial help, and is made good and preserved so at great expence, while much is incapable of any great improvement. But in the country we are describing, Nature reigns in her greatest luxuriance of vegetation, and varies little in the fertility of the soil. From the Don to the Danube, from Poland to the Black Sea, the soil is, with few exceptions, a dark putrid loam

162 The harem in the palace of the Khans at Bakhchisaray. From Clarke's *Travels in Various Countries of Europe, Asia and Africa.*

of great depth. This great colony likewise possesses the advantage of being traversed in almost every direction by some of the largest rivers in Europe – the Danube, the Dniester, the Bog, the Dnieper, the Don, and the Kuban; the smallest of which is in magnitude superior to the Thames or the Severn: the Danube, Dnieper, Bog, and Don are alone navigable; the remainder fertilize the colony through which they flow, but do not contribute to float its produce to the sea.

Upon this large and promising tract, the land measurers of the government, in the surveys which they were instructed to make, were ordered to set apart all the best spots, for the economical, or crown boors; and this was effected, by fixing upon all the land on both sides of the great rivers above mentioned, from ten to fifteen miles on either side, right and left of the same. The allotments to each village, were of course granted in proportion to the number of the colonists to be fixed there, but, universally speaking, the quantity of soil thrown to each village, would appear to us to be extremely large, and certainly out of all proportion to the population established upon it at the time, or even compared with what it has become since. The colony of Odessa, or the district around that city, consists of nearly five millions of acres of land; and as the whole contains only 180 lots, the size of each allotment averages 28,000 acres: many villages are much larger, and some of them have 100,000 acres, all of it fertile land. A village of the last named quantity, was generally considered capable of supporting at its establishment, from two, to three thousand revision souls, or twice that number of persons, or about forty acres per male; or, at three revision souls per family, one hundred and twenty acres per house. This proportion, if we consider the unvaried fertility of the soil, is unquestionably very great; and the more especially, when it is further considered, that the whole of it was a vast plain of pasture, to convert which into fields of corn, required no extraordinary exertion or expence.

The great misfortune which has appeared to operate in counteracting the beneficial effects, which might otherwise naturally have been expected to result from so munificent a distribution of the richest soil in a fine climate, contiguous to navigation, the sea, and great markets, has flowed from the mode of fixing these colonies. The feudal system being adopted, every house in a large village was consequently huddled and jammed together, with no other separation between house and house, than space just sufficient to enable the colonists to build their out-houses around a small yard. The evils resulting from this system, are in every point of view, great beyond calculation. To mention only two or three immediately affecting the colonist himself, we may observe, in seed, hay, and harvest-time, each family (leaving the old, and the very young at home), quit the village, with their teams, seed, provisions, fuel, &c., and take up their quarters from five, to ten, or fifteen miles distant, until the work which carried them there, be finished, when they remove back to it again.

During this interval, the shepherd, the herdsman, the hog-herd, each collect the live stock of the community, drive them to pasture, and back, and tend them in the field. Thus the murrain, and other distempers, have no chance of being confined to the spot where they first broke out, but ravage the herds and flocks of an entire village, in which it not unusually happens that three-fourths of the whole number are swept away. Fires (which frequently take place), destroy whole villages in a single night, and often, with immense quantities of corn in the straw.

At every revision or census of the inhabitants, the total quantity of land is regularly subdivided in such a manner amongst the whole number of revision males, that each has a part proportionate to the quantity to be distributed; but all of it is intermixed. No family has the right of securing to itself the allotted share for any greater length of time than the space of one revision, that is, three years; or for a fallow and two crops of corn. The population is then counted over again,

335

and a fresh distribution takes place. Notwithstanding this apparently equal arrangement, it always happens that some boors in every village, by superior industry and fortuitous circumstances, continue to be richer than the rest, and that others, by laziness, drunkenness, small families, and sundry accidents, remain in a state of comparative poverty: so that one boor frequently serves another, letting out his own labour and land to his more fortunate neighbours.

This very system, however, having subsisted throughout every part of the empire of Russia from the remotest antiquity, it was not to be expected that any other, or better plan of colonizing their fertile deserts, could have been adopted. Bigotted as the boors are universally allowed to be to their ancient customs in every country, here the whole power of government would have been utterly unavailing, to bring about so great an improvement as that of settling each family immediately on the land intended for cultivation. The advantages claimed in favour of the Russian plan of colonization, over that now alluded to, flows from the principles of despotic government. The cultivators of the soil are slaves, and as beasts of burden, their prosperity is no otherwise considered of consequence by the government or nobles, than as they contribute to pay poll-tax, and furnish recruits to the former, and labour the landed property of the latter. It is obvious that these services are much more easily exacted from the inhabitants of a village, whose houses are built contiguous to each other, than when they are remote, and dispersed over a wide extent of country. Added to which, is the superior facility of governing such villages; of calling them out to labour; of watching their motions; of receiving the orders of the government or their masters, and especially of calling out the recruits; very few of which would be procured, if each family did not watch his neighbours' actions, in this, as in many other of the above cases, and report their observations to the officers of government: all of which are objects of the very first magnitude. It is, however, equally clear, that agriculture cannot flourish under such conditions; and the extraordinary fertility of the soil, while liable to these and other objections flowing from the same source, has alone contributed to the support of this barbarous system.

The earliest establishment of the colonization of Russia may be dated from the beginning of Catherine the Second's reign. The revision of their numbers is taken every third year; and all who are registered on the day of the revision, (which is ascertained over the whole empire at the same time), are liable till the new revision, to a poll-tax of five rubles per male head, including all ages, whether any of them die or not in the intermediate time; but, on the other hand, all the new-born are exempt during the same period.

The boors are subject to many vexations, from the abuse

of power by the officers of the government belonging to the Landed Tribunal. Armed with the most absolute authority, they are chiefly men of low rank and humble estate, and receiving salaries of from two to three, or four guineas per annum, they have recourse to all the abundant means within their power of extending that income. *Apparently* to deliver the orders of the police, though often to live in free quarters, these men are seen at all times, and in all places, putting into requisition the boors and their horses, and galloping over the district, to the annoyance of the peasant, who is frequently called from the harvest field, or other important occupations, to furnish the required duty. They eat and drink wherever they go; and every pretext is laid hold of to oblige the boor to furnish contributions of whatever he possesses, for them to carry home to their families.

Mary Holderness, *Journey from Riga to the Crimea, with Some Account of the Manners and Customs of the Colonists of New Russia* (London 1827)

Through the Caucasus to Tbilisi

Some years after his stay in St Petersburg and Moscow Robert Ker Porter travelled extensively through Persia, on a journey which took him through the Caucasus to Georgia. The two selections from his account of this journey are typical, impressionistic descriptions, firstly of the famous pass through the Caucasus, as he leaves Vladikavkaz in the north and travels along the valley of the Terek towards the fortress at Lars; secondly, of Tiflis-Tbilisi, capital city of Georgia, lying beyond the mountain passes.

The convoy had been gone many hours; but confiding my letter for His Excellency to the commanding-officer of the fort, I was furnished with an escort of twelve Cossacks, and set forth on my way to Vladikavkaz.

The road lay over a continuation of the extensive plain, part of which we had crossed the day before: it bore a direction due east. On our right rolled the Terek, breaking over its stony bed, and washing with a surge, rather than a flowing stream, the rocky bases of the mountains which rise in progressive acclivities from its bold shores. The day had begun to clear about noon; and the dark curtain of vapours, which had so long shut these stupendous hills from my sight, broke away into a thousand masses of fleecy clouds; and, as they gradually glided downwards, exhaled into ether, or separated across the brows of the mountains, the vast piles of Caucasus were presented to my view; a world of themselves; rocky, rugged, and capped with snow; stretching east and west beyond the

Pass of the Caucasus.

WLADI CAUCAUSE

TIFLIS

Russian Wersts.

338

reach of vision, and shooting far into the skies. – It was a sight to make the senses pause; to oppress even respiration, by the weight of the impression on the mind, of such vast over-powering sublimity.

The proud head of Elbrus was yet far distant; but it rose in hoary majesty above all, the sovereign of these giant mountains; finely contrasting its silvery diadem, the snow of ages, with the blue misty brows of its immediate subject range; and they, being yet partially shrouded in the dissolving masses of white cloud, derived increased beauty from comparisons with the bold and black forms of the lower mountains, nearer the plain, whose rude and towering tops, and almost per-pendicular sides, sublimely carry the astonished eye along the awful picture; creating those feelings of terrific admiration, to which words can give no name.

After a ride of twenty-two versts, we reached the key of the celebrated pass into Georgia, where I rejoined my companions.

Vladikavkaz is one of the most important, and strongest military posts the Russians possess along the foot of the Caucasus. It generally has a whole regiment in garrison; and is the principal depot for supplying the various minor forts of the neighbouring stations in the mountains. It stands on some high ground on the banks of the Terek, sufficiently elevated to com-mand the approach to the pass, and not near enough to any other height, to be subject to the fire of the natives. The town increases rapidly, and so does the population in its vicinity; for here, as elsewhere along this frontier, the remark is verified, that wherever the Russians erect a fort, hundreds of Tartars draw near, and establish themselves in little villages. This voluntary proceeding, by bringing them in unsuspicious, and therefore amicable contact, with the Europeans, has tended greatly to the civilisation of this branch of the Tartar race; and hence, it is to be hoped, the influence of humane manners may gradually diffuse itself to more distant tribes. These establish-ments have already made considerable progress in domestic habits, and are become attentive to certain little comforts, regarded as necessaries in ordinary civilised life, but of which their still barbarous kindred tribes have not even an idea. The people, called Tartars, are remnants of the Huns, whose too-abundant population, centuries ago, overwhelmed Europe like a deluge. The ancient consequence of this nation may still be traced in the line of country they possessed, and which was yet too narrow to contain its people. Their dominion extended over the Crimea, and all the territory between the Don and Dnieper; stretching to the Black Sea, and looking towards the Caspian. They planted cities on the Terek and the Kuban; and that they were worthy of a great people, the ruins of Mtskheta, near the former river, nobly testify.

As from this point, Vladikavkaz, our road would be direct through the heart of the mountains, up and down acclivities

163 The famous pass through the Caucasus from Vladikavkaz to Tbilisi. From Robert Ker Porter, *Travels in Georgia*, 1821.

339

which would be termed precipices, in the more tameable Alps or Appenines of Europe, we here abandoned our piece of artillery, as well as the heavy part of the convoy; and, lightened of these two loads, set forth, with a more volant motion, under an escort of about forty soldiers, an officer, and a few Cossacks. At starting, our good commander of the fort particularly enjoined us to keep close together. Indeed, on no account to let any one of the party stray away, or lag behind the main body; for the path was so beset with lurking banditti, hid in all quarters of the rocks, that any straggler might instantly become their prize; and his liberty, if not his blood, pay the forfeit of his negligence.

At six o'clock in the morning, we began our march; taking as much military precaution as the nature of our route would admit. We crossed the Terek, over a bridge close to the town. The river there, at this season of the year, is not usually wide, but it was extremely rapid; and, from its course being impeded by numerous rocks in its channel, the noise with which it struggles for a passage, and rushes over them, may be heard at a great distance. Along the northern bank of the stream, the huts and little gardens of the settled Tartars, soften, with their forms of the gentler picturesque, the vast and terrible outlines of nature by which they are surrounded.

The valley, through which the Terek flows, was anciently denominated *Porta Caucausia,* from its being the great gate of communication between the nations on each side the mountains. Catherine the Second was the first European sovereign whose troops ever passed it from the north; a party of whom, under General Tottleben, penetrated into Georgia, and paved the way for those successes which afterwards determined the Empress to establish a high road direct from this pass to Tiflis. But this project, so pregnant with great consequences, was left to be begun and completed by her grandson, his present Imperial Majesty; who sent General Prince Tsitsianov, to commence the undertaking, about the beginning of the year 1804; and, by the most indefatigable labour on the side of the workmen, and attentive zeal on his, it is now finished: no less an achievement of incalculable utility, than it is one to be wondered at, and to command the lasting gratitude of all who have experienced its securities.

As we travelled onward, along the right bank of the river, we found it in many places full a quarter of a mile broad; and in others, where the cliffs projected very much, it was hardly thirty yards. Indeed, I am informed, there are points, where the opposite rocks draw so near, as to narrow the stream to less than half that width. When this is the case, the turbulence and rage of the waters increase with the difficulties, to a degree that covers the barrier rocks, and the stream itself, with foam.

For the first eight or ten versts of our march from Vladikavkaz, the slopes of the mountains, on both sides the

Terek, were clothed with trees and thick underwood; but, as we penetrated deeper into the valley, they gradually lost their verdure, becoming stony and barren. On reaching Balti, a small but strong fort about twelve versts forward, the hills assumed bolder forms, presenting huge protruding masses of rock, with very few spots of shrub or tree. The road here wears rather a face of danger, and must have been made, even thus passable, by the severest labour, aided by gun-powder. It runs beneath pendant archways of stone, which are merely high enough to allow the passage under them of a low carriage; but the path is so narrow as scarcely to admit two to move abreast, or pass each other, should they be so unlucky as to encounter; and on one side of the road is the edge of a precipice, which, in some places, is sixty feet deep; and in others, above one hundred. At the bottom of this abyss are the roaring waters of the Terek. In casting the eye upwards, still blacker, and terrible precipices are above us. We see large projections of rock, many thousand tons in weight, hanging from the beetling steep of the mountain, threatening destruction to all below: and it is not always a vain apprehension. Many of these huge masses have been launched downwards by the effect of a sudden thaw; and at various times, and various places, have so completely blocked up the regular road, as to compel the traveller to pass round them, often so near the brink of the precipice, as to be at the peril of his life.

At another military station, called Lars, where we were to change our escort, the scene becomes still wilder and more stupendous. The valley narrows to the appearance of a frightful chasm; so steep, so rugged, so walled in with rocks, as if cleft by the waters of the deluge. Its granite sides are almost perpendicular, and are many hundred feet in height. They are surmounted by summits lost in the clouds, which sweep along their ridges, or, rolling down the gloomy face of the abyss, form a sea of vapours, mingling with the rocks above our heads, as extraordinary as it is sublime. But, in short, that undescribable emotion of the soul, which instinctively acknowledges the presence of such amazing grandeur in Nature's works, is almost always our companion in these regions.

Most of the Russian posts here, are on stations formerly occupied by the ancients, for the same purpose; and the remains of these old fortresses may frequently be found in digging foundations for the new. At Lars, and about a verst from it, walls and towers of a commanding height, still rise in frowning, though decayed majesty, over the abrupt points of rock which defend the passage of the valley. By some, it is said to be one of the spots, where the locks or barriers, so much in use in times of antiquity, were erected; and indeed this part of the defile is so shut by nature, little trouble would be necessary to throw piles across, and close the whole with gates.

Evening came on, while we were yet some distance from our halting-place. I regretted it the more, as the darkness would deprive us of every sense of the scenery we were passing through, except its probable danger. The increasing gloom and indistinctness of the surrounding objects; the history of the place, in which we now silently and apprehensively travelled; the hoarse murmurs of the rushing waters at the foot of the ravine; and the vague musings which possess a man journeying

164 The pass at Derial and the River Terek. From Robert Ker Porter, *Travels in Georgia,* 1821.

in the blackness of night, through strange countries, desart and solitary; all, engendered sensations in the breast, more of terror than of fear,—an awe of something unknown.

Derial was our post for the night. As we drew near it, our road was rendered still more obscure, by its leading, for a considerable way, through a subterraneous passage cut in the solid rock. It is about a mile from the fort. We emerged on the side of the river, at the foot of a very steep precipice; thence crossed the stream on a wooden bridge; and, additionally guarded by a detachment from the fort, reached our quarters in safety. Thus closed our first day's advance into the Caucasus.

Information having been brought, that a marauding band of the natives were occupying a tract we must pass over next day; for the security of the convoy, the officer of the fort sent out a party of infantry, early in the morning, to dislodge them. Our march being therefore delayed, till news of the success of the expedition should arrive, I had time to observe some of the country through which we had passed the preceding night. The redoubt of the Russian post of Derial stands at the bottom of the gigantic chasm of that name, and is overhung by such enormous masses of rock as to make its situation terrible. On the summit of one of these promontories, impending over the left bank of the Terek, are to be seen the remains of a very ancient castle. With some difficulty I scrambled up to it, and found the ruins consisted of one strong square tower, with thick massive walls surrounding it, and encircling a space besides, sufficient to garrison several hundred soldiers. This seemed the citadel of the pass; but I observed, that on all the points where the rocks might have formed advantageous lodgements for any enemy who had been dexterous enough to gain them, the ruins of subordinate out-works were visible. The face of the mountain behind the tower had been hewn, with manifest great labour, into a kind of aqueduct, to convey water to the garrison. And, when we consider that there would be ground within its lines to supply themselves and cattle with food, we could not suppose a place better adapted for the purposes of such a station. A subterraneous passage runs down from the castle to the bank of the river, communicating, probably, with other works which might be below, to bar more immediately, the ingress of the valley. The pass, at this place, is not more than thirty yards across; which facility of nature, agreeing with the vestiges along its borders, leaves no doubt in my mind that this, from earliest times, has been one of the main doors of communication with the nations of the north, direct from Iberia . . .

The first syllable in the word Derial, as well as in that of Derbent, in the Asiatic languages, implies gate, door, or narrow pass; which confirms the other evidences, that here was the chief barrier of the valley, and that the castellated promontories of Lars, and other minor posts lower down, were probably the chain of communication from this great station, to others of different magnitude; but all to the same purport, ports of defence against the Barbarians.

I had time sufficient, before our detachment came in, to attempt making a sketch or two of the objects around me. I took my views from the old fortified height; and from the Russian redoubt below: but no pencil can convey, nor pen describe, the grandeur of the scene. At this one tremendous point, the chasm rises from the river's brink, upwards of a thousand feet. Its sides are broken into clefts and projections, dark and frowning; so high, so close, so overhanging, that even at mid-day the whole is covered with a shadow bordering on twilight. According to the calculations of Dr Renniggs, who visited the Caucasus in 1781, the elevation of the mountains directly opposite the castle of Derial, is not less than three thousand seven hundred and eighty-six feet. This measurement was the result of several observations; and it may be received as the common height of nearly the whole range, east and west, with the exception of Elbrus and Kazbek.

Our road from Derial lost nothing of its gloomy magnificence, all the way to the sort of gorge, whither the soldiers had been sent to dislodge its unwelcome guests; and there we found a spot peculiarly wild, and fitted to the uses of its late inhabitants. Vast quantities of low thick bushes, and brush-wood, occupied a suspicious-looking hollow on our left; which natural trench, so well covered from the eye of observation, terminated at a point that communicated its egress with the accesses of the mountain. But so difficult did they seem, that only one was visible, by which it appeared possible to us for the boldest adventurers to descend. But, descend they

165 Kalmuc and Cossack. From *La Russie, ou Moeurs, Usages et Costumes des habitants . . . de cet Empire.* M. Breton, Paris 1813.

do, and in no insufficient numbers; concealing themselves in the thickets till opportunity presents itself to spring upon their prey. Before the precaution was adopted, to send out a party of military, literally to beat the bushes, and clear the way, this road was one continued scene of bloodshed and robbery. These mountain-brigands being sure, from knowledge of their own paths and agility in gaining them, of always escaping pursuit, never failed to be in waiting on every approaching convoy; and keeping close behind their brush-wood, or broken rocks, fired on the unwary people as they passed; killing, or wounding numbers. The survivors, too often taking to flight, left the spoil to the leisurely collection of the victors.

Our escort was reinforced by those who had fulfilled the advance duty of the night before; and the whole moved on without molestation, though several times we could discern different parties of the banditti scrambling high amongst the rocks. Their desperate situations, and savage costume, heightened the Salvator-Rosa picture of the scene. But from the chance of the road not being quite free from them, I was always prevented though often induced to halt alone for a few minutes, to snatch a hasty sketch. The officer of the convoy would not allow it, as any single straggler might be cut off in a moment, by the sudden spring of one of the undiscovered ambushes. But I could not resist the temptation entirely; and, once or twice I detained a chasseur or two with me, while I

344

tried to catch some loose memorandums of those mighty mountains I might never see again.

As we followed the further progress of the Kura, the mountains gradually lost both their rocks and forest-scenery, presenting immense heights covered with beautiful verdure. The course of three or four versts brought us to a fine level expanse of country, in high cultivation, and traversed by a thousand sparkling rivulets from the hills on the western side of the plain. The river also added its waters to the refreshing beauties of the view. Our eyes turned, with a sense of repose, from the rugged wilds they had so long been contemplating, to the soft green which covered these noble hills; but ere we had pursued our way, for quite ten versts, over the luxuriant plain they bordered, we perceived the opening of a narrow, rocky valley. The river entered it, between two bold ranges of the mountains; and, at the extremity of the defile, we saw the capital of Georgia, the many towers of Tiflis, rising on the, then, precipitous and again sublime banks of the Kura. But the effect produced here, is of a deeper tinge. The town itself, stands at the foot of a line of dark and barren hills, whose high and caverned sides gloomily overshadow it. Every house, every building within its walls, seems to share the dismal hue of the surrounding heights; for a deep blackness, rests on all. The hoary battlements above, and the still majestic towers of the ancient citadel; the spires of Christian churches, and other marks of European residents; even their testimonies of past grandeur, and present conse- quence; and, what is more, present christian brotherhood; could not, for some time, erase the horrible dungeon- impression of Asiatic dirt and barbarism, received at first view of the town. On crossing a small stone bridge, we reached the guard-house of a quarantine, about three versts from Tiflis; but, on delivering our papers of health, we were allowed to proceed, without further detention, towards the gates of the city. Having entered them, (with the feeling of one going into the cave of Trophonius,) I took up my quarters at the house of Khoja Aratoon, an Armenian, whose father had served, as treasurer, several of our envoys and ambassadors, when resi- dent at the court of Persia. I was well pleased to hear the first information communicated to me by my host, that the Governor of Georgia, General Yermolov, was returned to Tiflis, from his embassy to the Persian monarch; and, accordingly, next morning, I presented myself to His Ex- cellency, and delivered my letters. His reception was in no respect like the gloom of his capital, and the sunshine within, soon spread its influence without doors.

Tiflis is distant from St Petersburg 2627 versts, in 42° 45′ N. lat., and 62° 40½′ E. long. according to Russian calculation. Chardin has placed it in lat. 43° and long. 64°. But Captain Monteith, of the Madras engineers, from an observation,

166 Seventeenth-century
Tiflis. From *Journal du
Voyage du Chevalier Chardin*.

found its latitude to be 41° 43'. The city has no claim to an
antiquity beyond the lapse of a few centuries; having been
founded in the year 1063, by the Tsar Liewvang, who wished
to derive personal benefit from certain warm springs in its
neighbourhood. Till that period, it could boast no habitation
in the form of a house; unless, perhaps, a few mud-hovels for
the convenience of the occupiers of a small fortress, which
stood on an adjacent height, and protected the valley. The
remains of this ancient bulwark are still to be seen on a hill to
the south of the town, at some distance from the station of the
more modern citadel, of Turkish origin. The position of the
old work of the native Tsars, completely commanded the road
along the western bank of the Kura; and its dark and frowning
towers, lonely as they are, still seem to threaten the passenger
below. A more intimate acquaintance with the town, gradually
effaced the impression of the general dreariness of its aspect;
but the effect of the circumjacent scenery always remained the
same; a vast prison, if I may so express myself, of high and
beetling rocks broken into deep clefts, black and bare, and
projecting in a thousand rugged and savage forms! And on
these bulwarks of nature, apparently sufficiently incarcerating
of themselves, we see every where the time-destroyed additions
of man: towers and battlements, lying in huge grey masses of
ruin on every pointed steep; while old mouldering walls,
track the declivities till their bases touch the town, or end in
the bed of the Kura. From the situation of the town, at the
bottom of a ravine like this, it cannot be supposed a very

346

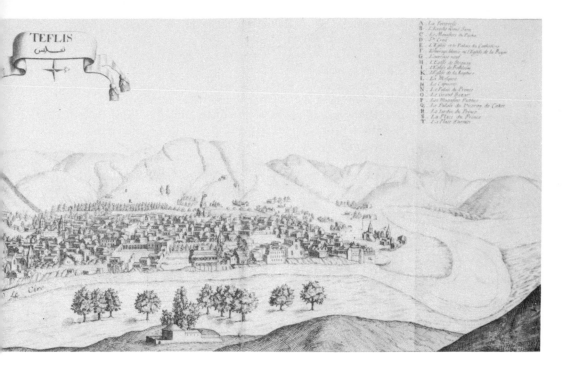

desirable abode for persons used to freer space, and wider
prospect. Hence the Governor-general has chosen his place
of residence at a short distance from the body of the city;
on the gentle slope of a hill, fronting the river, and a fine view
of the Caucasian mountains. When the house is finished, for it
is now undergoing a repair, it will be distinguished by a large
portico, and exterior ornamental figures sculptured in stone.

This building, with the arsenal, hospital, churches, and a few
villas in the neighbourhood, are the only erections, in or near
the place, that remind one at all of Europe. The rest is purely
Asiatic; but very different from the idea, commonly received
in Europe, of that term,—gay minarets, painted domes, and
gilded trellice-work. Here was a collection of low, flat-roofed
dwellings, built of dun brick, mingled with stones and mud;
the doors and windows exceedingly small; the latter covered
with paper, glass being in little use from its scarcity and dear-
ness: indeed, the natives have been so accustomed to live in a
kind of half-darkness, from the overshadowing of their
mountain, and the closeness of their abodes, that light seems
no way necessary to their vocations. As a proof, they hardly
ever apply to the effects of a little oil on the opacity of the paper.
The streets are, without exception, narrow; and, from the
primitive state of the pathways, intolerably filthy in wet
weather, and dusty in dry. However, His Excellency, the
Governor, is endeavouring to obviate this inconvenience, by
ordering them to be paved; which good work is already begun.
He is also establishing other improvements, by directing all

ruinous houses to be either repaired, or entirely pulled down, to make way for the erection of new ones, according to handsome and more salubrious plans. Amongst other works of this nature, carried on during his late absence in Persia, are alterations in the bazar, or great market-place for merchants. This has been totally roofed in, but with open circles left in the rafters, for the admission of air and light. Long colonnades unite it to the square of the city-guard; which place is also lined with shops, covered from the weather with a fine range of pillared arcades; and the natives themselves, thus sheltered in their own persons, and in that of their merchandise, from the injurious effects of rain or scorching heat, begin, though languidly, to acknowledge that these changes are improvements. The bazar is a narrow street, of a very long and winding extent. On each side of it are lines of shops of every description, such as fruiterers, grocers, barbers, cooks, mercers, sadlers, armourers, &c. &c. all open, whose various articles are spread and displayed to the best advantage. Notwithstanding the value of some of the merchandise they thus lay forth, subject to accident as well as purchase, the place is a free thoroughfare; not merely to pedestrians, but to horsemen, to asses with burthens, and even droves of buffaloes are not excluded. Hence it is often both disagreeable and dangerous to the foot-passenger; yet we never find it but full of people and bustle from morning until dusk. Not far from the bazar is the public caravansary, where merchant-travellers take up their quarters. Here you see, exposed on the stone or earthen floors, of dark and vaulted apartments, whatever goods the merchants who inhabit them may possess. The owner of each heap, sits cross-legged, in grave attendance, waiting the appearance of customers, or bargaining with those who arrive; and in one of them, I discovered an old fellow-traveller, an Armenian merchant, who had passed the Caucasus with me. He was pleased with the encounter, and treated me with a kaleon, sweetmeats, and some brandy, made at Yerevan. This building is circular, three stories in height with a sort of gallery running in front of each range of doors, from whence stone steps descend, to conduct passengers above or below. The centre of the court is filled with the horses and mules of the merchants in the caravansary.

At one extremity of the bazar we find a small bridge over a deep ravine, at the bottom of which flows a mountain-stream; pure and cold at its fountain-head, but mingling here with the hot-springs, which take their rise in the adjacent heights, it becomes warm, and derives all the medicinal properties, whose fame gave birth to Tiflis. Over this steaming flood we find the public baths erected. They form not only a resource in sickness, to the natives, and to travellers visiting them with the same object, but they are the daily resort of both sexes, as places of luxury and amusement. On one side of the bridge

348

stand those appropriated to the men; and on the other, immediately below the gloomy walls of the citadel, the range intended for the women. The water which supplies these distinct bath-houses is strongly impregnated with sulphur, having the usual offensive smell of such springs. Its degree of heat may be reckoned at from 15 to 36 degrees of Reaumur in the several basons. At the source of the hot stream it is about 42. The basons are excavated in the solid rock, over whose surface the water had originally flowed; and these are divided, under one immense vaulted roof, into different apartments, whence even the smallest egress of day-light is excluded; and which are merely rescued from total darkness by the faint glimmerings of a few twinkling lamps struggling with the vapours from the stream. The stench of the place, and the disorder and filth which this meagre illumination rendered visible, showed sufficient argument for the whole having been left in shade. I did not see a spot in any one of the apartments, where it was possible for a bather to lay his clothes down without the certainty of taking them up again drenched in wet and dirt. When, however, I considered that these baths are free to the entrance of all who will, and that they crowd, indiscriminately, into every chamber alike, I ceased some of my wonder at so great a dearth of order or cleanliness; though I did not the less mark the inconveniences of their absence, as we journeyed farther through the successive boiling caverns, and felt, at every remove, a more intense heat, a denser atmosphere of steam, and an increased accumulation of all that can disgust the senses of a man used to the retirement and comfort of European baths.

Robert Ker Porter, *Travels in Georgia, Persia, Armenia, Ancient Babylonia* (London 1821)

The Fair at Nizhniy-Novgorod

In 1818 the famous fair which had been held at Makaryev was transferred to the town of Nizhniy-Novgorod on the Volga. Robert Lyall, an English doctor who had lived a number of years in Russia, gives an informed, if rather dry, account of the scene which he encountered on his journey south to the Crimea and the Caucasus.

The bazars at Nizhniy-Novgorod, I believe, form the finest establishment of the kind in the world. The situation on which they stand was raised, as mentioned, ten, fifteen, and even twenty feet; and no less than 56,000 piles were driven into the earth so as to secure a foundation for extensive buildings.

The stone used in the new constructions, is partly the hard tuf of Pechersk, which is blasted by gunpowder; a white limestone from the upper Oka; and, in part, a red sandstone, which is quarried at Novinski, about sixteen versts up the Oka. The bazars are enclosed on three sides by canals, and on the fourth by an inlet of the Oka, into which ladened barges enter. The number of shops enclosed by the canals, and the oblong square formed by the government buildings, amounts to

167 The famous Fair on the sands at Makaryev on the Volga.

nearly 3000. The principal street, which runs between the church and the government buildings, is very spacious and elegant; and all the others are of a good breadth. All the edifices are two stories in height; the lower one being the shop, and the upper serving as a magazine; indeed many of the merchants fit up apartments in them for their temporary residence. Every shop fronts two streets. Nothing can be more simple and chaste than the general style of architecture, which well accords with the utility of the buildings. The Kitayskaya liniya, or Chinese Line, is so called because it is ornamented with pagodas, and other Eastern decorations. It is better known, however, by the name Sibirskaya liniya, or Siberian Line. But it must not be understood that the shops of this line are limited to the sale of Chinese or Siberian merchandise; at least, in 1822, we found all kinds of European manufactures

350

in them, and some of them were even hired by Englishmen. The best shops are in the spacious central street, in the Chinese Line, and at the corners of all the streets. For some of them 1000 and even 1500 rubles are paid; for others 200 to 500 or 1000 rubles, according to circumstances. They are only of use for the season, but are let for the whole year. Now they are all stuccoed, and painted yellow, and their roofs green or red. There are three government buildings, which are plain but handsome edifices, two stories high. The upper story of the central building is occupied as the residence of the governor during the fair, while the inferior story is let as an inn, for a very large sum. In the other two edifices are contained the courts of justice, the post-office, the bank, &c. all *pro tempore*.

Besides the stone edifices, here are 2220 wooden shops, which form a variety of markets on the town-side of the great bazar. They were erected in the year 1818, when the fair was transported from Makaryev. Some said that they were to be destroyed, so as to concentrate all the shops to the *grand bazar*: others reported that they were, on the contrary, to remain, and to be repaired in a more gaudy style.

Merchandise of all kinds, and from all the countries of Europe and Asia, is now transported to Nizhniy-Novgorod, by the Volga, the Oka, the Kama, and the other rivers which fall into them, as well as by land. The quantity of Russian produce disposed of is enormous; and, of course, the fair of this town is a national concern of the highest importance. Hence it deservedly merits the greatest attention of the crown. The individual who has been a frequent visitor of the 'Bargaining Shops,' or bazar, at Petersburg or Moscow, may easily conceive the appearance and the nature of that at Nizhniy-Novgorod, by supposing that the goods and wares of the former, were placed in the more beautiful and regular lines of shops of the latter, and that the same variety of nations crowded them and the streets. Here are seen the representatives of China, India, Tartary, Bucharia, Persia, Circassia, Armenia, Turkey, and Greece; besides Italians, Poles, Germans, French, English, Cossacks, Malo-Russians, and—the universal concomitants of traffic and money—Jews.

For many years past, the sale and exchange of goods at Makaryev, but especially since 1818, at Nizhniy-Novgorod, have amounted to immense sums; and now this fair, with great propriety, may be reckoned one of the most extensive in Europe. In consequence of the influx of merchants, and travellers in general, it is excessively busy; although in 1822, we heard heavy complaints of dull sales. But the markets acquired a new life after our departure, at an extraordinarily late period of the season, many of the Bucharians having been detained.

Among the objects at the bazars which excited our greatest curiosity, was an immense range of ironmongers' shops or stalls, called *balagany*, in which iron in the bar, as well as worked into every kind of instrument and utensil, was to be had. The table hereafter given, shows that the sale of iron, and iron articles alone, amounts to above 10,000,000 rubles. The fur-shops also merit particular notice; and the reader will be astonished at the value of their contents, the enormous sum of 36,000,000 rubles. As I have elsewhere enumerated the chief kinds of this commodity disposed of at Moscow, and as the same kinds are sold here, I shall refer to the work alluded to. The quantity of grey and black frizzled Tartar lamb-skins seen here is astonishing. The shops of the Bucharians are visited by all strangers. Their silk sashes, and gentlemen's silk morning-gowns, are greatly admired; and are sold at 100, 120, 150, and even 200 rubles each. They can be purchased cheaper at Moscow than at Nizhniy-Novgorod. In a line of small shops are displayed immense quantities of pearls, large and small, a great proportion of which, however, are of very inferior quality. Most of them are sold for the decoration of the holy images. Nothing can give a clearer idea of the extent to which image-worship is carried on in Russia, than the estimate of their value 1,300,000 rubles, at the fair of Nizhniy-Novgorod; while, probably, their real value was far above that sum. Artificial stones, beads, ear-rings, and similar ornaments, being low-priced, are seen in profusion. A great display is also made of the china of Russia, which has attained a considerable degree of perfection, both in the quality of the material, in the execution of the painting, and in the manner of gilding, and other decorations, &c. But the Russians fail greatly in giving a perfect regular form to most articles, and it is very difficult to get a set quite alike. One cause of this may be, that in the houses of the Russian nobles, almost every cup and saucer differs from another; while a peculiarly and highly ornamented couple are presented to the landlord and the lady of the house. The same custom is often observed at dinner. A finely cut and gilded wine-bottle, and a decorated tumbler and wine-glass, &c. are placed for the master and mistress of the mansion, far superior in appearance to those of the rest of the family, and (what is surprising) to those of the guests, even when they are of the highest rank – the Imperial family excepted. So it is, that what would be reckoned an insult in some countries is sanctioned by custom in others. The milliners' shops, which were well supplied with every kind of article, seemed to be the centre of fashion here, as at Moscow and Petersburg. The carriage-market contained a number of calashes, brichki, coaches, chaises, &c. of no imposing appearance, and many of them second-hand, but generally at a low price. A number of Kazan *kibitki,* which are famous over Russia, are annually sold here. In the horse-markets and temporary stables we saw a great number of horses, some of which were fine animals, and well deserved the examination of the amateur; but the greatest part were of very common breeds, and of very inferior appearance. Besides the traffic in the shops, much business is also transacted on board the barges in the Oka. Many of these were filled with the finest cured fish of the Don and the Volga. No barrels are employed, the boats being made on purpose to contain fish; and, of course, to retain their brine.

Robert Lyall, *Travels in Russia, the Krimea, the Caucasus and Georgia* (London 1825)

Moscow Markets and Merchants

Robert Lyall fires a whole broadside at the sharp practices and deceits of Russian merchants. Such detailed denunciations of the Russian character, not surprisingly, brought Lyall the wrath of the Russian government.

The Bargaining Shops, or Torgovyye Lavki, are commonly, though improperly, called Gostinnyy-Dvor. They form a great range of buildings on the east side of the Krasnaya ploshchad, and of the street called Moskvoretskaya Ulitsa, and on both sides of the Ilinskaya.

In Moscow, and in all the towns in Russia, the principal shops are all assembled together, as is the case in most kingdoms in the East, and at them may be bought almost every article to be had in the empire, except butcher's meat, fowls, fish, and vegetables, flour, and other provisions of this kind, all of which articles are sold in abundance at the Okhotnyy ryad, which is so near, though in the Belyy-Gorod, that it may be reckoned part of the great general market of Moscow, and is, indeed, the chief provision-market of the city.

Although at the markets in the different quarters of Moscow, you may find butcher's meat, fowls, fish, vegetables, and flour, and articles of coarse ware, tea, sugar, coffee, &c.; and although in some places there be shops, and magazines, where are sold articles of clothing, bed-linen, table drapery, &c.; yet when you wish to have a choice, and to buy a quantity, you go to the Okhotnyy ryad, and to the bargaining shops, it being well known that there you may purchase five or more per cent cheaper than in the smaller markets, or in the magazines.

The other chief place for articles of clothing, especially for ladies' dresses, is the Kuznetskiy Most, or Blacksmith's Bridge, which is, indeed, the furnishing place of the belles of Moscow, and is continually crowded with their equipages.

Different magazines, as the English magazine on the Tverskaya; the English magazine at the Kuznetskiy Most,

168 A street in the Mosk-vorechye district in Moscow, looking towards St Basil's. Water colour 1800–2 by a follower of F. Ye. Alekseyev.

are well-known places of fashion, and for the sale of British goods. The Gollandskaya Lavka, or Dutch shop, and the Nuremburgskiye Lavki, or Nuremberg shops, are celebrated for the sale of different articles.

The principal façade of the bargaining shops, with the two projecting wings bounding the east side of the Krasnaya ploshchad, is very long, and very handsome. Its centre is ornamented with twelve fluted Ionic columns, supporting a triangular pediment, on which are the arms of Moscow, and below them this inscription in Russ:

'Renewed in 1815.'

This façade is two stories high, and before each story runs a piazza with wide arcades, with small columns between them, and under which you may enter the shops, or take a walk.

The façade of the other range of shops in the Moskvoretskaya Ulitsa, presents nothing worthy of notice.

Behind the front buildings, are ranges of shops crowded together, with broad alleys between them; most of these alleys are covered over, and the light is admitted by windows in the roof. The shops have no windows, or rather their whole front

354

is windows; for the large doors when opened, serve in their place. Behind a long bench, or table, the merchant takes his station. The purchaser stands in the alley; he seldom enters the shops, or booths, some of which are of a moderate size, while others are so small that the merchant can scarcely find room to turn himself. The total number of shops here grouped together is said to amount to six thousand. The merchants are almost all Russian.

In these shops, placed in open alleys, with open doors, and no windows, and in the rigorous climate of Moscow, no fire is to be seen, no genial artificial heat is to be felt. Fires are not permitted, on account of the danger, and because, formerly, when a fire took place, the losses were enormous. Even candles are not permitted to be lighted, so that at twilight, in winter, all the shops are shut, and the centre of the city has a very dull appearance. They are shut about eight or nine o'clock in the evening in summer.

The disagreeableness and inconvenience of making bargains in these alleys and shops, even when well clothed, may be well conceived. The merchant, who is accustomed to his station, and who has provided clothes to counteract the cold, finds all the discomforts of these alleys to purchasers, great advantages to him. The shops not being over-lighted, his goods are not so well seen, and appear better than they are in reality; and the cold affecting the purchaser in the alley, often hurries him to the conclusion of a bargain, – no easy matter to arrange, if the merchant perceives that the value of his goods is not well known. The merchants generally live in distant quarters of the city; they come to the shops early in the morning, and remain till dusk, and then return to their homes. Thus in the Krasnaya ploshchad, where during day you might walk on the heads of thousands, in a winter evening often reigns the silence of death, interrupted only by passing equipages and bawling izvozchiki.

These shops are well entitled Bargaining Shops; and certainly the method of bargaining at them is peculiar to Russia: in them most of the retail commerce is carried on. At night, all these shops are locked, and doubly locked; but that is of small avail, they are besides all sealed up, a piece of small cord, or thread, being twined around the padlock, its ends are brought together, and then a kind of soft wax is applied over them, or on the door, on which an impression is made: this is sacred. A Russian will not readily break a seal, which he deems peculiarly entitled to respect, and therefore delinquencies of this kind are rare: to break a lock is of less consequence in his estimation . . .

At or near the bargaining shops, a person can provide himself with every article of clothing; of house furniture, and ornament; of food and drink; every thing that is necessary for the maintenance, comfort, or the luxury of life.

The stranger, in his promenades in the alleys of the bargaining shops, must be astonished at the numerous solicitations he meets with from the merchants and their boys, who are always stationed at the door, to enter their shops; at the continual cry 'Chto vam ugodno?'–'What do you wish to have?' These boys are like hawks, watching their prey; they observe all your movements in other shops, and if you quit them, will abuse the goods you have seen, and tell you they have much better articles, though they know them to be inferior; and use all the means in the world to seduce you, as it were, only to enter their master's shop. The greater volubility of tongue, address and cunning the boy has, in managing this affair, the more he is esteemed, and the more wages he will obtain.

These shops, as I have said, are well named Torgovyye Lavki, or Bargaining Shops; not only on account of the immense number of bargains daily made in them, but because not an article is bought without a great deal of discussion, and a peculiar mode of bargaining and transacting business, which I believe is peculiar to Russia . . .

169 Two tradesmen. From *La Russie, ou Moeurs, Usages et Costumes des habitants . . . de cet Empire,* M. Breton, Paris 1813.

The Russians themselves well know, and speak of the *roguery* of the merchants, contractors, and even workmen; for they are continually suffering by it, or must for ever be on the wing, watching, examining, and scolding; and after all, they often find themselves duped.

Contrary to the practice of other nations, the Russian merchants never expose to view their best articles, unless it be on the surface, to deceive. On the contrary, they expose only secondary commodities, and often the worst they have. They never shew you their best articles at first, although you ask them. You demand, for instance, a sight of the best hat;– the merchant shews you one, if you are content it is all well; if not, he shews you another; if that does not please, he brings out a third; every time proclaiming, before God, that it is his very best: you are still discontented, he produces a fourth, and a better hat, and with greater emphasis pronounces Yey Bogu, and boasts you will not find such a hat in any place in Moscow; declares that it is his best, and *that it is only* TO YOU that he would shew it. In bargaining with these merchants, we are almost forced to suppose that our physiognomy pleases them remarkably; that they have conceived something very favourably of us, and wish to oblige us. We are told it is only *to you,* and because he so esteems us, that he would sell his goods at the price; although we never saw the man before, and although he be as ignorant of us as we of him. This is so flattering to human nature, that very self-complacency pre-disposes us to be cheated; but no sooner have we concluded a bargain, than a servant or a peasant comes up; the same language and warm expressions are repeated to them, and to all who present themselves. The purse, and not the person is the

356

attraction.

A stranger, if he have some acquaintance with the Russian merchandising, is now at a stand, and comes to a bargain with the fifth hat. But one who is a little better acquainted, becomes angry, asks if the merchant takes you to be a fool, and departs, assured of being called back. The moment a Russian perceives that you know the articles and their value, and that you are going to another shop, he generally, though not always, brings forward his best commodities, but not till he is dragged to this step. This mode of acting holds with respect to all articles of clothing and provision, and indeed it is the general system to deceive in the quality, so far as I have seen or heard, throughout Russia. The reason of all this manœuvring is simple. In other countries the merchant justly demands a profit, regulated by the value of the article he sells; i.e. so much per cent., per shilling, or per pound: a Russian has no such calculation. On the contrary, he demands 3, 4, 5, 6, 7, 8, 10, 12 prices for his commodities; and his rule is to take as much as he can obtain; and he will tell you that your rule is to buy as cheap as you can. By this mode of acting he has often as much profit on a low-priced, as on a high-priced article; nay, frequently receives the price of the latter for the former.

170 Fish seller. Drawing by Le Prince.

The Russian cheats you in the price. He asks, for instance, for a shawl 500 rubles, and you buy it for 100 rubles, after he has descended to 450, 400, 350, 300, 250, 200; each time swearing that he gave more for it: you are departing, and offer a hundred, which he accepts, and probably you are duped. He then repeats that it is for you only he would give it at the price, and says he is sustaining a loss by the sale, although you may purchase the whole number of shawls in his shop for the same money, and if he should run short, he will find a supply from his neighbour.

Even after a number of years' residence in Russia, when a merchant demands of me 100 rubles for an article, with protestations that it is only *for me* at that price; that it is his *own price*; and crosses himself before the holy images, I feel reluctant to offer him 20 or 25 rubles, which is probably beyond its real value.

It is curious to see an adept in bargaining with Russians, or rather a Russian opposed to a Russian; after shewing and examining the article wanted, the combat thus begins: as the disposer always extravagantly praises his commodities, so the intending purchaser depreciates them in the same degree; though he may have found the very articles he wants, and though the quality be good, he says they are coarse, impure, mixed, or more commonly that they are *dryan,* i.e. dirt; on purpose to have a pretence for beating down their value, and offering a low price.

A Russian merchant always endeavours to obtain an offer: it is part of his system; it is often to his profit. You see his

357

commodities, and demand their price. He tells you. You are sure it is out of all character, and refuse. He then asks how much you will give. A stranger offers the third part, or fourth part, say 50 roubles; by far too much; but the Russian affects to refuse: you are departing, and he accepts. He then wishes to dupe you more, or to make you think you have made a good bargain: in fact, every part is practised to draw you into the snare. One who knows well the Russian character, hears of his friend's bargain, and undertakes, for the sake of amusement, to buy the same article for 25 rubles, and he has no difficulty in concluding his bargain with the same merchant. A stranger should buy nothing himself, unless he know the quality of the article, and its value.

There is another extraordinary feature in bargaining, which has often astonished me. After the usual manœuvres you buy a pair of common boots, for which 40 rubles had been asked, for 15 rubles; say on Thursday. You observe the shelf from which they were taken from among many other pairs of which you have had your choice; in the meantime the seller declaring that they are the *samyye luchshiye,* the very best in his shop. You return on Friday, and pick out another pair from the same shelves, and offer him 15 roubles. He refuses, and you must bargain again. He descends by 5 roubles at a time; he comes to 25 roubles; he assures you that they are better than the boots you bought yesterday; you assure yourself that they are every way the same, and remind him of his declaration, that those you bought yesterday were his very best. He laughs, and now tells you that he only said so to please you; displays the boots, and bids you look how superior is the leather, and the workmanship, and the tassels to *yesterday's,* all the time knowing them to be the very same; if he convinces you, so much the better for him: if not, you are displeased; you leave the shop; he calls you back: if you return, or even face to him, he will take 20, 18, 17, 16, 15 rubles; if you never regard him, but continue marching off, or going to another shop, he jumps from 25 to 15 rubles at once, and Izvolte, Izvolte, resounds in your ears. You return on Saturday, choose another pair; he again demands 40 rubles; and the same comedy is acted over again, as on Thursday or yesterday, which also finishes in the same manner.

For a Russian to jump by 50 rubles at a time, or by 25, 20, or 10 rubles, on articles amounting in real value to 100, 200, or 300 rubles, is nothing. He descends by hundreds on higher priced articles. But his comparative profit may be said to lessen as the real value of the articles advances: thus a merchant may obtain 30 or 40 rubles for a commodity which should only cost 10 or 20 rubles; or 100 rubles for what should only cost 30 or 40 rubles; because these are small sums, and such bargains are often made without due consideration. When the article amounts to a few hundred rubles, or when it comes to

171 Game seller. Drawing by Le Prince.

thousands, the bargain is then important, and being made with deliberation, and the value being ascertained, the merchant's profit runs less chance of being exorbitant. If the Russian fail, however, in cheating you in the price, he will try what is to be done in the quality and quantity: his roguery is not easily exhausted.

I have often heard it said, and there is little reason to doubt it, that false weights and measures are employed: as the same happens every where, it is not to be expected that a Russian will omit this part of his art. That the merchant will endeavour to satisfy you with unfilled measures I well know, as also that the Russian balance is generally suspended with the article-scale hung up, when not in use; or with a weight in the weight-scale; the weight-scale is always two, three, or more inches higher than the other, and leans upon a square piece of wood, or a box; so that allowing the balance to be just, it is always standing with the index at the equilibrium. You demand a pound of confectionary; it is put into the paper; it is let fall into the scale, which descends; the paper is most adroitly seized before the scale has time to rise or show whether it weighs a pound: if you insist upon its remaining, or being replaced, you almost invariably find it defective in weight. The merchant says it is nothing; adds a few more sweets, each time letting them fall with some force, and perhaps succeeds after all, to a certain degree, in his project. Beyond the equilibrium, a Russian says you have no right to claim, and his balance, when at rest, is always at this point. Should you dispute with him, and the index be on the commodity-side, he will take out to the last grain of tea.

172 A cooper. From J. A. Atkinson and J. Walker, *A Picturesque Representation of the Manners, Customs and Amusements of the Russians,* 1812.

The *Bezmen* is a kind of balance with a heavy end, and marks all along it, indicative of the pounds, when acting as a lever at different fulcrums, and is much used in Russia. Indeed it is nearly the steel-yard, except that the weight is reckoned by the length or shortness of the lever, and not by hanging weights. The *bezmen* may be false: if just, the merchant will only succeed in adding a quarter or half a pound to the weight by the mode of suspending the wire or string on which the beam moves, which being held in one hand, while the other hand adjusts the article in the scale or on the hook, he is prevented from giving any force to assist the descent. Almost every family provides itself with a just *bezmen,* and when they purchase articles from the hawkers, employ it in weighing them, and thus prevent much imposition. Most families also have an iron arshin-measure, for the same reasons.

You examine tea in the box, which you find good at the surface, and purchase; and on opening the parcel you find that it is mixed, or even sometimes adulterated with dried tea-leaves, which the servant maids dry after having been used at their master's table, roll up, and dispose of to the dealers for a trifle. If you buy a quantity of sugar, it is necessary to examine every loaf, or the merchant will, most probably, succeed in imposing a few loaves of inferior quality to the sample. You see fine prunes, raisins, figs, nuts, &c.: you purchase; he avoids giving those on the surface, and when you return home, you find that you have been duped. In winter, you buy *Chukhonskoye,* or butter made up in little wooden tubs, which is very hard and looks well, at forty or fifty kopeks per pound. In a warm room one-third of it melts into water. The manner of effecting this is by mixing plenty of water with the butter, while soft, and then exposing the whole to the cold, by which all is frozen into a mass. You often find good butter on the surface, while it is bad below; and in large barrels sometimes a heavy stone or two are introduced.

Good down and feathers are mixed beneath the surface with coarse feathers, stems, pieces of wood, nails, grains, powdered chalk, &c. If you buy a featherbed at the market, that is to say, the feathers in the tick, you are shamefully deceived; one-third of the weight is foreign materials, although the merchant has shewn you a few fine feathers as if taken by chance from the corner, the only such which exist in the bed. You buy a web of Holstein, a kind of coarse linen; of towelling; or of table napery, which has a fine appearance at the end shewn you; when it is cut up or examined, you discover that, except a few arshins, the quality of the interior is vastly inferior to what you saw, and are astonished, when it is too late. The same deceit is practised with Russian cloth, and stuffs of all kinds; with ribbons, tape, &c. Old furs are cleaned and sold for new, and new furs are dyed or coloured, so as to appear much darker than they are naturally, or indeed sometimes brown furs are made to appear black.

Wines are adulterated and counterfeited beyond all measure. An anecdote which I have often heard at Moscow, gives a just idea of this traffic. A gentleman wishing to call at a wine cellar, in order to make a purchase, met the young son of the proprietor opposite the door, and demanded if his father was at home. 'Yes, Sir,' he replied, *'he is down stairs making Don wine:'* a kind of wine, red and white, made on the banks of the Don, extremely brisk, like champagne, which, when of a fine quality, it a good deal resembles, and is sold at Moscow at 2, 2½, and 3 rubles a bottle. Wine is generally sold by the merchants in small bottles, and even when they appear large, it is only a deception, for the indentation or hollow in their bottom is so enormous, that one can almost thrust a fist into it. Rum, brandy, gin, &c. are all mixed and compounded; so that it is rare to taste them genuine, except at an enormous price. All kinds of mixed goods and damaged commodities are imposed on you. Counterfeited, or mixed gold and silver articles, ear-rings, rings, breast pins, brooches, false stones, are sold for genuine; wax and tallow candles are often sold by by the number, so many a pound, or a pood, which are defective

173 'Two Russian Boors who have just quitted a Kabak or Tippling House.' From Robert Lyall, *The Character of the Russians,* London 1823.

in weight.

To conclude, as we have seen, the Russian merchants, shop-keepers, and dealers, cheat in the quantity, the quality, and the price. If they miss their aim in the quantity, they succeed in the quality; and if they fail in both, it will be ten to one that they are successful in the price. The wary even are cheated in one or two of these ways, and the stranger is often duped by stratagem in all the three.

It is related of Peter the Great, that when demanded why he would not permit the Jews to come into Russia, that he jocularly replied, 'Because I am afraid my subjects will cheat them.'

174 The Kremlin from above the Stone Bridge. From Robert Lyall, *The Character of the Russians,* London 1823.

If you detect a Russian merchant openly cheating you, he does not blush, or show any mark of shame, – of shame he is not conscious in such affairs, he laughs and confesses it; or says he did not intend it, it was a mistake; or oftener, he avows it openly, and says it is my business to sell my articles as high as I can, it is yours to buy them as cheap as you can. The bargaining shops, commonly called the Gostinnyy Dvor, are the scene of the refinement of deception and roguery. A set of sharpers, whose very countenances are indicative of their pro-fession, assemble there every day, and with their flattery, lies, oaths, and villainy, deceive the public to an enormous extent, while they fill their own pockets. They seem to forget the saying of our Lord, 'With what measure ye mete, it shall be measured to you.' Indeed, the view is most painful to a mind imbued either with moral or religious principles. But the Russian modes of villainy, though general, are not singular in the world. Of this I am well convinced, by some experience in London among the lower merchants, and still more so by the accounts of the police of that metropolis, by Mr Colquhoun. There is one mighty difference, however, between Russia and other nations in this respect; for in Russia, it may be laid down as a fact, that the merchants, with a few exceptions, all act upon the nefarious system which we have endeavoured to develop: they are trained up to it from their very youth, and the expertness of boys of eight and ten years of age in the arts of his master is wonderful, is incredible; they are children in almost every thing, but men in deception: and even the peasant, who knows little beyond his field, his yard, his horse, and his *telega,* is a perfect knave when he comes to market; whereas, in other countries, it is principally among the lower and the lowest classes of merchants, and dealers, that the refinement of roguery exists. In Russia, it may be among all classes of merchants that dishonesty is the prominent feature.

Robert Lyall, *The Character of the Russians and a Detailed History of Moscow* (London 1823)

Down the Volga to Kazan *and* At the Sino-Russian Frontier

The following two extracts are taken from the account of a remarkable journey performed almost entirely on foot in the years 1820 and 1821 by a captain in the British navy, John Dundas Cochrane.

I AM now on the magnificent Volga. The lighter on board which I had embarked did not depart for thirty-six hours, and I felt too much of the sailor in me to quit her: in short, I considered myself as one of the crew, working my passage, and as such employed myself. Nothing was demanded of me but to row the boat ashore for the captain, and now and then a glass of vodka. This I was content to submit to, till I found that some grog and more tobacco, was followed by the demand of still more grog, which my purse could very ill bear. I was therefore very well pleased when the anchor was weighed, and we descended the stream; but so slow was our progress, that we kept the heights of Novgorod in sight for two days, being frequently obliged to anchor, with the ever-dunning sound of 'Vodka, Batyushka,' or gin, master. The vessel I was in measured about two hundred and fifty tons, perfectly flat-bottomed, and drawing but five feet water. At length, losing sight of Nizhniy Novgorod, we passed many islands and villages, the latter always on the right bank, and on the left an uninterrupted low moorish heath. The strength of the current I calculated at two knots and a half.

The variety and singular appearance of the different craft on the Volga, not a little surprised and amused me, as well as

the innumerable different ways in which they were propelled. The present season of the year, that immediately preceding the fair, is the best for the navigation of the Volga, when barks from one thousand tons to the size of a canoe, all promiscuously float together. They are generally provided with one mast, which, in the largest, may equal a frigate's main-mast. The weight of the mat-sail must be prodigious, having no fewer than a hundred and sixty breadths in it; and yet the facility with which it is managed will bear comparison with that of the Yankies, with their boom main-sail in the fore and aft clippers. They are generally worked by from fifteen to forty people. The rudder is a ponderous machine, in many cases suspended from the stern post, and yet towing astern twelve and fifteen feet; the tillers of which I have ascertained from measurement to be from thirty to forty feet long, and all worked by the hand.

The soil on either side is clay and chalk, and the wood fir and birch. The inhabitants of the villages are the inoffensive and ignorant Fins, a race of people more approximating to the character of the Gallegos in Lisbon, than any other class of people I have seen. Their great content, and small possessions, are in both a prominent feature. We reached Makaryev, after a tedious and vexatious voyage, vexatious from the annoyance of the horse-flies and mosquitoes. I was fairly put to the

175 A view of the city of Tver (renamed Kalinin in 1931) founded at the end of the eleventh century on the left bank of the Volga where it joins the Tvertsa.

alternative, whether, during my sleep, I would be suffocated or devoured. I preferred the former, as smacking more of humanity, wrapping myself up close in a spare sail, with three others of the crew.

Makaryev is the first inhabited spot, from Nizhniy Novgorod, on the left bank of the Volga; a straggling, and ill-built place, although a large monastery, at one extremity, appears to strive hard to acquire for it an appearance of respectability. The great fair, which is now held at Nizhniy Novgorod, was formerly held here; but was removed on the destruction of its site by fire, wilfully, as is supposed. Many vessels, loaded with tallow, hides, and iron, were then lying off it wind-bound, rather than work up between the numerous islands, shoals, and sand-banks, between this place and Novgorod. I remarked, with pleasure, the knowledge these otherwise ignorant fellows have of the power of the rudder, performing all the close shades, like a fleet of colliers in the Thames.

176 A barge carrying charcoal to the iron works in the region of the Urals. From J. A. Atkinson and J. Walker, *A Picturesque Representation of the Manners, Customs and Amusements of the Russians,* 1812.

At Makaryev I noticed the utmost height to which the Volga had risen last season–being eighteen feet perpendicular height, at one hundred and fifty feet distance from the nearest edge of the river, which is still going down. Having remained at anchor two days, and paid toll at a place called Vasilsursk which is a sort of sound, where loaded vessels pay one and a half, and those in ballast one ruble–(no slight sinecure)–we departed with a fresh and favourable gale, passing fleets of vessels, at anchor and under sail. If the trade of the place were to be computed from the number of vessels, without respect to their value, the Volga would indeed be a second Thames.

We soon reached Kozmodemyansk, a large and populous town, on the right bank of the river, with four neat churches, pleasantly situated at the base and extremity of that chain of lofty hills, which rise in succession from Nizhniy Novgorod, and here abruptly terminate. The left bank of the river still preserved its desolate and unhealthy appearance. The next halting-place was Cheboksary, where the river is very shallow, and encumbered with shifting banks; and here we were again detained by foul winds, as well as the negligence or laziness of the crew, till I began to feel tired of my aquatic excursion, the river offering so very little worthy of notice. I would fain have pursued my route by land, but was prevented by my bag of copper money, which, although its value was not a guinea, was, at least, sixty pounds weight. Leaving it was, of course, totally out of the question: I had, therefore, no remedy but patience.

At Cheboksary I again laid in a stock of provisions, conformably to agreement. It consisted of barley, rye, flour, with oil, and black bread. I had hitherto messed with the crew, whose diet was wholesome, although rather new to me, con-

364

sisting of the above flour, boiled, and stewed down with water and oil. He who likes burgoo, must relish *kasha*; and it was with extreme pleasure that I received the spoon into my hand, in my proper turn, to partake of this humble fare. This we did three times a day, and I had the happy consciousness of its perfect cleanliness, as I myself stood cook. Provisions, in general, may be here considered cheap; bread, a halfpenny per pound; beer, a halfpenny per bottle; eggs, three pence

177 The interior of a Tartar mosque in Kazan. From J. D. Cochrane, *Narrative of a Pedestrian Journey*, London 1824.

per dozen; and milk, a farthing per bottle. Animal food I know nothing about, not having bought any.

Passed the village of Vuchi, placed between two elevated table-hills. A monastery, with four churches, flanked with a thick forest of ever-greens, gave it a pleasing appearance. A boat came alongside from the monastery, with a poor-box, into which I put two pence, no small sum in this part of the world. Upon reaching the little hamlet of Kushuga, our crew quitted us, with bag and baggage, two long-bearded gentlemen taking charge of the craft to Kazan; a trifling incident, but which powerfully reminded me of the necessity of impressment. We were now anxiously looking out for Kazan, and the distant countries became more elevated, and well-wooded with lofty oaks. Sivyatski, with its remnant of an old stone castle, was the last interesting spot I observed, before I reached Kazan. The left bank of the river, except at the single town of Makaryev, is one universal waste. From the Volga to the city, is about three miles of a low flat; and this I walked on Tuesday the 22d of June, and the 12th day from Novgorod, being about the same time that I should have taken in going by land.

This celebrated city, on nearing it from the westward, greatly resembles Badajos on its approach from Elvas. The extended view, the river in front, the fortress on the left, and the distant elevated lands to the southward. The dirty suburbs, situate on a marshy swamp, the principal residence of the

365

Tartar inhabitants, is the next indication of Kazan; the last was after crossing the Kazanka, when the noblest part of this noble city fronts you in full view. I passed on to the hospitable abode of the learned professor Fuchs.

The extensive province of Kazan is watered by the noble Volga and beautiful Kama. Its population is reckoned at nine hundred thousand, composed of Tartars, Fins, Votyaki, Chuvash, and Russians, and a few Mordvas. Near five hundred

178 A view of the city of Kazan across the Volga. Drawing by Lespinasse (1767).

thousand of these inhabitants are peasants or slaves, four-fifths of whom belong to the crown, and the rest to the different nobility of Kazan. The trade of the province is said to be great, exporting vast quantities of tanned and untanned leather, besides about two hundred and fifty thousand poods [36 lbs English] of soap, made from the fat of the Astrakhan seals. Potash is also a thriving concern. The gold and silver embroidery of boots, shoes, slippers, bonnets, &c. employs a great number of people. The province is low and wet, and to its acknowledged unhealthiness the impurity of the water greatly contributes. The greatest heat is 29°, and the greatest cold 33° of Reaumur's scale. The Volga is navigable about two hundred days in the year. The province is in general well cultivated, and exports prodigious quantities of corn to the capitals. The revenue is estimated at sixteen millions of rubles [or about 700,000l, a ruble being 10d. of our money]; and of these, spirits alone furnish four millions, the consumption of which, in the city only, on a feast day, is said to amount to the value of five thousand rubles, and on ordinary days to about fifteen hundred.

The city of Kazan is considered as second only to the capitals, containing nearly forty thousand inhabitants, of which twelve thousand are Tartars. On the present state of the city, it is hardly fair to give an opinion, rising as it is from the ashes of a fire scarcely five years extinguished. It had formerly a cathedral on the site of the ancient mosque, as also a palace; both were destroyed by an explosion in the citadel. The

366

destruction of the city was indeed nearly complete, and it is difficult to conceive how any vestige could remain, a high wind driving a mass of flame over houses built, and streets absolutely paved, with wood. These wooden buildings and pavements have been discountenanced by the Emperor, who has held out many inducements to build with brick. The city is archiepiscopal, and the seat of an university. It has several handsome churches, four of which belong to the Raskolniki,

179 Verkhoturye on the Siberian side of the Urals was founded in 1598 on the River Tusa.

180 Yekaterinburg, now called Sverdlovsk, was founded in 1723 on the river Iset and soon became the principal metal-working town in the Urals.

besides many Tartar mosques, and some convents. The church of St Peter and St Paul is a handsome stone edifice, erected at the expense of a private gentleman in honour of Peter the Great, in consideration of that monarch's having made his residence a halting-place during one of his journeys. In Kazan also is a church, which gave rise to that beautiful building, the Kazan church, at Saint Petersburg, though its architecture would seem to denote a theatre. I dined with her eminence the abbess, for so she is styled. She had the benevolence to present me with an image of their saint, which was to act as a charm against otherwise inevitable mischief. I accepted it, of course, with due reverence, without any strong faith in its boasted virtues,—an estimate, which it will be seen by experience was fully vindicated. The lady, the original of this image, lives twelve miles from Kazan, to which, however, she makes an annual visit, and collects, from the bounty of her believers, sufficient to support her the ensuing year.

At the Sino-Russian Frontier

Having procured a guide, I left Bukhtarminsk for the line of demarcation on the Chinese and Russian frontiers. I first crossed the stream which gives name to the fortress, and then over a good path, entered upon a most romantic country, near the village of Voronye. It is impossible, without a poetical imagination, to conceive the beauties of such a country; the magnificent and bold sterile precipices which are seen rising from the great level pasture base, are, I should think, quite unparalleled; and the noble Irtysh forcing its way amongst the numerous islands near this part of the river, adds to the majesty of the scene. At the village, among other similar luxuries, I was treated with wild currants, melons, cassia, 'milk, and honey.' Surely this is the natural place for the habitation of man. The banks of the river are indented with numerous well formed artificial caves, used as ice-cellars. Fifteen miles farther I reached the picturesque village of Cheremshanka, remarkable as a great breeding place for cattle; thence along the banks of the Irtysh, on a good path, over a well cultivated corn country, I passed Krasnoyarskiy, and at eight in the evening reached Makariya, on the banks of the Narym, a small stream uniting with the Irtysh, in an abundant and fertile valley.

The night was so beautiful, the moon just ascending above the hills, that in spite of a good supper, which was ready and inviting my attack, I resumed my journey on horseback, in company with the landlord, to Malaya-Narymka, the last Russian spot on the frontier. An officer and a few men placed here, are all that are left to mark the boundaries of two such mighty empires as Russia and China. I forded the little stream which forms the actual limit, and seating myself on a stone on the left bank, was soon lost in a reverie. It was about midnight; the moon, apparently full, was near her meridian, and seemed to encourage a pensive inclination. What can surpass that scene I know not. Some of the loftiest granite mountains spreading in various directions, enclosing some of the most luxuriant valleys in the world; yet all deserted!—all this fair and fertile tract abandoned to wild beasts, merely to constitute a neutral territory!

To the first Chinese settlement it is eighty miles, I would fain have visited it, but durst not without previous notice, and for this ceremony could ill spare the time. Formerly their advanced post was where I am writing this account, and I felt something like pleasure to find myself within the *celestial* empire. Their guard was, it seems, removed by the Court of Pekin, from jealousy of her subjects holding any converse with foreigners. The commanding officer is a banished mandarin, who is compelled to live like the soldiers, being denied both money and assistance from his friends; but as the post is generally occupied by a person who has been condemned to death for some great crime, he is fain to accept his pardon on condition of serving ten years as chief of the guard. They have, I was informed, a neat village, with abundance of meat and vegetables, besides wild fruits.

At peep of dawn I re-crossed the Narym, and getting a canoe floated down to my deserted supper at Makariya, which the hostess had been desired by my companion to keep hot. I reached it at four in the morning, having been carried along by the stream with dangerous velocity. After some refreshment, I again entered the canoe, receiving a brick of tea, and a pound of tobacco from my obliging host. He is a voluntary settler, with twenty men under his command, who are all accumulating property. The velocity of the Irtyish soon carried me past Krasnoyarskiy, and I reached Bukhtarminsk at three in the morning of the following day, if possible still more delighted with the prospect; the ever-changing variety of the banks is as rich as the beauty of the inland scenery. The left bank consists generally of bold and lofty precipices crowned with wood, while the right presents a low, but beautiful plain, studded with rocky hills, and abounding in corn and hay.

The re-crossing of the Bukhtarma was certainly a hazardous adventure. The passage is hardly ever attempted but in the day time, as there are many shifting sand-banks, and a tremendous cross current, or rapid, to avoid. This is occasioned by four currents meeting at the same point of the Irtysh, near to the fortress; and so rapid is the collected stream that nothing but poling the canoe can cross it; and if once the boat be brought within the vortex of the centre, nothing can save it from being swamped.

It was with great difficulty that I prevailed on any of the Cossacks, who, at the best, are but indifferent boatmen, to take me across. After great toil and risk we reached in safety:– the fault was clearly mine had any accident occurred, but I was too impatient at the moment either to weigh the matter or to listen to remonstrance.

Arriving early, I roused up my old friend the collector of the customs, with whom I breakfasted and dined. The place is considered unhealthy, owing to the foulness of the water of the Bukhtarma; a mischief one would think easily remedied by the proximity of the Irtysh, which is only about two miles distant; but here Russian indolence supersedes most conveniences. I was informed that reindeer abound in the mountains, which also contain some sheep. The horns of the former are considered valuable, fetching two and three guineas a pair: when very young, the Chinese purchase them, and extract a favourite medicine; the younger the animal who has shed the horns, the greater the value. All sorts of diet were too cheap to be named, enough to hold out reasonable inducements to emigrate thither.

After dinner I embarked for Ustkamenogorsk, upon the Bukhtarma, descending which I rapidly entered the Irtysh, a noble river. The crew of the boat offered up thanks for their safe arrival: we had come through a close and mountainous bluff valley, and certainly there was something terrific in the passage. I need not observe that I was myself thankful, as really the mixing with military sailors was far from pleasant. At midnight when we reached fifty miles, several fishing-boats joined company; we left them, however, with courier haste, and I reached the fortress at six in the morning, having been about ten hours descending a distance of ninety miles. The scenery from Narym to Bukhtarminsk and Ustkameno-gorsk, a distance of one hundred and sixty miles, is upon the whole truly beautiful, though not a habitation is to be seen along the banks, which are lofty eminences, divided by tremendous and perpendicular ravines; there are, however, many delightful and romantic situations, but no means of holding a communication along the banks of the river, except by boats. Wild fowl and fish are in the utmost abundance, as observed before when speaking of Tobolsk.

Of the value of the Irtysh I need say nothing, it speaks for itself. Holding an almost uninterrupted communication from the frontiers of China to the frozen sea, a steam-boat might go from Bukhtarminsk to Tobolsk in a few days, and return in twice the time. Wood for fire is plentiful, and many establishments might be formed for the preparing and felling of it; while a water communication is ready formed with the Caspian, Baltic, and White Seas, and thence down even to Tobolsk. The soil, which is a black mould, is exceedingly rich. It is to the banks of the Bukhtarma that colonies of Scotch should be sent, and indeed such was the intention of the Emperor Paul, but it was set aside upon the breaking out of a war, and has not since been resumed, though there is no doubt that, at this moment, such settlers would be both protected and encouraged. No part of the world can offer greater or more certain advantages to the agriculturist, than the right bank of the Irtysh; nor rent, nor tax, nor war, will for ages disturb such a speculator . . .

In the early part of the evening I again embarked on the Irtysh for Ubinsk, the distance being eighty miles, – yet I arrived there early in the morning. The view of the country is various, the prospect more pleasant and open than higher up, and some prettily scattered hills on the plain, which attended me for thirty·miles, when the banks of the river became low and flat, and except some hills, very distant to the west, every thing reminded me that I had again entered upon the steppe desert.

John Dundas Cochrane, *Narrative of a Pedestrian Journey through Russia and Siberian Tartary, from the Frontiers of China to the Frozen Sea and Kamtchatka* (London 1824)

The Petersburg Flood of 1824

At the time Robert Lee was journeying from London to Odessa to take up an appointment as personal physician to Count Vorontsov, there occurred in St Petersburg that great inundation which is best remembered from the description in Pushkin's epic poem, *The Bronze Horseman.* The account in Lee's work came from an English eye-witness of the tragedy and is much more evocative than that in another English contemporary source, John Venning's *Memorials.*

A frightful and disastrous inundation also took place at this time at St. Petersburg, of which the following description has been furnished me by a medical friend, then residing at St. Petersburg:

181 The Palace of Pavlovsk, designed by Charles Cameron.

'The autumnal equinoctial gales most generally prevail at St. Petersburg from the south-west, by which the waters of the Gulf of Finland and Neva are much increased. So it was in 1824; and for some weeks the wind continued from nearly the same quarter. The night of the 18th of November was very stormy; and at daylight of the 19th it blew a hurricane from WSW, by which the stream of the river—the upper part at least—was reversed, and the waters, running higher than ever remembered, soon caused the lower parts of the city and neighbourhood of the embouchure to be inundated. At nine o'clock in the morning I attempted to cross the Voskresenkiy Bridge of boats, on my way to the General Naval Hospital, on the Vyborg side, but was unable owing to the great elevation. I then paid some professional visits; and at eleven called on Prince Naryshkin, who had already given orders to remove the furniture from his lower apartments, the water then being above the level of the Fontanka Canal, opposite to his residence. From this time the rise was rapid; and at half-past eleven, when I returned to my house, in the Great Millionaya, the water was gushing upwards through the gratings of the sewers, filling the streets and court-yards with which every house is provided. A servant took me on his back from the drozhki, my horses at that time being above their knees, and conveyed me to the landing of the staircase. The wind now blew in awful gusts; and the noise of the tempest with the cries of the people in the streets was terrific. It was not long ere boats were seen in the streets, with vast quantities of fire-wood and other articles floating about. As there was an ascent to my coach-house and stables, the water there attained but to four feet in depth; in most, however, it was necessary to get both horses and cows up to the landing-places of the stairs in order to save them, though the loss of animals was great. Now and then a horse was seen swimming across from one pavement to another, the deepest part of the streets of St. Petersburg being in the centre. The number of rats drowned on this occasion was inconceivable; and of dogs and cats not a few. The crisis seemed to be from one to three in the afternoon, at which hour the wind having veered round a couple of points to the northward, the waters began to abate; and by four o'clock the tops of the iron-posts, three feet in height, by the sides of the pavement, made their appearance. The reflux of the water was tremendous, causing much damage, and carrying off fire-wood, boards, lumber, and all sorts of rubbish, with various articles of furniture. From the commencement of the inundation the report of the signal cannon, fired first at the Galleyhaven, at the entrance of the river, then at the Admiralty dockyard, and lastly at the fortress, was continued at intervals as a warning to the inhabitants, and added not a little to the horror of the scene. At five o'clock persons were seen on the pavements carrying lanterns, and the rattling of equipages was heard an hour afterwards. The depth of water in the different parts of the city varied from four to nine and ten feet; but along the border of the Gulf of Finland, and especially in the low suburb of the Galleyhaven before alluded to, the depth was from fourteen to eighteen feet, and many of the small wooden houses built on piles were carried away, inmates and all. A few were floated up the Neva, rocking about with poor creatures clinging on the roof. Some of these perished; others were taken off, at a great risk, by boats from the Admiralty yard, which had been ordered out by the express command of His Imperial Majesty, who stood during the greatest part of the day on the balcony of the Winter Palace, giving the necessary orders. The government ironworks, near the shore of the gulf, and two miles distant, were almost annihilated, and the loss of life was great. This establishment was afterwards removed to the left and elevated bank of the Neva, five versts above the city. Vessels of various kinds, boats, timber, &c. floated over the parapets of the quays on the banks of the Neva and canals, into the streets and squares, and were for the most part afterwards broken up for fuel. As the lower part of most houses in St. Petersburg is occupied by shopkeepers and artizans of various descriptions, so these unfortunate people sustained much loss, and until their dwellings were considered to be sufficiently dried by means of stoves, found refuge and maintenance with their neighbours in the upper apartments. A German shoemaker with his family lived below me, and in this way became my guests for the space of eight days. The wind continued providentially to get round to the north during the night of the 19th, and a smart frost taking place on the following morning, rendered the roads and streets extremely slippery, but doing much good by the dryness it produced. On the 20th, the Emperor Alexander, ever benevolent and humane, visited those parts of the city and suburbs most afflicted by this catastrophe; and in person bestowed alms and consolation to the sufferers, for the most part of the lower classes, and in every way afforded such relief, both then and afterwards, as won for him the still greater love and admiration of his people and of the foreign residents in St. Petersburg. To assist the Emperor's benevolent views, a subscription was entered into, and the British residents came forward, as usual, with their wonted liberality. As nothing official was published as to the actual loss of lives on this melancholy occasion, it is impossible to state otherwise than by report. The authorities were shy on this subject; but from what information I could obtain, twelve or fifteen hundred persons must have perished. Owing to the damp and unwholesome state of the lower parts of the houses and cellars, the mortality during the subsequent winter was nearly doubled, from typhus chiefly, as also from affections of the lungs; and many dated

373

their rheumatic pains and various other maladies to the sufferings they then underwent.'

The effects of this calamity were still visible more than a year after, when I visited St. Petersburg, subsequent to the death of the Emperor Alexander. The red painted lines on the houses still remained to mark the height to which the waters had risen. In the inundation of 1752, the waters of the Neva rose eleven feet; and in that of 1777, the most extensive and destructive that had ever before occurred, they rose fourteen feet above the ordinary level of the river.

Robert Lee, *The Last Days of Alexander, and the First Days of Nicholas* (London 1854)

The Death of Alexander and the Decembrist Uprising

The death of Alexander at Taganrog on 19 November 1825 was followed by a period of uncertainty as to his successor. Oaths of allegiance were taken to the Grand Duke Constantine, who refused to accept the throne, which went to his younger brother, Nicholas. On 14 December there took place an abortive rebellion led by a group of young officers and aristocrats. The events of this time are vividly caught in the letters of Mrs Disbrowe, the wife of Edward, later Sir Edward, Disbrowe, who had been appointed British Minister Plenipotentiary to the Court at St Petersburg early in 1825 during the absence of the Ambassador.

St. Petersburg, 2/14 Dec, 1825

'Do not set me down as affected, dear folks, if I write in a melancholy mood. It is impossible to be otherwise in the midst of the general gloom that now prevails amongst these people.

Never was a monarch so mourned; but it is not as their Emperor that they deplore him, it is as a common friend. Every individual weeps as for the loss of their dearest, best friend. He was loved for himself; was so affable, so benevolent, interesting himself about his lowliest subjects; entered into the concerns of all around him in the most affectionate manner; and in short completely identified himself with his people. Mr Law (the English chaplain) gave us a most impressive sermon on Sunday, and passed a beautiful eulogium on the late monarch. The church was hung in black, and it was altogether extremely affecting. The only signs of life that the Emperor showed during the few last days was taking the

374

Empress's hand frequently and putting it to his heart and lips. He did this about half-an-hour before his death. He received the Communion on the 12/24, and then said: "I never felt so happy before; do with me as you like." His best friend – Prince Pierre Volkonsky – and the Empress never left him. After he died the Empress washed his hands, placed his feet together, and then threw herself on his body. I should think her cup of misery is now filled. She is wonderfully calm, and has had no particular attack since the sad event. The Empress-Mother is also very resigned. This is the fifth child she has lost, but of course this is the hardest blow of all. On the 17th there had been a slight amelioration of the fever. A courier was dispatched with the good news. Upon receiving it the poor old Empress immediately ordered a *Te Deum* to be celebrated. The ceremony was just begun when the fatal news arrived. The Grand Duke Nicholas repaired to the chapel, stopped the service, and made signs to the priest to take the cross to the Empress, saying to her: "My mother, look on that sign of suffering, and be resigned to the greatest misfortune you can meet on earth; the Emperor is dead!" She took the cross, clasped it to her breast, and dropped down as if she also was dead; and it was some time ere she recovered. The Grand Duke Nicholas was the first to swear allegiance to the Emperor Constantine. Constantine is Viceroy of Poland. It is uncertain when he will arrive, perhaps not this week. It is supposed he went to Taganrog upon hearing of his brother's illness. The mourning will last a year. The first part will be dreadfully dismal. The order is not yet announced, and so I do not know exactly what it is to be, except that gowns are to be common black flannel, quite frightful. I hear the length of the trains is to be fixed, and the quality of the stuff according to rank.

182 Mrs, later Lady, Disbrowe, wife of the British Minister Plenipotentiary in St Petersburg at the time of the Decembrist uprising.

Princess Sophie and Aline set off for Taganrog to join Prince Pierre Volkonsky on Saturday. He writes: "*C'en est fait; l'Empereur n'est plus, ma carrière est finie; j'ai servi cet Ange, je ne pourrais servir un autre Souverain. Dieu sait je l'ai servi comme Ami non seulement comme mon Empereur.*"

The Empress-Mother expresses great gratification at the way in which the English have solemnized the Emperor's death, and says: "*Remerciez ces bons Anglais pour moi.*" Since the sad news the towns have been entirely deserted, a remarkable trait of the grief of the people.'

St. Petersburg, 14/26 December, 1825

TO THE HONBLE. R. KENNEDY

'Long live the Emperor Nicholas! Ignoramuses that we were to suppose that Constantine meant to govern us. We were fifteen days in this pleasing error. Everyone took the oath of allegiance to him. All expected his arrival with impatience, but

375

he will have nothing to do with the crown, and so today his brother is declared. Lord Strangford says this ought to be called the Imperial year; two Emperors of Brazil, two of Russia. Constantine may say what he will; but he certainly is an ex. He got into a great passion when told he was Emperor; asked if they thought him a man to be frightened into making a declaration, or that he did not willingly resign the crown for himself and children, when he signed a document to that effect on his marrying Princess Lowitz! This resignation was formally drawn up and signed by the late Emperor Paul; one copy deposited here with the Empress-Mother and Council, and one at Moscow with the Senate and Metropolitan. In spite of this document he was proclaimed in both places as soon as the death of the Emperor Alexander was known, and all the troops and people took the oaths, and the Grand Duke Nicholas was the first to swear allegiance to him.

Messrs. Heckeren and Kielmansegge have arrived, and at their instigation I took off my mourning to go to see the ceremonies at the Kazan Church and hear the *Te Deum*. I had got to the top of the stairs, when, lo and behold! appeared Sir Daniel Bayley with a tremendously long face, to tell us not to stir, for one of the regiments had refused to take the oath to Nicholas, bayonetted two of their officers and a general; say that Constantine is shut up in Petersburg, and that they will have no other Emperor but him. They are now this very minute drawn up in square, on the Place d'Isaac, have loaded with ball, and Heaven knows what will follow! The Chevalier Guards took the oaths to Nicholas very quietly, and are assembling to quell this insubordination. The general is killed, but I believe the officers are only wounded . . . Half-past three. I have been walking on the Quay. The revolt is in the same state; frequent cheers are heard, but they will not receive the Emperor's aides-de-camp. It is said that even all the people declare for Constantine, but indeed I think the Government has been much to blame for trifling so long with the people, trying to keep them in ignorance of everything, and thus allowing them to become suspicious. It is said that General Miloradovich (Military Governor of the town) is wounded in the side. Troops are marching up from all sides to surround the rebels. They hardly deserve that name, poor misguided people. They (the Imperials) have just found among them they will retreat down this way most likely, poor creatures!

Half-past nine. It was dreadful to hear the firing. Every round went to my heart. I do not know particulars for certain, except that at this moment all is quiet, and some say the mutineers have retreated across the river and dispersed. They were the Moskovskiy Regiment, joined by a battalion of the Fin Regiment. Do you remember our listening to their band at the camp? More spectators than soldiers have been killed, about a hundred they say. There are no hopes of General

Miloradovich and a wounded officer who was carried to Count Laval's. Both the bridges close to our house were guarded, and the principal firing was down the back line, and all communication between this cut off. Every approach to the Place d'Isaac was prevented.

16/28 December. The poor soldiers seem to have been entirely misled by their officers, and soon returned to duty. They have received a general pardon; but of course a similar clemency

183 The Admiralty, reconstructed to the design of A. D. Zakharov (1806–23).

could not be extended to those who conducted them and excited them to revolt, and a great many officers are arrested; I am told upwards of thirty.

We are all in colours again during three days to cheer the accession of the Emperor Nicholas and his charming Empress Alexandrine, daughter of the King of Prussia. I grieve that he had such a melancholy inauguration on Monday; he was very much affected, and the Empress wept the whole afternoon. It put an end to all rejoicings; no illuminations nor public ceremonies. However, I trust that all is at an end, and everything will go on quietly. I went out in a *traineau* for the first time to-day. The town presented a curious spectacle. The traces of the sad event on Monday were horrid: pools of blood on the snow, and spattered up against the houses; the Senate House dreadfully battered. The whole took place on the Place d'Isaac. Poor General Miloradovich still lingers. He had escaped without a wound from forty-seven battles, but fell by the hand of an assassin at last. He was shot *à bout portant*. Only think how horrid! He was robbed of his watch and star as they carried him home dying.'

21 December, 1825
2 January, 1826

'We talk of and think of nothing but the unhappy event of Monday. Each day adds new names to the list of conspirators, and almost every family trembles lest some members of its own may not be implicated. It is a most unfortunate business, and brings great distress into the nation.

184 The Kazan cathedral (1801–11) on the Nevskiy Prospect built by A. B. Voronikhin (now the Museum of the History of Religion and Atheism). Lithograph by Karl Petrovich Beggrov (1799–1875).

The Emperor Nicholas has a melancholy commencement to his reign, but he has a fine opportunity of showing his talents, and considers himself happy in being the instrument of bringing the deep-laid conspiracy to light, and of saving his country from all the horrors that would have ensued had a discovery been delayed. Papa will be very sorry to hear that the Lavals are brought into distress by their son-in-law, Prince Trubetskoy, being one of the leading men in the affair. After the events of Monday he went to Count Lebzeltern, and without giving him the least suspicion of his connection with the revolt, asked leave to pass the night in his house, under pretext that Count Laval's was all in confusion in consequence of some soldiers having taken refuge in it. This was placing Count Lebzeltern in a most unpleasant situation, being a foreign Minister, and brother-in-law of the Prince. You may judge of his feelings when he was called up in the night and told that an officer was come to arrest his brother. Of course he could make no opposition, and Prince Trubetskoy has made the most important revelations. It is a frightful business, and

378

though all is quiet for the present, many families are in the deepest distress, and there is still cause for alarm. The soldiers were told to cry "Constantine and Constitutiaze," or some such Russian word for constitution. They asked the meaning of this, and were told: "Oh, it's the name of Constantine's wife." This sounds like a good story; but from all one hears of the deception practised upon the soldiers' simplicity, it is not at all impossible or improbable that this really happened. Some of the traits of the soldiers are quite affecting, and it has been so clearly proved that it was only by deceiving them that they were induced to revolt, and that they all evinced the deepest sorrow and repentance as soon as they perceived the

185 The entry into the square in front of the Winter Palace through the arch of the General Staff Building designed by Rossi (1829–34).

real state of things, and that Constantine's name was only a pretext to their own views, that all have been pardoned. I long to hear how you spent your Christmas. Mine is yet to come, but I do not expect a merry one. To try to be amused, I have invited myself to two children's parties on Christmas Eve, one at Madame Ludolf's, which, by-the-bye, begins with a meagre dinner, and the other at Madame de Gise's. They are to have a tree lighted up in the German way.'

23 December, 1825
4 January, 1826

'Charming to have two years at a time!'

St. Petersburg, 5/17 January, 1826

'We all look so dismal in our black cloth gowns, high with falling collars hemmed in white according to our rank; weepers of the same width, black caps; and last night we rehearsed the points, or schneps, a pointed black band across the forehead, hiding almost all the hair; it should be quite hid, but modern coquetry steals out a curl or two. Tomorrow there is to be a very extraordinary ceremony, and certainly very unseasonable, "the blessing of the waters." The whole court in general attends, but I suppose this year the ladies will not appear. The Emperor must, and all his attendants and priests— withouts hats, fifteen degrees below freezing-point, *imaginez,* in the open air on the river. A hole is cut in the ice, and formerly the devout used to plunge into the water and bring their children to be dipped. It has happened that the shivering priests let the unfortunate little creatures slip through their icy fingers under the ice. *"Mais quel bonheur l'enfant alloit tout droit au paradis,"* was the consoling reflection for the superstitious.

The sentence on the conspirators is not yet passed; it is expected next week. It is supposed that a few will be shot, although there is no existing law to condemn them to death; others to be branded, their ears and noses slit, and sent to Siberia. How horrible! The wife of one is a charming young woman just going to be confined of her first child. She came from Moscow to spend the New Year with her husband, not knowing that he was arrested or anything of what had happened. Her only brother, her husband, and brother-in-law are implicated, and her mother is lying paralysed in mind and body. What a complication of misery! It is said that a standard for the conspirators was found in Madame L.'s wardrobe, worked by her own hand.

Charlotte Disbrowe, *Old Days in Diplomacy* (London 1903)

THE AUTHORS

HERBERSTEIN, SIGISMUND von (1486-1566)
Herberstein was born in Vipava, east of Trieste and part of present-day
Yugoslavia. He studied law at the University of Vienna. His mother-
tongue was German, but he was proficient in Latin and Italian and had
some knowledge of Greek, French, Russian and Polish. He entered the
service of the Emperor Maximilian I in 1514 and over the next forty
years performed countless diplomatic missions which took him all over
Europe and twice to Russia in 1517 and 1526. He was made a Baron by
the Emperor Charles V and allowed to include in his amorial bearings
the representation of a Muscovite warrior complete with bow and whip.

CHANCELLOR, RICHARD (d. 1556)
Little is known about Chancellor's early life. In 1553, when he was
recommended by his friend Sir Henry Sidney, father-to-be of Sir
Philip Sidney, to take part in an expedition to find a northern sea route
to China, he was already a widower with two sons. He commanded the
Edward Bonaventure, the only one of the three ships under the overall
command of Sir Hugh Willoughby to make safe harbour in the White
Sea. This fortuitous landing led to Chancellor's visiting Moscow and
the establishment of an advantageous trading agreement with Ivan the
Terrible. Chancellor left Moscow in March 1554 and in the year following his return to England, the famous Muscovy, later Russia Company
was founded (February 1555). Chancellor returned to Russia in April
1555 and set off again for England in August 1556, accompanied by
Osip Nepeya, the first Russian ambassador to England. Only one of
the four ships reached Britain, and this foundered off the Scottish coast.
Nepeya was saved but Chancellor and one of his sons were drowned.

BEST, ROBERT
The account of the return of Osip Nepeya to Russia in 1557, which was
published anonymously in Hakluyt, has been attributed to the ambassador's English interpreter, Robert Best. Best came to Russia for the
first time with Chancellor in 1555 and was one of the few to survive the
return journey in the following year. He returned to Russia with Nepeya
and Anthony Jenkinson (d. 1611), who was to be the Muscovy Company's
agent until 1560 and made three further expeditions to Russia. Best was
very active on commercial and diplomatic errands over many years;
in 1571 he was the bearer of a letter from Elizabeth I of England to
Ivan the Terrible.

TURBERVILLE, GEORGE (d. 1597?)
Poet and scholar who published several translations from Latin and
works on falconry and hunting as well as two volumes of original verse,
the second of which, *Tragicall Tales,* contained his three epistles from

Muscovy. He went to Russia in 1568 as secretary to Sir Thomas Randolph (1523-1590), who was sent by Elizabeth I to discuss with Ivan the Terrible his request for asylum in England and the question of a political alliance between the two countries.

HORSEY, SIR JEROME (d. 1627)
He first went to Russia in 1573 as a clerk in the service of the Russia Company and returned to England in 1580 with a commission from Ivan the Terrible to purchase munitions. He was well received by Elizabeth and went again to Russia in 1581. In the course of the next decade he made further trips to England, succeeded in gaining special privileges for the Company but was then accused of fraud by the Russia Company. He left Russia finally in 1591 and spent the next thirty years of his life in Buckinghamshire. He was knighted in 1604. He was the author of several works on Russia, some of which appeared in the collections of Hakluyt and Purchas.

FLETCHER, GILES (1546-1611)
Born in Watford and educated at Eton and Cambridge, where he was a Fellow of King's College between 1568 and 1581, Fletcher turned to politics and entered Parliament in 1584, where he attracted the patronage of Sir Thomas Randolph, who had headed the embassy to Russia in 1568. He was a noted classical scholar with a facility for languages which allowed him to acquire a competent knowledge of Russian. Fletcher was sent to Russia by Elizabeth I in June 1588 and returned in the summer of 1589, after complex negotiations with Tsar Theodor and Boris Godunov to re-establish favourable trading privileges for the Muscovy Company. His book was published in 1591. The last years of his life were spent as treasurer of St Paul's.

OLEARIUS, ADAM (1603-1671)
Born in Aschersleben in the German principality of Anhalt. Studied at the University of Leipzig and continued academic pursuits until 1633, when he entered the service of Duke Frederick of Holstein. He went to Russia for the first time in that year in the capacity of secretary to the Holstein embassy, which was designed to set up commercial contacts with Russia and Persia. He visited the Russian Court on three further occasions, in 1636, 1639, and 1643, and on the last two was offered a position in the Russian service by Tsar Michael Fedorovich. From 1643 he occupied the positions of court mathematician and librarian to the Duke of Holstein. Apart from his famous work on Russia, Olearius, who was an eminent Persian scholar, published a translation of Saadi's *Gulistan*.

MIÈGE, GUY
Nothing is known about the author of *A Relation of Three Embassies . . .* apart from his name and the fact that he was a Swiss attendant to the Earl of Carlisle, who apparently read and approved his account. The Earl was sent as Ambassador Extraordinary to Muscovy with the purpose of restoring English trade privileges and was then to proceed to the Courts of Sweden and Denmark. The Embassy left England by ship on 19 August 1663 for Archangel and eventually returned to England in the following year.

COLLINS, SAMUEL (1619-1670)

Eldest son of an Essex vicar, Collins studied at Cambridge from 1635 but left without a degree. He later obtained his M.D. from Padua University. In 1660 he was recruited by an agent of Alexis Mikhaylovich for service in Russia and he acted as the Tsar's personal physician until 1669, when he finally left Russia for England. He died the following year during a visit to Paris. Collins is known to have supplied the Hon. Robert Boyle with much information (on Russian climatic conditions in particular) which was included in the latter's *New Experiments and Observations touching Cold.* and it is possible that Collins's work on Russia was concocted from a series of letters he had sent to Boyle during his stay in Russia.

FABRITIUS, LUDVIG (1648-1729)

Fabritius was born in Brasil, where his father, a former Leyden professor, was senior surgeon to the Dutch Company. His mother remarried after his father's death in 1657 and Fabritius went to Holland. In 1660 he and his stepfather Paul Rudolph Beem entered Russian service and saw action against the Poles. In 1667 they were posted to Astrakhan to help in the suppression of the Razin uprising; three years later they were captured and the stepfather put to death. Fabritius managed to escape to Persia and in 1672 returned to Astrakhan. In the following year he went to Moscow where he served in the Russian army until he retired with the rank of lieutenant colonel to Sweden in 1677. He then embarked on a diplomatic career which took him through Russia to Persia on three occasions between 1679 and 1697, and also to Holland and Constantinople. He was admitted to the Swedish nobility in 1696 and died in Stockholm at the age of eighty-one.

HEBDON, THOMAS

Hebdon was a prominent English merchant of the Russia Company and brother of Sir John Hebdon, who performed services both for the British and Russians. It was John Hebdon who recruited Dr Samuel Collins into Russian service in Holland in 1660 and may well have been involved in enlisting Ludvig Fabritius and his stepfather in the same year. Sir John Hebdon was certainly in England in 1666 where he was visited by General Patrick Gordon, who was by then a close friend of Collins and of other members of the Hebdon family.

IDES, YSBRANT

A merchant from Holstein who had traded in Russia from about 1677 and met the young tsar Peter the Great during the latter's frequent visits to the Foreign Quarter. Ides was appointed by Peter and his brother Ivan to lead an embassy to the Chinese Emperor to see if the conditions of the Treaty of Nerchinsk (which had been signed in 1689) were being observed and to organize trading links. He left Moscow on 14 March 1692 and arrived in Peking on 3 November. After difficult negotiations he arrived back in Moscow on 1 February 1695. He presented the Tsar with a detailed map and account of his journey. Another account of the embassy has been left by its secretary, Adam Brand.

KORB, JOHANN-GEORG

Korb was secretary to the Austrian Embassy sent by the Emperor Leopold I to Moscow in 1698. The Embassy remained in Moscow from

29 April 1698 until 27 September 1699, attempting to strengthen the existing Austro-Russian alliance against the Turks.

LE BRUN (DE BRUYN), CORNELIUS (1652-1726)

A painter who was born in The Hague. Much of his life was spent in travel, financed apparently by the Mayor of Amsterdam, Witsen. In 1674 he visited Rome, where he adopted the name of 'Adonis'. He subsequently travelled through Asia Minor and Egypt, before returning to Italy to spend eight years in Venice, studying under the artist Carlo Lotti. He returned to The Hague in 1693, and five years later published the account of his travels. In 1701 he set off for Moscow, where he met and painted Peter the Great, and then travelled on to Persia and India. Back in Holland he published in 1711 an account of his travels to Russia which he adorned as usual with his own engravings. He died at Utrecht.

PERRY, JOHN (1670-1732)

Born in Rodborough, Gloucestershire, Perry entered the British Navy at an early age and became a lieutenant in 1690. In 1693 he was given command of a fireship *Cygnet* which was captured by French privateers. Perry was court-martialled and fined £1,000 and sentenced to ten years' imprisonment. Released before his sentence expired, he met Peter the Great in 1698 during the Tsar's inspection and recruitment visit to England. He accepted a ten-year contract as an hydraulic engineer and arrived in Russia in the summer of 1698. He worked on various canal projects to link the Volga and the Don and St Petersburg and the Volga and on the construction of docks. Perry was unable to obtain the salary promised for his services and returned to England in 1712 after securing his release only with the greatest difficulty. In England he subsequently gained a reputation for his success in stopping a breach in the Thames Embankment at Dagenham, about which he published an account in 1721. His last years were spent in Lincolnshire and he died at Spalding whilst working on a project to drain the fens.

WEBER, FRIEDRICH CHRISTIAN

Weber was the Hanoverian Resident at the Court of Peter the Great, and after George I came to the English throne he also represented English interests in Russia. Weber arrived in St Petersburg in 1714 and remained until 1717 when he made a short visit to Hanover. He then returned to St Petersburg where he remained until October 1719. The first part of his book *Das Veränderte Russland* was published anonymously in Frankfurt in 1721 and translated into English almost immediately. Further parts of his work were published in 1738 and 1740 and were devoted primarily to the reigns of Catherine I and Peter II. It is thought that Weber served in Russia for another period of about five years in the late 1720s.

BELL, JOHN (1691-1780)

Born at the family estate at Antermony in Scotland. Having obtained his M.D., Bell resolved to enter Russian service and arrived in St Petersburg in 1714 with letters of recommendation to Peter the Great's chief physician, the Scot Dr Erskine. In 1715 Bell joined a Russian embassy to Persia, where it arrived in March 1717. At the end of 1718 he was back in St Petersburg and in the following year was appointed surgeon to the embassy of Lev Vasilevich Izmaylov which was to travel through Siberia to China. This embassy was away three years, but within months of its return Bell was off again to Derbent in 1722. Subsequently he lived in St Petersburg and acted as secretary to the British Consuls-General Thomas Ward and Claudius Rondeau. In 1737 he was sent on a diplomatic mission to Constantinople on behalf of both the Russians and the British. It was at Constantinople that he then spent a number of years as a merchant. In 1746 he married and returned to Scotland to pass the rest of his life at Antermony.

LOCATELLI, Count FRANCESCO (1691-?)

An Italian adventurer who was in French service before deciding to go to Russia in 1734. He presented himself to the Governor of Kazan who considered him a spy and despatched him under guard to St Petersburg where he was held for about a year before being expelled from the country. Locatelli vented his indignation in his book which appeared in Paris in 1735 and in London in the following year. Prince Antiokh Kantemir, who was at this time Russian ambassador in England, was concerned to restore a more favourable image of Russia in European eyes and decided to have a German translation of the work published along with a denunciation of its author. When Locatelli himself arrived in England in 1738, Kantemir suggested to his superior, Count Osterman, another measure frequently employed at this period—to hire men to beat up the unfortunate Italian. Whether the suggestion was acted upon is not known.

RONDEAU, LADY JANE (1700-1783)

The author of the anonymously published *Letters from a Lady* (1775) was at that time called Mrs Vigor, the widow of William Vigor, who had been a Quaker and a merchant of the Russia Company. Née Jane Goodwin, the daughter of a wealthy Yorkshire clergyman, she had gone to St Petersburg in 1728 on her marriage to Thomas Ward, who was the British Consul General to Russia. After Ward's death, in February 1731, she married within months Claudius Rondeau who was the English Resident at the Court of Russia. Again widowed, she returned to England at the end of Anna's reign, accompanied by Vigor, whom she was soon to marry. The last years of her life were spent at Taplow in Buckinghamshire and she died at Windsor.

COOK, JOHN

Little is known of Cook's life apart from the Russian episode which extended from 1735 until 1751. He was a Scottish doctor from Hamilton, who decided to go to Russia for reasons of health, but with letters of recommendation to his fellow-countryman Admiral Gordon and the President of the Russian College of Medicine. He served in St Petersburg until the middle of 1737 before setting off on travels which took him to Astrakhan. In the reign of Elizabeth he again travelled to Astrakhan as well as accompanying an embassy to Persia. He encountered typical difficulty in securing his release from Russian service but eventually arrived back in Dundee in the summer of 1751.

ALGAROTTI, Count FRANCESCO (1712-1764)

Born in Venice, the son of a rich merchant, and educated first at Rome. then at Venice and finally at Bologna, he was a widely educated man who combined a profound knowledge of the sciences with a love for belles-lettres. He gained the friendship of Frederick the Great who composed the epitaph for Algarotti's tomb in Pisa: 'Algarotto Ovidii aemulo, Newtoni discipulo, Fredericus rex.' Algarotti was in correspondence with notable scientists and writers in England, France and Germany, including Voltaire and Lord Hervey to whom his letters on Russia are addressed.

MANSTEIN, CHRISTOPH HERMAN von (1711-1757)

Born in St Petersburg, where his father, a scion of the Baltic German nobility, was in the service of Peter the Great, Manstein was educated in Germany before entering the Russian army. He achieved high rank under the Empress Anna Ivanovna and took part in the coup d'état which followed her death in 1740 to oust the regent Biron. He fell into disfavour under Elizabeth and was virtually banished to the provinces. He deserted the Russian service in 1744, for which he was sentenced to death. The last twelve years of his life were spent in the Prussian army and he was killed in action during the Seven Years' War.

MESSELIÈRE, Comte De La

In a work published nearly fifty years after the events it describes, La Messelière describes conditions at the court of the Empress Elizabeth at a time when the French were engaged in a diplomatic struggle to wrest influence in Russia away from the English. La Messelière was a member of the French Embassy, headed by the Marquis de l'Hôpital, which was in Russia between June 1757 and 1759.

CHAPPE D'AUTEROCHE, JEAN (1722-1769)

Born at Mauriac in Auvergne of a noble family. He took holy orders, but was dedicated also to the study of astronomy. In 1760 he was elected a member of the French Academy of Sciences and sent to Tobolsk to observe the transit of Venus over the sun, which was fixed for 6 June 1761. The tribulations of his trip as well as his success in observing the transit from a small observatory which he built are recorded in his book which was published seven years later and brought him the wrath of Catherine. In 1769 Chappe d'Auteroche again took part in an expedition to observe the passage of Venus; he journeyed to California and died there of a fever soon after completing his observations, which were published posthumously in 1772.

MACARTNEY, GEORGE First Earl (1737-1806)

Born at Lissanoure near Belfast and educated at Trinity College, Dublin. On 22 August 1764 was appointed envoy-extraordinary to Russia with the task of re-negotiating the trade agreement of 1735. He was knighted before leaving for St Petersburg where he successfully achieved his mission. He arrived back in June 1767 and on the next year published his *Account of Russia*. He entered Parliament briefly before being appointed to the chief secretaryship of Ireland on 1 January 1769 and serving in the Irish House of Commons. In 1775 Macartney became governor of the Caribee islands and was made a Baron in the following year. He later served in India for five years until 1786. In 1792, shortly after receiving an Earldom, he was sent as British plenipotentiary to China. In 1795 he was again employed on diplomatic business and sent to Italy to see the exiled Louis XVIII of France. Finally he became

386

governor of the colony of the Cape of Good Hope (1796-1798). He died at Chiswick.

RICHARDSON, WILLIAM (1743-1814)

Born at Aberfoyle in Perthshire, the son of a parish minister, he studied at the University of Glasgow before accepting in 1766 the position of tutor to the sons of Charles, Lord Cathcart. Two years later Richardson accompanied the Cathcarts to St Petersburg where Lord Cathcart was to be British Ambassador Extraordinary. He remained until 1772 and shortly after his return to Britain he was elected to the Chair of Humanity at Glasgow University, a position he was to hold until his death. Richardson indeed fully merited his position; he was both humanist and scholar; a poet as well as a philosopher, the author of numerous works including notable essays on Shakespeare.

COXE, Rev. WILLIAM (1747-1828)

Born in Piccadilly, the son of the Physician to the King's Household. Coxe was educated at Eton and King's College, Cambridge. He was ordained in 1771 and soon became tutor to the Duke of Marlborough's sons and chaplain at Blenheim. In 1775 he was appointed tutor and companion to George, Lord Herbert, the seventeen-year-old son of the Earl of Pembroke, and set off with him and a Captain Floyd on European travels which were planned to last five years and take them through Europe south to Italy and eventually north to Scandinavia and Russia. They entered Russia from Poland in August 1778 and were back in England a year later. In 1784 Coxe again went to St Petersburg as tutor to Samuel Whitbread, the son of the founder of the famous brewery. In 1803 fifty-six-year old Coxe married Elinore, the widowed sister of Stephen Shairp, the British Consul-General in St Petersburg and again visited the Russian capital in 1805. Coxe was the author of numerous books of biography and history; he composed several short works on Russian problems and his famous *Travels* went through six English editions between 1784 and 1803.

DIMSDALE, Baroness ELIZABETH

The third wife of Baron Thomas Dimsdale (1712-1800). Dimsdale was educated at St Thomas' Hospital and began practice in 1741 in Hertford. In 1767 he published a work on *The Present Method of Inoculation for the Small Pox* and in the following year was invited to Russia where he successfully inoculated Catherine and her son, the Grand-Duke Paul. He was made a Councillor of State and a Baron. In 1781 he was invited again to Russia, together with his wife, to inoculate the Grand-Dukes Alexander and Constantine. Later that year Dimsdale published in London his *Tracts on Inoculation* which included as its first chapter his account of his first journey to Russia.

CRAVEN, Lady ELIZABETH (1750-1828)

Née Lady Elizabeth Berkeley, the daughter of Augustus, fourth Earl of Berkeley, she married at the age of seventeen William Craven, later sixth Baron Craven. The marriage produced seven children in thirteen years, before Lady Craven embarked on a series of notorious liaisons in which, as Horace Walpole remarked at a later date, she was always *'infinitamente* indiscreet'. Lord Craven eventually broke with her in 1783, when she retired to France where she met the Margrave of

Anspach, a nephew of Frederick the Great. It was to the Margrave that she addressed the letters from France, Germany and Russia which she published in 1789. Lady Craven and the Margrave were eventually married in 1791, the year in which both Lord Craven and the Margravine had conveniently died within months of each other. At the end of 1791 the Margrave and the new Margarvine settled in Fulham in a home they called Brandenburgh House and in 1799 bought a country seat at Benham in Berkshire. From an early age Lady Craven had indulged her literary bent with a flood of poetry and dramas, and the 'Brandenburg theatricals' became a famous part of her new existence in playhouses which she set up both at Brandenburg House and at Benham. The Margrave died in 1806. The Margravine spent the last part of her life in Italy, at the Villa Craven, near Naples where she wrote her *Memoirs* (1826). She was buried in the old British cemetery at Naples.

DE LIGNE, Prince CHARLES JOSEPH (1735-1814)

Born in Brussels. He soon developed the ambition for a military career and at the age of seventeen wrote a discourse on the 'Profession of Arms' and became an ensign in his father's regiment. He was married in 1755 to Françoise Marie, Princess of Lichtenstein. De Ligne fought in the Seven Years' War with great distinction and in the following years his reputation as soldier, military tactician, man of letters and wit grew and he enjoyed the friendship of monarchs and writers such as Voltaire. In 1780 he set out on the tour of Europe which took him briefly to St Petersburg where he met Catherine the Great for the first time. He visited Russia again in December 1786 and was invited to join Catherine on her famous trip to the Crimea, which he did at Kiev, after a journey to Vienna to see the Emperor Joseph II. At the end of 1787 he entered Catherine's service and fought under Potemkin against the Turks. He returned to Vienna in 1791. In 1806 he was made a Field-Marshal by the Austrian Emperor.

LESSEPS, JEAN BAPTISTE DE (1766-1834)

Lesseps was the young interpreter to Jean François de Galaup, Comte de La Pérouse (1741-1788), the French explorer who had been instructed by Louis XVI to circumnavigate the world. The reached Kamchatka in September 1787 at which point Lesseps was detailed to carry dispatches about the expedition's progress to Versailles via Siberia, Moscow and St Petersburg. Lesseps took three and a half months on his journey from Yakutsk to France and escaped the fate which befell the rest of La Pérouse's expedition later in 1788. Lesseps was later to serve several terms as French consul in St Petersburg.

SWINTON, ANDREW

Although Swinton's account of his stay in St Petersburg and Moscow between late 1788 and early 1791 is well-known and often quoted for its lively pictures of social life, nothing is known about the author himself.

ANON. LETTERS FROM THE CONTINENT

The anonymity of the author of this work and the fact that it was printed only in 1812, long after the period it describes, have led to its being unjustly neglected. In its scathing pictures of European high society it is almost unique. The extant work is not complete, for many of the letters from Russia are missing and were apparently intercepted

388

by the Russian authorities on account of their negative portrayals of life and easily recognizable allusions to prominent figures such as Potemkin. It is possible that they still survive in some Russian archive. The letters were published by a friend long after the death of the author, who is described as 'an elegant classical scholar, and an accomplished gentleman'. He had resided several years in Germany, before making his tour. He arrived in St Petersburg at the end of 1790 and was in Warsaw by August 1791. From the lists of English gentlemen departing from the Russian capital in the summer of 1791, as printed in the *St Petersburg News,* a certain William Dennison, who was accompanied by his German servant Otto Schwartz, seems a possible candidate as the author.

MASSON, CHARLES-FRANÇOIS-PHILIBERT (1762-1807)

Born at Blamont in Franche-Comté. Was apprenticed to a watchmaker and went to Switzerland to continue his training, but was drawn to literature. He published his first verse in 1780. About 1785 he was called to St Petersburg by his elder brother, who was a colonel in Russian service. Masson was admitted in 1786 as an ensign into the Engineer Cadet Corps, of which the director was General P. I. Melissino, to whose niece his brother was married. Masson gained rapid promotion and entrée to the fashionable salons of the capital, where he was able to develop his literary talents. In 1795 he married Baroness Rozen, and was soon after entrusted with a mission to Germany by Catherine herself. In 1796 he became secretary to the Grand Duke Alexander. The accession of Paul brought his career to an abrupt end. He was dismissed, accused of excessive sympathy for recent French military triumphs and taken with his brother under escort to the frontier. It was at a retreat in Poland that he composed his memoirs on Russia, which were published anonymously in 1800. He eventually received permission to return to France in 1799, and died eight years later in Coblenz.

CLARKE, EDWARD DANIEL (1769-1822)

Born at Willingdon in Sussex, the son of the Reverend Edward Clarke, who was also noted as a traveller and author. He graduated from Cambridge in 1790 and in that year accompanied as tutor the Hon. Henry Tufton on a tour of Great Britain. This resulted in the first of Clarke's travel accounts. Throughout the 1790s Clarke travelled incessantly throughout Great Britain and on the Continent. In 1798 he took up residence at Cambridge where he was a Fellow and bursar of Jesus College. In the following year he set off on an extensive northern tour with a pupil, John Marten Cripps. In January 1800 Clarke and Cripps arrived in St Petersburg and had travelled down to the Sea of Azov by June. They left Russia to visit other places of antiquity including Rhodes, the Holy Land, Athens etc. In 1803 Clarke was awarded the degree of LL.D. at Cambridge and in 1805 was appointed as senior tutor at Jesus. He then married and was ordained. In 1808 he was appointed to the first professorship of mineralogy at Cambridge. He died in London and was buried in the Chapel of Jesus College.

CARR, Sir JOHN (1772-1832)

'Green Erin's knight and Europe's wandering star', as Lord Byron characterized Carr, gained a reputation in the first decade of the nineteenth century as the author of endless 'Tours' to all parts of Great Britain and Europe. *A Northern Summer* (1805), which described his travels through Scandinavia, Russia and Poland, was the second of the series. It received a kinder press than did many of those that followed. Carr also tried his hand at poetry and drama. He died in London.

PORTER, Sir ROBERT KER (1777-1842)

Born at Durham, he spent his boyhood in Edinburgh. In 1790 he was enrolled in the Academy of Arts at Somerset House under the supervision of the painter Benjamin West. By the time he was invited to Russia in 1804, he had established a reputation for immense battle scenes and dramatic historical canvases. He arrived in St Petersburg in the summer of 1805 and in the course of the next two years produced a number of historical paintings on the achievements of Peter the Great. His marriage to the Princess Maria Shcherbatova was deferred for four years when Porter was obliged to leave St Petersburg in 1807 because of the rupture with Britain which had followed the Franco-Russian alliance at Tilsit. He spent some time in Scandinavian capitals before accompanying Sir John Moore to Spain, where he was witness to that general's death. In 1811 he returned to Russia and was married the following year. He published his account of the 1812 campaign in 1813, the year in which he was knighted by the Prince Regent. Porter's extensive travels through Russia to the Caucasus and Persia began in 1817 and lasted until 1820. After yet another visit to Russia, he was appointed British consul in Venezuela and returned to England only in 1841. He died and was buried in St Petersburg, whilst on a visit in 1842 to see his only daughter, who had married a Russian officer.

STAËL-HOLSTEIN, GERMAINE, Baronne de (1766-1817)

The daughter of Genevois Necker, minister to Louis XVI. In 1786 she married Baron de Staël-Holstein, the Swedish Ambassador to France, from whom she separated finally in 1798. In the early days of the French Revolution her salon became one of the leading political and literary centres in Paris. With the fall of the monarchy she retired to Coppet in 1792 and in 1794 began her long and stormy liaison with Benjamin Constant. She was unable to gain the confidence of Napoleon and began in 1803 her 'ten years of exile' from the French capital, during which period she made numerous journeys to Weimar, Berlin, Italy, Russia, Sweden and England. Her literary talent, which had manifested itself since her earliest youth, came to fruition in the late 1790s and 1800s, when she produced such works as *De l'influence des passions* (1796), *De la littérature* (1800), *Delphine* (1802), *Corinne* (1807) and *De l'Allemagne* (1810). The account of her visit to Russia was published by her children after her death.

SÉGUR, Comte PHILIPPE-PAUL de (1780-1873)

The son of Count Louis Philippe de Ségur, who was French ambassador to Catherine's Court between 1784 and 1789 and the author of famous memoirs published in 1824. In that year Ségur *fils*, who had been to Russia in circumstances very different from those enjoyed by his father, published his own account of Napoleon and the Grand Army; his interpretation of Napoleon's motives led to a duel in which he was wounded. Ségur had achieved the rank of General in 1812 and became a 'Pair de France' in 1831. He gained a considerable reputation as a historian.

390

JOHNSTON, ROBERT

Moscow after the great events and the great conflagration of 1812 drew tourists like a magnet. Johnston, an Oxford graduate like J. T. James, who visited the Moscow ruins in 1813, and like William Macmichael, who was there in 1814 and again in 1817, shared the general British sympathy for the Russians at this period.

FREYGAN, FREDERICKA VON

The wife of Wilhelm von Freygan (1783-1849) who was the son of a court physician and was born in St Petersburg. He studied at Gottingen from 1802 to 1805 and received the degree of Doctor of Philosophy. He was appointed an aide to General Mikhelson, commander of the Russian army in Moldavia and in 1807 was sent to the Russian embassy in Vienna and later in Paris. In 1811 he accompanied the Governor-General of the Caucasus, the Marquis Paulucci, to Tiflis and in 1812 was sent to Persia to participate in the peace negotiations. The last thirty years of his life were spent in various diplomatic appointments abroad, including from 1834, Venice, where he died. Mme Freygan's letters from the Caucasus are followed in the English volume by extracts from her husband's account of his mission to Persia.

KLAPROTH, JULIUS HEINRICH (1783-1835)

Born in Berlin, the son of an eminent chemist Martin Klaproth, who attempted to dissuade him from his interests in languages, particularly oriental. He studied in Dresden in 1802 and published at the end of that year the first numbers of his *Asiatisches Magazin*. He was invited to St Petersburg in 1804 as an associate of the Academy of Sciences and managed to be included in an Embassy to China under Count Colovkin. He returned to St Petersburg in 1807, having amassed extensive material on the languages and habits of Eastern peoples. At the end of 1807 he was sent on a new expedition to the Caucasus to extend his studies to local languages, particularly Ossetian. The Academy recalled him to St Petersburg a year later and in 1811 Klaproth left Russia for ever, spending a few years in Germany before moving to Paris where he died. He was the author of numerous works, principally on geographical, ethnographical and linguistic subjects.

ADAMS, JOHN QUINCY (1767-1848)

Born at Braintree, Massachusetts. Attended several European universities and at the age of fourteen acted as secretary to Francis Dana, the first American envoy to the Russian court. He graduated from Harvard in 1787 and was admitted to the bar in 1790. He served as American minister to the Hague, London, Lisbon and Berlin before entering the U.S. Senate in 1803. In 1809 President Madison appointed Adams as the first recognized American minister to Russia and he chose to remain there to negotiate trade agreements, despite his election to the U.S. Supreme Court in 1811. In 1814 he was a member of the commission to negotiate peace between America and Great Britain and from 1815 to 1817 served in London as American minister. In 1825 he was elected sixth President of the United States, but was defeated by Andrew Jackson in 1828 and retired to his farm. From 1831 until his death he served as an independent Congressman.

PINKERTON, Rev. ROBERT (d. 1855)
In 1805 Pinkerton arrived at Karass, a missionary post among the Tartars in the North Caucasus which had been set up by the Edinburgh Missionary Society three years earlier. The deterioration in his wife's health obliged Pinkerton to go to St Petersburg where he became a tutor in certain noble families. In 1812 Pinkerton met the Revs. John Paterson and Ebernezer Henderson who had arrived in St Petersburg on business of the British and Foreign Bible Society and together they instigated moves which led to the establishment of the Russian Bible Society under Imperial patronage later that year. In the course of the next thirteen years Pinkerton worked incessantly to promote the aims of the Bible Society, travelling widely throughout Russia. The activities of the Russian Bible Society were brought to an end in 1825 and in that year Pinkerton undertook a tour of seven European states, visiting Bible establishments. In 1830 Pinkerton took up residence at Frankfurt-on-Main with jurisdiction over Bible Society affairs from France to the Russian border and in the following years travelled throughout Europe on many occasions. Whilst still in Russia Pinkerton had published in 1817 extracts of his letters during a tour in Russia, Poland and Germany, but the experiences of his many years in Russia were incorporated in his book published in 1833.

MACMICHAEL, WILLIAM (1784-1839)
Born at Bridgnorth, Shropshire and educated at Christ Church, Oxford, taking his B.A. in 1805 and M.D. in 1816. In 1811 he travelled to Russia, Turkey and Palestine. He paid further visits to Moscow in 1814 and 1817. He began his medical practice on his return in 1818 and was elected a Fellow of the College of Physicians. In 1829 he was appointed physician extraordinary to the King. He published a number of papers on diseases and some lively biographies of prominent doctors, in addition to his travel account. He died in London.

JOHNSON, JOHN
Johnson was a professional scholar, a lieutenant colonel, returning to England in 1817 from India, who took the opportunity to do some sightseeing en route. His knowledge of Russia was limited to the Caucasus and the Ukraine. Whilst in the South he managed to meet one of the heroes of 1812, General Yermolov, who was later visited there by Alexander Pushkin and courted by the future Decembrists.

HOLDERNESS, MARY
Mrs Holderness entered Russia at the end of 1815 and arrived in the Crimea in 1816. She was to spend four years in the village of Karagoz, where she made a detailed study of conditions in the new Russian territories. She published in 1821 shortly after her return to England her notes on the 'Crim Tartars', which she included two years later in her expanded, more intimate account of her stay. Her only other published work was *A Manual of Devotions* (1825).

LYALL, ROBERT (1790-1831)
Born at Paisley and educated at Edinburgh University where he took his M.D. in 1810. In 1815 he was in St Petersburg acting as a private physician to a member of the Russian nobility. He became a close friend of Sir Alexander Crichton, Alexander I's physician. Between 1815 and

1820 he was in the service of Countess Orlova-Chesmenskaya in Moscow and in 1821 attended General Nashchokin. In 1822 he made his trip to the south of Russia as guide and physician to Marquis Pucci, Count Salazar and Edward Penrhyn. In 1823 he returned to London and in the course of the next two years brought out his major works on Moscow and on his Crimean travels, which incurred the indignation of the Russian government. Lyall did not, or could not, return to Russia and in 1826 became British agent at Madagascar. He died of malaria at Port Louis, Mauritius.

COCHRANE, JOHN DUNDAS (1780-1825)

A member of a noble English family, Cochrane entered the Royal Navy at the age of ten and served until 1814. He then made the first of his pedestrian tours, through France, Spain and Portugal. In 1820 he left England to travel through Russia to America. Walking considerable distances but also using any means of transport available, Cochrane reached Okhotsk on the Pacific Coast in June 1821. His marriage to a native Kamchadal girl decided him against continuing his journey and he returned with her to England via St Petersburg. He published his travel account in 1824 and in the following year died in South America. His wife returned to Russia, where she married a Russian naval officer.

LEE, ROBERT (1793-1877)

Born at Melrose in Scotland and studied at Edinburgh, where he received his M.D. in 1814. Between 1817 and 1824 he practised in London, specializing in obstetrics. In 1824 he received on the recommendation of Dr A. B. Granville the position of physician to Prince Mikhail Voront-sov, the Governor-General of the Crimea and son of Count Semen Vorontsov who had been Russian ambassador to England. Lee left for Odessa in October 1824 and met Alexander I shortly before the latter's death at Taganrog. He returned to England in 1826 and resumed his earlier medical practice. In 1830 he was elected a Fellow of the Royal Society and in 1834 to the Professorship of Midwifery at Glasgow, from which he soon resigned. He died at Surbiton Hill in Surrey.

DISBROWE, Lady (d. 1855)

She was the eldest daughter of the Hon. Robert Kennedy and married Edward Cromwell Disbrowe (1790-1851) in October 1821 at Thun in Switzerland. By that time Disbrowe had enjoyed a successful career in the diplomatic service and had served in Lisbon, Copenhagen and Switzerland. He had already visited St Petersburg briefly in 1814 with Lord Cathcart, and in 1825 was appointed British Minister Pleni-potentiary to the Russian Court during the absence of the Ambassador. He arrived in St Petersburg in April and was followed in June by Mrs Disbrowe and her father and brother John, who became attaché to the Ambassador Lord Strangford. The Disbrowes remained in Russia until early in 1828. After service in Stuttgart, Copenhagen and Stockholm, the Disbrowes spent sixteen years in the Netherlands until Sir Edward's death in 1851. Lady Disbrowe lost her elder son Edward at the battle of Inkerman in 1854 and her younger son William died in Canada three years after his mother. Her eldest daughter Charlotte (b. 1822) pub-lished her parents' letters from Russia in a private edition in 1878 and incorporated them in a new volume in 1903.

393

Select bibliography

Contemporary interest in early travellers' accounts of Russia is reflected in the increase in reprints of works which were previously accessible only in major libraries and, more importantly, in new scholarly editions and translations. A reprint series which draws the majority of its titles from the period covered in the present work is *Russia through European Eyes*, Frank Cass, London. The works have no modern critical apparatus, although an original and important addition to the series will be W. Collier's edition of Parkinson's travel journal, a hitherto unknown but fascinating 'Northern Tour' during the age of Catherine II. Significant new editions of works written during the sixteenth and seventeenth centuries include the following:

Sigmund von Herberstein, *Description of Moscow and Muscovy 1557* (ed. Bertold Picard; tr. J. B. C. Grundy), Dent, London, 1969.

Heinrich von Staden, *The Land and Government of Muscovy: A Sixteenth Century Account* (ed. and tr. Thomas Esper), Stanford Univ. Press, Stanford, 1967.

Rude and Barbarous Kingdom: Russia in the Accounts of Sixteenth-Century English Voyagers (ed. Lloyd E. Berry and Robert O. Crummey), Univ. of Wisconsin Press, Madison, 1968.

Giles Fletcher, *Of the Russe Commonwealth* (ed. Richard Pipes and John V. A. Fine), Harvard Univ. Press, Cambridge, Mass., 1966. (Photomechanical reprint.)

Giles Fletcher, *Of the Rus Commonwealth* (ed. Albert J. Schmidt), Cornell Univ. Press, Ithaca, 1966. (Modernized text.)

The Travels of Olearius in Seventeenth-Century Russia (ed. and tr. Samuel H. Baron), Stanford Univ. Press, Stanford, 1967.

Eighteenth- and early nineteenth-century accounts which have recently been published are:

John Ledyard's Journey through Russia and Siberia 1787-1788: The Journal and Selected Letters (ed. Stephen D. Watrous), Univ. of Wisconsin Press, Madison, 1966.

General Wilson's Journal, 1812-1814 (ed. Antony Brett-James), William Kimber, London, 1964.

There are two anthologies of particular interest and value: *Seven Britons in Imperial Russia (1689-1812)* (ed. Peter Putnam), Princeton Univ. Press, Princeton, 1952. (This provides well-arranged and succinctly introduced extracts from the accounts of Perry, Hanway, Richardson, Harris, Coxe, Porter and Wilson.)

Antony Brett-James, *1812,* Macmillan, London, 1966. (Napoleon's ill-fated expedition to Russia is recreated in a mosaic of eye-witness accounts, many of which are rendered into English for the first time.)

Also to be noted is *Voyageurs en Russie, textes choisis du Xe au XXe siecle* (ed. Michel Forstetter), Vevey, 1947.

Bibliographic guides to travel literature exist, but are often incomplete or out of date, sometimes both. For travel accounts in all languages for the pre-Petrine period one should consult Friedrich von Adelung, *Kritisch-Literarische Übersicht der Reisenden in Russland bis 1700, deren Berichte bekannt sind,* St Petersburg, 1846 (reprint N. Israel, Amsterdam, 1960). For literature concerning Russia in most European languages, not merely travel accounts but also translations, pamphlets, historical and geographical works, the indispensable source is *Catalogue de la section des Russica, ou écrits sur la Russie en langues étrangères,* 2 vols, St Petersburg, 1873 (reprint P. Schippers, Amsterdam, 1964); this records works published up to 1869. A most welcome guide which has recently appeared in America is *To Russia and Return* (compiled by Harry W. Nerhood), Ohio State Univ. Press, 1968; its subtitle indicates the scope of Nerhood's undertaking: 'An annotated bibliography of Travelers' English-Language Accounts of Russia from the ninth century to the Present.' Nerhood catalogues 1422 books, originals and translations, but only 181 refer to the period up to 1825, although it must be said that quite a number of titles from this early period have been overlooked. An interesting bibliography of American eye-witness accounts of Russia, which is combined with an analysis of the major characteristics emerging from these writings, is Anna Babey, *Americans in Russia 1776-1917,* New York, 1938.

There is a rich secondary literature dealing with many aspects of Russia's contacts with the West. The list which follows is restricted to works in western European languages and includes primarily works which were consulted in the preparation of the present volume.

A provocative survey of Russia's indebtedness in all fields to the West is provided by Werner Keller's *Ost minus West = Null,* Hamburg, 1960 (English translation by Constantine Fitzgibbon: *Are the Russians Ten Feet Tall?,* Thames and Hudson, London, 1961). An outstanding study of early English writings on, and opinion of Russia is M. S. Anderson's *Britain's Discovery of Russia 1553-1815,* St Martin's Press, London, 1958. The impact of English culture is specifically treated in E. J. Simmons, *English Literature and Culture in Russia 1553-1815,* Harvard Univ. Press, Cambridge, Mass., 1935 (reprint Octagon Books, New York, 1964). A broader survey of the cultural interchange between the Anglo-American world and Russia is Dorothy Brewster's *East-West Passage,* George Allen and Unwin, London, 1954, whilst Max M. Laserson is specifically concerned with *The American Impact on Russia 1784-1917: Diplomatic and Ideological,* Macmillan, New York, 1950 (Collier Books, New York, 1962). Two early classic studies on Franco-Russian contacts are Émile Haumant, *La Culture française en Russie (1700-1900),* Paris, 1910 and Léonce Pingaud, *Les Français en Russie et les russes en France: l'ancien régime, l'émigration, les invasions,* Paris, 1886; two very informative later works on French knowledge of Russia specifically in the eighteenth century are Dimitri S. von Mohrenschildt, *Russia in the Intellectual Life of Eighteenth-Century France,* Columbia Univ. Press, New York, 1936 and Albert Lortholary, *Le Mirage russe en France au XVIIIe siècle,* Paris, 1951. The importance of the Italian contribution to Russia in the fields of architecture, painting and sculpture is underlined in E. Lo Gatto's *Gli Artisti Italiani in Russia,* Rome, 1934. It is a contribution particularly apparent in the creation of St Petersburg, and in this connection one might mention Christopher Marsden's entertaining *Palmyra of the North: The First Days of St Petersburg,* Faber and Faber, London, 1942. For many years Walther Kirschner has researched into Russia's economic and commercial contacts with the West and his collected essays have recently been published: *Commercial Relations between Russia and Europe 1400-1800,* Indiana Univ. Press, Bloomington, 1966. Finally, mention must be made of an invaluable study which takes account of Western travellers' writings on Russia and provides their essential historical and geographical context: W. H. Parker, *An Historical Geography of Russia,* Univ. of London Press, London, 1968.

Acknowledgements

The editor and publishers gratefully acknowledge the following sources of illustrations: Bibliothèque Nationale, Paris: 15, 16, 17, 43, 50, 92 (Sir David Solomon Collection), 109, 110, 113, 131, 179, 180, 183; The Trustees of the British Museum: Endpapers, 3, 5, 7, 8, 12, 14, 18, 19, 27, 29, 30, 33, 39, 41, 49, 51, 52, 53, 55, 66, 76, 77, 85, 101, 102, 103, 107, 117, 125, 129, 134, 136, 138, 139, 144, 161, 166, 173, 177, 178; Harold Cox Photos: 119; Ikon-Museum, Recklinghausen: 46, 47; Gottfried Keller-Stiftung, Kunstmuseum, Bern: 24, 74, 122, 126, 130; Gottfried Keller-Stiftung, Bernischer Historisches Museum: 65, 88, 120, 148, 181; Kungliga Biblioteket, Stockholm: 59, 73, 112, 114, 184; Metropolitan Museum of Art, New York: 83; Comune di Milano, Archivo Fotografico dei Civiti Musei Castello Sforzesco: 87; Nationalmuseet, Copenhagen: 26, 84; New York Public Library: 2, 4, 104; The Master and Fellows of Pembroke College, Cambridge: 25; The Queen's Collection: 58, 146, 147; Royal Library, Stockholm: 11, 21, 23, 111; Staatsbibliothek, Berlin: 62, 64, 90, 116; Thames and Hudson: 1; Thchuseve Museum of Architecture, Moscow: 99, 168; Victoria and Albert Museum, London: 157; Collection Viollet, Paris: 61, 63, 143.

The publishers wish to express especial gratitude for the personal assistance of Dr Ulla Ehrenswärd of the Kungliga Biblioteket, Stockholm, and Mrs Larissa Haskell, in obtaining illustrations.

INDEX

Abasses, 294-5
Adams, John Quincy, 289-93, 391
Age of Feeling, 45
Alexander I, Tsar, 14, 20, 27, 32, 33, 38, 43, 44, 46, 281, 293, 299-303, 306, 311, 321, 373, 374; death of, 14, 374-6
Alexandrine, Empress, 377
Alexis, Tsar, 18, 27, 28, 34
Algarotti, Count Francesco, 31, 34, 183-8, 385
Anna, Empress, 43, 188; and her Court, 188-92
Anne, Princess, 159, 189; wedding of, 159-63
Apraksin, Admiral, 155, 190
Arakcheyev, 255, 257, 258
Archangel, 142-3
Astrakhan, 17, 74, 100, 120, 122, 123, 180, 181, 182, 183
Atkinson, John, 46
Azov, 147, 232; Sea of, 322

Baykal, Lake, 170-4
Barboro, Giosofat, 20-1
Barnwell, George, 279
Basil III, Tsar, 14, 17, 22, 57
Bell, John, 30, 39, 170, 384
Best, Robert, 64, 381
Bestuzhev, Chancellor, 191, 193
Biron, Gustavus, 178, 188
Bogolyubsky, Andrey, 14
Bolsheretsk, 18, 235, 238, 239
Borovikovsky, 219
Borrow, George, 40
Bowles, Sir Jerome, 25
British and Foreign Bible Society, 36
Bukhtarminsk, 368, 369, 370
Burrough, Christopher, 24
Bush, Joseph, 219, 225

Carr, Sir John, 275, 389
Casanova, Giovanni Jacopo, 35
Catherine I, Empress, 31
Catherine II, the Great, Empress, 19, 20, 30, 34-5, 37, 38, 42, 43, 46, 196, 202, 247, 267, 279, 303, 332, 336; journey to the Crimea, 44; at Tsarskoye Selo, 219-27; in the Crimea, 232-5; physical description of, 250-3
Caviar, preparation of, 182-3
Chancellor, Richard, 13, 24, 60, 381
Chantreau, Pierre-Nicholas, 39
Chappe D'Auteroche, Jean, 37-40, 42, 43, 196, 386
Charles IX of Sweden, King, 87, 98
Cherkassky, Prince Ivan Borisovich, 91

Cherkassky, Prince Michael, 147
Cherny Yar, 121-2
Circassian Tartars, 74, 293-9; arms equipment of, 298-9
Clarke, Edward, 27, 32, 40, 45, 260, 266-74, 389
Cochrane, Captain John, 32, 41, 362, 393
Collins, Samuel, 27, 28, 90, 112, 116, 383
Constantine, Grand Duke, 374, 379
Contarini, Ambrosio, 21
Cook, John, 180, 385
Corporal punishment, forms of, 105-8
Court jesters, 190-2; names of, 190-2
Coxe, Rev. William, 29, 31, 38, 39, 40, 42, 47, 212-15, 243, 387
Craven, Lady Elizabeth, 32-3, 227, 387
Cronslot, 163-4, 183, 185
Cronstadt, 189

Danielovich, Grand Duke, 59
Danube, river, 333, 334
Dashkova, Princess, 32
Dashwood, Sir Francis, 31-2
Dawe, George, 46
Decembrist uprising, 44, 376-80
De Ligne, Prince Charles Joseph, 35, 196, 232, 388
Derial, 342-3
Deterson, Johann, 94
Diderot, Denis, 35, 37, 305
Dimsdale, Baroness Elizabeth, 219, 387
Disbrowe, Sir Edward, 374, 393
Disbrowe, Lady, 374, 393
Dnieper, river, 16, 51, 334, 339; crossing of, 325-6
Dniester, river, 16, 334
Don, river, 334, 339, 353
Dukhobortsky, 321-3

Elbrus, Mount, 339, 343
Elizabeth, Empress, 34, 43, 188, 189, 219, 225, 226, 227, 299; her reception of the French Ambassador, 193-6
Elphinstone, Captain, 280
Establishment of towns and cities, 18

Fabritius, Ludwig, 120, 383
False Demetrius, murder of, 26, 43, 83-6, 87
Fleming, Paul, 26
Fletcher, Giles, 24, 26, 37, 77, 382
Ford, Richard, 40

397

RUSSIA UNDER WESTERN EYES 1517-1825

Edited with an Introduction by Anthony Cross

The publication in 1549 of Sigmund von Herberstein's *Notes upon Russia (Rerum Moscoviticarum Commentarii)* was a major event in Western consciousness of the great and distant land of Russia. Within a decade the first English voyagers had reached the northern limits of a country ruled by the notorious Ivan the Terrible and penetrated into the heart of Muscovy. Over the following centuries foreigners poured into a country which was in a constant state of territorial and political flux. By the beginning of the nineteenth century the Tsars commanded an empire which stretched from the White Sea to the Black Sea and the Caspian, from the Baltic to the Pacific, and included vast territories populated by numerous and disparate peoples.

This volume provides a unique account of Russia over a period of three centuries, from the reign of Basil III to the death of Alexander I in 1825, drawn from the impressions of foreigners who differed widely in nationality, education, perceptiveness and sympathy. Diplomats, soldiers, doctors, engineers, tourists, English, Dutch, French, German, Italian and American, are all represented, and their accounts form a fascinating mosaic on Russian mores, peoples, places, rulers, which is given historical and cultural perspective in a wide-ranging introductory essay by Dr Cross.

Their descriptions form an important written record of westerners' reactions to Russia; a further dimension is provided by the wealth of contemporary paintings, drawings and engravings, from which a second rich chronicle has been created. The book includes nearly 200 illustrations, many of which are reproduced here for the first time.

Anthony Cross is Senior Lecturer in Russian in the School of European Studies, the University of East Anglia. He is the author of a book on the Russian author N. M. Karamzin and editor of a series of reprints of English-language travel accounts on Russia.

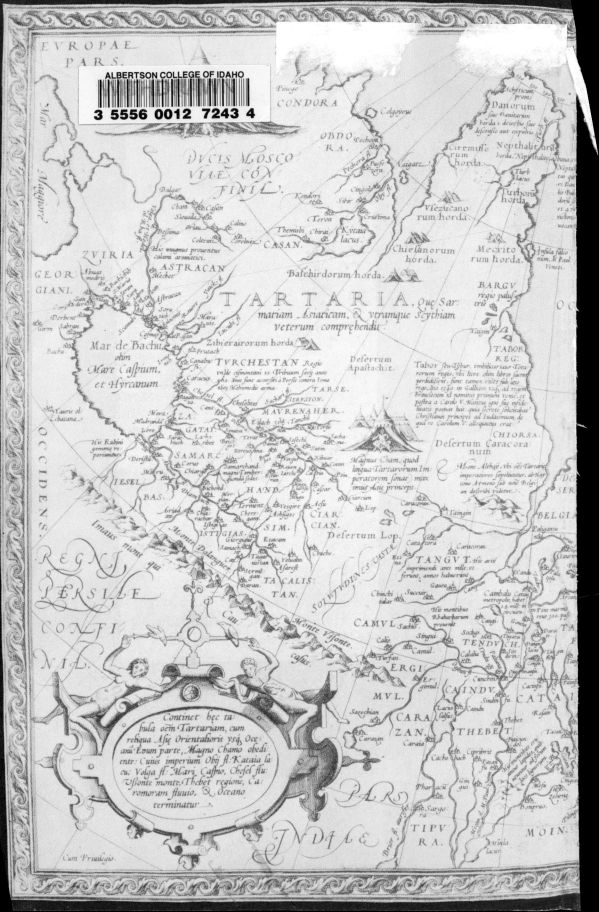

EVROPAE PARS.

Mar Maggiore?

Pincge

CONDORA

Colgoyeue

OBDO RA.

Pechora

DVCIS MOSCO VIAE CON FINIL.

Danorum siue Danatarium horda: detectio siue descensio aut expulsio

Schyticum prom?

Ciremisso rum horda.

Nephalit arum

Turchone horda

Vlezucano rum horda.

Chiesanorum horda.

Mecrito rum horda.

Insula falco num, S. Paul. Veneti.

ZVIRIA

GEOR GIANI.

ASTRACAN.

Baschirdorum horda.

BARGV regio palustris

Mar de Bachu, olim Mare Caspium, et Hyrcanum.

Zibierairorum horda

TARTARIA, Que Sar: matiam Asiaticam, & vtramque Scythiam veterum comprehendit:

TABOR REG.

TVRCHESTAN Regio

Desertum Apastachit.

Tabor seu Tybur, vmbihcus tuae Tartarorum regio, vbi licet olim libros sacros perdidissent, sunt tamen vsi sub vno rege, Stu 1560. in Galliam vsque ad regem Franciscum id nominis primum venit, et postea a Carolo V. Mantuae ipse sue infidelitatis poenas luit: qua secretis solicitabat Christianos principes ad Iudaismum, de qua re Carolum V. alloquutus erat

CHIORSA

OCCIDENS.

TARSE.

MAVRENAHER.

Desertum Caracora: num

Mons Althaii, vbi oes Tartarae imperatores sepeliuntur, ab Hay tone Armeno sub noie Belgi: an describi videtur.

GATAI.

SAMARC

IESEL BAS.

HAND.

SIM. ISTIGIAS.

CIAR CIAN.

Desertum Lop.

DESER

BELGIA

REGNI

PERSIDE

CONFI

NIL.

Imaus mons qui

Montes Dalanguier.

TACALIS: TAN.

SOLITVDINES CASTA.

TANGVT. Hic arte imprimendi ante mille. vt ferunt, annos habuerunt

Monte Vssonte.

Caucasus.

CAMVL.

ERGI

MVL.

CARA ZAN.

TENDVCH.

CAINDV.

THEBET

CATAI

PARS

TIPV RA.

MOIN.

INDIAE

Cum Priuilegio.